BRITISH LITERATURE

Middle Ages to the Eighteenth Century and Neoclassicism
Part Two

Edited by
Bonnie J. Robinson, Ph.D.
Laura J. Getty, Ph.D.

University System of Georgia
"Creating A More Educated Georgia"

UNG
UNIVERSITY *of*
NORTH GEORGIA™
UNIVERSITY PRESS
Blue Ridge | Cumming | Dahlonega | Gainesville | Oconee

ISBN: 978-1-940771-55-7

Produced by:
University System of Georgia

Published by:
University of North Georgia Press
Dahlonega, Georgia

Cover Design and Layout Design:
Corey Parson

For more information, please visit http://ung.edu/university-press
Or email ungpress@ung.edu

TABLE OF CONTENTS

Part Two: The Tudor Age (1485-1603) 599

PART 4: NEOCLASSICISM AND THE EIGHTEENTH CENTURY (1603-1688)   2120

2 The Tudor Age (1485-1603)

2.1 LEARNING OUTCOMES

After completing this chapter, you should be able to:

- Describe the economic, monarchic, and religious characteristics of Tudor rule
- Describe the reasons for the Reformation in England
- Characterize the Golden Age in England under the rule of Elizabeth I
- Analyze the causes for the growth of literature in vernacular, or native, English
- Compare Chaucer's influence with that of Edmund Spenser's on the development of literature in vernacular, or native, English
- Analyze the influence of classical and Italian literature on the English sonnet
- Analyze the influence of classical literature on English drama

2.2 INTRODUCTION

By deposing Richard II, Henry IV precipitated the dynastic wars, known as The Wars of the Roses, fought by the Lancasters and the Yorks, descendants of two brothers, John of Gaunt, the Duke of Lancaster (1340 -1399), and Edmund Langley, the Duke of York (1341-1402). These wars ended in 1485 with the Battle of Bosworth Field and the death of the last Plantagenet king, Richard III (b. 1452). The rule of the Tudors began when Henry Tudor, Earl of Richmond was crowned as King Henry VII (1457-1509) and then united the houses of Lancaster and York by marrying Elizabeth of York (1486-1503).

The rule of Henry VII oversaw a shift from a Medieval landlord and serf agricultural model to a commercial model. With the Parliament, Henry VII enacted laws and statutes that fostered England's economic growth, including protectionist and bullionist statutes, and giving supremacy to England's wool trade and cloth industry. Along with this shift came an increase in city populations, particularly that of London which would, over the course of the Tudor era, become the largest city in Europe and a leading port of trade.

Henry VII also oversaw a centralization of court power and the development of the King's Council, or Star Chamber, by which the monarchy wielded increasing authority over the nobility. The social upheaval of the Medieval era, with its vacuum of offices after the Black Death and resistance of hierarchy embodied in Chaucer's Miller, shifted to a new hierarchy and authority under Henry VII. He encouraged "New Men" at court, that is, men from relatively humble origins who gained increasing opportunities. And he limited the nobility, particularly by binding them through debts and obligations, or recognisances.

Henry VII used money to cement his authority; he accrued wealth through taxes, loans, benevolences, Church grants, and even feudal obligations. One instance of the latter was his receiving 30,000 pounds for knighting his son Arthur (1486-1502)—two years after Arthur's death. By many of these same streams, he financed wars in France and suppression of rebellions at home. England lost its claims to French territory, retaining Calais during Henry VII's reign but losing it during Henry VIII's (1491-1547). Although conflict diminished on the Continent, it increased at home, particularly with Scotland.

After Henry VII's death, the crown passed peacefully to Henry VIII. He corrected some of his father's monetary abuses, executing Sir Richard Empson (c. 1450-1510) and Edmund Dudley (c. 1462-1510), themselves New Men who collected taxes for Henry VII. Wars with Scotland, Ireland, France, and Spain marked Henry VIII's reign, as did his marrying six women. Although Henry VIII's wars depleted the wealth he inherited, he recovered it with the dissolution of the monasteries and the lands he consequently appropriated. The Reformation he initiated in England stemmed from Henry VIII's concern for succession (fear of another dynastic war) and desire to annul his marriage to Catherine of Aragon (1485-1536), who had not provided a male heir. When the Pope rejected his annulment, Henry VIII broke from the Roman Catholic Church and made himself head of the Church of England, confirmed by the Act of Supremacy in 1534.

From his marriages, Henry VIII gained three heirs. Their successive rules led to a short rebellion, after Edward VI's (1442-1483) death, and the execution of hundreds of Protestants during a counter-reformation under Mary I (1516-1558). Elizabeth I (1533-1603) ushered England into a Golden Age. She resolved the religious discord by becoming head of the Protestant (Anglican) Church of England. She navigated foreign affairs by considering various possible husbands, from Spain, Sweden, Austria, and France. Yet she remained married to England. Her position was threatened by her cousin Mary, Queen of Scots (1542-1587), who plotted Elizabeth I's assassination in hopes of ascending the throne and returning England to Catholicism. Elizabeth I had Mary executed before facing a long-threatened assault by the Spanish Armada. The last years of Elizabeth I's reign saw Irish rebellion under Hugh O'Neill, Earl of Tyrone (1550-1616).

Before Henry VII ascended the throne, William Caxton (c.1422-1491) introduced the printing press to England. The consequent increase in number and decrease in cost of books incentivized reading and fostered literacy. Under Henry

VII, England shifted from what had been a bilingual nation, with French or Latin as the courtly language and English the vernacular. The Renaissance, a movement coinciding with the reign of all the Tudors, fostered vernacular literatures spurred by the recovery and study of classical texts. The stability that Henry VII brought to England and that his son protected—even at the expense of Catherine of Aragon, Roman Catholicism, and Anne Boleyn (c. 1501-1536)—expanded individual learning (mainly for men) and intellectual thought. Renaissance humanism, particularly the English version of it, emphasized education of the individual, be he courtier or gentleman. But for the English, that education was linked to Christianity. And the individual's role in Christian faith, worship, understanding, and expression, shaped the religious controversies that marked the Tudor era. Humanist thinking influenced Thomas More's (1478-1535) political and theological critiques in *Utopia*. His understanding of Christianity determined his refusal to accept Henry VIII as supreme head of the church—and his consequent execution.

More wrote *Utopia* in Latin, reflecting thereby the humanist interest in classical learning. The Reformation, the beginning of which he witnessed, led to close and individual scrutiny of ideologies and theologies, a scrutiny which itself shaped England's consciousness as a nation. And the subordination of individual understanding and expression to the classical models in Latin of Cicero (106-43 BCE), Virgil (70-19 BCE), Terence (185-159 BCE), Plautus (c. 254-185 BCE), Seneca (4 BCE-65 CE) and others that formal education relied on unsurprisingly was countered by the development of a national literature not in Latin but in English, and in a variety of genres.

The Tudor era saw great development in English poetry and drama, with such modes as pastoral and lyric, and such forms as epic and tragedy. Edmund Spenser followed Chaucer by shaping ideal poetic diction, meter, and rhyme in English; he fashioned English sonnets in his *Amoretti*, drawing on Wyatt and Surrey's introduction of the Italian sonnet to England. Spenser also wrote an English epic, the most ambitious and weighty of classical genres. He intended his epic *The Faerie Queene* to be a national poem, comparable to Virgil's *Aeneid* (c. 29-19 BCE). And he used the great national myth/hero of King Arthur as his epic's model for the ideal gentleman or noble person, the epitome of Christian virtues. Elizabeth I also appears in this epic in many female roles, particularly Gloriana, the Faerie Queene, Arthur's beloved. And, starting with Henry VII, who named his first-born son Arthur, all the Tudors claimed descent from King Arthur.

English drama developed in part from classical and neoclassical drama. William Shakespeare's comedies owe much to Plautus and Seneca; indeed, his *Comedy of Errors* (1594) takes its plot from Plautus's *The Menaechmi, or The Twins*. English drama also developed in part from the Medieval cycles and morality plays. Like Everyman, Christopher Marlowe's Dr. Faustus struggles between good and evil. Shakespeare's tragedies similarly trace the Tudor era's growth of personal religion, with his characters demonstrating the shift from Medieval Fortuna, fate, or destiny to reason and responsibility. His characters are free to make choices but are held accountable for those choices, either by people or principles. And if a character/ individual has to make decisions and act accordingly, they always face the possibility of making wrong decisions. Like Faustus, Shakespeare's Hamlet fears behaving wrongly and suffers from a divided self as he tries to align his own actions and choices with divinity. Almost more than any other author, Shakespeare realizes the power of the English language to promote (or draw upon) a sense of national identity. Indeed, his use of the English language shapes a sense of humanity itself.

2.3 RECOMMENDED READING

Andrew Gurr, *Playgoing in Shakespeare's* London, 1987.

John Guy, *Tudor England*, 1988.

David Javitch, *Poetry and Courtliness in Renaissance*, 1976.

James Nohrnberg, *The Analogy of "The Faerie Queene,"* 1976.

J. A. Sharpe, *Early Modern England: A Social History*, 1987.

Murry Schwartz and Coppelia Kahn, eds., *Representing Shakespeare: New Psychoanalytic Essays*, 1980.

E. M. W. Tillyard, *The Elizabeth World Picture*, 1943.

Kim Walker, *Women Writers of the English Renaissance*, 1996.

2.4 THOMAS MORE

(1478-1535)

A martyr, humanist, historian, dramatist, and satirist, Thomas More was grandson to a baker. His father John More (1451-1530) married Agnes Graunger, whose father was a wealthy merchant and Sheriff of London. John More was a successful lawyer, ultimately knighted and serving on the Court of King's Bench. Thomas More received a gentleman's education, studying at St. Anthony's School in London before entering the household of John Morton (1420-1500), who was at that time both Archbishop of Canterbury and Lord Chancellor of England. Thomas More's learning, humanist scholarship, and writing defined his character, as did his statesmanship. He studied for two years at Oxford before he acceded to his father's

Image 2.1 | Sir Thomas More
Artist | Hans Holbein, the Younger
Source | Wikipedia
License | Public Domain

wishes by entering New Inn to study law, being called to the Bar in 1502. His own wishes had a more spiritual bent, for the next year saw him living near a Carthusian monastery, following that order's discipline, praying, fasting, self-flagellating, and abasing the flesh by wearing a hair shirt. According to his friend, the Humanist Desiderius Erasmus of Rotterdam (1466-1536), More considered joining the Franciscan order.

Instead, he entered Parliament, advocating government efficiency and denouncing heavy taxation. In 1505, he married Jane Colt; they had four children before she died in 1500. An exceptionally short thirty days later, he married Alice Harpur Middleton (1474-1546), a wealthy widow. Her daughter from her first marriage, along with More's daughters Margaret, Elizabeth, and Cicely received a classical education, with Margaret later gaining renown for her knowledge of Latin. More balanced a contented domestic life with an active public one. A successful barrister, he served as under-sherrif of the City of London, as Master of the Court of Requests, and as a Privy Counsellor. He traveled to Flanders as a delegate for Henry VIII and Cardinal Wolsey (1473-1530)—who recommended him as Speaker of the House of Commons—then became Chancellor of the Duchy of Lancaster.

He gained influence as Henry VIII's advisor, particularly through his condemnation of the Lutheran heresy (that is, the Reformation). Henry VIII granted More a pension, land, and sinecures. When Wolsey failed to obtain Henry VIII's annulment from Catherine of Aragon, Wolsey was removed as Lord Chancellor of England and expelled from court. Henry VIII then named More Wolsey's replacement as Lord Chancellor. In this position, More continued to support the Roman Catholic Church, possibly to the point of approving the torture and burning of Protestants. He certainly suppressed William Tyndale's English translation of the New Testament (1526), one that turned directly to the Hebrew and Greek, as challenging the power of the Roman Catholic Church in England. Tyndale's *The Obedience of a Christian Man, and how Christian rulers ought to govern* (1528) probably helped to encourage Henry VIII to become head of the Church in England, replacing the Pope, and breaking with the Roman Catholic Church. He then divorced Catherine of Aragon to marry Anne Boleyn and had several acts passed to secure the legitimacy of their issue. More resigned as Lord Chancellor and refused to take the Succession Oath. He was imprisoned then beheaded for high treason.

Seemingly far away from these political and religious controversies, More's *Utopia* ("No Place" or "Nowhere," in English) depicts a fictional good place located somewhere in the New World whose citizens practice a form of communism, welfare, and undenominational theism. To the classical model of Plato's *The Republic*, More added the contemporary contrast of New World and Old World cultures. In Utopia, some women could be priests, and all priests are chosen for their holiness. All citizens work, for a limited time on farms, and then in various trades, such as carpentry and masonry; they use their leisure time for learning. The ethical basis of their lives satirically critiques the corruption and immorality of

More's society. It's difficult to attribute any particular Utopian practice to More's own held beliefs, especially considering their religious tolerance and his actions against Protestants. Their ethical behavior seems superior to England's. But that may not be More's main point. His main critique may be wonder at a society that can do so much good—without Christian revelation. And condemnation of the pride that keeps his society from emulating such goodness—despite having that revelation.

Image 2.2 | Map of Utopia
Artist | Abraham Ortelius
Source | Wikimedia Commons
License | Public Domain

2.4.1 *Utopia*

(1516)

THE PREFACE

There is no way of writing so proper, for the refining and polishing a Language, as the translating of Books into it, if he that undertakes it, has a competent skill of the one Tongue, and is a Master of the other. When a Man writes his own Thoughts, the heat of his Fancy, and the quickness of his Mind, carry him so much after the Notions themselves, that for the most part he is too warm to judge of the aptness of Words, and the justness of Figures; so that he either neglects these too much, or overdoes them: But when a Man translates, he has none of these Heats about him: and therefore the French took no ill Method, when they intended to reform and beautify their Language, in setting their best Writers on Work to translate the Greek and Latin Authors into it. There is so little praise got by Translations, that a Man cannot be engaged to it out of Vanity, for it has passed for a sign of a slow Mind, that can amuse it self with so mean an Entertainment; but we begin to grow wiser, and tho ordinary Translators must succeed ill in the esteem of the World, yet some have appeared of late that will, I hope, bring that way of writing in credit. The English Language has wrought it self out, both of the fulsome Pedantry under which it laboured long ago, and the trifling way of dark and unintelligible Wit that came after that, and out of the course extravagance of Canting that succeeded this: but as one Extream commonly produces another, so we were beginning to fly into a sublime pitch, of a strong but false Rhetorick, which had much corrupted, not only the Stage, but even the Pulpit; two places, that tho they ought not to be named together, much less to resemble one another; yet it cannot be denied, but the Rule and Measure of Speech is generally taken from them: but that florid strain is almost quite worn out, and is become now as ridiculous as it was once admired. So that without either the Expence or Labour that the French have undergone, our Language has, like a rich Wine, wrought out its Tartar, and [has] insensibly brought to a Purity that could not have been compassed without much labour, had it not been for the great advantage that we have of a Prince, who is so great a Judge, that his single approbation or dislike has almost as great an Authority over our Language, as his Prerogative gives him over our Coin. We are now so much refined, that how defective soever our Imaginations or Reasonings may be, yet our Language has fewer Faults, and is more natural and proper, than it was ever at any time before. When one compares the best Writers of the last Age, with these that excel in this, the difference is very discernable: even the great Sir Francis Bacon, that was the first that writ our Language correctly; as he is still our best Author, yet in some places has Figures so strong, that they could not pass now before a severe Judg. I will not provoke the present Masters of the Stage, by preferring the Authors of the last Age to them: for tho they all acknowledg that they come far short of B. Iohnson, Beamont and Fletcher, yet I believe they are better pleased to say this themselves, than to have it observed by others. Their Language is now certainly properer, and more natural than it was formerly, chiefly since the correction that was given by the Rehearsal; and it is to be hoped, that the Essay on Poetry, which may be well matched with the best Pieces of its kind that even Augustus's Age produced, will have a more powerful Operation, if clear sense, joined with home but gentle Reproofs, can work more on our Writers, than that unmerciful exposing of them has done.

I have now much leisure, and want diversion, so I have bestowed some of my hours upon Translations, in which I have proposed no ill Patterns to my self: but the Reader will be best able to judge whether I have copied skilfully after such

Originals. This small Volume which I now publish, being writ by one of the greatest Men that this Island has produced, seemed to me to contain so many fine and well-digested Notions, that I thought it might be no unkind nor ill entertainment to the Nation, to put a Book in their Hands, to which they have so good a Title, and which has a very common fate upon it, to be more known and admired all the World over, than here at Home. It was once translated into English not long after it was written; and I was once apt to think it might have been done by Sir Thomas More himself: for as it is in the English of his Age, and not unlike his Stile; so the Translator has taken a liberty that seems too great for any but the Author himself, who is Master of his own Book, and so may leave out or alter his Original as he pleases: which is more than a Translator ought to do, I am sure it is more than I have presumed to do.

It was writ in the Year 1516, as appears by the Date of the Letter of Peter Giles's, in which he says, That it was sent him but a few days before from the Author, and that bears date the first of November that Year; but I cannot imagine how he comes to be called Sheriff of London in the Title of the Book, for in all our printed Catalogues of Sheriffs, his Name is not to be found. I do not think my self concerned in the Matter of his Book, no more than any other Translator is in his Author: nor do I think More himself went in heartily to that which is the chief Basis of his Utopia, the taking away of all Property, and the levelling the World; but that he only intended to set many Notions in his Reader's way; and that he might not seem too much in earnest, he went so far out of all Roads to do it the less suspected: the earnestness with which he recommends the precaution used in Marriages among the Utopians, makes one think that he had a misfortune in his own choice, and that therefore he was so cautious on that Head; for the strictness of his Life covers him from severe Censures: His setting out so barbarous a practice, as the hiring of Assassinates to take off Enemies, is so wild and so immoral both, that it does not admit of any thing to soften or excuse it, much less to justify it; and the advising Men in some Cases to put an end to their Lives, notwithstanding all the Caution with which he guards it, is a piece of rough and fierce Philosophy. The tenderest part of the whole Work, was the representation he gives of Henry the Seventh's Court; and his Discourses upon it, towards the end of the first Book, in which his Disguise is so thin, that the Matter would not have been much plainer if he had named him: But when he ventured to write so freely of the Father in the Son's Reign, and to give such an Idea of Government under the haughtiest Prince, and the most impatient of uneasy Restraints that ever reigned in England, who yet was so far from being displeased with him for it, that as he made him long his particular Friend, so he employed him in all his Affairs afterwards, and raised him to be L. Chancellor, I thought I might venture to put it in more Modern English: for as the Translators of Plutarch's Hero's, or of Tullies Offices, are not concerned, either in the Maxims, or in the Actions that they relate; so I, who only tell, in the best English I can, what Sir Thomas More writ in very Elegant Latin, must leave his Thoughts and Notions to the Reader's censure, and do think my self liable for nothing but the fidelity of the Translation, and the correctness of the English; and for that I can only say, that I have writ as carefully, and as well as I can.

THE AUTHOR'S EPISTLE TO PETER GILES

I Am almost ashamed, my dearest Peter Giles, to send you this Book of the Utopian Common-Wealth, after almost a Years delay; whereas no doubt you look›d for it within six Weeks: for as you know I had no occasion for using my Invention, or for taking pains to put things into any method, because I had nothing to do, but to repeat exactly those things that I heard Raphael relate in your presence; so neither was there any occasion given for a studied Eloquence: since as he delivered things to us of the sudden, and in a careless Stile; so he being, as you know, a greater Master of the Greek, than of the Latin; the plainer my words are, they will resemble his simplicity the more: and will be by consequence the nearer to the Truth, and that is all that I think lies on me: and it is indeed the only thing in which I thought my self concerned. I confess, I had very little left on me in this Matter, for otherwise the inventing and ordering of such a Scheme, would have put a Man of an ordinary pitch, either of Capacity, or of Learning, to some pains, and have cost him some time; but if it had been necessary that this Relation should have been made, not only truly, but eloquently, it could never have been performed by me, even after all the pains and time that I could have bestowed upon it. My part in it was so very small, that it could not give me much trouble, all that belonged to me being only to give a true and full account of the things that I had heard: but although this required so very little of my time; yet even that little was long denied me by my other Affairs, which press much upon me: for while in pleading, and hearing, and in judging or composing of Causes, in waiting on some Men upon Business, and on others out of Respect, the greatest part of the Day is spent on other Mens Affairs, the remainder of it must be given to my Family at home: So that I can reserve no part of it to my self, that is, to my Study: I must talk with my Wife, and chat with my Children, and I have somewhat to say to my Servants; for all these things I reckon as a part of Business, except a Man will resolve to be a Stranger at Home: and with whomsoever either Nature, Chance, or Choice has engaged a Man, in any Commerce, he must endeavour to make himself as acceptable to these about him, as he possibly can; using still such a temper in it, that he may not spoil them by an excessive gentleness, so that his Servants may not become his Masters. In such things as I have named to you, do Days, Months, and Years slip away; what is then left for Writing? and yet I have said nothing of that time that must go for Sleep, or for Meat: in which many do waste almost as much of their time, as in Sleep, which consumes very near the half of our Life; and indeed all the time which I can gain to my self, is that which I steal from my Sleep and my Meals; and because that is not much, I have made but a slow progress; yet because it is somewhat, I have at last got to an end of my Utopia, which I now send to you, and expect that after you have read it, you will let me know if you can put me in mind of any thing that has escaped me; for tho I would think my self very happy, if

I had but as much Invention and Learning as I know I have Memory, which makes me generally depend much upon it, yet I do not relie so entirely on it, as to think I can forget nothing.

My Servant John Clement has started some things that shake me: You know he was present with us, as I think he ought to be at every Conversation that may be of use to him, for I promise my self great Matters from the progress he has so early made in the Greek and Roman Learning. As far as my Memory serves me, the Bridg over Anider at Amaurot, was 500 paces broad, according to Raphael's account; but John assures me, he spoke only of 300 paces; therefore I pray you recollect what you can remember of this, for if you agree with him, I will believe that I have been mistaken; but if you remember nothing of it, I will not alter what I have written, because it is according to the best of my remembrance: for as I will take care that there may be nothing falsly set down; so if there is any thing doubtful, tho I may perhaps tell a lie, yet I am sure I will not make one; for I would rather pass for a good Man, than for a wise Man: but it will be easy to correct this Mistake, if you can either meet with Raphael himself, or know how to write to him.

I have another Difficulty that presses me more, and makes your writing to him the more necessary: I know not whom I ought to blame for it, whether Raphael, you, or my self; for as we did not think of asking it, so neither did he of telling us, in what part of the newfound World Utopia is situated; this was such an omission that I would gladly redeem it at any rate: I am ashamed, that after I have told so many things concerning this Island, I cannot let my Readers know in what Sea it lies. There are some among us that have a mighty desire to go thither, and in particular, one pious Divine is very earnest on it, not so much out of a vain curiosity of seeing unknown Countries, as that he may advance our Religion, which is so happily begun to be planted there; and that he may do this regularly, he intends to procure a Mission from the Pope, and to be sent thither as their Bishop. In such a case as this, he makes no scruple of aspiring to that Character, and thinks it is rather meritorious to be ambitious of it, when one desires it only for advancing the Christian Religion, and not for any Honour or Advantage that may be had by it, but is acted meerly by a pious Zeal. Therefore I earnestly beg it of you, if you can possibly meet with Raphael, or if you know how to write to him, that you will be pleased to inform your self of these things, that there may be no falshood left in my Book, nor any important Truth wanting. And perhaps it will not be unfit to let him see the Book it self: for as no Man can correct any Errors that may be in it, so well as he; so by reading it, he will be able to give a more perfect judgment of it than he can do upon any Discourse concerning it: and you will be likewise able to discover whether this Undertaking of mine is acceptable to him or not; for if he intends to write a Relation of his Travels, perhaps he will not be pleased that I should prevent him, in that part that belongs to the Utopian Common-Wealth; since if I should do so, his Book will not surprize the World with the pleasure which this new Discovery will give the Age. And I am so little fond of appearing in print upon this occasion, that if he dislikes it, I will lay it aside;

And even though he should approve of it, I am not positively determined as to the publishing of it. Mens tastes differ much; some are of so morose a Temper, so sour a Disposition, and make such absurd Iudgments of Things, that Men of chearful and lively Tempers, who indulge their Genius, seem much more happy, than those who waste their time and strength in order to the publishing some Book, that tho of it self it might be useful or pleasant, yet instead of being well received, will be sure to be either loathed at, or censured. Many know nothing of Learning, and others despise it: a Man that is accustomed to a course and harsh Sile, thinks every thing is rough that is not barbarous. Our trifling Pretenders to Learning, think all is slight that is not drest up in words that are worn out of use; some love only old things, and many like nothing but what is their own. Some are so sour, that they can allow no Jests, and others are so dull that they can endure nothing that is sharp; and some are as much afraid of any thing that is quick or lively, as a Man bit with a mad Dog is of Water; others are so light and unsetled, that their Thoughts change as quick as they do their Postures: and some, when they meet in Taverns, take upon them among their Cups to pass Censures very freely on all Writers; and with a supercilious liberty to condemn every thing that they do not like: in which they have the advantage that a bald Man has, who can catch hold of another by the Hair, while the other cannot return the like upon him. They are safe as it were of Gunshot, since there is nothing in them considerable enough to be taken hold of. And some are so unthankful, that even when they are well pleased with a Book, yet they think they owe nothing to the Author; and are like those rude Guests, who after they have been well entertained at a good Dinner, go away when they have glutted their Appetites, without so much as thanking him that treated them. But who would put himself to the charge of making a Feast for Men of such nice Palats, and so different Tastes; who are so forgetful of the Civilities that are done them? But do you once clear those Points with Raphael, and then it will be time enough to consider whether it be fit to publish it or not; for since I have been at the pains to write it, if he consents to the publishing it, I will follow my Friend's Advice, and chiefly yours. Farewel my dear Peter, commend me kindly to your good Wise, and love me still as you use to do, for I assure you I love you daily more and more.

THE DISCOURSES OF RAPHAEL HYTHLODAY, OF THE BEST STATE OF A COMMON-WEALTH

Written by Sir Thomas More, Citizen and Sheriff of London.

Henry the 8th, the unconquered King of England, a Prince adorned with all the Vertues that become a great Monarch; having some Differences of no small Consequence with Charles the most serene Prince of Castile, sent me into Flanders as his Ambassador, for treating and composing Matters between them. I was Collegue and Companion to that incomparable Man Cuthbert Tonstal, whom the King made lately Master of the Rolls, with such an Universal Applause; of whom I will say nothing, not because I fear that the Testimony of a Friend will be suspected, but rather because his Learning and Vertues are greater than that they can be set forth with advantage by me, and they are so well known, that they need not my Commendations, unless I would, according to the Proverb, Shew the Sun with a Lanthorn. Those that were appointed by the Prince to treat with us, met us at Bruges, according to Agreement: they were all worthy Men. The Markgrave of Bruges was their Head, and the chief Man among them; but he that was esteemed the wisest, and that spoke for the rest, was George Temse the Provost of Casselsee; both Art and Nature had concurred to make him eloquent: He was very learned in the Law; and as he had a great Capacity, so by a long practice in Affairs, he was very dextrous at them. After we had met once and again, and could not come to an Agreement, they went to Brussels for some days to receive the Prince's Pleasure. And since our Business did admit of it, I went to Antwerp: While I was there, among many that visited me, there was one that was more acceptable to me than any other; Peter Giles born at Antwerp, who is a Man of great Honour, and of a good Rank in his Town; yet it is not such as he deserves: for I do not know if there be any where to be found a learneder and a better bred young Man: for as he is both a very worthy Person, and a very knowing Man; so he is so civil to all Men, and yet so particularly kind to his Friends, and is so full of Candor and Affection, that there is not perhaps above one or two to be found any where, that is in all respects so perfect a Friend as he is: He is extraordinarily modest, there is no artifice in him; and yet no Man has more of a prudent simplicity than he has: His Conversation was so pleasant and so innocently chearful, that his Company did in a great measure lessen any longings to go back to my Country, and to my Wife and Children, which an absence of four months had quickned very much. One day as I was returning home from Mass at St. Maries, which is the chief Church, and the most frequented of any in Antwerp, I saw him by accident talking with a Stranger, that seemed past the flower of his Age; his Face was tanned, he had a long Beard, and his Cloak was hanging carelessly about him, so that by his Looks and Habit, I concluded he was a Seaman. As soon as Peter saw me, he came and saluted me; and as I was returning his Civility, he took me aside, and pointing to him with whom he had been discoursing, he said, Do you see that Man? I was just thinking to bring him to you. I answered, He should have been very welcome on your account: And on his own too, replied he, if you knew the Man; for there is none alive that can give you so copious an account of unknown Nations and Countries as he can do; which I know you very much desire. Then said I, I did not guess amiss, for at first sight I took him for a Seaman: But you are much mistaken, said he, for he has not sailed as a Seaman, but as a Traveller, or rather as a Philosopher; for this Raphael, who from his Family carries the Name of Hythloday, as he is not ignorant of the Latine Tongue, so he is eminently learned in the Greek, having applied himself more particularly to that than to the former, because he had given himself much to Philosophy, in which he knew that the Romans have left us nothing that is valuable, except what is to be found in Seneca and Cicero. He is a Portuguese by birth, and was so desirous of seeing the World, that he divided his Estate among his Brothers, and run Fortunes with Americus Vesputius, and bore a share in three of his four Voyages, that are now published: only he did not return with him in his last, but obtained leave of him almost by force, that he might be one of those four and twenty who were left at the farthest place at which they touched, in their last Voyage to New Castile. The leaving him thus, did not a little gratify one that was more fond of travelling than of returning home, to be buried in his own Country: for he used often to say, That the way to Heaven was the same from all places; and he that had no Grave, had the Heavens still over him. Yet this disposition of Mind had cost him dear, if God had not been very gracious to him; for after he, with five Castilians, had travelled over many Countries, at last, by a strange good fortune, he got to Ceylon, and from thence to Calicut, and there he very happily found some Portuguese Ships; and so, beyond all Mens expectations, he came back to his own Country. When Peter had said this to me, I thanked him for his kindness, in intending to give me the acquaintance of a Man, whose Conversation he knew would be so acceptable to me; and upon that Raphael and I embraced one another: And after those Civilities were past, which are ordinary for Strangers upon their first meeting, We went all to my House, and entring into the Garden, sat down on a green Bank, and entertained one another in Discourse. He told us, that when Vesputius had sailed away, he and his Companions that staid behind in New-Castile, did by degrees insinuate themselves into the People of the Country, meeting often with them, and treating them gently: and at last they grew not only to live among them without danger, but to converse familiarly with them; and got so far into the Heart of a Prince, whose Name and Country I have forgot, that he both furnished them plentifully with all things necessary, and also with the conveniences of travelling; both Boats when they went by Water, and Wagons when they travelled over Land; and he sent with them a very faithful Guide, who was to introduce and recommend them to such other Princes as they had a mind to see: and after many days Journey, they came to Towns, and Cities, and to Common-Wealths, that were both happily governed, and well-peopled. Under the Aequator, and as far on both sides of it as the Sun moves, there lay vast Deserts that were parched with the perpetual heat of the Sun; the Soil was withered, all Things look'd dismally, and all Places were either quite uninhabited, or abounded with Wild Beasts and Serpents, and some few Men, that were neither less wild, nor less cruel than the Beasts themselves. But as they went farther, a new Scene opened, all things grew milder, the Air less burning, the Soil more verdant, and even the Beasts were less wild: And at last there are Nations, Towns, and Cities, that have not only mutual commerce among themselves, and with their Neighbours, but trade both by Sea and Land, to very remote Countries. There they found the Conveniencies of seeing many Countries on all Hands, for no Ship went any Voyage into which he and his Companions were not very welcome. The first Vessels that they saw were Flat-bottomed, their Sails were made of Reeds and Wicker woven close together, only some were made of Leather; but afterwards they found Ships made with round Keels, and Canvass Sails, and in all things like our Ships: and the Seamen understood both Astronomy and Navigation. He got wonderfully into their favour, by shewing them the use of the Needle, of which till then they were utterly ignorant; and whereas they sailed before with great caution, and only in Summer-time, now they count all Seasons alike, trusting wholly to the Loadstone, in which they are perhaps more secure than safe; so that there is reason to fear, that this Discovery which was thought would prove so much to their Advantage, may by their imprudence become an occasion of much Mischief to them. But it were too long to dwell on all that he told us he had observed in every place, it would be too great a digression from our present purpose: and what-ever is necessary to be told, chiefly concerning the wise and prudent Institutions that he observed among civilized Nations, may perhaps be related by us on a more proper occasion. We ask'd him many questions concerning all these things, to which he answered very willingly; only we made no enquiries after Monsters, than which nothing is more common; for every where one may hear of ravenous Dogs and Wolves, and cruel Men-eaters; but it is not so easy to find States that are well and wisely governed.

But as he told us of many things that were amiss in those New-found Nations, so he reckoned up not a few things, from which Patterns might be taken for correcting the Errors of these Nations among whom we live; of which an account may be given, as I have already promised, at some other time; for at present I intend only to relate these Particulars that he told us of the Manners and Laws of the Utopians: but I will begin with the Occasion that led us to speak of that Common-Wealth. After Raphael had discoursed with great judgment of the Errors that were both among us and these Nations, of which there was no small number, and had treated of the wise Institutions both here and there, and had spoken as distinctly of the Customs and Government of every Nation through which he had past, as if he had spent his whole Life in it; Peter being struck with admiration, said, I wonder, Raphael, how it comes that you enter into no King›s Service, for I am sure there are none to whom you would not be very acceptable: for your Learning and Knowledg, both of Men and Things, is such, that you would not only entertain them very pleasantly, but be of good use to them, by the Examples that you could set before them, and the Advices that you could give them; and by this means you would both serve your own Interest, and be of great use to all your Friends. As for my Friends, answered he, I need not be much concerned, having already done all that was incumbent on me toward them; for when I was not only in good Health, but fresh and young, I distributed that among my Kindred and Friends, which other People do not part with till they are old and sick; and then they unwillingly give among them, that which they can enjoy no longer themselves. I think my Friends ought to rest contented with this, and not to expect that for their sakes I should enslave my self to any King whatsoever. Soft and fair, said Peter, I do not mean that you should be a Slave to any King, but only that you should assist them, and be useful to them. The change of the Word, said he, does not alter the Matter. But term it as you will, replied Peter, I do not see any other way in which you can be so useful, both in private to your Friends, and to the Publick, and by which you can make your own Condition happier. Happier! answered Raphael, is that to

be compassed in a way so abhorrent to my Genius? Now I live as I will, to which
I believe few Courtiers can pretend: and there are so very many that court the
Favour of great Men, that there will be no great loss, if they are not troubled either
with me, or with others of my temper. Upon this, I said, I perceive Raphael that
you neither desire Wealth nor Greatness; and indeed I value and admire such a
Man much more than I do any of the great Men in the World. Yet I think you
would do a thing well-becoming so generous and so philosophical a Soul as yours
is, if you would apply your Time and Thoughts to Publick Affairs, even though
you may happen to find that a little uneasy to your self; and this you can never do
with so much advantage, as by being taken into the Council of some great Prince,
and by setting him on to noble and worthy Things, which I know you would do
if you were in such a Post; for the Springs, both of Good and Evil, flow over a
whole Nation, from the Prince, as from a lasting Fountain. So much Learning as
you have, even without practice in Affairs; or so great a practice as you have had,
without any other Learning, would render you a very fit Counsellor to any King
whatsoever, You are doubly mistaken, said he, Mr. More, both in your Opinion of
me, and in the Judgment that you make of things: for as I have not that Capacity
that you fancy to be in me; so if I had it, the Publick would not be one jot the better,
when I had sacrificed my quiet to it. For most Princes apply themselves more to
warlike Matters, than to the useful Arts of Peace; and in these I neither have any
knowledg, nor do I much desire it: They are generally more set on acquiring new
Kingdoms, right or wrong, than on governing those well that they have: and among
the Ministers of Princes, there are none that either are not so wise as not to need
any assistance, or at least that do not think themselves so wise, that they imagine
they need none; and if they do court any, it is only those for whom the Prince has
much personal Favour, whom by their Faunings and Flatteries they endeavour to
fix to their own Interests: and indeed Nature has so made us, that we all love to
be flattered, and to please our selves with our own Notions. The old Crow loves
his Young, and the Ape his Cubs. Now if in such a Court, made up of Persons that
envy all others, and do only admire themselves, one should but propose any thing
that he had either read in History, or observed in his Travels, the rest would think
that the Reputation of their Wisdom would sink, and that their Interests would be
much depressed, if they could not run it down: And if all other things failed, then
they would fly to this, That such or such things pleased our Ancestors, and it were
well for us if we could but match them. They would set up their Rest on such an
Answer, as a sufficient confutation of all that could be said; as if this were a great
Mischief, that any should be found wiser than his Ancestors: But tho they willingly
let go all the good Things that were among those of former Ages; yet if better things
are proposed, they cover themselves obstinately with this excuse, of reverence to
past Times. I have met with these proud, morose, and absurd Judgments of Things
in many places, particularly once in England. Was you ever there, said I? Yes, I was,
answered he, and staid some months there, not long after the Rebellion in the West
was suppressed, with a great slaughter of the poor People that were engaged in it.

I was then much obliged to that reverend Prelate Iohn Morton Archbishop of Canterbury, Cardinal, and Chancellor of England; a Man, said he, Peter (for Mr. More knows well what he was) that was not less venerable for his Wisdom and Vertues, than for the high Character he bore: He was of a middle stature, not broken with Age; his looks begot Reverence rather than Fear; his Conversation was easy, but serious and grave; he took pleasure sometimes to try the force of those that came as Suiters to him upon Business, by speaking sharply, tho decently to them, and by that he discovered their Spirit and presence of Mind; with which he was much delighted, when it did not grow up to an impudence, as bearing a great resemblance to his own temper; and he look'd on such Persons as the fittest Men for Affairs. He spoke both gracefully and weightily; he was eminently skilled in the Law, and had a vast Understanding, and a prodigious Memory: and those excellent Talents with which Nature had furnished him, were improved by Study and Experience. When I was in England, the King depended much on his Councils, and the Government seemed to be chiefly supported by him; for from his Youth up, he had been all along practised in Affairs; and having passed through many Traverses of Fortune, he had acquired to his great cost, a vast stock of Wisdom: which is not soon lost, when it is purchased so dear. One day when I was dining with him, there hapned to be at Table one of the English Lawyers, who took occasion to run out in a high commendation of the severe execution of Justice upon Thieves, who, as he said, were then hanged so fast, that there were sometimes 20 on one Gibbet; and upon that he said, he could not wonder enough how it came to pass, that since so few escaped, there were yet so many Thieves left who were still robbing in all places. Upon this, I who took the boldness to speak freely before the Cardinal, said, There was no reason to wonder at the Matter, since this way of punishing Thieves, was neither just in it Self, nor good for the Publick; for as the Severity was too great, so the Remedy was not effectual; simple Theft not being so great a Crime, that it ought to cost a Man his Life; and no Punishment how severe soever, being able to restrain those from robbing, who can find out no other way of livelihood; and in this, said I, not only you in England, but a great part of the World, imitate some ill Masters, that are readier to chastise their Scholars, than to teach them. There are dreadful Punishments enacted against Thieves, but it were much better to make such good Provisions, by which every Man might be put in a Method how to live, and so be preserved from the fatal necessity of stealing, and of dying for it. There has been care enough taken for that, said he, there are many Handycrafts, and there is Husbandry, by which they may make a shift to live, unless they have a greater mind to follow ill Courses. That will not serve your turn, said I, for many lose their Limbs in Civil or Forreign Wars, as lately in the Cornish Rebellion, and some time ago in your Wars with France, who being thus mutilated in the Service of their King and Country, can no more follow their old Trades, and are too old to learn new Ones: But since Wars are only accidental Things, and have Intervals, let us consider those Things that fall out every day. There is a great number of Noble Men among you, that live not only idle themselves as Drones, subsisting by other

Mens Labours, who are their Tenants, and whom they pare to the quick, and thereby raise their Revenues; this being the only instance of their Frugality, for in all other things they are Prodigal, even to the beggering of themselves: But besides this, they carry about with them a huge number of idle Fellows, who never learn'd any Art by which they may gain their Living; and these, as soon as either their Lord dies, or they themselves fall sick, are turned out of Doors; for your Lords are readier to feed idle People, than to take care of the sick; and often the Heir is not able to keep together so great a Family as his Predecessor did: Now when the Stomachs of those that are thus turned out of Doors, grow keen, they rob no less keenly; and what else can they do? for after that, by wandring about, they have worn out both their Health and their Cloaths, and are tattered, and look ghastly, Men of Quality will not entertain them, and poor Men dare not do it; knowing that one who has been bred up in Idleness and Pleasure, and who was used to walk about with his Sword and Buckler, despising all the Neighbourhood with an insolent Scorn, as far below him, is not fit for the Spade and Mattock: Nor will he serve a poor Man for so small a Hire, and in so low a Diet as he can afford. To this he answered, This sort of Men ought to be particularly cherished among us, for in them consists the Force of the Armies for which we may have occasion; since their Birth inspires them with a nobler sence of Honour, than is to be found among Tradesmen or Ploughmen. You may as well say, replied I, that you must cherish Thieves on the account of Wars, for you will never want the one, as long as you have the other; and as Robbers prove sometimes gallant Souldiers, so Souldiers prove often brave Robbers; so near an Alliance there is between those two sorts of Life. But this bad custom of keeping many Servants, that is so common among you, is not peculiar to this Nation. In France there is yet a more pestiferous sort of People, for the whole Country is full of Souldiers, that are still kept up in time of Peace; if such a state of a Nation can be called a Peace: and these are kept in Pay upon the same account that you plead for those Idle Retainers about Noble Men: this being a Maxim of those pretended Statesmen, That it is necessary for the Publick Safety, to have a good Body of Veteran Souldiers ever in readiness. They think raw Men are not to be depended on, and they sometimes seek Occasions for making War, that they may train up their Souldiers in the Art of cutting Throats, or as Salust observed, for keeping their Hands in use, that they may not grow dull by too long an intermission. But France has learn'd, to its cost, how dangerous it is to feed such Beasts. The Fate of the Romans, Carthaginians, and Syrians, and many other Nations, and Cities, which were both overturned, and quite ruined by those standing Armies, should make others wiser: and the folly of this Maxim of the French, appears plainly even from this, that their trained Souldiers find your raw Men prove often too hard for them; of which I will not say much, lest you may think I flatter the English Nation. Every day's Experience shews, that the Mechanicks in the Towns, or the Clowns in the Country, are not afraid of fighting with those idle Gentlemen, if they are not disabled by some Misfortune in their Body, or dispirited by extream Want. So that you need not fear, that those well-shaped and strong Men, (for it is only such that

Noblemen love to keep about them, till they spoil them) who now grow feeble with ease, and are softned with their effeminate manner of Life, would be less fit for Action if they were well bred and well employed. And it seems very unreasonable, that for the prospect of a War, which you need never have but when you please, you should maintain so many idle Men, as will always disturb you in time of Peace, which is ever to be more considered than War. But I do not think that this necessity of Stealing, arises only from hence, there is another Cause of it that is more peculiar to England. What is that? said the Cardinal: The encrease of Pasture, said I, by which your Sheep, that are naturally mild, and easily kept in order, may be said now to devour Men, and unpeople, not only Villages, but Towns: For where-ever it is found, that the Sheep of any Soil yield a softer and richer Wool than ordinary, there the Nobility and Gentry, and even those Holy Men the Abbots, not contented with the old Rents which their Farms yielded, nor thinking it enough that they living at their ease, do no good to the Publick, resolve to do it Hurt instead of Good. They stop the course of Agriculture, inclose Grounds, and destroy Houses and Towns, reserving only the Churches, that they may lodg their Sheep in them: And as if Forrests and Parks had swallowed up too little Soil, those worthy Country-Men turn the best inhabited Places into Solitudes; for when any unsatiable Wretch, who is a Plague to this Country, resolves to inclose many thousand Acres of Ground, the Owners, as well as Tenants, are turned out of their Possessions, by Tricks, or by main Force, or being wearied out with ill Usage, they are forced to sell them. So those miserable People, both Men and Women, Married, Unmarried, Old and Young, with their Poor, but numerous Families, (since Country-Business requires many Hands) are all forced to change their Seats, not knowing whither to go; and they must sell for almost nothing, their Houshold-stuff, which could not bring them much Mony, even tho they might stay for a Buyer: when that little Mony is at an end, for it will be soon spent; what is left for them to do, but either to steal, and so to be hanged, (God knows how justly) or to go about and beg? And if they do this, they are put in Prison as idle Vagabonds; whereas they would willingly work, but can find none that will hire them; for there is no more occasion for Country Labour, to which they have been bred, when there is no Arable Ground left. One Shepherd can look after a Flock, which will stock an extent of Ground that would require many hands, if it were to be ploughed and reaped. This likewise raises the price of Corn in many places. The price of Wool is also so risen, that the poor People who were wont to make Cloth, are no more able to buy it; and this likewise makes many of them idle: For since the increase of Pasture, God has punished the Avarice of the Owners, by a Rot among the Sheep, which has destroyed vast numbers of them, but had been more justly laid upon the Owners themselves. But suppose the Sheep should encrease ever so much, their Price is not like to fall; since tho they cannot be called a Monopoly, because they are not engrossed by one Person, yet they are in so few hands, and these are so rich, that as they are not prest to sell them sooner than they have a mind to it, so they never do it till they have raised the Price as high as is possible. And on the same account it is, that the other kinds of Cattel are so dear, and so much the more, because that many Villages being pulled down, and all Country-Labour being much neglected, there are none that look after the breeding of them. The Rich do not breed Cattel as they do Sheep, but buy them Lean, and at low Prices; and after they have fatned them on their Grounds, they sell them again at high rates. And I do not think that all the Inconveniences that this will produce, are yet observed; for as they sell the Cattle dear, so if they are consumed faster then the breeding Countries from which they are brought, can afford them; then the stock most decrease, and this must needs end in a great Scarcity; and by these means this your Island, that seemed as to this particular, the happiest in the World, will suffer much by the cursed Avarice of a few Persons; besides that, the rising of Corn makes all People lessen their Families as much as they can; and what can those who are dismissed by them do, but either Beg or Rob? And to this last, a Man of a great Mind is much sooner drawn than to the former. Luxury likewise breaks in apace upon you, to set forward your Poverty and Misery; there is an excessive Vanity in Apparel, and great Cost in Diet; and that not only in Noblemens Families, but even among Tradesmen, and among the Farmers themselves, and among all Ranks of Persons. You have also many infamous Houses, and besides those that are known, the Taverns and Alehouses are no better; add to these, Dice, Cards, Tables, Football, Tennis, and Coits, in which Mony runs fast away; and those that are initiated into them, must in conclusion betake themselves to robbing for a supply. Banish those Plagues, and give order that these who have dispeopled so much Soil, may either rebuild the Villages that they have pulled down, or let out their Grounds to such as will do it: Restrain those engrossings of the Rich, that are as bad almost as Monopolies; leave fewer Occasions to Idleness; let Agriculture be set up again, and the Manufacture of the Wooll be regulated, that so there may be Work found for these Companies of Idle People, whom want Forces to be Thieves, or who now being idle Vagabonds, or useless Servants, will certainly grow Thieves at last. If you do not find a Remedy to these Evils, it is a vain thing to boast of your Severity of punishing Theft; which tho it may have the appearance of Justice, yet in it self it is neither just nor convenient: for if you suffer your People to be ill Educated, and their Manners to be corrupted from their Infancy, and then punish them for those Crimes to which their first Education disposed them, what else is to be concluded from this, but that you first make Thieves, and then punish them?

[Two missing pages] . . . allow of it; upon the same Grounds, Laws may be made to allow of Adultery and Perjury in some Cases: for God having taken from us the Right of disposing, either of our own, or of other Peoples Lives, if it is pretended that the mutual Consent of Men in making Laws, allowing of Manslaughter in Cases in which God has given us no Example, frees People from the Obligation of the Divine Law, and so makes Murder a lawful Action; What is this, but to give a preference to Humane Laws before the Divine? And if this is once admitted, by the same Rule Men may in all other things put what Restrictions they please upon the Laws of God. If by the Mosaical Law, tho it was rough and severe, as being a Yoke laid on an obstinate and servile Nation, Men were only fined, and not put to death for Theft; we cannot imagine that in this new Law of Mercy, in which God treats us with the tenderness of a Father, he has given us a greater License to Cruelty, than he did to the Jews. Upon these Reasons it is, that I think the putting Thieves to death is not lawful; and it is plain and obvious that it is absurd, and of ill Consequence to the Common-Wealth, that a Thief and a Murderer should be equally punished: for if a Robber sees that his Danger is the same, if he is convicted of Theft, as if he were guilty of Murder, this will naturally set him on to kill the Person whom otherwise he would only have robbed, since if the Punishment is the same, there is more security, and less danger of discovery, when he that can best make it is put out of the way; so that the terrifying Thieves too much, provokes them to cruelty.

But as to the Question, What more convenient way of Punishment can be found? I think it is much easier to find out that, than to invent any thing that is worse; Why should we doubt but the way that was so long in use among the old Romans, who understood so well the Arts of Government, was very proper for their Punishment? they condemned such as they found guilty of great Crimes, to work their whole Lives in Quarries, or to dig in Mines with Chains about them. But the Method that I liked best, was that which I observed in my Travels in Persia, among the Polylerits, who are a considerable and well-governed People. They pay a yearly Tribute to the King of Persia; but in all other respects they are a free Nation, and governed by their own Laws. They lie far from the Sea, and are environed with Hills; and being contented with the Productions of their own Country, which is very fruitful, they have little commerce with any other Nation; and as they, according to the Genius of their Country, have no appetite of inlarging their Borders; so their Mountains, and the Pension that they pay to the Persian, secure them from all Invasions. Thus they have no Wars among them; they live rather conveniently than splendidly, and may be rather called a Happy Nation, than either Eminent or Famous; for I do not think that they are known so much as by Name to any but their next Neighbours. Those that are found guilty of Theft among them, are bound to make restitution to the Owner, and not as it is in other places, to the Prince, for they reckon that the Prince has no more right to the stollen Goods than the Thief; but if that which was stollen is no more in being, then the Goods of the Thieves are estimated, and Restitution being made out of them, the Remainder is given to their Wives, and Children: And they themselves are condemned to serve in the Publick Works, but are neither imprisoned, nor chained, unless there hapned to be some extraordinary Circumstances in their Crimes. They go about loose and free, working for the Publick: If they are Idle or backward to work, they are whipp'd; but if they work hard, they are well used and treated without any mark of Reproach, only the Lists of them are called always at Night, and then they are shut up, and they suffer no other uneasiness, but this of constant Labour; for as they work for the Publick, so they are well entertained out of the Publick Stock, which is done differently in different places: In some places, that which is bestowed on them, is raised by a charitable Contribution; and tho this way may seem uncertain, yet so merciful are the Inclinations of that People, that they are plentifully supplied by it; but in other places Publick Revenues are set aside for them; or there is a constant Tax of a Poll-mony raised for their Maintenance. In some places they are set to no Publick Work, but every privat Man that has occasion to hire Workmen, goes to the Market-places and hires them of the Publick, a little lower than he would do a Free-man: If they go lazily about their Task, he may quicken them with the Whip. By this means there is always some piece of Work or other to be done by them; and beside their Livelyhood, they earn somewhat still to the Publick. They wear all a peculiar Habit, of one certain colour, and their Hair is cropt a little above their Ears, and a little of one of their Ears is cut off. Their Friends are allowed to give them either Meat, Drink, or Clothes, so they are of their proper Colour; but it is Death, both to the Giver and Taker, if they give them Mony; nor is it less penal for any Free-man to take Mony from them, upon any account whatsoever: And it is also Death for any of these Slaves (so they are called) to handle Arms. Those of every Division of the Country, are distinguished by a peculiar Mark: And it is capital to lay that aside, and so it is also to go out of their Bounds, or to talk with a Slave of another Jurisdiction; and the very attempt of an escape, is no less penal than an escape it self; it is Death for any other Slave to be accessary to it: If a Free-man engages in it, he is condemned to slavery: Those that discover it are rewarded; if Free-men, in Mony; and if Slaves, with Liberty, together with a Pardon for being accessary to it; that so they may find their Account, rather in repenting of their accession to such a design, than in persisting in it.

These are their Laws and Rules in this Matter; in which both the Gentleness and the Advantages of them are very obvious; since by these Means, as Vices are destroyed, so Men are preserved; but are so treated, that they see the necessity of being good: and by the rest of their Life they make reparation for the Mischief they had formerly done. Nor is there any hazard of their falling back to their old Customs: And so little do Travellers apprehend Mischief from them, that they generally make use of them for Guides, from one Jurisdiction to another; for there is nothing left them by which they can rob, or be the better for it, since as they are disarmed, so the very having of Mony is a sufficient Conviction: and as they are certainly punished if discovered, so they cannot hope to escape: for their Habit being in all the parts of it different from what is commonly worn, they cannot fly away, unless they should go naked, and even then their crop'd Ear would betray them. The only danger to be feared from them, is their conspiring against the Government: but those of one Division and Neighbourhood can do nothing to any purpose, unless a general Conspiracy were laid amongst all the Slaves of the several Jurisdictions, which cannot be done, since they cannot meet or talk together; nor will any venture on a Design where the Concealment would be so dangerous, and the Discovery so profitable: and none of them is quite hopeless of recovering his Freedom, since by their Obedience and Patience, and by giving grounds to believe that they will change their manner of Life for the future, they may expect at last to obtain their Liberty: and some are every Year restored to it, upon the good Character that is given of them. When I had related all this, I added, That I did not see why such a Method might not be followed with more advantage, than could ever be expected from that severe Justice which the Counsellor magnified so much. To all this he answered, That it could never be so setled in England, without endangering the whole Nation by it; and as he said that, he shook his Head, and made some grimaces, and so held his peace; and all the Company seemed to be of his mind: only the Cardinal said, It is not easy to guess whether it would succeed well or ill, since no trial has been made of it: But if when the Sentence of Death were past upon a Thief, the Prince would reprieve him for a while, and make the Experiment upon him, denying him the privilege of a Sanctuary; then if it had a good effect upon him, it might take place; and if it succeeded not, the worst would be, to execute the Sentence on the condemned Persons at last. And I do not see, said he, why it would be either injust or inconvenient, or at all dangerous, to admit of such a delay: And I think the Vagabonds ought to be treated in the same manner, against whom tho we have made many Laws, yet we have not been able to gain our end by them all. When the Cardinal had said this, then they all fell to commend the Motion, tho they had despised it when it came from me; but they did more particularly commend that concerning the Vagabonds, because it had been added by him.

I do not know whether it be worth the while to tell what followed, for it was very ridiculous; but I shall venture at it, for as it is not forreign to this Matter, so some good use may be made of it. There was a Jester standing by, that counterfeited the Fool so naturally, that he seemed to be really one. The Jests at which he offered were so cold and dull, that we laughed more at him than at them; yet sometimes he said, as it were by chance, things that were not unpleasant; so as to justify the old Proverb, That he who throws the Dice often, will sometimes have a lucky Hit. When one of the Company had said, that I had taken care of the Thieves, and the Cardinal had taken care of the Vagabonds, so that there remained nothing but that some publick Provision might be made for the Poor, whom Sickness or Old Age had disabled from Labour: Leave that to me, said the Fool, and I shall take care of them; for there is no sort of People whose sight I abhor more, having been so often vexed with them, and with their sad Complaints; but as dolefully soeveras they have told their Tale to me, they could never prevail so far as to draw one Penny of Mony from me: for either I had no mind to give them any thing, or when I had a mind to it, I had nothing to give them: and they now know me so well, that they will not lose their labour on me, but let me pass without giving me any trouble, because they hope for nothing from me, no more in faith than if I were a Priest: But I would have a Law made, for sending all these Beggars to Monasteries, the Men to the Benedictines to be Lay-Brothers, and the Women to be Nuns. The Cardinal smiled, and approved of it in jest; but the rest liked it in earnest. There was a Divine present, who tho he was a grave morose Man, yet he was so pleased with this Reflection that was made on the Priests and the Monks, that he began to play with the Fool, and said to him, This will not deliver you from all Beggers, except you take care of us Friars. That is done already, answered the Fool, for the Cardinal has provided for you, by what he proposed for the restraining Vagabonds, and setting them to work, for I know no Vagabonds like you. This was well entertained by the whole Company, who looking at the Cardinal, perceived that he was not ill pleased at it; only the Friar himself was so bit, as may be easily imagined, and fell out into such a passion, that he could not forbear railing at the Fool, and called him Knave, Slanderer, Backbiter, and Son of Perdition, and cited some dreadful Threatnings out of the Scriptures against him. Now the Jester thought he was in his Element, and laid about him freely: he said, Good Friar be not angry, for it is written, In patience possess your Soul. The Friar answered, (for I shall give you his own words) I am not angry, you Hangman; at least I do not sin in it, for the Psalmist says, Be ye angry, and sin not. Upon this the Cardinal admonished him gently, and wished him to govern his Passions. No, my Lord, said he, I speak not but from a good Zeal, which I ought to have; for Holy Men have had a good Zeal, as it is said, The Zeal of thy House hath eaten me up; and we sing in our Church, that those who mock'd Elisha as he went up to the House of God, felt the Effects of his Zeal; which that Mocker, that Rogue, that Scoundrel, will perhaps feel. You do this perhaps with a good intention, said the Cardinal; but in my Opinion, it were wiser in you, not to say better for you, not to engage in so ridiculous a Contest with a Fool. No, my Lord, answered he, that were not wisely done; for Solomon, the wisest of Men, said, Answer a Fool according to his folly; which I now do, and shew him the Ditch into which he will fall, if he is not aware of it; for if the many Mockers of Elisha, who was but one bald Man, felt the Effect of his Zeal, What will become of one Mocker of so many Friars, among whom there are so many bald Men? We have likewise a Bull, by which all that jeer us are excommunicated. When the Cardinal saw that there was no end of this Matter, he made a sign to the Fool to withdraw, and turned the Discourse another way; and soon after he rose from the Table, and dismissing us, he went to hear Causes.

Thus, Mr. More, I have run out into a tedious Story, of the length of which I had been ashamed, if, as you earnestly begged it of me, I had not observed you to hearken to it, as if you had no mind to lose any part of it: I might have contracted it, but I resolved to give it you at large, that you might observe how those that had despised what I had proposed, no sooner perceived that the Cardinal did not dislike it, but they presently approved of it, and fawned so on him, and flattered him to such a degree, that they in good earnest applauded those things that he only liked in jest. And from hence you may gather, how little Courtiers would value either me or my Counsels.

To this I answered, You have done me a great kindness in this Relation; for as every thing has been related by you, both wisely and pleasantly, so you have made me imagine, that I was in my own Country, and grown young again, by recalling that good Cardinal into my thoughts, in whose Family I was bred from my Childhood: And tho you are upon other accounts very dear to me, yet you are the dearer, because you honour his Memory so much: but after all this I cannot change my Opinion, for I still think that if you could overcome that aversion which you have to the Courts

of Princes, you might do a great deal of good to Mankind, by the Advices that you
would give; and this is the chief Design that every good Man ought to propose to
himself in living: for whereas your Friend Plato thinks that then Nations will be
happy, when either Philosophers become Kings, or Kings become Philosophers.
No wonder if we are so far from that Happiness, if Philosophers will not think
it fit for them to assist Kings with their Councels. They are not so base minded,
said he, but that they would willingly do it: many of them have already done it
by their Books, if these that are in Power would hearken to their good Advices.
But Plato judged right, that except Kings themselves became Philosophers, it could
never be brought about, that they who from their Childhood are corrupted with
false Notions, should fall in intirely with the Counsels of Philosophers, which he
himself found to be true in the Person of Dionysius.

Do not you think, that if I were about any King, and were proposing good Laws
to him, and endeavouring to root out of him all the cursed Seeds of Evil that I
found in him, I should either be turned out of his Court, or at least be laughed
at for my pains? For Instance, What could I signify if I were about the King
of France, and were called into his Cabinet-Council, where several wise Men do in
his hearing propose many Expedients; as by what Arts and Practices Milan may
be kept; and Naples, that has so oft slip'd out of their hands, recovered; and
how the Venetians, and after them the rest of Italy may be subdued; and then
how Flanders, Brabant, and all Burgundy, and some other Kingdoms which he
has swallowed already in his Designs, may be added to his Empire. One proposes
a League with the Venetians, to be kept as long as he finds his account in it, and
that he ought to communicate Councils with them, and give them some share of
the Spoil, till his Success makes him need or fear them less, and then it will be
easily taken out of their Hands. Another proposes the hireing the Germans, and
the securing the Switzers by Pensions. Another proposes the gaining the Emperor
by Mony, which is Omnipotent with him. Another proposes a Peace with the King
of Arragon, and in order to the cementing it, the yielding up the King of Navar's
Pretensions. Another thinks the Prince of Castile is to be wrought on, by the hope
of an Alliance; and that some of his Courtiers are to be gained to the French Faction
by Pensions. The hardest Point of all is, what to do with England: a Treaty of Peace
is to be set on foot, and if their Alliance is not to be depended on, yet it is to be made
as firm as can be; and they are to be called Friends, but suspected as Enemies:
Therefore the Scots are to be kept in readiness, to be let loose upon England on
every occasion; and some banished Nobleman is to be supported underhand, (for
by the League it cannot be done avowedly) who has a pretension to the Crown, by
which means that suspected Prince may be kept in awe. Now when things are in so
great a Fermentation, and so many gallant Men are joining Councils, how to carry
on the War, if so mean a Man as I am should stand up, and wish them to change all
their Councils, to let Italy alone, and stay at home, since the Kingdom of France was
indeed greater than that it could be well governed by one Man; So that he ought
not to think of adding others to it: And if after this, I should propose to them the

Resolutions of the Achorians, a People that lie over against the Isle of Utopia to the South-east, who having long ago engaged in a War, that they might gain another Kingdom to their King, who had a Pretension to it by an old Alliance, by which it had descended to him; and having conquered it, when they found that the trouble of keeping it, was equal to that of gaining it; for the conquered People would be still apt to rebel, or be exposed to Forreign Invasions, so that they must always be in War, either for them, or against them; and that therefore they could never disband their Army: That in the mean time Taxes lay heavy on them, that Mony went out of the Kingdom; that their Blood was sacrificed to their King's Glory, and that they were nothing the better by it, even in time of Peace; their Manners being corrupted by a long War; Robbing and Murders abounding every where, and their Laws falling under contempt, because their King being distracted with the Cares of the Kingdom, was less able to apply his Mind to any one of them; when they saw there would be no end of those Evils, they by joint Councils made an humble Address to their King, desiring him to chuse which of the two Kingdoms he had the greatest mind to keep, since he could not hold both; for they were too great a People to be governed by a divided King, since no Man would willingly have a Groom that should be in common between him and another. Upon which the good Prince was forced to quit his new Kingdom to one of his Friends, (who was not long after dethroned) and to be contented with his old One. To all this I would add, that after all those Warlike Attempts, and the vast Confusions, with the Consumptions both of Treasure and of People, that must follow them; perhaps upon some Misfortune, they might be forced to throw up all at last; therefore it seemed much more eligible that the King should improve his ancient Kingdom all he could, and make it flourish as much as was possible; that he should love his People, and be beloved of them; that he should live among them, and govern them gently; and that he should let other Kingdoms alone, since that which had fallen to his share was big enough, if not too big for him. Pray how do you think would such a Speech as this be heard? I confess, said I, I think not very well.

But what said he, if I should sort with another kind of Ministers, whose chief Contrivances and Consultations were, by what Art Treasure might be heaped up? Where one proposes, the crying up of Mony, when the King had a great Debt on him, and the crying it down as much when his Revenues were to come in, that so he might both pay much with a little, and in a little receive a great deal: Another proposes a pretence of a War, that so Money might be raised in order to the carrying it on, and that a Peace might be concluded as soon as that was done; and this was to be made up with such appearances of Religion as might work on the People, and make them impute it to the piety of their Prince, and to his tenderness of the Lives of his Subjects. A third offers some old musty Laws, that have been antiquated by a long disuse; and which, as they had been forgotten by all the Subjects, so they had been also broken by them; and that the levying of the Penalties of these Laws, as it would bring in a vast Treasure, so there might be a very good Pretence for it, since it would look like the executing of Law, and the doing of Justice. A fourth proposes the prohibiting of many things under severe Penalties, especially such things as were against the Interest of the People, and then the dispensing with these Prohibitions upon great Compositions, to those who might make Advantages by breaking them. This would serve two ends, both of them acceptable to many; for as those whose Avarice led them to transgress, would be severely fined; so the selling Licences dear, would look as if a Prince were tender of his People, and would not easily, or at low Rates, dispense with any thing that might be against the Publick Good. Another proposes, that the Judges must be made sure, that they may declare always in favor of the Prerogative, that they must be often sent for to Court, that the King may hear them argue those Points in which he is concerned; since that how unjust soever any of his Pretensions may be, yet still some one or other of them, either out of contradiction to others, or the pride of singularity, or that they may make their Court, would find out some Pretence or other to give the King a fair colour to carry the Point: For if the Judges but differ in Opinion, the clearest thing in the World is made by that means disputable, and Truth being once brought in question, the King upon that may take advantage to expound the Law for his own profit: the Judges that stand out will be brought over, either out of fear or modesty; and they being thus gained, all of them may be sent to the Bench to give Sentence boldly, as the King would have it: for fair Pretences will never be wanting when Sentence is to be given in the Prince's Favor: it will either be said, that Equity lies of his side, or some words in the Law will be found sounding that way, or some forced sence will be put on them; and when all other things fail, the King's undoubted Prerogative will be pretended, as that which is above all Law; and to which a Religious Judg ought to have a special regard. Thus all consent to that Maxim of Grassus, That a Prince cannot have Treasure enough, since he must maintain his Armies out of it: that a King, even tho he would, can do nothing unjustly; that all Property is in him, not excepting the very Persons of his Subjects: And that no Man has any other Property, but that which the King out of his goodness thinks fit to leave him: and they think it is the Prince's Interest, that there be as little of this left as may be, as if it were his advantage that his People should have neither Riches nor Liberty; since these things make them less easy and tame to a cruel and injust Government; whereas Necessity and Poverty blunts them, makes them patient, and bears them down, and breaks that height of Spirit, that might otherwise dispose them to rebel. Now what if after all these Propositions were made, I should rise up and assert, That such Councels were both unbecoming a King, and mischievous to him: and that not only his Honor but his Safety consisted more in his Peoples Wealth, than in his own; if I should shew, that they choose a King for their own sake, and not for his; that by his care and endeavors they may be both easy and safe: and that therefore a Prince ought to take more care of his Peoples Happiness, than of his own, as a Shepherd is to take more care of his Flock than of himself. It is also certain, that they are much mistaken, that think the Poverty of a Nation is a means of the Publick Safety: Who quarrel more than Beggers do? who does more earnestly long for a change, than he that is uneasy in his present Circumstances? and who run in to create Confusions with so desperate a boldness, as those who having nothing to lose, hope to gain by them? If a King should fall under so much contempt or envy, that he could not keep his Subjects in their Duty, but by Oppression and ill Usage, and by impoverishing them, it were certainly better for him to quit his Kingdom, than to retain it by such Methods, by which tho he keeps the Name of Authority, yet he loses the Majesty due to it. Nor is it so becoming the Dignity of a King to reign over Beggars, as to reign over rich and happy Subjects. And therefore Fabritius, that was a Man of a noble and exalted Temper, said, He would rather govern rich Men, than be rich himself; and for one Man to abound in Wealth and Pleasure, when all about him are mourning and groaning, is to be a Goaler and not a King. He is an unskilful Physician, that cannot cure a Disease, but by casting his Patient into another: So he that can find no other way for correcting the Errors of his People, but by taking from them the Conveniences of Life, shews that he knows not what it is to govern a free Nation. He himself ought rather to shake off his Sloth, or to lay down his Pride; for the Contempt or Hatred that his People have for him, takes its rise from the Vices in himself. Let him live upon what belongs to himself, without wronging others, and accommodate his Expence to his Revenue. Let him punish Crimes, and by his wise Conduct let him endeavour to prevent them, rather than be severe when he has suffered them to be too common: Let him not rashly revive Laws that are abbrogated by disuse, especially if they have been long forgotten, and never wanted. And let him never take any Penalty for the breach of them, to which a Judg would not give way in a private Man, but would look on him as a crafty and unjust Person for pretending to it. To these things I would add, that Law among the Macarians, that lie not far from Utopia, by which their King, in the day on which he begins to reign, is tied by an Oath confirmed by solemn Sacrifices, never to have at once above a thousand Pounds of Gold in his Treasures, or so much Silver as is equal to that in value. This Law, as they say, was made by an excellent King, who had more regard to the Riches of his Country, than to his own Wealth; and so provided against the heaping up of so much Treasure, as might impoverish the People: he thought that moderate Sum might be sufficient for any Accident; if either the King had occasion for it against Rebels, or the Kingdom against the Invasion of an Enemy, but that it was not enough to encourage a Prince to invade other Mens Rights, which was the chief cause of his making that Law. He also thought, that it was a good Provision for a free circulation of Mony, that is necessary for the course of Commerce and Exchange: And when a King must distribute all these extraordinary Accessions that encrease Treasure beyond the due pitch, it makes him less disposed to oppress his Subjects. Such a King as this is, will be the terror of ill Men, and will be beloved of all good Men.

If, I say, I should talk of these or such like things, to Men that had taken their biass another way, how deaf would they be to it all? No doubt, very deaf, answered I; and no wonder, for one is never to offer at Propositions or Advices, that he is certain will not be entertained. Discourses so much out of the road could not avail any thing, nor have any effect on Men, whose Minds were prepossessed with different Sentiments. This Philosophical way of Speculation, is not unpleasant among Friends in a free Converrsation; but there is no room for it in the Courts of Princes, where great Affairs are carried on by Authority. That is what I was saying, replied he, that there is no room for Philosophy in the Courts of Princes. Yes, there is, said I, but not for this Speculative Philosophy, that makes every thing to be alike fitting at all times: But there is another Philosophy that is more pliable, that knows its proper Scene, and accommodates it self to it; and that teaches a Man to act that part which has fallen to his share, fitly and decently. If when one of Plautus's Comedies is upon the Stage, and a Company of Servants are acting their parts, you should come out in the Garb of a Philosopher, and repeat out of Octavia, a Discourse of Seneca's to Nero, had it not been better for you to have said nothing, than by mixing things of such different Natures, to have made such an impertinent Tragi-Comedy? for you spoil and corrupt the Play that is in hand, when you mix with it things disagreeing to it, even tho they were better than it is: therefore go through with the Play that is acting, the best you can; and do not confound it, because another that is pleasanter comes into your thoughts. It is even so in a Common-Wealth, and in the Councils of Princes; if ill Opinions cannot be quite rooted out; and if you cannot cure some received Vices according to your wishes, you must not therefore abandon the Common-Wealth; or forsake the Ship in a Storm, because you cannot command the Winds; nor ought you to assault People with Discourses that are out of their Road, when you see their Notions are such that you can make no impression on them: but you ought to cast about, and as far as you can to manage things dextrously, that so if you cannot make Matters go well, they may be as little ill as is possible; for except all Men were good, all things cannot go well; which I do not hope to see in a great while. By this, answered he, all that I shall do shall be to preserve my self from being mad, while I endeavour to cure the madness of other People: for if I will speak truth, I must say such things as I was formerly saying; and for lying, whether a Philosopher can do it or not, I cannot tell; I am sure I cannot do it. But tho these Discourses may be uneasy and ungrateful to them, I do not see why they should seem foolish or extravagant: indeed if I should either propose such things as Plato has contrived in his Common-Wealth, or as the Utopians practise in theirs, tho they might seem better, as certainly they are, yet they are so quite different from our Establishment, which is founded on Property, there being no such thing among them, that I could not expect that it should have any effect on them: But such Discourses as mine, that only call past Evils to mind, and give warning of what may follow, have nothing in them that is so absurd, that they may not be used at any time; for they can only be unpleasant to those who are resolved to run headlong the contrary way: and if we must let alone every thing as absurd or extravagant, which by reason of the wicked Lives of many may seem uncouth, we must, even among Christians, give over pressing the greatest part of those things that Christ hath taught us: tho he has commanded us not to conceal them, but to proclaim on the House-tops that which he taught in secret. The greatest parts of his Precepts are more disagreeing to the Lives of the Men of this Age, than any part of my Discourse has been: But the Preachers seem to have learn'd that craft to which you advise me; for they observing that the World would not willingly sute their Lives to the Rules that Christ has given, have fitted his Doctrine, as if it had been a leaden Rule, to their Lives; that so some way or other they might agree with one another. But I see no other effect of this compliance, except it be that Men become more secure in their wickedness by it. And this is all the success that I can have in a Court; for I must always differ from the rest, and then I will signify nothing; or if I agree with them, then I will only help forward their madness. I do not comprehend what you mean by your casting about, or by the bending and handling things so dextrously, that if they go not well, they may go as little ill as may be: for in Courts they will not bear with a Man's holding his peace, or conniving at them: a Man must bare-facedly approve of the worst Councils, and consent to the blackest Designs: So that one would pass for a Spy, or possibly for a Traitor, that did but coldly approve of such wicked Practices: And when a Man is engaged in such a Society, he will be so far from being able to mend Matters by his casting about, as you call it, that he will find no occasions of doing any good: the ill Company will sooner corrupt him, than be the better for him: or if notwithstanding all their ill Company, he remains still entire and innocent, yet their Follies and Knavery will be imputed to him; and by mixing Councils with them, he must bear his share of all the blame that belongs wholly to others.

It was no ill Simily, by which Plato set forth the unreasonableness of a Philosopher›s medling with Government: If one, says he, shall see a great company run out into the Rain every day, and delight to be wet in it; and if he knows that it will be to no purpose for him to go and perswade them to come into their Houses, and avoid the Rain; so that all that can be expected from his going to speak to them, will be, that he shall be wet with them; when it is so, he does best to keep within Doors, and preserve himself, since he cannot prevail enough to correct other Peoples Folly.

Tho to speak plainly what is my Heart, I must freely own to you, that as long as there is any Property, and while Mony is the Standard of all other things, I cannot think that a Nation can be governed either Justly or Happily: Not Justly, because the best things will fall to the share of the worst of Men: Nor Happily, because all things will be divided among a few, (and even these are not in all respects happy) the rest being left to be absolutely miserable. Therefore when I reflect on the wise and good Constitutions of the Utopians, among whom all things are so well governed, and with so few Laws; and among whom as Vertue hath its due reward, yet there is such an equality, that every Man lives in plenty; and when I compare with them so many other Nations that are still making new Laws, and yet can never bring their Constitution to a right Regulation, among whom tho every one has his Property; yet all the Laws that they can invent, cannot prevail so far, that Men can either obtain or preserve it, or be certainly able to distinguish what is their own, from what is another Man›s; of which the many Law Suits that every day break out, and depend without any end, give too plain a demonstration: When, I say, I ballance all these things in my thoughts, I grow more favourable to Plato, and do not wonder that he resolved, not to make any Laws for such as would not submit to a community of all things: For so wise a Man as he was, could not but foresee that the setting all upon the Level, was the only way to make a Nation happy; which cannot be obtained so long as there is Property: for when every Man draws to himself all that he can compass, by one Title or another, it must needs follow, that how plentiful soever a Nation may be, yet a few dividing the Wealth of it among themselves, the rest must fall under Poverty. So that there will be two sorts of People among them, that deserve that their Fortunes should be interchanged; the former being useless, but wicked and ravenous; and the latter, who by their constant industry serve the Publick more than themselves, being sincere and modest Men. From whence I am perswaded, that till Property is taken away, there can be no equitable or just distribution made of things, nor can the World be happily governed: for as long as that is maintained, the greatest and the far best part of Mankind, will be still oppressed with a load of Cares and Anxieties. I confess, without the taking of it quite away, those Pressures that lie on a great part of Mankind, may be made lighter; but they can never be quite removed. For if Laws were made, determining at how great an extent in Soil, and at how much Mony every Man must stop, and limiting the Prince that he may not grow too great, and restraining the People that they may not become too insolent, and that none might factiously aspire to publick Employments; and that they might neither be sold, nor made burdensome by a great expence; since otherwise those that serve in them, will be tempted to reimburse themselves by Cheats and Violence, and it will become necessary to find out rich Men for undergoing those Employments for which wise Men ought rather to be sought out; these Laws, I say, may have such Effects, as good Diet and Care may have on a Sick Man, whose recovery is desperate: they may allay and mitigate the Disease, but it can never be quite healed, nor the Body Politick be brought again to a good Habit, as long as Property remains; and it will fall out as in a complication of Diseases, that by applying a Remedy to one Sore, you will provoke another; and that which removes one ill Symptom, produces others, while the strengthning of one part of the Body weakens the rest. On the contrary, answered I, it seems to me that Men cannot live conveniently, where all things are common: How can there be any Plenty, where every Man will excuse himself from Labour? For as the hope of Gain doth not excite him, so the confidence that he has in other Mens Industry, may make him slothful: And if People come to be pinched with Want, and yet cannot dispose of any thing as their own; what can follow upon this, but perpetual Sedition and Bloodshed, especially when the Reverence and Authority due to Magistrates falls to the Ground? For I cannot imagine how that can be kept up among those that are in all things equal to one another. I do not wonder, said he, that it appears so to you, since you have no Notion, or at least no right one, of such a Constitution: But if you had been in Utopia with me, and had seen their Laws and Rules as I did, for the space of five Years, in which I lived among them;

and during which time I was so delighted with them, that indeed I would never have left them, if it had not been to make the discovery of that new World to the Europeans; you would then confess that you had never seen a People so well constituted as they are. You will not easily perswade me, said Peter, that any Nation in that New World, is better governed than those among us are. For as our Understandings are not worse than theirs, so our Government, if I mistake not, being ancienter, a long practice has helped us to find out many Conveniences of Life: And some happy Chances have discovered other things to us, which no Man›s Understanding could ever have invented. As for the Antiquity, either of their Government, or of ours, said he, you cannot pass a true Judgment of it, unless you had read their Histories; for if they are to be believed, they had Towns among them, before these parts were so much as inhabited: And as for these Discoveries, that have been either hit on by chance, or made by ingenious Men, these might have hapned there as well as here. I do not deny but we are more ingenious than they are, but they exceed us much in Industry and Application: They knew little concerning us, before our arrival among them; they call us all by a general Name of the Nations that lie beyond the Equinoctial Line; for their Chronicle mentions a Shipwrack that was made on their Coast 1200 Years ago; and that some Romans and Egyptians that were in the Ship, getting safe a Shore, spent the rest of their days amongst them; and such was their Ingenuity, that from this single Opportunity, they drew the advantage of Learning from those unlook›d for Guests, all the useful Arts that were then among the Romans, which those Shipwrack›d Men knew: And by the Hints that they gave them, they themselves found out even some of those Arts which they could not fully explain to them; so happily did they improve that Accident, of having some of our People cast upon their shore: But if any such Accident have at any time brought any from thence into Europe, we have been so far from improving it, that we do not so much as remember it; as in after Times perhaps it will be forgot by our People that I was ever there. For tho they from one such Accident, made themselves Masters of all the good Inventions that were among us; yet I believe it would be long before we would learn or put in practice any of the good Institutions that are among them: And this is the true Cause of their being better governed, and living happier than we do, tho we come not short of them in point of Understanding, or outward Advantages. Upon this I said to him, I do earnestly beg of you, that you would describe that Island very particularly to us. Be not too short in it, but set out in order all things relating to their Soil, their Rivers, their Towns, their People, their Manners, Constitution, Laws, and in a word, all that you imagine we desire to know: and you may well imagine that we desire to know every thing concerning them, of which we are hitherto ignorant. I will do it very willingly, said he, for I have digested the whole Matter carefully; but it will take up some time. Let us go then, said I, first and dine, and then we shall have leasure enough. Be it so, said he. So we went in and dined, and after Dinner we came back, and sat down in the same place. I ordered my Servants to take care that none might come and interrupt us: and both Peter and I desired Raphael to be as good as his word: So when he saw that we were very intent upon it, he paused a little to recollect himself, and began in this manner.

THE SECOND BOOK

The Island of Utopia, in the middle of it, where it is broadest, is 200 miles broad, and holds almost at the same breadth over a great part of it; but it grows narrower towards both ends. Its Figure is not unlike a Crescent: between its Horns, the Sea comes in eleven miles broad, and spreads it self into a great Bay, which is environed with Land to the compass of about 500 miles, and is well secured from Winds: There is no great Current in the Bay, and the whole Coast is, as it were, one continued Harbour, which gives all that live in the Island great convenience for mutual Commerce: but the entry into the Bay, what by Rocks on one hand, and Shallows on the other, is very dangerous. In the middle of it there is one single Rock which appears above Water, and so is not dangerous; on the top of it there is a Tower built, in which a Garrison is kept. The other Rocks lie under Water, and are very dangerous. The Channel is known only to the Natives, so that if any Stranger should enter into the Bay, without one of their Pilates, he would run a great danger of Shipwrack: for even they themselves could not pass it safe, if some marks that are on their Coast did not direct their way; and if these should be but a little shifted, any Fleet that might come against them, how great soever it were, would be certainly lost. On the other side of the Island, there are likewise many Harbours; and the Coast is so fortified, both by Nature and Art, that a small number of Men can hinder the descent of a great Army. But they report (and there remains good marks of it to make it credible) that this was no Island at first, but a part of the Continent. Utopus that conquered it (whose Name it still carries, for Abraxa was its first Name) and brought the rude and uncivilized Inhabitants into such a good Government, and to that measure of Politeness, that they do now far excel all the rest of mankind; having soon subdued them, he designed to separate them from the Continent, and and to bring the Sea quite about them, and in order to that he made a deep Channel to be digged fifteen miles long: He not only forced the Inhabitants to work at it, but likewise his own Souldiers, that the Natives might not think he treated them like Slaves; and having set vast numbers of Men to work, he brought it to a speedy conclusion beyond all Mens expectations: By this their Neighbours, who laughed at the folly of the Undertaking at first, were struck with admiration and terror, when they saw it brought to perfection. There are 54 Cities in the Island, all large and well built: the Manners, Customs, and Laws of all their Cities are the same, and they are all contrived as near in the same manner, as the Ground on which they stand will allow: The nearest lie at least 24 miles distant from one another, and the most remote are not so far distant, but that a Man can go on foot in one day from it, to that which lies next it. Every City sends three of their wisest Senators once a Year to Amaurot, for consulting about their common Concerns; for that is the cheif Town of the Island, being situated near the Center of it, so that it is the most convenient place for their Assemblies.

Every City has so much Ground set off for its Jurisdiction, that there is twenty miles of Soil round it, assigned to it: and where the Towns lie wider, they have much more Ground: no Town desires to enlarge their Bounds, for they consider themselves rather as Tenants than Landlords of their Soil. They have built over all the Country, Farmhouses for Husbandmen, which are well contrived, and are furnished with all things necessary for Countey-labour. Inhabitants are sent by turns from the Cities to dwell in them; no Country-family has fewer than fourty Men and Women in it, besides two Slaves. There is a Master and a Mistress set over every Family; and over thirty Families there is a Magistrate setled. Every Year twenty of this Family come back to the Town, after they have stayed out two Years in the Country: and in their room there are other twenty sent from the Town, that they may learn Country-work, from those that have been already one Year in the Country, which they must teach those that come to them the next Year from the Town. By this means such as dwell in those Country-Farms, are never ignorant of Agriculture, and so commit no Errors in it, which might otherwise be fatal to them, and bring them under a scarcity of corn. But tho there is every Year such a shifting of the Husbandmen, that none may be forced against his mind to follow that hard course of life too long; yet many among them take such pleasure in it, that they desire leave to continue many Years in it. These Husbandmen labour the Ground, breed Cattel, hew Wood, and convey it to the Towns, either by Land or Water, as is most convenient. They breed an infinite multitude of Chickens in a very curious manner: for the Hens do not sit and hatch them, but they lay vast numbers of Eggs in a gentle and equal heat, in which they are hatched; and they are no sooner out of the Shell, and able to stir about, but they seem to consider those that feed them as their Mothers, and follow them as other Chickens do the Hen that hatched them. They breed very few Horses, but those they have, are full of Mettle, and are kept only for exercising their Youth in the Art of sitting and riding of them; for they do not put them to any Work, either of Plowing or Carriage, in which they imploy Oxen; for tho Horses are stronger, yet they find Oxen can hold out longer; and as they are not subject to so many Diseases, so they are kept upon a less charge, and with less trouble: And when they are so worn out, that they are no more fit for labour, they are good Meat at last. They sow no Corn, but that which is to be their Bread; for they drink either Wine, Cider, or Perry, and often Water, sometimes pure, and sometimes boiled with Hony or Liquorish, with which they abound: and tho they know exactly well how much Corn will serve every Town, and all that tract of Country which belongs to it, yet they sow much more, and breed more Cattel than are necessary for their consumption: and they give that overplus of which they make no use to their Neighbours. When they want any thing in the Country which it does not produce, they fetch that from the Town, without carrying any thing in exchange for it: and the Magistrates of the Town take care to see it given them: for they meet generally in the Town once a month, upon a Festival-Day. When the time of Harvest comes, the Magistrates in the Country send to those in the Towns, and let them know how many hands they will need for reaping the

Harvest; and the number they call for being sent to them, they commonly dispatch it all in one day.

Of their Towns, particularly of Amaurot

He that knows one of their Towns, knows them all, they are so like one another, except where the scituation makes some difference. I shall therefore describe one of them, and it is no matter which; but none is so proper as Amaurot: for as none is more eminent, all the rest yielding in precedence to this, because it is the Seat of their Supream Council; so there was none of them better known to me, I having lived five Years altogether in it.

It lies upon the side of a Hill, or rather a rising Ground: its Figure is almost square, for from the one side of it, which shoots up almost to the top of the Hill, it runs down in a descent for two miles to the River Anider; but it is a little broader the other way that runs along by the Bank of that River. The Anider rises about 80 miles above Amaurot, in a small Spring at first; but other Brooks falling into it, of which two are more considerable, as it runs by Amaurot, it is grown half a mile broad, but it still grows larger and larger, till after sixty miles course below, it is buried in the Ocean. Between the Town and the Sea, and for some miles above the Town, it ebbs and flows every six hours, with a strong Current. The Tide comes up for about thirty miles so full, that there is nothing but Salt-water in the River, the fresh Water being driven back with its force; and above that, for some miles, the Water is brackish, but a little higher, as it runs by the Town, it is quite fresh; and when the Tide ebbs, it continues fresh all along to the Sea. There is a Bridg cast over the River, not of Timber, but of fair Stone, consisting of many stately Arches; it lies at that part of the Town which is farthest from the Sea, so that Ships without any hindrance lie all along the side of the Town. There is likewise another River that runs by it, which tho it is not great, yet it runs pleasantly, for it rises out of the same Hill on which the Town stands, and so runs down throw it, and falls into the Anider. The Inhabitants have fortified the Fountain-head of this River, which springs a little without the Towns; that so if they should happen to be besieged, the Enemy might not be able to stop or divert the course of the Water, nor poison it; from thence it is carried in earthen Pipes to the lower Streets: and for those places of the Town to which the Water of that small River cannot be conveyed, they have great Cisterns for receiving the Rain-water, which supplies the want of the other. The Town is compassed with a high and thick Wall, in which there are many Towers and Forts; there is also a broad and deep dry Ditch, set thick with Thorns, cast round three sides of the Town, and the River is instead of a Ditch on the fourth side. The Streets are made very convenient for all Carriage, and are well sheltred from the Winds. Their Buildings are good, and are so uniform, that a whole side of a Street looks like one House. The Streets are twenty foot broad; there lie Gardens behind all their Houses; these are large, but enclosed with Buildings, that on all Hands face the Streets; so that every House has both a Door to the Street, and a back Door to the Garden: their Doors have all two Leaves, which as they are easily opened, so they shut of their own accord; and there being no Property among them, every Man may freely enter into any House whatsoever. At every ten Years ends, they shift their Houses by Lots. They cultivate their Gardens with great care, so that they have both Vines, Fruits, Herbs, and Flowers in them; and all is so well ordered, and so finely kept, that I never saw Gardens any where that were both so fruitful and so beautiful as theirs are. And this humor of ordering their Gardens so well, is not only kept up by the pleasure they find in it, but also by an emulation between the Inhabitants of the several Streets, who vie with one another in this Matter; and there is indeed nothing belonging to the whole Town, that is both more useful, and more pleasant. So that he who founded the Town, seems to have taken care of nothing more than of their Gardens; for they say, the whole Scheme of the Town was designed at first by Utopus, but he left all that belonged to the Ornament and Improvement of it, to be added by those that should come after him, that being too much for one Man to bring to perfection. Their Records, that contain the History of their Town and State, are preserved with an exact care, and run backwards 1760 Years. From these it appears, that their Houses were at first low and mean, like Cottages made of any sort of Timber, and were built with mud Walls, and thatch'd with Straw: but now their Houses are three Stories high, the Fronts of them are faced either with Stone, Plaistering, or Brick; and between the facings of their Walls, they throw in their Rubbish; their Roofs are flat, and on them they lay a sort of Plaister which costs very little, and yet is so tempered, that as it is not apt to take Fire, so it resists the Weather more than Lead does. They have abundance of Glass among them, with which they glaze their Windows: they use also in their Windows, a thin linnen Cloth, that is so oiled or gummed, that by that means it both lets in the Light more freely to them, and keeps out the Wind the better.

Of their Magistrates

Thirty Families chuse every Year a Magistrate, who was called anciently the Syphogrant, but is now called the Philarch: and over every ten Syphogrants, with the Families subject to them, there is another Magistrate, who was anciently called the Tranibore, but of late the Archphilarch. All the Syphogrants, who are in number 200, chuse the Prince out of a List of four, whom the People of the four Divisions of the City name to them; but they take an Oath before they proceed to an Election, that they will chuse him whom they think meetest for the Office: They give their Voices secretly, so that it is not known for whom every one gives his Suffrage. The Prince is for Life, unless he is removed upon suspicion of some design to enslave the People. The Tranibors are new chosen every Year, but yet they are for the most part still continued: All their other Magistrates are only Annual. The Tranibors meet every third day, and oftner if need be, and consult with the Prince, either concerning the Affairs of the State in general, or such private Differences as may arise sometimes among the People; tho that falls out but seldom. There are always two Syphogrants called into the Council-Chamber, and these are changed every day. It is a fundamental Rule of their Government, that no Conclusion can be made in any thing that relates to the Publick, till it has been first debated three several days in their Council. It is Death for any to meet and consult concerning the State, unless it be either in their ordinary Council, or in the Assembly of the whole Body of the People.

These things have been so provided among them, that the Prince and the Tranibors may not conspire together to change the Government, and enslave the People; and therefore when any thing of great importance is set on foot, it is sent to the Syphogrants; who after they have communicated it with the Families that belong to their Divisions, and have considered it among themselves, make report to the Senate; and upon great Occasions, the Matter is referred to the Council of the whole Island. One Rule observed in their Council, is, never to debate a thing on the same day in which is first proposed; for that is always referred to the next meeting, that so Men may not rashly, and in the heat of Discourse, engage themselves too soon, which may biass them so much, that instead of considering the Good of the Publick, they will rather study to maintain their own Notions; and by a perverse and preposterous sort of shame, hazard their Country, rather than endanger their own Reputation, or venture the being suspected to have wanted foresight in the Expedients that they proposed at first. And therefore to prevent this, they take care that they may rather be deliberate, than sudden in their Motions.

Of their Trades, and manner of Life

Agriculture is that which is so universally understood among them all, that no Person, either Man or Woman, is ignorant of it; from their Childhood they are instructed in it, partly by what they learn at School, and partly by practice, they being led out often into the Fields, about the Town, where they not only see others at work, but are likewise exercised in it themselves. Besides Agriculture, which is so common to them all, every Man has some peculiar Trade to which he applies himself, such as the Manufacture of Wool, or Flax, Masonry, Smiths Work, or Carpenters Work; for there is no other sort of Trade that is in great esteem among them. All the Island over, they wear the same sort of Clothes without any other distinction, except that which is necessary for marking the difference between the two Sexes, and the married and unmarried. The fashion never alters; and as it is not ungrateful nor uneasy, so it is fitted for their Climate, and calculated both for their Summers and Winters. Every Family makes their own Clothes; but all among them, Women as well as Men, learn one or other of the Trades formerly mentioned. Women, for the most part, deal in Wool and Flax, which sute better with their feebleness, leaving the other ruder Trades to the Men. Generally the same Trade passes down from Father to Son, Inclination often following Descent: but if any Man's Genius lies another way, he is by Adoption translated into a Family that deals in the Trade to which he is inclined: And when that is to be done, care is taken, not only by his Father, but by the Magistrate, that he may be put to a discreet and good Man. And if after a Man has learn'd one Trade, he desires to acquire another, that is also allowed, and is managed in the same manner as the former. When he has learn'd both, he follows that which he likes best, unless the Publick has more occasion for the other.

The chief, and almost the only Business of the Syphogrants, is to take care that no Man may live idle, but that every one may follow his Trade diligently: yet they do not wear themselves out with perpetual Toil, from Morning to Night, as if they were Beasts of Burden; which as it is indeed a heavy slavery, so it is the common course of Life of all Tradesmen every where, except among the Utopians: But they dividing the Day and Night into twenty four hours, appoint six of these for Work, three of them are before Dinner; and after that they dine, and interrupt their Labour for two hours, and then they go to work again for other three hours; and after that they sup, and at eight a Clock, counting from Noon, they go to bed and sleep eight hours: and for their other hours, besides those of Work, and those that go for eating and sleeping, they are left to every Man's discretion; yet they are not to abuse that Interval to Luxury and Idleness, but must imploy it in some proper Exercise according to their various Inclinations, which is for the most part Reading. It is ordinary to have Publick Lectures every Morning before day-break; to which none are obliged to go, but those that are mark'd out for Literature; yet a great many, both Men and Women of all Ranks, go to hear Lectures of one sort or another, according to the variety of their Inclinations. But if others, that are not made for Contemplation, chuse rather to imploy themselves at that time in their Trade, as many of them do, they are not hindred, but are commended rather, as Men that take care to serve their Country. After Supper, they spend an hour in some Diversion: In Summer it is in their Gardens, and in Winter it is in the Halls where they eat; and thy entertain themselves in them, either with Musick or Discourse. They do not so much as know Dice, or suchlike foolish and mischievous Games: They have two sorts of Games not unlike our . . . [2 missing pages] . . . profitable Trades; and if all that number that languishes out their Life in sloth and idleness, of whom every one consumes as much as any two of the Men that are at work do, were forced to labour, you may easily imagine that a small proportion of time would serve for doing all that is either necessary, profitable, or pleasant to Mankind, pleasure being still kept within its due bounds: Which appears very plainly in Utopia, for there, in a great City, and in all the Territory that lies round it, you can scarce find five hundred, either Men or Women, that by their Age and Strength, are capable of Labour, that are not engaged in it; even the Syphogrants themselves, tho the Law excuses them, yet do not excuse themselves, that so by their Examples they may excite the industry of the rest of the People; the like exemption is allowed to those, who being recommended to the People by the Priests, are by the secret Suffrages of the Syphogrants, priviledged from Labour, that they may apply themselves wholly to study; and if any of these falls short of those Hopes that he seemed to give at first, he is obliged to go to work. And sometimes a Mechanick, that does so imploy his leisure hours, that he makes a considerable advancement in Learning, is eased from being a Tradesman, and ranked among their Learned Men. Out of these they chuse their Ambassadors, their Priests, their Tranibors, and the Prince himself; who was anciently called their Barzenes, but is called of late their Ademus. And thus from the great numbers among them, that are neither suffered to be idle, nor to be imployed in any fruitless Labour; you may easly make the estimate, how much good Work may be done in those few hours in which they are obliged to labour. But besides all that has been already said, this is to be considered, that those needful Arts which are among them, are managed with less labour than any where else. The building, or the repairing of Houses among us, employs many hands, because often a thriftless Heir suffers a House that his Father built, to fall into decay, so that his Successor must, at a great cost, repair that which he might have kept up with a small charge: and often it falls out, that the same House which one built at a vast expence, is neglected by another, that thinks he has a more delicate sense of such things; and he suffering it to fall to ruin, builds another at no less charge. But among the Utopians, all things are so regulated, that Men do very seldom build upon any new piece of Ground; and they are not only very quick in repairing their Houses, but shew their foresight in preventing their decay: So that their Buildings are preserved very long, with very little labour: And thus the Craftsmen to whom that care belongs, are often without any Imploiment, except it be the hewing of Timber, and the squaring of Stones, that so the Materials may be in readiness for raising a Building very suddenly, when there is any occasion for it. As for their Clothes, observe how little work goes for them: While they are at labour, they are cloathed with Leather and Skins, cast carelesly about them, which will last seven Years; and when they appear in publick, they put on an upper Garment, which hides the other: and these are all of one colour, and that is the natural colour of the Wool: and as they need less Woollen Cloth than is used any where else, so that which they do need, is much less costly. They use Linnen Cloth more; but that is prepared with less labour, and they value Cloth only by the whiteness of the Linnen, or the cleanness of the Wool, without much regard to the fineness of the Thread; and whereas in other places, four or five upper Garments of Woollen Cloth, and of different Colours, and as many Vests of Silk will scarce serve one Man; and those that are nicer, think ten too few; every Man there is contented with one which very oft serves him two Years. Nor is there any thing that can tempt a Man to desire more; for if he had them, he would neither be the warmer, nor would he make one jot the better appearance for it. And thus since they are all imploied in some useful Labour; and since they content themselves with fewer things, it falls out that there is a great abundance of all things among them: So that often, for want of other Work, if there is any need of mending their High Ways at any time, you will see marvellous numbers of people brought out to work at them; and when there is no occasion of any publick work, the hours of working are lessened by publick Proclamation; for the Magistrates do not engage the people into any needless Labour, since by their constitution they aim chiefly at this, that except in so far as publick necessity requires it, all the people may have as much free time for themselves as may be necessary for the improvement of their minds, for in this they think the happiness of Life consists.

Of their Traffick

But it is now time to explain to you the mutual Intercourse of this People, their Commerce, and the Rules by which all things are distributed among them. As their Cities are composed of Families, so their Families are made up of those that are nearly related to one another. Their Women, when they grow up, are married out; but all the Males, both Children and Grandchildren, live still in the same House, in great obedience to their common Parent, unless Age has weakned his Understanding; and in that case he that is next to him in Age, comes in his room. But lest any City should become either out of measure great, or fall under a dispeopling by any accident, provision is made that none of their Cities may have above six thousand Families in it, besides those of the Country round it; and that no Family may have less than ten, and more than sixteen Persons in it; but there can be no determined number for the Children under Age: And this Rule is easily observed, by removing some of the Children of a more fruitful Couple, to any other Family that does not abound so much in them. By the same Rule, they supply Cities that do not encrease so fast, by others that breed faster: And if there is any encrease over the whole Island, then they draw out a number of their Citizens out of the several Towns, and send them over to the Neighbouring Continent; where, if they find that the Inhabitants have more Soil than they can well cultivate, they fix a Colony, taking in the Inhabitants to their Society, if they will live with them; and where they do that of their own accord, they quickly go into their method of Life, and to their Rules, and this proves a happiness to both the Nations: for according to their constitution, such care is taken of the Soil, that it becomes fruitful enogh for both, tho it might be otherwise too narrow and barren for any one of them.

But if the Natives refuse to conform themselves to their Laws, they drive them out of those Bounds which they mark out for themselves, and use force if they resist. For they account it a very just cause of War, if any Nation will hinder others to come and possess a part of their Soil, of which they make no use, but let it lie idle and uncultivated; since every Man has by the Law of Nature a right to such a waste Portion of the Earth, as is necessary for his subsistence. If any Accident has so lessened the number of the Inhabitants of any of their Towns, that it cannot be made up from the other Towns of the Island, without diminishing them too much, which is said to have fallen out but twice, since they were first a People, by two Plagues that were among them; then the number is filled up, by recalling so many out of their Colonies, for they will abandon their Colonies, rather than suffer any of their Towns to sink too low.

But to return to the manner of their living together; the Ancientest of every Family governs it, as has been said. Wives serve their Husbands, and Children their Parents, and always the Younger serves the Elder. Every City is divided into four equal Parts, and in the middle of every part there is a Market-place: that which is brought thither manufactured by the several Families, is carried from thence to Houses appointed for that purpose, in which all things of a sort are laid by themselves; and every Father of a Family goes thither, and takes whatsoever he or his Family stand in need of, without either paying for it, or laying in any thing in pawn or exchange for it. There is no reason for denying any thing to any Person, since there is such plenty of every thing among them: and there is no danger of any Man's asking more than he needs; for what should make any do that, since they are all sure that they will be always supplied? It is the fear of want that makes any of the whole Race of Animals, either greedy or ravenous; but besides Fear, there is in Man a vast Pride, that makes him fancy it a particular Glory for him to excel other in Pomp and Excess. But by the Laws of the Utopians, there is no room for these things among them. Near these Markets there are also others for all sorts of Victuals, where there are not only Herbs, Fruits, and Bread, but also Fish, Fowl, and Cattel. There are also without their Towns, places appointed near some running Water, for killing their Beasts, and for washing away their filth; which is done by their Slaves, for they suffer none of their Citizens to kill their Cattel, becaues they think, that Pity and good Nature, which are among the best of those Affections that are born with us, are much impaired by the butchering of Animals: Nor do they suffer any thing that is foul or unclean to be brought within their Towns, lest the Air should be infected by ill smells which might prejudice their Health. In every Street there are great Halls that lie at an equal distance from one another, which are marked by particular Names. The Syphogrants dwell in these, that are set over thirty Families, fifteen lying on one side of it, and as many on the other. In these they do all meet and eat. The Stewards of every one of them come to the Market-place at an appointed hour; and according to the number of those that belong to their Hall, they carry home Provisions. But they take more care of their Sick, than of any others, who are looked after and lodged in public Hospitals: They have belonging to every Town four Hospitals, that are built without their Walls, and are so large, that they may pass for little Towns: By this means, if they had ever such a number of sick Persons, they could lodg them conveniently, and at such a distance, that such of them as are sick of infectious Diseases, may be kept so far from the rest, that there can be no danger of Contagion. The Hospitals are so furnished and stored with all things that are convenient for the ease and recovery of their Sick; and those that are put in them, are all looked after with so tender and watchful a care, and are so constantly treated by their skilful Physicians; that as none is sent to them against their will, so there is scarce one in a whole Town, that if he should fall ill, would not chuse rather to go thithither, than lie sick at home.

After the Steward of the Hospitals has taken for them whatsoever the Physician does prescribe at the Market-place, then the best things that remain, are distributed equally among the Halls, in proportion to their numbers, only, in the first place, they serve the Prince, the chief Priest, the Tranibors and Ambassadors, and Strangers, (if there are any, which indeed falls out but seldom, and for whom there are Houses well furnished, particularly appointed when they come among them). At the hours of Dinner and Supper, the whole Syphogranty being called together by sound of Trumpet, meets and eats together, except only such as are in the Hospitals, or lie sick at home. Yet after the Halls are served, no Man is hindred to carry Provisions home from the Market-place; for they know that none does that but for some good reason for tho any that will may eat at home, yet none does it willingly, since it is both an indecent and foolish thing, for any to give themselves the trouble to make ready an ill Dinner at home, when there is a much more plentiful one made ready for him so near hand. All the uneasy and sordid Services about these Halls, are performed by their Slaves; but the dressing and cooking their Meat, and the ordering their Tables, belongs only to the Women; which goes round all the Women of every Family by turns. They sit at three or more Tables, according to their numbers; the Men sit towards the Wall, and the Women sit on the other side, that if any of them should fall suddenly ill, which is ordinary to Women with Child, she may, without disturbing the rest, rise and go to the Nurses Room, who are there with the suckling Children; where there is always Fire, and clean Water at hand, and some Cradles in which they may lay the young Children, if there is occasion for it, and that they may shift and dress them before the Fire. Every Child is nursed by its own Mother, if Death or Sickness does not intervene; and in that case the Syphogrants Wives find out a Nurse quickly, which is no hard matter to do; for any one that can do it, offers her self chearfully: for as they are much inclined to that piece of Mercy, so the Child whom they nurse, considers the Nurse as its Mother. All the Children under five Years old, sit among the Nurses, the rest of the younger sort of both Sexes, till they are fit for Marriage, do either serve those that sit at Table; or if they are not strong enough for that, they stand by them in great silence, and eat that which is given them, by those that sit at Table; nor have they any other formality of dining. In the middle of the first Table, which stands in the upper end of the Hall, a— [2 pages missing] . . . trey, where they live at a greater distance, every one eats at home, and no Family wants any necessary sort of Provision, for it is from them that Provisions are sent unto those that live in the Towns.

Of the Travelling of the Utopians

If any of them has a mind to visit his Friends that live in some other Town, or desires to travel and see the rest of the Country, he obtains leave very easily from the Syphogrant and Tranibors to do it, when there is no particular occasion for him at home: such as travel, carry with them a Passport from the Prince, which both certifies the Licence that is granted for travvelling, and limits the Time of their return. They are furnished with a Wagon and a Slave, who drives the Oxen, and looks after them: but unless there are Women in the Company, the Wagon is sent back at the end of the Journey as a needless trouble: While they are on the Road, they carry no Provisions with them; yet they want nothing, but are every way treated as if they were at home. If they stay in any place longer then a Night, every one follows his proper Occupation, and is very well used by those of his own Trade: but if any Man goes out of the City to which he belongs, without leave, and is found going about without a Passport, he is roughly handled, and is punished as a Fugitive, and sent home disgracefully; and if he falls again into the like Fault, he is condemned to slavery. If any Man has a mind to travel only over the Precinct of his own City, he may freely do it, obtaining his Father's Permission, and his Wives Consent; but when he comes into any of the Countrey-houses, he must labour with them according to their Rules, if he expects to be entertain'd by them: and if he does this, he may freely go over the whole Precinct, being thus as useful to the City to which he belongs, as if he were still within it. Thus you see that there are no idle Persons among them, nor pretences of excusing any from Labour. There are no Taverns, no Alehouses, nor Stews among them; nor any other occasions of corrupting themselves, or of getting into Corners, or forming themselves into Parties: All Men live in full view, so that all are obliged, both to perform their ordinary Task, and to employ themselves well in their spare hours. And it is certain, that a People thus ordered, must live in great abundance of all things; and these being equally distributed among them, no Man can want any thing, or be put to beg.

In their great Council at Amaurot, to which there are three sent from every Town once every Year, they examine what Towns abound in Provisions, and what are under any Scarcity, that so the one may be furnished from the other; and this is done freely, without any sort of exchange; for according to their Plenty or Scarcity, they supply, or are supplied from one another; so that indeed the whole Island is, as it were, one Family. When they have thus taken care of their whole Country, and laid up stores for two Years, which they do in case that an ill Year should happen to come, then they order an Exportation of the Overplus, both of Corn, Honey, Wool, Flax, Wood, Scarlet, and Purple; Wax, Tallow, Leather, and Cattel, which they send out commonly in great quantities to other Countries. They order a seventh part of all these Goods to be freely given to the Poor of the Countries to which they send them, and they sell the rest at moderate Rates. And by this exchange, they not only bring back those few things that they need at home, for indeed they scarce need any thing but Iron, but likewise a great deal of Gold and Silver; and by their driving this trade so long, it is not to be imagined how vast a Treasure they have got among them: so that now they do not much care whether they sell off their Merchandize for Mony in hand, or upon trust. A great part of their Treasure is now in Bonds; but in all their Contracts no private Man stands bound, but the Writing runs in Name of the Town; and the Towns that owe them Mony, raise it from those private hands that owe it to them, and lay it up in their publick Chamber, or enjoy the profit of it till the Utopians call for it; and they chuse rather to let the greatest part of it lie in their hands, who make advantage by it, then to call for it themselves: but if they see that any of their other Neighbours stand more in need of it, then they raise it, and lend it to them; or use it themselves, if they are engaged in a War, which is the only occasion that they can have for all that Treasure that they have laid up; that so either in great Extremities, or sudden Accidents, they may serve themselves by it; cheifly for hiring Foreign Souldiers, whom they more willingly expose to danger than their own People: They give them great Pay, knowing well that this will work even on their Enemies, and engage them either to betray their own side, or at least to desert it, or will set them on to mutual Factions among themselves: for this end they have an incredible Treasure; but they do not keep it as a Treasure, but in such a manner as I am almost affraid to tell it, lest you think it so extravagant, that you can hardly believe it; which I have the more reason to apprehend from others, because if I had not seen it my self, I could not have been easily perswaded to have beleived it upon any Man's Report.

It is certain, that all things appear so far incredible to us, as they differ from our own Customs: but one who can judg aright, will not wonder to find, that since their other Constitutions differ so much from ours, their value of Gold and Silver should be measured, not by our Standard, but by one that is very different from it; for since they have no use of Mony among themselves, but keep it for an accident; that tho, as it may possibly fall out, it may have great intervals; they value it no further than it deserves, or may be useful to them. So that it is plain, that they must prefer Iron either to Gold or Silver: for Men can no more live without Iron, than without Fire or Water; but Nature has markt out no use for the other Metals, with which we may not very well dispence. The folly of Man has enhansed the value of Gold and Silver, because of their scarcity: whereas on the contrary they reason, that Nature, as an indulgent Parent, has given us all the best things very freely, and in great abundance, such as are Water and Earth, but has laid up and hid from us the things that are vain and useless. If those Metals were laid up in any Tower among them, it would give jealousy of the Prince and Senate, according to that foolish mistrust into which the Rabble is apt to fall, as if they intended to cheat the People, and make advantages to themselves by it; or if they should work it into Vessels, or any sort of Plate, they fear that the People might grow too fond of it, and so be unwilling to let the Plate be run down, if a War made it necessary to pay their Souldiers with it: Therefore to prevent all these inconveniences, they have fallen upon an expedient, which as it agrees with their other Policy, so is very different from ours, and will scarce gain belief among us, who value Gold so much, and lay it up so carefully: for whereas they eat and drink out of Vessels of Earth, or Glass, that tho they look very prety, yet are of very slight Materials; they make their Chamber-pots and Close-stools of Gold and Silver; and that not only in their publick Halls, but in their private Houses: Of the same Mettals they likewise make Chains and Fetters for their Slaves; and as a Badge of Infamy, they hang an Ear-ring of Gold to some, and make others wear a Chain or a Coronet of Gold; and thus they take care, by all manner of ways, that Gold and Silver may be of no esteem among them; And from hence it is, that whereas other Nations part with their Gold and their Silver, as unwillingly as if one tore out their Bowels, those of Utopia would look on their giving in all their Gold or Silver, when there were any use for it, but as the parting with a Trifle, or as we would estimate the loss of a Penny. They find Pearls on their Coast; and Diamonds, and Carbuncles on their Rocks: they do not look after them, but if they find them by chance, they polish them, and with them they adorn their Children, who are delighted with them, and glory in them during their Childhood; but when they grow to Years, and see that none but Children use such Baubles, they of their own accord, without being bid by their Parents, lay them aside; and would be as much ashamed to use them afterwards, as Children among us, when they come to Years, are of their Nuts, Puppets, and other Toies.

I never saw a clearer Instance of the different impressions that different Customs make on People, than I observed in the Ambassadors of the Anemolians who came to Amaurot when I was there: and because they came to treat of Affairs of great Consequence, the Deputies from the several Towns had met to wait for their coming. The Ambassadours of the Nations that lie near Utopia, knowing their Customs, and that fine Cloaths are in no esteem among them; that Silk is despised, and Gold is a Badg of Infamy, use to come very modestly cloathed; but the Anemolians that lay more remote, and so had little commerce with them, when they understood that they were coursly cloathed, and all in the same manner, they took it for granted that they had none of those fine Things among them of which they made no use; and they being a vain-glorious, rather than a wise People, resolved to set themselves out with so much pomp, that they should look like Gods, and so strike the Eyes of the poor Utopians with their splendor. Thus three Ambassadors made their entry with an hundred Attendants, that were all clad in Garments of different colours, and the greater part in Silk; the Ambassadors themselves, who were of the Nobility of their Country, were in Cloth of Gold, and adorned with massy Chains, Ear-rings and Rings of Gold: Their Caps were covered with Bracelets set full of Pearls and other Gems: In a word, they were set out with all those things, that among the Utopians were either the Badges of Slavery, the Marks of Infamy, or Childrens Rattels. It was not unpleasant to see on the one side how they lookt big, when they compared their rich Habits with the plain Cloaths of the Utopians, who were come out in great numbers to see them make their Entry: And on the other side, to observe how much they were mistaken in the Impression which they hoped this Pomp would have made on them: It appeared so ridiculous a shew to all that had never stirred out of their Country, and so had not seen the Customs of other Nations; that tho they paid some reverence to those that were the most meanly clad, as if they had been the Ambassadors, yet when they saw the Ambassadors themselves, so full of Gold Chains, they looking upon them as Slaves, made them no reverence at all. You might have seen their Children, who were grown up to that bigness, that they had thrown away their Jewels, call to their Mothers, and push them gently, and cry out, See that great Fool that wears Pearls and Gems, as if he were yet a Child. And their Mothers answered them in good earnest, Hold your Peace, this is, I believe, one of the Ambassador's Fools. Others censured the fashion of their Chains, and observed that they were of no use, for they were too slight to bind their Slaves, who could easily break them; and they saw them hang so loose about them, that they reckoned they could easily throw them away, and so get from them. But after the Ambassadors had staid a day among them, and saw so vast a quantity of Gold in their Houses, which was as much despised by them, as it was esteemed in other Nations, and that there was more Gold and Silver in the Chains and Fetters of one Slave, than all their Ornaments amounted to, their Plumes fell, and they were ashamed of all that Glory for which they had formerly valued themselves, and so laid it aside: to which they were the more determined, when upon their engaging into some free Discourse with the Utopians, they discovered their sense of such things, and their other Customs. The Utopians wonder how any Man should be so much taken with the glaring doubtful lustre of a Jewel or Stone, that can look up to a Star, or to the Sun himself; or how any should value himself, because his Cloth is made of a finer Thread: for how fine soever that Thread may be, it was once no better than the Fleece of a Sheep, and that Sheep was a Sheep still for all its wearing it. They wonder much to hear, that Gold which it self is so useless a thing, should be every where so much esteemed, that even Men for whom it was made, and by whom it has its value, should yet be thought of less value than it is: So that a Man of Lead, who has no more sence than a Log of Wood, and is as bad as he is foolish, should have many wise and good Men serving him, only because he has a great heap of that Metal; and if it should so happen, that by some Accident, or Trick of Law, (which does sometimes produce as great Changes as Chance it self) all this Wealth should pass from the Master to the meanest Varlet of his whole Family, he himself would very soon become one of his Servants, as if he were a thing that belonged to his Wealth, and so were bound to follow its Fortune. But they do much more admire and detest their folly, who when they see a rich Man, tho they neither owe him any thing, nor are in any sort obnoxious to him, yet meerly because he is rich, they give him little less than Divine Honours; even tho they know him to be so covetous and base minded, that notwithstanding all his Wealth, he will not part with one Farthing of it to them as long as he lives. These and such like Notions has that People drunk in, partly from their Education, being bred in a Country, whose Customs and Constitutions are very opposite to all such foolish Maxims: and partly from their Learning and Studies; for tho there are but few in any Town that are excused from Labour, so that they may give themselves wholly to their Studies, these being only such Persons as discover from their Childhood an extraordinary capacity and disposition for Letters, yet their Children, and a great part of the Nation, both Men and Women, are taught to spend those hours in which they are not obliged to work, in Reading: and this they do their whole Life long. They have all their Learning in their own Tongue; which is both a copious and pleasant Language, and in which a Man can fully express his Mind: It runs over a great Tract of many Countries, but it is not equally pure in all places: They had never so much as heard of the Names of any of those Philosophers that are so famous in these parts of the World, before we went among them: and yet they had made the same Discoveries that the Greeks had done, both in Musick, Logick, Arithmetick, and Geometry. But as they are equal to the Ancient Philosophers almost in all things, so they far exceed our Modern Logicians, for they have never yet fallen upon the barbarous Nicities that our Youth are forced to learn in those trifling Logical Schools that are among us; and they are so far from minding Chimera's, and Fantastical Images made in the Mind, that none of them could comprehend what we meant, when we talked to them of a Man in the Abstract, as common to all Men in particular, (so that tho we spoke of him as a thing that we could point at with our Fingers, yet none of them could perceive him) and yet distinct from every one, as if he were some monstrous Colossus or Giant. Yet for all this ignorance of these empty Notions, they knew Astronomy, and all the Motions of the Orbs exactly; and they have many Instruments, well contrived and divided, by which they do very accurately compute the Course and Positions of the Sun, Moon, and Stars. But for the Cheat, of divining by the Stars, and by their Oppositions or Conjunctions, it has not so much as entred into their Thoughts. They . . . [2 pages missing] . . . this caution, that a lesser Pleasure might not stand in the way of a greater, and that no pleasure ought to be pursued, that should draw a great deal of pain after it: for they think it the maddest thing in the World to pursue Vertue, that is a sour and difficult thing; and not only to renounce the pleasures of Life, but willingly to undergo much pain and trouble, if a Man has no prospect of a Reward. And what Reward can there be, for one that has passed his whole Life, not only without pleasure, but in pain, if there is nothing to be expected after death? Yet they do not place Happiness in all sorts of Pleasures, but only in those that in themselves are good and honest: for whereas there is a Party among them that places Happiness in bare Vertue, others think that our Natures are conducted by Vertue to Happiness, as that which is the chief Good of Man. They define Vertue thus, that it is a living according to Nature; and think that we are made by God for that end: They do believe that a Man does then follow the Dictates of Nature, when he pursues or avoids things according to the direction of Reason: they say, that the first dictate of Reason is, the kindling in us a love and reverence for the Divine Majesty, to whom we owe both all that we have, and all that we can ever hope for. In the next place, Reason directs us, to keep our Minds as free of Passion, and as chearful as we can; and that we should consider our selves as bound by the ties of good Nature and Humanity, to use our utmost endeavours to help forward the Happiness of all other Persons; for there was never any Man that was such a morose and severe pursuer of Vertue, and such an Enemy to Pleasure, that tho he set hard Rules to Men to undergo, much pain, many watchings, and other rigors, yet did not at the same time advise them to do all they could in order to the relieving and easing such People as were miserable; and did not represent it as a mark of a laudable temper, that it was gentle and good natured: And they infer from thence, that if a Man ought to advance the welfare and comfort of the rest of Mankind, there being no Vertue more proper and peculiar to our Nature, than to ease the miseries of others, to free them from trouble & anxiety, in furnishing them with the Comforts of Life, that consist in Pleasure; Nature does much more vigorously lead him to do all this for himself. A Life of Pleasure, is either a real Evil; and in that case we ought not only, not to assist others in their pursuit of it, but on the contrary, to keep them from it all we can, as from that which is hurtful and deadly to them; or if it is a good thing, so that we not only may, but ought to help others to it, Why then ought not a Man to begin with himself? since no Man can be more bound to look after the good of another, than after his own: for Nature cannot direct us to be good and kind to others, and yet at the same time to be unmerciful and cruel to our selves. Thus as they define Vertue to be a living according to Nature, so they reckon that Nature sets all People on to seek after Pleasure, as the end of all they do. They do also observe, that in order to the supporting the Pleasures of Life, Nature inclines us to enter into Society; for there is no Man so much raised above the rest of mankind, that he should be the only Favorite of Nature, which on the contrary seems to have levelled all those together that belong to the same Species. Upon this they infer, that no Man ought to seek his own Conveniences so eagerly, that thereby he should prejudice others; and therefore they think, that not only all Agreements between private Persons ought to be observed; but likewise, that all those Laws ought to be kept, which either a good Prince has published in due form, or to which a People, that is neither oppressed with Tyranny, nor circumvented by Fraud, has consented, for distributing those Conveniences of Life which afford us all our Pleasures. They think it is an evidence of true Wisdom, for a Man to pursue his own Advantages, as far as the Laws allow it. They account it Piety, to prefer the Publick Good to one's Private Concerns; but they think it unjust, for a Man to seek for his own Pleasure, by snatching another Man's Pleasures from him. And on the contrary, they think it a sign of a gentle and good Soul, for a Man to dispence with his own Advantage for the good of others; and that by so doing, a good Man finds as much pleasure one way, as he parts with another; for as he may expect the like from others when he may come to need it, so if that should fail him, yet the Sense of a good Action, and the Reflections that one makes on the Love and Gratitude of those whom he has so obliged, gives the Mind more Pleasure, than the Body could have found in that from which it had restrained it self: they are also perswaded that God will make up the loss of those small Pleasures, with a vast and endless Joy, of which Religion does easily convince a good Soul. Thus upon an enquiry into the whole Matter, they reckon that all our Actions, and even all our Vertues terminate in Pleasure, as in our chief End and greatest Happiness; and they call every Motion or State, either of Body or Mind, in which Nature teaches us to delight, a Pleasure. And thus they cautiously limit Pleasure, only to those Appetites to which Nature leads us; for they reckon that Nature leads us only to those Delights to which Reason as well as Sense carries us, and by which we neither injure any other Person, nor let go greater Pleasures for it; and which do not draw troubles on us after them: but they look upon those Delights which Men, by a foolish tho common Mistake, call Pleasure, as if they could change the Nature of Things, as well as the use of Words, as things that not only do not advance our Happiness, but do rather obstruct it very much, because they do so entirely possess the Minds of those that once go into them, with a false Notion of Pleasure, that there is no room left for truer and purer Pleasures.

There are many things that in themselves have nothing that is truly delighting: On the contrary, they have a good deal of bitterness in them; and yet by our perverse Appetites after forbidden Objects, are not only ranked among the Pleasures, but are made even the greatest Designs of Life. Among those who pursue these sophisticated Pleasures, they reckon those whom I mentioned before, who think themselves really the better for having fine Clothes; in which they think they are doubly mistaken, both in the Opinion that they have of their Clothes, and in the Opinion that they have of themselves; for if you consider the use of Clothes, why should a fine Thread be thought better than a course one? And yet that sort of Men, as if they had some real Advantages beyond others, and did not owe it wholly to their Mistakes, look big, and seem to fancy themselves to be the more valuable on that account, and imagine that a respect is due to them for the sake of a rich Garment, to which they would not have pretended, if they had been more meanly cloathed; and they resent it as an Affront, if that respect is not paid them. It is also a great folly to be taken with these outward Marks of Respect, which signify nothing: For what true or real Pleasure can one find in this, that another Man stands bare, or makes Legs to him? Will the bending another Man's Thighs give yours an ease? And will his Head's being bare, cure the madness of yours? And yet it is wonderful to see how this false Notion of Pleasure bewitches many, who delight themselves with the fancy of their Nobility, and are pleased with this Conceit, that they are descended from Ancestors, who have been held for some Successions rich, and that they have had great Possessions; for this is all that makes Nobility at present; yet they do not think themselves a whit the less noble, tho their immediate Parents have left none of this Wealth to them; or tho they themselves have squandred it all away. The Utopians have no better Opinion of those, who are much taken with Gems and Precious Stones, and who account it a degree of Happiness, next to a Divine one, if they can purchase one that is very extraordinary; especially if it be of that sort of Stones, that is then in greatest request; for the same sort is not at all times of the same value with all sorts of People; nor will Men buy it, unless it be dismounted and taken out of the Gold: And then the Jeweller is made to give good Security, and required solemnly to swear that the Stone is true, that by such an exact Caution, a false one may not be bought instead of a true: Whereas if you were to examine it, your Eye could find no difference between that which is counterfeit, and that which is true; so that they are all one to you as much as if you were blind: And can it be thought that they who heap up an useless Mass of Wealth, not for any use that it is to bring them, but meerly to please themselves with the contemplation of it, enjoy any true Pleasure in it? The Delight they find, is only a false shadow of Joy: those are no better, whose Error is somewhat different from the former, and who hide it, out of their fear of losing it; for what other Name can fit the hiding it in the Earth, or rather the restoring it to it again, it being thus cut off from being useful, either to its Owner, or to the rest of Mankind? and yet the Owner having hid it carefully, is glad, because he thinks he is now sure of it. And in case one should come to steal it, the Owner, tho he might live perhaps ten Years after that, would all that while after the Theft, of which he knew nothing, find no difference between his having it, or losing it, for both ways it was equally useless to him.

Among those foolish pursuers of Pleasure, they reckon all those that delight in Hunting, or Birding, or Gaming: Of whose madness they have only heard, for they have no such things among them: but they have asked us; What sort of Pleasure is it that Men can find in throwing the Dice? for if there were any pleasure in it, they think the doing it so often should give one a Surfeit of it: And what pleasure can one find in hearing the barking and howling of Dogs, which seem rather odious than pleasant sounds? Nor can they comprehend the pleasure of seeing Dogs run after a Hare, more than of seeing one Dog run after another; for you have the same entertainment to the Eye on both these Occasions; if the seeing them run is that which gives the pleasure, since that is the same in both cases: but if the Pleasure lies in seeing the Hare killed and torn by the Dogs, this ought rather to stir pity, when a weak, harmless, and fearful Hare, is devoured by a strong, fierce, and cruel Dog. Therefore all this business of hunting, is among the Utopians turned over to their Butchers; and those are all Slaves, as was formerly said: and they look on Hunting, as one of the basest parts of a Butcher's work: for they account it both more profitable, and more decent to kill those Beasts that are more necessary and useful to Mankind; whereas the killing and tearing of so small and miserable an Animal, which a Huntsman proposes to himself, can only attract him with the false shew of Pleasure; for it is of little use to him: they look on the desire of the Bloodshed, even of Beasts, as a mark of a Mind that is already corrupted with cruelty, or that at least by the frequent returns of so brutal a pleasure, must degenerate into it.

Thus tho the Rabble of Mankind looks upon these, and all other things of this kind, which are indeed innumerable, as Pleasures; the Utopians on the contrary observing, that there is nothing in the nature of them that is truly pleasant, conclude that they are not to be reckoned among Pleasures: for tho these things may create some tickling in the Senses, (which seems to be a true Notion of Pleasure) yet they reckon that this does not arise from the thing it self, but from a depraved Custom, which may so vitiate a Man's taste, that bitter things may pass for sweet; as Women with Child think Pitch or Tallow taste sweeter than Hony; but as a Man's Sense when corrupted, either by a Disease, or some ill Habit, does not change the nature of other things, so neither can it change the nature of Pleasure.

They reckon up several sorts of these Pleasures, which they call true Ones: Some belong to the Body, and others to the Mind. The Pleasures of the Mind lie in Knowledg, and in that delight which the contemplation of Truth carries with it; to which they add the joyful Reflections on a well-spent Life, and the assured hopes of a future Happiness. They divide the Pleasures of the Body into two sorts; the one is that which gives our Senses some real delight, and is performed, either by the recruiting of Nature, and supplying those parts on which the internal heat of Life feeds; and that is done by eating or drinking: Or when Nature is eased of any surcharge that oppresses it, as when we empty our Guts, beget Children, or free any of the parts of our Body from Aches or Heats by friction. There is another kind of this sort of Pleasure, that neither gives us any thing that our Bodies require, nor frees us from any thing with which we are overcharged; and yet it excites our Senses by a secret unseen Vertue, and by a generous Impression, it so tickles and affects them, that it turns them inwardly upon themselves; and this is the Pleasure begot by Musick. Another sort of bodily Pleasure is, that which consists in a quiet and good constitution of Body, by which there is an entire healthiness spread over all the parts of the Body, not allayed with any Disease. This, when it is free from all mixture of pain, gives an inward pleasure of it self, even tho it should not be excited by any external and delighting Object; and altho this Pleasure does not so vigorously affect the Sense, nor act so strongly upon it; yet as it is the greatest of all Pleasures, so almost all the Utopians reckon it the Foundation and Basis of all the other Joys of Life; since this alone makes one's state of Life to be easy and desirable; and when this is wanting, a Man is really capable of no other Pleasure. They look upon indolence and freedom from Pain, if it does not rise from a perfect Health, to be a state of Stupidity rather than of Pleasure. There has been a Controversy in this Matter very narrowly canvassed among them; Whether a firm and entire Health could be called a Pleasure, or not? Some have thought that there was no Pleasure, but that which was excited by some sensible Motion in the Body. But this Opinion has been long ago run down among them, so that now they do almost all agree in this, That Health is the greatest of all bodily Pleasures; and that as there is a Pain in Sickness, which is as opposite in its nature to Pleasure, as Sickness it self is to Health, so they hold that Health carries a Pleasure along with it: And if any should say, that Sickness is not really a Pain, but that it only carries a Pain along with it, they look upon that as a fetch of subtilty, that does not much alter the Matter. So they think it is all one, whether it be said, that Health is in it self a Pleasure, or that it begets a Pleasure, as Fire gives Heat; so it be granted, that all those whose Health is entire, have a true pleasure in it: And they reason thus, What is the Pleasure of eating, but that a Man's Health which had been weakned, does, with the assistance of Food, drive away Hunger, and so recruiting it self, recovers its former Vigour? And being thus refresh'd, it finds a pleasure in that Conflict: and if the Conflict is Pleasure, the Victory must yet breed a greater Pleasure, except we will fancy that it becomes stupid as soon as it has obtained that which it pursued, and so does neither know nor rejoice in its own welfare. If it is said, that Health cannot be felt, they absolutely deny that, for what Man is in Health, that does not perceive it when he is awake? Is there any Man that is so dull and stupid, as not to acknowledg that he feels a delight in Health? And what is Delight, but another name for Pleasure?

But of all Pleasures, they esteem those to be the most valuable that lie in the Mind; and the chief of these, are those that arise out of true Vertue, and the witness of a good Conscience: They account Health the chief Pleasure that belongs to the Body; for they think that the pleasure of eating and drinking, and all the other delights of the Body, are only so far desirable, as they give or maintain Health: but they are not pleasant in themselves, otherwise than as they resist those Impressions that our natural Infirmity is still making upon us: And as a wise Man desires rather to avoid Diseases, than to take Physick; and to be freed from pain, rather than to find ease by Remedies: so it were a more desirable state, not to need this sort of Pleasure, than to be obliged to indulge it: And if any Man imagines that there is a real Happiness in this Pleasure, he must then confess that he would be the happiest of all Men, if he were to lead his life in a perpetual hunger, thirst, and itching, and by consequence in perpetual eating, drinking, and scratching himself, which any one may easily see would be not only a base, but a miserable state of Life. These are indeed the lowest of Pleasures, and the least pure: for we can never relish them, but when they are mixed with the contrary pains. The pain of Hunger, must give us the pleasure of Eating; and here the Pain outballances the Pleasure: and as the Pain is more vehement, so it lasts much longer; for as it is upon us before the Pleasure comes, so it does not cease, but with the Pleasure that extinguishes it, and that goes off with it: So that they think none of those Pleasures are to be valued, but as they are necessary. Yet they rejoice in them, and with due gratitude acknowledg the tenderness of the great Author of Nature, who has planted in us Appetites, by which those things that are necessary for our preservation, are likewise made pleasant to us. For how miserable a thing would Life be, if those daily Diseases of Hunger and Thirst, were to be carried off by such bitter Drugs, as we must use for those Diseases that return seldomer upon us? and thus these pleasant, as well as proper Gifts of Nature, do maintain the strength and the sprightliness of our Bodies.

They do also entertain themselves with the other Delights that they let in at their Eyes, their Ears, and their Nostrils, as the pleasant relishes and seasonings of Life, which Nature seems to have marked out . . . [2 page missing] . . . to be seen a greater encrease, both of Corn and Cattel, nor are there any where healthier Men to be found, and freer from Diseases than among them: for one may see there, not only such things put in practice, that Husbandmen do commonly for manuring and improving an ill Soil, but in some places a whole Wood is plucked up by the Roots, as well as whole ones planted in other places, where there were formerly none: In doing of this the cheif consideration they have is of carriage, that their Timber may be either near their Towns, or lie upon the Sea, or some Rivers, so that it may be floated to them; for it is a harder work to carry Wood at any distance over Land, then Corn. The People are industrious, apt to learn, as well as chearful and pleasant; and none can endure more labour, when it is necessary, than they; but except in that case they love their ease. They are unwearied pursuers of knowledg; for when we had given them some hints of the Learning and Discipline of the Greeks, concerning whom we only instructed them, (for we know that there was nothing among the Romans, except their, Historians and their Poets, that they would value much) it was strange to see how eagerly they were set on learning that Language: We began to read a little of it to them, rather in compliance with their importunity, than out of any hopes of their profiting much by it: But after a very short trial, we found they made such a progress in it, that we saw our labour was like to be more successful than we could have expected. They learned to write their Characters, and to pronounce their Language so right, and took up all so quick, they remembered it so faithfully, and became so ready and correct in the use of it, that it would have look'd like a Miracle, if the greater part of those whom we taught had not been Men, both of extraordinay Capacity, and of a fit Age for it: They were for the greatest part chosen out among their learned Men, by their cheif Council, tho some learn'd it of their own accord. In three Years time they became Masters of the whole Language, so that they read the best of the Greek Authors very exactly. I am indeed apt to think, that they learned that Language the more easily, because it seems to be of kin to their own: I believe that they were a Colony of the Greeks; for tho their Language comes nearer the Persian, yet they retain many Names, both for their Towns and Magistrates, that are of Greek Origination. I had happened to carry a great many Books with me, instead of Merchandise, when I failed my fourth Voyage; for I was so far from thinking of coming back soon, that I rather thought never to have returned at all, and I gave them all my Books, among which many of Plato's and some of Aristotle's works were. I had also Theophrastus of the Plants, which to my great regret, was imperfect; for having laid it carelessly by, while we were at Sea, a Monkey had fallen upon it and had torn out leaves in many places. They have no Books of Grammar, but Lascares, for I did not carry Theodorus with me; nor have they any Dictionaries but Hesichius and Dioscorides. They esteem Plutarch highly, and were much taken with Lucian's Wit, and with his pleasant way of writing. As for the Poets, they have Aristophanes, Homer, Euripides, and Sophocles of Aldus's Edition; and for Historians, they have Thucidydes, Herodotus and Herodian. One of my Companions, Thricius Apinatus, happened to carry with him some of Hippocrates's Works, and Galen's Microtechne, which they hold in great estimation; for tho there is no Nation in the World, that needs Physick so little as they do, yet there is not any that honours it so much: They reckon the knowledg of it to be one of the pleasantest and profitablest parts of Philosophy, by which, as they search into the Secrets of Nature, so they not only find marvellous pleasure in it, but think that in making such enquiries, they do a most acceptable thing to the Author of Nature; and imagine that he, as all Inventers of curious Engines, has exposed to our view this great Machine of the Universe, we being the only Creatures capable of contemplating it: and that therefore an exact and curious Observer and Admirer of his Workmanship, is much more acceptable to him, than one of the Herd; who as if he were a Beast, and not capable of Reason, looks on all this glorious Scene, only as a dull and unconcerned Spectator.

The Minds of the Utopians, when they are once excited by Learning, are very ingenious in finding out all such Arts as tend to the conveniences of Life. Two things they owe to us, which are the Art of Printing, and the Manufacture of Paper: yet they do not owe these so entirely to us, but that a great part of the invention was their own; for after we had shewed them some Paper-books of Aldus's Impression, and began to explain to them the way of making Paper, and of printing, tho we spake but very crudely of both these, not being practised in either of them, they presently took up the whole matter from the hints that we gave them: and whereas before they only writ on Parchment, or on the Barks of Trees, or Reeds; they have now set up the Manufacture of Paper, and Printing presses: and tho at first they could not arrive at a perfection in them, yet by making many essays, they at last found out, and corrected all their Errors, and brought the whole thing to perfection; so that if they had but a good number of Greek Authors, they would be quickly supplied with many Copies of them: at present; tho they have no more than those I have mentioned, yet by several Impressions, they have multiplied them into many thousands. If any Man should go among them, that had some extraordinary Talent, or that by much travelling had observed the Customs of many Nations, (which made us to be so well received) he would be very welcome to them; for they are very desirous to know the state of the whole World. Very few go among them on the account of Traffick, for what can a Man carry to them but Iron, or Gold, or Silver, which Merchants desire rather to export, than import to any strange Country: and as for their Exportation, they think it better to manage that themselves, than to let Forraigners come and deal in it, for by this means, as they understand the state of the neighbouring Countries better, so they keep up the Art of Navigation, which cannot be maintained but by much practise in it.

Of their Slaves, and of their Marriages

They do not make Slaves of Prisoners of War, except those that are taken fighting against them; nor of the Sons of their Slaves, nor of the Slaves of other Nations: the Slaves among them, are only such as are condemned to that state of Life for some Crime that they had committed, or which is more common, such as their Merchants find condemned to die in those parts to which they trade, whom they redeem sometimes at low rates; and in other places they have them for nothing; and so they fetch them away. All their Slaves are kept at perpetual labour, and are always chained, but with this difference, that they treat their own Natives much worse, looking on them as a more profligate sort of People; who not being restrained from Crimes, by the advantages of so excellent an Education, are judged worthy of harder usage than others. Another sort of Slaves, is, when some of the poorer sort in the neighbouring Countries, offer of their own accord to come and serve them; they treat these better, and use them in all other respects, as well as their own Country Men, except that they impose more labour upon them, which is no hard task to them that have been accustomed to it; and if any of these have a mind to go back to their own Country, which indeed falls out but seldom, as they do not force them to stay▪ so they do not send them away empty handed.

I have already told you with what care they look after their Sick, so that nothing is left undone that can contribute either to their Ease or Health: and for those who are taken with fixed and incurable Diseases, they use all possible ways to cherish them, and to make their Lives as comfortable as may be: they visit them often, and take great pains to make their time pass off easily: but when any is taken with a torturing and lingering pain, so that there is no hope, either of recovery or ease, the Priests and Magistrates come and exhort them, that since they are now unable to go on with the business of Life, and are become a burden to themselves, and to all about them, so that they have really out-lived themselves, they would no longer nourish such a rooted Distemper, but would chuse rather to die, since they cannot live, but in much misery: being assured, that if they either deliver themselves from their Prison and Torture, or are willing that others should do it, they shall be happy after their Deaths: And since by their dying thus, they lose none of the Pleasures, but only the Troubles of Life; they think they act, not only reasonably in so doing, but religiously and piously; because they follow the Advices that are given them by the Priests, who are the Expounders of the Will of God to them. Such as are wrought on by these Perswasions, do either starve themselves of their own accord, or they take Opium, and so they die without pain. But no Man is forced on this way of ending his Life; and if they cannot be perswaded to it, they do not for that fail in their attendance and care of them: But as they believe that a voluntary Death, when it is chosen upon such an Authority, is very honourable; so if any Man takes away his own Life, without the approbation of the Priests and the Senate, they give him none of the Honours of a decent Funeral, but throw his Body into some Ditch.

Their Women are not married before eighteen, nor their Men before two and twenty; and if any of them run into forbidden Embraces before their Marriage, they are severely punished, and the privilege of Marriage is denied them, unless there is a special Warrant obtained for it afterward from the Prince. Such Disorders cast a great reproach upon the Master and Mistress of the Family in which they fall out; for it is supposed, that they have been wanting to their Duty. The reason of punishing this so severely, is, because they think that if they were not so strictly restrained from all vagrant Appetites, very few would engage in a married state, in which Men venture the quiet of their whole Life, being restricted to one Person; besides many other Inconveniences that do accompany it. In the way of chusing of their Wives, they use a method that would appear to us very absurd and ridiculous, but is constantly observed among them, and accounted a wise and good Rule. Before Marriage, some grave Matron presents the Bride naked, whether she is a Virgin or a Widow, to the Bridegroom; and after that, some grave Man presents the Bridegroom naked to the Bride. We indeed both laughed at this, and condemned it as a very indecent thing. But they, on the other hand, wondered at the folly of the Men of all other Nations; who if they are but to buy a Horse of a small value, are so cautious, that they will see every part of him, and take off both his Sadle, and all his other Tackle, that there may be no secret Ulcer hid under under any of them; and that yet in the choice of a Wife, on which depends the happiness or unhappiness of the rest of his Life, a Man should venture upon trust, and only see about an handbreadth of the Face, all the rest of the Body being covered; under which there may lie hid that which may be contagious, as well as loathsome. All Men are not so wise, that they chuse a Woman only for her good Qualities; and even wise Men consider the Body, as that which adds not a little to the Mind: And it is certain, there may be some such deformity covered with ones Clothes, as may totally alienate a Man from his Wife, when it is too late to part with her: for if such a thing is discovered after Marriage, a Man has no remedy but patience: So they think it is reasonable, that there should be a good provision made against such mischievous Frauds.

There was so much the more reason in making a regulation in this Matter, because they are the only People of those parts that do neither allow of Polygamy, nor of Divorces, except in the cases of Adultery, or insufferable Perversness: for in these Cases the Senate dissolves the Marriage, and grants the injured Person leave to marry again; but the Guilty are made infamous, and are never allowed the privilege of a second Marriage. None are suffered to put away their Wives against their Wills, because of any great Calamity that may have fallen on their Person; for they look on it as the height of Cruelty and Treachery to abandon either of the married Persons, when they need most the tender care of their Consort; and that chiefly in the case of old Age, which as it carries many Diseases along with it, so it is a Disease of it self. But it falls often out, that when a married Couple do not agree well together, they by mutual consent separate, and find out other Persons with whom they hope they may live more happily: yet this is not done, without obtaining leave of the Senate; which never admits of a Divorce, but upon a strict enquiry made, both by the Senators and their Wives, into the Grounds upon which it proceeds: and even when they are satisfied concerning the Reasons of it, they go on but slowly, for they reckon that too great easiness, in granting leave for new Marriages, would very much shake the kindness of married Persons. They punish severely those that defile the Marriage-Bed: If both Parties are married, they are divorced, and the injured Persons may marry one another, or whom they please; but the Adulterer, and the Adulteress are condemned to slavery. Yet if either of the injured Persons cannot shake off the Love of the married Person, they may live with them still in that state; but they must follow them to that Labour to which the Slaves are condemned; and sometimes the Repentance of the condemned Person, together with the unshaken kindness of the innocent and injured Person, has prevailed so far with the Prince, that he has taken off the Sentence. But those that relapse, after they are once pardoned, are punished with Death. Their Law does not determine the Punishment for other Crimes; but that is left to the Senate, to temper it according to the Circumstances of the Fact. Husbands have power to correct their Wives, and Parents to correct their Children, unless the Fault is so great, that a publick Punishment is thought necessary for the striking terror into others. For the most part, Slavery is the punishment even of the greatest Crimes; for as that is no less terrible to the Criminals themselves than Death; so they think the preserving them in a state of servitude, is more for the Interest of the Common-Wealth, than the killing them outright; since as their Labour is a greater benefit to the Publick, than their Death could be; so the sight of their Misery is a more lasting terror to other Men, than that which would be given by their Death. If their Slaves rebel, and will not bear their Yoke, and submit to the Labour that is enjoined them, they are treated as wild Beasts that cannot be kept in order, neither by a Prison, nor by their Chains; and are at last put to death. But those who bear their Punishment patiently, and are so much wrought on by that pressure, that lies so hard on them, that it appears they are really more troubled for the Crimes they have committed, than for the Miseries they suffer, are not out of hope, but that at last either the Prince will, by his Prerogative, or the People will by their intercession restore them again to their liberty, or at least very much mitigate their slavery. He that tempts a married Woman to Adultery, is no less severely punished, than he that commits it; for they reckon that a laid and studied Design of committing any Crime, is equal to the Fact it self; since its not taking effect does not make the Person that did all that in him lay in order to it, a whit the less guilty.

They take great pleasure in Fools, and as it is thought a base and unbecoming thing to use them ill, so they do not think it amiss for People to divert themselves with their Folly: and they think this is a great advantage to the Fools themselves: For if Men were so sullen and severe, as not at all to please themselves with their ridiculous behaviour, and foolish sayings, which is all that they can do to recommend themselves to others, it could not be expected that they would be so well look'd to, nor so tenderly used as they must otherwise be. If any Man should reproach another for his being mishaped or imperfect in any part of his Body, it would not at all be thought a reflection on the Person that were so treated, but it would be accounted a very unworthy thing for him that had upbraided another with that which he could not help. It is thought a sign of a sluggish and sordid Mind, not to preserve carefully one's natural Beauty; but it is likewise an infamous thing among them to use Paint or Fard. And they all see that no Beauty recommends a Wife so much to her Husband, as the probity of her Life, and her Obedience: for as some few are catched and held only by Beauty, so all People are held by the other Excellencies which charm all the World.

As they fright Men from committing Crimes by Punishments, so they invite them to the love of Vertue, by publick Honours: therefore they erect Statues in honour to the memories of such worthy Men as have deserved well of their Country, and set these in their Market-places, both to perpetuate the remembrance of their Actions, and to be an incitement to their Posterity to follow their example.

If any Man aspires to any Office, he is sure never to compass it: They live all easily together, for none of the Magistrates are either insolent or cruel to the People; but they affect rather to be called Fathers, and by being really so, they well deserve that Name; and the People pay them all the marks of Honour the more freely, because none are exacted of them. The Prince himself has no distinction, either of Garments, or of a Crown; but is only known by a Sheaf of Corn that is carried before him, as the High Priest is also known by a Wax Light that is carried before him.

They have but few Laws, and such is their Constitution, that they need not many. They do very much condemn other Nations, whose Laws, together with the Commentaries on them, swell up to so many Volumes; for they think it an unreasonable thing to oblige Men to obey a Body of Laws, that are both of such a bulk, and so dark, that they cannot be read or understood by every one of the Subjects.

They have no Lawyers among them, for they consider them as a sort of People, whose Profession it is to disguise Matters, as well as to wrest Laws; and therefore they think it is much better that every Man should plead his own Cause, and trust it to the Judg, as well as in other places the Client does it to a Counsellor. By this means they both cut off many delays, and find out Truth more certainly: for after the Parties have laid open the Merits of their Cause, without those Artifices which Lawyers are apt to suggest, the Judg examines the whole Matter, and supports the simplicity of such well-meaning Persons, whom otherwise crafty Men would be sure to run down: And thus they avoid those Evils, which appear very remarkably among all those Nations that labour under a vast load of Laws. Every one of them is skilled in their Law, for as it is a very short study, so the plainnest meaning of which words are capable, is always the sense of their Laws. And they argue thus; All Laws are promulgated for this end, that every Man may know his Duty; and therefore the plainest and most obvious sense of the words, is that which must be put on them; since a more refined Exposition cannot be easily comprehended, and Laws become thereby useless to the greater part of Mankind, who need most the direction of them: for to them it is all one, not to make a Law at all, and to couch it in such tearms, that without a quick apprehension, and much study, a Man cannot find out the true meaning of it; and the generality of Mankind are both so dull, and so much imployed in their several Trades, that they have neither the leisure nor the capacity requisite for such an enquiry.

Some of their Neighbours, who are Masters of their own Liberties, having long ago, by the assistance of the Utopians, shaken off the Yoke of Tyranny; and being much taken with those Vertues that they observe among them, have come to them, and desired that they would send Magistrates among them to govern them; some changing them every Year, and others every five Years. At the end of their Government, they bring them back to Utopia, with great expressions of honour and esteem, and carry away others to govern in their stead. In this they seem to have fallen upon a very good Expedient for their own happiness and safety: For since the good or ill Condition of a Nation depends so much upon their Magistrates, they could not have made a better choice, than by pitching on Men whom no Advantages can biass; for Wealth is of no use to them, since they must go so soon back to their own Country; and they being strangers among them, are not engaged in any of their Heats or Animosities: And it is certain, that when Publick Judicatories are swayed, either by partial Affections, or by Avarice, there must follow upon it a dissolution of all Justice, which is the chief Sinew of Society.

The Utopians call those Nations that come and ask Magistrates from them, Neighbours; but they call those to whom they have been more particularly assisting, Friends. And whereas all other Nations are perpetually either making Leagues, or breaking them, they never enter into any Alliance with any other State. They think Leagues are useless things, and reckon, that if the common Ties of Humane Nature do not knit Men together, the Faith of Promises will have no great effect on them: And they are the more confirmed in this, by that which they see among the Nations round about them, who are no strict observers of Leagues and Treaties. We know how religiously they are observed in Europe; more particularly where the Christian Doctrine is received, among whom they are sacred and inviolable. Which is partly owing to the Justice and Goodness of the Princes themselves, and partly to their Reverence that they pay to the Popes: who as they are most religious observers of their own Promises, so they exhort all other Princes to perform theirs; and when fainter Methods do not prevail, they compel them to it by the severity of the Pastoral Censure; and think that it would be the most indecent thing possible, if Men who are particularly designed by the title of the Faithful, should not religiously keep the Faith of their Treaties. But in that new found World, which is not more distant from us in Scituation, than it is disagreeing from us in their Manners, and course of Life, there is no trusting to Leagues, even tho they were made with all the pomp of the most Sacred Ceremonies that is possible: On the contrary, they are the sooner broken for that, some slight Pretence being found in the words of the Treaties, which are contrived in such ambiguous Terms, and that on design, that they can never be so strictly bound, but they will always find some Loop-hole to escape at; and so they break both their Leagues and their Faith. And this is done with that impudence, that those very Men who value themselves on having suggested these Advices to their Princes, would yet, with a haughty scorn, declaim against such Craft, or to speak plainer, such Fraud and Deceit, if they found private Men make use of it in their Bargains; and would readily say, that they deserved to be hanged for it.

By this means it is, that all sort of Justice passes in the World, but for a low-spirited and vulgar Vertue, which is far below the dignity of Royal Greatness Or at least, there are two sorts of Justice set up: the one is mean, and creeps on the Ground, and therefore becomes none but the baser sort of Men, and so must be kept in severely by many restraints, that it may not break out beyond the Bounds that are set to it. The other is, the peculiar Vertue of Princes, which as it is more majestick than that which becomes the, Rabble, so takes a freer compass; and lawful or unlawful, are only measured by Pleasure and Interest. These practices among the Princes that lie about Utopia, who make so little account of their Faith, seem to be the Reasons that determine them to engage in no Confederacies: perhaps they would change their mind if they lived among us: but yet tho Treaties were more religiously observed, they would still dislike the custom of making them; since the World has taken up a false Maxim upon it, as if there were no tie of Nature knitting one Nation to another, that are only separated perhaps by a Mountain, or a River, and that all were born in a state of Hostility, and so might lawfully do all that mischief to their Neighbours, against which there is no provision made by Treaties: And that when Treaties are made, they do not cut off the Enmity, or restrain the License of preying upon one another, if by the unskilfulness of wording them, there are not effectual Proviso's made against them. They on the other hand judg, that no Man is to be esteemed our Enemy that has never injured us; and that the Partnership of the Humane Nature, that is among all Men, is instead of a League. And that kindness and good Nature unite Men more effectually, and more forcibly than any Agreements whatsoever; since thereby the Engagements of Mens Hearts become stronger, than any thing can be to which a few words can bind them.

Of their Military Discipline

They detest War as a very brutal thing; and which, to the reproach of Humane Nature, is more practised by Men, than by any sort of Beasts: and they, against the custom of almost all other Nations, think that there is nothing more inglorious than that Glory that is gained by War: And therefore tho they accustom themselves daily to Military Exercises, and the Discipline of War, in which not only their Men, but their Women likewise, are trained up, that so in cases of Necessity, they may not be quite useless: Yet they do not rashly engage in War, unless it be either to defend themselves, or their Friends, from any unjust Aggressors; or out of good Nature, or in compassion to an oppressed Nation, that they assist them to the shaking off the Yoke Tyranny. They indeed help their Friends, not only in Defensive, but also in Offensive Wars: but they never do that, unless they had been consulted with while the Matter was yet entire; and that being satisfied with the Grounds on which they went, they had found that all Demands of Reparation were rejected, so that a War was necessary: which they do not think to be only just, when one Neighbour makes an inrode on another, by publick Order, and carries away their Spoils; but when the Merchants of one Country are oppressed in another, either under the pretence of some unjust Laws, or by the perverse wresting of good ones: this they count a juster cause of War than the other, because those Injuries are done under some colour of Laws. This was the only Ground of that War, in which they engaged with the Nephelogetes against the Aleopolitanes, a little before our time: for the Merchants of the former, having, as they thought, met with great injustice among the latter, that, whether it was in it self right or wrong, did draw on a terrible War, many of their Neighbours being engaged in it; and their keenness in carrying it on, being supported by their strength in maintaining it; it not only shook some very flourishing States, and very much afflicted others; but after a series of much Mischief, it ended in the entire conquest and slavery of the Aleopolitanes, who tho before the War, they were in all respects much superior to the Nephelogetes, yet by it they fell under their Empire; But the Utopians, tho they had assisted them in the War, yet pretended to no share of the spoil.

But tho they assist their Friends so vigorously, in taking reparation for Injuries that are done them in such Matters; yet if they themselves should meet with any such fraud, provided there were no violence done to their Persons, they would only carry it so far, that unless satisfaction were made, they would give over trading with such a People. This is not done, because they consider their Neighbours more than their own Citizens; but since their Neighbours trade every one upon his own Stock, Fraud is a more sensible injury to them, than it is to the Utopians, among whom the Publick only suffers in such a case: And since they expect nothing in return for the Merchandize that they export; but that in which they abound so much, and is of little use to them, the loss does not much affect them; therefore they think it would be too severe a thing to revenge a Loss that brings so little inconvenience with it, either to their Life, or their Livelihood, with the death of many People: but if any of their People is either killed or wounded wrongfully, whether that be done by Publick Authority, or only by private Men, as soon as they hear of it, they send Ambassadors, and demand, that the Guilty Persons may be delivered up to them; and if that is denied, they declare War; but if that is done, they condemn those either to Death or Slavery.

They would be both troubled and ashamed of a bloody Victory over their Enemies; and think it would be as foolish a Purchase, as to buy the most valuable Goods at too high a Rate. And in no Victory do they glory so much, as in that which is gained by dexterity and good conduct, without Bloodshed. They appoint publick Triumphs in such Cases, and erect Trophies to the honour of those who have succeeded well in them; for then do they reckon that a Man acts sutably to his Nature, when he conquers his Enemy in such a way, that no other Creature but a Man could be capable of it, and that is, by the strength of his Understanding. Bears, Lions, Boars, Wolves, and Dogs, and other Animals, imploy their bodily Force one against another, in which as many of them are superior to Man, both in strength and fierceness, so they are all subdued by the reason and understanding that is in him.

The only Design of the Utopians in War, is to obtain that by Force, which if it had been granted them in time, would have prevented the War; or if that cannot be done, to take so severe a Revenge of those that have injured them, that they may be terrified from doing the like in all time coming. By these Ends they measure all their Designs, and manage them so, that it is visible that the Appetite of Fame or Vain-glory, does not work so much on them, as a just care of their own Security.

As soon as they declare War, they take care to have a great many Schedules, that are sealed with their Common Seal, affixed in the most conspicuous places of their Enemies Country. This is carried secretly, and done in many places all at once. In those they promise great Rewards to such as shall kill the Prince, and lesser in proportion to such as shall kill any other Persons, who are those on whom, next to the Prince himself, they cast the chief blame of the War. And they double the Sum to him, that instead of killing the Person so marked out, shall take him alive, and put him in their hands. They offer not only Indemnity, but Rewards, to such of the Persons themselves that are so marked, if they will act against their Countrymen: By this means those that are named in their Schedules, become not only distrustful of their Fellow-Citizens, but are jealous of one another: and are much distracted by Fear and Danger; for it has often fallen out, that many of them, and even the Prince himself, have been betrayed by those in whom they have trusted most: for the Rewards that the Utopians offer, are so unmeasurably great, that there is no sort of Crime to which Men cannot be drawn by them. They consider the Risque that those run, who undertake such Services, and offer a Recompence proportioned to the danger; not only a vast deal of Gold, but great Revenues in Lands that lie among other Nations that are their Friends, where they may go and enjoy them very securely; and they observe the Promises they make of this kind most religiously. They do very much approve of this way of corrupting their Enemies, tho it appears to others to be a base and cruel thing; but they look on it as a wise course, to make an end of that which would be otherwise a great War, without so much as hazarding one Battel to decide it. They think it likewise an Act of Mercy and Love to Mankind, to prevent the great slaughter of those that must otherwise be killed in the progress of the War, both of their own side, and of their Enemies, by the death of a few that are most guilty; and that in so doing, they are kind even to their Enemies, and pity them no less than their own People, as knowing that the greater part of them do not engage in the War of their own accord, but are driven into it by the Passions of their Prince.

If this Method does not succeed with them, then they sow Seeds of Contention among their Enemies, and animate the Prince's Brother, or some of the Nobility, to aspire to the Crown. If they cannot disunite them by Domestick Broils, then they engage their Neighbours against them, and make them set on foot some old Pretensions, which are never wanting to Princes, when they have occasion for them. And they supply them plentifully with Mony, tho but very sparingly with any Auxiliary Troops: for they are so render of their own People, that they would not willingly exchange one of them, even with the Prince of their Enemies Country. But as they keep their Gold and Silver only for such an occasion, so when that offers it self, they easily part with it, since it would be no inconvenience to them, tho they should reserve nothing of it to themselves. For besides the Wealth that they have among them at home, they have a vast Treasure abroad; Many Nations round about them, being deep in their Debt: so that they hire Souldiers from all Places for carrying on their Wars; but chiefly from the Zapolets, who lie five hundred miles from Utopia eastward. They are a rude, wild, and fierce Nation, who delight in the Woods and Rocks, among which they were born and bred up. They are hardned both against Heat, Cold, and Labour, and know nothing of the delicacies of Life. They do not apply themselves to Agriculture, nor do they care either for their Houses or their Clothes. Cattel is all that they look after; and for the greatest part, they live either by their Hunting, or upon Rapine; and are made, as it were, only for War. They watch all opportunities of engaging in it, and very readily embrace such as are offered them. Great numbers of them will often go out, and offer themselves upon a very low Pay, to serve any that will employ them: they know none of the Arts of Life, but those that lead to the taking it away; they serve those that hire them, both with much courage and great Fidelity; but will not engage to serve for any determin'd time, and agree upon such Terms, that the next day they may go over to the Enemies of those whom they serve, if they offer them a greater pay: and they will perhaps return to them the day after that, upon a higher advance of their Pay. There are few Wars in which they make not a considerable part of the Armies of both sides: so it falls often out, that they that are of kin to one another, and were hired in the same Country, and so have lived long and familiarly together; yet they forgetting both their Relation and former Friendship, kill one another upon no other consideration, but because they are hired to it for a little Mony, by Princes of different Interests: and so great regard have they to Mony, that they are easily wrought on by the difference of one Penny a Day, to change sides. So entirely does their Avarice turn them, and yet this Mony on which they are so much set, is of little use to them; for what they purchase thus with their Blood, they quickly waste it on Luxury, which among them is but of a poor and miserable form.

This Nation serves the Utopians against all People whatsoever, for they pay higher than any other. The Utopians hold this for a Maxim, that as they seek out the best sort of Men for their own use at home, so they make use of this worst sort of Men for the Consumption of War, and therefore they hire them with the offers of vast Rewards, to expose themselves to all sorts of hazards, out of which the greater part never returns to claim their Promises. Yet they make them good most religiously to such as escape. And this animates them to adventure again, when there is occasion for it; for the Utopians are not at all troubled how many of them soever happen to be killed; and reckon it a service done to Mankind, if they could be a mean to deliver the World from such a leud and vicious sort of People, that seem to have run together, as to the Drain of Humane Nature. Next to these they are served in their Wars, with those upon whose account they undertake them, and with the Auxiliary Troops of their other Friends, to whom they join some few of their own People, and send some Man of eminent and approved Vertue to command in chief. There are two sent with him, who during his Command, are but private Men, but the first is to succeed him if he should happen to be either killed or taken; and in case of the like misfortune to him, the third comes in his place; and thus they provide against ill Events, that such Accidents as may befal their Generals, may not endanger their Armies. When they draw out Troops of their own People, they take such out of every City as freely offer themselves, for none are forced to the Laws of the Country, and their Learning, add more vigor to their Minds: for as they do not undervalue Life to the degree of throwing it away too prodigally; so they are not so indecently fond of it, that when they see they must sacrifice it honourably, they will preserve it by base and unbecoming Methods. In the greatest heat of Action, the bravest of their Youth, that have jointly devoted themselves for that piece of Service, single out the General of their Enemies, and set on him either openly, or lay an Ambuscade for him: if any of them are spent and wearied in the Attempt, others come in their stead, so that they never give over pursuing him, either by close Weapons, when they can get near him, or those that wound at a distance, when others get in between: thus they seldom fail to kill or take him at last, if he does not secure himself by flight. When they gain the Day in any Battel, they kill as few as possibly they can; and are much more set on taking many Prisoners, than on killing those that fly before them: nor do they ever let their Men so loose in the pursuit of their Enemies, that they do not retain an entire Body still in order; so that if they have been forced to engage the last of their Battalions, before they could gain the day, they will rather let their Enemies all escape than pursue them, when their own Army is in disorder; remembering well what has often fallen out to themselves; that when the main Body of their Army has been quite defeated and broken, so that their Enemies reckoning the Victory was sure and in their hands, have let themselves loose into an irregular pursuit, a few of them that lay for a reserve, waiting a fit opportunity, have fallen on them while they were in this chase, stragling and in disorder, apprehensive of no danger, but counting the Day their own; and have turned the whole Action, and so wresting out of their hands a Victory that seemed certain and undoubted, the vanquished have of a sudden become victorious.

It is hard to tell whether they are more dextrous in laying or avoiding Ambushes: they sometimes seem to fly when it is far from their thoughts; and when they intend to give Ground, they do it so, that it is very hard to find out their Design. If they see they are ill posted, or are like to be overpowred by numbers, then they . . . [2 pages missing] . . . their Friends to reimburse them of their expence in it; but they take that from the conquered, either in Mony which they keep for the next occasion, or in Lands, out of which a constant Revenue is to be paid them; by many increases, the Revenue which they draw out from several Countries on such Occasions, is now risen to above 700000 Ducats a Year. They send some of their own People to receive these Revenues, who have orders to live magnificently, and like Princes, and so they consume much of it upon the place; and either bring over the rest to Utopia, or lend it to that Nation in which it lies. This they most commonly do, unless some great occasion which falls out, but very seldom, should oblige them to call for it all. It is out of these Lands that they assign those Rewards to such as they encourage to adventure on desperate Attempts, which was mentioned formerly. If any Prince that engages in War with them, is making preparations for invading their Country, they prevent him, and make his Country the Seat of the War; for they do not willingly suffer any War to break in upon their Island; and if that should happen, they would only defend themselves by their own People; but would not at all call for Auxiliary Troops to their assistance.

Of the Religions of the Utopians

There are several sorts of Religions, not only in different parts of the Island, but even in every Town; some worshipping the Sun, others the Moon, or one of the Planets: some worship such Men as have been eminent in former times for Vertue, or Glory, not only as ordinary Deities, but as the supream God: yet the greater and wiser sort of them worship none of these, but adore one Eternal, Invisible, Infinite, and Incomprehensible Deity; as a Being that is far above all our Apprehensions, that is spread over the whole Universe, not by its Bulk, but by its Power and Vertue; him they call the Father of all, and acknowledg that the beginnings, the encrease, the progress, the vicissitudes, and the end of all things come only from him; nor do they offer divine honouts to any but to him alone. And indeed, tho they differ concerning other things, yet all agree in this; that they think there is one supream Being that made and governs the World, whom they call in the Language of their Country, Mithras. They differ in this, that one thinks the God whom he worships is this Supream Being, and another thinks that his Idol is that God; but they all agree in one principle, that whatever is this Supream Being, is also that Great Essence, to whose Glory and Majesty all honours are ascribed by the consent of all Nations.

By degrees, they all fall off from the various Superstitions that are among them, and grow up to that one Religion that is most in request, and is much the best: and there is no doubt to be made, but that all the others had vanished long ago, if it had not happned that some unlucky Accidents, falling on those who were advising the change of those superstitious ways of Worship; these have been ascribed not to Chance, but to somewhat from Heaven; and so have raised in them a fear, that the God, whose Worship was like to be abandoned, has interposed and revenged himself on those that designed it.

After they had heard from us, an account of the Doctrine, the course of Life, and the Miracles of Christ, and of the wonderful constancy of so many Martyrs, whose **Blood, that was so willingly offered up by them, was the chief occasion of spreading** their Religion over a vast number of Nations; it is not to be imagined how inclined they were to receive it. I shall not determine whether this proceeded from any secret inspiration of God, or whether it was because it seemed so favorable to that community of Goods, which is an opinion so particular, as well as so dear to them; since they perceived that Christ and his Followers lived by that Rule; and that it was still kept up in some Communities among the sincerest sort of Christians, from which soever of these Motives it might be true it is, that many of them came over to our Religion, and were initiated into it by Baptism. But as two of our number were dead, so none of the four that survived, were in Priests Orders; therefore we could do no more but baptize them; so that to our great regret, they could not partake of the other Sacraments, that can only be administred by Priests: but they are instructed concerning them, and long most vehemently for them; and they were disputing very much among themselves, Whether one that were chosen by **them to be a Preist, would not be thereby qualified to do all the things that belong** to that Character, even tho he had no Authority derived from the Pope; and they seemed to be resolved to chuse some for that Imployment, but they had not done it when I left them

Those among them that have not received our Religion, yet do not fright any from it, and use none ill that goes over to it; so that all the while I was there, one Man was only punished on this occasion. He being newly baptized, did, notwithstanding all that we could say to the contrary, dispute publickly concerning the Christian Religion, with more zeal than discretion; and with so much heat, that he not only preferred our Worship to theirs, but condemned all their Rites as profane; and cried out against all that adhered to them, as impious and sacrilegious Persons, that were to be damned to everlasting Burnings. Upon this he, having preached these things often, was seized on, and after a Trial, he was condemned to banishment, not **for having disparaged their Religion, but for his inflaming the People to Sedition:** for this is one of their ancientest Laws, that no Man ought to be punished for his **Religion. At the first constitution of their Goverment, Utopus having understood,** that before his coming among them, the old Inhabitants had been engaged in grtat quarrels concerning Religion, by which they were so broken among themselves, that he found it an easy thing to conquer them, since they did not unite their

Forces against him, but every different Party in Religion fought by themselves: upon that, after he had subdued them, he made a Law that every Man might be of what Religion he pleased, and might endeavor to draw others to it by the force of Argument, and by amicable and modest ways, but without bitterness against those of other Opinions; but that he ought to use no other Force but that of Persuasion; and was neither to mixt Reproaches nor Violence with it; and such as did otherwise, were to be condemned to Banishment or Slavery.

This Law was made by Utopus, not only for preserving the Publick Peace, which he saw suffered much by daily Contentions and Irreconcilable Heats in these Matters, but because he thought the Interest of Religion it self required it.

He judged it was not fit to determine any thing rashly in that Matter; and seemed to doubt whether those different Forms of Religion might not all come from God, who might inspire Men differently, he being possibly pleased with a variety in it: and so he thought it was a very indecent and foolish thing for any Man to frighten and threaten other Men to believe any thing because it seemed true to him; and in case that one Religion were certainly true, and all the rest false, he reckoned that the native Force of Truth would break forth at last, and shine bright, if it were managed only by the strength of Argument, and with a winning gentleness; whereas if such Matters were carried on by Violence and Tumults, then, as the wickedest sort of Men is always the most obstinate, so the holiest and best Religion in the World might be overlaid with so much foolish superstition, that it would be quite choaked with it, as Corn is with Briars and Thorns; therefore he left Men wholly to their liberty in this matter, that they might be free to beleive as they should see cause; only he made a solemn and severe Law against such as should so far degenerate from the dignity of humane Nature, as to think that our Souls died with our Bodies, or that the World was governed by Chance, without a wise over-ruling Providence: for they did all formerly believe that there was a state of Rewards and Punishments to the Good and Bad after this Life; and they look on those that think otherwise, as scarce fit to be counted Men, since they degrade so noble a Being as our Soul is, and reckon it to be no better than a Beast's; so far are they from looking on such Men as fit for humane society, or to be Citizens of a well-ordered Common-Wealth; since a Man of such Principles must needs, as oft as he dares do it, despise all their Laws and Customs: for there is no doubt to be made, that a Man who is affraid of nothing but the Law, and apprehends nothing after death, will not stand to break through all the Laws of his Country, either by fraud or force, that so he may satisfy his Appetites. They never raise any that hold these Maxims, either to Honours or Offices, nor imploy them in any publick Trust, but despise them, as Men of base and sordid Minds: yet they do not punish them, because they lay this doun for a ground, that a Man cannot make himself beleive any thing he pleases; nor do they drive any to dissemble their thoughts by threatnings, so that Men are not tempted to lie or disguise their Opinions among them; which being a sort of Fraud, is abhorred by the Utopians: they take indeed care that they may not argue for these Opinions, especially before the common

People: But they do suffer, and even encourage them to dispute concerning them in private with their Priests, and and other grave Men, being confident that they will be cured of those mad Opinions, by having reason laid before them. There are many among them that run far to the other extream, tho it is neither thought an ill nor unreasonable Opinion, and therfore is not at all discouraged. They think that the Souls of Beasts are immortal, tho far inferior to the dignity of the humane Soul, and not capable of so great a happiness. They are almost all of them very firmly perswaded, that good Men will be infinitely happy in another state; so that tho they are compassionate to all that are sick, yet they lament no Man's Death, except they see him part with Life uneasy, and as if he were forced to it; For they look on this as a very ill persage, as if the Soul being conscious to it self of Guilt, and quite hopeless, were affraid to die, from some secret hints of approaching misery. They think that such a Man's appearance before God, cannot be acceptable to him, who being called on, does not go out chearfully, but is backward and unwilling, and is, as it were, dragged to it. They are struck with horror, when they see any die in this manner, and carry them out in silence, and with sorrow, and praying God that he would be merciful to the Errors of the departed Soul, they lay the Body in the Ground: but when any die chearfully, and full of hope, they do not mourn for them, but sing Hymns when they carry out their Bodies, and commending their Souls very earnestly to God, in such a manner, that their whole behaviour is rather grave then sad, they burn their Body, and set up a Pillar where the Pile was made, with an Inscription to the honour of such Mens memory; And when they come from the Funeral, they discourse of their good Life, and worthy Actions, but speak of nothing oftner and with more . . . [2 pages missing] . . . himself that happiness that comes after Death. Some of these visit the Sick; others mend High-ways, cleanse Ditches, or repair Bridges, and dig Turf, Gravel, or Stones. Others fell and cleave Timber, and bring Wood, Corn, and other Necessaries, on Carts, into their Towns. Nor do these only serve the Publick, but they serve even Private Men, more than the Slaves themselves do: for if there is any where a rough, hard, and sordid piece of work to be done, from which many are frightned by the labour and loathsomeness of it, if not the despair of accomplishing it, they do chearfully, and of their own accord, take that to their share; and by that means, as they ease others very much, so they afflict themselves, and spend their whole life in hard Labor: and yet they do not value themselves upon that, nor lessen other peoples credit, that by so doing they may raise their own; but by their stooping to such sevile Employments, they are so far from being despised, that they are so much the more esteemed by the whole Nation.

Of these there are two sorts: Some live unmarried and chast, and abstain from eating any sort of Flesh; and thus weaning themselves from all the pleasures of the present Life, which they account hurtful, they pursue, even by the hardest and painfullest methods possible, that blessedness which they hope for hereafter; and the nearer they approach to it, they are the more chearful and earnest in their endeavours after it. Another sort of them is less willing to put themselves to much toil, and so they prefer a married state to a single one; and as they do not deny themselves the pleasure of it, so they think the begetting of Children is a debt which they owe to Humane Nature, and to their Country: nor do they avoid any Pleasure that does not hinder Labour; and therefore they eat Flesh so much the more willingly, because they find themselves so much the more able for work by it: The Utopians look upon these as the wiser Sect, but they esteem the others as the holier. They would indeed laugh at any Man, that upon the Principles of Reason, would prefer an unmarried state to a married, or a Life of Labour to an easy Life: but they reverence and admire such as do it upon a Motive of Religion. There is nothing in which they are more cautious, than in giving their Opinion positively concerning any sort of Religion. The Men that lead those severe Lives, are called in the Language of their Country Brutheskas, which answers to those we call Religious Orders.

Their Priests are Men of eminent Piety, and therefore they are but few, for there are only thirteen in every Town, one for every Temple in it; but when they go to War, seven of these go out with their Forces, and seven others are chosen to supply their room in their absence; but these enter again upon their Employment when they return; and those who served in their absence, attend upon the High Priest, till Vacancies fall by Death; for there is one that is set over all the rest. They are chosen by the People, as the other Magistrates are, by Suffrages given in secret, for preventing of Factions: and when they are chosen, they are consecrated by the College of Priests. The care of all Sacred Things, and the Worship of God, and an inspection into the Manners of the People, is committed to them. It is a reproach to a Man to be sent for by any of them, or to be even spoke to in secret by them, for that always gives some suspicions: all that is incumbent on them, is only to exhort and admonish People; for the power of correcting and punishing ill Men, belongs wholly to the Prince, and to the other Magistrates: The severest thing that the Priest does, is the excluding of Men that are desperately wicked from joining in their Worship: There's not any sort of Punishment that is more dreaded by them than this, for as it loads them with Infamy, so it fills them with secret Horrors, such is their reverence to their Religion; nor will their Bodies be long exempted from their share of trouble; for if they do not very quickly satisfy the Priests of the truth of their Repentance, they are seized on by the Senate, and punished for their Impiety. The breeding of the Youth belongs to the Priests, yet they do not take so much care of instructing them in Letters, as of forming their Minds and Manners aright; and they use all possible Methods to infuse very early in the tender and flexible Minds of Children, such Opinions as are both good in themselves, and will be useful to their Country: for when deep impressions of these things are made at that Age, they follow Men through the whole course of their Lives, of much Blood on either side; and when the Victory turns to their side, they run in among their own Men to restrain their Fury; and if any of their Enemies see them, or call to them, they are preserved by that means: and such as can come so near them as to touch their Garments, have not only their Lives, but their Fortunes secured to them: It is upon this account, that all the Nations round about consider them so much, and pay them so great reverence, that they have been often no less able to preserve their own People from the fury of their Enemies, than to save their Enemies from their rage: for it has sometimes fallen out, that when their Armies have been in disorder, and forced to fly, so that their Enemies were running upon the slaughter and spoil, the Priests by interposing, have stop'd the shedding of more Blood, and have separated them from one another; so that by their Mediation, a Peace has been concluded on very reasonable Terms; nor is there any Nation about them so fierce, cruel, or barbarous, as not to look upon their Persons as Sacred and Inviolable The first and the last day of the Month, and of the Year, is a Festival: they measure their Months by the course of the Moon; and their Years by the course of the Sun: The first days are called in their Language the Cynemernes, and the last the Trapemernes, which answers in our Language to the Festival that begins, or ends the Season.

They have magnificent Temples, that are not only nobly built, but are likewise of great Reception: which is necessary, since they have so few of them: They are a little dark within, which flows not from any Error in their Architecture, but is done on design; for their Priests think that too much light dissipates the thoughts, and that a more moderate degree of it, both recollects the Mind, and raises Devotion. Tho there are many different Forms of Religion among them, yet all these, how various soever, agree in the main Point, which is the worshipping the Divine Essence; and therefore there is nothing to be seen or heard in their Temples, in which the several Perswasions among them may not agree; for every Sect performs those Rites that are peculiar to it, in their private Houses, nor is there any thing in the Publick Worship, that contradicts the particular ways of those different Sects. There are no Images for God in their Temples, so that every one may represent him to his thoughts, according to the way of his Religion; nor do they call this one God by any other Name, but that of Mithras, which is the common Name by which they all express the Divine Essence, whatsoever otherwise they think it to be; nor are there any Prayers among them, but such as every one of them may use without prejudice to his own Opinion.

They meet in their Temples on the Evening of the Festival that concludes a Season: and not having yet broke their Fast, they thank God for their good success during that Year or Month, which is then at an end: and the next day, being that which begins the new Season, they meet early in their Temples, to pray for the happy Progress of all their Affairs during that Period, upon which they then enter. In the Festival which concludes the Period, before they go to the Temple, both Wives and Children fall on their Knees before their Husbands or Parents, and confess every thing in which they have either erred or failed in their Duty, and beg pardon for it: Thus all little Discontents in Families are removed, that so they may offer up their Devotions with a pure and serene mind; for they hold it a great impiety to enter upon them with disturbed thoughts; or when they are conscious to themselves that they bear Hatred or Anger in their Hearts to any Person; and think that they should become liable to severe Punishments, if they presumed to offer

Sacrifices without cleansing their Hearts, and reconciling all their Differences. In the Temples, the two Sexes are separated, the Men go to the right hand, and the Women to the left: and the Males and Females do all place themselves before the Head, and Master or Mistress of that Family to which they belong; so that those who have the Government of them at home, may see their deportment in publick: and they intermingle them so, that the younger and the older may be set by one another; for if the younger sort were all set together, they would perhaps trifle away that time too much, in which they ought to beget in themselves a most religious dread of the Supream Being, which is the greatest, and almost the only incitement to Vertue.

They offer up no living Creature in Sacrifice, nor do they think it suitable to the Divine Being, from whose Bounty it is that these Creatures have derived their Lives, to take pleasure in their Death, or the offering up their Blood. They burn Incense, and other sweet Odours, and have a great number of Wax Lights during their Worship; not out of any Imagination that such Oblations can add any thing to the Divine Nature, for even Prayers do not that; but as it is a harmless and pure way of worshipping God, so they think those sweet Savors and Lights, together with some other Ceremonies, do, by a secret and unaccountable Vertue, elevate Mens Souls, and inflame them with more force and chearfulness during the Divine Worship.

The People appear all in the Temples in white Garments; but the Priest's Vestments are particoloured; both the Work and Colours are wonderful: they are made of no rich Materials, for they are neither embroidered, nor set with precious Stones, but are composed of the Plumes of several Birds, laid together with so much Art, and so neatly, that the true value of them is far beyond the costliest Materials. They say, that in the ordering and placing those Plumes, some dark Mysteries are represented, which pass down among their Priests in a secret Tradition concerning them; and that they are as Hieroglyphicks, putting them in mind of the Blessings that they have received from God, and of their Duties, both to him and to their Neighbours. As soon as the Priest appears in those Ornaments, they all fall prostrate on the Ground, with so much reverence and so deep a silence, that such as look on, cannot but be struck with it, as if it were the effect of the appearance of a Deity. After they have been for some time in this posture, they all stand up, upon a sign given by the Priest, and sing some Hymns to the Honour of God, some musical Instruments playing all the while. These are quite of another form than those that are used among us: but, as many of them are much sweeter than ours, so others are not to be compared to those that we have. Yet in one thing they exceed us much, which is, that all their Musick, both Vocal and Instrumental, does so imitate and express the Passions, and is so fitted to the present occasion, whether the subject matter of the Hymn is chearful, or made to appease, or troubled, doleful, or angry; that the Musick makes an impression of that which is represented, by which it enters deep into the Hearers, and does very much affect and kindle them. When this is done, both Priests and People offer up very solemn Prayers to God in a set

Form of Words; and these are so composed, that whatsoever is pronounced by the whole Assembly, may be likewise applied by every Man in particular to his own condition; in these they acknowledg God to be the Author and Governor of the World, and the Fountain of all the Good that they receive; for which they offer up their Thanksgivings to him; and in particular, they bless him for his Goodness in ordering it so, that they are born under a Government that is the happiest in the World, and are of a Religion that they hope is the truest of all others: but if they are mistaken, and if there is either a better Government, or a Religion more acceptable to God, they implore his Goodness to let them know it, vowing, that they resolve to follow him whithersoever he leads them: but if their Government is the best, and their Religion the truest, then they pray that he may fortify them in it, and bring all the World, both to the same Rules of Life, and to the same Opinions concerning himself; unless, according to the unsearchableness of his Mind, he is pleased with a variety of Religions. Then they pray that God may give them an easy passage at last to himself; not presuming to set limits to him, how early or late it should be; but if it may be wish'd for, without derogating from his Supream Authority, they desire rather to be quickly delivered, and to go to God, tho by the terriblest sort of Death, than to be detained long from seeing him, in the most prosperous course of Life possible. When this Prayer is ended, they all fall down again upon the Ground, and after a little while they rise up, and go home to Dinner; and spend the rest of the day in diversion or Military Exercises. Thus have I described to you, as particularly as I could, the Constitution of that Common-Wealth, which I do not only think to be the best in the World, but to be indeed the only Common-Wealth that truly deserves that name. In all other places, it is visible, that whereas People talk of a Common-Wealth, every Man only seeks his own Wealth; but there where no Man has any Property, all Men do zealously pursue the good of the Publick: and indeed, it is no wonder to see Men act so differently, for in other Common-Wealths, every Man knows, that unless he provides for himself, how flourishing soever the Common-Wealth may be, he must die of Hunger; so that he sees the necessity of preferring his own Concerns to the Publick; but in Utopia, where every Man has a right to every thing, they do all know, that if care is taken to keep the Publick Stores full, no private Man can want any thing; for among them there is no unequal distribution, so that no Man is poor, nor in any necessity; and tho no Man has any thing, yet they are all rich; for what can make a Man so rich, as to lead a serene and chearful Life, free from anxieties; neither apprehending want himself, nor vexed with the endless complaints of his Wife? he is not affraid of the misery of his Children, nor is he contriving how to raise a Portion for his Daughters, but is secure in this, that both he and his Wife, his Children and Grand-Children, to as many Generations as he can fancy, will all live, both plentifully and happily, since among them there is no less care taken of those who were once engaged in Labour, but grow afterwards unable to follow it, than there is elsewhere for these that continue still at it. I would gladly hear any Man compare the Justice that is among them, with that which is among all other Nations; among whom, may I perish, if I see any thing that looks either like Justice, or Equity; for what Justice is there in this, that a Noble-man, a Goldsmith, or a Banquer, or any other Man, that either does nothing at all, or at best is imployed in things that are of no use to the Publick, should live in great luxury and splendor, upon that which is so ill acquired; and a mean Man, a Carter, a Smith, or a Ploughman, that works harder, even than the Beasts themselves, and is imployed in Labours that are so necessary, that no Common-Wealth could hold out an Year to an end without them, can yet be able to earn so poor a livelihood out of it, and must lead so miserable a Life in it, that . . . [2 pages missing] . . . whole People, then they are accounted Laws: and yet these wicked Men after they have, by a most insatiable covetousness, divided that among themselves, with which all the rest might have been well supplied, are far from that happiness, that is enjoyed among the Utopians: for the use as well as the desire of Mony being extinguished, there is much anxiety and great occasions of Mischief cut off with it: and who does not see that Frauds, Thefts, Robberies, Quarrels, Tumults, Contentions, Seditions, Murders, Treacheries, and Witchrafts, that are indeed rather punished than restrained by the severities of Law, would all fall off, if Mony were not any more valued by the World? Mens Fears, Solicitudes, Cares, Labours, and Watchings, would all perish in the same moment, that the value of Mony did sink: even Poverty it self, for the relief of which Mony seems most necessary, would fall, if there were no Mony in the World. And in order to the apprehending this aright, take one instance.

Consider any Year that has been so unfruitful, that many thousands have died of Hunger; and yet if at the end of that Year a survey were made of the Granaries of all the rich Men, that have hoarded up the Corn, it would be found that there was enough among them, to have prevented all that consumption of Men that perished in that Misery: and that if it had been distributed among them, none would have felt the terrible effects of that scarcity; so easy a thing would it be to supply all the necessities of Life, if that blessed thing called Mony, that is pretended to be invented for procuring it, were not really the only thing that obstructed it.

I do not doubt but rich Men are sensible of this, and that they know well how much a greater happiness it were to want nothing that were necessary, than to abound in many superfluities; and to be rescued out of so much Misery, than to abound with so much Wealth: and I cannot think but the sense of every Man's Interest, and the Authority of Christ's Commands, who as he was infinitely wise, and so knew what was best, so was no less good in discovering it to us, would have drawn all the World over to the Laws of the Utopians, if Pride, that plague of Humane Nature, that is the source of so much misery, did not hinder . . . [2 pages missing] . . . count the had given of it in general; and so taking him by the hand, I carried him to supper, and told him I would find out some other time for examining that matter more particularly, and for discoursing more copiously concerning it; for which I wish I may find a good opportunity. In the mean while, tho I cannot perfectly agree to every thing that was related by Raphael, yet there are many things in the Common-Wealth of Utopia, that I rather wish than hope to see followed in our Governments; tho it must be confessed, that he is both a very learned Man, and has had a great practice in the World.

FINIS

2.4.2 Reading and Review Questions

1. Why does More insist on the factuality of this fiction, with himself being a character in the text who firsthand witnesses Hythloday's account of Utopia? How does his self-characterization compare with that of Chaucer's in his Tale of Sir Thopas?

2. What human qualities does More suggest are innate to human beings of all races, places, times, and classes? What are the adverse effects of these innate human qualities? How do the Utopians overcome these adverse effects?

3. How do the Utopians treat gender matters? What qualities does he suggest are innate to all women, to all men? What qualities does he suggest are conditioned by society? What conditioned behaviors of both men and women do the Utopians overcome, and how, and to what effect?

4. Why does More have the Utopians require every person to work on a farm? Why does he not have the Utopians require institutionalized learning?

5. In terms of religion, how tolerant are the Utopians, do you think? Why do they require faith in a divine figure—regardless of which figure?

2.5 THOMAS WYATT

(1503-1542)

The life of Thomas Wyatt, son of minor nobleman Sir Henry Wyatt, modeled the capriciousness of medieval Fortuna—in a Renaissance courtier. Educated at St. John's College, Cambridge, married to the daughter of Lord Cobham, and early serving as a court official, Wyatt followed the expected paths of the successful courtier. In his official capacity, he traveled to France and Italy where studied literature, including Petrarch's sonnets and Pietro Aretino's poems in ottava rima (poems with eight-line stanzas, ten or eleven syllables per line, and ABABABCC rhyme scheme). Wyatt won official posts as Marshal of Calais, Commissioner of the Peace in Essex, and ambassador to Spain.

Image 2.3 | Sir Thomas Wyatt
Artist | Unknown
Source | Wikimedia Commons
License | Public Domain

While in Italy, though, Wyatt was captured by Spanish troops, from whom he escaped. While serving as Commissioner of Peace, he was briefly imprisoned—for uncertain cause. Perhaps a quarrel with the duke of Suffolk led to this misfortune. Perhaps his unverified relationship with Anne Boleyn prior to her marrying Henry VIII won Wyatt disfavor. As ambassador to Spain, he certainly had to face the ire of Emperor Charles V, nephew of Catherine of Aragon, then divorced from Henry VIII. And in 1541, Wyatt was accused of treason by Thomas Bonner, the bishop of London. His masterful self-defense attests to his rhetorical skills, for he won full pardon and resumed his role of ambassador. And en route to meet the Spanish ambassador, Wyatt caught fever and died.

His writing similarly embodies opposing trends. A complete courtier and gentleman, Wyatt was adept at learned pursuits; his prose translation of Plutarch's essay *Quiet of the Mind* was published during his lifetime and well-received. His poetry circulated at court but was not published until 1557 when several of his poems were included in Tottel's important *Songes and Sonettes,* also known as *Tottel's Miscellany.* Wyatt's native English lyrics reflect the influence of medieval popular song and Chaucer's poetry. His metrical stanzas, including terza rima (three-line stanza with chained rhyme scheme of ABA BCB CDC, etc.), ottava rima, rondeau (lyric poems with refrains), and sonnets, reflect the influence of Italian and French literature. Indeed, his translations of Petrarch's sonnets led to Wyatt's introducing the sonnet into English. And he is credited with inventing the fourteen-line poem with ABBA ABBA CDDC EE rhyme scheme known as the English (or Shakespearian) sonnet.

He did not invent but certainly helped popularize sonnet conventions (or conceits), including the disdainful lady, the agonized lover, and the idealized mistress. He added to traditional sonnet imagery—such as comparing love to sickness, servitude, and war—his unique perspective on life's instabilities and uncertainties. And to the metrical regularity he brought to English poetry, he added his own irregular metric patterns and rough, often colloquial, speech patterns and language.

2.5.1 "The Long Love That in My Thought Doth Harbor"

(1557)

The long love that in my thought doth harbour
And in mine hert doth keep his residence,
Into my face presseth with bold pretence
And therein campeth, spreading his banner.
She that me learneth to love and suffer
And will that my trust and lustës negligence
Be rayned by reason, shame, and reverence,
With his hardiness taketh displeasure.
Wherewithall unto the hert's forest he fleeth,

Leaving his enterprise with pain and cry,
And there him hideth and not appeareth.
What may I do when my master feareth
But in the field with him to live and die?
For good is the life ending faithfully.

2.5.2 "My Galley"

(1557)

My galley, chargèd with forgetfulness,
Thorough sharp seas in winter nights doth pass
'Tween rock and rock; and eke mine en'my, alas,
That is my lord, steereth with cruelness;
And every owre a thought in readiness,
As though that death were light in such a case.
An endless wind doth tear the sail apace
Of forced sighs and trusty fearfulness.
A rain of tears, a cloud of dark disdain,
Hath done the weared cords great hinderance;
Wreathèd with error and eke with ignorance.
The stars be hid that led me to this pain;
Drownèd is Reason that should me comfort,
And I remain despairing of the port.

2.5.3 "Whoso List to Hunt"

(1557)

Whoso list to hunt, I know where is an hind,
But as for me, hélas, I may no more.
The vain travail hath wearied me so sore,
I am of them that farthest cometh behind.
Yet may I by no means my wearied mind
Draw from the deer, but as she fleeth afore
Fainting I follow. I leave off therefore,
Sithens in a net I seek to hold the wind.
Who list her hunt, I put him out of doubt,
As well as I may spend his time in vain.
And graven with diamonds in letters plain
There is written, her fair neck round about:
Noli me tangere, for Caesar's I am,
And wild for to hold, though I seem tame.

2.5.4 "My Lute, Awake!"

(1557)

My labor that thou and I shall waste
And end that I have now begun,
For when this song is sung and past,
My lute, be still, for I have done.

As to be heard where ear is none,
As lead to grave in marble stone,
My song may pierce her heart as soon.
Should we then sigh or sing or moan?
No, no, my lute, for I have done.

Proud of the spoil that thou hast got
Of simple hearts through love's shot,
By whom, unkind, thou hast them won,
Think not he hath his bow forgot,
Although my lute and I have done.

Vengance shall fall on thy disdain
That makest but game on earnest pain;
Think not alone under the sun
Unquit to cause thy lovers plain
Although my lute and I have done.

Perchance thee lie withered and old
The winter nights that are so cold,
Plaining in vain unto the moon;
Thy wishes then dare not be told.
Care then who list, for I have done.

And then may chance thee to repent
The time that thou hast lost and spnt
To cause thy lovers sigh and swoon;
Then shalt thou know beauty but lent,
And wish and want as I have done.

Now cease, my lute, this is the last
Labor that thou and I shall waste
And ended is that we begun.
Now is the song both sung and past;
My lute, be still, for I have done.

2.5.5 "They Flee From Me"

(1557)

They flee from me that sometime did me seek
With naked foot, stalking in my chamber.
I have seen them gentle, tame, and meek,
That now are wild and do not remember
That sometime they put themself in danger
To take bread at my hand; and now they range,
Busily seeking with a continual change.

Thanked be fortune it hath been otherwise
Twenty times better; but once in special,
In thin array after a pleasant guise,
When her loose gown from her shoulders did fall,
And she me caught in her arms long and small;
Therewithall sweetly did me kiss
And softly said, 'dear heart, how like you this?'

It was no dream: I lay broad waking.
But all is turned thorough my gentleness
Into a strange fashion of forsaking;
And I have leave to go of her goodness,
And she also, to use newfangleness.
But since that I so kindly am served
I would fain know what she hath deserved.

2.5.6 "And Wilt Thou Leave Me Thus?"

(1557)

And wilt thou leave me thus?
Say nay, say nay, for shame,
To save thee from the blame
Of all my grief and grame;
And wilt thou leave me thus?
Say nay, say nay!

And wilt thou leave me thus,
That hath loved thee so long
In wealth and woe among?
And is thy heart so strong

As for to leave me thus?
Say nay, say nay!

And wilt thou leave me thus,
That hath given thee my heart
Never for to depart,
Nother for pain nor smart;
And wilt thou leave me thus?
Say nay, say nay!

And wilt thou leave me thus
And have no more pity
Of him that loveth thee?
Hélas, thy cruelty!
And wilt thou leave me thus?
Say nay, say nay!

2.5.7 Reading and Review Questions

1. How consistent, or logically-developed, are the metaphors in Wyatt's poetry? Consider, for example, the following metaphors in "The Long Love:" love harbors in his heart and keeps residence there; love camps and spreads a banner; love is like a deer taking refuge in a forest, etc.

2. In "My Galley," how effective, if at all, is the extended comparison of the speaker to a storm-tossed ship?

3. "Whoso List to Hunt" is a translation of a Petrarchan sonnet. Yet, some scholars perceive in it autobiographical references to Wyatt's supposed relationship with Anne Boleyn ("Noli me tangere, for Caesar's I am,/ And wild for to hold, though I seem tame"). How, if at all, does Wyatt introduce personal elements in his sonnets? How sincere are his sonnets? How do you know?

4. In "My Lute, Awake!" Wyatt seems to be displaying his own artfulness. His song is his complaint to an unnamed desired lady, and when he ends the song, his lute will be silent. What is the purpose of this art, do you think? Between the lady and his art, which is more important to Wyatt, do you think? How do you know?

5. "And Wilt Thou Leave Me Thus?" repeats lines almost like a song. Do these repetitions add meaning to the poem, or are they ornamental? How do you know?

2.6 HENRY HOWARD, EARL OF SURREY

(1517-1547)

Henry Howard had a some-what ostentatious childhood, as his friends and blood relations tied him to Henry VIII. He was first cousin to both Queens Anne Boleyn and Catherine Howard (1523-1542), respectively the second and fifth wives of Henry VIII, both of whom he had beheaded. He was also childhood comrade and close friend to Henry FitzRoy, 1st Duke of Richmond and Somerset (1519-1536), Henry VIII's illegitimate son.

He served as Lieutenant General of the King on Sea and Land, fighting in the wars against France. He also participated in the suppression of the Pilgrimage of Grace, the Yorkshire uprising

Image 2.4 | Henry Howard, Earl of Surrey
Artist | Unknown
Source | Wikimedia Commons
License | Public Domain

against the dissolution of the monasteries. These official activities were offset by more unruly and imperious behavior, including striking a courtier and destroying property by rapping with pebbles on the windows of houses in London, for both of which actions he was imprisoned. He was beheaded for the prideful and treasonable act of quartering the arms of Edward the Confessor (1003-1066). Though he was entitled to bear Edward the Confessor's arms, Surrey's doing so posed a threat to Henry VIII who had him tried for desiring to usurp the crown from Henry's only male heir, the future Edward VI. Surrey was condemned and executed on Tower Hill on January 19, 1547.

He was survived by five children by his wife Frances de Vere, daughter of John de Vere, 15th Earl of Oxford; memorialized by an opulent painted alabaster tomb in St. Michael's at Framlingham; and immortalized in literature by joining Wyatt as one of the first poets to write sonnets in English. He most commonly used Wyatt's English or Shakespearean sonnet form. These formal restraints release an intimate, emotional expression and responsiveness. In his translations of Virgil's *Aeneid* Books 2 and 4, Surrey was the first to use blank verse, or lines of iambic pentameter, that has been deemed uniquely appropriate to the English language. His literary output included love poems, elegies, and translations of Psalms and Ecclesiastes from the Bible.

Image 2.5 | Tomb of Henry Howard, Earl of Surrey and his wife Frances de Vere
Artist | Steve Parker
Source | Wikimedia Commons
License | CC BY 2.0

2.6.1 "The soote season"

(1557)

The soote season, that bud and bloom forth brings,
With green hath clad the hill and eke the vale.
The nightingale with feathers new she sings;
The turtle to her make hath told her tale.
Summer is come, for every spray now springs.
The hart hath hung his old head on the pale;
The buck in brake his winter coat he flings;
The fishes float with new repairèd scale;
The adder all her slough away she slings;
The swift swallow pursueth the fliès small;
The busy bee her honey now she mings.
Winter is worn, that was the flowers' bale.
And thus I see among these pleasant things,
Each care decays, and yet my sorrow springs.

2.6.2 "Love, that doth reign and live within my thought"

(1557)

Love, that doth reign and live within my thought,
And built his seat within my captive breast,
Clad in the arms wherein with me he fought,
Oft in my face he doth his banner rest.
But she that taught me love and suffer pain,
My doubtful hope and eke my hot desir
With shamefast look to shadow and refrain,
Her smiling grace converteth straight to ire.
And coward Love then to the heart apace
Taketh his flight, where he doth lurk and plain,
His purpose lost, and dare not show his face.
For my lord's guilt thus faultless bide I pain,
Yet from my lord shall not my foot remove:
Sweet is the death that taketh end by love.

2.6.3 "Alas! so all things now do hold their peace"

(1557)

Alas! so all things now do hold their peace,
Heaven and earth disturbèd in no thing.
The beast, the air, the birds their song do cease;
The nightès chare the stars about doth bring;
Calm is the sea, the waves work less and less.
So am not I, whom love, alas, doth wring,
Bringing before my face the great increase
Of my desires, whereat I weep and sing,
In joy and woe, as in a doubtful ease:
For my sweet thoughts sometime do pleasure bring,
But by and by the cause of my disease
Gives me a pang that inwardly doth sting,
When that I think what grief it is, again,
To live, and lack the thing should rid my pain.

2.6.4 "So cruel prison how could betide"

(1557)

So cruel prison how could betide, alas,
As proud Windsor, where I in lust and joy
With a king's son my childish years did pass
In greater feast than Priam's sons of Troy?

Where each sweet place returns a taste full sour:
The large green courts, where we were wont to hove,
With eyes cast up unto the Maidens' Tower,
And easy sighs, such as folk draw in love.

The stately sales, the ladies bright of hue,
The dances short, long tales of great delight,
With words and looks that tigers could but rue,
Where each of us did plead the other's right.

The palm play where, dispoilèd for the game,
With dazed eyes oft we by gleams of love
Have missed the ball and got sight of our dame,
To bait her eyes, which kept the leads above.

The graveled ground, with sleeves tied on the helm,
On foaming horse, with swords and friendly hearts,
With cheer as though the one should overwhelm,
Where we have fought and chasèd oft with darts.

With silver drops the meads yet spread for ruth,
In active games of nimbleness and strength,
Where we did strain, trailèd by swarms of youth,
Our tender limbs that yet shot up in length.

The secret groves which oft we made resound
Of pleasant plaint and of our ladies' praise,
Recording soft what grace each one had found,
What hope of speed, what dread of long delays.

The wild forest, the clothèd holts with green,
With reins availed and swift breathèd horse,
With cry of hounds and merry blasts between,
Where we did chase the fearful hart a force.

The void walls eke that harbored us each night,
Wherewith, alas, revive within my breast
The sweet accord, such sleeps as yet delight,
The pleasant dreams, the quiet bed of rest,

The secret thoughts imparted with such trust,
The wanton talk, the divers change of play,

The friendship sworn, each promise kept so just,
Wherewith we passed the winter nights away.

And with this thought, the blood forsakes my face,
The tears berain my cheeks of deadly hue,
The which as soon as sobbing sighs, alas,
Upsuppèd have, thus I my plaint renew:

"O place of bliss, renewer of my woes,
Give me accompt, where is my noble fere,
Whom in thy walls thou didst each night enclose,
To other lief, but unto me must dear."

Each stone, alas, that doth my sorrow rue,
Returns thereto a hollow sound of plaint.
Thus I alone, where all my freedom grew,
In prison pine with bondage and restraint.

And with remembrance of the greater grief
To banish the less, I find my chief relief.

2.6.5 "O happy dames, that may embrace"

(1557)

O happy dames, that may embrace
The fruit of your delight,
Help to bewail the woeful case
And eke the heavy plight
Of me, that wonted to rejoice
The fortune of my pleasant choice:
Good ladies, help to fill my mourning voice.

In ship, freight with rememberance
Of thoughts and pleasures past,
He sails, that hath in governance
My life, while it will last;
With scalding sighs, for lack of gale,
Futhering his hope, that is his sail,
Toward me, the sweet port of his avail.

Alas, how oft in dreams I see
Those eyes, that were my food,
Which sometime so delighted me,

That yet they do me good;
Wherewith I wake with his return,
Whose absent flame did make me burn:
But when I find the lack, Lord how I mourn!

When other lovers in arms across
Rejoice their chief delight,
Drowned in tears to mourn my loss
I stand the bitter night
In my window, where I may see
Before the winds how the clouds flee.
Lo, what a mariner love hath made me!

And in green waves when the salt flood
Doth rise by rage of wind,
A thousand fancies in that mood
Assail my restless mind.
Alas, now drencheth my sweet foe,
That with the spoil of my heart did go
And left me; but, alas, why did he so?

And when the seas wax calm again,
To chese from me annoy,
My doubtful hope doth cause my plain,
So dread cuts off my joy.
Thus is my wealth mingled with woe,
And of each thought a doubt doth grow:
Now he comes! Will he come? Alas, no, no!

2.6.6 Reading and Review Questions

1. To what effect does Surrey use sounds, like consonance and assonance? How does his use of sounds compare to Wyatt's?

2. What seems characteristically English in the sonnets' nature imagery, especially considering that their source is Italian (Petrarch's Sonnets)? How does his use of sonnet conventions compare with Wyatt's?

3. How do Surrey's closing couplet's complete their respective sonnets' meaning and intent?

4. To Surrey, what makes Windsor a more than physical prison, and why?

5. The speaker in "O happy dames, that may embrace," is a female. What attitudes towards and expectations of women does Surrey reveal through his speaker's words?

2.7 QUEEN ELIZABETH

(1533-1603)

Queen Elizabeth I was the daughter of Henry VIII and Anne Boleyn, who was beheaded when Elizabeth was two years old. After Henry and his third wife Jane Seymour (c. 1508-1537) had Edward, Henry's longed-for male heir, Elizabeth and her half sister Mary were declared illegitimate. As Henry's daughter, legitimate or otherwise, Elizabeth was tutored in music and in the French, Spanish, Greek, and Latin languages. Her tutors included the classicists William Grindal (d. 1548) and Roger Ascham (c. 1515-1568).

Although she lost her biological mother at an early age, Elizabeth received care from her step-mothers, particularly Catherine Parr (1512-1548), who survived Henry. After Henry's death, Catherine married Thomas

Image 2.6 | The Coronation of Queen Elizabeth
Artist | Unknown
Source | Wikimedia Commons
License | Public Domain

Seymour, who used his proximity to Elizabeth to influence her and possibly to angle for her hand in a future marriage. Her half-brother Edward's brief reign had little effect on Elizabeth's life. The reign of his successor, Elizabeth's half-sister Mary, however, caused dangerous upheaval, to Elizabeth proper and to the country as a whole. Protestant rebels rallied against the Roman Catholic Mary's succession, first for Jane Grey (1537-1554), a legitimate daughter of Henry's sister, then for Elizabeth. Although she herself did not encourage or conspire with the rebels, Elizabeth was briefly imprisoned in the Tower of London under suspicion of treason.

Elizabeth succeeded Mary to rule a country straitened by Continental war and internal religious strife. With the Act of Supremacy (1558), Elizabeth reestablished the Church of England; with the Act of Uniformity (1558), she established the Book of Common Prayer. She also maintained a tenuous peace with the Continent, particularly France and Spain, for the greater part of her reign. Prudent, cautious, and extremely wise in her choice of advisors, Elizabeth used her single status to her advantage. Nations that might have warred with her instead sent her suitors, including the Dukes of Saxony, Holstein, Anjou and Savoy; Prince Frederick of Denmark; Don Carlos of Spain; and King Charles IX of France. Only when she supported the Protestant rebellion against Spain in the Netherlands did she trigger the long-threatened attack of the Spanish Armada in 1588. Its defeat heralded a golden age for her realm and her rule.

Religious strife again threatened when her cousin Mary Stuart, Queen of the Scots, married the future King of France. His early death brought the threats closer to home with several assassination attempts made against Elizabeth in hopes of making Mary Queen of England as well as Scotland. When Mary took refuge in England, Elizabeth had her imprisoned in Fotheringhay Castle, keeping the threat at bay for nineteen years. From her imprisonment, Mary encouraged rebellion and was implicated in the Babington Plot against Elizabeth's life and was consequently beheaded.

In her later years, Elizabeth faced riots at home due to food shortages and rebellion in Ireland. The latter gave armed troops to a court favorite, Robert Devereaux, 2nd Earl of Essex (b. 1565). His troops did not suppress the Irish rebellion but instead supported his own against Elizabeth. He was beheaded for treason in 1601. Elizabeth I's long reign fostered England's economic growth, military strength, and, most importantly, artistic and literary immortality. To the end of her life, she refused to soothe her nation's fears against her own mortality by marrying and then bearing an heir. She wedded herself to England and her subjects.

Her writing reflects the emotional weight of the political challenges she faced as a female and as a sovereign—as a woman, who was both an individual and a symbol, who always had too much to lose. She wrote in many forms, including speeches for state occasions, translations, and poems. In her poems, we hear her voice—poignant and strong, emotional and moral—and can appreciate her complexity.

2.7.1 "The Doubt of Future Foes"

(ca. 1568)

The doubt of future foes exiles my present joy,
And wit me warns to shun such snares as threatens mine annoy.
For falsehood now doth flow, and subjects faith doth ebb,
Which should not be, if reason ruled or wisdom weaved the web.
But clouds of toys untried do cloak aspiring minds,
Which turns to rain of late repent, by course of changèd winds.
The top of hope supposed, the root of rue shall be,
And fruitless all their grafted guile, as shortly you shall see.
Their dazzled eyes with pride, which great ambition blinds,
Shall be unsealed by worthy wights whose foresight falsehood finds.
The daughter of debate, that discord aye doth sow,
Shall reap no gain where former rule still peace hath taught to grow.

No foreign banished wight shall anchor in this port:
Our realm brooks no seditious sects--let them elsewhere resort.
My rusty sword through rest shall first his edge employ
To poll their tops who seek such change or gape for future joy.

2.7.2 "On Monsieur's Departure"

(ca. 1582)

I grieve and dare not show my discontent,
I love and yet am forced to seem to hate,
I do, yet dare not say I ever meant,
I seem stark mute but inwardly do prate.
    I am and not, I freeze and yet am burned,
    Since from myself another self I turned.

My care is like my shadow in the sun,
Follows me flying, flies when I pursue it,
Stands and lies by me, doth what I have done.
His too familiar care doth make me rue it.
    No means I find to rid him from my breast,
    Till by the end of things it be supprest.

Some gentler passion slide into my mind,
For I am soft and made of melting snow;
Or be more cruel, love, and so be kind.
Let me or float or sink, be high or low.
    Or let me live with some more sweet content,
    Or die and so forget what love ere meant.

2.7.3 "The Golden Speech"

(1601)

Mr Speaker,

    We have heard your declaration and perceive your care of our estate. I do assure you there is no prince that loves his subjects better, or whose love can countervail our love. There is no jewel, be it of never so rich a price, which I set before this jewel: I mean your love. For I do esteem it more than any treasure or riches; for that we know how to prize, but love and thanks I count invaluable. And, though God hath raised me high, yet this I count the glory of my Crown, that I have reigned with your loves. This makes me that I do not so much rejoice that God hath made me to be a Queen, as to be a Queen over so thankful a people. Therefore I have cause to wish nothing more than to content the subject and that is a duty which I owe.

Neither do I desire to live longer days than I may see your prosperity and that is my only desire. And as I am that person still yet, under God, hath delivered you and so I trust by the almighty power of God that I shall be his instrument to preserve you from every peril, dishonour, shame, tyranny and oppression, partly by means of your intended helps which we take very acceptably because it manifesteth the largeness of your good loves and loyalties unto your sovereign.

Of myself I must say this: I never was any greedy, scraping grasper, nor a strait fast-holding Prince, nor yet a waster. My heart was never set on any worldly goods. What you bestow on me, I will not hoard it up, but receive it to bestow on you again. Therefore render unto them I beseech you Mr Speaker, such thanks as you imagine my heart yieldeth, but my tongue cannot express. Mr Speaker, I would wish you and the rest to stand up for I shall yet trouble you with longer speech. Mr Speaker, you give me thanks but I doubt me I have greater cause to give you thanks, than you me, and I charge you to thank them of the Lower House from me. For had I not received a knowledge from you, I might have fallen into the lapse of an error, only for lack of true information.

Since I was Queen, yet did I never put my pen to any grant, but that upon pretext and semblance made unto me, it was both good and beneficial to the subject in general though a private profit to some of my ancient servants, who had deserved well at my hands. But the contrary being found by experience, I am exceedingly beholden to such subjects as would move the same at first. And I am not so simple to suppose but that there be some of the Lower House whom these grievances never touched. I think they spake out of zeal to their countries and not out of spleen or malevolent affection as being parties grieved. That my grants should be grievous to my people and oppressions to be privileged under colour of our patents, our kingly dignity shall not suffer it. Yea, when I heard it, I could give no rest unto my thoughts until I had reformed it. Shall they, think you, escape unpunished that have oppressed you, and have been respectless of their duty and regardless our honour? No, I assure you, Mr Speaker, were it not more for conscience' sake than for any glory or increase of love that I desire, these errors, troubles, vexations and oppressions done by these varlets and lewd persons not worthy of the name of subjects should not escape without condign punishment. But I perceive they dealt with me like physicians who, ministering a drug, make it more acceptable by giving it a good aromatical savour, or when they give pills do gild them all over.

I have ever used to set the Last Judgement Day before mine eyes and so to rule as I shall be judged to answer before a higher judge, and now if my kingly bounties have been abused and my grants turned to the hurt of my people contrary to my will and meaning, and if any in authority under me have neglected or perverted what I have committed to them, I hope God will not lay their culps and offenses in my charge. I know the title of a King is a glorious title, but assure yourself that the shining glory of princely authority hath not so dazzled the eyes of our understanding, but that we well know and remember that we also are to yield an account of our actions before the great judge. To be a king and wear a crown is a thing more glorious to them that see it than it is pleasant to them that bear it. For myself I was never so much enticed with the glorious name of a King or royal authority of a Queen as delighted that God hath made me his instrument to maintain his truth and glory and to defend his kingdom as I said from peril, dishonour, tyranny and oppression. There will never Queen sit in my seat with more zeal to my country, care to my subjects and that will sooner with willingness venture her life for your good and safety than myself. For it is my desire to live nor reign no longer than my life and reign shall be for your good. And though you have had, and may have, many princes more mighty and wise sitting in this seat, yet you never had nor shall have, any that will be more careful and loving.

For I, oh Lord, what am I, whom practices and perils past should not fear? Or what can I do? That I should speak for any glory, God forbid. And I pray to you Mr Comptroller, Mr Secretary and you of my Council, that before these gentlemen go into their countries, you bring them all to kiss my hand.

2.7.4 Reading and Review Questions

1. "The doubt of future foes" takes as its subject a woman, Mary Queen of Scots, the "daughter of debate." Does this poem attribute any womanly qualities to its subject? Why, or why not?

2. Many Elizabethan love poems lament and deplore the beloved who is often portrayed as deceptive and untrustworthy. How does "On Monsieur's Departure" both repeat and reevaluate this depiction of a beloved woman? How does this depiction compare with that of Wyatt's?

3. In the Elizabethan era, women were considered weak and passive. To what degree, if any, does "On Monsieur's Departure" rely on this view, and why?

4. What virtues, if any, does Elizabeth attribute to herself in her "Golden Speech" (given to members of Parliament after she revoked patents that gave disproportionate wealth to their holders)? What societal values, if any, does she claim to uphold, and why?

5. What heroic qualities, if any, does Elizabeth attribute to herself in her poems, in her "Golden Speech," and why?

2.8 EDMUND SPENSER

(1552-1599)

Although connected to a "house of auncient fame," that of the Spencers of Althorpe, Northampton, Edmund Spenser entered Pembroke College, Cambridge as a poor scholar. There he benefitted from the Renaissance concept of the perfect courtier and studied Hebrew, Greek, Latin, French, vernacular English, and vocal and instrumental music. He also acquired proper deportment by acting in annual plays performed for the court.

He published his first poetry while at Cambridge, including translations from Petrarch (1304-1374) and Joachim du Bellay (1522-1560). He also became friends with the poet and scholar Gabriel Harvey (c. 1552-1631) who later published his correspondence with Spenser and whom

Image 2.7 | Edmund Spenser
Artist | Unknown
Source | Wikimedia Commons
License | Public Domain

Spenser later portrayed as Hobinol in *Shepheardes Calendar* (1579). After earning his Master of Art degree, he returned to London where Harvey introduced Spenser to Sir Philip Sidney (1554-1586) and secured him a place in the household of Robert Dudley, 1ˢᵗ Earl of Leicester (1532-1588). Although he may have traveled to various places, including Ireland—likely serving as private messenger to Leicester—Spenser spent most of his time at the homes of either Sidney or Leicester. Sidney's *Defense of Poesy* as well as his Protestant advocacy seem especially to have influenced Spenser. And it is Sidney to whom Spenser dedicated his pastoral eclogue (classically-styled poem on a pastoral subject) *Shepheardes Calendar*.

This work was modeled on Greek, Italian, and French pastorals but was particularly indebted to Chaucer, as appears in its use of archaic language. It establishes and builds on the growing interest in native poetry. Interest in native, or vernacular, English literature was growing due to increased education, Renaissance learning, and increased nationalism. Spenser's poetic fame grew as he circulated several of his poetic works among friends. For a short time, Spenser was a member of the "Areopagus," a group of writers including Fulke Greville, 1ˢᵗ Baron Brooke (1554-162) that promoted English as a literary language. Among Spenser's important contributions to this endeavor are the ABAB BCBC CDCD EE rhyme scheme of what came to be known as the Spenserian sonnet as well as the Spenserian stanza, comprising eight lines in iambic pentameter with the final line in iambic hexameter.

In 1580, Spenser was appointed private secretary by Arthur Grey, Baron Grey de Wilton (1536-1593), the new Lord Deputy, with whom Spenser traveled to

Ireland. Grey actively suppressed Irish rebels and attempted to do the same to Roman Catholicism in Ireland. After Grey left Ireland, Spenser remained there as a civil servant, acquiring property in County Kildare, Cork, and Munster. Sir Walter Raleigh, who had extensive property in Munster, visited Spenser in 1589. Raleigh encouraged Spenser's literary ambitions, and the two returned to London where Raleigh presented Spenser to Elizabeth I. In 1590, Spenser published the first installment of *The Faerie Queene,* dedicated to "the most mighty and magnificent Empresse Elizabeth, by the grace of God, Queene of England, France, and Ireland; Defender of the Faith, &c." He prefaced his epic with sonnets commended to such important figures of his day as William Cecil, 1st Baron Burghley (1520-1598), Raleigh, and Mary (Sidney) Herbert, the Countess of Pembroke.

The Faerie Queene won Spenser immediate acclaim and a pension of fifty pounds a year, but not the preferment at Court to which he aspired. He returned to Ireland, to his duties as clerk, to the management of his estate, and to his writing. In 1594, he married Elizabeth Boyle, who was related to Sir Richard Boyle, later created the first Earl of Cork. The next year, Spenser commemorated his courtship and marriage in his *Amoretti* and *Epithalamion,* the latter after the classical celebration of a bride and bridegroom.

In 1596, he published the second instalment of *The Faeirie Queene* at the Stationers' Hall. The following year, Elizabeth I recommended him as Sheriff of Cork in Ireland. The tone of his Mutability Cantos, the last cantos of *The Faerie*

Queene he wrote, was justified by the final events of his life. During Tyrone's Rebellion, his castle at Kilcolman was sacked and burnt to the ground. Spenser and his family escaped to Cork. He then traveled to Westminster with dispatches for Elizabeth I, including his own policy statement on the "recovery of the Realme of Ireland." Whatever role he may have played in that recovery was cut short by his death, following a sudden illness soon after his arrival in Westminster. He died on January 16, 1599. He was buried at Westminster Abbey, next to Chaucer.

Envisaged as a national epic, *The Faerie Queene* draws on Arthurian legend and includes elements of romance, fable, and allegory. Although he completed only six of the twenty-four books he projected, Spenser seems to have offered a completed poem through which he declared himself to be a Poet, that is, his country's Virgil.

Image 2.8 | *The Faerie Queene* Title Page
Artist | Edmund Spenser
Source | Wikimedia Commons
License | Public Domain

Indeed, the body of Spenser's work as a whole follows Virgil's, who wrote in the order of the creation of the arts: pastoral, romances, and epics. The opening of *The Faerie Queene* echoes Virgil's *Aeneid,* as does also its overall structure with twelve cantos similar to the *Aeneid's* twelve books. Each book of the *Faerie Queene* is dedicated to a single virtue: Holiness, Temperance, Chastity, Friendship, Justice, and Courtesy. As a national epic, *The Faerie Queene* is also a religious and moral work, an embodiment of its dedicated virtues, the forms of which we cannot actually see. However, we can see beauty (with which we can fall in love), so Spenser presents these virtues as beauties, as abstract ideals made concrete.

Each book also has its own hero, beginning with the Redcrosse Knight, the knight of holiness. The technical hero is Prince Arthur, who connects with each book's hero, traveling through their lives and assisting them as he searches for his beloved, Gloriana, who first joined him in a dream. Prince Arthur represents the complete gentleman, for each virtue is magnified in him in the appropriate book, and at the epic's end, Arthur will be the perfect (or perfected) knight. The real virtue needed to read the epic is constancy, which is the virtue announced in the Mutability Cantos, the fragment that "completes" the epic.

The conception of the poem, the twelve virtues formed in Prince Arthur, is found in Sidney's *Defense of Poesy* which declares the intent of poetry to be making the reader virtuous. Prince Arthur models the perfect gentleman and courtier for England, and the grand intent and effect of Spenser's poem is to produce a similarly-perfected reader.

The Faerie Queene is also an allegory, writing in which the subject and object are both divided and brought together. One of the first people we meet in Book I, Canto I is a beautiful virgin named Una whose parents (Adam and Eve) are held captive by a dragon (death); Una represents Veiled Truth, and allegory is a form of Veiled Truth. The allegory in Canto I represents not only the one true (Protestant) church—that frees all sons of Adam and daughters of Eve from death—but also Spenser's literary art. The Redcrosse Knight mistakenly defends unveiled truth in the figure of (the Roman Catholic, Whore of Babylon) Duessa, the "two-faced," not-at-all virgin, false mirror of Una. Veiled and unveiled Truth thus represent how allegory can be two things at the same time: truth and fiction (or "lie"). Like a labyrinth, this epic leads the reader past images and symbols of art to truth itself.

2.8.1 from *The Faerie Queene*

Book I

Canto I

> *The Patron of true Holinesse*
> *foule Errour doth defeate;*
> *Hypocrisie him to entrappe*
> *doth to his home entreate.*

I

A GENTLE Knight was pricking on the plaine,
Ycladd in mightie armes and silver shielde,
Wherein old dints of deepe wounds did remaine,
The cruel markes of many'a bloudy fielde;
Yet armes till that time did he never wield:
His angry steede did chide his foming bitt,
As much disdayning to the curbe to yield:
Full jolly knight he seemd, and faire did sitt,
As one for knightly giusts and fierce encounters fitt.

II

And on his brest a bloudie Crosse he bore,
The deare remembrance of his dying Lord,
For whose sweete sake that glorious badge he wore,
And dead as living ever him ador'd:
Upon his shield the like was also scor'd,
For soveraine hope, which in his helpe he had:
Right faithfull true he was in deede and word,
But of his cheere did seeme too solemne sad;
Yet nothing did he dread, but ever was ydrad.

III

Upon a great adventure he was bond,
That greatest Gloriana to him gave,
That greatest Glorious Queene of Faerie lond,
To winne him worship, and her grace to have,
Which of all earthly things he most did crave;
And ever as he rode, his hart did earne
To prove his puissance in battell brave
Upon his foe, and his new force to learne;
Upon his foe, a Dragon horrible and stearne.

IV

A lovely Ladie rode him faire beside,
Upon a lowly Asse more white then snow,
Yet she much whiter, but the same did hide
Under a vele, that wimpled was full low,
And over all a blacke stole she did throw,
As one that inly mournd: so was she sad,
And heavie sat upon her palfrey slow;
Seemed in heart some hidden care she had,
And by her in a line a milke white lambe she lad.

V

So pure and innocent, as that same lambe,
She was in life and every vertuous lore,
And by descent from Royall lynage came
Of ancient Kings and Queenes, that had of yore
Their scepters stretcht from East to Westerne shore,
And all the world in their subjection held;
Till that infernall feend with foule uprore
Forwasted all their land, and them expeld:
Whom to avenge, she had this Knight from far compeld.

VI

Behind her farre away a Dwarfe did lag,
That lasie seemd in being ever last,
Or wearied with bearing of her bag
Of needments at his backe. Thus as they past,
The day with cloudes was suddeine overcast,
And angry Jove an hideous storme of raine
Did poure into his Lemans lap so fast,
That everie wight to shrowd it did constrain,
And this faire couple eke to shroud themselves were fain.

VII

Enforst to seeke some covert nigh at hand,
A shadie grove not far away they spide,
That promist ayde the tempest to withstand:
Whose loftie trees yclad with sommers pride
Did spred so broad, that heavens light did hide,
Not perceable with power of any starre:
And all within were pathes and alleies wide,
With footing worne, and leading inward farre:
Faire harbour that them seemes; so in they entred arre.

VIII

And foorth they passe, with pleasure forward led,
Joying to heare the birdes sweete harmony,
Which therein shrouded from the tempest dred,
Seemd in their song to scorne the cruell sky.
Much can they prayse the trees so straight and hy,
The sayling Pine, the Cedar proud and tall,
The vine-prop Elme, the Poplar never dry,
The builder Oake, sole king of forrests all,
The Aspine good for staves, the Cypresse funerall.

IX

The Laurell, meed of mightie Conquerours
And Poets sage, the firre that weepeth still,
The Willow worne of forlorne Paramours,
The Eugh obedient to the benders will,
The Birch for shaftes, the Sallow for the mill,
The Mirrhe sweete bleeding in the bitter wound,
The warlike Beech, the Ash for nothing ill,
The fruitfull Olive, and the Platane round,
The carver Holme, the Maple seeldom inward sound.

X

Led with delight, they thus beguile the way,
Untill the blustring storme is overblowne;
When weening to returne, whence they did stray,
They cannot finde that path, which first was showne,
But wander too and fro in wayes unknowne,
Furthest from end then, when they neerest weene,
That makes them doubt their wits be not their owne:
So many pathes, so many turnings seene,
That which of them to take, in diverse doubt they been.

XI

At last resolving forward still to fare,
Till that some end they finde or in or out,
That path they take, that beaten seemd most bare,
And like to lead the labyrinth about;
Which when by tract they hunted had throughout,
At length it brought them to a hollow cave
Amid the thickest woods. The Champion stout
Eftsoones dismounted from his courser brave,
And to the Dwarfe awhile his needlesse spere he gave.

XII

Be well aware, quoth then that Ladie milde,
Least suddaine mischiefe ye too rash provoke:
The danger hid, the place unknowne and wilde,
Breedes dreadfull doubts: Oft fire is without smoke,
And perill without show: therefore your stroke,
Sir Knight, with-hold, till further triall made.
Ah Ladie, (said he) shame were to revoke
The forward footing for an hidden shade:
Vertue gives her selfe light, through darkenesse for to wade.

XIII

Yea but (quoth she) the perill of this place
I better wot then you, though now too late
To wish you backe returne with foule disgrace,
Yet wisedome warnes, whilest foot is in the gate,
To stay the steppe, ere forced to retrate.
This is the wandring wood, this Errours den,
A monster vile, whom God and man does hate:
Therefore I read beware. Fly fly (quoth then
The fearefull Dwarfe) this is no place for living men.

XIV

But full of fire and greedy hardiment,
The youthfull knight could not for ought be staide,
But forth unto the darksome hole he went,
And looked in: his glistring armor made
A litle glooming light, much like a shade,
By which he saw the ugly monster plaine,
Halfe like a serpent horribly displaide,
But th'other halfe did womans shape retaine,
Most lothsom, filthie, foule, and full of vile disdaine.

XV

And as she lay upon the durtie ground,
Her huge long taile her den all overspred,
Yet was in knots and many boughtes upwound,
Pointed with mortall sting. Of her there bred
A thousand yong ones, which she dayly fed,
Sucking upon her poisnous dugs, eachone
Of sundry shapes, yet all ill favored:
Soone as that uncouth light upon them shone,
Into her mouth they crept, and suddain all were gone.

XVI

Their dam upstart, out of her den effraide,
And rushed forth, hurling her hideous taile
About her cursed head, whose folds displaid
Were stretcht now forth at length without entraile.
She lookt about, and seeing one in mayle
Armed to point, sought backe to turne againe;
For light she hated as the deadly bale,
Ay wont in desert darknesse to remaine,
Where plain none might her see, nor she see any plaine.

XVII

Which when the valiant Elfe perceiv'd, he lept
As Lyon fierce upon the flying pray,
And with his trenchand blade her boldly kept
From turning backe, and forced her to stay:
Therewith enrag'd she loudly gan to bray,
And turning fierce, her speckled taile advaunst,
Threatning her angry sting, him to dismay:
Who nought aghast his mightie hand enhaunst:
The stroke down from her head unto her shoulder glaunst.

XVIII

Much daunted with that dint, her sence was dazd,
Yet kindling rage, her selfe she gathered round,
And all attonce her beastly body raizd
With doubled forces high above the ground:
Tho wrapping up her wrethed sterne arownd,
Lept fierce upon his shield, and her huge traine
All suddenly about his body wound,
That hand or foot to stirre he strove in vaine:
God helpe the man so wrapt in Errours endlesse traine.

XIX

His Lady sad to see his sore constraint,
Cride out, Now now Sir knight, shew what ye bee,
Add faith unto your force, and be not faint:
Strangle her, else she sure will strangle thee.
That when he heard, in great perplexitie,
His gall did grate for griefe and high disdaine,
And knitting all his force got one hand free,
Wherewith he grypt her gorge with so great paine,
That soone to loose her wicked bands did her constraine.

XX

Therewith she spewd out of her filthy maw
A floud of poyson horrible and blacke,
Full of great lumpes of flesh and gobbets raw,
Which stunck so vildly, that it forst him slacke
His grasping hold, and from her turne him backe:
Her vomit full of bookes and papers was,
With loathly frogs and toades, which eyes did lacke,
And creeping sought way in the weedy gras:
Her filthy parbreake all the place defiled has.

XXI

As when old father Nilus gins to swell
With timely pride above the Aegyptian vale,
His fattie waves do fertile slime outwell,
And overflow each plaine and lowly dale:
But when his later spring gins to avale,
Huge heapes of mudd he leaves, wherein there breed
Ten thousand kindes of creatures, partly male
And partly female of his fruitful seed;
Such ugly monstrous shapes elswhere may no man reed.

XXII

The same so sore annoyed has the knight,
That welnigh choked with the deadly stinke,
His forces faile, ne can no lenger fight.
Whose corage when the feend perceiv'd to shrinke,
She poured forth out of her hellish sinke
Her fruitfull cursed spawne of serpents small,
Deformed monsters, fowle, and blacke as inke,
With swarming all about his legs did crall,
And him encombred sore, but could not hurt at all.

XXIII

As gentle Shepheard in sweete even-tide,
When ruddy Phoebus gins to welke in west,
High on an hill, his flocke to vewen wide,
Markes which do byte their hasty supper best,
A cloud of combrous gnattes do him molest,
All striving to infixe their feeble stings,
That from their noyance he no where can rest,
But with his clownish hands their tender wings
He brusheth oft, and oft doth mar their murmurings.

XXIV

Thus ill bestedd, and fearefull more of shame,
Then of the certeine perill he stood in,
Halfe furious unto his foe he came,
Resolv'd in minde all suddenly to win,
Or soone to lose, before he once would lin
And strooke at her with more then manly force,
That from her body full of filthie sin
He raft her hatefull head without remorse;
A streame of cole black bloud forth gushed from her corse.

XXV

Her scattred brood, soone as their Parent deare
They saw so rudely falling to the ground,
Groning full deadly, all with troublous feare,
Gathred themselves about her body round,
Weening their wonted entrance to have found
At her wide mouth: but being there withstood
They flocked all about her bleeding wound,
And sucked up their dying mothers blood,
Making her death their life, and eke her hurt their good.

XXVI

That detestable sight him much amazde,
To see th' unkindly Impes, of heaven accurst,
Devoure their dam; on whom while so he gazd,
Having all satisfide their bloudy thurst,
Their bellies swolne he saw with fulnesse burst,
And bowels gushing forth: well worthy end
Of such as drunke her life, the which them nurst;
Now needeth him no lenger labour spend,
His foes have slaine themselves, with whom he should contend.

XXVII

His Ladie seeing all that chaunst, from farre
Approcht in hast to greet his victorie,
And said, Faire knight, borne under happy starre,
Who see your vanquisht foes before you lye:
Well worthie be you of that Armorie,
Wherin ye have great glory wonne this day,
And proov'd your strength on a strong enimie,
Your first adventure: many such I pray,
And henceforth ever wish that like succeed it may.

XXVIII

Then mounted he upon his Steede againe,
And with the Lady backward sought to wend;
That path he kept which beaten was most plaine,
Ne ever would to any by-way bend,
But still did follow one unto the end,
The which at last out of the wood them brought.
So forward on his way (with God to frend)

He passed forth, and new adventure sought;
Long way he travelled, before he heard of ought.

XXIX

At length they chaunst to meet upon the way
An aged Sire, in long blacke weedes yclad,
His feete all bare, his beard all hoarie gray
And by his belt his booke he hanging had;
Sober he seemde, and very sagely sad,
And to the ground his eyes were lowly bent,
Simple in shew, and voyde of malice bad,
And all the way he prayed, as he went,
And often knockt his brest, as one that did repent.

XXX

He faire the knight saluted, louting low,
Who faire him quited, as that courteous was:
And after asked him, if he did know
Of straunge adventures, which abroad did pas.
Ah my deare Sonne (quoth he) how should, alas,
Silly old man, that lives in hidden cell,
Bidding his beades all day for his trespas,
Tydings of warre and worldly trouble tell?
With holy father sits not with such things to mell.

XXXI

But if of daunger which hereby doth dwell,
And homebred evil ye desire to heare,
Of a straunge man I can you tidings tell,
That wasteth all this countrey farre and neare.
Of such (said he) I chiefly do inquere,
And shall you well reward to shew the place,
In which that wicked wight his dayes doth weare:
For to all knighthood it is foule disgrace,
That such a cursed creature lives so long a space.

XXXII

Far hence (quoth he) in wastfull wildernesse
His dwelling is, by which no living wight
May ever passe, but thorough great distresse.
Now (sayd the Lady) draweth toward night,
And well I wote, that of your later fight
Ye all forwearied be: for what so strong,

Page | 697

But wanting rest will also want of might?
The Sunne that measures heaven all day long,
At night doth baite his steedes the Ocean waves emong.

XXXIII

Then with the Sunne take Sir, your timely rest,
And with new day new worke at once begin:
Untroubled night they say gives counsell best.
Right well Sir knight ye have advised bin,
(Quoth then that aged man;) the way to win
Is wisely to advise: now day is spent;
Therefore with me ye may take up your In
For this same night. The knight was well content:
So with that godly father to his home they went.

XXXIV

A little lowly Hermitage it was,
Downe in a dale, hard by a forests side,
Far from resort of people, that did pas
In travell to and froe: a little wyde
There was an holy Chappell edifyde,
Wherein the Hermite dewly wont to say
His holy things each morne and eventyde:
Thereby a Christall streame did gently play,
Which from a sacred fountaine welled forth alway.

XXXV

Arrived there, the little house they fill,
Ne looke for entertainement, where none was:
Rest is their feast, and all things at their will:
The noblest mind the best contentment has.
With faire discourse the evening so they pas:
For that old man of pleasing wordes had store,
And well could file his tongue as smooth as glas,
He told of Saintes and Popes, and evermore
He strowd an *Ave-Mary* after and before.

XXXVI

The drouping Night thus creepeth on them fast,
And the sad humour loading their eye liddes,
As messenger of Morpheus on them cast
Sweet slombring deaw, the which to sleepe them biddes.
Unto their lodgings then his guestes he riddes:

Where when all drownd in deadly sleepe he findes,
He to this study goes, and there amiddes
His Magick bookes and artes of sundry kindes,
He seekes out mighty charmes, to trouble sleepy mindes.

XXXVII

Then choosing out few words most horrible,
(Let none them read) thereof did verses frame,
With which and other spelles like terrible,
He bad awake blacke Plutoes griesly Dame,
And cursed heaven and spake reprochfull shame
Of highest God, the Lord of life and light;
A bold bad man, that dar'd to call by name
Great Gorgon, Prince of darknesse and dead night,
At which Cocytus quakes, and Styx is put to flight.

XXXVIII

And forth he cald out of deepe darknesse dred
Legions of Sprights, the which like little flyes
Fluttring about his ever damned hed,
Awaite whereto their service he applyes,
To aide his friends, or fray his enimies:
Of those he chose out two, the falsest twoo,
And fittest for to forge true-seeming lyes;
The one of them he gave a message too,
The other by him selfe staide other worke to doo.

XXXIX

He making speedy way through spersed ayre,
And through the world of waters wide and deepe,
To Morpheus house doth hastily repaire.
Amid the bowels of the earth full steepe,
And low, where dawning day doth never peepe,
His dwelling is; there Tethys his wet bed
Doth ever wash, and Cynthia still doth steepe
In silver deaw his ever-drouping hed,
Whiles sad Night over him her mantle black doth spred.

XL

Whose double gates he findeth locked fast,
The one faire fram'd of burnisht Yvory,
The other all with silver overcast;
And wakeful dogges before them farre do lye,

Watching to banish Care their enimy,
Who oft is wont to trouble gentle Sleepe.
By them the Sprite doth passe in quietly,
And unto Morpheus comes, whom drowned deepe
In drowsie fit he findes: of nothing he takes keepe.

XLI

And more, to lulle him in his slumber soft,
A trickling streame from high rock tumbling downe,
And ever-drizling raine upon the loft,
Mixt with a murmuring winde, much like the sowne
Of swarming Bees, did cast him in a swowne:
No other noyse, nor peoples troublous cryes,
As still are wont t'annoy the walled towne,
Might there be heard: but carelesse Quiet lyes,
Wrapt in eternall silence farre from enemyes.

XLII

The messenger approching to him spake,
But his wast wordes returnd to him in vaine:
So sound he slept, that nought mought him awake.
Then rudely he him thrust, and pusht with paine
Whereat he gan to stretch: but he againe
Shooke him so hard, that forced him to speake.
As one then in a dreame, whose dryer braine
Is tost with troubled sights and fancies weake,
He mumbled soft, but would not all his silence breake.

XLIII

The Sprite then gan more boldly him to wake,
And threatned unto him the dreaded name
Of Hecate: whereat he gan to quake,
And lifting up his lumpish head, with blame
Halfe angry asked him, for what he came.
Hither (quoth he) me Archimago sent,
He that the stubborne Sprites can wisely tame,
He bids thee to him send for his intent
A fit false dreame, that can delude the sleepers sent.

XLIV

The God obayde, and, calling forth straightway
A diverse dreame out of his prison darke,
Delivered it to him, and downe did lay

Page | 700

His heavie head, devoide of carefull carke,
Whose sences all were straight benumbed and starke.
He backe returning by the Yvorie dore,
Remounted up as light as chearefull Larke,
And on his litle winges the dreame he bore
In hast unto his Lord, where he him left afore.

XLV

Who all this while with charmes and hidden artes,
Had made a Lady of that other Spright,
And fram'd of liquid ayre her tender partes
So lively, and so like in all mens sight,
That weaker sence it could have ravisht quight:
The maker selfe, for all his wondrous witt,
Was nigh beguiled with so goodly sight:
Her all in white he clad, and over it
Cast a black stole, most like to seeme for Una fit.

XLVI

Now when that ydle dreame was to him brought,
Unto that Elfin knight he bad him fly,
Where he slept soundly void of evill thought,
And with false shewes abuse his fantasy,
In sort as he him schooled privily:
And that new creature, borne without her dew,
Full of the makers guile, with usage sly
He taught to imitate that Lady trew,
Whose semblance she did carrie under feigned hew.

XLVII

Thus well instructed, to their worke they hast,
And coming where the knight in slomber lay,
The one upon his hardy head him plast
And made him dreame of loves and lustfull play,
That nigh his manly hart did melt away,
Bathed in wanton blis and wicked joy:
Then seemed him his Lady by him lay,
And to him playnd, how that false winged boy,
Her chast hart had subdewd, to learne Dame Pleasures toy.

XLVIII

And she herselfe of beautie soveraigne Queene,
Fayre Venus seemde unto his bed to bring

Her, whom he waking evermore did weene,
To bee the chastest flowre, that ay did spring
On earthly braunch, the daughter of a king,
Now a loose Leman to vile service bound:
And eke the Graces seemed all to sing,
Hymen Iö Hymen dauncing all around,
Whilst freshest Flora her with Yvie girlond crownd.

XLIX

In this great passion of unwonted lust,
Or wonted feare of doing ought amis,
He started up, as seeming to mistrust
Some secret ill, or hidden foe of his:
Lo there before his face his Lady is,
Under blake stole hyding her bayted hooke;
And as halfe blushing offred him to kis,
With gentle blandishment and lovely looke,
Most like that virgin true, which for her knight him took.

L

All cleane dismayd to see so uncouth sight,
And half enraged at her shamelesse guise,
He thought have slaine her in his fierce despight:
But hasty heat tempring with suffrance wise,
He stayde his hand, and gan himselfe advise
To prove his sense, and tempt her faigned truth.
Wringing her hands in womans pitteous wise,
Tho can she weepe, to stirre up gentle ruth,
Both for her noble bloud, and for her tender youth.

LI

And said, Ah Sir, my liege Lord and my love,
Shall I accuse the hidden cruell fate,
And mightie causes wrought in heaven above,
Or the blind God, that doth me thus amate,
For hoped love to winne me certaine hate?
Yet thus perforce he bids me do, or die.
Die is my dew; yet rew my wretched state
You, whom my hard avenging destinie
Hath made judge of my life or death indifferently.

LII

Your owne deare sake forst me at first to leave
My Fathers kingdome—There she stopt with teares;
Her swollen hart her speech seemd to bereave,
And then againe begun; My weaker yeares
Captiv'd to fortune and frayle worldly feares,
Fly to your fayth for succour and sure ayde:
Let me not dye in languor and long teares.
Why Dame (quoth he) what hath ye thus dismayd?
What frayes ye, that were wont to comfort me affrayd?

LIII

Love of your selfe, she saide, and deare constraint,
Lets me not sleepe, but wast the wearie night
In secret anguish and unpittied plaint,
Whiles you in carelesse sleepe are drowned quight.
Her doubtfull words made that redoubted knight
Suspect her truth: yet since no' untruth he knew,
Her fawning love with foule disdainefull spight
He would not shend; but said, Deare dame I rew,
That for my sake unknowne such griefe unto you grew.

LIV

Assure your selfe, it fell not all to ground;
For all so deare as life is to my hart,
I deeme your love, and hold me to you bound:
Ne let vaine feares procure your needlesse smart,
Where cause is none, but to your rest depart.
Not all content, yet seemd she to appease
Her mournefull plaintes, beguiled of her art,
And fed with words that could not chuse but please,
So slyding softly forth, she turned as to her ease.

LV

Long after lay he musing at her mood,
Much griev'd to thinke that gentle Dame so light,
For whose defence he was to shed his blood.
At last, dull wearinesse of former fight
Having yrockt asleepe his irkesome spright,
That troublous dreame gan freshly tosse his braine,
With bowres, and beds, and Ladies deare delight:
But when he saw his labour all was vaine,
With that misformed spright he backe returnd againe.

Canto II

The guilefull great Enchaunter parts
the Redcrosse Knight from truth,
Into whose stead faire Falshood steps,
and workes him wofull ruth.

I

BY this the Northerne wagoner had set
His sevenfold teme behind the stedfast starre,
That was in Ocean waves yet never wet,
But firme is fixt, and sendeth light from farre
To all that in the wide deepe wandring arre:
And chearefull Chaunticlere with his note shrill
Had warned once, that Phœbus fiery carre
In hast was climbing up the Easterne hill,
Full envious that night so long his roome did fill.

II

When those accursed messengers of hell,
That feigning dreame, and that faire-forged Spright
Came to their wicked maister, and gan tell
Their bootelesse paines, and ill succeeding night:
Who all in rage to see his skilfull might
Deluded so, gan threaten hellish paine
And sad Proserpines wrath, them to affright.
But when he saw his threatning was but vaine,
He cast about, and searcht his baleful bookes againe.

III

Eftsoones he tooke that miscreated faire,
And that false other Spright, on whom he spred
A seeming body of the subtile aire,
Like a young Squire, in loves and lustybed
His wanton dayes that ever loosely led,
Without regard of armes and dreaded fight:
Those two he tooke, and in a secret bed,
Coverd with darknesse and misdeeming night,
Them both together laid, to joy in vaine delight.

IV

Forthwith he runnes with feigned faithfull hast
Unto his guest, who after troublous sights
And dreames, gan now to take more sound repast,

Whom suddenly he wakes with fearfull frights,
As one aghast with feends or damned sprights,
And to him cals, Rise, rise, unhappy Swaine
That here wex old in sleepe, whiles wicked wights
Have knit themselves in Venus shameful chaine,
Come see where your false Lady doth her honour staine.

V

All in amaze he suddenly upstart
With sword in hand, and with the old man went
Who soone him brought into a secret part
Where that false couple were full closely ment
In wanton lust and leud embracement:
Which when he saw, he burnt with gealous fire,
The eye of reason was with rage yblent,
And would have slaine them in his furious ire,
But hardly was restreined of that aged sire.

VI

Returning to his bed in torment great,
And bitter anguish of his guiltie sight,
He could not rest, but did his stout heart eat,
And wast his inward gall with deepe despight,
Yrkesome of life, and too long lingring night.
At last faire Hesperus in highest skie
Had spent his lampe and brought forth dawning light,
Then up he rose, and clad him hastily;
The Dwarfe him brought his steed: so both away do fly.

VII

Now when the rosy-fingred Morning faire,
Weary of aged Tithones saffron bed,
Had spread her purple robe through deawy aire,
And the high hils Titan discovered,
The royall virgin shooke off drowsy-hed;
And rising forth out of her baser bowre,
Lookt for her knight, who far away was fled,
And for her Dwarfe, that wont to wait each houre:
Then gan she waile and weepe, to see that woefull stowre.

VIII

And after him she rode with so much speede
As her slow beast could make; but all in vaine:

For him so far had borne his light-foot steede,
Pricked with wrath and fiery fierce disdaine,
That him to follow was but fruitlesse paine;
Yet she her weary limbes would never rest,
But every hill and dale, each wood and plaine,
Did search, sore grieved in her gentle brest,
He so ungently left her, whom she loved best.

IX

But subtill Archimago, when his guests
He saw divided into double parts,
And Una wandring in woods and forrests,
Th' end of his drift, he praisd his divelish arts,
That had such might over true meaning harts:
Yet rests not so, but other meanes doth make,
How he may worke unto her further smarts:
For her he hated as the hissing snake,
And in her many troubles did most pleasure take.

X

He then devisde himselfe how to disguise;
For by his mightie science he could take
As many formes and shapes in seeming wise,
As ever Proteus to himselfe could make:
Sometime a fowle, sometime a fish in lake,
Now like a foxe, now like a dragon fell,
That of himselfe he ofte for feare would quake,
And oft would flie away. O who can tell
The hidden power of herbes and might of Magicke spell?

XI

But now seemde best the person to put on
Of that good knight, his late beguiled guest:
In mighty armes he was yclad anon:
And silver shield, upon his coward brest
A bloudy crosse, and on his craven crest
A bounch of haires discolourd diversly:
Full jolly knight he seemde, and well addrest,
And when he sate upon his courser free,
Saint George himself ye would have deemed him to be.

XII

But he the knight, whose semblaunt he did beare,
The true Saint George, was wandred far away,
Still flying from his thoughts and gealous feare;
Will was his guide, and griefe led him astray.
At last him chaunst to meete upon the way
A faithless Sarazin all arm'd to point,
In whose great shield was writ with letters gay
Sans foy: full large of limbe and every joint
He was, and cared not for God or man a point.

XIII

He had a faire companion of his way,
A goodly Lady clad in scarlot red,
Purfled with gold and pearle of rich assay,
And like a Persian mitre on her hed
She wore, with crowns and owches garnished,
The which her lavish lovers to her gave;
Her wanton palfrey all was overspred
With tinsell trappings, woven like a wave,
Whose bridle rung with golden bels and bosses brave.

XIV

With faire disport and courting dalliaunce
She intertainde her lover all the way:
But when she saw the knight his speare advaunce,
She soone left off her mirth and wanton play,
And bade her knight addresse him to the fray:
His foe was nigh at hand. He prickt with pride
And hope to winne his Ladies heart that day,
Forth spurred fast: adowne his coursers side
The red bloud trickling staind the way, as he did ride.

XV

The knight of the Redcrosse when him he spide,
Spurring so hote with rage dispiteous,
Gan fairely couch his speare, and towards ride:
Soone meete they both, both fell and furious,
That daunted with their forces hideous,
Their steeds do stagger, and amazed stand,
And eke themselves, too rudely rigorous,
Astonied with the stroke of their owne hand
Doe backe rebut, and each to other yeeldeth land.

XVI

As when two rams stird with ambitious pride,
Fight for the rule of the rich fleeced flocke,
Their horned fronts so fierce on either side
Do meete, that with the terrour of the shocke
Astonied both, stand sencelesse as a blocke,
Forgetfull of the hanging victory:
So stood these twaine, unmoved as a rocke,
Both staring fierce, and holding idely
The broken reliques of their former cruelty.

XVII

The Sarazin sore daunted with the buffe
Snatcheth his sword, and fiercely to him flies;
Who well it wards, and quyteth cuff with cuff:
Each others equall puissaunce envies,
And through their iron sides with cruell spies
Does seeke to perce: repining courage yields
No foote to foe. The flashing fier flies
As from a forge out of their burning shields,
And streams of purple bloud new dies the verdant fields.

XVIII

Curse on that Crosse (quoth then the Sarazin),
That keepes thy body from the bitter fit;
Dead long ygoe I wote thou haddest bin,
Had not that charme from thee forwarned it:
But yet I warne thee now assured sitt,
And hide thy head. Therewith upon his crest
With rigour so outrageous he smitt,
That a large share it hewd out of the rest,
And glauncing down his shield from blame him fairly blest.

XIX

Who thereat wondrous wroth, the sleeping spark
Of native vertue gan eftsoones revive,
And at his haughtie helmet making mark,
So hugely stroke, that it the steele did rive,
And cleft his head. He tumbling downe alive,
With bloudy mouth his mother earth did kis.
Greeting his grave: his grudging ghost did strive
With the fraile flesh; at last it flitted is,
Whither the soules do fly of men that live amis.

XX

The Lady when she saw her champion fall,
Like the old ruines of a broken towre,
Staid not to waile his woefull funerall,
But from him fled away with all her powre;
Who after her as hastily gan scowre,
Bidding the Dwarfe with him to bring away
The Sarazins shield, signe of the conqueroure.
Her soone he overtooke, and bad to stay,
For present cause was none of dread her to dismay.

XXI

She turning backe with ruefull countenaunce,
Cride, Mercy mercy Sir vouchsafe to show
On silly Dame, subject to hard mischaunce,
And to your mighty will. Her humblesse low
In so ritch weedes and seeming glorious show,
Did much emmove his stout heroicke heart,
And said, Deare dame, your suddin overthrow
Much rueth me; but now put feare apart,
And tell, both who ye be, and who that tooke your part.

XXII

Melting in teares, then gan she thus lament;
The wretched woman, whom unhappy howre
Hath now made thrall to your commandement,
Before that angry heavens list to lowre,
And fortune false betraide me to your powre,
Was, (O what now availeth that I was!)
Borne the sole daughter of an Emperour,
He that the wide West under his rule has,
And high hath set his throne, where Tiberis doth pas.

XXIII

He in the first flowre of my freshest age,
Betrothed me unto the onely haire
Of a most mighty king, most rich and sage;
Was never Prince so faithfull and so faire,
Was never Prince so meeke and debonaire;
But ere my hoped day of spousall shone,
My dearest Lord fell from high honours staire
Into the hands of his accursed fone,
And cruelly was slaine, that shall I ever mone.

XXIV

His blessed body spoild of lively breath,
Was afterward, I know not how, convaid
And fro me hid: of whose most innocent death
When tidings came to me, unhappy maid,
O how great sorrow my sad soule assaid.
Then forth I went his woefull corse to find,
And many yeares throughout the world I straid,
A virgin widow, whose deepe wounded mind
With love long time did languish as the striken hind.

XXV

At last it chaunced this proud Sarazin
To meete me wandring, who perforce me led
With him away, but yet could never win
The Fort, that Ladies hold in soveraigne dread;
There lies he now with foule dishonour dead,
Who whiles he livde, was called proud Sansfoy,
The eldest of three brethren, all three bred
Of one bad sire, whose youngest is Sansjoy;
And twixt them both was born the bloudy bold Sansloy.

XXVI

In this sad plight, friendlesse, unfortunate,
Now miserable I Fidessa dwell,
Craving of you in pitty of my state,
To do none ill, if please ye not do well.
He in great passion all this while did dwell,
More busying his quicke eyes, her face to view,
Then his dull eares, to heare what she did tell;
And said, Faire Lady hart of flint would rew
The undeserved woes and sorrowes which ye shew.

XXVII

Henceforth in safe assuraunce may ye rest,
Having both found a new friend you to aid,
And lost an old foe that did you molest:
Better new friend then an old foe is said.
With chaunge of cheare the seeming simple maid
Let fall her eyen, as shamefast to the earth,
And yeelding soft, in that she nought gain-said,
So forth they rode, he feining seemely merth,
And she coy lookes: so dainty they say maketh derth.

XXVIII

Long time they thus together traveiled,
Till weary of their way, they came at last
Where grew two goodly trees, that faire did spred
Their armes abroad, with gray mosse overcast,
And their greene leaves trembling with every blast,
Made a calme shadow far in compasse round:
The fearfull Shepheard often there aghast
Under them never sat, ne wont there sound
His mery oaten pipe, but shund th' unlucky ground.

XXIX

But this good knight soone as he them can spie,
For the cool shade him thither hastly got:
For golden Phœbus now ymounted hie,
From fiery wheeles of his faire chariot
Hurled his beame so scorching cruell hot,
That living creature mote it not abide;
And his new Lady it endured not.
There they alight, in hope themselves to hide
From the fierce heat, and rest their weary limbs a tide.

XXX

Faire seemely pleasaunce each to other makes,
With goodly purposes there as they sit:
And in his falsed fancy he her takes
To be the fairest wight that lived yit;
Which to expresse he bends his gentle wit,
And thinking of those braunches greene to frame
A girlond for her dainty forehead fit,
He pluckt a bough; out of whose rift there came
Small drops of gory bloud, that trickled down the same.

XXXI

Therewith a piteous yelling voyce was heard,
Crying, O spare with guilty hands to teare
My tender sides in this rough rynd embard,
But fly, ah fly far hence away, for feare
Least to you hap, that happened to me heare,
And to this wretched Lady, my deare love,
O too deare love, love bought with death too deare.
Astond he stood, and up his haire did hove,
And with that suddein horror could no member move.

XXXII

At last whenas the dreadfull passion
Was overpast, and manhood well awake,
Yet musing at the straunge occasion,
And doubting much his sence, he thus bespake;
What voyce of damned Ghost from Limbo lake,
Or guilefull spright wandring in empty aire,
Both which fraile men do oftentimes mistake,
Sends to my doubtfull eares these speaches rare,
And ruefull plaints, me bidding guiltlesse bloud to spare?

XXXIII

Then groning deepe, Nor damned Ghost, (quoth he,)
Nor guileful sprite to thee these wordes doth speake,
But once a man Fradubio, now a tree,
Wretched man, wretched tree; whose nature weake
A cruell witch her cursed will to wreake,
Hath thus transformd, and plast in open plaines,
Where Boreas doth blow full bitter bleake,
And scorching Sunne does dry my secret vaines:
For though a tree I seeme, yet cold and heat me paines.

XXXIV

Say on Fradubio then, or man, or tree,
Quoth then the knight, by whose mischievous arts
Art thou misshaped thus, as now I see?
He oft finds med'cine, who his griefe imparts;
But double griefs afflict concealing harts,
As raging flames who striveth to suppresse.
The author then (said he) of all my smarts,
Is one Duessa a false sorceresse,
That many errant knights hath brought to wretchednesse.

XXXV

In prime of youthly yeares, when corage hot
The fire of love and joy of chevalree
First kindled in my brest, it was my lot
To love this gentle Lady, whom ye see,
Now not a Lady, but a seeming tree;
With whom as once I rode accompanyde,
Me chaunced of a knight encountred bee,
That had a like faire Lady by his syde,
Like a faire Lady, but did fowle Duessa hyde.

XXXVI

Whose forged beauty he did take in hand,
All other Dames to have exceeded farre;
I in defence of mine did likewise stand,
Mine, that did then shine as the Morning starre.
So both to battell fierce arraunged arre,
In which his harder fortune was to fall
Under my speare: such is the dye of warre:
His Lady left as a prise martiall,
Did yield her comely person to be at my call.

XXXVII

So doubly lov'd of Ladies unlike faire,
Th' one seeming such, the other such indeede,
One day in doubt I cast for to compare,
Whether in beauties glorie did exceede;
A Rosy girlond was the victors meede:
Both seemde to win, and both seemde won to bee,
So hard the discord was to be agreede.
Fraelissa was as faire, as faire mote bee,
And ever false Duessa seemde as faire as shee.

XXXVIII

The wicked witch now seeing all this while
The doubtfull ballaunce equally to sway,
What not by right, she cast to win by guile,
And by her hellish science raisd streightway
A foggy mist, that overcast the day,
And a dull blast, that breathing on her face,
Dimmed her former beauties shining ray,
And with foule ugly forme did her disgrace:
Then was she faire alone, when none was faire in place.

XXXIX

Then cride she out, Fye, fye, deformed wight,
Whose borrowed beautie now appeareth plaine
To have before bewitched all mens sight;
O leave her soone, or let her soone be slaine.
Her loathly visage viewing with disdaine,
Eftsoones I thought her such, as she me told,
And would have kild her; but with faigned paine
The false witch did my wrathfull hand with-hold;
So left her, where she now is turnd to treen mould.

XL

Then forth I tooke Duessa for my Dame,
And in the witch unweeting joyd long time,
Ne ever wist but that she was the same,
Till on a day (that day is every Prime,
When Witches wont do penance for their crime)
I chaunst to see her in her proper hew,
Bathing her selfe in origane and thyme:
A filthy foule old woman I did vew,
That ever to have toucht her I did deadly rew.

XLI

Her neather parts misshapen, monstruous,
Were hidd in water, that I could not see.
But they did seeme more foule and hideous,
Then womans shape man would beleeve to bee.
Thensforth from her most beastly companie
I gan refraine, in minde to slip away,
Soone as appeard safe opportunitie:
For danger great, if not assur'd decay,
I saw before mine eyes, if I were knowne to stray.

XLII

The divelish hag by chaunges of my cheare
Perceiv'd my thought, and drownd in sleepie night,
With wicked herbs and ointments did besmeare
My body all, through charms and magicke might,
That all my senses were bereaved quight:
Then brought she me into this desert waste,
And by my wretched lovers side me pight,
Where now enclosd in wooden wals full faste,
Banisht from living wights, our wearie dayes we waste.

XLIII

But how long time, said then the Elfin knight,
Are you in this misformed house to dwell?
We may not chaunge (quoth he) this evil plight,
Till we be bathed in a living well;
That is the terme prescribed by the spell.
O how, said he, mote I that well out find,
That may restore you to your wonted well?
Time and suffised fates to former kynd
Shall us restore, none else from hence may us unbynd.

XLIV

The false Duessa, now Fidessa hight,
Heard how in vaine Fradubio did lament,
And knew well all was true. But the good knight
Full of sad feare and ghastly dreriment,
When all this speech the living tree had spent,
The bleeding bough did thrust into the ground,
That from the bloud he might be innocent,
And with fresh clay did close the wooden wound:
Then turning to his Lady, dead with feare her found.

XLV

Her seeming dead he found with feigned feare,
As all unweeting of that well she knew,
And paynd himselfe with busie care to reare
Her out of carelesse swowne. Her eyelids blew
And dimmed sight with pale and deadly hew
At last she up gan lift: with trembling cheare
Her up he tooke, too simple and too trew,
And oft her kist. At length all passed feare,
He set her on her steede, and forward forth did beare.

Canto III

Forsaken Truth long seekes her love,
and makes the Lyon mylde,
Marres blind Devotions mart, and fals
in hand of leachour vylde.

I

NOUGHT is there under heav'ns wide hollownesse,
That moves more deare compassion of mind,
Then beautie brought t' unworthy wretchednesse
Through envies snares, or fortunes freakes unkind.
I, whether lately through her brightnesse blind,
Or through alleageance and fast fealtie,
Which I do owe unto all woman kind,
Feele my hart perst with so great agonie,
When such I see, that all for pittie I could die.

II

And now it is empassioned so deepe,
For fairest Unaes sake, of whom I sing,
That my fraile eyes these lines with teares do steepe,

To thinke how she through guilefull handeling,
Though true as touch, though daughter of a king,
Though faire as ever living wight was faire,
Though nor in word nor deede ill meriting,
Is from her knight divorced in despaire,
And her due loves deriv'd to that vile witches share.

III

Yet she most faithfull Ladie all this while
Forsaken, wofull, solitarie mayd
Far from all peoples prease, as in exile,
In wildernesse and wastfull deserts strayd,
To seeke her knight; who subtilly betrayd
Through that late vision, which th' Enchaunter wrought,
Had her abandond. She of nought affrayd,
Through woods and wastnesse wide him daily sought;
Yet wished tydings none of him unto her brought.

IV

One day nigh wearie of the yrkesome way,
From her unhastie beast she did alight,
And on the grasse her daintie limbes did lay
In secret shadow, farre from all mens sight:
From her faire head her fillet she undight,
And laid her stole aside. Her angels face
As the great eye of heaven shyned bright,
And made a sunshine in the shadie place;
Did never mortall eye behold such heavenly grace.

V

It fortuned out of the thickest wood
A ramping Lyon rushed suddainly,
Hunting full greedy after salvage blood;
Soone as the royall virgin he did spy,
With gaping mouth at her ran greedily,
To have attonce devourd her tender corse:
But to the pray when as he drew more ny,
His bloody rage asswaged with remorse,
And with the sight amazd, forgat his furious forse.

VI

In stead thereof he kist her wearie feet,
And lickt her lilly hands with fawning tong,

As he her wronged innocence did weet.
O how can beautie maister the most strong,
And simple truth subdue avenging wrong?
Whose yeelded pride and proud submission,
Still dreading death, when she had marked long,
Her hart gan melt in great compassion,
And drizling teares did shed for pure affection.

VII

The Lyon Lord of every beast in field,
Quoth she, his princely puissance doth abate,
And mightie proud to humble weake does yield,
Forgetfull of the hungry rage, which late
Him prickt, in pittie of my sad estate:
But he my Lyon, and my noble Lord,
How does he find in cruell hart to hate,
Her that him lov'd, and ever most adord,
As the God of my life? why hath he me abhord?

VIII

Redounding teares did choke th' end of her plaint,
Which softly ecchoed from the neighbour wood;
And sad to see her sorrowfull constraint
The kingly beast upon her gazing stood;
With pittie calmd, downe fell his angry mood.
At last in close hart shutting up her paine,
Arose the virgin borne of heavenly brood,
And to her snowy Palfrey got againe,
To seeke her strayed Champion, if she might attaine.

IX

The Lyon would not leave her desolate,
But with her went along, as a strong gard
Of her chast person, and a faithfull mate
Of her sad troubles and misfortunes hard:
Still when she slept, he kept both watch and ward,
And when she wakt, he waited diligent,
With humble service to her will prepard:
From her faire eyes he tooke commaundement,
And ever by her lookes conceived her intent.

X

Long she thus traveiled through deserts wyde,
By which she thought her wandring knight shold pas,
Yet never shew of living wight espyde;
Till that at length she found the troden gras,
In which the tract of peoples footing was,
Under the steepe foot of a mountaine hore;
The same she followes, till at last she has
A damzell spyde slow footing her before,
That on her shoulders sad a pot of water bore.

XI

To whom approching she to her gan call,
To weet, if dwelling place were nigh at hand;
But the rude wench her answerd nought at all;
She could not heare, nor speake, nor understand;
Till seeing by her side the Lyon stand,
With suddaine feare her pitcher downe she threw,
And fled away: for never in that land
Face of faire Ladie she before did vew,
And that dread Lyons looke her cast in deadly hew.

XII

Full fast she fled, ne never lookt behynd,
As if her life upon the wager lay,
And home she came, whereas her mother blynd
Sate in eternall night: nought could she say,
But suddaine catching hold, did her dismay
With quaking hands, and other signes of feare;
Who full of ghastly fright and cold affray,
Gan shut the dore. By this arrived there
Dame Una, wearie Dame, and entrance did requere.

XIII

Which when none yeelded, her unruly Page
With his rude claws the wicket open rent,
And let her in; where of his cruell rage
Nigh dead with feare, and faint astonishment,
She found them both in darkesome corner pent;
Where that old woman day and night did pray
Upon her beads devoutly penitent;
Nine hundred *Pater nosters* every day,
And thrise nine hundred *Aves* she was wont to say.

XIV

And to augment her painefull pennance more,
Thrise every weeke in ashes she did sit,
And next her wrinkled skin rough sackcloth wore,
And thrise three times did fast from any bit:
But now for feare her beads she did forget.
Whose needlesse dread for to remove away,
Faire Una framed words and count'nance fit:
Which hardly doen, at length she gan them pray,
That in their cotage small that night she rest her may.

XV

The day is spent, and commeth drowsie night,
When every creature shrowded is in sleepe;
Sad Una downe her laies in wearie plight,
And at her feete the Lyon watch doth keepe:
In stead of rest, she does lament, and weepe
For the late losse of her deare loved knight,
And sighes, and grones, and ever more does steepe
Her tender brest in bitter teares all night,
All night she thinks too long, and often lookes for light.

XVI

Now when Aldeboran was mounted hie
Above the shynie Cassiopeias chaire,
And all in deadly sleepe did drowned lie,
One knocked at the dore, and in would fare;
He knocked fast, and often curst, and sware,
That readie entrance was not at his call:
For on his backe a heavy load he bare
Of nightly stelths, and pillage severall,
Which he had got abroad by purchase criminall.

XVII

He was, to weete, a stout and sturdy thiefe,
Wont to robbe Churches of their ornaments,
And poore mens boxes of their due reliefe,
Which given was to them for good intents;
The holy Saints of their rich vestiments
He did disrobe, when all men carelesse slept,
And spoild the Priests of their habiliments,
Whiles none the holy things in safety kept;
Then he by conning sleights in at the window crept.

XVIII

And all that he by right or wrong could find,
Unto this house he brought, and did bestow
Upon the daughter of this woman blind,
Abessa, daughter of Corceca slow,
With whom he whoredome usd, that few did know,
And fed her fat with feast of offerings,
And plentie, which in all the land did grow;
Ne spared he to give her gold and rings:
And now he to her brought part of his stolen things.

XIX

Thus long the dore with rage and threats he bet,
Yet of those fearfull women none durst rize,
The Lyon frayed them, him in to let:
He would no longer stay him to advize,
But open breakes the dore in furious wize,
And entring is; when that disdainfull beast
Encountring fierce, him suddaine doth surprize,
And seizing cruell clawes on trembling brest,
Under his Lordly foot him proudly hath supprest.

XX

Him booteth not resist, nor succour call,
His bleeding hart is in the vengers hand,
Who streight him rent in thousand peeces small,
And quite dismembred hath: the thirsty land
Drunke up his life; his corse left on the strand.
His fearefull friends weare out the wofull night,
Ne dare to weepe, nor seeme to understand
The heavie hap, which on them is alight,
Affraid, least to themselves the like mishappen might.

XXI

Now when broad day the world discovered has,
Up Una rose, up rose the Lyon eke,
And on their former journey forward pas,
In wayes unknowne, her wandring knight to seeke,
With paines farre passing that long wandring Greeke,
That for his love refused deitie;
Such were the labours of his Lady meeke,
Still seeking him, that from her still did flie;
Then furthest from her hope, when most she weened nie.

XXII

Soone as she parted thence, the fearfull twaine,
That blind old woman and her daughter deare,
Came forth, and finding Kirkrapine there slaine,
For anguish great they gan to rend their heare,
And beat their brests, and naked flesh to teare.
And when they both had wept and wayld their fill,
Then forth they ran like two amazed deare,
Halfe mad through malice, and revenging will,
To follow her, that was the causer of their ill.

XXIII

Whom overtaking, they gan loudly bray,
With hollow howling, and lamenting cry,
Shamefully at her rayling all the way,
And her accusing of dishonesty,
That was the flowre of faith and chastity;
And still amidst her rayling, she did pray,
That plagues, and mischiefs, and long misery
Might fall on her, and follow all the way,
And that in endlesse error she might ever stray.

XXIV

But when she saw her prayers nought prevaile,
She backe returned with some labour lost;
And in the way as shee did weepe and waile,
A knight her met in mighty armes embost,
Yet knight was not for all his bragging bost,
But subtill Archimag, that Una sought
By traynes into new troubles to have tost:
Of that old woman tidings he besought,
If that of such a Ladie she could tellen ought.

XXV

Therewith she gan her passion to renew,
And cry, and curse, and raile, and rend her heare,
Saying, that harlot she too lately knew,
That caused her shed so many a bitter teare,
And so forth told the story of her feare:
Much seemed he to mone her haplesse chaunce,
And after for that Ladie did inquere;
Which being taught, he forward gan advaunce
His fair enchaunted steed, and eke his charmed launce.

XXVI

Ere long he came where Una traveild slow,
And that wilde Champion wayting her besyde:
Whom seeing such, for dread he durst not show
Himselfe too nigh at hand, but turned wyde
Unto an hill; from whence when she him spyde,
By his like seeming shield, her knight by name
She weend it was, and towards him gan ryde:
Approaching nigh, she wist it was the same,
And with faire fearefull humblesse towards him shee came:

XXVII

And weeping said, Ah my long lacked Lord,
Where have ye bene thus long out of my sight?
Much feared I to have bene quite abhord,
Or ought have done, that ye displeasen might,
That should as death unto my deare heart light:
For since mine eye your joyous sight did mis,
My chearefull day is turnd to chearelesse night,
And eke my night of death the shadow is;
But welcome now my light, and shining lampe of blis.

XXVIII

He thereto meeting said, My dearest Dame,
Farre be it from your thought, and fro my will,
To thinke that knighthood I so much should shame,
As you to leave, that have me loved still,
And chose in Faery court of meere goodwill,
Where noblest knights were to be found on earth:
The earth shall sooner leave her kindly skill,
To bring forth fruit, and make eternall derth,
Then I leave you, my liefe, yborne of heavenly berth.

XXIX

And sooth to say, why I left you so long,
Was for to seeke adventure in strange place,
Where Archimago said a felon strong
To many knights did daily worke disgrace;
But knight he now shall never more deface:
Good cause of mine excuse; that mote ye please
Well to accept, and evermore embrace
My faithfull service, that by land and seas
Have vowd you to defend: now then your plaint appease.

XXX

His lovely words her seemd due recompence
Of all her passed paines: one loving howre
For many yeares of sorrow can dispence:
A dram of sweet is worth a pound of sowre:
She has forgot, how many a woful stowre
For him she late endurd; she speakes no more
Of past: true is, that true love hath no powre
To looken backe; his eyes be fixt before.
Before her stands her knight, for whom she toyld so sore.

XXXI

Much like, as when the beaten marinere,
That long hath wandred in the Ocean wide,
Oft soust in swelling Tethys saltish teare,
And long time having tand his tawney hide
With blustring breath of heaven, that none can bide,
And scorching flames of fierce Orions hound,
Soone as the port from farre he has espide,
His chearefull whistle merrily doth sound,
And Nereus crownes with cups; his mates him pledg around.

XXXII

Such joy made Una, when her knight she found;
And eke th' enchaunter joyous seemd no lesse,
Then the glad marchant, that does vew from ground
His ship farre come from watrie wildernesse,
He hurles out vowes, and Neptune oft doth blesse:
So forth they past, and all the way they spent
Discoursing of her dreadful late distresse,
In which he askt her, what the Lyon ment:
Who told her all that fell in journey as she went.

XXXIII

They had not ridden farre, when they might see
One pricking towards them with hastie heat,
Full strongly armd, and on a courser free,
That through his fiercenesse fomed all with sweat,
And the sharpe yron did for anger eat,
When his hot ryder spurd his chauffed side;
His looke was sterne, and seemed still to threat
Cruell revenge, which he in hart did hyde,
And on his shield *Sans loy* in bloudie lines was dyde.

XXXIV

When nigh he drew unto this gentle payre
And saw the Red-crosse, which the knight did beare,
He burnt in fire, and gan eftsoones prepare
Himselfe to battell with his couched speare.
Loth was that other, and did faint through feare,
To taste th' untryed dint of deadly steele;
But yet his Lady did so well him cheare,
That hope of new goodhap he gan to feele;
So bent his speare, and spurd his horse with yron heele.

XXXV

But that proud Paynim forward came so fierce,
And full of wrath, that with his sharp-head speare,
Through vainly crossed shield he quite did pierce,
And had his staggering steede not shrunke for feare,
Through shield and bodie eke he should him beare:
Yet so great was the puissance of his push,
That from his saddle quite he did him beare:
He tombling rudely downe to ground did rush,
And from his gored wound a well of bloud did gush.

XXXVI

Dismounting lightly from his loftie steed,
He to him lept, in mind to reave his life,
And proudly said, Lo there the worthie meed
Of him that slew Sansfoy with bloudie knife;
Henceforth his ghost freed from repining strife,
In peace may passen over Lethe lake,
When mourning altars purgd with enemies life,
The blacke infernall Furies doen aslake:
Life from Sansfoy thou tookst, Sansloy shall from thee take.

XXXVII

Therewith in haste his helmet gan unlace,
Till Una cried, O hold that heavie hand,
Deare Sir, what ever that thou be in place:
Enough is, that thy foe doth vanquisht stand
Now at thy mercy: Mercie not withstand:
For he is one the truest knight alive,
Though conquered now he lie on lowly land,
And whilest him fortune favourd, faire did thrive
In bloudie field: therefore of life him not deprive.

XXXVIII

Her piteous words might not abate his rage,
But rudely rending up his helmet, would
Have slaine him straight: but when he sees his age,
And hoarie head of Archimago old,
His hasty hand he doth amazed hold,
And halfe ashamed, wondred at the sight:
For that old man well knew he, though untold,
In charmes and magicke to have wondrous might,
Ne ever wont in field, ne in round lists to fight;

XXXIX

And said, Why Archimago, lucklesse syre,
What doe I see? what hard mishap is this,
That hath thee hither brought to taste mine yre?
Or thine the fault, or mine the error is,
Instead of foe to wound my friend amis?
He answered nought, but in a traunce still lay,
And on those guilefull dazed eyes of his
The cloude of death did sit. Which doen away,
He left him lying so, ne would no lenger stay:

XL

But to the virgin comes, who all this while
Amased stands, her selfe so mockt to see
By him, who has the guerdon of his guile,
For so misfeigning her true knight to bee:
Yet is she now in more perplexitie,
Left in the hand of that same Paynim bold,
From whom her booteth not at all to flie;
Who, by her cleanly garment catching hold,
Her from her Palfrey pluckt, her visage to behold.

XLI

But her fierce servant, full of kingly awe
And high disdaine, whenas his soveraine Dame
So rudely handled by her foe he sawe,
With gaping jawes full greedy at him came,
And ramping on his shield, did weene the same
Have reft away with his sharpe rending clawes:
But he was stout, and lust did now inflame
His corage more, that from his griping pawes
He hath his shield redeem'd, and foorth his swerd he drawes.

XLII

O then too weake and feeble was the forse
Of salvage beast, his puissance to withstand:
For he was strong, and of so mightie corse,
As ever wielded speare in warlike hand,
And feates of armes did wisely understand.
Eftsoones he perced through his chaufed chest
With thrilling point of deadly yron brand,
And launcht his Lordly hart: with death opprest
He roar'd aloud, whiles life forsooke his stubborne brest.

XLIII

Who now is left to keepe the forlorne maid
From raging spoile of lawlesse victors will?
Her faithfull gard remov'd, her hope dismaid,
Her selfe a yielded pray to save or spill.
He now Lord of the field, his pride to fill,
With foule reproches, and disdainfull spight
Her vildly entertaines, and will or nill,
Beares her away upon his courser light:
Her prayers nought prevaile, his rage is more of might.

XLIV

And all the way, with great lamenting paine,
And piteous plaints she filleth his dull eares,
That stony hart could riven have in twaine,
And all the way she wets with flowing teares:
But he enrag'd with rancor, nothing heares.
Her servile beast yet would not leave her so,
But followes her farre off, ne ought he feares,
To be partaker of her wandring woe,
More mild in beastly kind, then that her beastly foe.

Canto IV

To sinfull house of Pride, Duessa
guides the faithfull knight,
Where brother's death to wreak Sansjoy
doth chalenge him to fight.

I

YOUNG knight whatever that dost armes professe,
And through long labours huntest after fame,
Beware of fraud, beware of ficklenesse,

In choice, and change of thy deare loved Dame,
Least thou of her beleeve too lightly blame,
And rash misweening doe thy hart remove:
For unto knight there is no greater shame,
Then lightnesse and inconstancie in love;
That doth this Redcrosse knights ensample plainly prove.

II

Who after that he had faire Una lorne,
Through light misdeeming of her loialtie,
And false Duessa in her sted had borne,
Called Fidess', and so supposd to bee;
Long with her traveild, till at last they see
A goodly building, bravely garnished,
The house of mightie Prince it seemd to bee:
And towards it a broad high way that led,
All bare through peoples feet, which thither traveiled.

III

Great troupes of people traveild thitherward
Both day and night, of each degree and place,
But few returned, having scaped hard,
With balefull beggerie, or foule disgrace;
Which ever after in most wretched case,
Like loathsome lazars, by the hedges lay.
Thither Duessa bad him bend his pace:
For she is wearie of the toilesome way,
And also nigh consumed is the lingring day.

IV

A stately Pallace built of squared bricke,
Which cunningly was without morter laid,
Whose wals were high, but nothing strong, nor thick,
And golden foile all over them displaid,
That purest skye with brightnesse they dismaid:
High lifted up were many loftie towres,
And goodly galleries farre over laid,
Full of faire windowes and delightful bowres;
And on the top a Diall told the timely howres.

V

It was a goodly heape for to behould,
And spake the praises of the workmans wit;

But full great pittie, that so faire a mould
Did on so weake foundation ever sit:
For on a sandie hill, that still did flit
And fall away, it mounted was full hie,
That every breath of heaven shaked it:
And all the hinder parts, that few could spie,
Were ruinous and old, but painted cunningly.

VI

Arrived there, they passed in forth right;
For still to all the gates stood open wide:
Yet charge of them was to a Porter hight
Cald Malvenù, who entrance none denide:
Thence to the hall, which was on every side
With rich array and costly arras dight:
Infinite sorts of people did abide
There waiting long, to win the wished sight
Of her that was the Lady of that Pallace bright.

VII

By them they passe, all gazing on them round,
And to the Presence mount; whose glorious vew
Their frayle amazed senses did confound:
In living Princes court none ever knew
Such endlesse richesse, and so sumptuous shew;
Ne Persia selfe, the nourse of pompous pride
Like ever saw. And there a noble crew
Of Lordes and Ladies stood on every side,
Which with their presence faire the place much beautifide.

VIII

High above all a cloth of State was spred,
And a rich throne, as bright as sunny day,
On which there sate most brave embellished
With royall robes and gorgeous array,
A mayden Queene, that shone as Titans ray,
In glistring gold, and peerelesse pretious stone:
Yet her bright blazing beautie did assay
To dim the brightnesse of her glorious throne,
As envying her selfe, that too exceeding shone.

IX

Exceeding shone, like Phœbus fairest childe,
That did presume his fathers firie wayne,
And flaming mouthes of steedes unwonted wilde
Through highest heaven with weaker hand to rayne;
Proud of such glory and advancement vaine,
While flashing beames do daze his feeble eyen,
He leaves the welkin way most beaten plaine,
And rapt with whirling wheeles, inflames the skyen,
With fire not made to burne, but fairely for to shyne.

X

So proud she shyned in her Princely state,
Looking to heaven; for earth she did disdayne:
And sitting high; for lowly she did hate:
Lo underneath her scornefull feete was layne
A dreadfull Dragon with an hideous trayne,
And in her hand she held a mirrhour bright,
Wherein her face she often vewed fayne,
And in her selfe-lov'd semblance tooke delight;
For she was wondrous faire, as any living wight.

XI

Of griesly Pluto she the daughter was,
And sad Proserpina the Queene of hell;
Yet did she thinke her pearlesse worth to pas
That parentage, with pride so did she swell;
And thundring Jove, that high in heaven doth dwell,
And wield the world, she claymed for her syre,
Or if that any else did Jove excell:
For to the highest she did still aspyre,
Or if ought higher were then that, did it desyre.

XII

And proud Lucifera men did her call,
That made her selfe a Queene, and crownd to be,
Yet rightfull kingdome she had none at all,
Ne heritage of native soveraintie,
But did usurpe with wrong and tyrannie
Upon the scepter, which she now did hold:
Ne ruld her Realmes with lawes, but pollicie,
And strong advizement of six wisards old,
That with their counsels bad her kingdome did uphold.

XIII

Soone as the Elfin knight in presence came,
And false Duessa seeming Lady faire,
A gentle Husher, Vanitie by name
Made rowme, and passage for them did prepaire:
So goodly brought them to the lowest staire
Of her high throne, where they on humble knee
Making obeyssance, did the cause declare,
Why they were come, her royall state to see,
To prove the wide report of her great Majestee.

XIV

With loftie eyes, halfe loth to looke so low,
She thanked them in her disdainefull wise;
Ne other grace vouchsafed them to show
Of Princesse worthy, scarse them bad arise.
Her Lordes and Ladies all this while devise
Themselves to setten forth to straungers sight:
Some frounce their curled haire in courtly guise,
Some prancke their ruffes, and others trimly dight
Their gay attire: each others greater pride does spight.

XV

Goodly they all that knight do entertaine,
Right glad with him to have increast their crew:
But to Duess' each one himselfe did paine
All kindnesse and faire courtesie to shew;
For in that court whylome her well they knew:
Yet the stout Faerie mongst the middest crowd
Thought all their glorie vaine in knightly vew,
And that great Princesse too exceeding prowd,
That to strange knight no better countenance allowd.

XVI

Suddein upriseth from her stately place
The royall Dame, and for her coche did call:
All hurtlen forth, and she with Princely pace,
As faire Aurora in her purple pall,
Out of the east the dawning day doth call:
So forth she comes: her brightnesse brode doth blaze;
The heapes of people thronging in the hall,
Do ride each other, upon her to gaze:
Her glorious glitterand light doth all mens eyes amaze.

XVII

So forth she comes, and to her coche does clyme,
Adorned all with gold, and girlonds gay,
That seemd as fresh as Flora in her prime,
And strove to match, in royall rich array,
Great Junoes golden chaire, the which they say
The Gods stand gazing on, when she does ride
To Joves high house through heavens bras-paved way
Drawne of faire Pecocks, that excell in pride,
And full of Argus eyes their tailes dispredden wide.

XVIII

But this was drawne of six unequall beasts,
On which her six sage Counsellours did ryde,
Taught to obay their bestiall beheasts,
With like conditions to their kinds applyde:
Of which the first, that all the rest did guyde,
Was sluggish Idlenesse the nourse of sin;
Upon a slouthful Asse he chose to ryde,
Arayd in habit blacke, and amis thin,
Like to an holy Monck, the service to begin.

XIX

And in his hand his Portesse still he bare,
That much was worne, but therein little red,
For of devotion he had little care,
Still drownd in sleepe, and most of his dayes ded;
Scarse could he once uphold his heavie hed,
To looken, whether it were night or day:
May seeme the wayne was very evill led,
When such an one had guiding of the way,
That knew not, whether right he went, or else astray.

XX

From worldly cares himselfe he did esloyne,
And greatly shunned manly exercise,
From every worke he chalenged essoyne,
For contemplation sake: yet otherwise,
His life he led in lawlesse riotise;
By which he grew to grievous malady;
For in his lustlesse limbs through evill guise
A shaking fever raignd continually:
Such one was Idlenesse, first of this company.

XXI

And by his side rode loathsome Gluttony,
Deformed creature, on a filthie swyne;
His belly was up-blowne with luxury,
And eke with fatnesse swollen were his eyne,
And like a Crane his necke was long and fyne,
With which he swallowed up excessive feast,
For want whereof poore people oft did pyne;
And all the way, most like a brutish beast,
He spued up his gorge, that all did him deteast.

XXII

In greene vine leaves he was right fitly clad;
For other clothes he could not weare for heat,
And on his head an yvie girland had,
From under which fast trickled downe the sweat:
Still as he rode, he somewhat still did eat,
And in his hand did beare a bouzing can,
Of which he supt so oft, that on his seat
His dronken corse he scarse upholden can,
In shape and life more like a monster, then a man.

XXIII

Unfit he was for any worldly thing,
And eke unhable once to stirre or go,
Not meet to be of counsell to a king,
Whose mind in meat and drinke was drowned so,
That from his friend he seldome knew his fo:
Full of diseases was his carcas blew,
And a dry dropsie through his flesh did flow:
Which by misdiet daily greater grew:
Such one was Gluttony, the second of that crew.

XXIV

And next to him rode lustfull Lechery,
Upon a bearded Goat, whose rugged haire,
And whally eyes (the signe of gelosy),
Was like the person selfe, whom he did beare:
Who rough, and blacke, and filthy did appeare,
Unseemely man to please faire Ladies eye;
Yet he of Ladies oft was loved deare,
When fairer faces were bid standen by:
O who does know the bent of womens fantasy?

XXV

In a greene gowne he clothed was full faire,
Which underneath did hide his filthinesse,
And in his hand a burning hart he bare,
Full of vaine follies, and new fanglenesse,
For he was false, and fraught with ficklenesse;
And learned had to love with secret lookes;
And well could daunce, and sing with ruefulnesse,
And fortunes tell, and read in loving bookes,
And thousand other wayes, to bait his fleshly hookes.

XXVI

Inconstant man, that loved all he saw,
And lusted after all that he did love;
Ne would his looser life be tide to law,
But joyd weak wemens hearts to tempt and prove,
If from their loyall loves he might them move;
Which lewdnesse fild him with reprochfull paine
Of that fowle evill, which all men reprove,
That rots the marrow and consumes the braine:
Such one was Lecherie, the third of all this traine.

XXVII

And greedy Avarice by him did ride,
Upon a Camell loaden all with gold;
Two iron coffers hong on either side,
With precious mettall full as they might hold;
And in his lap an heape of coine he told;
For of his wicked pelfe his God he made,
And unto hell him selfe for money sold;
Accursed usurie was all his trade,
And right and wrong ylike in equall ballaunce waide.

XXVIII

His life was nigh unto deaths doore yplast,
And thred-bare cote, and cobled shoes he ware,
Ne scarse good morsell all his life did tast,
But both from backe and belly still did spare,
To fill his bags, and richesse to compare;
Yet chylde ne kinsman living had he none
To leave them to; but thorough daily care
To get, and nightly feare to lose his owne,
He led a wretched life unto him selfe unknowne.

XXIX

Most wretched wight, whom nothing might suffise,
Whose greedy lust did lacke in greatest store,
Whose need had end, but no end covetise,
Whose wealth was want, whose plenty made him pore,
Who had enough, yet wished ever more;
A vile disease, and eke in foote and hand
A grievous gout tormented him full sore,
That well he could not touch, nor go, nor stand;
Such one was Avarice, the fourth of this faire band.

XXX

And next to him malicious Envie rode,
Upon a ravenous wolfe, and still did chaw
Betweene his cankred teeth a venemous tode,
That all the poison ran about his chaw;
But inwardly he chawed his owne maw
At neighbours wealth, that made him ever sad;
For death it was when any good he saw,
And wept, that cause of weeping none he had,
But when he heard of harme, he wexed wondrous glad.

XXXI

All in a kirtle of discolourd say
He clothed was, ypainted full of eyes;
And in his bosome secretly there lay
An hatefull Snake, the which his taile uptyes
In many folds, and mortall sting implyes.
Still as he rode, he gnasht his teeth, to see
Those heapes of gold with griple Covetyse;
And grudged at the great felicitie
Of proud Lucifera, and his owne companie.

XXXII

He hated all good workes and vertuous deeds,
And him no lesse, that any like did use,
And who with gracious bread the hungry feeds,
His almes for want of faith he doth accuse;
So every good to bad he doth abuse:
And eke the verse of famous Poets witt
He does backebite, and spightfull poison spues
From leprous mouth on all that ever writt:
Such one vile Envie was, that fifte in row did sitt.

XXXIII

And him beside rides fierce revenging Wrath,
Upon a Lion, loth for to be led;
And in his hand a burning brond he hath,
The which he brandisheth about his hed;
His eyes did hurle forth sparkles fiery red,
And stared sterne on all that him beheld,
As ashes pale of hew and seeming ded;
And on his dagger still his hand he held,
Trembling through hasty rage, when choler in him sweld.

XXXIV

His ruffin raiment all was staind with blood,
Which he had spilt, and all to rags yrent,
Through unadvized rashnesse woxen wood;
For of his hands he had no governement,
Ne car'd for bloud in his avengement:
But when the furious fit was overpast,
His cruell facts he often would repent;
Yet wilfull man he never would forecast,
How many mischieves should ensue his heedlesse hast.

XXXV

Full many mischiefes follow cruell Wrath;
Abhorred bloodshed and tumultuous strife,
Unmanly murder, and unthrifty scath,
Bitter despight, with rancours rusty knife,
And fretting griefe the enemy of life;
All these, and many evils moe haunt ire,
The swelling Splene, and Frenzy raging rife,
The shaking Palsey, and Saint Fraunces fire:
Such one was Wrath, the last of this ungodly tire.

XXXVI

And after all, upon the wagon beame
Rode Sathan, with a smarting whip in hand,
With which he forward lasht the laesie teme,
So oft as Slowth still in the mire did stand.
Hugh routs of people did about them band,
Showting for joy, and still before their way
A foggy mist had covered all the land;
And underneath their feet, all scattered lay
Dead sculs and bones of men, whose life had gone astray.

XXXVII

So forth they marchen in this goodly sort,
To take the solace of the open aire,
And in fresh flowring fields themselves to sport;
Emongst the rest rode that false Lady faire,
The foule Duessa, next unto the chaire
Of proud Lucifera, as one of the traine:
But that good knight would not so nigh repaire,
Him selfe estraunging from their joyaunce vaine,
Whose fellowship seemd far unfit for warlike swaine.

XXXVIII

So having solaced themselves a space
With pleasaunce of the breathing fields yfed,
They backe retourned to the Princely Place;
Whereas an errant knight in armes ycled,
And heathnish shield, wherein with letters red
Was writ *Sans joy*, they new arrived find:
Enflam'd with fury and fiers hardy-hed
He seemd in hart to harbour thoughts unkind,
And nourish bloudy vengeaunce in his bitter mind.

XXXIX

Who when the shamed shield of slaine Sansfoy
He spide with that same Faery champions page,
Bewraying him, that did of late destroy
His eldest brother, burning all with rage
He to him leapt, and that same envious gage
Of victors glory from him snatcht away:
But th' Elfin knight, which ought that warlike wage
Disdaind to loose the meed he wonne in fray,
And him rencountring fierce, reskewd the noble pray.

XL

Therewith they gan to hurtlen greedily,
Redoubted battaile ready to darrayne,
And clash their shields, and shake their swords on hy,
That with their sturre they troubled all the traine;
Till that great Queene upon eternall paine
Of high displeasure that ensewen might,
Commaunded them their fury to refraine,
And if that either to that shield had right,
In equall lists they should the morrow next it fight.

XLI

Ah dearest Dame, (quoth then the Paynim bold,)
Pardon the error of enraged wight,
Whom great griefe made forget the raines to hold
Of reasons rule, to see this recreant knight,
No knight, but treachour full of false despight
And shamefull treason, who through guile hath slayn
The prowest knight that ever field did fight,
Even stout Sansfoy (O who can then refrayn?)
Whose shield he beares renverst, the more to heape disdayn.

XLII

And to augment the glorie of his guile,
His dearest love, the faire Fidessa, loe
Is there possessed of the traytour vile,
Who reapes the harvest sowen by his foe,
Sowen in bloudy field, and bought with woe:
That brothers hand shall dearely well requight,
So be, O Queene, you equall favour showe.
Him litle answerd th' angry Elfin knight;
He never meant with words, but swords to plead his right.

XLIII

But threw his gauntlet as a sacred pledge,
His cause in combat the next day to try:
So been they parted both, with harts on edge
To be aveng'd each on his enimy.
That night they pas in joy and jollity,
Feasting and courting both in bowre and hall;
For Steward was excessive Gluttonie,
That of his plenty poured forth to all;
Which doen, the Chamberlain Slowth did to rest them call.

XLIV

Now whenas darkesome night had all displayed
Her coleblacke curtein over brightest skye,
The warlike youthes on dayntie couches layd,
Did chace away sweet sleepe from sluggish eye,
To muse on meanes of hoped victory.
But whenas Morpheus had with leaden mace
Arrested all that courtly company,
Up-rose Duessa from her resting place,
And to the Paynims lodging comes with silent pace.

XLV

Whom broad awake she finds, in troublous fit,
Forecasting, how his foe he might annoy,
And him amoves with speaches seeming fit:
Ah deare Sansjoy, next dearest to Sansfoy,
Cause of my new griefe, cause of my new joy,
Joyous, to see his ymage in mine eye,
And greev'd, to thinke how foe did him destroy,
That was the flowre of grace and chevalrye;
Lo his Fidessa to thy secret faith I flye.

XLVI

With gentle wordes he can her fairely greet,
And bad say on the secret of her hart.
Then sighing soft, I learne that litle sweet
Oft tempred is (quoth she) with muchell smart:
For since my brest was launcht with lovely dart
Of deare Sans foy, I never joyed howre,
But in eternall woes my weaker hart
Have wasted, loving him with all my powre,
And for his sake have felt full many an heavie stowre.

XLVII

At last when perils all I weened past,
And hop'd to reape the crop of all my care,
Into new woes unweeting I was cast,
By this false faytor, who unworthy ware
His worthy shield, whom he with guilefull snare
Entrapped slew, and brought to shamefull grave.
Me silly maid away with him he bare,
And ever since hath kept in darksome cave,
For that I would not yeeld, that to Sans foy I gave.

XLVIII

But since faire Sunne hath sperst that lowring clowd,
And to my loathed life now shewes some light,
Under your beames I will me safely shrowd,
From dreaded storme of his disdainfull spight:
To you th' inheritance belongs by right
Of brothers prayse, to you eke longs his love.
Let not his love, let not his restlesse spright,
Be unreveng'd, that calles to you above
From wandring Stygian shores, where it doth endlesse move.

XLIX

Thereto said he, Faire Dame, be nought dismaid
For sorrowes past; their griefe is with them gone:
Ne yet of present perill be affraid;
For needlesse feare did never vantage none
And helplesse hap it booteth not to mone.
Dead is Sansfoy, his vitall paines are past,
Though greeved ghost for vengeance deepe do grone:
He lives, that shall him pay his dewties last,
And guiltie Elfin blood shall sacrifice in hast.

L

O but I feare the fickle freakes (quoth shee)
Of fortune false, and oddes of armes in field.
Why Dame (quoth he) what oddes can ever bee,
Where both do fight alike, to win or yield?
Yea but (quoth she) he beares a charmed shield,
And eke enchaunted armes, that none can perce,
Ne none can wound the man that does them wield.
Charmd or enchaunted (answerd he then ferce)
I no whit reck, ne you the like need to reherce.

LI

But faire Fidessa, sithens fortunes guile,
Or enimies powre, hath now captived you,
Returne from whence ye came, and rest a while
Till morrow next, that I the Elfe subdew,
And with Sansfoyes dead dowry you endew.
Ay me, that is a double death (she said)
With proud foes sight my sorrow to renew:
Where ever yet I be, my secret aid
Shall follow you. So passing forth she him obaid.

Canto V

The faithfull knight in equall field
subdewes his faithlesse foe,
Whom false Duessa saves, and for
his cure to hell does goe.

I

THE noble hart, that harbours vertuous thought,
And is with child of glorious great intent,
Can never rest, untill it forth have brought

Th' eternall brood of glorie excellent.
Such restlesse passion did all night torment
The flaming corage of that Faery knight,
Devizing, how that doughtie turnament
With greatest honour he atchieven might;
Still did he wake, and still did watch for dawning light.

II

At last the golden Orientall gate,
Of greatest heaven gan to open faire,
And Phoebus fresh, as bridegrome to his mate,
Came dauncing forth, shaking his deawie haire:
And hurls his glistring beams through gloomy aire.
Which when the wakeful Elfe perceiv'd, streightway
He started up, and did him selfe prepaire,
In sunbright armes, and battailous array:
For with that Pagan proud he combat will that day.

III

And forth he comes into the commune hall,
Where earely waite him many a gazing eye,
To weet what end to straunger knights may fall.
There many Minstrales maken melody,
To drive away the dull melancholy,
And many Bardes, that to the trembling chord
Can tune their timely voyces cunningly,
And many Chroniclers that can record
Old loves, and warres for Ladies doen by many a Lord.

IV

Soone after comes the cruell Sarazin,
In woven maile all armed warily,
And sternly lookes at him, who not a pin
Does care for looke of living creatures eye.
They bring them wines of Greece and Araby,
And daintie spices fetcht from furthest Ynd,
To kindle heat of corage privily:
And in the wine a solemne oth they bynd
T' observe the sacred lawes of armes, that are assynd.

V

At last forth comes that far renowmed Queene,
With royall pomp and Princely majestie;

She is ybrought unto a paled greene,
And placed under stately canapee,
The warlike feates of both those knights to see.
On th' other side in all mens open vew
Duessa placed is, and on a tree
Sans-foy his shield is hangd with bloody hew:
Both those the lawrell girlonds to the victor dew.

VI

A shrilling trompet sownded from on hye,
And unto battaill bad them selves addresse:
Their shining shieldes about their wrestes they tye,
And burning blades about their heads do blesse,
The instruments of wrath and heavinesse:
With greedy force each other doth assayle,
And strike so fiercely, that they do impresse
Deepe dinted furrowes in the battred mayle;
The yron walles to ward their blowes are weak and fraile.

VII

The Sarazin was stout, and wondrous strong,
And heaped blowes like yron hammers great;
For after bloud and vengeance he did long.
The knight was fiers, and full of youthly heat,
And doubled strokes, like dreaded thunders threat:
For all for prayse and honour he did fight.
Both stricken strike, and beaten both do beat,
That from their shields forth flyeth firie light,
And helmets hewen deepe show marks of eithers might.

VIII

So th' one for wrong, the other strives for right;
As when a Gryfon seized of his pray,
A Dragon fiers encountreth in his flight,
Through widest ayre making his ydle way,
That would his rightfull ravine rend away;
With hideous horror both together smight,
And souce so sore that they the heavens affray:
The wise Soothsayer seeing so sad sight,
Th' amazed vulgar tels of warres and mortall fight.

IX

So th' one for wrong, the other strives for right,
And each to deadly shame would drive his foe:
The cruell steele so greedily doth bight
In tender flesh that streames of bloud down flow,
With which the armes, that earst so bright did show,
Into a pure vermillion now are dyde:
Great ruth in all the gazers harts did grow,
Seeing the gored woundes to gape so wyde,
That victory they dare not wish to either side.

X

At last the Paynim chaunst to cast his eye,
His suddein eye, flaming with wrathful fyre,
Upon his brothers shield, which hong thereby:
Therewith redoubled was his raging yre,
And said, Ah wretched sonne of wofull syre,
Doest thou sit wayling by blacke Stygian lake,
Whilest here thy shield is hangd for victors hyre,
And sluggish german doest thy forces slake
To after-send his foe, that him may overtake?

XI

Goe caytive Elfe, him quickly overtake,
And soone redeeme from his long wandring woe;
Goe guiltie ghost, to him my message make,
That I his shield have quit from dying foe.
Therewith upon his crest he stroke him so,
That twise he reeled, readie twise to fall;
End of the doubtfull battell deemed tho
The lookers on, and lowd to him gan call
The false Duessa, Thine the shield, and I, and all.

XII

Soone as the Faerie heard his Ladie speake,
Out of his swowning dreame he gan awake,
And quickning faith, that earst was woxen weake,
The creeping deadly cold away did shake:
Tho mov'd with wrath, and shame, and Ladies sake,
Of all attonce he cast avengd to bee,
And with so' exceeding furie at him strake,
That forced him to stoupe upon his knee;
Had he not stouped so, he should have cloven bee.

XIII

And to him said, Goe now proud Miscreant,
Thy selfe thy message do to german deare;
Alone he wandring thee too long doth want:
Goe say, his foe thy shield with his doth beare.
Therewith his heavie hand he high gan reare,
Him to have slaine; when loe a darkesome clowd
Upon him fell: he no where doth appeare,
But vanisht is. The Elfe him calls alowd,
But answer none receives: the darkness him does shrowd.

XIV

In haste Duessa from her place arose,
And to him running said, O prowest knight,
That ever Ladie to her love did chose,
Let now abate the terror of your might,
And quench the flame of furious despight,
And bloudie vengeance; lo th' infernall powres,
Covering your foe with cloud of deadly night,
Have borne him hence to Plutoes balefull bowres.
The conquest yours, I yours, the shield, the glory yours.

XV

Not all so satisfide, with greedie eye
He sought all round about, his thristie blade
To bath in bloud of faithlesse enemy;
Who all that while lay hid in secret shade:
He standes amazed, how he thence should fade.
At last the trumpets Triumph sound on hie,
And running Heralds humble homage made,
Greeting him goodly with new victorie,
And to him brought the shield, the cause of enmitie.

XVI

Wherewith he goeth to that soveraine Queene,
And falling her before on lowly knee,
To her makes present of his service seene:
Which she accepts, with thankes, and goodly gree,
Greatly advauncing his gay chevalree.
So marcheth home, and by her takes the knight,
Whom all the people follow with great glee,
Shouting, and clapping all their hands on hight,
That all the aire it fils, and flyes to heaven bright.

XVII

Home is he brought, and laid in sumptuous bed:
Where many skilfull leaches him abide,
To salve his hurts, that yet still freshly bled.
In wine and oyle they wash his woundes wide,
And softly can embalme on every side.
And all the while, most heavenly melody
About the bed sweet musicke did divide,
Him to beguile of griefe and agony:
And all the while Duessa wept full bitterly.

XVIII

As when a wearie traveller that strayes
By muddy shore of broad seven-mouthed Nile,
Unweeting of the perillous wandring wayes,
Doth meete a cruell craftie Crocodile,
Which in false griefe hyding his harmefull guile,
Doth weepe full sore, and sheddeth tender teares:
The foolish man, that pitties all this while
His mournefull plight, is swallowed up unawares,
Forgetfull of his owne, that mindes anothers cares.

XIX

So wept Duessa untill eventide,
That shyning lampes in Joves high house were light:
Then forth she rose, ne lenger would abide,
But comes unto the place, where th' Hethen knight
In slombring swownd nigh voyd of vitall spright,
Lay cover'd with inchaunted cloud all day:
Whom when she found, as she him left in plight,
To wayle his woefull case she would not stay,
But to the easterne coast of heaven makes speedy way.

XX

Where griesly Night, with visage deadly sad,
That Phœbus chearefull face durst never vew,
And in a foule blacke pitchie mantle clad,
She findes forth comming from her darkesome mew,
Where she all day did hide her hated hew.
Before the dore her yron charet stood,
Alreadie harnessed for journey new;
And coleblacke steedes yborne of hellish brood,
That on their rustie bits did champ, as they were wood.

XXI

Who when she saw Duessa sunny bright,
Adornd with gold and jewels shining cleare,
She greatly grew amazed at the sight,
And th' unacquainted light began to feare:
For never did such brightnesse there appeare,
And would have backe retyred to her cave,
Until the witches speech she gan to heare,
Saying, Yet, O thou dreaded Dame, I crave
Abide, till I have told the message which I have.

XXII

She stayd, and foorth Duessa gan proceede
O thou most auncient Grandmother of all,
More old then Jove, whom thou at first didst breede,
Or that great house of Gods cælestiall,
Which wast begot in Daemogorgons hall,
And sawst the secrets of the world unmade,
Why suffredst thou thy Nephewes deare to fall
With Elfin sword, most shamefully betrade?
Lo where the stout Sansjoy doth sleepe in deadly shade.

XXIII

And him before, I saw with bitter eyes
The bold Sansfoy shrinke underneath his speare;
And now the pray of fowles in field he lyes,
Nor wayld of friends, nor layd on groning beare,
That whylome was to me too dearely deare.
O what of Gods then boots it to be borne,
If old Aveugles sonnes so evill heare?
Or who shall not great Nightes children scorne,
When two of three her Nephews are so fowle forlorne?

XXIV

Up then, up dreary Dame, of darknesse Queene,
Go gather up the reliques of thy race,
Or else goe them avenge, and let be seene,
That dreaded Night in brightest day hath place,
And can the children of faire light deface.
Her feeling speeches some compassion moved
In hart, and chaunge in that great mothers face:
Yet pittie in her hart was never proved
Till then: for evermore she hated, never loved.

XXV

And said, Deare daughter rightly may I rew
The fall of famous children borne of mee,
And good successes, which their foes ensew:
But who can turne the streame of destinee,
Or breake the chayne of strong necessitee,
Which fast is tyde to Joves eternall seat?
The sonnes of Day he favoureth, I see,
And by my ruines thinkes to make them great:
To make one great by others losse, is bad excheat.

XXVI

Yet shall they not escape so freely all;
For some shall pay the price of others guilt:
And he the man that made Sansfoy to fall,
Shall with his owne bloud price that he has spilt.
But what art thou, that telst of Nephews kilt?
I that do seeme not I, Duessa am,
(Quoth she) how ever now in garments gilt,
And gorgeous gold arrayd I to thee came;
Duessa I, the daughter of Deceipt and Shame.

XXVII

Then bowing downe her aged backe, she kist
The wicked witch, saying; In that faire face
The false resemblance of Deceipt I wist
Did closely lurke; yet so true-seeming grace
It carried, that I scarce in darkesome place
Could it discerne, though I the mother bee
Of falshood, and roote of Duessaes race.
O welcome child, whom I have longd to see,
And now have seene unwares. Lo now I go with thee.

XXVIII

Then to her yron wagon she betakes,
And with her beares the fowle welfavourd witch:
Through mirkesome aire her readie way she makes.
Her twyfold Teme, of which two blacke as pitch,
And two were browne, yet each to each unlich,
Did softly swim away, ne ever stampe,
Unlesse she chaunst their stubborne mouths to twitch;
Then foming tarre, their bridles they would champe,
And trampling the fine element would fiercely rampe.

XXIX

So well they sped, that they be come at length
Unto the place, whereas the Paynim lay,
Devoid of outward sense, and native strength,
Coverd with charmed cloud from vew of day
And sight of men, since his late luckelesse fray.
His cruell wounds with cruddy bloud congeald
They binden up so wisely, as they may,
And handle softly, till they can be healed:
So lay him in her charet close in night concealed.

XXX

And all the while she stood upon the ground,
The wakefull dogs did never cease to bay,
As giving warning of th' unwonted sound,
With which her yron wheeles did them affray,
And her darke griesly looke them much dismay:
The messenger of death, the ghastly Owle
With drery shriekes did also her bewray;
And hungry Wolves continually did howle,
At her abhorred face, so filthy and so fowle.

XXXI

Thence turning backe in silence soft they stole,
And brought the heavie corse with easie pace
To yawning gulfe of deepe Avernus hole.
By that same hole an entrance darke and bace
With smoake and sulphure hiding all the place,
Descends to hell: there creature never past,
That backe returned without heavenly grace;
But dreadfull Furies which their chaines have brast,
And damned sprights sent forth to make ill men aghast.

XXXII

By that same way the direfull dames doe drive
Their mournefull charet, fild with rusty blood,
And downe to Plutoes house are come bilive:
Which passing through, on every side them stood
The trembling ghosts with sad amazed mood,
Chattring their yron teeth, and staring wide
With stonie eyes; and all the hellish brood
Of feends infernall flockt on every side,
To gaze on earthly wight that with the Night durst ride.

XXXIII

They pas the bitter waves of Acheron,
Where many soules sit wailing woefully,
And come to fiery flood of Phlegeton,
Whereas the damned ghosts in torments fry,
And with sharpe shrilling shriekes doe bootlesse cry,
Cursing high Jove, the which them thither sent.
The house of endlesse paine is built thereby,
In which ten thousand sorts of punishment
The cursed creatures doe eternally torment.

XXXIV

Before the threshold dreadfull Cerberus
His three deformed heads did lay along,
Curled with thousand adders venemous,
And lilled forth his bloudie flaming tong:
At them he gan to reare his bristles strong,
And felly gnarre, until Dayes enemy
Did him appease; then downe his taile he hong
And suffred them to passen quietly:
For she in hell and heaven had power equally.

XXXV

There was Ixion turned on a wheele,
For daring tempt the Queene of heaven to sin;
And Sisyphus an huge round stone did reele
Against an hill, ne might from labour lin;
There thirsty Tantalus hong by the chin;
And Tityus fed a vulture on his maw;
Typhœus joynts were stretched on a gin,
Theseus condemnd to endlesse slouth by law,
And fifty sisters water in leake vessels draw.

XXXVI

They all beholding worldly wights in place,
Leave off their worke, unmindfull of their smart,
To gaze on them; who forth by them doe pace,
Till they be come unto the furthest part;
Where was a Cave ywrought by wondrous art,
Deepe, darke, uneasie, dolefull, comfortlesse,
In which sad Aesculapius farre apart
Emprisond was in chaines remedilesse,
For that Hippolytus rent corse he did redresse.

XXXVII

Hippolytus a jolly huntsman was
That wont in charett chace the foming Bore:
He all his Peeres in beauty did surpas,
But Ladies love as losse of time forbore:
His wanton stepdame loved him the more,
But when she saw her offred sweets refused,
Her love she turnd to hate, and him before
His father fierce of treason false accused,
And with her gealous termes his open eares abused.

XXXVIII

Who all in rage his Sea-god syre besought,
Some cursed vengeaunce on his sonne to cast,
From surging gulf two monsters straight were brought,
With dread whereof his chasing steedes aghast,
Both charet swift and huntsman overcast.
His goodly corps on ragged cliffs yrent,
Was quite dismembred, and his members chast
Scattered on every mountaine, as he went,
That of Hippolytus was left no moniment.

XXXIX

His cruell step-dame seeing what was donne,
Her wicked dayes with wretched knife did end,
In death avowing th' innocence of her sonne,
Which hearing, his rash Syre began to rend
His haire, and hastie tongue that did offend.
Tho gathering up the relicks of his smart,
By Dianes meanes, who was Hippolyts frend,
Them brought to Æsculape, that by his art
Did heale them all againe, and joyned every part.

XL

Such wondrous science in mans wit to raine
When Jove avizd, that could the dead revive,
And fates expired could renew againe,
Of endlesse life he might him not deprive,
But unto hell did thrust him downe alive,
With flashing thunderbolt ywounded sore:
Where long remaining, he did alwaies strive
Himselfe with salves to health for to restore,
And slake the heavenly fire, that raged evermore.

XLI

There auncient Night arriving, did alight
From her nigh wearie waine, and in her armes
To Æsculapius brought the wounded knight:
Whom having softly disarayd of armes,
Tho gan to him discover all his harmes,
Beseeching him with prayer, and with praise,
If either salves, or oyles, or herbes, or charmes
A fordonne wight from dore of death mote raise,
He would at her request prolong her nephews daies.

XLII

Ah Dame (quoth he) thou temptest me in vaine,
To dare the thing, which daily yet I rew,
And the old cause of my continued paine
With like attempt to like end to renew.
Is not enough, that thrust from heaven dew
Here endlesse penance for one fault I pay,
But that redoubled crime with vengeance new
Thou biddest me to eeke? can Night defray
The wrath of thundring Jove that rules both night and day?

XLIII

Not so (quoth she) but sith that heavens king
From hope of heaven hath thee excluded quight,
Why fearest thou, that canst not hope for thing;
And fearest not, that more thee hurten might,
Now in the powre of everlasting Night?
Goe to then, O thou farre renowmed sonne
Of great Apollo, shew thy famous might
In medicine, that else hath to thee wonne
Great paines, and greater praise, both never to be donne.

XLIV

Her words prevaild: And then the learned leach
His cunning hand gan to his wounds to lay,
And all things else, the which his art did teach:
Which having seene, from thence arose away
The mother of dread darknesse, and let stay
Aveugles sonne there in the leaches cure,
And backe returning tooke her wonted way,
To runne her timely race, whilst Phœbus pure,
In westerne waves his weary wagon did recure.

XLV

The false Duessa leaving noyous Night,
Returnd to stately pallace of Dame Pride;
Where when she came, she found the Faery knight
Departed thence, albe his woundes wide
Not throughly heald, unreadie were to ride.
Good cause he had to hasten thence away;
For on a day his wary Dwarfe had spide
Where in a dongeon deepe huge numbers lay
Of caytive wretched thrals, that wayled night and day.

XLVI

A ruefull sight, as could be seene with eie;
Of whom he learned had in secret wise
The hidden cause of their captivitie,
How mortgaging their lives to Covetise,
Through wastfull Pride and wanton Riotise,
They were by law of that proud Tyrannesse,
Provokt with Wrath, and Envies false surmise,
Condemned to that Dongeon mercilesse,
Where they should live in woe, and die in wretchednesse.

XLVII

There was that great proud king of Babylon,
That would compell all nations to adore,
And him as onely God to call upon,
Till through celestiall doome throwne out of dore,
Into an Oxe he was transform'd of yore:
There also was king Croesus, that enhaunst
His hart too high through his great riches store;
And proud Antiochus, the which advaunst
His cursed hand gainst God and on his altars daunst.

XLVIII

And them long time before, great Nimrod was,
That first the world with sword and fire warrayd;
And after him old Ninus farre did pas
In princely pompe, of all the world obayd;
There also was that mightie Monarch layd
Low under all, yet above all in pride,
That name of native syre did fowle upbrayd,
And would as Ammons sonne be magnifide,
Till scornd of God and man a shamefull death he dide.

XLIX

All these together in one heape were throwne,
Like carkases of beasts in butchers stall.
And in another corner wide were strowne
The antique ruines of the Romaines fall:
Great Romulus the Grandsyre of them all,
Proud Tarquin, and too lordly Lentulus,
Stout Scipio, and stubborne Hanniball,
Ambitious Sylla, and sterne Marius,
High Caesar, great Pompey, and fierce Antonius.

L

Amongst these mightie men were wemen mixt,
Proud wemen, vaine, forgetfull of their yoke:
The bold Semiramis, whose sides transfixt
With sonnes own blade, her fowle reproches spoke;
Faire Sthenoboea, that her selfe did choke
With wilfull cord, for wanting of her will;
High minded Cleopatra, that with stroke
Of Aspes sting her selfe did stoutly kill:
And thousands moe the like, that did that dongeon fill;

LI

Besides the endlesse routs of wretched thralles,
Which thither were assembled day by day,
From all the world after their wofull falles
Through wicked pride, and wasted wealthes decay.
But most of all, which in the Dongeon lay,
Fell from high Princes courts, or Ladies bowres;
Where they in idle pompe, or wanton play,
Consumed had their goods, and thriftlesse howres,
And lastly throwne themselves into these heavy stowres.

LII

Whose case when as the carefull Dwarfe had tould,
And made ensample of their mournefull sight
Unto his maister, he no lenger would
There dwell in perill of like painefull plight,
But early rose, and ere that dawning light
Discovered had the world to heaven wyde,
He by a privie Posterne tooke his flight,
That of no envious eyes he mote be spyde:
For doubtlesse death ensewd, if any him descryde.

LIII

Scarse could he footing find in that fowle way,
For many corses, like a great Lay-stall,
Of murdred men which therein strowed lay,
Without remorse, or decent funerall:
Which all through that great Princesse pride did fall
And came to shamefull end. And them beside
Forth ryding underneath the castell wall,
A donghill of dead carkases he spide,
The dreadfull spectacle of that sad house of Pride.

Canto VI

From lawlesse lust by wondrous grace
fayre Una is releast:
Whom salvage nation does adore,
and learnes her wise beheast.

I

AS when a ship, that flyes faire under saile,
An hidden rocke escaped hath unwares,
That lay in waite her wrack for to bewaile,
The Marriner yet halfe amazed stares
At perill past, and yet in doubt ne dares
To joy at his foole-happie oversight:
So doubly is distrest twixt joy and cares
The dreadlesse courage of this Elfin knight,
Having escapt so sad ensamples in his sight.

II

Yet sad he was that his too hastie speede
The faire Duess' had forst him leave behind;
And yet more sad, that Una his deare dreed
Her truth had staind with treason so unkind;
Yet crime in her could never creature find,
But for his love, and for her owne selfe sake,
She wandred had from one to other Ynd,
Him for to seeke, ne ever would forsake,
Till her unwares the fiers Sansloy did overtake.

III

Who, after Archimagoes fowle defeat,
Led her away into a forest wilde,
And turning wrathfull fyre to lustfull heat,

With beastly sin thought her to have defilde,
And made the vassal of his pleasures wilde.
Yet first he cast by treatie, and by traynes,
Her to persuade that stubborne fort to yilde:
For greater conquest of hard love he gaynes,
That workes it to his will, then he that it constraines.

IV

With fawning words he courted her awhile,
And looking lovely, and oft sighing sore,
Her constant hart did tempt with diverse guile,
But wordes and lookes, and sighes she did abhore;
As rocke of Diamond steadfast evermore,
Yet for to feed his fyrie lustfull eye,
He snatcht the vele that hong her face before;
Then gan her beautie shyne, as brightest skye
And burnt his beastly hart t'efforce her chastitye.

V

So when he saw his flatt'ring artes to fayle,
And subtile engines bett from batteree;
With greedy force he gan the fort assayle,
Whereof he weend possessed soone to bee,
And with rich spoile of ransackt chastitee.
Ah heavens! that do this hideous act behold,
And heavenly virgin thus outraged see,
How can ye vengeance just so long withold
And hurle not flashing flames upon that Paynim bold?

VI

The pitteous maiden carefull comfortlesse,
Does throw out thrilling shriekes, and shrieking cryes,
The last vaine helpe of womens great distresse,
And with loud plaints importuneth the skyes,
That molten starres do drop like weeping eyes;
And Phœbus flying so most shameful sight,
His blushing face in foggy cloud implyes,
And hides for shame. What wit of mortall wight
Can now devise to quit a thrall from such a plight?

VII

Eternal providence exceeding thought,
Where none appeares can make herselfe a way:

A wondrous way it for this Lady wrought,
From Lyons clawes to pluck the griped pray.
Her shrill outcryes and shriekes so loud did bray,
That all the woodes and forestes did resownd;
A troupe of Faunes and Satyres far away
Within the wood were dauncing in a rownd,
Whiles old Sylvanus slept in shady arber sownd:

VIII

Who when they heard that pitteous strained voice,
In haste forsooke their rurall meriment,
And ran towards the far rebownded noyce,
To weet, what wight so loudly did lament.
Unto the place they come incontinent:
Whom when the raging Sarazin espide,
A rude, mishapen, monstrous rablement,
Whose like he never saw, he durst not bide,
But got his ready steed, and fast away gan ride.

IX

The wyld woodgods arrived in the place,
There find the virgin dolefull desolate,
With ruffled rayments, and faire blubbred face,
As her outrageous foe had left her late;
And trembling yet through feare of former hate:
All stand amazed at so uncouth sight,
And gin to pittie her unhappie state;
All stand astonied at her beautie bright,
In their rude eyes unworthy of so wofull plight.

X

She more amaz'd, in double dread doth dwell;
And every tender part for feare doth shake:
As when a greedie Wolfe, through hunger fell,
A seely Lambe farre from the flocke does take,
Of whom he meanes his bloudie feast to make,
A Lyon spyes fast running towards him,
The innocent pray in hast he does forsake,
Which quit from death yet quakes in every lim
With chaunge of feare, to see the Lyon looke so grim.

XI

Such fearefull fit assaid her trembling hart,
Ne word to speake, ne joynt to move she had:
The salvage nation feele her secret smart,
And read her sorrow in her count'nance sad;
Their frowning forheads with rough hornes yclad,
And rustick horror all a side doe lay;
And gently grenning, show a semblance glad
To comfort her, and feare to put away,
Their backward bent knees teach her humbly to obay.

XII

The doubtfull Damzell dare not yet commit
Her single person to their barbarous truth;
But still twixt feare and hope amazd does sit,
Late learnd what harme to hasty trust ensu'th:
They in compassion of her tender youth,
And wonder of her beautie soveraine,
Are wonne with pitty and unwonted ruth,
And all prostrate upon the lowly plaine,
Do kisse her feete, and fawne on her with count'nance faine.

XIII

Their harts she ghesseth by their humble guise,
And yieldes her to extremitie of time;
So from the ground she fearlesse doth arise,
And walketh forth without suspect of crime:
They all as glad, as birdes of joyous Prime,
Thence lead her forth, about her dauncing round,
Shouting, and singing all a shepheards ryme,
And with greene braunches strowing all the ground,
Do worship her, as Queene, with olive girlond cround.

XIV

And all the way their merry pipes they sound,
That all the woods with doubled Eccho ring,
And with their horned feet do weare the ground,
Leaping like wanton kids in pleasant Spring.
So towards old Sylvanus they her bring;
Who with the noyse awaked commeth out
To weet the cause, his weake steps governing,
And aged limbs on Cypresse stadle stout;
And with an yvie twyne his wast is girt about.

XV

Far off he wonders, what them makes so glad,
Or Bacchus merry fruit they did invent,
Or Cybeles franticke rites have made them mad,
They drawing nigh, unto their God present
That flowre of faith and beautie excellent.
The God himselfe, vewing that mirrhour rare,
Stood long amazd, and burnt in his intent;
His owne faire Dryope now he thinkes not faire,
And Pholoe fowle when her to this he doth compaire.

XVI

The woodborne people fall before her flat,
And worship her as Goddesse of the wood;
And old Sylvanus selfe bethinkes not, what
To thinke of wight so faire, but gazing stood,
In doubt to deeme her borne of earthly brood;
Sometimes Dame Venus selfe he seemes to see,
But Venus never had so sober mood;
Sometimes Diana he her takes to bee,
But misseth bow, and shaftes, and buskins to her knee.

XVII

By vew of her he ginneth to revive
His ancient love, and dearest Cyparisse,
And calles to mind his pourtraiture alive,
How faire he was, and yet not faire to this,
And how he slew with glauncing dart amisse
A gentle Hynd, the which the lovely boy
Did love as life, above all worldly blisse;
For griefe whereof the lad n'ould after joy,
But pynd away in anguish and selfe-wild annoy.

XVIII

The wooddy Nymphes, faire Hamadryades,
Her to behold do thither runne apace,
And all the troupe of light-foot Naiades
Flocke all about to see her lovely face:
But when they vewed have her heavenly grace,
They envy her in their malitious mind,
And fly away for feare of fowle disgrace:
But all the Satyres scorne their woody kind,
And henceforth nothing faire but her on earth they find.

XIX

Glad of such lucke, the luckelesse lucky maid,
Did her content to please their feeble eyes,
And long time with that salvage people staid,
To gather breath in many miseries.
During which time her gentle wit she plyes,
To teach them truth, which worshipt her in vaine,
And made her th' Image of Idolatryes;
But when their bootlesse zeale she did restraine
From her own worship, they her Asse would worship fayn.

XX

It fortuned a noble warlike knight
By just occasion to that forrest came,
To seeke his kindred, and the lignage right,
From whence he tooke his well deserved name:
He had in armes abroad wonne muchell fame,
And fild far lands with glorie of his might,
Plaine, faithfull, true, and enimy of shame,
And ever lov'd to fight for Ladies right:
But in vaine glorious frayes he litle did delight.

XXI

A Satyres sonne yborne in forrest wyld,
By straunge adventure as it did betyde,
And there begotten of a Lady myld,
Faire Thyamis the daughter of Labryde,
That was in sacred bands of wedlocke tyde
To Therion, a loose unruly swayne;
Who had more joy to raunge the forrest wyde,
And chase the salvage beast with busie payne,
Then serve his Ladies love, and wast in pleasures vayne.

XXII

The forlorne mayd did with loves longing burne
And could not lacke her lovers company,
But to the wood she goes, to serve her turne,
And seeke her spouse that from her still does fly,
And followes other game and venery:
A Satyre chaunst her wandring for to finde,
And kindling coles of lust in brutish eye,
The loyall links of wedlocke did unbind,
And made her person thrall unto his beastly kind.

XXIII

So long in secret cabin there he held
Her captive to his sensuall desire,
Till that with timely fruit her belly sweld,
And bore a boy unto that salvage sire:
Then home he suffred her for to retyre,
For ransome leaving him the late borne childe;
Whom till to ryper yeares he gan aspire,
He noursled up in life and manners wilde,
Emongst wild beasts and woods, from lawes of men exilde.

XXIV

For all he taught the tender ymp, was but
To banish cowardize and bastard feare;
His trembling hand he would him force to put
Upon the Lyon and the rugged Beare;
And from the she Beares teats her whelps to teare;
And eke wyld roaring Buls he would him make
To tame, and ryde their backes not made to beare;
And the Robuckes in flight to overtake,
That every beast for feare of him did fly and quake.

XXV

Thereby so fearlesse, and so fell he grew,
That his owne sire and maister of his guise
Did often tremble at his horrid vew,
And oft for dread of hurt would him advise,
The angry beasts not rashly to despise,
Nor too much to provoke; for he would learne
The Lyon stoup to him in lowly wise,
(A lesson hard) and make the Libbard sterne
Leave roaring, when in rage he for revenge did earne.

XXVI

And for to make his powre approved more,
Wyld beasts in yron yokes he would compell;
The spotted Panther, and the tusked Bore,
The Pardale swift, and the tigre cruell,
The Antelope, and Wolfe both fierce and fell;
And them constraine in equall teme to draw.
Such joy he had, their stubborne harts to quell,
And sturdie courage tame with dreadfull aw,
That his beheast they feared, as a tyrans law.

XXVII

His loving mother came upon a day
Unto the woods, to see her little sonne;
And chaunst unwares to meet him in the way,
After his sportes, and cruell pastime donne;
When after him a Lyonesse did runne,
That roaring all with rage, did lowd requere
Her children deare, whom he away had wonne:
The Lyon whelpes she saw how he did beare,
And lull in rugged armes, withouten childish feare.

XXVIII

The fearefull Dame all quaked at the sight,
And turning backe, gan fast to fly away,
Untill with love revokt from vaine affright,
She hardly yet perswaded was to stay,
And then to him these womanish words gan say;
Ah Satyrane, my dearling, and my joy,
For love of me leave off this dreadfull play;
To dally thus with death is no fit toy,
Go find some other play-fellowes, mine own sweet boy.

XXIX

In these and like delights of bloudy game
He trayned was, till ryper yeares he raught;
And there abode, whilst any beast of name
Walkt in that forest, whom he had not taught
To feare his force: and then his courage haught
Desird of forreine foemen to be knowne,
And far abroad for straunge adventures sought;
In which his might was never overthrowne;
But through all Faery lond his famous worth was blown.

XXX

Yet evermore it was his manner faire,
After long labours and adventures spent,
Unto those native woods for to repaire,
To see his sire and offspring auncient.
And now he thither came for like intent;
Where he unwares the fairest Una found,
Straunge Lady, in so straunge habiliment,
Teaching the Satyres, which her sat around,
Trew sacred lore, which from her sweet lips did redound.

XXXI

He wondred at her wisedome heavenly rare,
Whose like in womens wit he never knew;
And when her curteous deeds he did compare,
Gan her admire, and her sad sorrowes rew,
Blaming of Fortune, which such troubles threw,
And joyd to make proofe of her crueltie,
On gentle Dame, so hurtlesse, and so trew:
Thenceforth he kept her goodly company,
And learnd her discipline of faith and veritie.

XXXII

But she all vowd unto the Redcrosse knight,
His wandring perill closely did lament,
Ne in this new acquaintaunce could delight,
But her deare heart with anguish did torment,
And all her wit in secret counsels spent,
How to escape. At last in privie wise
To Satyrane she shewed her intent;
Who glad to gain such favour, gan devise
How with that pensive Maid he best might thence arise.

XXXIII

So on a day when Satyres all were gone
To do their service to Sylvanus old,
The gentle virgin left behind alone
He led away with courage stout and bold.
Too late it was, to Satyres to be told,
Or ever hope recover her againe:
In vaine he seekes that having cannot hold.
So fast he carried her with carefull paine,
That they the woods are past, and come now to the plaine.

XXXIV

The better part now of the lingring day,
They traveild had, whenas they farre espide
A weary wight forwandring by the way,
And towards him they gan in haste to ride,
To weete of newes, that did abroad betide,
Or tydings of her knight of the Redcrosse.
But he them spying, gan to turne aside,
For feare as seemd, or for some feigned losse;
More greedy they of newes, fast towards him do crosse.

XXXV

A silly man, in simple weedes forworne,
And soild with dust of the long dried way;
His sandales were with toilsome travell torne,
And face all tand with scorching sunny ray,
As he had traveild many a sommers day,
Through boyling sands of Arabie and Ynde;
And in his hand a Jacobs staffe, to stay
His wearie limbes upon: and eke behind,
His scrip did hang, in which his needments he did bind.

XXXVI

The knight approaching nigh, of him inquerd
Tidings of warre, and of adventures new;
But warres, nor new adventures none he herd.
Then Una gan to aske, if ought he knew,
Or heard abroad of that her champion trew,
That in his armour bare a croslet red.
Aye me, Deare dame (quoth he) well may I rew
To tell the sad sight which mine eies have red.
These eies did see that knight both living and eke ded.

XXXVII

That cruell word her tender hart so thrild,
That suddein cold did runne through every vaine,
And stony horrour all her sences fild
With dying fit, that downe she fell for paine.
The knight her lightly reared up againe,
And comforted with curteous kind reliefe:
Then, wonne from death, she bad him tellen plaine
The further processe of her hidden griefe:
The lesser pangs can beare, who hath endur'd the chiefe.

XXXVIII

Then gan the Pilgrim thus, I chaunst this day,
This fatall day, that shall I ever rew,
To see two knights in travell on my way
(A sory sight) arraung'd in battell new,
Both breathing vengeaunce, both of wrathfull hew:
My fearefull flesh did tremble at their strife,
To see their blades so greedily imbrew,
That drunke with bloud, yet thristed after life:
What more? the Redcrosse knight was slaine with Paynim knife.

XXXIX

Ah dearest Lord (quoth she) how might that bee,
And he the stoughtest knight, that ever wonne?
Ah dearest dame (quoth he) how might I see
The thing, that might not be, and yet was donne?
Where is (said Satyrane) that Paynims sonne,
That him of life, and us of joy hath reft?
Not far away (quoth he) he hence doth wonne
Foreby a fountaine, where I late him left
Washing his bloudy wounds, that through the steele were cleft.

XL

Therewith the knight thence marched forth in hast,
Whiles Una with huge heavinesse opprest,
Could not for sorrow follow him so fast;
And soone he came, as he the place had ghest,
Whereas that Pagan proud him selfe did rest,
In secret shadow by a fountaine side:
Even he it was, that earst would have supprest
Faire Una: whom when Satyrane espide,
With fowle reprochfull words he boldly him defide.

XLI

And said, Arise thou cursed Miscreaunt,
That hast with knightlesse guile and trecherous train
Faire knighthood fowly shamed, and doest vaunt
That good knight of the Redcrosse to have slain:
Arise, and with like treason now maintain
Thy guilty wrong, or els thee guilty yield.
The Sarazin this hearing, rose amain,
And catching up in hast his three-square shield,
And shining helmet, soone him buckled to the field.

XLII

And drawing nigh him said, Ah misborne Elfe,
In evill houre thy foes thee hither sent,
Anothers wrongs to wreake upon thy selfe:
Yet ill thou blamest me, for having blent
My name with guile and traiterous intent:
That Redcrosse knight, perdie, I never slew,
But had he beene, where earst his arms were lent,
Th' enchaunter vaine his errour should not rew:
But thou his errour shalt, I hope, now proven trew.

XLIII

Therewith they gan, both furious and fell,
To thunder blowes, and fiersly to assaile
Each other bent his enimy to quell,
That with their force they perst both plate and maile,
And made wide furrowes in their fleshes fraile,
That it would pitty any living eie.
Large floods of bloud adowne their sides did raile;
But floods of bloud could not them satisfie:
Both hungred after death: both chose to win, or die.

XLIV

So long they fight, and fell revenge pursue,
That fainting each, themselves to breathen let,
And oft refreshed, battell oft renue:
As when two Bores with rancling malice met,
Their gory sides fresh bleeding fiercely fret,
Til breathlesse both them selves aside retire,
Where foming wrath, their cruell tuskes they whet,
And trample th' earth, the whiles they may respire;
Then backe to fight againe, new breathed and entire.

XLV

So fiersly, when these knights had breathed once,
They gan to fight returne, increasing more
Their puissant force, and cruell rage attonce.
With heaped strokes more hugely then before,
That with their drerie wounds and bloudy gore
They both deformed, scarsely could be known.
By this, sad Una fraught with anguish sore,
Led with their noise, which through the aire was thrown:
Arriv'd, wher they in erth their fruitles bloud had sown.

XLVI

Whom all so soone as that proud Sarazin
Espide, he gan revive the memory
Of his lewd lusts, and late attempted sin,
And left the doubtfull battell hastily,
To catch her, newly offred to his eie:
But Satyrane with strokes him turning, staid,
And sternely bad him other businesse plie,
Then hunt the steps of pure unspotted Maid:
Wherewith he all enrag'd, these bitter speaches said.

XLVII

O foolish faeries son, what fury mad
Hath thee incenst, to hast thy doefull fate?
Were it not better I that Lady had,
Then that thou hadst repented it too late?
Most senseless man he, that himselfe doth hate
To love another. Lo then for thine ayd
Here take thy lovers token on thy pate.
So they two fight; the whiles the royall Mayd
Fledd farre away, of that proud Paynim sore afrayd.

XLVIII

But that false Pilgrim, which that leasing told,
Being in deed old Archimage, did stay
In secret shadow, all this to behold,
And much rejoiced in their bloudy fray:
But when he saw the Damsell passe away,
He left his stond, and her pursewd apace,
In hope to bring her to her last decay,
But for to tell her lamentable cace,
And eke this battels end, will need another place.

Canto VII

*The Redcrosse knight is captive made
by Gyaunt proud opprest,
Prince Arthur meets with Una greatly with those newes distrest.*

I

WHAT man so wise, what earthly wit so ware,
As to discry the crafty cunning traine,
By which deceipt doth maske in visour faire,
And cast her colours dyed deepe in graine,
To seeme like Truth, whose shape she well can faine,
And fitting gestures to her purpose frame;
The guiltlesse man with guile to entertaine?
Great maistresse of her art was that false Dame,
The false Duessa, cloked with Fidessaes name.

II

Who when returning from the drery Night,
She fownd not in that perilous house of Pryde,
Where she had left, the noble Redcrosse knight,

Her hoped pray; she would no lenger bide,
But forth she went, to seeke him far and wide.
Ere long she fownd, whereas he wearie sate
To rest him selfe, foreby a fountaine side,
Disarmed all of yron-coted Plate,
And by his side his steed the grassy forage ate.

III

He feedes upon the cooling shade, and bayes
His sweatie forehead in the breathing wind,
Which through the trembling leaves full gently playes,
Wherein the cherefull birds of sundry kind
Do chaunt sweet musick, to delight his mind:
The Witch approaching gan him fairely greet,
And with reproch of carelesnesse unkind
Upbrayd, for leaving her in place unmeet,
With fowle words tempring faire, soure gall with hony sweet.

IV

Unkindnesse past, they gan of solace treat,
And bathe in pleasaunce of the joyous shade,
Which shielded them against the boyling heat,
And with greene boughes decking a gloomy glade,
About the fountaine like a girlond made;
Whose bubbling wave did ever freshly well,
Ne ever would through fervent sommer fade:
The sacred Nymph, which therein wont to dwell,
Was out of Dianes favour, as it then befell.

V

The cause was this: One day, when Phœbe fayre
With all her band was following the chace,
This Nymph, quite tyr'd with heat of scorching ayre,
Sat downe to rest in middest of the race:
The goddesse wroth gan fowly her disgrace,
And bad the waters, which from her did flow,
Be such as she her selfe was then in place.
Thenceforth her waters waxed dull and slow,
And all that drinke thereof do faint and feeble grow.

VI

Hereof this gentle knight unweeting was,
And lying downe upon the sandie graile,

Drunke of the streame, as cleare as cristall glas:
Eftsoones his manly forces gan to faile,
And mightie strong was turned to feeble fraile.
His chaunged powres at first them selves not felt,
Till crudled cold his corage gan assaile,
And cheareful bloud in faintnesse chill did melt,
Which like a fever fit through all his body swelt.

VII

Yet goodly court he made still to his Dame,
Pourd out in loosnesse on the grassy grownd,
Both carelesse of his health, and of his fame:
Till at the last he heard a dreadfull sownd,
Which through the wood loud bellowing did rebownd,
That all the earth for terrour seemd to shake,
And trees did tremble. Th' Elfe therewith astownd,
Upstarted lightly from his looser make,
And his unready weapons gan in hand to take.

VIII

But ere he could his armour on him dight,
Or get his shield, his monstrous enimy
With sturdie steps came stalking in his sight,
An hideous Geant, horrible and hye,
That with his tallnesse seemd to threat the skye,
The ground eke groned under him for dreed;
His living like saw never living eye,
Ne durst behold: his stature did exceed
The hight of three the tallest sonnes of mortall seed.

IX

The greatest Earth his uncouth mother was,
And blustering Æolus his boasted syre,
Who with his breath, which through the world doth pas,
Her hollow womb did secretly inspire,
And fild her hidden caves with stormie yre,
That she conceived; and trebling the dew time,
In which the wombes of women do expire,
Brought forth this monstrous masse of earthly slime
Puft up with emptie wind, and fild with sinfull crime.

X

So growen great through arrogant delight
Of th' high descent, whereof he was yborne,
And through presumption of his matchlesse might,
All other powres and knighthood he did scorne.
Such now he marcheth to this man forlorne,
And left to losse: his stalking steps are stayde
Upon a snaggy Oke, which he had torne
Out of his mothers bowelles, and it made
His mortall mace, wherewith his foeman he dismayde.

XI

That when the knight he spide, he gan advance
With huge force and insupportable mayne,
And towardes him with dreadfull fury praunce;
Who haplesse, and eke hopelesse, all in vaine
Did to him pace, sad battaile to darrayne,
Disarmd, disgrast, and inwardly dismayde,
And eke so faint in every joynt and vaine,
Through that fraile fountaine, which him feeble made,
That scarsely could he weeld his bootlesse single blade.

XII

The Geaunt strooke so maynly mercilesse,
That could have overthrowne a stony towre,
And were not heavenly grace, that did him blesse,
He had beene pouldred all, as thin as flowre:
But he was wary of that deadly stowre,
And lightly lept from underneath the blow:
Yet so exceeding was the villeins powre,
That with the wind it did him overthrow,
And all his sences stound, that still he lay full low.

XIII

As when that divelish yron Engin wrought
In deepest Hell, and framd by Furies skill,
With windy Nitre and quick Sulphur fraught,
And ramd with bullet round, ordaind to kill,
Conceiveth fire, the heavens it doth fill
With thundring noyse, and all the ayre doth choke,
That none can breath, nor see, nor heare at will,
Through smouldry cloud of duskish stincking smoke,
That th' onely breath him daunts, who hath escapt the stroke.

XIV

So daunted when the Geaunt saw the knight,
His heavie hand he heaved up on hye,
And him to dust thought to have battred quight,
Untill Duessa loud to him gan crye;
O great Orgoglio, greatest under skye,
O hold thy mortall hand for Ladies sake,
Hold for my sake, and do him not to dye,
But vanquisht thine eternall bondslave make,
And me, thy worthy meed, unto thy Leman take.

XV

He hearkned, and did stay from further harmes,
To gayne so goodly guerdon, as she spake:
So willingly she came into his armes,
Who her as willingly to grace did take,
And was possessed of his new found make.
Then up he tooke the slombred sencelesse corse,
And ere he could out of his swowne awake,
Him to his castle brought with hastie forse,
And in a Dongeon deepe him threw without remorse.

XVI

From that day forth Duessa was his deare,
And highly honourd in his haughtie eye,
He gave her gold and purple pall to weare,
And triple crowne set on her head full hye,
And her endowd with royall majestye:
Then for to make her dreaded more of men,
And peoples harts with awfull terrour tye,
A monstrous beast ybred in filthy fen
He chose, which he had kept long time in darksome den.

XVII

Such one it was, as that renowmed Snake
Which great Alcides in Stremona slew,
Long fostred in the filth of Lerna lake,
Whose many heads out budding ever new
Did breed him endlesse labour to subdew:
But this same Monster much more ugly was;
For seven great heads out of his body grew,
An yron brest, and back of scaly bras,
And all embrewd in bloud, his eyes did shine as glas.

XVIII

His tayle was stretched out in wondrous length,
That to the house of heavenly gods it raught,
And with extorted powre, and borrow'd strength,
The ever-burning lamps from thence it braught,
And prowdly threw to ground, as things of naught;
And underneath his filthy feet did tread
The sacred things, and holy heasts foretaught.
Upon this dreadfull Beast with sevenfold head
He sett the false Duessa, for more aw and dread.

XIX

The wofull Dwarfe, which saw his maisters fall,
Whiles he had keeping of his grasing steed,
And valiant knight become a caytive thrall,
When all was past, tooke up his forlorne weed,
His mightie armour, missing most at need;
His silver shield, now idle maisterlesse;
His poynant speare, that many made to bleed,
The rueful moniments of heavinesse,
And with them all departes, to tell his great distresse.

XX

He had not travaild long, when on the way
He wofull Ladie, wofull Una met,
Fast flying from that Paynims greedy pray,
Whilest Satyrane him from pursuit did let:
Who when her eyes she on the Dwarfe had set,
And saw the signes, that deadly tydings spake,
She fell to ground for sorrowfull regret,
And lively breath her sad brest did forsake,
Yet might her pitteous hart be seene to pant and quake.

XXI

The messenger of so unhappie newes,
Would faine have dyde: dead was his hart within,
Yet outwardly some little comfort shewes:
At last recovering hart, he does begin
To rub her temples, and to chaufe her chin,
And everie tender part does tosse and turne.
So hardly he the flitted life does win,
Unto her native prison to retourne:
Then gins her grieved ghost thus to lament and mourne.

XXII

Ye dreary instruments of dolefull sight,
That doe this deadly spectacle behold,
Why do ye lenger feed on loathed light,
Or liking find to gaze on earthly mould,
Sith cruell fates the carefull threeds unfould,
The which my life and love together tyde?
Now let the stony dart of senselesse cold
Perce to my hart, and pas through every side,
And let eternall night so sad sight fro me hide.

XXIII

O lightsome day, the lampe of highest Jove,
First made by him, mens wandring wayes to guyde,
When darkenesse he in deepest dongeon drove,
Henceforth thy hated face for ever hyde,
And shut up heavens windowes shyning wyde:
For earthly sight can nought but sorrow breed,
And late repentance, which shall long abyde.
Mine eyes no more on vanitie shall feed,
But seeled up with death, shall have their deadly meed.

XXIV

Then downe againe she fell unto the ground;
But he her quickly reared up againe:
Thrise did she sinke adowne in deadly swownd
And thrise he her reviv'd with busie paine,
At last when life recover'd had the raine,
And over-wrestled his strong enemie,
With foltring tong, and trembling every vaine,
Tell on (quoth she) the wofull Tragedie,
The which these reliques sad present unto mine eie.

XXV

Tempestuous fortune hath spent all her spight,
And thrilling sorrow throwne his utmost dart;
Thy sad tongue cannot tell more heavy plight,
Then that I feele, and harbour in mine hart:
Who hath endur'd the whole, can beare each part.
If death it be, it is not the first wound,
That launched hath my brest with bleeding smart.
Begin, and end the bitter balefull stound;
If lesse then that I feare, more favour I have found.

XXVI

Then gan the Dwarfe the whole discourse declare,
The subtill traines of Archimago old;
The wanton loves of false Fidessa faire,
Bought with the blood of vanquisht Paynim bold;
The wretched payre transformed to treen mould;
The house of Pride, and perils round about;
The combat, which he with Sansjoy did hould;
The lucklesse conflict with the Gyant stout,
Wherein captiv'd, of life or death he stood in doubt.

XXVII

She heard with patience all unto the end,
And strove to maister sorrowfull assay,
Which greater grew, the more she did contend,
And almost rent her tender hart in tway;
And love fresh coles unto her fire did lay:
For greater love, the greater is the losse.
Was never Lady loved dearer day,
Then she did love the knight of the Redcrosse;
For whose deare sake so many troubles her did tosse.

XXVIII

At last when fervent sorrow slaked was,
She up arose, resolving him to find
Alive or dead: and forward forth doth pas,
All as the Dwarfe the way to her assynd:
And evermore, in constant carefull mind,
She fed her wound with fresh renewed bale;
Long tost with stormes, and bet with bitter wind,
High over hills, and low adowne the dale,
She wandred many a wood, and measurd many a vale.

XXIX

At last she chaunced by good hap to meet
A goodly knight, faire marching by the way
Together with his Squire, arrayed meet:
His glitterand armour shined farre away,
Like glauncing light of Phœbus brightest ray;
From top to toe no place appeared bare,
That deadly dint of steele endanger may:
Athwart his brest a bauldrick brave he ware,
That shynd, like twinkling stars, with stons most pretious rare.

XXX

And in the midst thereof one pretious stone
Of wondrous worth, and eke of wondrous mights,
Shapt like a Ladies head, exceeding shone,
Like Hesperus emongst the lesser lights,
And strove for to amaze the weaker sights:
Thereby his mortall blade full comely hong
In yvory sheath, ycarv'd with curious slights;
Whose hilts were burnisht gold, and handle strong
Of mother pearle, and buckled with a golden tong.

XXXI

His haughtie helmet, horrid all with gold,
Both glorious brightnesse, and great terrour bred;
For all the crest a Dragon did enfold
With greedie pawes, and over all did spred
His golden wings: his dreadfull hideous hed
Close couched on the bever, seem'd to throw
From flaming mouth bright sparkles fierie red,
That suddeine horror to faint harts did show,
And scaly tayle was stretcht adowne his backe full low.

XXXII

Upon the top of all his loftie crest,
A bunch of haires discolourd diversly,
With sprincled pearle, and gold full richly drest,
Did shake, and seemd to daunce for jollity,
Like to an Almond tree ymounted hye
On top of greene Selinis all alone,
With blossoms brave bedecked daintily;
Whose tender locks do tremble every one
At every little breath that under heaven is blowne.

XXXIII

His warlike shield all closely cover'd was,
Ne might of mortall eye be ever seene;
Not made of steele, nor of enduring bras,
Such earthly mettals soone consumed beene;
But all of Diamond perfect pure and cleene
It framed was, one massie entire mould,
Hewen out of Adamant rocke with engines keene,
That point of speare it never percen could,
Ne dint of direfull sword divide the substance would.

XXXIV

The same to wight he never wont disclose,
But when as monsters huge he would dismay,
Or daunt unequall armies of his foes,
Or when the flying heavens he would affray;
For so exceeding shone his glistring ray,
That Phœbus golden face it did attaint,
As when a cloud his beames doth over-lay;
And silver Cynthia wexed pale and faint,
As when her face is staynd with magicke arts constraint.

XXXV

No magicke arts hereof had any might,
Nor bloudie wordes of bold Enchaunters call;
But all that was not such as seemd in sight,
Before that shield did fade, and suddeine fall;
And, when him list the raskall routes appall,
Men into stones therewith he could transmew,
And stones to dust, and dust to nought at all;
And when him list the prouder lookes subdew,
He would them gazing blind, or turne to other hew.

XXXVI

Ne let it seeme, that credence this exceedes,
For he that made the same, was knowne right well
To have done much more admirable deedes.
It Merlin was, which whylome did excell
All living wightes in might of magicke spell:
Both shield, and sword, and armour all he wrought
For this young Prince, when first to armes he fell;
But when he dyde, the Faerie Queene it brought
To Faerie lond, where yet it may be seene, if sought.

XXXVII

A gentle youth, his dearely loved Squire,
His speare of heben wood behind him bare,
Whose harmefull head, thrice heated in the fire,
Had riven many a brest with pikehead square:
A goodly person, and could menage faire
His stubborne steed with curbed canon bit,
Who under him did trample as the aire,
And chauft, that any on his backe should sit;
The yron rowels into frothy fome he bit.

XXXVIII

When as this knight nigh to the Ladie drew,
With lovely court he gan her entertaine;
But when he heard her answeres loth, he knew
Some secret sorrow did her heart distraine:
Which to allay, and calme her storming paine,
Faire feeling words he wisely gan display,
And for her humour fitting purpose faine,
To tempt the cause it selfe for to bewray;
Wherewith emmov'd, these bleeding words she gan to say.

XXXIX

What worlds delight, or joy of living speach
Can heart, so plung'd in sea of sorrowes deep,
And heaped with so huge misfortunes, reach?
The carefull cold beginneth for to creepe,
And in my heart his yron arrow steepe,
Soone as I thinke upon my bitter bale:
Such helplesse harmes yts better hidden keepe,
Then rip up griefe, where it may not availe,
My last left comfort is, my woes to weepe and waile.

XL

Ah Ladie deare, quoth then the gentle knight,
Well may I weene your griefe is wondrous great;
For wondrous great griefe groneth in my spright,
Whiles thus I heare you of your sorrowes treat.
But wofull Ladie, let me you intrete
For to unfold the anguish of your hart:
Mishaps are maistred by advice discrete,
And counsell mittigates the greatest smart;
Found never helpe who never would his hurts impart.

XLI

O but (quoth she) great griefe will not be tould,
And can more easily be thought then said.
Right so (quoth he), but he that never would,
Could never: will to might gives greatest aid.
But griefe (quoth she) does greater grow displaid,
If then it find not helpe, and breedes despaire.
Despaire breedes not (quoth he) where faith is staid.
No faith so fast (quoth she) but flesh does paire.
Flesh may empaire (quoth he) but reason can repaire.

XLII

His goodly reason, and well guided speach,
So deepe did settle in her gracious thought,
That her perswaded to disclose the breach,
Which love and fortune in her heart had wrought,
And said; Faire Sir, I hope good hap hath brought
You to inquire the secrets of my griefe,
Or that your wisedome will direct my thought,
Or that your prowesse can me yield reliefe:
Then heare the storie sad, which I shall tell you briefe.

XLIII

The forlorne Maiden, whom your eyes have seene
The laughing stocke of fortunes mockeries,
Am th' only daughter of a King and Queene,
Whose parents deare, whilest equal destinies
Did runne about, and their felicities
The favourable heavens did not envy,
Did spread their rule through all the territories,
Which Phison and Euphrates floweth by,
And Gehons golden waves doe wash continually.

XLIV

Till that their cruell cursed enemy,
An huge great Dragon horrible in sight,
Bred in the loathly lakes of Tartary,
With murdrous ravine, and devouring might
Their kingdome spoild, and countrey wasted quight:
Themselves, for feare into his jawes to fall,
He forst to castle strong to take their flight,
Where fast embard in mighty brasen wall,
He has them now foure yeres besiegd to make them thrall.

XLV

Full many knights adventurous and stout
Have enterpriz'd that Monster to subdew;
From every coast that heaven walks about,
Have thither come the noble Martiall crew,
That famous hard atchievements still pursew;
Yet never any could that girlond win,
But all still shronke, and still he greater grew:
All they for want of faith, or guilt of sin,
The pitteous pray of his fierce crueltie have bin.

XLVI

At last yledd with farre reported praise,
Which flying fame throughout the world had spred,
Of doughty knights, whom Faery land did raise,
That noble order hight of Maidenhed,
Forthwith to court of Gloriane I sped
Of Gloriane great Queene of glory bright,
Whose Kingdomes seat Cleopolis is red,
There to obtaine some such redoubted knight,
The Parents deare from tyrants powre deliver might.

XLVII

It was my chance (my chance was faire and good)
There for to find a fresh unproved knight,
Whose manly hands imbrew'd in guiltie blood
Had never bene, ne ever by his might
Had throwne to ground the unregarded right:
Yet of his prowesse proofe he since hath made
(I witnesse am) in many a cruell fight;
The groning ghosts of many one dismaide
Have felt the bitter dint of his avenging blade.

XLVIII

And ye the forlorne reliques of his powre,
His byting sword, and his devouring speare,
Which have endured many a dreadfull stowre,
Can speake his prowesse, that did earst you beare,
And well could rule: now he hath left you heare
To be the record of his ruefull losse,
And of my dolefull disaventurous deare:
O heavie record of the good Redcrosse,
Where have you left your Lord, that could so well you tosse?

XLIX

Well hoped I, and faire beginnings had,
That he my captive languor should redeeme,
Till all unweeting, an Enchaunter bad
His sence abusd, and made him to misdeeme
My loyalty, not such as it did seeme;
That rather death desire, then such despight.
Be judge ye heavens, that all things right esteeme,
How I him lov'd, and love with all my might,
So thought I eke of him, and thinke I thought aright.

L

Thenceforth me desolate he quite forsooke,
To wander, where wilde fortune would me lead,
And other bywaies he himselfe betooke,
Where never foot of living wight did tread,
That brought not backe the balefull body dead;
In which him chaunced false Duessa meete,
Mine onely foe, mine onely deadly dread,
Who with her witchcraft, and misseeming sweete,
Inveigled him to follow her desires unmeete.

LI

At last by subtill sleights she him betraid
Unto his foe, a Gyant huge and tall,
Who him disarmed, dissolute, dismaid,
Unwares surprised, and with mighty mall
The monster mercilesse him made to fall,
Whose fall did never foe before behold;
And now in darkesome dungeon, wretched thrall,
Remedilesse, for aie he doth him hold;
This is my cause of griefe, more great then may be told.

LII

Ere she had ended all, she gan to faint:
But he her comforted and faire bespake,
Certes, Madame, ye have great cause of plaint,
The stoutest heart, I weene, could cause to quake.
But be of cheare, and comfort to you take:
For till I have acquit your captive knight,
Assure your selfe, I will you not forsake.
His chearefull wordes reviv'd her chearelesse spright,
So forth they went, the Dwarfe them guiding ever right.

Canto VIII

Faire virgin, to redeeme her deare
brings Arthur to the fight:
Who slayes that Gyant, woundes the beast,
and strips Duessa quight.

I

AY me, how many perils doe enfold
The righteous man, to make him daily fall,
Were not that heavenly grace doth him uphold,

And stedfast truth acquite him out of all.
Her love is firme, her care continuall,
So oft as he through his owne foolish pride,
Or weaknesse is to sinfull bands made thrall:
Else should this Redcrosse knight in bands have dydd
For whose deliverance she this Prince doth thither guide.

II

They sadly traveild thus, until they came
Nigh to a castle builded strong and hie:
Then cryde the Dwarfe, Lo yonder is the same,
In which my Lord my liege doth lucklesse lie,
Thrall to that Gyants hateful tyrannie:
Therefore, deare Sir, your mightie powres assay.
The noble knight alighted by and by
From loftie steede, and bad the Ladie stay,
To see what end of fight should him befall that day.

III

So with the Squire, th' admirer of his might,
He marched forth towards that castle wall;
Whose gates he found fast shut, ne living wight
To ward the same, nor answere commers call.
Then tooke that Squire an horne of bugle small.
Which hong adowne his side in twisted gold
And tassels gay. Wyde wonders over all
Of that same hornes great vertues weren told,
Which had approved bene in uses manifold.

IV

Was never wight that heard that shrilling sownd,
But trembling feare did feel in every vaine;
Three miles it might be easie heard around,
And Ecchoes three answerd it selfe againe:
No false enchauntment, nor deceiptfull traine,
Might once abide the terror of that blast,
But presently was voide and wholly vaine:
No gate so strong, no locke so firme and fast,
But with that percing noise flew open quite, or brast.

V

The same before the Geants gate he blew,
That all the castle quaked from the ground,

And every dore of freewill open flew.
The Gyant selfe dismaied with that sownd,
Where he with his Duessa dalliance fownd,
In hast came rushing forth from inner bowre,
With staring countenance sterne, as one astownd,
And staggering steps, to weet, what suddein stowre,
Had wrought that horror strange, and dar'd his dreaded powre.

VI

And after him the proud Duessa came
High mounted on her many-headed beast;
And every head with fyrie tongue did flame,
And every head was crowned on his creast,
And bloody mouthed with late cruell feast.
That when the knight beheld, his mightie shild
Upon his manly arme he soone addrest,
And at him fiercely flew, with courage fild,
And eger greedinesse through every member thrild.

VII

Therewith the Gyant buckled him to fight,
Inflam'd with scornefull wrath and high disdaine,
And lifting up his dreadfull club on hight,
All arm'd with ragged snubbes and knottie graine,
Him thought at first encounter to have slaine.
But wise and wary was that noble Pere,
And lightly leaping from so monstrous maine,
Did faire avoide the violence him nere;
It booted nought to thinke such thunderbolts to beare.

VIII

Ne shame he thought to shunne so hideous might:
The idle stroke, enforcing furious way,
Missing the marke of his misaymed sight
Did fall to ground, and with his heavie sway
So deepely dinted in the driven clay,
That three yardes deepe a furrow up did throw:
The sad earth wounded with so sore assay,
Did grone full grievous underneath the blow,
And trembling with strange feare, did like an earthquake show.

IX

As when almightie Jove, in wrathfull mood,
To wreake the guilt of mortall sins is bent,
Hurles forth his thundring dart with deadly food,
Enrold in flames, and smouldring dreriment,
Through riven cloudes and molten firmament;
The fierce threeforked engin making way
Both loftie towres and highest trees hath rent,
And all that might his angry passage stay,
And shooting in the earth, casts up a mount of clay.

X

His boystrous club, so buried in the ground,
He could not rearen up againe so light,
But that the knight him at avantage found,
And whiles he strove his combred clubbe to quight
Out of the earth, with blade all burning bright
He smote off his left arme, which like a blocke
Did fall to ground, depriv'd of native might;
Large streames of bloud out of the truncked stocke
Forth gushed, like fresh water streame from riven rocke.

XI

Dismayed with so desperate deadly wound,
And eke impatient of unwonted paine,
He lowdly brayd with beastly yelling sound,
That all the fields rebellowed againe;
As great a noyse, as when in Cymbrian plaine
An heard of Bulles, whom kindly rage doth sting,
Do for the milkie mothers want complaine,
And fill the fields with troublous bellowing,
The neighbour woods around with hollow murmur ring.

XII

That when his deare Duessa heard, and saw
The evil stownd, that daungerd her estate,
Unto his aide she hastily did draw
Her dreadfull beast, who swolne with blood of late
Came ramping forth with proud presumpteous gate,
And threatned all his heads like flaming brands.
But him the Squire made quickly to retrate,
Encountring fierce with single sword in hand,
And twixt him and his Lord did like a bulwarke stand.

XIII

The proud Duessa, full of wrathfull spight,
And fierce disdaine, to be affronted so,
Enforst her purple beast with all her might
That stop out of the way to overthroe,
Scorning the let of so unequall foe:
But nathemore would that courageous swayne
To her yeeld passage, gainst his Lord to goe,
But with outrageous strokes did him restraine,
And with his bodie bard the way atwixt them twaine.

XIV

Then tooke the angrie witch her golden cup,
Which still she bore, replete with magick artes;
Death and despeyre did many thereof sup,
And secret poyson through their inner parts,
Th' eternall bale of heavie wounded harts;
Which after charmes and some enchauntments said
She lightly sprinkled on his weaker parts;
Therewith his sturdie courage soone was quayd,
And all his senses were with suddeine dread dismayd.

XV

So downe he fell before the cruell beast,
Who on his neck his bloody clawes did seize,
That life nigh crusht out of his panting brest:
No powre he had to stirre, nor will to rize.
That when the carefull knight gan well avise,
He lightly left the foe, with whom he fought,
And to the beast gan turne his enterprise;
For wondrous anguish in his hart it wrought,
To see his loved Squire into such thraldome brought.

XVI

And high advauncing his blood-thirstie blade,
Stroke one of those deformed heads so sore,
That of his puissance proud ensample made;
His monstrous scalpe downe to his teeth it tore,
And that misformed shape mis-shaped more:
A sea of blood gusht from the gaping wound,
That her gay garments staynd with filthy gore,
And overflowed all the field around;
That over shoes in bloud he waded on the ground.

XVII

Thereat he roared for exceeding paine,
That to have heard great horror would have bred,
And scourging th' emptie ayre with his long traine,
Through great impatience of his grieved hed
His gorgeous ryder from her loftie sted
Would have cast downe, and trod in durtie myre,
Had not the Gyant soone her succoured;
Who all enrag'd with smart and franticke yre,
Came hurtling in full fierce, and forst the knight retyre.

XVIII

The force which wont in two to be disperst,
In one alone left hand he now unites,
Which is through rage more strong than both were erst;
With which his hideous club aloft he dites,
And at his foe with furious rigour smites,
That strongest Oake might seeme to overthrow:
The stroke upon his shield so heavie lites,
That to the ground it doubleth him full low:
What mortall wight could ever beare so monstrous blow?

XIX

And in his fall his shield, that covered was,
Did loose his vele by chaunce, and open flew:
The light whereof, that heavens light did pas,
Such blazing brightnesse through the aier threw,
That eye mote not the same endure to vew.
Which when the Gyaunt spyde with staring eye,
He downe let fall his arme, and soft withdrew
His weapon huge, that heaved was on hye
For to have slaine the man, that on the ground did lye.

XX

And eke the fruitfull-headed beast, amazd
At flashing beames of that sunshiny shield,
Became starke blind, and all his sences daz'd,
That downe he tumbled on the durtie field,
And seem'd himselfe as conquered to yield.
Whom when his maistresse proud perceiv'd to fall,
Whiles yet his feeble feet for faintnesse reeld,
Unto the Gyant loudly she gan call,
O helpe Orgoglio, helpe, or else we perish all.

XXI

At her so pitteous cry was much amoov'd
Her champion stout, and for to ayde his frend,
Againe his wonted angry weapon proov'd:
But all in vaine: for he has read his end
In that bright shield, and all their forces spend
Themselves in vaine: for since that glauncing sight,
He had no powre to hurt, nor to defend;
As where th' Almighties lightning brond does light,
It dimmes the dazed eyen, and daunts the senses quight.

XXII

Whom when the Prince, to battell new addrest,
And threatning high his dreadfull stroke did see,
His sparkling blade about his head he blest,
And smote off quite his right leg by the knee,
That downe he tombled; as an aged tree,
High growing on the top of rocky clift,
Whose hartstrings with keene steele nigh hewen be,
The mightie trunck halfe rent, with ragged rift
Doth roll adowne the rocks, and fall with fearefull drift.

XXIII

Or as a Castle reared high and round,
By subtile engins and malitious slight
Is undermined from the lowest ground,
And her foundation forst, and feebled quight,
At last downe falles, and with her heaped hight
Her hastie ruine does more heavie make,
And yields it selfe unto the victours might;
Such was this Gyants fall, that seemd to shake
The stedfast globe of earth, as it for feare did quake.

XXIV

The knight then lightly leaping to the pray,
With mortall steele him smot againe so sore,
That headlesse his unweldy bodie lay,
All wallowd in his owne fowle bloudy gore,
Which flowed from his wounds in wondrous store.
But soone as breath out of his breast did pas,
That huge great body, which the Gyaunt bore,
Was vanisht quite, and of that monstrous mas
Was nothing left, but like an emptie bladder was.

XXV

Whose grievous fall, when false Duessa spide,
Her golden cup she cast unto the ground,
And crowned mitre rudely threw aside;
Such percing griefe her stubborne hart did wound,
That she could not endure that dolefull stound,
But leaving all behind her, fled away;
The light-foot Squire her quickly turnd around,
And by hard meanes enforcing her to stay,
So brought unto his Lord, as his deserved pray.

XXVI

The royall Virgin which beheld from farre,
In pensive plight, and sad perplexitie,
The whole atchievement of this doubtfull warre,
Came running fast to greet his victorie,
With sober gladnesse, and myld modestie,
And with sweet joyous cheare him thus bespake:
Faire braunch of noblesse, flowre of chevalrie,
That with your worth the world amazed make,
How shall I quite the paines ye suffer for my sake?

XXVII

And you fresh budd of vertue springing fast,
Whom these sad eyes saw nigh unto deaths dore,
What hath poore Virgin for such perill past
Wherewith you to reward? Accept therefore
My simple selfe, and service evermore;
And he that high does sit, and all things see
With equall eyes, their merites to restore,
Behold what ye this day have done for mee,
And what I cannot quite, requite with usuree.

XXVIII

But sith the heavens, and your faire handeling
Have made you master of the field this day,
Your fortune maister eke with governing,
And well begun end all so well, I pray.
Ne let that wicked woman scape away;
For she it is, that did my Lord bethrall,
My dearest Lord, and deepe in dongeon lay,
Where he his better dayes hath wasted all.
O heare, how piteous he to you for ayd does call.

XXIX

Forthwith he gave in charge unto his Squire,
That scarlot whore to keepen carefully;
Whiles he himselfe with greedie great desire
Into the Castle entred forcibly,
Where living creature none he did espye;
Then gan he lowdly through the house to call:
But no man car'd to answere to his crye.
There raignd a solemne silence over all,
Nor voice was heard, nor wight was seene in bowre or hall.

XXX

At last with creeping crooked pace forth came
An old old man, with beard as white as snow,
That on a staffe his feeble steps did frame,
And guide his wearie gate both to and fro:
For his eye sight him failed long ygo,
And on his arme a bounch of keyes he bore,
The which unused rust did overgrow:
Those were the keyes of every inner dore,
But he could not them use, but kept them still in store.

XXXI

But very uncouth sight was to behold,
How he did fashion his untoward pace,
For as he forward moov'd his footing old,
So backward still was turnd his wrincled face,
Unlike to men, who ever as they trace,
Both feet and face one way are wont to lead.
This was the auncient keeper of that place,
And foster father of the Gyant dead;
His name Ignaro did his nature right aread.

XXXII

His reverend haires and holy gravitie
The knight much honord, as beseemed well,
And gently askt, where all the people bee,
Which in that stately building wont to dwell.
Who answerd him full soft, he could not tell.
Again he askt, where that same knight was layd,
Whom great Orgoglio with his puissance fell
Had made his caytive thrall, againe he sayde,
He could not tell: ne ever other answere made.

XXXIII

Then asked he, which way he in might pas:
He could not tell, againe he answered.
Thereat the curteous knight displeased was,
And said, Old sire, it seemes thou hast not red
How ill it sits with that same silver hed,
In vaine to mocke, or mockt in vaine to bee:
But if thou be, as thou art pourtrahed
With natures pen, in ages grave degree,
Aread in graver wise, what I demaund of thee.

XXXIV

His answere likewise was, he could not tell.
Whose sencelesse speach, and doted ignorance
When as the noble Prince had marked well,
He ghest his nature by his countenance,
And calmd his wrath with goodly temperance.
Then to him stepping, from his arme did reach
Those keyes, and made himselfe free enterance.
Each dore he opened without any breach;
There was no barre to stop, nor foe him to empeach.

XXXV

There all within full rich arrayd he found,
With royall arras and resplendent gold.
And did with store of every thing abound,
That greatest Princes presence might behold.
But all the floore (too filthy to be told)
With bloud of guiltlesse babes, and innocents trew,
Which there were slaine, as sheepe out of the fold,
Defiled was, that dreadfull was to vew,
And sacred ashes over it was strowed new.

XXXVI

And there beside of marble stone was built
An Altare, carv'd with cunning ymagery,
On which true Christians bloud was often spilt,
And holy Martyrs often doen to dye,
With cruell malice and strong tyranny:
Whose blessed sprites from underneath the stone
To God for vengeance cryde continually,
And with great griefe were often heard to grone,
That hardest heart would bleede, to hear their piteous mone.

XXXVII

Through every rowme he sought, and every bowr,
But no where could he find that woful thrall:
At last he came unto an yron doore,
That fast was lockt, but key found not at all
Emongst that bounch, to open it withall;
But in the same a little grate was pight,
Through which he sent his voyce, and lowd did call
With all his powre, to weet, if living wight
Were housed there within, whom he enlargen might.

XXXVIII

Therewith an hollow, dreary, murmuring voyce
These pitteous plaints and dolours did resound;
O who is that, which brings me happy choyce
Of death, that here lye dying every stound,
Yet live perforce in balefull darkenesse bound?
For now three Moones have changed thrice their hew,
And have been thrice hid underneath the ground,
Since I the heavens chearfull face did vew,
O welcome thou, that doest of death bring tydings trew.

XXXIX

Which when that Champion heard, with percing point
Of pitty deare his hart was thrilled sore,
And trembling horrour ran through every joynt
For ruth of gentle knight so fowle forlore:
Which shaking off, he rent that yron dore,
With furious force, and indignation fell;
Where entred in, his foot could find no flore,
But all a deepe descent, as darke as hell,
That breathed ever forth a filthie banefull smell.

XL

But neither darkenesse fowle, nor filthy bands,
Nor noyous smell his purpose could withhold,
(Entire affection hateth nicer hands)
But that with constant zeale, and courage bold,
After long paines and labours manifold,
He found the meanes that Prisoner up to reare;
Whose feeble thighes, unhable to uphold
His pined corse, him scarse to light could beare.
A ruefull spectacle of death and ghastly drere.

XLI

His sad dull eyes deepe sunck in hollow pits,
Could not endure th' unwonted sunne to view;
His bare thin cheekes for want of better bits,
And empty sides deceived of their dew,
Could make a stony hart his hap to rew;
His rawbone armes, whose mighty brawned bowrs
Were wont to rive steele plates, and helmets hew,
Were cleane consum'd, and all his vitall powres
Decayd, and all his flesh shronk up like withered flowres.

XLII

Whom when his Lady saw, to him she ran
With hasty joy: to see him made her glad,
And sad to view his visage pale and wan,
Who earst in flowres of freshest youth was clad.
Tho when her well of teares she wasted had,
She said, Ah dearest Lord, what evill starre
On you hath frownd, and pourd his influence bad,
That of your selfe ye thus berobbed arre,
And this misseeming hew your manly looks doth marre?

XLIII

But welcome now my Lord, in wele or woe,
Whose presence I have lackt too long a day;
And fie on Fortune mine avowed foe,
Whose wrathful wreakes them selves doe now alay.
And for these wrongs shall treble penaunce pay
Of treble good: good growes of evils priefe.
The chearelesse man, whom sorrow did dismay,
Had no delight to treaten of his griefe;
His long endured famine needed more reliefe.

XLIV

Faire Lady, then said that victorious knight,
The things, that grievous were to do, or beare,
Them to renew, I wote, breeds no delight;
Best musicke breeds delight in loathing eare:
But th' onely good, that growes of passed feare,
Is to be wise, and ware of like agein.
This dayes ensample hath this lesson deare
Deepe written in my heart with yron pen,
That blisse may not abide in state of mortall men.

XLV

Henceforth sir knight, take to you wonted strength,
And maister these mishaps with patient might;
Loe where your foe lyes stretcht in monstrous length,
And loe that wicked woman in your sight,
The roote of all your care, and wretched plight,
Now in your powre, to let her live, or dye.
To do her dye (quoth Una) were despight,
And shame t'avenge so weake an enimy;
But spoile her of her scarlot robe, and let her fly.

XLVI

So as she bad, that witch they disaraid,
And robd of royall robes, and purple pall,
And ornaments that richly were displaid;
Ne spared they to strip her naked all.
Then when they had despoiled her tire and call,
Such as she was, their eyes might her behold,
That her misshaped parts did them appall,
A loathly, wrinckled hag, ill favoured, old,
Whose secret filth good manners biddeth not be told.

XLIX

Which when the knights beheld, amazd they were,
And wondred at so fowle deformed wight.
Such then (said Una) as she seemeth here,
Such is the face of falshood, such the sight
Of fowle Duessa, when her borrowed light
Is laid away, and counterfesaunce knowne.
Thus when they had the witch disrobed quight,
And all her filthy feature open showne,
They let her goe at will, and wander wayes unknowne.

L

She flying fast from heavens hated face,
And from the world that her discovered wide,
Fled to the wastfull wildernesse apace,
From living eyes her open shame to hide,
And lurkt in rocks and caves long unespide.
But that faire crew of knights, and Una faire
Did in that castle afterwards abide,
To rest them selves, and weary powres repaire,
Where store they found of all that dainty was and rare.

Canto IX

His loves and lignage Arthur tells:
the Knights knit friendly hands:
Sir Trevisan flies from Despayre,
whom Redcrosse Knight withstands.

I

O GOODLY golden chaine, wherewith yfere
The vertues linked are in lovely wize:
And noble mindes of yore allyed were,
In brave poursuit of chevalrous emprize,
That none did others safety despize,
Nor aid envy to him, in need that stands,
But friendly each did others prayse devize,
How to advaunce with favourable hands,
As this good Prince redeemd the Redcrosse knight from bands.

II

Who when their powres empaird through labour long,
With dew repast they had recured well,
And that weake captive wight now wexed strong,
Them list no lenger there at leasure dwell,
But forward fare, as their adventures fell,
But ere they parted, Una faire besought
That straunger knight his name and nation tell;
Least so great good, as he for her had wrought,
Should die unknown, and buried be in thanklesse thought.

III

Faire virgin (said the Prince) ye me require
A thing without the compas of my wit:
For both the lignage and the certain Sire,
From which I sprong, from me are hidden yit.
For all so soone as life did me admit
Into this world, and shewed heavens light,
From mothers pap I taken was unfit:
And streight deliver'd to a Faery knight,
To be upbrought in gentle thewes and martiall might.

IV

Unto old Timon he me brought bylive,
Old Timon, who in youthly yeares hath beene
In warlike feates th'expertest man alive,

Page | 791

And is the wisest now on earth I weene;
His dwelling is low in a valley greene,
Under the foot of Rauran mossy hore,
From whence the river Dee as silver cleene,
His tombling billowes roll with gentle rore:
There all my dayes he traind me up in vertuous lore.

V

Thither the great magicien Merlin came,
As was his use, ofttimes to visit me:
For he had charge my discipline to frame,
And Tutours nouriture to oversee.
Him oft and oft I askt in privitie,
Of what loines and what lignage I did spring:
Whose aunswere bad me still assured bee,
That I was sonne and heire unto a king,
As time in her just terme the truth to light should bring.

VI

Well worthy impe, said then the Lady gent,
And pupill fit for such a Tutours hand.
But what adventure, or what high intent
Hath brought you hither into Faery land,
Aread Prince Arthur, crowne of Martiall band?
Full hard it is (quoth he) to read aright
The course of heavenly cause, or understand
The secret meaning of th' eternall might,
That rules mens wayes, and rules the thoughts of living wight.

VII

For whether he through fatall deepe foresight
Me hither sent, for cause to me unghest,
Or that fresh bleeding wound, which day and night
Whilome doth rancle in my riven brest,
With forced fury following his behest,
Me hither brought by wayes yet never found;
You to have helpt I hold myself yet blest.
Ah curteous knight (quoth she) what secret wound
Could ever find, to grieve the gentlest hart on ground?

VIII

Deare dame (quoth he) you sleeping sparkes awake,
Which troubled once, into huge flames will grow,

Ne ever will their fervent fury slake,
Till living moysture into smoke do flow,
And wasted life do lye in ashes low.
Yet sithens silence lesseneth not my fire,
But told it flames, and hidden it does glow;
I will revele what ye so much desire:
Ah Love, lay down thy bow, the whiles I may respire.

IX

It was in freshest flowre of youthly yeares,
When courage first does creepe in manly chest,
Then first the coale of kindly heat appeares
To kindle love in every living brest;
But me had warnd old Timons wise behest,
Those creeping flames by reason to subdew,
Before their rage grew to so great unrest,
As miserable lovers use to rew,
Which still wex old in woe, whiles woe still wexeth new.

X

That idle name of love, and lovers life,
As losse of time, and vertues enimy,
I ever scornd, and joyd to stirre up strife,
In middest of their mournfull Tragedy,
Ay wont to laugh, when them I heard to cry,
And blow the fire, which them to ashes brent:
Their God himselfe, griev'd at my libertie,
Shot many a dart at me with fiers intent,
But I them warded all with wary government.

XI

But all in vaine: no fort can be so strong,
Ne fleshly brest can armed be so sound,
But will at last be wonne with battrie long,
Or unawares at disadvantage found:
Nothing is sure, that growes on earthly ground:
And who most trustes in arme of fleshly might,
And boasts in beauties chaine not to be bound,
Doth soonest fall in disaventrous fight,
And yeeldes his caytive neck to victours most despight.

XII

Ensample make of him your haplesse joy,
And of my selfe now mated, as ye see;
Whose prouder vaunt that proud avenging boy
Did soone pluck downe and curbd my libertie.
For on a day, prickt forth with jollitie
Of looser life, and heat of hardiment,
Raunging the forest wide on courser free,
The fields, the floods, the heavens with one consent
Did seeme to laugh on me, and favour mine intent.

XIII

For-wearied with my sports, I did alight
From loftie steed, and downe to sleepe me layd;
The verdant gras my couch did goodly dight,
And pillow was my helmet faire displayd:
Whiles every sence the humour sweet embayd,
And slombring soft my hart did steale away,
Me seemed, by my side a royall Mayd
Her daintie limbes full softly down did lay:
So faire a creature yet saw never sunny day.

XIV

Most goodly glee and lovely blandishment
She to me made, and bad me love her deare;
For dearely sure her love was to me bent,
As when just time expired should appeare.
But whether dreames delude, or true it were,
Was never hart so ravisht with delight,
Ne living man like words did ever heare,
As she to me delivered all that night;
And at her parting said, She Queene of Faeries hight.

XV

When I awoke, and found her place devoyd,
And nought but pressed gras, where she had lyen,
I sorrowed all so much as earst I joyd,
And washed all her place with watry eyen.
From that day forth I lov'd that face divine;
From that day forth I cast in carefull mind
To seeke her out with labour, and long tyne,
And never vowd to rest till her I find,
Nine monethes I seeke in vain, yet ni'll that vow unbind.

XVI

Thus as he spake, his visage wexed pale,
And chaunge of hew great passion did bewray;
Yet still he strove to cloke his inward bale,
And hide the smoke that did his fire display,
Till gentle Una thus to him gan say;
O happy Queene of Faeries, that has found
Mongst many, one that with his prowesse may
Defend thine honour, and thy foes confound:
True Loves are often sown, but seldom grow on ground.

XVII

Thine, O then, said the gentle Recrosse knight,
Next to that Ladies love, shal be the place,
O fairest virgin, full of heavenly light,
Whose wondrous faith exceeding earthly race,
Was firmest fixt in mine extremest case.
And you, my Lord, the Patrone of my life,
Of that great Queene may well gaine worthy grace:
For onely worthy you through prowes priefe,
Yf living man mote worthie be, to be her liefe.

XVIII

So diversly discoursing of their loves,
The golden Sunne his glistring head gan shew,
And sad remembraunce now the Prince amoves
With fresh desire his voyage to pursew;
Als Una earnd her traveill to renew.
Then those two knights, fast friendship for to bynd,
And love establish each to other trew,
Gave goodly gifts, the signes of gratefull mynd,
And eke the pledges firme, right hands together joynd.

XIX

Prince Arthur gave a boxe of Diamond sure,
Embowd with gold and gorgeous ornament,
Wherein were closd few drops of liquor pure,
Of wondrous worth, and vertue excellent,
That any wound could heale incontinent:
Which to requite, the Redcrosse knight him gave
A booke, wherein his Saveours testament
Was writ with golden letters rich and brave;
A worke of wondrous grace, and able soules to save.

XX

Thus beene they parted, Arthur on his way
To seeke his love, and th' other for to fight
With Unaes foe, that all her realme did pray.
But she now weighing the decayed plight,
And shrunken synewes of her chosen knight,
Would not a while her forward course pursew,
Ne bring him forth in face of dreadfull fight,
Till he recovered had his former hew:
For him to be yet weake and wearie well she knew.

XXI

So as they traveild, lo they gan espy
An armed knight towards them gallop fast,
That seemed from some feared foe to fly,
Or other griesly thing, that him aghast.
Still as he fled, his eye was backward cast,
As if his feare still followed him behind;
Als flew his steed, as he his bands had brast,
And with his winged heeles did tread the wind,
As he had beene a fole of Pegasus his kind.

XXII

Nigh as he drew, they might perceive his head
To be unarmd, and curld uncombed heares
Upstaring stiffe, dismayd with uncouth dread;
Nor drop of bloud in all his face appeares
Nor life in limbe: and to increase his feares
In fowle reproch of knighthoods faire degree,
About his neck an hempen rope he weares,
That with his glistring armes does ill agree;
But he of rope or armes has now no memoree.

XXIII

The Redcrosse knight toward him crossed fast,
To weet, what mister wight was so dismayd:
There him he finds all sencelesse and aghast,
That of him selfe he seemd to be afrayd;
Whom hardly he from flying forward stayd,
Till he these wordes to him deliver might;
Sir knight, aread who hath ye thus arayd,
And eke from whom make ye this hasty flight:
For never knight I saw in such misseeming plight.

XXIV

He answerd nought at all, but adding new
Feare to his first amazment, staring wide
With stony eyes, and hartlesse hollow hew,
Astonisht stood, as one that had aspide
Infernall furies, with their chaines untide.
Him yet againe, and yet againe bespake
The gentle knight; who nought to him replide,
But trembling every joint did inly quake,
And foltring tongue at last these words seemd forth to shake.

XXV

For Gods deare love, Sir knight, do me not stay;
For loe he comes, he comes fast after mee.
Eft looking back would faine have runne away;
But he him forst to stay, and tellen free
The secret cause of his perplexitie:
Yet nathemore by his bold hartie speach
Could his bloud-frosen hart emboldned bee,
But through his boldnesse rather feare did reach,
Yet forst, at last he made through silence suddein breach.

XXVI

And am I now in safetie sure (quoth he)
From him, that would have forced me to dye?
And is the point of death now turnd fro mee,
That I may tell this haplesse history?
Feare nought: (quoth he) no daunger now is nye.
Then shall I you recount a ruefull cace,
(Said he) the which with this unlucky eye
I late beheld, and had not greater grace
Me reft from it, had bene partaker of the place.

XXVII

I lately chaunst (would I had never chaunst)
With a faire knight to keepen companee,
Sir Terwin hight, that well himselfe advaunst
In all affaires, and was both bold and free,
But not so happy as mote happy bee:
He lov'd, as was his lot, a Ladie gent,
That him againe lov'd in the least degree:
For she was proud, and of too high intent,
And joyd to see her lover languish and lament.

XXVIII

From whom returning sad and comfortlesse,
As on the way together we did fare,
We met that villen (God from him me blesse)
That cursed wight, from whom I scapt whyleare,
A man of hell, that cals himselfe Despaire:
Who first us greets, and after faire areedes
Of tydings strange, and of adventures rare:
So creeping close, as Snake in hidden weedes,
Inquireth of our states, and of our knightly deedes.

XXIX

Which when he knew, and felt our feeble harts
Embost with bale, and bitter byting griefe,
Which love had launched with his deadly darts,
With wounding words and termes of foule repriefe,
He pluckt from us all hope of due reliefe,
That earst us held in love of lingring life;
Then hopelesse hartlesse, gan the cunning thiefe
Perswade us die, to stint all further strife:
To me he lent this rope, to him a rustie knife.

XXX

With which sad instrument of hasty death,
That wofull lover, loathing lenger light,
A wide way made to let forth living breath.
But I more fearfull, or more luckie wight,
Dismayd with that deformed dismall sight,
Fled fast away, halfe dead with dying feare:
Ne yet assur'd of life by you, Sir knight,
Whose like infirmitie like chaunce may beare:
But God you never let his charmed speeches heare.

XXXI

How may a man (said he) with idle speach
Be wonne, to spoyle the Castle of his health?
I wote (quoth he) whom triall late did teach,
That like would not for all this worldes wealth:
His subtill tongue, like dropping honny, mealt'h
Into the hart, and searcheth every vaine;
That ere one be aware, by secret stealth
His powre is reft, and weaknesse doth remaine.
O never Sir desire to try his guilefull traine.

XXXII

Certes (said he) hence shall I never rest,
Till I that treacherours art have heard and tride;
And you Sir knight, whose name mote I request,
Of grace do me unto his cabin guide.
I that hight Trevisan (quoth he) will ride,
Against my liking backe, to do you grace:
But not for gold nor glee will I abide
By you, when ye arrive in that same place
For lever had I die, then see his deadly face.

XXXIII

Ere long they come, where that same wicked wight
His dwelling has, low in an hollow cave,
Farre underneath a craggie clift ypight,
Darke, dolefull, drearie, like a greedy grave,
That still for carrion carcases doth crave:
On top whereof aye dwelt the ghastly Owle,
Shrieking his balefull note, which ever drave
Far from that haunt all other chearefull fowle;
And all about it wandring ghostes did waile and howle.

XXXIV

And all about old stockes and stubs of trees,
Whereon nor fruit nor leafe was ever seene,
Did hang upon the ragged rocky knees;
On which had many wretches hanged beene,
Whose carcases were scattered on the greene,
And throwne about the clifts. Arrived there,
That bare-head knight for dread and dolefull teene,
Would faine have fled, ne durst approchen neare,
But th' other forst him stay, and comforted in feare.

XXXV

That darkesome cave they enter, where they find
That cursed man, low sitting on the ground,
Musing full sadly in his sullein mind;
His griesie lockes, long growen, and unbound,
Disordred hong about his shoulders round,
And hid his face; through which his hollow eyne
Lookt deadly dull, and stared as astound;
His raw-bone cheekes, through penurie and pine,
Were shronke into his jawes, as he did never dine.

Page | 799

XXXVI

His garment nought but many ragged clouts,
With thornes together pind and patched was,
The which his naked sides he wrapt abouts;
And him beside there lay upon the gras
A drearie corse, whose life away did pas,
All wallowed in his owne yet luke-warme blood,
That from his wound yet welled fresh alas;
In which a rustie knife fast fixed stood,
And made an open passage for the gushing flood.

XXXVII

Which piteous spectacle, approving trew
The wofull tale that Trevisan had told,
When as the gentle Redcrosse knight did vew,
With firie zeale he burnt in courage bold,
Him to avenge, before his bloud were cold,
And to the villein said, Thou damned wight,
The author of this fact we here behold,
What justice can but judge against thee right,
With thine owne bloud to price his bloud, here shed in sight.

XXXVIII

What franticke fit (quoth he) hath thus distraught
Thee, foolish man, so rash a doome to give?
What justice ever other judgement taught,
But he should die, who merites not to live?
None else to death this man despayring drive,
But his owne guiltie mind deserving death.
Is then unjust to each his due to give?
Or let him die, that loatheth living breath?
Or let him die at ease, that liveth here uneath?

XXXIX

Who travels by the wearie wandring way,
To come unto his wished home in haste,
And meetes a flood, that doth his passage stay,
Is not great grace to helpe him over past,
Or free his feet that in the myre sticke fast?
Most envious man, that grieves at neighbours good,
And fond, that joyest in the woe thou hast,
Why wilt not let him passe, that long hath stood
Upon the banke, yet wilt thy selfe not passe the flood?

XL

He there does now enjoy eternall rest
And happy ease, which thou dost want and crave,
And further from it daily wanderest:
What if some little paine the passage have,
That makes fraile flesh to feare the bitter wave?
Is not short paine well borne, that brings long ease,
And layes the soule to sleepe in quiet grave?
Sleepe after toyle, port after stormie seas,
Ease after warre, death after life does greatly please.

XLI

The knight much wondred at his suddeine wit,
And said, The terme of life is limited,
Ne may a man prolong, nor shorten it;
The souldier may not move from watchfull sted,
Nor leave his stand, untill his Captaine bed.
Who life did limit by almightie doome
(Quoth he) knowes best the termes established;
And he, that points the Centonell his roome,
Doth license him depart at sound of morning droome.

XLII

Is not his deed, what ever thing is donne
In heaven and earth? did not he all create
To die againe? all ends that was begonne.
Their times in his eternall booke of fate
Are written sure, and have their certaine date.
Who then can strive with strong necessitie,
That holds the world in his still chaunging state,
Or shunne the death ordaynd by destinie?
When houre of death is come, let none aske whence, nor why.

XLIII

The lenger life, I wote the greater sin,
The greater sin, the greater punishment:
All those great battels, which thou boasts to win,
Through strife, and blood-shed, and avengement,
Now praysd, hereafter deare thou shalt repent:
For life must life, and blood must blood repay.
Is not enough thy evill life forespent?
For he that once hath missed the right way,
The further he doth goe, the further he doth stray.

XLIV

Then do no further goe, no further stray,
But here lie downe, and to thy rest betake,
Th' ill to prevent, that life ensewen may.
For what hath life, that may it loved make,
And gives not rather cause it to forsake?
Feare, sicknesse, age, losse, labour, sorrow, strife,
Paine, hunger, cold, that makes the hart to quake;
And ever fickle fortune rageth rife,
All which, and thousands mo do make a loathsome life.

XLV

Thou wretched man, of death hast greatest need,
If in true ballance thou wilt weigh thy state:
For never knight, that dared warlike deede,
More lucklesse disaventures did amate:
Witnesse the dungeon deepe, wherein of late
Thy life shut up, for death so oft did call;
And though good lucke prolonged hath thy date,
Yet death then would the like mishaps forestall,
Into the which hereafter thou maiest happen fall.

XLVI

Why then doest thou, O man of sin, desire
To draw thy dayes forth to their last degree?
Is not the measure of thy sinfull hire
High heaped up with huge iniquitie,
Against the day of wrath, to burden thee?
Is not enough, that to this Ladie milde
Thou falsed hast thy faith with perjurie,
And sold thy selfe to serve Duessa vilde,
With whom in all abuse thou hast thy selfe defilde?

XLVII

Is not he just, that all this doth behold
From highest heaven, and beares an equall eye?
Shall he thy sins up in his knowledge fold,
And guilty be of thine impietie?
Is not his law, Let every sinner die:
Die shall all flesh? what then must needs be donne,
Is it not better to doe willinglie,
Then linger, till the glasse be all out ronne?
Death is the end of woes: die soone, O faeries sonne.

XLVIII

The knight was much enmoved with his speach,
That as a swords point through his hart did perse,
And in his conscience made a secret breach,
Well knowing true all that he did reherse,
And to his fresh remembraunce did reverse
The ugly vew of his deformed crimes,
That all his manly powres it did disperse,
As he were charmed with inchaunted rimes,
That oftentimes he quakt, and fainted oftentimes.

XLIX

In which amazement, when the Miscreant
Perceived him to waver weake and fraile,
Whiles trembling horror did his conscience dant,
And hellish anguish did his soule assaile,
To drive him to despaire, and quite to quaile,
He shew'd him painted in a table plaine,
The damned ghosts, that doe in torments waile,
And thousand feends that doe them endlesse paine
With fire and brimstone, which for ever shall remaine.

L

The sight whereof so throughly him dismaid,
That nought but death before his eyes he saw,
And ever burning wrath before him laid,
By righteous sentence of th' Almighties law.
Then gan the villein him to overcraw,
And brought unto him swords, ropes, poison, fire,
And all that might him to perdition draw;
And bad him choose, what death he would desire:
For death was due to him, that had provokt Gods ire.

LI

But when as none of them he saw him take,
He to him raught a dagger sharpe and keene,
And gave it him in hand: his hand did quake,
And tremble like a leafe of Aspin greene,
And troubled bloud through his pale face was seene
To come, and goe with tidings from the heart,
As it a running messenger had beene.
At last resolv'd to worke his finall smart,
He lifted up his hand, that backe againe did start.

LII

Which whenas Una saw, through every vaine
The crudled cold ran to her well of life,
As in a swowne: but soone reliv'd againe,
Out of his hand she snatcht the cursed knife,
And threw it to the ground, enraged rife,
And to him said, Fie, fie, faint harted knight,
What meanest thou by this reprochfull strife?
Is this the battell, which thou vauntst to fight
With that fire-mouthed Dragon, horrible and bright?

LIII

Come, come away, fraile, seely, fleshly wight,
Ne let vaine words bewitch thy manly hart,
Ne divelish thoughts dismay thy constant spright.
In heavenly mercies hast thou not a part?
Why shouldst thou then despeire, that chosen art?
Where justice growes, there grows eke greater grace,
The which doth quench the brond of hellish smart,
And that accurst hand-writing doth deface.
Arise, Sir knight, arise, and leave this cursed place.

LIV

So up he rose, and thence amounted streight.
Which when the carle beheld, and saw his guest
Would safe depart for all his subtill sleight,
He chose an halter from among the rest,
And with it hung himselfe, unbid unblest.
But death he could not worke himselfe thereby;
For thousand times he so himselfe had drest,
Yet nathelesse it could not doe him die,
Till he should die his last, that is, eternally.

Canto X

*Her faithfull knight faire Una brings
to house of Holinesse,
Where he is taught repentance, and
the way to heavenly blesse.*

I

WHAT man is he, that boasts of fleshly might
And vaine assurance of mortality,
Which all so soone as it doth come to fight

Against spirituall foes, yeelds by and by,
Or from the field most cowardly doth fly?
Ne let the man ascribe it to his skill,
That thorough grace hath gained victory.
If any strength we have, it is to ill,
But all the good is Gods, both power and eke will.

II

But that, which lately hapned, Una saw,
That this her knight was feeble, and too faint;
And all his sinews woxen weake and raw,
Through long enprisonment, and hard constraint,
Which he endured in his late restraint,
That yet he was unfit for bloudy fight:
Therefore to cherish him with diets daint,
She cast to bring him, where he chearen might.
Till he recovered had his late decayed plight.

III

There was an auntient house not farre away,
Renowmd throughout the world for sacred lore,
And pure unspotted life: so well they say
It governd was, and guided evermore,
Through wisedome of a matrone grave and hore
Whose onely joy was to relieve the needes
Of wretched soules, and helpe the helpelesse pore:
All night she spent in bidding of her bedes,
And all the day in doing good and godly deedes.

IV

Dame Cœlia men did her call, as thought
From heaven to come, or thither to arise,
The mother of three daughters, well upbrought
In goodly thewes, and godly exercise:
The eldest two, most sober, chast, and wise,
Fidelia and Speranza virgins were,
Though spousd, yet wanting wedlocks solemnize:
But faire Charissa to a lovely fere
Was lincked, and by him had many pledges dere.

V

Arrived there, the dore they find fast lockt;
For it was warely watched night and day,

For feare of many foes: but when they knockt,
The Porter opened unto them streight way:
He was an aged syre, all hory gray,
With lookes full lowly cast, and gate full slow,
Wont on a staffe his feeble steps to stay,
Hight Humiltà. They passe in stouping low;
For streight and narrow was the way which he did show.

VI

Each goodly thing is hardest to begin,
But entred in a spacious court they see,
Both plaine, and pleasant to be walked in,
Where them does meete a francklin faire and free,
And entertaines with comely courteous glee,
His name was Zele, that him right well became,
For in his speeches and behaviour hee
Did labour lively to expresse the same,
And gladly did them guide, till to the Hall they came.

VII

There fairely them receives a gentle Squire,
Of milde demeanure, and rare courtesie,
Right cleanly clad in comely sad attire;
In word and deede that shew'd great modestie,
And knew his good to all of each degree,
Hight Reverence. He them with speeches meet
Does faire entreat; no courting nicetie,
But simple true, and eke unfained sweet,
As might become a Squire so great persons to greet.

VIII

And afterwards them to his Dame he leades,
That aged Dame, the Ladie of the place:
Who all this while was busy at her beades:
Which doen, she up arose with seemely grace,
And toward them full matronely did pace.
Where when that fairest Una she beheld,
Whom well she knew to spring from heavenly race,
Her hart with joy unwonted inly sweld,
As feeling wondrous comfort in her weaker eld.

IX

And her embracing said, O happie earth,
Whereon thy innocent feet doe ever tread,
Most vertuous virgin borne of heavenly berth,
That, to redeeme thy woefull parents head,
From tyrans rage, and ever dying dread,
Hast wandred through the world now long a day;
Yet ceasest not thy weary soles to lead,
What grace hath thee now hither brought this way?
Or doen thy feeble feet unweeting hither stray?

X

Strange thing it is an errant knight to see
Here in this place, or any other wight,
That hither turnes his steps. So few there bee
That chose the narrow path, or seeke the right:
All keepe the broad high way, and take delight
With many rather for to go astray,
And be partakers of their evill plight,
Then with a few to walke the rightest way;
O foolish men, why haste ye to your owne decay?

XI

Thy selfe to see, and tyred limbes to rest,
O matrone sage (quoth she) I hither came;
And this good knight his way with me addrest,
Led with thy prayses and broad-blazed fame,
That up to heaven is blowne. The auncient Dame
Him goodly greeted in her modest guise,
And entertaynd them both, as best became,
With all the court'sies that she could devise,
Ne wanted ought, to shew her bounteous or wise.

XII

Thus as they gan of sundry things devise,
Loe two most goodly virgins came in place,
Ylinked arme in arme in lovely wise,
With countenance demure, and modest grace,
They numbred even steps and equall pace:
Of which the eldest, that Fidelia hight,
Like sunny beames threw from her christall face,
That could have dazd the rash beholders sight,
And round about her head did shine like heavens light.

XIII

She was araied all in lilly white,
And in her right hand bore a cup of gold,
With wine and water fild up to the hight,
In which a Serpent did himselfe enfold,
That horrour made to all that did behold;
But she no whit did chaunge her constant mood:
And in her other hand she fast did hold
A booke, that was both signd and seald with blood:
Wherin darke things were writ, hard to be understood.

XIV

Her younger sister, that Speranza hight,
Was clad in blew, that her beseemed well;
Not all so chearefull seemed she of sight,
As was her sister; whether dread did dwell,
Or anguish in her hart, is hard to tell:
Upon her arme a silver anchor lay,
Whereon she leaned ever, as befell:
And ever up to heaven, as she did pray,
Her stedfast eyes were bent, ne swarved other way.

XV

They seeing Una, towards her gan wend,
Who them encounters with like courtesie;
Many kind speeches they betwene them spend,
And greatly joy each other well to see:
Then to the knight with shamefast modestie
They turne themselves, at Unaes meeke request,
And him salute with well beseeming glee;
Who faire them quites, as him beseemed best,
And goodly gan discourse of many a noble gest.

XVI

Then Una thus; But she your sister deare,
The deare Charissa where is she become?
Or wants she health, or busie is elsewhere?
Ah no, said they, but forth she may not come:
For she of late is lightned of her wombe,
And hath encreast the world with one sonne more,
That her to see should be but troublesome.
Indeed (quoth she) that should be trouble sore;
But thankt be God, and her encrease so evermore.

XVII

Then said the aged Cœlia, Deare dame,
And you good Sir, I wote that of youre toyle,
And labours long, through which ye hither came,
Ye both forwearied be: therefore a whyle
I read you rest, and to your bowres recoyle.
Then called she a Groome, that forth him led
Into a goodly lodge, and gan despoile
Of puissant armes, and laid in easie bed;
His name was meeke Obedience rightfully ared.

XVIII

Now when their wearie limbes with kindly rest,
And bodies were refresht with due repast,
Faire Una gan Fidelia faire request,
To have her knight into her schoolehouse plaste,
That of her heavenly learning he might taste,
And heare the wisedom of her words divine.
She graunted, and that knight so much agraste,
That she him taught celestiall discipline,
And opened his dull eyes, that light mote in them shine.

XIX

And that her sacred Booke, with blood ywrit,
That none could read, except she did them teach,
She unto him disclosed every whit,
And heavenly documents thereout did preach,
That weaker wit of man could never reach,
Of God, of grace, of justice, of free will,
That wonder was to heare her goodly speach:
For she was able with her words to kill,
And raise againe to life the hart that she did thrill.

XX

And when she list poure out her larger spright,
She would commaund the hastie Sunne to stay,
Or backward turne his course from heavens hight;
Sometimes great hostes of men she could dismay;
Dry-shod to passe, she parts the flouds in tway;
And eke huge mountaines from their native seat
She would commaund, themselves to beare away,
And throw in raging sea with roaring threat.
Almightie God her gave such powre, and puissaunce great.

XXI

The faithfull knight now grew in litle space,
By hearing her, and by her sisters lore,
To such perfection of all heavenly grace,
That wretched world he gan for to abhore,
And mortall life gan loath, as thing forlore,
Greevd with remembrance of his wicked wayes,
And prickt with anguish of his sinnes so sore,
That he desirde to end his wretched dayes:
So much the dart of sinfull guilt the soule dismayes.

XXII

But wise Speranza gave him comfort sweet,
And taught him how to take assured hold
Upon her silver anchor, as was meet;
Else had his sinnes so great and manifold
Made him forget all that Fidelia told.
In this distressed doubtfull agonie,
When him his dearest Una did behold,
Disdeining life, desiring leave to die,
She found her selfe assayld with great perplexitie.

XXIII

And came to Cœlia to declare her smart,
Who well acquainted with that commune plight,
Which sinfull horror workes in wounded hart,
Her wisely comforted all that she might,
With goodly counsell and advisement right;
And streightway sent with carefull diligence,
To fetch a Leach, the which had great insight
In that disease of grieved conscience,
And well could cure the same; his name was Patience.

XXIV

Who comming to that soule-diseased knight,
Could hardly him intreat to tell his griefe:
Which knowne, and all that noyd his heavie spright
Well searcht, eftsoones he gan apply relief
Of salves and med'cines, which had passing priefe,
And thereto added words of wondrous might;
By which to ease he him recured briefe,
And much aswag'd the passion of his plight,
That he his paine endur'd, as seeming now more light.

XXV

But yet the cause and root of all his ill,
Inward corruption and infected sin,
Not purg'd nor heald, behind remained still,
And festring sore did rankle yet within,
Close creeping twixt the marrow and the skin.
Which to extirpe, he laid him privily
Downe in a darkesome lowly place farre in,
Whereas he meant his corrosives to apply,
And with streight diet tame his stubborne malady.

XXVI

In ashes and sackcloth he did array
His daintie corse, proud humors to abate,
And dieted with fasting every day,
The swelling of his wounds to mitigate,
And made him pray both earely and eke late:
And ever as superfluous flesh did rot
Amendment readie still at hand did wayt,
To pluck it out with pincers firie whot,
That soone in him was left no one corrupted jot.

XXVII

And bitter Penance with an yron whip,
Was wont him once to disple every day:
And sharpe Remorse his hart did pricke and nip,
That drops of blood thence like a well did play:
And sad Repentance used to embay
His bodie in salt water smarting sore,
The filthy blots of sinne to wash away.
So in short space they did to health restore
The man that would not live, but earst lay at deathes dore.

XXVIII

In which his torment often was so great,
That like a Lyon he would cry and rore,
And rend his flesh, and his owne synewes eat.
His owne deare Una hearing evermore
His ruefull shriekes and gronings, often tore
Her guiltlesse garments, and her golden heare,
For pitty of his paine and anguish sore;
Yet all with patience wisely she did beare;
For well she wist his crime could else be never cleare.

XXIX

Whom thus recover'd by wise Patience
And trew Repentaunce they to Una brought:
Who joyous of his cured conscience,
Him dearely kist, and fairely eke besought
Himselfe to chearish, and consuming thought
To put away out of his carefull brest.
By this Charissa, late in child-bed brought,
Was woxen strong, and left her fruitfull nest;
To her faire Una brought this unacquainted guest.

XXX

She was a woman in her freshest age,
Of wondrous beauty, and of bountie rare,
With goodly grace and comely personage,
That was on earth not easie to compare;
Full of great love, but Cupid's wanton snare
As hell she hated, chast in worke and will;
Her necke and breasts were ever open bare,
That ay thereof her babes might sucke their fill;
The rest was all in yellow robes arayed still.

XXXI

A multitude of babes about her hong,
Playing their sports, that joyd her to behold,
Whom still she fed, whiles they were weake and young,
But thrust them forth still as they wexed old:
And on her head she wore a tyre of gold,
Adornd with gemmes and owches wondrous faire,
Whose passing price uneath was to be told:
And by her side there sate a gentle paire
Of turtle doves, she sitting in an yvorie chaire.

XXXII

The knight and Una entring faire her greet,
And bid her joy of that her happie brood;
Who them requites with court'sies seeming meet,
And entertaines with friendly chearefull mood.
Then Una her besought, to be so good
As in her vertuous rules to schoole her knight,
Now after all his torment well withstood,
In that sad house of Penaunce, where his spright
Had past the paines of hell, and long enduring night.

XXXIII

She was right joyous of her just request,
And taking by the hand that Faeries sonne,
Gan him instruct in every good behest,
Of love, and righteousnesse, and well to donne,
And wrath, and hatred warely to shonne,
That drew on men Gods hatred and his wrath,
And many soules in dolours had fordonne:
In which when him she well instructed hath,
From thence to heaven she teacheth him the ready path.

XXXIV

Wherein his weaker wandring steps to guide,
An auncient matrone she to her does call,
Whose sober lookes her wisedome well describe:
Her name was Mercie, well knowne over all,
To be both gratious, and eke liberall:
To whom the carefull charge of him she gave,
To lead aright, that he should never fall
In all his wayes through this wide worldes wave,
That Mercy in the end his righteous soule might save.

XXXV

The godly Matrone by the hand him beares
Forth from her presence, by a narrow way,
Scattred with bushy thornes, and ragged breares,
Which still before him she remov'd away,
That nothing might his ready passage stay:
And ever when his feet encombred were,
Or gan to shrinke, or from the right to stray,
She held him fast, and firmely did upbeare,
As carefull Nourse her child from falling oft does reare.

XXXVI

Eftsoones unto an holy Hospitall,
That was fore by the way, she did him bring,
In which seven Bead-men that had vowed all
Their life to service of high heavens king,
Did spend their dayes in doing godly thing:
Their gates to all were open evermore,
That by the wearie way were traveiling,
And one sate wayting ever them before,
To call in commers by, that needy were and pore.

XXXVII

The first of them that eldest was, and best,
Of all the house had charge and governement,
As Guardian and Steward of the rest:
His office was to give entertainement
And lodging, unto all that came, and went:
Not unto such, as could him feast againe,
And double quite, for that he on them spent,
But such, as want of harbour did constraine:
Those for Gods sake his dewty was to entertaine.

XXXVIII

The second was as Almner of the place,
His office was, the hungry for to feed,
And thristy give to drinke, a worke of grace:
He feard not once him selfe to be in need,
Ne car'd to hoord for those whom he did breede:
The grace of God he layd up still in store,
Which as a stocke he left unto his seede;
He had enough, what need him care for more?
And had he lesse, yet some he would give to the pore.

XXXIX

The third had of their wardrobe custodie,
In which were not rich tyres, nor garments gay,
The plumes of pride, and wings of vanitie,
But clothes meet to keepe keene could away,
And naked nature seemely to aray;
With which bare wretched wights he dayly clad,
The images of God in earthly clay;
And if that no spare cloths to give he had,
His owne coate he would cut, and it distribute glad.

XL

The fourth appointed by his office was,
Poore prisoners to relieve with gratious ayd,
And captives to redeeme with price of bras,
From Turkes and Sarazins, which them had stayd,
And though they faultie were, yet well he wayd,
That God to us forgiveth every howre
Much more then that why they in bands were layd,
And he that harrowd hell with heavie stowre,
The faultie soules from thence brought to his heavenly bowre.

XLI

The fift had charge sicke persons to attend,
And comfort those, in point of death which lay;
For them most needeth comfort in the end,
When sin, and hell, and death do most dismay
The feeble soule departing hence away.
All is but lost, that living we bestow,
If not well ended at our dying day.
O man have mind of that last bitter throw
For as the tree does fall, so lyes it ever low.

XLII

The sixt had charge of them now being dead,
In seemely sort their corses to engrave,
And deck with dainty flowres their bridall bed,
That to their heavenly spouse both sweet and brave
They might appeare, when he their soules shall save.
The wondrous workmanship of Gods owne mould,
Whose face he made all beasts to feare, and gave
All in his hand, even dead we honour should.
Ah dearest God me graunt, I dead be not defould.

XLIII

The seventh, now after death and buriall done,
Had charge the tender orphans of the dead
And widowes ayd, least they should be undone:
In face of judgement he their right would plead,
Ne ought the powre of mighty men did dread
In their defence, nor would for gold or fee
Be wonne their rightfull causes downe to tread:
And, when they stood in most necessitee,
He did supply their want, and gave them ever free.

XLIV

There when the Elfin knight arrived was,
The first and chiefest of the seven, whose care
Was guests to welcome, towardes him did pas:
Where seeing Mercie, that his steps upbare,
And alwayes led, to her with reverence rare
He humbly louted in meeke lowlinesse,
And seemely welcome for her did prepare:
For of their order she was Patronesse,
Albe Charissa were their chiefest founderesse.

XLV

There she awhile him stayes, him selfe to rest,
That to the rest more able he might bee:
During which time, in every good behest
And godly worke of almes and charitee,
She him instructed with great industree;
Shortly therein so perfect he became,
That from the first unto the last degree,
His mortall life he learned had to frame
In holy righteousnesse, without rebuke or blame.

XLVI

Thence forward by that painfull way they pas,
Forth to an hill, that was both steepe and hy;
On top whereof a sacred chappell was,
And eke a little Hermitage thereby,
Wherein an aged holy man did lye,
That day and night said his devotion,
Ne other worldly busines did apply;
His name was heavenly Contemplation;
Of God and goodnesse was his meditation.

XLVII

Great grace that old man to him given had;
For God he often saw from heavens hight,
All were his earthly eyen both blunt and bad,
And through great age had lost their kindly sight,
Yet wondrous quick and persant was his spright,
As Eagles eye, that can behold the Sunne:
That hill they scale with all their powre and might,
That his fraile thighes nigh weary and fordonne
Gan faile, but by her helpe the top at last he wonne.

XLVIII

There they do finde that godly aged Sire,
With snowy lockes adowne his shoulders shed,
As hoarie frost with spangles doth attire
The mossy braunches of an Oke halfe ded.
Each bone might through his body well be red,
And every sinew seene through his long fast:
For nought he car'd his carcas long unfed;
His mind was full of spirituall repast,
And pyn'd his flesh, to keepe his body low and chast.

XLIX

Who when these two approaching he aspide,
At their first presence grew agrieved sore,
That forst him lay his heavenly thoughts aside;
And had he not that Dame respected more,
Whom highly he did reverence and adore,
He would not once have moved for the knight.
They him saluted, standing far afore;
Who well them greeting, humbly did requight,
And asked, to what end they clomb that tedious height.

L

What end (quoth she) should cause us take such paine,
But that same end which every living wight
Should make his marke, high heaven to attaine?
Is not from hence the way, that leadeth right
To that most glorious house that glistreth bright
With burning starres and everliving fire,
Whereof the keyes are to thy hand behight
By wise Fidelia? She doth thee require,
To show it to his knight, according his desire.

LI

Thrise happy man, said then the father grave,
Whose staggering steps thy steady hand doth lead,
And shewes the way, his sinfull soule to save.
Who better can the way to heaven aread,
Then thou thy selfe, that was both borne and bred
In heavenly throne, where thousand Angels shine?
Thou doest the prayers of the righteous sead
Present before the majestie divine,
And his avenging wrath to clemencie incline.

LII

Yet since thou bidst, thy pleasure shal be donne.
Then come thou man of earth, and see the way,
That never yet was seene of Faeries sonne,
That never leads the traveiler astray,
But after labors long, and sad delay,
Brings them to joyous rest and endlesse blis.
But first thou must a season fast and pray,
Till from her bands the spright assoiled is,
And have her strength recur'd from fraile infirmitis.

LIII

That donne, he leads him to the highest Mount;
Such one as that same mighty man of God,
That blood-red billowes like a walled front
On either side disparted with his rod,
Till that his army dry-foot through them yod,
Dwelt forty dayes upon; where writ in stone
With bloudy letters by the hand of God,
The bitter doome of death and balefull mone
He did receive, whiles flashing fire about him shone.

LIV

Or like that sacred hill, whose head full hie,
Adornd with fruitfull Olives all arownd,
Is, as it were for endlesse memory
Of that deare Lord who oft thereon was fownd,
For ever with a flowring girlond crownd:
Or like that pleasaunt Mount, that is for ay
Through famous Poets verse each where renownd,
On which the thrise three learned Ladies play
Their heavenly notes, and make full many a lovely lay.

LV

From thence, far off he unto him did shew
A litle path, that was both steepe and long,
Which to a goodly Citie led his vew;
Whose wals and towres were builded high and strong
Of perle and precious stone, that earthly tong
Cannot describe, nor wit of man can tell;
Too high a ditty for my simple song;
The Citie of the great king hight it well,
Wherein eternall peace and happinesse doth dwell.

LVI

As he thereon stood gazing, he might see
The blessed Angels to and fro descend
From highest heaven in gladsome companee,
And with great joy into that Citie wend,
As commonly as friend does with his frend.
Whereat he wondred much, and gan enquere,
What stately building durst so high extend
Her loftie towres unto the starry sphere,
And what unknowen nation there empeopled were.

LVII

Faire knight (quoth he) Hierusalem that is,
The new Hierusalem, that God has built
For those to dwell in, that are chosen his,
His chosen people purg'd from sinfull guilt
With pretious blood, which cruelly was spilt
On cursed tree, of that unspotted lam,
That for the sinnes of al the world was kilt:
Now are they Saints all in that Citie sam,
More dear unto their God then younglings to their dam.

LVIII

Till now, said then the knight, I weened well,
That great Cleopolis, where I have beene,
In which that fairest Faerie Queene doth dwell,
The fairest citie was that might be seene;
And that bright towre all built of christall cleene,
Panthea, seemd the brightest thing that was:
But now by proofe all otherwise I weene;
For this great Citie that does far surpas,
And this bright Angels towre quite dims that towre of glas.

LIX

Most trew, then said the holy aged man;
Yet is Cleopolis, for earthly frame,
The fairest peece that eye beholden can;
And well beseemes all knights of noble name,
That covett in th' immortall booke of fame
To be eternized, that same to haunt,
And doen their service to that soveraigne dame,
That glorie does to them for guerdon graunt:
For she is heavenly borne, and heaven may justly vaunt.

LX

And thou faire ymp, sprong out from English race,
How ever now accompted Elfins sonne,
Well worthy doest thy service for her grace,
To aide a virgin desolate fordonne.
But when thou famous victory hast wonne,
And high emongst all knights hast hong thy shield,
Thenceforth the suit of earthly conquest shonne,
And wash thy hands from guilt of bloudy field:
For blood can nought but sin, and wars but sorrowes yield.

LXI

Then seek this path, that I to thee presage,
Which after all to heaven shall thee send;
Then peaceably thy painefull pilgrimage
To yonder same Hierusalem do bend,
Where is for thee ordaind a blessed end:
For thou emongst those Saints, whom thou doest see,
Shall be a Saint, and thine owne nations frend
And Patrone: thou Saint George shalt called bee,
Saint George of mery England, the signe of victoree.

LXII

Unworthy wretch (quoth he) of so great grace,
How dare I thinke such glory to attaine?
These that have it attaind, were in like cace,
(Quoth he) as wretched, and liv'd in like paine.
But deeds of armes must I at last be faine
And Ladies love to leave so dearely bought?
What need of armes, where peace doth ay remaine,
(Said he,) and battailes none are to be fought?
As for loose loves, they're vain, and vanish into nought.

LXIII

O let me not (quoth he) then turne againe
Backe to the world, whose joyes so fruitlesse are;
But let me here for aye in peace remaine,
Or streight way on that last long voyage fare,
That nothing may my present hope empare.
That may not be, (said he) ne maist thou yit
Forgo that royall maides bequeathed care,
Who did her cause into thy hand commit,
Till from her cursed foe thou have her freely quit.

LXIV

Then shall I soone (quoth he) so God me grace,
Abet that virgins cause disconsolate,
And shortly backe returne unto this place,
To walke this way in Pilgrims poore estate.
But now aread, old father, why of late
Didst thou behight me borne of English blood,
Whom all a Faeries sonne doen nominate?
That word shall I (said he) avouchen good,
Sith to thee is unknowne the cradle of thy blood.

LXV

For well I wote thou springst from ancient race
Of Saxon kings, that have with mightie hand
And many bloody battailes fought in place
High reard their royall throne in Britane land,
And vanquisht them, unable to withstand:
From thence a Faerie thee unweeting reft,
There as thou slepst in tender swadling band,
And her base Elfin brood there for thee left.
Such men do Chaungelings call, so chang'd by Faeries theft.

LXVI

Thence she thee brought into this Faerie lond,
And in an heaped furrow did thee hyde,
Where thee a Ploughman all unweeting fond,
As he his toylesome teme that way did guyde,
And brought thee up in ploughmans state to byde
Whereof Georgos he gave thee to name;
Till prickt with courage, and thy forces pryde,
To Faerie court thou cam'st to seeke for fame,
And prove thy puissaunt armes, as seemes thee best became.

LXVII

O holy Sire (quoth he) how shall I quight
The many favours I with thee have found,
That hast my name and nation red aright,
And taught the way that does to heaven bound?
This said, adowne he looked to the ground,
To have returnd, but dazed were his eyne
Through passing brightnesse, which did quite confound
His feeble sence and too exceeding shyne.
So darke are earthly things compard to things divine.

LXVIII

At last whenas himselfe he gan to find,
To Una back he cast him to retire;
Who him awaited still with pensive mind.
Great thankes and goodly meed to that good syre
He thence departing gave for his paines hyre.
So came to Una, who him joyd to see,
And after little rest, gan him desire
Of her adventure mindfull for to bee.
So leave they take of Cœlia, and her daughters three.

Canto XI

The knight with that old Dragon fights
two dayes incessantly;
The third him overthrowes, and gayns
most glorious victory.

I

HIGH time now gan it wex for Una faire
To thinke of those her captive Parents deare,
And their forwasted kingdome to repaire:
Whereto whenas they now approched neare,
With hartie wordes her knight she gan to cheare,
And in her modest manner thus bespake;
Deare knight, as deare as ever knight was deare,
That all these sorrowes suffer for my sake,
High heaven behold the tedious toyle ye for me take.

II

Now are we come unto my native soyle,
And to the place where all our perils dwell;
Here haunts that feend, and does his dayly spoyle;
Therefore henceforth be at your keeping well,
And ever ready for your foeman fell.
The sparke of noble courage now awake,
And strive your excellent selfe to excell:
That shall ye evermore renowmed make,
Above all knights on earth that batteill undertake.

III

And pointing forth, Lo yonder is (said she)
The brasen towre in which my parents deare
For dread of that huge feend emprisond be,
Whom I from far, see on the walles appeare,
Whose sight my feeble soule doth greatly cheare:
And on the top of all I do espye
The watchman wayting tydings glad to heare,
That O my parents might I happily
Unto you bring, to ease you of your misery.

IV

With that they heard a roaring hideous sound,
That all the ayre with terrour filled wide,
And seemd uneath to shake the stedfast ground.

Eftsoones that dreadful Dragon they espide,
Where stretcht he lay upon the sunny side,
Of a great hill, himselfe like a great hill.
But all so soone as he from far descride
Those glistring armes, that heaven with light did fill,
He rousd himselfe full blith, and hastned them untill.

V

Then bad the knight his Lady yede aloofe,
And to an hill her selfe withdraw aside:
From whence she might behold that battailles proof,
And eke be safe from daunger far descryde:
She him obayd, and turnd a little wyde.
Now O thou sacred muse, most learned Dame,
Faire ympe of Phœbus and his aged bride,
The Nourse of time and everlasting fame,
That warlike hands ennoblest with immortall name;

VI

O gently come into my feeble brest
Come gently, but not with that mighty rage,
Wherewith the martiall troupes thou doest infest,
And harts of great Heroës doest enrage,
That nought their kindled courage may aswage,
Soone as thy dreadfull trompe begins to sownd,
The God of warre with his fiers equipage
Thou doest awake, sleepe never he so sownd,
All scared nations doest with horrour sterne astownd.

VII

Faire Goddesse, lay that furious fit aside,
Till I of warres and bloody Mars do sing,
And Briton fields with Sarazin bloud bedyde,
Twixt that great Faery Queene, and Paynim king,
That with their horrour heaven and earth did ring;
A worke of labour long and endlesse prayse:
But now a while let downe that haughtie string
And to my tunes thy second tenor rayse,
That I this man of God his godly armes may blaze.

VIII

By this the dreadfull Beast drew nigh to hand,
Halfe flying, and halfe footing in his haste,

That with his largenesse measured much land,
And made wide shadow under his huge wast,
As mountaine doth the valley overcast.
Approching nigh, he reared high afore
His body monstrous, horrible, and vaste,
Which to increase his wondrous greatnesse more,
Was swoln with wrath, and poyson, and with bloudy gore.

IX

And over, all with brasen scales was armd,
Like plated coate of steele, so couched neare,
That nought mote perce, ne might his corse be harmd
With dint of sword, nor push of pointed speare;
Which, as an Eagle, seeing pray appeare,
His aery plumes doth rouze, full rudely dight;
So shaked he, that horrour was to heare,
For as the clashing of an Armour bright,
Such noyse his rouzed scales did send unto the knight.

X

His flaggy wings when forth he did display,
Were like two sayles, in which the hollow wynd
Is gathered full, and worketh speedy way:
And eke the pennes, that did his pineons bynd,
Were like mayne-yards, with flying canvas lynd;
With which whenas him list the ayre to beat,
And there by force unwonted passage find,
The cloudes before him fled for terrour great,
And all the heavens stood still amazed with his threat.

XI

His huge long tayle wound up in hundred foldes,
Does overspred his long bras-scaly backe,
Whose wreathed boughts when ever he unfoldes,
And thicke entangled knots adown does slacke,
Bespotted as with shields of red and blacke,
It sweepeth all the land behind him farre,
And of three furlongs does but litle lacke;
And at the point two stings in-fixed arre,
Both deadly sharpe, that sharpest steele exceeden farre.

XII

But stings and sharpest steele did far exceed
The sharpnesse of his cruell rending clawes;
Dead was it sure, as sure as death in deed,
What ever thing does touch his ravenous pawes,
Or what within his reach he ever drawes.
But his most hideous head my toung to tell
Does tremble: for his deepe devouring jawes
Wide gaped, like the griesly mouth of hell,
Through which into his darke abisse all ravin fell.

XIII

And that more wondrous was, in either jaw
Threeranckes of yron teeth enraunged were,
In which yet trickling blood, and gobbets raw
Of late devoured bodies did appeare,
That sight thereof bred cold congealed feare:
Which to increase, and as atonce to kill,
A cloud of smoothering smoke and sulphure seare,
Out of his stinking gorge forth steemed still,
That all the ayre about with smoke and stench did fill.

XIV

His blazing eyes, like two bright shining shields,
Did burne with wrath, and sparkled living fyre:
As two broad Beacons, set in open fields,
Send forth their flames far off to every shyre,
And warning give, that enemies conspyre
With fire and sword the region to invade;
So flam'd his eyne with rage and rancorous yre:
But farre within, as in a hollow glade,
Those glaring lampes were set, that made a dreadfull shade.

XV

So dreadfully he towards him did pas,
Forelifting up aloft his speckled brest,
And often bounding on the brused gras,
As for great joyance of his newcome guest.
Eftsoones he gan advance his haughtie crest,
As chauffed Bore his bristles doth upreare,
And shoke his scales to battell ready drest;
That made the Redcrosse knight nigh quake for feare,
As bidding bold defiance to his foeman neare.

XVI

The knight gan fairely couch his steadie speare,
And fiercely ran at him with rigorous might:
The pointed steele arriving rudely theare,
His harder hide would neither perce, nor bight,
But glauncing by forth passed forward right;
Yet sore amoved with so puissaunt push,
The wrathfull beast about him turned light,
And him so rudely passing by, did brush
With his long tayle, that horse and man to ground did rush.

XVII

Both horse and man up lightly rose againe,
And fresh encounter towards him addrest:
But th'idle stroke yet backe recoyld in vaine,
And found no place his deadly point to rest.
Exceeding rage enflam'd the furious beast,
To be avenged of so great despight;
For never felt his imperceable brest
So wondrous force, from hand of living wight;
Yet had he prov'd the powre of many a puissant knight.

XVIII

Then with his waving wings displayed wyde,
Himselfe up high he lifted from the ground,
And with strong flight did forcibly divide
The yielding aire, which nigh too feeble found
Her flitting parts, and element unsound,
To beare so great a weight: he cutting way
With his broad sayles, about him soared round:
At last low stouping with unweldie sway,
Snatcht up both horse and man, to beare them quite away.

XIX

Long he them bore above the subject plaine,
So far as Ewghen bow a shaft may send,
Till struggling strong did him at last constraine
To let them downe before his flightes end:
As hagard hauke, presuming to contend
With hardie fowle, above his hable might,
His wearie pounces all in vaine doth spend
To trusse the pray too heavy for his flight;
Which comming downe to ground, does free it selfe by fight.

XX

He so disseized of his gryping grosse,
The knight his thrillant speare again assayd
In his bras-plated body to embosse,
And three mens strength unto the stroke he layd;
Wherewith the stiffe beame quaked, as affrayd,
And glauncing from his scaly necke, did glyde
Close under his left wing, then broad displayd:
The percing steele there wrought a wound full wyde,
That with the uncouth smart the Monster lowdly cryde.

XXI

He cryde, as raging seas are wont to rore,
When wintry storme his wrathfull wreck does threat
The roaring billowes beat the ragged shore,
As they the earth would shoulder from her seat,
And greedy gulfe does gape, as he would eat
His neighbour element in his revenge:
Then gin the blustring brethren boldly threat
To move the world from off his steadfast henge,
And boystrous battell make, each other to avenge.

XXII

The steely head stucke fast still in his flesh,
Till with his cruell clawes he snatcht the wood,
And quite a sunder broke. Forth flowed fresh
A gushing river of blacke goarie blood,
That drowned all the land, whereon he stood;
The streame thereof would drive a water-mill:
Trebly augmented was his furious mood
With bitter sence of his deepe rooted ill,
That flames of fire he threw forth from his large nosethrill.

XXIII

His hideous tayle then hurled he about,
And therewith all enwrapt the nimble thyes
Of his froth-fomy steed, whose courage stout
Striving to loose the knot that fast him tyes,
Himselfe in streighter bandes too rash implyes,
That to the ground he is perforce constraynd
To throw his rider: who can quickly ryse
From off the earth, with durty blood distaynd,
For that reprochfull fall right fowly he disdaynd.

XXIV

And fiercely tooke his trenchand blade in hand,
With which he stroke so furious and so fell,
That nothing seemd the puissaunce could withstand:
Upon his crest the hardned yron fell,
But his more hardned crest was armd so well,
That deeper dint therein it would not make;
Yet so extremely did the buffe him quell,
That from thenceforth he shund the like to take,
But when he saw them come, he did them still forsake.

XXV

The knight was wroth to see his stroke beguyld,
And smote againe with more outrageous might;
But backe againe the sparckling steele recoyld,
And left not any marke, where it did light,
As if in Adamant rocke it had bene pight.
The beast impatient of his smarting wound,
And of so fierce and forcible despight,
Thought with his wings to stye above the ground;
But his late wounded wing unserviceable found.

XXVI

Then full of griefe and anguish vehement,
He lowdly brayd, that like was never heard,
And from his wide devouring oven sent
A flake of fire, that, flashing in his beard,
Him all amazd, and almost made affeard:
The scorching flame sore swinged all his face,
And through his armour all his body seard,
That he could not endure so cruell cace,
But thought his armes to leave, and helmet to unlace.

XXVII

Not that great Champion of the antique world,
Whom famous Poetes verse so much doth vaunt,
And hath for twelve huge labours high extold,
So many furies and sharpe fits did haunt,
When him the poysond garment did enchaunt,
With Centaures bloud and bloudie verses charm'd;
As did this knight twelve thousand dolours daunt,
Whom fyrie steele now burnt, that earst him arm'd,
That erst him goodly arm'd, now most of all him harm'd.

XXVIII

Faint, wearie, sore, emboyled, grieved, brent
With heat, toyle, wounds, armes, smart, and inward fire,
That never man such mischiefes did torment;
Death better were, death did he oft desire,
But death will never come, when needes require.
Whom so dismayd when that his foe beheld,
He cast to suffer him no more respire,
But gan his sturdy sterne about to weld,
And him so strongly stroke, that to the ground him feld.

XXIX

It fortuned, (as faire it then befell,)
Behind his backe unweeting, where he stood,
Of auncient time there was a springing well,
From which fast trickled forth a silver flood,
Full of great vertues, and for med'cine good.
Whylome, before that cursed Dragon got
That happy land, and all with innocent blood
Defyld those sacred waves, it rightly hot
The well of life, ne yet his vertues had forgot.

XXX

For unto life the dead it could restore,
And guilt of sinfull crimes cleane wash away,
Those that with sicknesse were infected sore
It could recure, and aged long decay
Renew, as one were borne that very day.
Both Silo this, and Jordan did excell,
And th' English Bath, and eke the German Spau;
Ne can Cephise, nor Hebrus match this well:
Into the same the knight back overthrowen, fell.

XXXI

Now gan the golden Phœbus for to steepe
His fierie face in billowes of the west,
And his faint steedes watred in Ocean deepe,
Whiles from their journall labours they did rest,
When that infernall Monster, having kest
His wearie foe into that living well,
Can high advance his broad discoloured brest
Above his wonted pitch, with countenance fell,
And clapt his yron wings, as victor he did dwell.

XXXII

Which when his pensive Ladie saw from farre,
Great woe and sorrow did her soule assay,
As weening that the sad end of the warre,
And gan to highest God entirely pray,
That feared chance from her to turne away;
With folded hands and knees full lowly bent,
All night she watcht, ne once adowne would lay
Her daintie limbs in her sad dreriment,
But praying still did wake, and waking did lament.

XXXIII

The morrow next gan early to appeare,
That Titan rose to runne his daily race;
But early ere the morrow next gan reare
Out of the sea faire Titans deawy face,
Up rose the gentle virgin from her place,
And looked all about, if she might spy
Her loved knight to move his manly pace:
For she had great doubt of his safety,
Since late she saw him fall before his enemy.

XXXIV

At last she saw, where he upstarted brave
Out of the well, wherein he drenched lay:
As Eagle fresh out of the Ocean wave,
Where he hath left his plumes all hoary gray,
And deckt himselfe with feathers youthly gay,
Like Eyas hauke up mounts unto the skies,
His newly budded pineons to assay,
And marveiles at himselfe, still as he flies:
So new this new-borne knight to battell new did rise.

XXXV

Whom when the damned feend so fresh did spy,
No wonder if he wondred at the sight,
And doubted, whether his late enemy
It were, or other new supplied knight.
He, now to prove his late renewed might,
High brandishing his bright deaw-burning blade,
Upon his crested scalpe so sore did smite,
That to the scull a yawning wound it made;
The deadly dint his dulled senses all dismaid.

XXXVI

I wote not, whether the revenging steele
Were hardned with that holy water dew,
Wherein he fell, or sharper edge did feele,
Or his baptized hands now greater grew;
Or other secret vertue did ensew;
Else never could the force of fleshly arme,
Ne molten mettall in his blood embrew;
For till that stownd could never wight him harme,
By subtilty, nor slight, nor might, nor mighty charme.

XXXVII

The cruell wound enraged him so sore,
That loud he yelded for exceeding paine;
As hundred ramping Lyons seem'd to rore,
Whom ravenous hunger did thereto constraine:
Then gan he tosse aloft his stretched traine,
And therewith scourge the buxome aire so sore,
That to his force to yeelden it was faine;
Ne ought his sturdy strokes might stand afore,
That high trees overthrew, and rocks in peeces tore.

XXXVIII

The same advauncing high above his head,
With sharpe intended sting so rude him smot,
That to the earth him drove, as stricken dead,
Ne living wight would have him life behot:
The mortall sting his angry needle shot
Quite through his shield, and in his shoulder seasd,
Where fast it stucke, ne would there out be got:
The griefe thereof him wondrous sore diseasd,
Ne might his ranckling paine with patience be appeasd.

XXXIX

But yet more mindfull of his honour deare,
Then of the grievous smart, which him did wring,
From loathed soile he can him lightly reare,
And strove to loose the far infixed sting:
Which when in vaine he tryde with struggeling,
Inflam'd with wrath, his raging blade he heft,
And strooke so strongly, that the knotty string
Of his huge taile he quite a sunder cleft,
Five joints thereof he hewd, and but the stump him left.

XL

Hart cannot thinke, what outrage, and what cryes,
With foule enfouldred smoake and flashing fire,
The hell-bred beast threw forth unto the skyes,
That all was covered with darkenesse dire:
Then fraught with rancour, and engorged ire,
He cast at once him to avenge for all,
And gathering up himselfe out of the mire,
With his uneven wings did fiercely fall,
Upon his sunne-bright shield, and gript it fast withall.

XLI

Much was the man encombred with his hold,
In feare to lose his weapon in his paw,
Ne wist yet, how his talaunts to unfold;
For harder was from Cerberus greedy jaw
To plucke a bone, then from his cruell claw
To reave by strength the griped gage away:
Thrise he assayd it from his foot to draw,
And thrise in vaine to draw it did assay,
It booted nought to thinke to robbe him of his pray.

XLII

Tho when he saw no power might prevaile,
His trustie sword he cald to his last aid,
Wherewith he fiercely did his foe assaile,
And double blowes about him stoutly laid,
That glauncing fire out of the yron plaid;
As sparckles from the Andvile use to fly,
When heavy hammers on the wedge are swaid;
Therewith at last he forst him to unty
One of his grasping feete, him to defend thereby.

XLIII

The other foot, fast fixed on his shield,
Whenas no strength, nor stroks mote him constraine
To loose, ne yet the warlike pledge to yield,
He smot thereat with all his might and maine,
That nought so wondrous puissaunce might sustaine;
Upon the joint the lucky steele did light,
And made such way, that hewd it quite in twaine;
The paw yett missed not his minisht might,
But hong still on the shield, as it at first was pight.

XLIV

For griefe thereof and divelish despight,
From his infernall fournace forth he threw
Huge flames, that dimmed all the heavens light,
Enrold in duskish smoke and brimstone blew:
As burning Aetna from his boyling stew
Doth belch out flames, and rockes in peeces broke,
And ragged ribs of mountains molten new,
Enwrapt in coleblacke clouds and filthy smoke,
That all the land with stench, and heaven with horror chokc.

XLV

The heate whereof, and harmefull pestilence
So sore him noyd, that forst him to retire
A little backward for his best defence,
To save his body from the scorching fire,
Which he from hellish entrailes did expire.
It chaunst (eternall God that chaunce did guide,)
As he recoiled backward, in the mire
His nigh forwearied feeble feet did slide,
And downe he fell, with dread of shame sore terrifide.

XLVI

There grew a goodly tree him faire beside,
Loaden with fruit and apples rosie red,
As they in pure vermilion had beene dide,
Whereof great vertues over all were red:
For happy life to all which thereon fed,
And life eke everlasting did befall:
Great God it planted in that blessed sted
With his Almighty hand, and did it call
The tree of life, the crime of our first fathers fall.

XLVII

In all the world like was not to be found,
Save in that soile, where all good things did grow,
And freely sprong out of the fruitfull ground,
As incorrupted Nature did them sow,
Till that dread Dragon all did overthrow.
Another like faire tree eke grew thereby,
Whereof whoso did eat, eftsoones did know
Both good and ill: O mornefull memory:
That tree through one mans fault hath doen us all to dy.

XLVIII

From that first tree forth flowd, as from a well,
A trickling streame of Balme, most soveraine
And dainty deare, which on the ground, still fell,
And overflowed all the fertile plaine,
As it had deawed bene with timely raine:
Life and long health that gratious ointment gave,
And deadly wounds could heale and reare againe
The senselesse corse appointed for the grave.
Into that same he fell: which did from death him save.

XLIX

For nigh thereto the ever damned beast
Durst not approch, for he was deadly made,
And all that life preserved did detest:
Yet he is oft adventur'd to invade.
By this the drouping day-light gan to fade,
And yield his roome to sad succeeding night,
Who with her sable mantle gan to shade
The face of earth, and wayes of living wight,
And high her burning torch set up in heaven bright.

L

When gentle Una saw the second fall
Of her deare knight, who wearie of long fight,
And faint through losse of blood, mov'd not at all,
But lay, as in a dreame of deepe delight,
Besmeard with pretious Balme, whose vertuous might
Did heale his wounds, and scorching heat alay,
Againe she stricken was with sore affright,
And for his safetie gan devoutly pray,
And watch the noyous night, and wait for joyous day.

LI

The joyous day gan early to appeare,
And faire Aurora from the deawy bed
Of aged Tithone gan herselfe to reare
With rosy cheekes, for shame as blushing red;
Her golden locks for haste were loosely shed
About her eares, when Una her did marke
Clymbe to her charet, all with flowers spred;
From heaven high to chase the chearelesse darke,
With merry note her loud salutes the mounting larke.

LII

Then freshly up arose the doughtie knight,
All healed of his hurts and woundes wide,
And did himselfe to battell ready dight;
Whose early foe awaiting him beside
To have devourd, so soone as day he spyde,
When now he saw himselfe so freshly reare,
As if late fight had nought him damnifyde,
He woxe dismayd, and gan his fate to feare;
Nathlesse with wonted rage he him advaunced neare.

LIII

And in his first encounter, gaping wide,
He thought attonce him to have swallowd quight,
And rusht upon him with outragious pride;
Who him r'encountring fierce, as hauke in flight
Perforce rebutted backe. The weapon bright
Taking advantage of his open jaw,
Ran through his mouth with so importune might,
That deepe emperst his darksome hollow maw,
And back retyrd, his life blood forth with all did draw.

LIV

So downe he fell, and forth his life did breath,
That vanisht into smoke and cloudes swift;
So downe he fell, that th' earth him underneath
Did grone, as feeble so great load to lift;
So downe he fell, as an huge rockie clift,
Whose false foundation waves have washt away,
With dreadfull poyse is from the mayneland rift,
And rolling downe, great Neptune doth dismay;
So downe he fell, and like an heaped mountaine lay.

LV

The knight himselfe even trembled at his fall,
So huge and horrible a masse it seem'd,
And his deare Ladie, that beheld it all,
Durst not approch for dread, which she misdeem'd;
But yet at last, whenas the direfull feend
She saw not stirre, off-shaking vaine affright,
She nigher drew, and saw that joyous end:
Then God she praysd, and thankt her faithfull knight,
That had atchieved so great a conquest by his might.

Canto XII

Faire Una to the Redcrosse knight,
betrouthed is with joy:
Though false Duessa it to barre
her false sleights doe imploy.

I

BEHOLD I see the haven nigh at hand,
To which I meane my wearie course to bend;
Vere the maine shete, and beare up with the land,
The which afore is fairely to be kend,
And seemeth safe from storms that may offend;
There this faire virgin wearie of her way
Must landed be, now at her journeyes end:
There eke my feeble barke a while may stay
Till merry wind and weather call her thence away.

II

Scarsely had Phœbus in the glooming East
Yet harnessed his firie-footed teeme,
Ne reard above the earth his flaming creast;
When the last deadly smoke aloft did steeme
That signe of last outbreathed life did seeme
Unto the watchman on the castle wall,
Who thereby dead that balefull Beast did deeme,
And to his Lord and Ladie lowd gan call,
To tell how he had seene the Dragons fatall fall.

III

Uprose with hastie joy, and feeble speed
That aged Sire, the Lord of all that land,
And looked forth, to weet if true indeede
Those tydings were, as he did understand,
Which whenas true by tryall he out found,
He bad to open wyde his brazen gate,
Which long time had bene shut, and out of hond
Proclaymed joy and peace through all his state;
For dead now was their foe which them forrayed late.

IV

Then gan triumphant Trompets sound on hie,
That sent to heaven the ecchoed report
Of their new joy, and happie victorie

Gainst him, that had them long opprest with tort,
And fast imprisoned in sieged fort.
Then all the people, as in solemne feast,
To him assembled with one full consort,
Rejoycing at the fall of that great beast,
From whose eternall bondage now they were releast.

V

Forth came that auncient Lord and aged Queene,
Arayd in antique robes downe to the ground,
And sad habiliments right well beseene;
A noble crew about them waited round
Of sage and sober Peres, all gravely gownd;
Whom farre before did march a goodly band
Of tall young men, all hable armes to sownd,
But now they laurell braunches bore in hand;
Glad signe of victorie and peace in all their land.

VI

Unto that doughtie Conquerour they came,
And him before themselves prostrating low,
Their Lord and Patrone loud did him proclame,
And at his feet their laurell boughes did throw.
Soone after them all dauncing on a row
The comely virgins came, with girlands dight,
As fresh as flowres in medow greene do grow,
When morning deaw upon their leaves doth light:
And in their hands sweet Timbrels all upheld on hight.

VII

And them before, the fry of children young
Their wanton sports and childish mirth did play,
And to the Maydens sounding tymbrels sung,
In well attuned notes, a joyous lay,
And made delightfull musicke all the way,
Untill they came, where that faire virgin stood;
As faire Diana in fresh sommers day,
Beholds her Nymphes enraung'd in shadie wood,
Some wrestle, some do run, some bathe in christall flood:

VIII

So she beheld those maydens meriment
With chearefull vew; who when to her they came,

Themselves to ground with gracious humblesse bent,
And her ador'd by honorable name,
Lifting to heaven her everlasting fame:
Then on her head they set a girland greene,
And crowned her twixt earnest and twixt game;
Who in her self-resemblance well beseene,
Did seeme such, as she was, a goodly maiden Queene.

IX

And after, all the raskall many ran,
Heaped together in rude rablement,
To see the face of that victorious man:
Whom all admired, as from heaven sent,
And gazd upon with gaping wonderment.
But when they came where that dead Dragon lay,
Stretcht on the ground in monstrous large extent,
The sight with idle feare did them dismay,
Ne durst approch him nigh, to touch, or once assay.

X

Some feard, and fled; some feard and well it faynd;
One that would wiser seeme then all the rest,
Warnd him not touch, for yet perhaps remaynd
Some lingring life within his hollow brest,
Or in his wombe might lurke some hidden nest
Of many Dragonets, his fruitfull seed;
Another said, that in his eyes did rest
Yet sparckling fire, and bad thereof take heed;
Another said, he saw him move his eyes indeed.

XI

One mother, when as her foolehardie chyld
Did come too neare, and with his talants play,
Halfe dead through feare, her little babe revyld,
And to her gossips gan in counsell say;
How can I tell, but that his talants may
Yet scratch my sonne, or rend his tender hand?
So diversly themselves in vaine they fray;
Whiles some more bold, to measure him nigh stand,
To prove how many acres he did spread of land.

XII

Thus flocked all the folke him round about,
The whiles that hoarie king, with all his traine,
Being arrived where that champion stout
After his foes defeasance did remaine,
Him goodly greetes, and faire does entertaine
With princely gifts of yvorie and gold,
And thousand thankes him yeelds for all his paine.
Then when his daughter deare he does behold,
Her dearely doth imbrace, and kisseth manifold.

XIII

And after to his Pallace he them brings,
With shaumes, and trompets, and with Clarions sweet;
And all the way the joyous people sings,
And with their garments strowes the paved street:
Whence mounting up, they find purveyance meet
Of all that royall Princes court became,
And all the floore was underneath their feet
Bespred with costly scarlot of great name,
On which they lowly sit, and fitting purpose frame.

XIV

What needs me tell their feast and goodly guize,
In which was nothing riotous nor vaine?
What needs of dainty dishes to devize,
Of comely services, or courtly trayne?
My narrow leaves cannot in them containe
The large discourse of royall Princes state.
Yet was their manner then but bare and plaine:
For th' antique world excesse and pride did hate;
Such proud luxurious pompe is swollen up but late.

XV

Then when with meates and drinkes of every kinde
Their fervent appetites they quenched had,
That auncient Lord gan fit occasion finde,
Of straunge adventures, and of perils sad,
Which in his travell him befallen had,
For to demaund of his renowmed guest:
Who then with utt'rance grave, and count'nance sad,
From point to point, as is before exprest,
Discourst his voyage long, according his request.

XVI

Great pleasures mixt with pittiful regard,
That godly King and Queene did passionate,
Whiles they his pittifull adventures heard,
That oft they did lament his lucklesse state,
And often blame the too importune fate,
That heaped on him so many wrathfull wreakes:
For never gentle knight, as he of late,
So tossed was in fortunes cruell freakes;
And all the while salt teares bedeawd the hearers cheaks.

XVII

Then sayd the royall Pere in sober wise;
Deare Sonne, great beene the evils which ye bore
From first to last in your late enterprise,
That I note whether prayse, or pitty more:
For never living man, I weene, so sore
In sea of deadly daungers was distrest;
But since now safe ye seised have the shore,
And well arrived are, (high God be blest)
Let us devize of ease and everlasting rest.

XVIII

Ah, dearest Lord, said then that doughty knight,
Of ease or rest I may not yet devize,
For by the faith, which I to armes have plight,
I bounden am streight after this emprize,
As that your daughter can ye well advize,
Backe to returne to that great Faerie Queene,
And her to serve six yeares in warlike wize,
Gainst that proud Paynim king that workes her teene
Therefore I ought crave pardon, till I there have beene.

XIX

Unhappie falles that hard necessitie,
(Quoth he) the troubler of my happie peace,
And vowed foe of my felicitie;
Ne I against the same can justly preace:
But since that band ye cannot now release,
Nor doen undo; (for vowes may not be vaine,)
Soone as the terme of those six yeares shall cease,
Ye then shall hither backe returne againe,
The marriage to accomplish vowd betwixt you twain.

XX

Which for my part I covet to performe,
In sort as through the world I did proclame,
That whoso kild that monster most deforme,
And him in hardy battaile overcame,
Should have mine onely daughter to his Dame,
And of my kingdome heyre apparaunt bee:
Therefore since now to thee perteines the same,
By dew desert of noble chevalree,
Both daughter and eke kingdome, lo, I yield to thee.

XXI

Then forth he called that his daughter faire,
The fairest Un' his onely daughter deare,
His onely daughter, and his onely heyre;
Who forth proceeding with sad sober cheare,
As bright as doth the morning starre appeare
Out of the East, with flaming lockes bedight,
To tell that dawning day is drawing neare,
And to the world does bring long wished light:
So faire and fresh that Lady shewd her selfe in sight.

XXII

So faire and fresh, as freshest flowre in May;
For she had layd her mournefull stole aside,
And widow-like sad wimple throwne away,
Wherewith her heavenly beautie she did hide,
Whiles on her wearie journey she did ride;
And on her now a garment she did weare,
All lilly white, withoutten spot, or pride,
That seemd like silke and silver woven neare,
But neither silke nor silver therein did appeare.

XXIII

The blazing brightnesse of her beauties beame,
And glorious light of her sunshyny face,
To tell, were as to strive against the streame;
My ragged rimes are all too rude and bace,
Her heavenly lineaments for to enchace.
Ne wonder; for her owne deare loved knight,
All were she dayly with himselfe in place,
Did wonder much at her celestiall sight:
Oft had he seene her faire, but never so faire dight.

XXIV

So fairely dight, when she in presence came,
She to her Sire made humble reverence,
And bowed low, that her right well became,
And added grace unto her excellence:
Who with great wisedome and grave eloquence
Thus gan to say. But eare he thus had said,
With flying speede, and seeming great pretence
Came running in, much like a man dismaid,
A Messenger with letters, which his message said.

XXV

All in the open hall amazed stood
At suddeinnesse of that unwarie sight,
And wondred at his breathlesse hastie mood.
But he for nought would stay his passage right,
Till fast before the king he did alight;
Where falling flat, great humblesse he did make,
And kist the ground, whereon his foot was pight;
Then to his hands that writ he did betake,
Which he disclosing, red thus, as the paper spake.

XXVI

To thee, most mighty king of Eden faire,
Her greeting sends in these sad lines addrest,
The wofull daughter, and forsaken heire
Of that great Emperour of all the West;
And bids thee be advized for the best,
Ere thou thy daughter linck in holy band
Of wedlocke to that new unknowen guest:
For he already plighted his right hand
Unto another love, and to another land.

XXVII

To me sad mayd, or rather widow sad,
He was affiaunced long time before,
And sacred pledges he both gave, and had,
False erraunt knight, infamous, and forswore:
Witnesse the burning Altars, which he swore,
And guiltie heavens of his bold perjury,
Which though he hath polluted oft of yore,
Yet I to them for judgement just do fly,
And them conjure t'avenge this shamefull injury.

XXVIII

Therefore since mine he is, or free or bond,
Or false or trew, or living or else dead,
Withhold, O soveraine Prince, your hasty hond
From knitting league with him, I you aread;
Ne weene my right with strength adowne to tread,
Through weaknesse of my widowhed, or woe;
For truth is strong her rightfull cause to plead,
And shall find friends, if need requireth soe.
So bids thee well to fare, Thy neither friend, nor foe, *Fidessa*.

XXIX

When he these bitter byting wordes had red,
The tydings straunge did him abashed make,
That still he sate long time astonished,
As in great muse, ne word to creature spake.
At last his solemne silence thus he brake,
With doubtfull eyes fast fixed on his guest;
Redoubted knight, that for mine onely sake
Thy life and honour late adventurest,
Let nought be hid from me, that ought to be exprest.

XXX

What meane these bloody vowes, and idle threats,
Throwne out from womanish impatient mind?
What heavens? what altars? what enraged heates
Here heaped up with termes of love unkind,
My conscience cleare with guilty bands would bind?
High God be witnesse, that I guiltlesse ame.
But if your selfe, Sir knight, ye faultie find,
Or wrapped be in loves of former Dame,
With crime do not it cover, but disclose the same.

XXXI

To whom the Redcrosse knight this answere sent
My Lord, my King, be nought hereat dismayd,
Till well ye wote by grave intendiment,
What woman, and wherefere doth me upbrayd
With breach of love, and loyalty betrayd.
It was in my mishaps, as hitherward
I lately traveild, that unwares I strayd
Out of my way, through perils straunge and hard;
That day should faile me, ere I had them all declard.

XXXII

There did I find, or rather I was found
Of this false woman, that Fidessa hight,
Fidessa hight the falsest Dame on ground,
Most false Duessa, royall richly dight,
That easy was to invegle weaker sight:
Who by her wicked arts, and wylie skill,
Too false and strong for earthly skill or might,
Unwares me wrought unto her wicked will,
And to my foe betrayd, when least I feared ill.

XXXIII

Then stepped forth the goodly royall Mayd,
And on the ground her selfe prostrating low,
With sober countenaunce thus to him sayd;
O pardon me, my soveraigne Lord, to show
The secret treasons, which of late I know
To have bene wroght by that false sorceresse.
She onely she it is, that earst did throw
This gentle knight into so great distresse,
That death him did awaite in dayly wretchednesse.

XXXIV

And now it seemes, that she suborned hath
This craftie messenger with letters vaine,
To worke new woe and unprovided scath,
By breaking of the band betwixt us twaine;
Wherein she used hath the practicke paine
Of this false footman, clokt with simplenesse,
Whom if ye please for to discover plaine,
Ye shall him Archimago find, I ghesse,
The falsest man alive; who tries shall find no lesse.

XXXV

The king was greatly moved at her speach,
And, all with suddein indignation fraight,
Bad on that Messenger rude hands to reach.
Eftsoones the Gard, which on his state did wait,
Attacht that faitor false, and bound him strait:
Who seeming sorely chauffed at his band,
As chained Beare, whom cruell dogs do bait,
With idle force did faine them to withstand,
And often semblaunce made to scape out of their hand.

XXXVI

But they him layd full low in dungeon deepe,
And bound him hand and foote with yron chains
And with continual watch did warely keepe:
Who then would thinke, that by his subtile trains
He could escape fowle death or deadly paines?
Thus when that princes wrath was pacifide,
He gan renew the late forbidden bains,
And to the knight his daughter dear he tyde,
With sacred rites and vowes for ever to abyde.

XXXVII

His owne two hands the holy knots did knit,
That none but death for ever can devide;
His owne two hands, for such a turne most fit,
The housling fire did kindle and provide,
And holy water thereon sprinckled wide;
At which the bushy Teade a groome did light,
And sacred lamp in secret chamber hide,
Where it should not be quenched day nor night,
For feare of evill fates, but burnen ever bright.

XXXVIII

Then gan they sprinckle all the posts with wine,
And made great feast to solemnize that day;
They all perfumde with frankencense divine,
And precious odours fetcht from far away,
That all the house did sweat with great aray:
And all the while sweete Musicke did apply
Her curious skill, the warbling notes to play,
To drive away the dull Melancholy;
The whiles one sung a song of love and jollity.

XXXIX

During the which there was an heavenly noise
Heard sound through all the Pallace pleasantly,
Like as it had bene many an Angels voice
Singing before th' eternall Majesty,
In their trinall triplicities on hye;
Yet wist no creature whence that heavenly sweet
Proceeded, yet eachone felt secretly
Himselfe thereby reft of his sences meet,
And ravished with rare impression in his sprite.

XL

Great joy was made that day of young and old,
And solemne feast proclaimd throughout the land,
That their exceeding merth may not be told:
Suffice it heare by signes to understand
The usuall joyes at knitting of loves band.
Thrise happy man the knight himselfe did hold,
Possessed of his Ladies hart and hand,
And ever, when his eye did her behold,
His heart did seeme to melt in pleasures manifold.

XLI

Her joyous presence, and sweet company
In full content he there did long enjoy;
Ne wicked envie, ne vile gealosy,
His deare delights were able to annoy:
Yet swimming in that sea of blissfull joy,
He nought forgot how he whilome had sworne,
In case he could that monstrous beast destroy,
Unto his Faerie Queene backe to returne;
The which he shortly did, and Una left to mourne.

XLII

Now strike your sailes ye jolly Mariners,
For we be come unto a quiet rode,
Where we must land some of our passengers,
And light this wearie vessell of her lode.
Here she a while may make her safe abode,
Till she repaired have her tackles spent,
And wants supplide. And then againe abroad
On the long voyage whereto she is bent:
Well may she speede and fairely finish her intent.

Book II

Canto VII

> *Guyon findes Mamon in a delue,*
> *Sunning his threasure hore:*
> *Is by him tempted, and led downe,*
> *To see his secret store.*

I

AS Pilot well expert in perilous waue,
That to a stedfast starre his course hath bent,

When foggy mistes, or cloudy tempests haue
The faithfull light of that faire lampe yblent,
And couer'd heauen with hideous dreriment,
Vpon his card and compas firmes his eye,
The maisters of his long experiment,
And to them does the steddy helme apply,
Bidding his winged vessell fairely forward fly.

III

So *Guyon* hauing lost his trusty guide,
Late left beyond that *Ydle lake*, proceedes
Yet on his way, of none accompanide;
And euermore himselfe with comfort feedes,
Of his owne vertues, and prayse-worthy deedes.
So long he yode, yet no aduenture found,
Which fame of her shrill trompet worthy reedes:
For still he traueild through wide wastfull ground,
That nought but desert wildernesse shew'd all around.

III

At last he came vnto a gloomy glade,
Couer'd with boughes and shrubs from heauens light,
Whereas he sitting found in secret shade
An vncouth, saluage, and vnciuile wight,
Of griesly hew, and fowle ill fauour'd sight;
His face with smoke was tand, and eyes were bleard,
His head and beard with sout were ill bedight,
His cole-blacke hands did seeme to haue beene seard
In smithes fire-spitting forge, and nayles like clawes appeard.

IV

His yron coate all ouergrowne with rust,
Was vnderneath enueloped with gold,
Whose glistring glosse darkned with filthy dust,
Well yet appeared, to haue beene of old
A worke of rich entayle, and curious mould,
Wouen with antickes and wild Imagery:
And in his lap a masse of coyne he told,
And turned vpsidowne, to feede his eye
And couetous desire with his huge threasury.

V

And round about him lay on euery side
Great heapes of gold, that neuer could be spent:
Of which some were rude owre, not purifide
Of *Mulcibers* deuouring element;
Some others were new driuen, and distent
Into great Ingoes, and to wedges square;
Some in round plates withouten moniment;
But most were stampt, and in their metall bare
The antique shapes of kings and kesars straunge and rare.

VI

Soone as he *Guyon* saw, in great affright
And hast he rose, for to remoue aside
Those pretious hils from straungers enuious sight,
And downe them poured through an hole full wide,
Into the hollow earth, them there to hide.
But *Guyon* lightly to him leaping, stayd
His hand, that trembled, as one terrifyde;
And though him selfe were at the sight dismayd,
Yet him perforce restraynd, and to him doubtfull sayd.

VII

What art thou man, (if man at all thou art)
That here in desert hast thine habitaunce,
And these rich heapes of wealth doest hide apart
From the worldes eye, and from her right vsaunce?
Thereat with staring eyes fixed askaunce,
In great disdaine, he answerd; Hardy Elfe,
That darest vew my direfull countenaunce,
I read thee rash, and heedlesse of thy selfe,
To trouble my still seate, and heapes of pretious pelfe.

VIII

God of the world and worldlings I me call,
Great *Mammon*, greatest god below the skye,
That of my plenty poure out vnto all,
And vnto none my graces do enuye:
Riches, renowme, and principality,
Honour, estate, and all this worldes good,
For which men swinck and sweat incessantly,
Fro me do flow into an ample flood,
And in the hollow earth haue their eternall brood.

IX

Wherefore if me thou deigne to serue and sew,
At thy commaund lo all these mountaines bee;
Or if to thy great mind, or greedy vew
All these may not suffise, there shall to thee
Ten times so much be numbred francke and free.
 Mammon (said he) thy godheades vaunt is vaine,
And idle offers of thy golden fee;
To them, that couet such eye-glutting gaine,
Proffer thy giftes, and fitter seruaunts entertaine.

X

Me ill besits, that in der-doing armes,
And honours suit my vowed dayes do spend,
Vnto thy bounteous baytes, and pleasing charmes,
With which weake men thou witchest, to attend:
Regard of worldly mucke doth fowly blend,
And low abase the high heroicke spright,
That ioyes for crownes and kingdomes to contend;
Faire shields, gay steedes, bright armes be my delight:
Those be the riches fit for an aduent'rous knight.

XI

Vaine glorious Elfe (said he) doest not thou weet,
That money can thy wantes at will supply?
Sheilds, steeds, and armes, and all things for thee meet
It can puruay in twinckling of an eye;
And crownes and kingdomes to thee multiply.
Do not I kings create, and throw the crowne
Sometimes to him, that low in dust doth ly?
And him that raignd, into his rowme thrust downe,
And whom I lust, do heape with glory and renowne?

XII

All otherwise (said he) I riches read,
And deeme them roote of all disquietnesse;
First got with guile, and then preseru'd with dread,
And after spent with pride and lauishnesse,
Leauing behind them griefe and heauinesse.
Infinite mischiefes of them do arize,
Strife, and debate, bloudshed, and bitternesse,
Outrageous wrong, and hellish couetize,
That noble heart as great dishonour doth despize.

XIII

Ne thine be kingdomes, ne the scepters thine;
But realmes and rulers thou doest both confound,
And loyall truth to treason doest incline;
Witnesse the guiltlesse bloud pourd oft on ground,
The crowned often slaine, the slayer cround,
The sacred Diademe in peeces rent,
And purple robe gored with many a wound;
Castles surprizd, great cities sackt and brent:
So mak'st thou kings, and gaynest wrongfull gouernement.

XIV

Long were to tell the troublous stormes, that tosse
The priuate state, and make the life vnsweet:
Who swelling sayles in Caspian sea doth crosse,
And in frayle wood on *Adrian* gulfe doth fleet,
Doth not, I weene, so many euils meet.
Then *Mammon* wexing wroth, And why then, said,
Are mortall men so fond and vndiscreet,
So euill thing to seeke vnto their ayd,
And hauing not complaine, and hauing it vpbraid?

XV

Indeede (quoth he) through fowle intemperaunce,
Frayle men are oft captiu'd to couetise:
But would they thinke, with how small allowaunce
Vntroubled Nature doth her selfe suffise,
Such superfluities they would despise,
Which with sad cares empeach our natiue ioyes:
At the well head the purest streames arise:
But mucky filth his braunching armes annoyes,
And with vncomely weedes the gentle waue accloyes.

XVI

The antique world, in his first flowring youth,
Found no defect in his Creatours grace,
But with glad thankes, and vnreproued truth,
The gifts of soueraigne bountie did embrace:
Like Angels life was then mens happy cace;
But later ages pride, like corn-fed steed,
Abusd her plenty, and fat swolne encreace
To all licentious lust, and gan exceed
The measure of her meane, and naturall first need.

XVII

Then gan a cursed hand the quiet wombe
Of his great Grandmother with steele to wound,
And the hid treasures in her sacred tombe,
With Sacriledge to dig. Therein he found
Fountaines of gold and siluer to abound,
Of which the matter of his huge desire
And pompous pride eftsoones he did compound;
Then auarice gan through his veines inspire
His greedy flames, and kindled life-deuouring fire.

XVIII

Sonne (said he then) let be thy bitter scorne,
And leaue the rudenesse of that antique age
To them, that liu'd therein in state forlorne;
Thou that doest liue in later times, must wage
Thy workes for wealth, and life for gold engage.
If then thee list my offred grace to vse,
Take what thou please of all this surplusage;
If thee list not, leaue haue thou to refuse:
But thing refused, do not afterward accuse.

XIX

Me list not (said the Elfin knight) receaue
Thing offred, till I know it well be got,
Ne wote I, but thou didst these goods bereaue
From rightfull owner by vnrighteous lot,
Or that bloud guiltinesse or guile them blot.
Perdy (quoth he) yet neuer eye did vew,
Ne toung did tell, ne hand these handled not,
But safe I haue them kept in secret mew,
From heauens sight, and powre of all which them pursew.

XX

What secret place (quoth he) can safely hold
So huge a masse, and hide from heauens eye?
Or where hast thou thy wonne, that so much gold
Thou canst preserue from wrong and robbery?
Come thou (quoth he) and see. So by and by
Through that thicke couert he him led, and found
A darkesome way, which no man could descry,
That deepe descended through the hollow ground,
And was with dread and horrour compassed around.

XXI

At length they came into a larger space,
That stretcht it selfe into an ample plaine,
Through which a beaten broad high way did trace,
That streight did lead to *Plutoes* griesly raine:
By that wayes side, there sate infernall Payne,
And fast beside him sat tumultuous Strife:
The one in hand an yron whip did straine,
The other brandished a bloudy knife,
And both did gnash their teeth, and both did threaten life.

XXII

On thother side in one consort there sate,
Cruell Reuenge, and rancorous Despight,
Disloyall Treason, and hart-burning Hate,
But gnawing Gealosie out of their sight
Sitting alone, his bitter lips did bight,
And trembling Feare still to and fro did fly,
And found no place, where safe he shroud him might,
Lamenting Sorrow did in darknesse lye,
And Shame his vgly face did hide from liuing eye.

XXIII

And ouer them sad Horrour with grim hew,
Did alwayes sore, beating his yron wings;
And after him Owles and Night-rauens flew,
The hatefull messengers of heauy things,
Of death and dolour telling sad tidings;
Whiles sad *Celeno*, sitting on a clift,
A song of bale and bitter sorrow sings,
That hart of flint a sunder could haue rift:
Which hauing ended, after him she flyeth swift.

XXIV

All these before the gates of *Pluto* lay,
By whom they passing, spake vnto them nought.
But th'Elfin knight with wonder all the way
Did feed his eyes, and fild his inner thought.
At last him to a litle dore he brought,
That to the gate of Hell, which gaped wide,
Was next adioyning, ne them parted ought:
Betwixt them both was but a litle stride,
That did the house of Richesse from hell-mouth diuide.

XXV

Before the dore sat selfe-consuming Care,
Day and night keeping wary watch and ward,
For feare least Force or Fraud should vnaware
Breake in, and spoile the treasure there in gard:
Ne would he suffer Sleepe once thither-ward
Approch, albe his drowsie den were next;
For next to death is Sleepe to be compard:
Therefore his house is vnto his annext;
Here Sleep, there Richesse, and Hel-gate them both betwext.

XXVI

So soone as *Mammon* there arriu'd, the dore
To him did open, and affoorded way;
Him followed eke Sir *Guyon* euermore,
Ne darkenesse him, ne daunger might dismay.
Soone as he entred was, the dore streight way
Did shut, and from behind it forth there lept
An vgly feend, more fowle then dismall day,
The which with monstrous stalke behind him stept,
And euer as he went, dew watch vpon him kept.

XXVII

Well hoped he, ere long that hardy guest,
If euer couetous hand, or lustfull eye,
Or lips he layd on thing, that likt him best,
Or euer sleepe his eye-strings did vntye,
Should be his pray. And therefore still on hye
He ouer him did hold his cruell clawes,
Threatning with greedy gripe to do him dye
And rend in peeces with his rauenous pawes,
If euer he transgrest the fatall *Stygian* lawes.

XXVIII

That houses forme within was rude and strong,
Like an huge caue, hewne out of rocky clift,
From whose rough vaut the ragged breaches hong,
Embost with massy gold of glorious gift,
And with rich metall loaded euery rift,
That heauy ruine they did seeme to threat;
And ouer them *Arachne* high did lift
Her cunning web, and spred her subtile net,
Enwrapped in fowle smoke and clouds more blacke then Iet.

XXIX

Both roofe, and floore, and wals were all of gold,
But ouergrowne with dust and old decay,
And hid in darkenesse, that none could behold
The hew thereof: for vew of chearefull day
Did neuer in that house it selfe display,
But a faint shadow of vncertain light;
Such as a lamp, whose life does fade away:
Or as the Moone cloathed with clowdy night,
Does shew to him, that walkes in feare and sad affright.

XXX

In all that rowme was nothing to be seene,
But huge great yron chests and coffers strong,
All bard with double bends, that none could weene
Them to efforce by violence or wrong;
On euery side they placed were along.
But all the ground with sculs was scattered,
And dead mens bones, which round about were flong,
Whose liues, it seemed, whilome there were shed,
And their vile carcases now left vnburied.

XXXI

They forward passe, ne *Guyon* yet spoke word,
Till that they came vnto an yron dore,
Which to them opened of his owne accord,
And shewd of richesse such exceeding store,
As eye of man did neuer see before;
Ne euer could within one place be found,
Though all the wealth, which is, or was of yore,
Could gathered be through all the world around,
And that aboue were added to that vnder ground.

XXXII

The charge thereof vnto a couetous Spright
Commaunded was, who thereby did attend,
And warily awaited day and night,
From other couetous feends it to defend,
Who it to rob and ransacke did intend.
Then *Mammon* turning to that warriour, said;
Loe here the worldes blis, loe here the end,
To which all men do ayme, rich to be made:
Such grace now to be happy, is before thee laid.

XXXIII

Certes (said he) I n'ill thine offred grace,
Ne to be made so happy do intend:
Another blis before mine eyes I place,
Another happinesse, another end.
To them, that list, these base regardes I lend:
But I in armes, and in atchieuements braue,
Do rather choose my flitting houres to spend,
And to be Lord of those, that riches haue,
Then them to haue my selfe, and be their seruile sclaue.

XXXIV

Thereat the feend his gnashing teeth did grate,
And grieu'd, so long to lacke his greedy pray;
For well he weened, that so glorious bayte
Would tempt his guest, to take thereof assay:
Had he so doen, he had him snatcht away,
More light then Culuer in the Faulcons fist.
Eternall God thee saue from such decay.
But whenas *Mammon* saw his purpose mist,
Him to entrap vnwares another way he wist.

XXXV

Thence forward he him led, and shortly brought
Vnto another rowme, whose dore forthright,
To him did open, as it had beene taught:
Therein an hundred raunges weren pight,
And hundred fornaces all burning bright;
By euery fornace many feends did bide,
Deformed creatures, horrible in sight,
And euery feend his busie paines applide,
To melt the golden metall, ready to be tride.

XXXVI

One with great bellowes gathered filling aire,
And with forst wind the fewell did inflame;
Another did the dying bronds repaire
With yron toungs, and sprinckled oft the same
With liquid waues, fiers *Vulcans* rage to tame,
Who maistring them, renewd his former heat;
Some scumd the drosse, that from the metall came;
Some stird the molten owre with ladles great;
And euery one did swincke, and euery one did sweat.

XXXVII

But when as earthly wight they present saw,
Glistring in armes and battailous aray,
From their whot worke they did themselues withdraw
To wonder at the sight: for till that day,
They neuer creature saw, that came that way.
Their staring eyes sparckling with feruent fire,
And vgly shapes did nigh the man dismay,
That were it not for shame, he would retire,
Till that him thus bespake their soueraigne Lord and sire.

XXXVIII

Behold, thou Faeries sonne, with mortall eye,
That liuing eye before did neuer see:
The thing, that thou didst craue so earnestly,
To weet, whence all the wealth late shewd by mee,
Proceeded, lo now is reueald to thee.
Here is the fountaine of the worldes good:
Now therefore, if thou wilt enriched bee,
Auise thee well, and chaunge thy wilfull mood,
Least thou perhaps hereafter wish, and be withstood.

XXXIX

Suffise it then, thou Money God (quoth hee)
That all thine idle offers I refuse.
All that I need I haue; what needeth mee
To couet more, then I haue cause to vse?
With such vaine shewes thy worldlings vile abuse:
But giue me leaue to follow mine emprise.
Mammon was much displeasd, yet no'te he chuse,
But beare the rigour of his bold mesprise,
And thence him forward led, him further to entise.

XL

He brought him through a darksome narrow strait,
To a broad gate, all built of beaten gold:
The gate was open, but therein did wait
A sturdy villein, striding stiffe and bold,
As if that highest God defie he would;
In his right hand an yron club he held,
But he himselfe was all of golden mould,
Yet had both life and sence, and well could weld
That cursed weapon, when his cruell foes he queld.

XLI

Disdayne he called was, and did disdaine
To be so cald, and who so did him call:
Sterne was his looke, and full of stomacke vaine,
His portaunce terrible, and stature tall,
Far passing th'hight of men terrestriall;
Like an huge Gyant of the *Titans* race,
That made him scorne all creatures great and small,
And with his pride all others powre deface:
More fit amongst blacke fiendes, then men to haue his place.

XLII

Soone as those glitterand armes he did espye,
That with their brightnesse made that darknesse light,
His harmefull club he gan to hurtle hye,
And threaten batteill to the Faery knight;
Who likewise gan himselfe to batteill dight,
Till *Mammon* did his hasty hand withhold,
And counseld him abstaine from perilous fight:
For nothing might abash the villein bold,
Ne mortall steele emperce his miscreated mould.

XLIII

So hauing him with reason pacifide,
And the fiers Carle commaunding to forbeare,
He brought him in. The rowme was large and wide,
As it some Gyeld or solemne Temple weare:
Many great golden pillours did vpbeare
The massy roofe, and riches huge sustayne,
And euery pillour decked was full deare
With crownes and Diademes, and titles vaine,
Which mortall Princes wore, whiles they on earth did rayne.

XLIV

A route of people there assembled were,
Of euery sort and nation vnder skye,
Which with great vprore preaced to draw nere
To th'vpper part, where was aduaunced hye
A stately siege of soueraigne maiestye;
And thereon sat a woman gorgeous gay,
And richly clad in robes of royaltye,
That neuer earthly Prince in such aray
His glory did enhaunce, and pompous pride display.

XLV

Her face right wondrous faire did seeme to bee,
That her broad beauties beam great brightnes threw
Through the dim shade, that all men might it see:
Yet was not that same her owne natiue hew,
But wrought by art and counterfetted shew,
Thereby more louers vnto her to call;
Nath'lesse most heauenly faire in deed and vew
She by creation was, till she did fall;
Thenceforth she sought for helps, to cloke her crime withall.

XLVI

There, as in glistring glory she did sit,
She held a great gold chaine ylincked well,
Whose vpper end to highest heauen was knit,
And lower part did reach to lowest Hell;
And all that preace did round about her swell,
To catchen hold of that long chaine, thereby
To clime aloft, and others to excell:
That was *Ambition*, rash desire to sty,
And euery lincke thereof a step of dignity.

XLVII

Some thought to raise themselues to high degree,
By riches and vnrighteous reward,
Some by close shouldring, some by flatteree;
Others through friends, others for base regard;
And all by wrong wayes for themselues prepard.
Those that were vp themselues, kept others low,
Those that were low themselues, held others hard,
Ne suffred them to rise or greater grow,
But euery one did striue his fellow downe to throw.

XLVIII

Which whenas *Guyon* saw, he gan inquire,
What meant that preace about that Ladies throne,
And what she was that did so high aspire.
Him *Mammon* answered; That goodly one,
Whom all that folke with such contention,
Do flocke about, my deare, my daughter is;
Honour and dignitie from her alone
Deriued are, and all this worldes blis
For which ye men do striue: few get, but many mis.

XLIX

And faire *Philotime* she rightly hight,
The fairest wight that wonneth vnder skye,
But that this darksome neather world her light
Doth dim with horrour and deformitie,
Worthy of heauen and hye felicitie,
From whence the gods haue her for enuy thrust:
But sith thou hast found fauour in mine eye,
Thy spouse I will her make, if that thou lust,
That she may thee aduance for workes and merites iust.

L

Gramercy *Mammon* (said the gentle knight)
For so great grace and offred high estate;
But I, that am fraile flesh and earthly wight,
Vnworthy match for such immortall mate
My selfe well wote, and mine vnequall fate;
And were I not, yet is my trouth yplight,
And loue auowd to other Lady late,
That to remoue the same I haue no might:
To chaunge loue causelesse is reproch to warlike knight.

LI

Mammon emmoued was with inward wrath;
Yet forcing it to faine, him forth thence led
Through griesly shadowes by a beaten path,
Into a gardin goodly garnished
With hearbs and fruits, whose kinds mote not be red:
Not such, as earth out of her fruitfull woomb
Throwes forth to men, sweet and well sauoured,
But direfull deadly blacke both leafe and bloom,
Fit to adorne the dead, and decke the drery toombe.

LII

There mournfull *Cypresse* grew in greatest store,
And trees of bitter *Gall*, and *Heben* sad,
Dead sleeping *Poppy*, and blacke *Hellebore*,
Cold *Coloquintida*, and *Tetra* mad,
Mortall *Samnitis*, and *Cicuta* bad,
Which with th'vniust *Atheniens* made to dy
Wise *Socrates*, who thereof quaffing glad
Pourd out his life, and last Philosophy
To the faire *Critias* his dearest Belamy.

LIII

The *Gardin* of *Proserpina* this hight;
And in the midst thereof a siluer seat,
With a thicke Arber goodly ouer dight,
In which she often vsd from open heat
Her selfe to shroud, and pleasures to entreat.
Next thereunto did grow a goodly tree,
With braunches broad dispred and body great,
Clothed with leaues, that none the wood mote see
And loaden all with fruit as thicke as it might bee.

LIV

Their fruit were golden apples glistring bright,
That goodly was their glory to behold,
On earth like neuer grew, ne liuing wight
Like euer saw, but they from hence were sold;
For those, which *Hercules* with conquest bold
Got from great *Atlas* daughters, hence began,
And planted there, did bring forth fruit of gold:
And those with which th'*Eubaean* young man wan
Swift *Atalanta*, when through craft he her out ran.

LV

Here also sprong that goodly golden fruit,
With which *Acontius* got his louer trew,
Whom he had long time sought with fruitlesse suit:
Here eke that famous golden Apple grew,
The which emongst the gods false *Ate* threw;
For which th'*Idaean* Ladies disagreed,
Till partiall *Paris* dempt it *Venus* dew,
And had of her, faire *Helen* for his meed,
That many noble *Greekes* and *Troians* made to bleed.

LVI

The warlike Elfe much wondred at this tree,
So faire and great, that shadowed all the ground,
And his broad braunches, laden with rich fee,
Did stretch themselues without the vtmost bound
Of this great gardin, compast with a mound,
Which ouer-hanging, they themselues did steepe,
In a blacke flood which flow'd about it round;
That is the riuer of *Cocytus* deepe,
In which full many soules do endlesse waile and weepe.

LVII

Which to behold, he clomb vp to the banke,
And looking downe, saw many damned wights,
In those sad waues, which direfull deadly stanke,
Plonged continually of cruell Sprights,
That with their pitteous cryes, and yelling shrights,
They made the further shore resounden wide:
Emongst the rest of those same ruefull sights,
One cursed creature he by chaunce espide,
That drenched lay full deepe, vnder the Garden side.

LVIII

Deepe was he drenched to the vpmost chin,
Yet gaped still, as coueting to drinke
Of the cold liquor, which he waded in,
And stretching forth his hand, did often thinke
To reach the fruit, which grew vpon the brincke:
**But both the fruit from hand, and floud from mouth
Did flie abacke, and made him vainely swinke:**
The whiles he steru'd with hunger and with drouth
He daily dyde, yet neuer throughly dyen couth.

LIX

The knight him seeing labour so in vaine,
Askt who he was, and what he ment thereby:
Who groning deepe, thus answerd him againe;
Most cursed of all creatures vnder skye,
Lo *Tantalus*, I here tormented lye:
Of whom high *Ioue* wont whylome feasted bee,
Lo here I now for want of food doe dye:
But if that thou be such, as I thee see,
Of grace I pray thee, giue to eat and drinke to mee.

LX

Nay, nay, thou greedie *Tantalus* (quoth he)
Abide the fortune of thy present fate,
And vnto all that liue in high degree,
Ensample be of mind intemperate,
To teach them how to vse their present state.
Then gan the cursed wretch aloud to cry,
Accusing highest *Ioue* and gods ingrate,
And eke blaspheming heauen bitterly,
As authour of vniustice, there to let him dye.

LXI

He lookt a little further, and espyde
Another wretch, whose carkasse deepe was drent
Within the riuer, which the same did hyde:
But both his hands most filthy feculent,
Aboue the water were on high extent,
And faynd to wash themselues incessantly;
Yet nothing cleaner were for such intent,
But rather fowler seemed to the eye;
So lost his labour vaine and idle industry.

LXII

The knight him calling, asked who he was,
Who lifting vp his head, him answerd thus:
I *Pilate* am the falsest Iudge, alas,
And most vniust, that by vnrighteous
And wicked doome, to Iewes despiteous
Deliuered vp the Lord of life to die,
And did acquite a murdrer felonous;
The whiles my hands I washt in puritie,
The whiles my soule was soyld with foule iniquitie.

LXIII

Infinite moe, tormented in like paine
He there beheld, too long here to be told:
Ne *Mammon* would there let him long remaine,
For terrour of the tortures manifold,
In which the damned soules he did behold,
But roughly him bespake. Thou fearefull foole,
Why takest not of that same fruit of gold,
Ne sittest downe on that same siluer stoole,
To rest thy wearie person, in the shadow coole.

LXIV

All which he did, to doe him deadly fall
In frayle intemperance through sinfull bayt;
To which if he inclined had at all,
That dreadfull feend, which did behind him wayt,
Would him haue rent in thousand peeces strayt:
But he was warie wise in all his way,
And well perceiued his deceiptfull sleight,
Ne suffred lust his safetie to betray;
So goodly did beguile the Guyler of the pray.

LXV

And now he has so long remained there,
That vitall powres gan wexe both weake and wan,
For want of food, and sleepe, which two vpbeare,
Like mightie pillours, this fraile life of man,
That none without the same enduren can.
For now three dayes of men were full outwrought,
Since he this hardie enterprize began:
For thy great *Mammon* fairely he besought,
Into the world to guide him backe, as he him brought.

LXVI

The God, though loth, yet was constraind t'obay,
For lenger time, then that, no liuing wight
Below the earth, might suffred be to stay:
So backe againe, him brought to liuing light.
But all so soone as his enfeebled spright
Gan sucke this vitall aire into his brest,
As ouercome with too exceeding might,
The life did flit away out of her nest,
And all his senses were with deadly fit opprest.

Canto IX

The house of Temperance, in which
doth sober Alma dwell,
Besiegd of many foes, whom straunger
knightes to flight compell.

I

OF all Gods workes, which do this world adorne,
There is no one more faire and excellent,
Then is mans body both for powre and forme,
Whiles it is kept in sober gouernment;
But none then it, more fowle and indecent,
Distempred through misrule and passions bace:
It growes a Monster, and incontinent
Doth loose his dignitie and natiue grace.
Behold, who list, both one and other in this place.

II

After the Paynim brethren conquer'd were,
The *Briton* Prince recou'ring his stolne sword,
And *Guyon* his lost shield, they both yfere

Forth passed on their way in faire accord,
Till him the Prince with gentle court did bord;
Sir knight, mote I of you this curt'sie read,
To weet why on your shield so goodly scord
Beare ye the picture of that Ladies head?
Full liuely is the semblaunt, though the substance dead.

III

Faire Sir (said he) if in that picture dead
Such life ye read, and vertue in vaine shew,
What mote ye weene, if the trew liuely-head
Of that most glorious visage ye did vew?
But if the beautie of her mind ye knew,
That is her bountie, and imperiall powre,
Thousand times fairer then her mortall hew,
O how great wonder would your thoughts deuoure,
And infinite desire into your spirite poure!

IV

She is the mighty Queene of *Faerie*,
Whose faire retrait I in my shield do beare;
She is the flowre of grace and chastitie,
Throughout the world renowmed far and neare,
My liefe, my liege, my Soueraigne, my deare,
Whose glory shineth as the morning starre,
And with her light the earth enlumines cleare;
Far reach her mercies, and her prayses farre,
As well in state of peace, as puissaunce in warre.

V

Thrise happy man, (said then the *Briton* knight)
Whom gracious lot, and thy great valiaunce
Haue made thee souldier of that Princesse bright,
Which with her bounty and glad countenance
Doth blesse her seruaunts, and them high aduaunce.
How may straunge knight hope euer to aspire,
By faithfull seruice, and meet amenance,
Vnto such blisse? sufficient were that hire
For losse of thousand liues, to dye at her desire.

VI

Said *Guyon*, Noble Lord, what meed so great,
Or grace of earthly Prince so soueraine,

But by your wondrous worth and warlike feat
Ye well may hope, and easely attaine?
But were your will, her sold to entertaine,
And numbred be mongst knights of *Maydenhed*,
Great guerdon, well I wote, should you remaine,
And in her fauour high be reckoned,
As *Arthegall*, and *Sophy* now beene honored.

VII

Certes (then said the Prince) I God auow,
That sith I armes and knighthood first did plight,
My whole desire has beene, and yet is now,
To serue that Queene with all my powre and might.
Now hath the Sunne with his lamp-burning light,
Walkt round about the world, and I no lesse,
Sith of that Goddesse I haue sought the sight,
Yet no where can her find: such happinesse
Heauen doth to me enuy, and fortune fauourlesse.

VIII

Fortune, the foe of famous cheuisaunce
Seldome (said *Guyon*) yields to vertue aide,
But in her way throwes mischiefe and mischaunce,
Whereby her course is stopt, and passage staid.
But you, faire Sir, be not herewith dismaid,
But constant keepe the way, in which ye stand;
Which were it not, that I am else delaid
With hard aduenture, which I haue in hand,
I labour would to guide you through all Faery land.

IX

Gramercy Sir (said he) but mote I weete,
What straunge aduenture do ye now pursew?
Perhaps my succour, or aduizement meete
Mote stead you much your purpose to subdew.
Then gan Sir *Guyon* all the story shew
Of false *Acrasia*, and her wicked wiles,
Which to auenge, the Palmer him forth drew
From Faery court. So talked they, the whiles
They wasted had much way, and measurd many miles.

X

And now faire *Phœbus* gan decline in hast

His weary wagon to the Westerne vale,
Whenas they spide a goodly castle, plast
Foreby a riuer in a pleasaunt dale,
Which choosing for that euenings hospitale,
They thither marcht: but when they came in sight,
And from their sweaty Coursers did auale,
They found the gates fast barred long ere night,
And euery loup fast lockt, as fearing foes despight.

XI

Which when they saw, they weened fowle reproch
Was to them doen, their entrance to forstall,
Till that the Squire gan nigher to approch;
And wind his horne vnder the castle wall,
That with the noise it shooke, as it would fall:
Eftsoones forth looked from the highest spire
The watch, and lowd vnto the knights did call,
To weete, what they so rudely did require.
Who gently answered, They entrance did desire.

XII

Fly, fly, good knights, (said he) fly fast away
If that your liues ye loue, as meete ye should;
Fly fast, and saue your selues from neare decay,
Here may ye not haue entraunce, though we would:
We would and would againe, if that we could;
But thousand enemies about vs raue,
And with long siege vs in this castle hould:
Seuen yeares this wize they vs besieged haue,
And many good knights slaine, that haue vs sought to saue.

XIII

Thus as he spoke, loe with outragious cry
A thousand villeins round about them swarmd
Out of the rockes and caues adioyning nye,
Vile caytiue wretches, ragged, rude, deformd,
All threatning death, all in straunge manner armd,
Some with vnweldy clubs, some with long speares,
Some rusty kniues, some staues in fire warmd.
Sterne was their looke, like wild amazed steares,
Staring with hollow eyes, and stiffe vpstanding heares.

XIV

Fiersly at first those knights they did assaile,
And droue them to recoile: but when againe
They gaue fresh charge, their forces gan to faile,
Vnhable their encounter to sustaine;
For with such puissaunce and impetuous maine
Those Champions broke on them, that forst them fly,
Like scattered Sheepe, whenas the Shepheards swaine
A Lyon and a Tigre doth espye,
With greedy pace forth rushing from the forest nye.

XV

A while they fled, but soone returnd againe
With greater fury, then before was found;
And euermore their cruell Captaine
Sought with his raskall routs t'enclose them round,
And ouerrun to tread them to the ground.
But soone the knights with their bright-burning blades
Broke their rude troupes, and orders did confound,
Hewing and slashing at their idle shades;
For though they bodies seeme, yet substance from them fades.

XVI

As when a swarme of Gnats at euentide
Out of the fennes of Allan do arise,
Their murmuring small trompets sounden wide,
Whiles in the aire their clustring army flies,
That as a cloud doth seeme to dim the skies;
Ne man nor beast may rest, or take repast,
For their sharpe wounds, and noyous iniuries,
Till the fierce Northerne wind with blustring blast
Doth blow them quite away, and in the *Ocean* cast.

XVII

Thus when they had that troublous rout disperst,
Vnto the castle gate they come againe,
And entraunce crau'd, which was denied erst.
Now when report of that their perilous paine,
And combrous conflict, which they did sustaine,
Came to the Ladies eare, which there did dwell,
She forth issewed with a goodly traine
Of Squires and Ladies equipaged well,
And entertained them right fairely, as befell.

XVIII

Alma she called was, a virgin bright;
That had not yet felt *Cupides* wanton rage,
Yet was she woo'd of many a gentle knight,
And many a Lord of noble parentage,
That sought with her to lincke in marriage:
For she was faire, as faire mote euer bee,
And in the flowre now of her freshest age;
Yet full of grace and goodly modestee,
That euen heauen reioyced her sweete face to see.

XIX

In robe of lilly white she was arayd,
That from her shoulder to her heele downe raught,
The traine whereof loose far behind her strayd,
Braunched with gold and pearle, most richly wrought,
And borne of two faire Damsels, which were taught
That seruice well. Her yellow golden heare
Was trimly wouen, and in tresses wrought,
Ne other tyre she on her head did weare,
But crowned with a garland of sweete Rosiere.

XX

Goodly she entertaind those noble knights,
And brought them vp into her castle hall;
Where gentle court and gracious delight
She to them made, with mildnesse virginall,
Shewing her selfe both wise and liberall:
There when they rested had a season dew,
They her besought of fauour speciall,
Of that faire Castle to affoord them vew;
She graunted, and them leading forth, the same did shew.

XXI

First she them led vp to the Castle wall,
That was so high, as foe might not it clime,
And all so faire, and fensible withall,
Not built of bricke, ne yet of stone and lime,
But of thing like to that *Ægyptian* slime,
Whereof king *Nine* whilome built *Babell* towre;
But O great pitty, that no lenger time
So goodly workemanship should not endure:
Soone it must turne to earth; no earthly thing is sure.

XXII

The frame thereof seemd partly circulare,
And part triangulare, O worke diuine;
Those two the first and last proportions are,
The one imperfect, mortall, fœminine;
Th'other immortall, perfect, masculine,
And twixt them both a quadrate was the base,
Proportioned equally by seuen and nine;
Nine was the circle set in heauens place,
All which compacted made a goodly diapase.

XXIII

Therein two gates were placed seemly well:
The one before, by which all in did pas,
Did th'other far in workmanship excell;
For not of wood, nor of enduring bras,
But of more worthy substance fram'd it was;
Doubly disparted, it did locke and close,
That when it locked, none might thorough pas,
And when it opened, no man might it close,
Still open to their friends, and closed to their foes.

XXIV

Of hewen stone the porch was fairely wrought,
Stone more of valew, and more smooth and fine,
Then Iet or Marble far from Ireland brought;
Ouer the which was cast a wandring vine,
Enchaced with a wanton yuie twine.
And ouer it a faire Portcullis hong,
Which to the gate directly did incline,
With comely compasse, and compacture strong,
Neither vnseemely short, nor yet exceeding long.

XXV

Within the Barbican a Porter sate,
Day and night duely keeping watch and ward,
Nor wight, nor word mote passe out of the gate,
But in good order, and with dew regard;
Vtterers of secrets he from thence debard,
Bablers of folly, and blazers of crime.
His larumbell might lowd and wide be hard,
When cause requird, but neuer out of time;
Early and late it rong, at euening and at prime.

XXVI

And round about the porch on euery side
Twise sixteen warders sat, all armed bright
In glistring steele, and strongly fortifide:
Tall yeomen seemed they, and of great might,
And were enraunged ready, still for fight.
By them as *Alma* passed with her guestes,
They did obeysaunce, as beseemed right,
And then againe returned to their restes:
The Porter eke to her did lout with humble gestes.

XXVII

Thence she them brought into a stately Hall,
Wherein were many tables faire dispred,
And ready dight with drapets festiuall,
Against the viaundes should be ministred.
At th'upper end there sate, yclad in red
Downe to the ground, a comely personage,
That in his hand a white rod menaged,
He Steward was hight *Diet*; rype of age,
And in demeanure sober, and in counsell sage.

XXVIII

And through the Hall there walked to and fro
A iolly yeoman, Marshall of the same,
Whose name was *Appetite*; he did bestow
Both guestes and meate, when euer in they came,
And knew them how to order without blame,
As him the Steward bad. They both attone
Did dewty to their Lady, as became;
Who passing by, forth led her guestes anone
Into the kitchin rowme, ne spard for nicenesse none.

XXIX

It was a vaut ybuilt for great dispence,
With many raunges reard along the wall;
And one great chimney, whose long tonnell thence,
The smoke forth threw. And in the midst of all
There placed was a caudron wide and tall,
Vpon a mighty furnace, burning whot,
More whot, then *Aetn'*, or flaming *Mongiball*:
For day and night it brent, ne ceased not,
So long as any thing it in the caudron got.

XXX

But to delay the heat, least by mischaunce
It might breake out, and set the whole on fire,
There added was by goodly ordinaunce,
An huge great paire of bellowes, which did styre
Continually, and cooling breath inspyre.
About the Caudron many Cookes accoyld,
With hookes and ladles, as need did require;
The whiles the viandes in the vessell boyld
They did about their businesse sweat, and sorely toyld.

XXXI

The maister Cooke was cald *Concoction*,
A carefull man, and full of comely guise:
The kitchin Clerke, that hight *Digestion*,
Did order all th'Achates in seemely wise,
And set them forth, as well he could deuise.
The rest had seuerall offices assind,
Some to remoue the scum, as it did rise;
Others to beare the same away did mind;
And others it to vse according to his kind.

XXXII

But all the liquour, which was fowle and wast,
Not good nor seruiceable else for ought,
They in another great round vessell plast,
Till by a conduit pipe it thence were brought:
And all the rest, that noyous was, and nought,
By secret wayes, that none might it espy,
Was close conuaid, and to the back-gate brought,
That cleped was *Port Esquiline*, whereby
It was auoided quite, and throwne out priuily.

XXXIII

Which goodly order, and great workmans skill
Whenas those knights beheld, with rare delight,
And gazing wonder they their minds did fill;
For neuer had they seene so straunge a sight.
Thence backe againe faire *Alma* led them right,
And soone into a goodly Parlour brought,
That was with royall arras richly dight,
In which was nothing pourtrahed, nor wrought,
Not wrought, nor pourtrahed, but easie to be thought.

Page | 871

XXXIV

And in the midst thereof vpon the floure,
A louely beuy of faire Ladies sate,
Courted of many a iolly Paramoure,
The which them did in modest wise amate,
And eachone sought his Lady to aggrate:
And eke emongst them litle *Cupid* playd
His wanton sports, being returned late
From his fierce warres, and hauing from him layd
His cruell bow, wherewith he thousands hath dismayd.

XXXV

Diuerse delights they found them selues to please;
Some song in sweet consort, some laught for ioy,
Some plaid with strawes, some idly sat at ease;
But other some could not abide to toy,
All pleasaunce was to them griefe and annoy:
This frownd, that faund, the third for shame did blush,
Another seemed enuious, or coy,
Another in her teeth did gnaw a rush:
But at these straungers presence euery one did hush.

XXXVI

Soone as the gracious *Alma* came in place,
They all attonce out of their seates arose,
And to her homage made, with humble grace:
Whom when the knights beheld, they gan dispose
Themselues to court, and each a Damsell chose:
The Prince by chaunce did on a Lady light,
That was right faire and fresh as morning rose,
But somwhat sad, and solemne eke in sight,
As if some pensiue thought constraind her gentle spright.

XXXVII

In a long purple pall, whose skirt with gold,
Was fretted all about, she was arayd;
And in her hand a Poplar braunch did hold:
To whom the Prince in curteous manner said;
Gentle Madame, why beene ye thus dismaid,
And your faire beautie do with sadnesse spill?
Liues any, that you hath thus ill apaid?
Or doen you loue, or doen you lacke your will?
What euer be the cause, it sure beseemes you ill.

XXXVIII

Faire Sir, (said she halfe in disdainefull wise,)
How is it, that this word in me ye blame,
And in your selfe do not the same aduise?
Him ill beseemes, anothers fault to name,
That may vnwares be blotted with the same:
Pensiue I yeeld I am, and sad in mind,
Through great desire of glory and of fame;
Ne ought I weene are ye therein behind,
That haue twelue moneths sought one, yet no where can her find.

XXXIX

The Prince was inly moued at her speach,
Well weeting trew, what she had rashly told;
Yet with faire semblaunt sought to hide the breach,
Which chaunge of colour did perforce vnfold,
Now seeming flaming whot, now stony cold.
Tho turning soft aside, he did inquire,
What wight she was, that Poplar braunch did hold:
It answered was, her name was *Prays-desire*,
That by well doing sought to honour to aspire.

XL

The whiles, the *Faerie* knight did entertaine
Another Damsell of that gentle crew,
That was right faire, and modest of demaine,
But that too oft she chaung'd her natiue hew:
Straunge was her tyre, and all her garment blew,
Close round about her tuckt with many a plight:
Vpon her fist the bird, which shonneth vew,
And keepes in couerts close from liuing wight,
Did sit, as yet ashamd, how rude *Pan* did her dight.

XLI

So long as *Guyon* with her commoned,
Vnto the ground she cast her modest eye,
And euer and anone with rosie red
The bashfull bloud her snowy cheekes did dye,
That her became, as polisht yuory,
Which cunning Craftesman hand hath ouerlayd
With faire vermilion or pure Castory.
Great wonder had the knight, to see the mayd
So straungely passioned, and to her gently sayd,

XLII

Faire Damzell, seemeth, by your troubled cheare,
That either me too bold ye weene, this wise
You to molest, or other ill to feare
That in the secret of your hart close lyes,
From whence it doth, as cloud from sea arise.
If it be I, of pardon I you pray;
But if ought else that I mote not deuise,
I will, if please you it discure, assay,
To ease you of that ill, so wisely as I may.

XLIII

She answerd nought, but more abasht for shame,
Held downe her head, the whiles her louely face
The flashing bloud with blushing did inflame,
And the strong passion mard her modest grace,
That *Guyon* meruayld at her vncouth cace:
Till *Alma* him bespake, why wonder yee
Faire Sir at that, which ye so much embrace?
She is the fountaine of your modestee;
You shamefast are, but *Shamefastnesse* it selfe is shee.

XLIV

Thereat the Elfe did blush in priuitee,
And turnd his face away; but she the same
Dissembled faire, and faynd to ouersee.
Thus they awhile with court and goodly game,
Themselues did solace each one with his Dame,
Till that great Ladie thence away them sought,
To vew her castles other wondrous frame.
Vp to a stately Turret she them brought,
Ascending by ten steps of Alablaster wrought.

XLV

That Turrets frame most admirable was,
Like highest heauen compassed around,
And lifted high aboue this earthly masse,
Which it suruew'd, as hils doen lower ground;
But not on ground mote like to this be found,
Not that, which antique *Cadmus* whylome built
In *Thebes*, which *Alexander* did confound;
Nor that proud towre of *Troy*, though richly guilt,
From which young *Hectors* bloud by cruell *Greekes* was spilt.

XLVI

The roofe hereof was arched ouer head,
And deckt with flowers and herbars daintily;
Two goodly Beacons, set in watches stead,
Therein gaue light, and flam'd continually:
For they of liuing fire most subtilly
Were made, and set in siluer sockets bright,
Couer'd with lids deuiz'd of substance sly,
That readily they shut and open might.
O who can tell the prayses of that makers might!

XLVII

Ne can I tell, ne can I stay to tell
This parts great workmanship, and wondrous powre,
That all this other worlds worke doth excell,
And likest is vnto that heauenly towre,
That God hath built for his owne blessed bowre.
Therein were diuerse roomes, and diuerse stages,
But three the chiefest, and of greatest powre,
In which there dwelt three honorable sages,
The wisest men, I weene, that liued in their ages.

XLVIII

Not he, whom *Greece*, the Nourse of all good arts,
By *Phœbus* doome, the wisest thought aliue,
Might be compar'd to these by many parts:
Nor that sage *Pylian* syre, which did suruiue
Three ages, such as mortall men contriue,
By whose aduise old *Priams* cittie fell,
With these in praise of pollicies mote striue.
These three in these three roomes did sundry dwell,
And counselled faire *Alma*, how to gouerne well.

XLIX

The first of them could things to come foresee:
The next could of things present best aduize;
The third things past could keepe in memoree,
So that no time, nor reason could arize,
But that the same could one of these comprize.
For thy the first did in the forepart sit,
That nought mote hinder his quicke preiudize:
He had a sharpe foresight, and working wit,
That neuer idle was, ne once could rest a whit.

Page | 875

L

His chamber was dispainted all within,
With sundry colours, in the which were writ
Infinite shapes of things dispersed thin;
Some such as in the world were neuer yit,
Ne can deuized be of mortall wit;
Some daily seene, and knowen by their names,
Such as in idle fantasies doe flit:
Infernall Hags, *Centaurs*, feendes, *Hippodames*,
Apes, Lions, AEgles, Owles, fooles, louers, children, Dames.

LI

And all the chamber filled was with flyes,
Which buzzed all about, and made such sound,
That they encombred all mens eares and eyes,
Like many swarmes of Bees assembled round,
After their hiues with honny do abound:
All those were idle thoughts and fantasies,
Deuices, dreames, opinions vnsound,
Shewes, visions, sooth-sayes, and prophesies;
And all that fained is, as leasings, tales, and lies.
And all the chamber filled was with flies,
Which buzzed all about, and made such sound,
That they encumbered all men's ears and eyes,
Like many swarms of bees assembled round,

LII

Emongst them all sate he, which wonned there,
That hight *Phantastes* by his nature trew;
A man of yeares yet fresh, as mote appere,
Of swarth complexion, and of crabbed hew,
That him full of melancholy did shew;
Bent hollow beetle browes, sharpe staring eyes,
That mad or foolish seemd: one by his vew
Mote deeme him borne with ill disposed skyes,
When oblique *Saturne* sate in the house of agonyes.

LIII

Whom *Alma* hauing shewed to her guestes,
Thence brought them to the second roome, whose wals
Were painted faire with memorable gestes,
Of famous Wisards, and with picturals
Of Magistrates, of courts, of tribunals,

Of commen wealthes, of states, of pollicy,
Of lawes, of iudgements, and of decretals;
All artes, all science, all Philosophy,
And all that in the world was aye thought wittily.

LIV

Of those that roome was full, and them among
There sate a man of ripe and perfect age,
Who did them meditate all his life long,
That through continuall practise and vsage,
He now was growne right wise, and wondrous sage.
Great pleasure had those stranger knights, to see
His goodly reason, and graue personage,
That his disciples both desir'd to bee;
But *Alma* thence them led to th'hindmost roome of three.

LV

That chamber seemed ruinous and old,
And therefore was remoued farre behind,
Yet were the wals, that did the same vphold,
Right firme and strong, though somewhat they declind,
And therein sate an old oldman, halfe blind,
And all decrepit in his feeble corse,
Yet liuely vigour rested in his mind,
And recompenst him with a better scorse:
Weake body well is chang'd for minds redoubled forse.

LVI

This man of infinite remembrance was,
And things foregone through many ages held,
Which he recorded still, as they did pas,
Ne suffred them to perish through long eld,
As all things else, the which this world doth weld,
But laid them vp in his immortall scrine,
Where they for euer incorrupted dweld:
The warres he well remembred of king *Nine*,
Of old *Assaracus*, and *Inachus* diuine.

LVII

The yeares of *Nestor* nothing were to his,
Ne yet *Mathusalem*, though longest liu'd;
For he remembred both their infancies:
Ne wonder then, if that he were depriu'd

Of natiue strength now, that he them suruiu'd.
His chamber all was hangd about with rolles,
And old records from auncient times deriu'd,
Some made in books, some in long parchment scrolles,
That were all worme-eaten, and full of canker holes.

LVIII

Amidst them all he in a chaire was set,
Tossing and turning them withouten end;
But for he was vnhable them to fet,
A litle boy did on him still attend,
To reach, when euer he for ought did send;
And oft when things were lost, or laid amis,
That boy them sought, and vnto him did lend.
Therefore he *Anamnestes* cleped is,
And that old man *Eumnestes*, by their propertis.

LIX

The knights there entring, did him reuerence dew
And wondred at his endlesse exercise,
Then as they gan his Librarie to vew,
And antique Registers for to auise,
There chaunced to the Princes hand to rize,
An auncient booke, hight *Briton moniments*,
That of this lands first conquest did deuize,
And old diuision into Regiments,
Till it reduced was to one mans gouernments.

LX

Sir *Guyon* chaunst eke on another booke,
That hight *Antiquitie* of *Faerie* lond,
In which when as he greedily did looke,
Th'off-spring of Elues and Faries there he fond,
As it deliuered was from hond to hond:
Whereat they burning both with feruent fire,
Their countries auncestry to vnderstond,
Crau'd leaue of *Alma*, and that aged sire,
To read those bookes; who gladly graunted their desire.

Book III

Canto I

Guyon encountreth Britomart,
faire Florimell is chaced:
Duessaes traines and Malecastaes
champions are defaced.

I

THe famous Briton Prince and Faerie knight,
After long wayes and perilous paines endured,
Hauing their wearie limbes to perfect plight
Restord, and sory wounds right well recured,
Of the faire *Alma* greatly were procured,
To make there lenger soiourne and abode;
But when thereto they might not be allured,
From seeking praise, and deeds of armes abrode,
They courteous conge tooke, and forth together yode.

II

But the captiu'd *Acrasia* he sent,
Because of trauell long, a nigher way,
With a strong gard, all reskew to preuent,
And her to Faerie court safe to conuay,
That her for witnesse of his hard assay,
Vnto his *Faerie* Queene he might present:
But he himselfe betooke another way,
To make more triall of his hardiment,
And seeke aduentures, as he with Prince *Arthur* went.

III

Long so they trauelled through wastefull wayes,
Where daungers dwelt, and perils most did wonne,
To hunt for glorie and renowmed praise;
Full many Countries they did ouerronne,
From the vprising to the setting Sunne,
And many hard aduentures did atchieue;
Of all the which they honour euer wonne,
Seeking the weake oppressed to relieue,
And to recouer right for such, as wrong did grieue.

IV

At last as through an open plaine they yode,
They spide a knight, that towards pricked faire,

And him beside an aged Squire there rode,
That seem'd to couch vnder his shield three-square,
As if that age bad him that burden spare,
And yield it those, that stouter could it wield:
He them espying, gan himselfe prepare,
And on his arme addresse his goodly shield
That bore a Lion passant in a golden field.

V

Which seeing good Sir *Guyon*, deare besought
The Prince of grace, to let him runne that turne.
He graunted: then the Faery quickly raught
His poinant speare, and sharpely gan to spurne
His fomy steed, whose fierie feete did burne
The verdant grasse, as he thereon did tread;
Ne did the other backe his foot returne,
But fiercely forward came withouten dread,
And bent his dreadfull speare against the others head.

VI

They bene ymet, and both their points arriued,
But *Guyon* droue so furious and fell,
That seem'd both shield and plate it would haue riued;
Nathelesse it bore his foe not from his sell,
But made him stagger, as he were not well:
But *Guyon* selfe, ere well he was aware,
Nigh a speares length behind his crouper fell,
Yet in his fall so well him selfe he bare,
That mischieuous mischance his life and limbes did spare.

VII

Great shame and sorrow of that fall he tooke;
For neuer yet, sith warlike armes he bore,
And shiuering speare in bloudie field first shooke,
He found himselfe dishonored so sore.
Ah gentlest knight, that euer armour bore,
Let not thee grieue dismounted to haue beene,
And brought to ground, that neuer wast before;
For not thy fault, but secret powre vnseene,
That speare enchaunted was, which layd thee on the greene.

VIII

But weenedst thou what wight thee ouerthrew,
Much greater griefe and shamefuller regret
For thy hard fortune then thou wouldst renew,
That of a single damzell thou wert met
On equall plaine, and there so hard beset;
Euen the famous *Britomart* it was,
Whom straunge aduenture did from *Britaine* fet,
To seeke her louer (loue farre sought alas,)
Whose image she had scene in *Venus* looking glas.

IX

Full of disdainefull wrath, he fierce vprose,
For to reuenge that foule reprochfull shame,
And snatching his bright sword began to close
With her on foot, and stoutly forward came;
Die rather would he, then endure that same.
Which when his Palmer saw, he gan to feare
His toward perill and vntoward blame,
Which by that new rencounter he should reare:
For death sate on the point of that enchaunted speare.

X

And hasting towards him gan faire perswade,
Not to prouoke misfortune, nor to weene
His speares default to mend with cruell blade;
For by his mightie Science he had seene
The secret vertue of that weapon keene,
That mortall puissance mote not withstond:
Nothing on earth mote alwaies happie beene.
Great hazard were it, and aduenture fond,
To loose long gotten honour with one euill hond.

XI

By such good meanes he him discounselled,
From prosecuting his reuenging rage;
And eke the Prince like treaty handeled,
His wrathfull will with reason to asswage,
And laid the blame, not to his carriage,
But to his starting steed, that swaru'd asyde,
And to the ill purueyance of his page,
That had his furnitures not firmely tyde:
So is his angry courage fairely pacifyde.

XII

Thus reconcilement was betweene them knit,
Through goodly temperance, and affection chaste,
And either vowd with all their power and wit,
To let not others honour be defaste,
Of friend or foe, who euer it embaste,
Ne armes to beare against the others syde:
In which accord the Prince was also plaste,
And with that golden chaine of concord tyde.
So goodly all agreed, they forth yfere did ryde.

XIII

O goodly vsage of those antique times,
In which the sword was seruant vnto right;
When not for malice and contentious crimes,
But all for praise, and proofe of manly might,
The martiall brood accustomed to fight:
Then honour was the meed of victorie,
And yet the vanquished had no despight:
Let later age that noble vse enuie,
Vile rancour to auoid, and cruell surquedrie.

XIV

Long they thus trauelled in friendly wise,
Through countries waste, and eke well edifyde,
Seeking aduentures hard, to exercise
Their puissance, whylome full dernely tryde:
At length they came into a forrest wyde,
Whose hideous horror and sad trembling sound
Full griesly seem'd: Therein they long did ryde,
Yet tract of liuing creatures none they found,
Saue Beares, Lions, and Buls, which romed them around.

XV

All suddenly out of the thickest brush,
Vpon a milke-white Palfrey all alone,
A goodly Ladie did foreby them rush,
Whose face did seeme as cleare as Christall stone,
And eke through feare as white as whales bone:
Her garments all were wrought of beaten gold,
And all her steed with tinsell trappings shone,
Which fled so fast, that nothing mote him hold,
And scarse them leasure gaue, her passing to behold.

XVI

Still as she fled, her eye she backward threw,
As fearing euill, that pursewd her fast;
And her faire yellow locks behind her flew,
Loosely disperst with puffe of euery blast:
All as a blazing starre doth farre outcast
His hearie beames, and flaming lockes dispred,
At sight whereof the people stand aghast:
But the sage wisard telles, as he has red,
That it importunes death and dolefull drerihed.

XVII

So as they gazed after her a while,
Lo where a griesly Foster forth did rush,
Breathing out beastly lust her to defile:
His tyreling iade he fiercely forth did push,
Through thicke and thin, both ouer banke and bush
In hope her to attaine by hooke or crooke,
That from his gorie sides the bloud did gush:
Large were his limbes, and terrible his looke,
And in his clownish hand a sharp bore speare he shooke.

XVIII

Which outrage when those gentle knights did see,
Full of great enuie and fell gealosy,
They stayd not to auise, who first should bee,
But all spurd after fast, as they mote fly,
To reskew her from shamefull villany.
The Prince and *Guyon* equally byliue
Her selfe pursewd, in hope to win thereby
Most goodly meede, the fairest Dame aliue:
But after the foule foster *Timias* did striue.

XIX

The whiles faire *Britomart*, whose constant mind,
Would not so lightly follow beauties chace,
Ne reckt of Ladies Loue, did stay behind,
And them awayted there a certaine space,
To weet if they would turne backe to that place:
But when she saw them gone, she forward went,
As lay her iourney, through that perlous Pace,
With stedfast courage and stout hardiment;
Ne euill thing she fear'd, ne euill thing she ment.

XX

At last as nigh out of the wood she came,
A stately Castle farre away she spyde,
To which her steps directly she did frame.
That Castle was most goodly edifyde,
And plaste for pleasure nigh that forrest syde:
But faire before the gate a spatious plaine,
Mantled with greene, it selfe did spredden wyde,
On which she saw sixe knights, that did darraine
Fierce battell against one, with cruell might and maine.

XXI

Mainly they all attonce vpon him laid,
And sore beset on euery side around,
That nigh he breathlesse grew, yet nought dismaid,
Ne euer to them yielded foot of ground
All had he lost much bloud through many a wound,
But stoutly dealt his blowes, and euery way
To which he turned in his wrathfull stound,
Made them recoile, and fly from dred decay,
That none of all the sixe before, him durst assay.

XXII

Like dastard Curres, that hauing at a bay
The saluage beast embost in wearie chace,
Dare not aduenture on the stubborne pray,
Ne byte before, but rome from place to place,
To get a snatch, when turned is his face.
In such distresse and doubtfull ieopardy,
When *Britomart* him saw, she ran a pace
Vnto his reskew, and with earnest cry,
Bad those same sixe forbeare that single enimy.

XXIII

But to her cry they list not lenden eare,
Ne ought the more their mightie strokes surceasse,
But gathering him round about more neare,
Their direfull rancour rather did encreasse;
Till that she rushing through the thickest preasse,
Perforce disparted their compacted gyre,
And soone compeld to hearken vnto peace:
Tho gan she myldly of them to inquyre
The cause of their dissention and outrageous yre.

XXIV

Whereto that single knight did answere frame;
These six would me enforce by oddes of might,
To chaunge my liefe, and loue another Dame,
That death me liefer were, then such despight,
So vnto wrong to yield my wrested right:
For I loue one, the truest one on ground,
Ne list me chaunge; she th'*Errant Damzell* hight,
For whose deare sake full many a bitter stownd,
I haue endur'd, and tasted many a bloudy wound.

XXV

Certes (said she) then bene ye sixe to blame,
To weene your wrong by force to iustifie:
For knight to leaue his Ladie were great shame,
That faithfull is, and better were to die.
All losse is lesse, and lesse the infamie,
Then losse of loue to him, that loues but one;
Ne may loue be compeld by maisterie;
For soone as maisterie comes, sweete loue anone
Taketh his nimble wings, and soone away is gone.

XXVI

Then spake one of those sixe, There dwelleth here
Within this castle wall a Ladie faire,
Whose soueraine beautie hath no liuing pere,
Thereto so bounteous and so debonaire,
That neuer any mote with her compaire.
She hath ordaind this law, which we approue,
That euery knight, which doth this way repaire,
In case he haue no Ladie, nor no loue,
Shall doe vnto her seruice neuer to remoue.

XXVII

But if he haue a Ladie or a Loue,
Then must he her forgoe with foule defame,
Or else with vs by dint of sword approue,
That she is fairer, then our fairest Dame,
As did this knight, before ye hither came.
Perdie (said *Britomart*) the choise is hard:
But what reward had he, that ouercame?
He should aduaunced be to high regard,
(Said they) and haue our Ladies loue for his reward.

XXVIII

Therefore a read Sir, if thou haue a loue.
Loue haue I sure, (quoth she) but Lady none;
Yet will I not fro mine owne loue remoue,
Ne to your Lady will I seruice done,
But wreake your wrongs wrought to this knight alone,
And proue his cause. With that her mortall speare
She mightily auentred towards one,
And downe him smot, ere well aware he weare,
Then to the next she rode, and downe the next did beare.

XXIX

Ne did she stay, till three on ground she layd,
That none of them himselfe could reare againe;
The fourth was by that other knight dismayd,
All were he wearie of his former paine,
That now there do but two of six remaine;
Which two did yield, before she did them smight.
Ah (said she then) now may ye all see plaine,
That truth is strong, and trew loue most of might,
That for his trusty seruaunts doth so strongly fight.

XXX

Too well we see, (said they) and proue too well
Our faulty weaknesse, and your matchlesse might:
For thy faire Sir, yours be the Damozell,
Which by her owne law to your lot doth light,
And we your liege men faith vnto you plight.
So vnderneath her feet their swords they mard,
And after her besought, well as they might,
To enter in, and reape the dew reward:
She graunted, and then in they all together far'd.

XXXI

Long were it to describe the goodly frame,
And stately port of *Castle Ioyeous*,
(For so that Castle hight by commune name)
Where they were entertaind with curteous
And comely glee of many gracious
Faire Ladies, and many a gentle knight,
Who through a Chamber long and spacious,
Eftsoones them brought vnto their Ladies sight,
That of them cleeped was the *Lady of delight*.

XXXII

But for to tell the sumptuous aray
Of that great chamber, should be labour lost:
For liuing wit, I weene, cannot display
The royall riches and exceeding cost,
Of euery pillour and of euery post;
Which all of purest bullion framed were,
And with great pearles and pretious stones embost,
That the bright glister of their beames cleare
Did sparckle forth great light, and glorious did appeare.

XXXIII

These straunger knights through passing, forth were led
Into an inner rowme, whose royaltee
And rich purueyance might vneath be red;
Mote Princes place beseeme so deckt to bee.
Which stately manner when as they did see,
The image of superfluous riotize,
Exceeding much the state of meane degree,
They greatly wondred, whence so sumptuous guize
Might be maintaynd, and each gan diuersely deuize.

XXXIV

The wals were round about apparelled
With costly clothes of *Arras* and of *Toure*,
In which with cunning hand was pourtrahed
The loue of *Venus* and her Paramoure
The faire *Adonis*, turned to a flowre,
A work of rare deuice, and wondrous wit.
First did it shew the bitter balefull stowre,
Which her assayd with many a feruent fit,
When first her tender hart was with his beautie smit.

XXXV

Then with what sleights and sweet allurements she
Entyst the Boy, as well that art she knew,
And wooed him her Paramoure to be;
Now making girlonds of each flowre that grew,
To crowne his golden lockes with honour dew;
Now leading him into a secret shade
From his Beauperes, and from bright heauens vew,
Where him to sleepe she gently would perswade,
Or bathe him in a fountaine by some couert glade.

XXXVI

And whilst he slept, she ouer him would spred
Her mantle, colour'd like the starry skyes,
And her soft arme lay vnderneath his hed,
And with ambrosiall kisses bathe his eyes;
And whilest he bath'd, with her two crafty spyes,
She secretly would search each daintie lim,
And throw into the well sweet Rosemaryes,
And fragrant violets, and Pances trim,
And euer with sweet Nectar she did sprinkle him.

XXXVII

So did she steale his heedelesse hart away,
And ioyd his loue in secret vnespyde.
But for she saw him bent to cruell play,
To hunt the saluage beast in forrest wyde,
Dreadfull of daunger, that mote him betyde,
She oft and oft aduiz'd him to refraine
From chase of greater beasts, whose brutish pryde
Mote breede him scath vnwares: but all in vaine;
For who can shun the chaunce, that dest'ny doth ordaine?

XXXVIII

Lo, where beyond he lyeth languishing,
Deadly engored of a great wild Bore,
And by his side the Goddesse groueling
Makes for him endlesse mone, and euermore
With her soft garment wipes away the gore,
Which staines his snowy skin with hatefull hew:
But when she saw no helpe might him restore,
Him to a dainty flowre she did transmew,
Which in that cloth was wrought, as if it liuely grew.

XXXIX

So was that chamber clad in goodly wize,
And round about it many beds were dight,
As whilome was the antique worldes guize,
Some for vntimely ease, some for delight,
As pleased them to vse, that vse it might:
And all was full of Damzels, and of Squires,
Dauncing and reueling both day and night,
And swimming deepe in sensuall desires,
And *Cupid* still emongst them kindled lustfull fires.

XL

And all the while sweet Musicke did diuide
Her looser notes with *Lydian* harmony;
And all the while sweet birdes thereto applide
Their daintie layes and dulcet melody,
Ay caroling of loue and iollity,
That wonder was to heare their trim consort.
Which when those knights beheld, with scornefull eye,
They sdeigned such lasciuious disport,
And loath'd the loose demeanure of that wanton sort.

XLI

Thence they were brought to that great Ladies vew,
Whom they found sitting on a sumptuous bed,
That glistred all with gold and glorious shew,
As the proud *Persian* Queenes accustomed:
She seemd a woman of great bountihed,
And of rare beautie, sauing that askaunce
Her wanton eyes, ill signes of womanhed,
Did roll too lightly, and too often glaunce,
Without regard of grace, or comely amenaunce.

XLII

Long worke it were, and needlesse to deuize
Their goodly entertainement and great glee:
She caused them be led in curteous wize
Into a bowre, disarmed for to bee,
And cheared well with wine and spiceree:
The *Redcrosse* Knight was soone disarmed there,
But the braue Mayd would not disarmed bee,
But onely vented vp her vmbriere,
And so did let her goodly visage to appere.

XLIII

As when faire *Cynthia*, in darkesome night,
Is in a noyous cloud enueloped,
Where she may find the substaunce thin and light,
Breakes forth her siluer beames, and her bright hed
Discouers to the world discomfited;
Of the poore traueller, that went astray,
With thousand blessings she is heried;
Such was the beautie and the shining ray,
With which faire *Britomart* gaue light vnto the day.

XLIV

And eke those six, which lately with her fought,
Now were disarmd, and did them selues present
Vnto her vew, and company vnsoght;
For they all seemed curteous and gent,
And all sixe brethren, borne of one parent,
Which had them traynd in all ciuilitee,
And goodly taught to tilt and turnament;
Now were they liegemen to this Lady free,
And her knights seruice ought, to hold of her in fee.

XLV

The first of them by name *Gardante* hight,
A iolly person, and of comely vew;
The second was *Parlante*, a bold knight,
And next to him *Iocante* did ensew;
Basciante did him selfe most curteous shew;
But fierce *Bacchante* seemd too fell and keene;
And yet in armes *Noctante* greater grew:
All were faire knights, and goodly well beseene,
But to faire *Britomart* they all but shadowes beene.

XLVI

For she was full of amiable grace,
And manly terrour mixed therewithall,
That as the one stird vp affections bace,
So th'other did mens rash desires apall,
And hold them backe, that would in errour fall;
As he, that hath espide a vermeill Rose,
To which sharpe thornes and breres the way forstall,
Dare not for dread his hardy hand expose,
But wishing it far off, his idle wish doth lose.

XLVII

Whom when the Lady saw so faire a wight,
All ignoraunt of her contrary sex,
(For she her weend a fresh and lusty knight)
She greatly gan enamoured to wex,
And with vaine thoughts her falsed fancy vex:
Her fickle hart conceiued hasty fire,
Like sparkes of fire, which fall in sclender flex,
That shortly brent into extreme desire,
And ransackt all her veines with passion entire.

XLVIII

Eftsoones she grew to great impatience
And into termes of open outrage brust,
That plaine discouered her incontinence,
Ne reckt she, who her meaning did mistrust;
For she was giuen all to fleshly lust,
And poured forth in sensuall delight,
That all regard of shame she had discust,
And meet respect of honour put to flight:
So shamelesse beauty soone becomes a loathly sight.

XLIX

Faire Ladies, that to loue captiued arre,
And chaste desires do nourish in your mind,
Let not her fault your sweet affections marre,
Ne blot the bounty of all womankind;
‹Mongst thousands good one wanton Dame to find:
Emongst the Roses grow some wicked weeds;
For this was not to loue, but lust inclind;
For loue does alwayes bring forth bounteous deeds,
And in each gentle hart desire of honour breeds.

L

Nought so of loue this looser Dame did skill,
But as a coale to kindle fleshly flame,
Giuing the bridle to her wanton will,
And treading vnder foote her honest name:
Such loue is hate, and such desire is shame.
Still did she roue at her with crafty glaunce
Of her false eyes, that at her hart did ayme,
And told her meaning in her countenaunce;
But *Britomart* dissembled it with ignoraunce.

LI

Supper was shortly dight and downe they sat,
Where they were serued with all sumptuous fare,
Whiles fruitfull *Ceres*, and *Lyaeus* fat
Pourd out their plenty, without spight or spare:
Nought wanted there, that dainty was and rare;
And aye the cups their bancks did ouerflow,
And aye betweene the cups, she did prepare
Way to her loue, and secret darts did throw;
But *Britomart* would not such guilfull message know.

LII

So when they slaked had the feruent heat
Of appetite with meates of euery sort,
The Lady did faire *Britomart* entreat,
Her to disarme, and with delightfull sport
To loose her warlike limbs and strong effort,
But when she mote not thereunto be wonne,
(For she her sexe vnder that straunge purport
Did vse to hide, and plaine apparaunce shonne:)
In plainer wise to tell her grieuaunce she begonne.

LIII

And all attonce discouered her desire
With sighes, and sobs, and plaints, and piteous griefe,
The outward sparkes of her in burning fire;
Which spent in vaine, at last she told her briefe,
That but if she did lend her short reliefe,
And do her comfort, she mote algates dye.
But the chaste damzell, that had neuer priefe
Of such malengine and fine forgerie,
Did easily beleeue her strong extremitie.

LIV

Full easie was for her to haue beliefe,
Who by self-feeling of her feeble sexe,
And by long triall of the inward griefe,
Wherewith imperious loue her hart did vexe,
Could iudge what paines do louing harts perplexe.
Who meanes no guile, be guiled soonest shall,
And to faire semblaunce doth light faith annexe;
The bird, that knowes not the false fowlers call,
Into his hidden net full easily doth fall.

LV

For thy she would not in discourteise wise,
Scorne the faire offer of good will profest;
For great rebuke it is, loue to despise,
Or rudely sdeigne a gentle harts request;
But with faire countenaunce, as beseemed best,
Her entertaynd; nath'lesse she inly deemd
Her loue too light, to wooe a wandring guest:
Which she misconstruing, thereby esteemd
That from like inward fire that outward smoke had steemd.

LVI

Therewith a while she her flit fancy fed,
Till she mote winne fit time for her desire,
But yet her wound still inward freshly bled,
And through her bones the false instilled fire
Did spred it selfe, and venime close inspire.
Tho were the tables taken all away,
And euery knight, and euery gentle Squire
Gan choose his dame with *Basciomani* gay,
With whom he meant to make his sport and courtly play.

LVII

Some fell to daunce, some fell to hazardry,
Some to make loue, some to make meriment,
As diuerse wits to diuers things apply;
And all the while faire *Malecasta* bent
Her crafty engins to her close intent.
By this th'eternall lampes, wherewith high *Ioue*
Doth light the lower world, were half yspent,
And the moist daughters of huge *Atlas* stroue
Into the *Ocean* deepe to driue their weary droue.

LVIII

High time it seemed then for euery wight
Them to betake vnto their kindly rest;
Eftsoones long waxen torches weren light,
Vnto their bowres to guiden euery guest:
Tho when the Britonesse saw all the rest
Auoided quite, she gan her selfe despoile,
And safe commit to her soft fethered nest,
Where through long watch, and late dayes weary toile,
She soundly slept, and carefull thoughts did quite assoile.

LIX

Now whenas all the world in silence deepe
Yshrowded was, and euery mortall wight
Was drowned in the depth of deadly sleepe,
Faire *Malecasta*, whose engrieued spright
Could find no rest in such perplexed plight,
Lightly arose out of her wearie bed,
And vnder the blacke vele of guilty Night,
Her with a scarlot mantle couered,
That was with gold and Ermines faire enueloped.

LX

Then panting soft, and trembling euery ioynt,
Her fearfull feete towards the bowre she moued;
Where she for secret purpose did appoynt
To lodge the warlike mayd vnwisely loued,
And to her bed approching, first she prooued,
Whether she slept or wakt, with her soft hand
She softly felt, if any member mooued,
And lent her weary eare to vnderstand,
If any puffe of breath, or signe of sence she fond.

LXI

Which whenas none she fond, with easie shift,
For feare least her vnwares she should abrayd,
Th'embroderd quilt she lightly vp did lift,
And by her side her selfe she softly layd,
Of euery finest fingers touch affrayd;
Ne any noise she made, ne word she spake,
But inly sigh'd. At last the royall Mayd
Out of her quiet slomber did awake,
And chaungd her weary side, the better ease to take.

LXII

Where feeling one close couched by her side,
She lightly lept out of her filed bed,
And to her weapon ran, in minde to gride
The loathed leachour. But the Dame halfe ded
Through suddein feare and ghastly drerihed,
Did shrieke alowd, that through the house it rong,
And the whole family therewith adred,
Rashly out of their rouzed couches sprong,
And to the troubled chamber all in armes did throng.

LXIII

And those six Knights that Ladies Champions,
And eke the *Redcrosse* knight ran to the stownd,
Halfe armd and halfe vnarmd, with them attons:
Where when confusedly they came, they fownd
Their Lady lying on the sencelesse grownd;
On th'other side, they saw the warlike Mayd
All in her snow-white smocke, with locks vnbownd,
Threatning the point of her auenging blade,
That with so troublous terrour they were all dismayde.

LXIV

About their Lady first they flockt arownd,
Whom hauing laid in comfortable couch,
Shortly they reard out of her frosen swownd;
And afterwards they gan with fowle reproch
To stirre vp strife, and troublous contecke broch:
But by ensample of the last dayes losse,
None of them rashly durst to her approch,
Ne in so glorious spoile themselues embosse;
Her succourd eke the Champion of the bloudy Crosse.

LXV

But one of those sixe knights, *Gardante* hight,
Drew out a deadly bow and arrow keene,
Which forth he sent with felonous despight,
And fell intent against the virgin sheene:
The mortall steele stayd not, till it was seene
To gore her side, yet was the wound not deepe,
But lightly rased her soft silken skin,
That drops of purple bloud thereout did weepe,
Which did her lilly smock with staines of vermeil steepe.

LXVI

Wherewith enrag'd she fiercely at them flew,
And with her flaming sword about her layd,
That none of them foule mischiefe could eschew,
But with her dreadfull strokes were all dismayd:
Here, there, and euery where about her swayd
Her wrathfull steele, that none mote it abide;
And eke the *Redcrosse* knight gaue her good aid,
Ay ioyning foot to foot, and side to side,
That in short space their foes they haue quite terrifide.

LXVII

Tho whenas all were put to shamefull flight,
The noble *Britomartis* her arayd,
And her bright armes about her body dight:
For nothing would she lenger there be stayd,
Where so loose life, and so vngentle trade
Was vsd of Knights and Ladies seeming gent:
So earely ere the grosse Earthes gryesy shade,
Was all disperst out of the firmament,
They tooke their steeds, and forth vpon their iourney went.

Canto II

*The Redcrosse knight to Britomart
describeth Artegall:
The wondrous myrrhour, by which she
in loue with him did fall.*

I

HEre haue I cause, in men iust blame to find,
That in their proper prayse too partiall bee,
And not indifferent to woman kind,
To whom no share in armes and cheualrie
They do impart, ne maken memorie
Of their braue gestes and prowesse martiall;
Scarse do they spare to one or two or three,
Rowme in their writs; yet the same writing small
Does all their deeds deface, and dims their glories all.

II

But by record of antique times I find,
That women wont in warres to beare most sway,
And to all great exploits them selues inclind:
Of which they still the girlond bore away,
Till enuious Men fearing their rules decay,
Gan coyne streight lawes to curb their liberty;
Yet sith they warlike armes haue layd away,
They haue exceld in artes and pollicy,
That now we foolish men that prayse gin eke t'enuy.

III

Of warlike puissaunce in ages spent,
Be thou faire *Britomart*, whose prayse I write,
But of all wisedome be thou precedent,
O soueraigne Queene, whose prayse I would endite,
Endite I would as dewtie doth excite;
But ah my rimes too rude and rugged arre,
When in so high an obiect they do lite,
And striuing, fit to make, I feare do marre:
Thy selfe thy prayses tell, and make them knowen farre.

IV

She trauelling with *Guyon* by the way,
Of sundry things faire purpose gan to find,
T'abridg their iourney long, and lingring day;

Mongst which it fell into that Faeries mind,
To aske this Briton Mayd, what vncouth wind,
Brought her into those parts, and what inquest
Made her dissemble her disguised kind:
Faire Lady she him seemed, like Lady drest,
But fairest knight aliue, when armed was her brest.

V

Thereat she sighing softly, had no powre
To speake a while, ne ready answere make,
But with hart-thrilling throbs and bitter stowre,
As if she had a feuer fit, did quake,
And euery daintie limbe with horrour shake;
And euer and anone the rosy red,
Flasht through her face, as it had beene a flake
Of lightning, through bright heauen fulmined;
At last the passion past she thus him answered.

VI

Faire Sir, I let you weete, that from the howre
I taken was from nourses tender pap,
I haue beene trained vp in warlike stowre,
To tossen speare and shield, and to affrap
The warlike ryder to his most mishap;
Sithence I loathed haue my life to lead,
As Ladies wont, in pleasures wanton lap,
To finger the fine needle and nyce thread;
Me leuer were with point of foemans speare be dead.

VII

All my delight on deedes of armes is set,
To hunt out perils and aduentures hard,
By sea, by land, where so they may be met,
Onely for honour and for high regard,
Without respect of richesse or reward.
For such intent into these parts I came,
Withouten compasse, or withouten card,
Far fro my natiue soyle, that is by name
The greater *Britaine*, here to seeke for prayse and fame.

VIII

Fame blazed hath, that here in Faery lond
Do many famous Knightes and Ladies wonne,

And many straunge aduentures to be fond,
Of which great worth and worship may be wonne;
Which I to proue, this voyage haue begonne.
But mote I weet of you, right curteous knight,
Tydings of one, that hath vnto me donne
Late foule dishonour and reprochfull spight,
The which I seeke to wreake, and *Arthegall* he hight.

IX

The word gone out, she backe againe would call,
As her repenting so to haue missayd,
But that he it vp-taking ere the fall,
Her shortly answered; Faire martiall Mayd
Certes ye misauised beene, t'vpbrayd
A gentle knight with so vnknightly blame:
For weet ye well of all, that euer playd
At tilt or tourney, or like warlike game,
The noble *Arthegall* hath euer borne the name.

X

For thy great wonder were it, if such shame
Should euer enter in his bounteous thought,
Or euer do, that mote deseruen blame:
The noble courage neuer weeneth ought,
That may vnworthy of it selfe be thought.
Therefore, faire Damzell, be ye well aware,
Least that too farre ye haue your sorrow sought:
You and your countrey both I wish welfare,
And honour both; for each of other worthy are.

XI

The royall Mayd woxe inly wondrous glad,
To heare her Loue so highly magnifide,
And ioyd that euer she affixed had,
Her hart on knight so goodly glorifide,
How euer finely she it faind to hide:
The louing mother, that nine monethes did beare,
In the deare closet of her painefull side,
Her tender babe, it seeing safe appeare,
Doth not so much reioyce, as she reioyced theare.

XII

But to occasion him to further talke,
To feed her humour with his pleasing stile,
Her list in strifull termes with him to balke,
And thus replide, How euer, Sir, ye file
Your curteous tongue, his prayses to compile,
It ill beseemes a knight of gentle sort,
Such as ye haue him boasted, to beguile
A simple mayd, and worke so haynous tort,
In shame of knighthood, as I largely can report.

XIII

Let be therefore my vengeaunce to disswade,
And read, where I that faytour false may find.
Ah, but if reason faire might you perswade,
To slake your wrath, and mollifie your mind,
(Said he) perhaps ye should it better find:
For hardy thing it is, to weene by might,
That man to hard conditions to bind,
Or euer hope to match in equall fight,
Whose prowesse paragon saw neuer liuing wight.

XIV

Ne soothlich is it easie for to read,
Where now on earth, or how he may be found;
For he ne wonneth in one certaine stead,
But restlesse walketh all the world around,
Ay doing things, that to his fame redound,
Defending Ladies cause, and Orphans right,
Where so he heares, that any doth confound
Them comfortlesse, through tyranny or might;
So is his soueraine honour raisde to heauens hight.

XV

His feeling words her feeble sence much pleased,
And softly sunck into her molten hart;
Hart that is inly hurt, is greatly eased
With hope of thing, that may allegge his smart;
For pleasing words are like to Magick art,
That doth the charmed Snake in slomber lay:
Such secret ease felt gentle *Britomart*,
Yet list the same efforce with faind gainesay;
So dischord oft in Musick makes the sweeter lay.

XVI

And said, Sir knight, these idle termes forbeare,
And sith it is vneath to find his haunt,
Tell me some markes, by which he may appeare,
If chaunce I him encounter parauaunt;
For perdie one shall other slay, or daunt:
What shape, what shield, what armes, what steed, what sted,
And what so else his person most may vaunt?
All which the *Redcrosse* knight to point ared,
And him in euery part before her fashioned.

XVII

Yet him in euery part before she knew,
How euer list her now her knowledge faine,
Sith him whilome in *Britaine* she did vew,
To her reuealed in a mirrhour plaine,
Whereof did grow her first engraffed paine;
Whose root and stalke so bitter yet did tast,
That but the fruit more sweetnesse did containe,
Her wretched dayes in dolour she mote wast,
And yield the pray of loue to lothsome death at last.

XVIII

By strange occasion she did him behold,
And much more strangely gan to loue his sight,
As it in bookes hath written bene of old.
In *Deheubarth* that now South-wales is hight,
What time king *Ryence* raign'd, and dealed right,
The great Magitian *Merlin* had deuiz'd,
By his deepe science, and hell-dreaded might,
A looking glasse, right wondrously aguiz'd,
Whose vertues through the wyde world soone were solemniz'd.

XIX

It vertue had, to shew in perfect sight,
What euer thing was in the world contaynd,
Betwixt the lowest earth and heauens hight,
So that it to the looker appertaynd;
What euer foe had wrought, or frend had faynd,
Therein discouered was, ne ought mote pas,
Ne ought in secret from the same remaynd;
For thy it round and hollow shaped was,
Like to the world it selfe, and seem'd a world of glas.

XX

Who wonders not, that reades so wonderous worke?
But who does wonder, that has red the Towre,
Wherein th' Egyptian *Phao* long did lurke
From all mens vew, that none might her discoure,
Yet she might all men vew out of her bowre?
Great *Ptolomǽe* it for his lemans sake
Ybuilded all of glasse, by Magicke powre,
And also it impregnable did make;
Yet when his loue was false, he with a peaze it brake.

XXI

Such was the glassie globe that *Merlin* made,
And gaue vnto king *Ryence* for his gard,
That neuer foes his kingdome might inuade,
But he it knew at home before he hard
Tydings thereof, and so them still debar'd.
It was a famous Present for a Prince,
And worthy worke of infinite reward,
That treasons could bewray, and foes conuince;
Happie this Realme, had it remained euer since.

XXII

One day it fortuned, faire *Britomart*
Into her fathers closet to repayre;
For nothing he from her reseru'd apart,
Being his onely daughter and his hayre:
Where when she had espyde that mirrhour fayre,
Her selfe a while therein she vewd in vaine;
Tho her auizing of the vertues rare,
Which thereof spoken were, she gan againe
Her to bethinke of, that mote to her selfe pertaine.

XXIII

But as it falleth, in the gentlest harts
Imperious Loue hath highest set his throne,
And tyrannizeth in the bitter smarts
Of them, that to him buxome are and prone:
So thought this Mayd (as maydens vse to done)
Whom fortune for her husband would allot,
Not that she lusted after any one;
For she was pure from blame of sinfull blot,
Yet wist her life at last must lincke in that same knot.

XXIV

Eftsoones there was presented to her eye
A comely knight, all arm'd in complete wize,
Through whose bright ventayle lifted vp on hye
His manly face, that did his foes agrize,
And friends to termes of gentle truce entize,
Lookt foorth, as *Phœbus* face out of the east,
Betwixt two shadie mountaines doth arize;
Portly his person was, and much increast
Through his Heroicke grace, and honorable gest.

XXV

His crest was couered with a couchant Hound,
And all his armour seem'd of antique mould,
But wondrous massie and assured sound,
And round about yfretted all with gold,
In which there written was with cyphers old,
  Achilles armes, which Arthegall did win.
And on his shield enueloped seuenfold
He bore a crowned litle Ermilin,
That deckt the azure field with her faire pouldred skin.

XXVI

The Damzell well did vew his personage,
And liked well, ne further fastned not,
But went her way; ne her vnguilty age
Did weene, vnwares, that her vnlucky lot
Lay hidden in the bottome of the pot;
Of hurt vnwist most daunger doth redound:
But the false Archer, which that arrow shot
So slyly, that she did not feele the wound,
Did smyle full smoothly at her weetlesse wofull stound.

XXVII

Thenceforth the feather in her loftie crest,
Ruffed of loue, gan lowly to auaile,
And her proud portance, and her princely gest,
With which she earst tryumphed, now did quaile:
Sad, solemne, sowre, and full of fancies fraile
She woxe; yet wist she neither how, nor why,
She wist not, silly Mayd, what she did aile,
Yet wist, she was not well at ease perdy,
Yet thought it was not loue, but some melancholy.

XXVIII

So soone as Night had with her pallid hew
Defast the beautie of the shining sky,
And reft from men the worlds desired vew,
She with her Nourse adowne to sleepe did lye;
But sleepe full farre away from her did fly:
In stead thereof sad sighes, and sorrowes deepe
Kept watch and ward about her warily,
That nought she did but wayle, and often steepe
Her daintie couch with teares, which closely she did weepe.

XXIX

And if that any drop of slombring rest
Did chaunce to still into her wearie spright,
When feeble nature felt her selfe opprest,
Streight way with dreames, and with fantasticke sight
Of dreadfull things the same was put to flight,
That oft out of her bed she did astart,
As one with vew of ghastly feends affright:
Tho gan she to renew her former smart,
And thinke of that faire visage, written in her hart.

XXX

One night, when she was tost with such vnrest,
Her aged Nurse, whose name was *Glauce* hight,
Feeling her leape out of her loathed nest,
Betwixt her feeble armes her quickly keight,
And downe againe in her warme bed her dight;
Ah my deare daughter, ah my dearest dread,
What vncouth fit (said she) what euill plight
Hath thee opprest, and with sad drearyhead
Chaunged thy liuely cheare, and liuing made thee dead?

XXXI

For not of nought these suddeine ghastly feares
All night afflict thy naturall repose,
And all the day, when as thine equall peares
Their fit disports with faire delight doe chose,
Thou in dull corners doest thy selfe inclose,
Ne tastest Princes pleasures, ne doest spred
Abroad thy fresh youthes fairest flowre, but lose
Both leafe and fruit, both too vntimely shed,
As one in wilfull bale for euer buried.

XXXII

The time, that mortall men their weary cares
Do lay away, and all wilde beastes do rest,
And euery riuer eke his course forbeares,
Then doth this wicked euill thee infest,
And riue with thousand throbs thy thrilled brest;
Like an huge *Aetn'* of deepe engulfed griefe,
Sorrow is heaped in thy hollow chest,
Whence forth it breakes in sighes and anguish rife,
As smoke and sulphure mingled with confused strife.

XXXIII

Aye me, how much I feare, least loue it bee;
But if that loue it be, as sure I read
By knowen signes and passions, which I see,
Be it worthy of thy race and royall sead,
Then I auow by this most sacred head
Of my deare foster child, to ease thy griefe,
And win thy will: Therefore away doe dread;
For death nor daunger from thy dew reliefe
Shall me debarre, tell me therefore my liefest liefe.

XXXIV

So hauing said, her twixt her armes twaine
She straightly straynd, and colled tenderly,
And euery trembling ioynt, and euery vaine
She softly felt, and rubbed busily,
To doe the frosen cold away to fly;
And her faire deawy eies with kisses deare
She oft did bath, and oft againe did dry;
And euer her importund, not to feare
To let the secret of her hart to her appeare.

XXXV

The Damzell pauzd, and then thus fearefully;
Ah Nurse, what needeth thee to eke my paine?
Is not enough, that I alone doe dye,
But it must doubled be with death of twaine?
For nought for me but death there doth remaine.
O daughter deare (said she) despaire no whit;
For neuer sore, but might a salue obtaine:
That blinded God, which hath ye blindly smit,
Another arrow hath your louers hart to hit.

XXXVI

But mine is not (quoth she) like others wound;
For which no reason can find remedy.
Was neuer such, but mote the like be found,
(Said she) and though no reason may apply
Salue to your sore, yet loue can higher stye,
Then reasons reach, and oft hath wonders donne.
But neither God of loue, nor God of sky
Can doe (said she) that, which cannot be donne.
Things oft impossible (quoth she) seeme, ere begonne.

XXXVII

These idle words (said she) doe nought asswage
My stubborne smart, but more annoyance breed,
For no no vsuall fire, no vsuall rage
It is, O Nurse, which on my life doth feed,
And suckes the bloud, which from my hart doth bleed.
But since thy faithfull zeale lets me not hyde
My crime, (if crime it be) I will it reed.
Nor Prince, nor pere it is, whose loue hath gryde
My feeble brest of late, and launched this wound wyde.

XXXVIII

Nor man it is, nor other liuing wight;
For then some hope I might vnto me draw,
But th'only shade and semblant of a knight,
Whose shape or person yet I neuer saw,
Hath me subiected to loues cruell law:
The same one day, as me misfortune led,
I in my fathers wondrous mirrhour saw,
And pleased with that seeming goodly-hed,
Vnwares the hidden hooke with baite I swallowed.

XXXIX

Sithens it hath infixed faster hold
Within my bleeding bowels, and so sore
Now ranckleth in this same fraile fleshly mould,
That all mine entrailes flow with poysnous gore,
And th'vlcer groweth daily more and more;
Ne can my running sore find remedie,
Other then my hard fortune to deplore,
And languish as the leafe falne from the tree,
Till death make one end of my dayes and miserie.

XL

Daughter (said she) what need ye be dismayd,
Or why make ye such Monster of your mind?
Of much more vncouth thing I was affrayd;
Of filthy lust, contrarie vnto kind:
But this affection nothing straunge I find;
For who with reason can you aye reproue,
To loue the semblant pleasing most your mind,
And yield your heart, whence ye cannot remoue?
No guilt in you, but in the tyranny of loue.

XLI

Not so th'*Arabian Myrrhe* did set her mind;
Nor so did *Biblis* spend her pining hart,
But lou'd their natiue flesh against all kind,
And to their purpose vsed wicked art:
Yet playd *Pasiphae* a more monstrous part,
That lou'd a Bull, and learnd a beast to bee;
Such shamefull lusts who loaths not, which depart
From course of nature and of modestie?
Sweet loue such lewdnes bands from his faire companie.

XLII

But thine my Deare (welfare thy heart my deare)
Though strange beginning had, yet fixed is
On one, that worthy may perhaps appeare;
And certes seemes bestowed not amis:
Ioy thereof haue thou and eternall blis.
With that vpleaning on her elbow weake,
Her alablaster brest she soft did kis,
Which all that while she felt to pant and quake,
As it an Earth-quake were; at last she thus bespake.

XLIII

Beldame, your words doe worke me litle ease;
For though my loue be not so lewdly bent,
As those ye blame, yet may it nought appease
My raging smart, ne ought my flame relent,
But rather doth my helpelesse griefe augment.
For they, how euer shamefull and vnkind,
Yet did possesse their horrible intent:
Short end of sorrowes they thereby did find;
So was their fortune good, though wicked were their mind.

XLIV

But wicked fortune mine, though mind be good,
Can haue no end, nor hope of my desire,
But feed on shadowes, whiles I die for food,
And like a shadow wexe, whiles with entire
Affection, I doe languish and expire.
I fonder, then *Cephisus* foolish child,
Who hauing vewed in a fountaine shere
His face, was with the loue thereof beguild;
I fonder loue a shade, the bodie farre exild.

XLV

Nought like (quoth she) for that same wretched boy
Was of himselfe the idle Paramoure;
Both loue and louer, without hope of ioy,
For which he faded to a watry flowre.
But better fortune thine, and better howre,
Which lou'st the shadow of a warlike knight;
No shadow, but a bodie hath in powre:
That bodie, wheresoeuer that it light,
May learned be by cyphers, or by Magicke might.

XLVI

But if thou may with reason yet represse
The growing euill, ere it strength haue got,
And thee abandond wholly doe possesse,
Against it strongly striue, and yield thee not,
Till thou in open field adowne be smot.
But if the passion mayster thy fraile might,
So that needs loue or death must be thy lot,
Then I auow to thee, by wrong or right
To compasse thy desire, and find that loued knight.

XLVII

Her chearefull words much cheard the feeble spright
Of the sicke virgin, that her downe she layd
In her warme bed to sleepe, if that she might;
And the old-woman carefully displayd
The clothes about her round with busie ayd;
So that at last a little creeping sleepe
Surprisd her sense: She therewith well apayd,
The drunken lampe downe in the oyle did steepe,
And set her by to watch, and set her by to weepe.

XLVIII

Earely the morrow next, before that day
His ioyous face did to the world reueale,
They both vprose and tooke their readie way
Vnto the Church, their prayers to appeale,
With great deuotion, and with litle zeale:
For the faire Damzell from the holy herse
Her loue-sicke hart to other thoughts did steale;
And that old Dame said many an idle verse,
Out of her daughters hart fond fancies to reuerse.

XLIX

Returned home, the royall Infant fell
Into her former fit; for why, no powre
Nor guidance of her selfe in her did dwell.
But th'aged Nurse her calling to her bowre,
Had gathered Rew, and Sauine, and the flowre
Of *Camphora*, and Calamint, and Dill,
All which she in a earthen Pot did poure,
And to the brim with Colt wood did it fill,
And many drops of milke and bloud through it did spill.

L

Then taking thrise three haires from off her head,
Them trebly breaded in a threefold lace,
And round about the pots mouth, bound the thread,
And after hauing whispered a space
Certaine sad words, with hollow voice and bace,
She to the virgin said, thrise said she it;
Come daughter come, come; spit vpon my face,
Spit thrise vpon me, thrise vpon me spit;
Th'vneuen number for this businesse is most fit.

LI

That sayd, her round about she from her turnd,
She turned her contrarie to the Sunne,
Thrise she her turnd contrary, and returnd,
All contrary, for she the right did shunne,
And euer what she did, was streight vndonne.
So thought she to vndoe her daughters loue:
But loue, that is in gentle brest begonne,
No idle charmes so lightly may remoue,
That well can witnesse, who by triall it does proue.

LII

Ne ought it mote the noble Mayd auayle,
Ne slake the furie of her cruell flame,
But that she still did waste, and still did wayle,
That through long languour, and hart-burning brame
She shortly like a pyned ghost became,
Which long hath waited by the Stygian strond.
That when old *Glauce* saw, for feare least blame
Of her miscarriage should in her be fond,
She wist not how t'amend, nor how it to withstond.

Canto III

> *Merlin bewrayes to Britomart,*
> *the state of Artegall.*
> *And shewes the famous Progeny*
> *which from them springen shall.*

I

Most sacred fire, that burnest mightily
In liuing brests, ykindled first aboue,
Emongst th'eternall spheres and lamping sky,
And thence pourd into men, which men call Loue;
Not that same, which doth base affections moue
In brutish minds, and filthy lust inflame,
But that sweet fit, that doth true beautie loue,
And choseth vertue for his dearest Dame,
Whence spring all noble deeds and neuer dying fame:

II

Well did Antiquitie a God thee deeme,
That ouer mortall minds hast so great might,
To order them, as best to thee doth seeme,
And all their actions to direct aright;
The fatall purpose of diuine foresight,
Thou doest effect in destined descents,
Through deepe impression of thy secret might,
And stirredst vp th'Heroes high intents,
Which the late world admyres for wondrous moniments.

III

But thy dread darts in none doe triumph more,
Ne brauer proofe in any, of thy powre
Shew'dst thou, then in this royall Maid of yore,

Making her seeke an vnknowne Paramoure,
From the worlds end, through many a bitter stowre:
From whose two loynes thou afterwards did rayse
Most famous fruits of matrimoniall bowre,
Which through the earth haue spred their liuing prayse,
That fame in trompe of gold eternally displayes.

IV

Begin then, O my dearest sacred Dame,
Daughter of *Phœbus* and of *Memorie*,
That doest ennoble with immortall name
The warlike Worthies, from antiquitie,
In thy great volume of Eternitie:
Begin, O *Clio*, and recount from hence
My glorious Soueraines goodly auncestrie,
Till that by dew degrees and long protense,
Thou haue it lastly brought vnto her Excellence.

V

Full many wayes within her troubled mind,
Old *Glauce* cast, to cure this Ladies griefe:
Full many waies she sought, but none could find,
Nor herbes, nor charmes, nor counsell, that is chiefe
And choisest med'cine for sicke harts reliefe:
For thy great care she tooke, and greater feare,
Least that it should her turne to foule repriefe,
And sore reproch, when so her father deare
Should of his dearest daughters hard misfortune heare.

VI

At last she her auisd, that he, which made
That mirrhour, wherein the sicke Damosell
So straungely vewed her straunge louers shade,
To weet, the learned *Merlin*, well could tell,
Vnder what coast of heauen the man did dwell,
And by what meanes his loue might best be wrought:
For though beyond the *Africk Ismaell*,
Or th'Indian *Peru* he were, she thought
Him forth through infinite endeuour to haue sought.

VII

Forthwith themselues disguising both in straunge
And base attyre, that none might them bewray,

To *Maridunum*, that is now by chaunge
Of name *Cayr-Merdin* cald, they tooke their way:
There the wise *Merlin* whylome wont (they say)
To make his wonne, low vnderneath the ground,
In a deepe delue, farre from the vew of day,
That of no liuing wight he mote be found,
When so he counseld with his sprights encompast round.

VIII

And if thou euer happen that same way
To trauell, goe to see that dreadfull place:
It is an hideous hollow caue (they say)
Vnder a rocke that lyes a litle space
From the swift *Barry*, tombling downe apace,
Emongst the woodie hilles of *Dyneuowre*:
But dare thou not, I charge, in any cace,
To enter into that same balefull Bowre,
For fear the cruell Feends should thee vnwares deuowre.

IX

But standing high aloft, low lay thine eare,
And there such ghastly noise of yron chaines,
And brasen Caudrons thou shalt rombling heare,
Which thousand sprights with long enduring paines
Doe tosse, that it will stonne thy feeble braines,
And oftentimes great grones, and grieuous stounds,
When too huge toile and labour them constraines:
And oftentimes loud strokes, and ringing sounds
From vnder that deepe Rocke most horribly rebounds.

X

The cause some say is this: A litle while
Before that *Merlin* dyde, he did intend,
A brasen wall in compas to compile
About *Cairmardin*, and did it commend
Vnto these Sprights, to bring to perfect end.
During which worke the Ladie of the Lake,
Whom long he lou'd, for him in hast did send,
Who thereby forst his workemen to forsake,
Them bound till his returne, their labour not to slake.

XI

In the meane time through that false Ladies traine,
He was surprisd, and buried vnder beare,
Ne euer to his worke returnd againe:
Nath'lesse those feends may not their worke forbeare,
So greatly his commaundement they feare,
But there doe toyle and trauell day and night,
Vntill that brasen wall they vp doe reare:
For *Merlin* had in Magicke more insight,
Then euer him before or after liuing wight.

XII

For he by words could call out of the sky
Both Sunne and Moone, and make them him obay:
The land to sea, and sea to maineland dry,
And darkesome night he eke could turne to day:
Huge hostes of men he could alone dismay,
And hostes of men of meanest things could frame,
When so him list his enimies to fray:
That to this day for terror of his fame,
The feends do quake, when any him to them does name.

XIII

And sooth, men say that he was not the sonne
Of mortall Syre, or other liuing wight,
But wondrously begotten, and begonne
By false illusion of a guilefull Spright,
On a faire Ladie Nonne, that whilome hight
 Matilda, daughter to *Pubidius*,
Who was the Lord of *Mathrauall* by right,
And coosen vnto king *Ambrosius*:
Whence he indued was with skill so maruellous.

XIV

They here ariuing, staid a while without,
Ne durst aduenture rashly in to wend,
But of their first intent gan make new dout
For dread of daunger, which it might portend:
Vntill the hardie Mayd (with loue to frend)
First entering, the dreadfull Mage there found
Deepe busied bout worke of wondrous end,
And writing strange characters in the ground,
With which the stubborn feends he to his seruice bound.

XV

He nought was moued at their entrance bold:
For of their comming well he wist afore,
Yet list them bid their businesse to vnfold,
As if ought in this world in secret store
Were from him hidden, or vnknowne of yore.
Then *Glauce* thus, let not it thee offend,
That we thus rashly through thy darkesome dore,
Vnwares haue prest: for either fatall end,
Or other mightie cause vs two did hither send.

XVI

He bad tell on; And then she thus began.
Now haue three Moones with borrow'd brothers light,
Thrice shined faire, and thrice seem'd dim and wan,
Sith a sore euill, which this virgin bright
Tormenteth, and doth plonge in dolefull plight,
First rooting tooke; but what thing it mote bee,
Or whence it sprong, I cannot read aright:
But this I read, that but if remedee,
Thou her afford, full shortly I her dead shall see.

XVII

Therewith th'Enchaunter softly gan to smyle
At her smooth speeches, weeting inly well,
That she to him dissembled womanish guyle,
And to her said, Beldame, by that ye tell,
More need of leach-craft hath your Damozell,
Then of my skill: who helpe may haue elsewhere,
In vaine seekes wonders out of Magicke spell.
Th'old woman wox half blanck, those words to heare;
And yet was loth to let her purpose plaine appeare.

XVIII

And to him said, If any leaches skill,
Or other learned meanes could haue redrest
This my deare daughters deepe engraffed ill,
Certes I should be loth thee to molest:
But this sad euill, which doth her infest,
Doth course of naturall cause farre exceed,
And housed is within her hollow brest,
That either seemes some cursed witches deed,
Or euill spright, that in her doth such torment breed.

XIX

The wisard could no lenger beare her bord,
But brusting forth in laughter, to her sayd;
Glauce, what needs this colourable word,
To cloke the cause, that hath it selfe bewrayd?
Ne ye faire *Britomartis*, thus arayd,
More hidden are, then Sunne in cloudy vele;
Whom thy good fortune, hauing fate obayd,
Hath hither brought, for succour to appele:
The which the powres to thee are pleased to reuele.

XX

The doubtfull Mayd, seeing her selfe descryde,
Was all abasht, and her pure yuory
Into a cleare Carnation suddeine dyde;
As faire *Aurora* rising hastily,
Doth by her blushing tell, that she did lye
All night in old *Tithonus* frosen bed,
Whereof she seemes ashamed inwardly.
But her old Nourse was nought dishartened,
But vauntage made of that, which *Merlin* had ared.

XXI

And sayd, Sith then thou knowest all our griefe,
(For what doest not thou know?) of grace I pray,
Pitty our plaint, and yield vs meet reliefe.
With that the Prophet still awhile did stay,
And then his spirite thus gan forth display;
Most noble Virgin, that by fatall lore
Hast learn'd to loue, let no whit thee dismay
The hard begin, that meets thee in the dore,
And with sharpe fits thy tender hart oppresseth sore.

XXII

For so must all things excellent begin,
And eke enrooted deepe must be that Tree,
Whose big embodied braunches shall not lin,
Till they to heauens hight forth stretched bee.
For from thy wombe a famous Progenie
Shall spring, out of the auncient *Troian* blood,
Which shall reuiue the sleeping memorie
Of those same antique Peres, the heauens brood,
Which *Greeke* and *Asian* riuers stained with their blood.

XXIII

Renowmed kings, and sacred Emperours,
Thy fruitfull Ofspring, shall from thee descend;
Braue Captaines, and most mighty warriours,
That shall their conquests through all lands extend,
And their decayed kingdomes shall amend:
The feeble Britons, broken with long warre,
They shall vpreare, and mightily defend
Against their forrein foe, that comes from farre,
Till vniuersall peace compound all ciuill iarre.

XXIV

It was not, *Britomart*, thy wandring eye,
Glauncing vnwares in charmed looking glas,
But the streight course of heauenly destiny,
Led with eternall prouidence, that has
Guided thy glaunce, to bring his will to pas:
Ne is thy fate, ne is thy fortune ill,
To loue the prowest knight, that euer was.
Therefore submit thy wayes vnto his will,
And do by all dew meanes thy destiny fulfill.

XXV

But read (said *Glauce*) thou Magitian
What meanes shall she out seeke, or what wayes take?
How shall she know, how shall she find the man?
Or what needs her to toyle, sith fates can make
Way for themselues, their purpose to partake?
Then *Merlin* thus; **Indeed the fates are firme,**
And may not shrinck, though all the world do shake:
Yet ought mens good endeuours them confirme,
And guide the heauenly causes to their constant terme.

XXVI

The man whom heauens haue ordaynd to bee
The spouse of *Britomart*, is *Arthegall*:
He wonneth in the land of *Fayeree*,
Yet is no *Fary* borne, ne sib at all
To Elfes, but sprong of seed terrestriall,
And whilome by false *Faries* stolne away,
Whiles yet in infant cradle he did crall;
Ne other to himselfe is knowne this day,
But that he by an Elfe was gotten of a *Fay*.

XXVII

But sooth he is the sonne of *Gorlois*,
And brother vnto *Cador* Cornish king,
And for his warlike feates renowmed is,
From where the day out of the sea doth spring,
Vntill the closure of the Euening.
From thence, him firmely bound with faithfull band,
To this his natiue soyle thou backe shalt bring,
Strongly to aide his countrey, to withstand
The powre of forrein Paynims, which inuade thy land.

XXVIII

Great aid thereto his mighty puissaunce,
And dreaded name shall giue in that sad day:
Where also proofe of thy prow valiaunce
Thou then shalt make, t'increase thy louers pray.
Long time ye both in armes shall beare great sway,
Till thy wombes burden thee from them do call,
And his last fate him from thee take away,
Too rathe cut off by practise criminall
Of secret foes, that him shall make in mischiefe fall.

XXIX

With thee yet shall he leaue for memory
Of his late puissaunce, his Image dead,
That liuing him in all actiuity
To thee shall represent. He from the head
Of his coosin *Constantius* without dread
Shall take the crowne, that was his fathers right,
And therewith crowne himselfe in th'others stead:
Then shall he issew forth with dreadfull might,
Against his Saxon foes in bloudy field to fight.

XXX

Like as a Lyon, that in drowsie caue
Hath long time slept, himselfe so shall he shake,
And comming forth, shall spred his banner braue
Ouer the troubled South, that it shall make
The warlike *Mertians* for feare to quake:
Thrise shall he fight with them, and twise shall win,
But the third time shall faire accordaunce make:
And if he then with victorie can lin,
He shall his dayes with peace bring to his earthly In.

XXXI

His sonne, hight *Vortipore*, shall him succeede
In kingdome, but not in felicity;
Yet shall he long time warre with happy speed,
And with great honour many battels try:
But at the last to th'importunity
Of froward fortune shall be forst to yield.
But his sonne *Malgo* shall full mightily
Auenge his fathers losse, with speare and shield,
And his proud foes discomfit in victorious field.

XXXII

Behold the man, and tell me *Britomart*,
If ay more goodly creature thou didst see;
How like a Gyaunt in each manly part
Beares he himselfe with portly maiestee,
That one of th'old *Heroes* seemes to bee:
He the six Islands, comprouinciall
In auncient times vnto great Britainee,
Shall to the same reduce, and to him call
Their sundry kings to do their homage seuerall.

XXXIII

All which his sonne *Careticus* awhile
Shall well defend, and *Saxons* powre suppresse,
Vntill a straunger king from vnknowne soyle
Arriuing, him with multitude oppresse;
Great *Gormond*, hauing with huge mightinesse
Ireland subdewd, and therein fixt his throne,
Like a swift Otter, fell through emptinesse,
Shall ouerswim the sea with many one
Of his Norueyses, to assist the Britons fone.

XXXIV

He in his furie all shall ouerrunne,
And holy Church with faithlesse hands deface,
That thy sad people vtterly fordonne,
Shall to the vtmost mountaines fly apace:
Was neuer so great wast in any place,
Nor so fowle outrage doen by liuing men:
For all thy Cities they shall sacke and race,
And the greene grasse, that groweth, they shall bren,
That euen the wild beast shall dy in starued den.

XXXV

Whiles thus thy Britons do in languour pine,
Proud *Etheldred* shall from the North arise,
Seruing th'ambitious will of *Augustine*,
And passing *Dee* with hardy enterprise,
Shall backe repulse the valiaunt *Brockwell* twise,
And *Bangor* with massacred Martyrs fill;
But the third time shall rew his foolhardise:
For *Cadwan* pittying his peoples ill,
Shall stoutly him defeat, and thousand *Saxons* kill.

XXXVI

But after him, *Cadwallin* mightily
On his sonne *Edwin* all those wrongs shall wreake;
Ne shall auaile the wicked sorcery
Of false *Pellite*, his purposes to breake,
But him shall slay, and on a gallowes bleake
Shall giue th'enchaunter his vnhappy hire;
Then shall the Britons, late dismayd and weake,
From their long vassalage gin to respire,
And on their Paynim foes auenge their ranckled ire.

XXXVII

Ne shall he yet his wrath so mitigate,
Till both the sonnes of *Edwin* he haue slaine,
Offricke and *Osricke*, twinnes vnfortunate,
Both slaine in battell vpon Layburne plaine,
Together with the king of *Louthiane*,
Hight *Adin*, and the king of *Orkeny*,
Both ioynt partakers of their fatall paine:
But *Penda*, fearefull of like desteny,
Shall yield him selfe his liegeman, and sweare fealty.

XXXVIII

Him shall he make his fatall Instrument,
T'afflict the other *Saxons* vnsubdewd;
He marching forth with fury insolent
Against the good king *Oswald*, who indewd
With heauenly powre, and by Angels reskewd,
All holding crosses in their hands on hye,
Shall him defeate withouten bloud imbrewd:
Of which, that field for endlesse memory,
Shall *Heuenfield* be cald to all posterity.

XXXIX

Whereat *Cadwallin* wroth, shall forth issew,
And an huge hoste into Northumber lead,
With which he godly *Oswald* shall subdew,
And crowne with martyrdome his sacred head.
Whose brother *Oswin*, daunted with like dread,
With price of siluer shall his kingdome buy,
And *Penda*, seeking him adowne to tread,
Shall tread adowne, and do him fowly dye,
But shall with gifts his Lord *Cadwallin* pacify.

XL

Then shall *Cadwallin* dye, and then the raine
Of *Britons* eke with him attonce shall dye;
Ne shall the good *Cadwallader* with paine,
Or powre, be hable it to remedy,
When the full time prefixt by destiny,
Shalbe expird of *Britons* regiment.
For heauen it selfe shall their successe enuy,
And them with plagues and murrins pestilent
Consume, till all their warlike puissaunce be spent.

XLI

Yet after all these sorrowes, and huge hills
Of dying people, during eight yeares space,
Cadwallader not yielding to his ills,
From *Armoricke*, where long in wretched cace
He liu'd, returning to his natiue place,
Shalbe by vision staid from his intent:
For th'heauens haue decreed, to displace
The *Britons*, for their sinnes dew punishment,
And to the *Saxons* ouer-giue their gouernment.

XLII

Then woe, and woe, and euerlasting woe,
Be to the Briton babe, that shalbe borne,
To liue in thraldome of his fathers foe;
Late King, now captiue, late Lord, now forlorne,
The worlds reproch, the cruell victours scorne,
Banisht from Princely bowre to wastfull wood:
O who shall helpe me to lament, and mourne
The royall seed, the antique *Troian* blood,
Whose Empire lenger here, then euer any stood.

XLIII

The Damzell was full deepe empassioned,
Both for his griefe, and for her peoples sake,
Whose future woes so plaine he fashioned,
And sighing sore, at length him thus bespake;
Ah but will heauens fury neuer slake,
Nor vengeaunce huge relent it selfe at last?
Will not long misery late mercy make,
But shall their name for euer be defast,
And quite from of the earth their memory be rast?

XLIV

Nay but the terme (said he) is limited,
That in this thraldome *Britons* shall abide,
And the iust reuolution measured,
That they as Straungers shalbe notifide.
For twise foure hundredth yeares shalbe supplide,
Ere they to former rule restor'd shalbee,
And their importune fates all satisfide:
Yet during this their most obscuritee,
Their beames shall oft breake forth, that men them faire may see.

XLV

For *Rhodoricke*, whose surname shalbe Great,
Shall of him selfe a braue ensample shew,
That Saxon kings his friendship shall intreat;
And *Howell Dha* shall goodly well indew
The saluage minds with skill of iust and trew;
Then *Griffyth Conan* also shall vp reare
His dreaded head, and the old sparkes renew
Of natiue courage, that his foes shall feare,
Least backe againe the kingdome he from them should beare.

XLVI

Ne shall the Saxons selues all peaceably
Enioy the crowne, which they from Britons wonne
First ill, and after ruled wickedly:
For ere two hundred yeares be full outronne,
There shall a Rauen far from rising Sunne,
With his wide wings vpon them fiercely fly,
And bid his faithlesse chickens ouerronne
The fruitfull plaines, and with fell cruelty,
In their auenge, tread downe the victours surquedry.

XLVII

Yet shall a third both these, and thine subdew;
There shall a Lyon from the sea-bord wood
Of *Neustria* come roring, with a crew
Of hungry whelpes, his battailous bold brood,
Whose clawes were newly dipt in cruddy blood,
That from the Daniske Tyrants head shall rend
Th'vsurped crowne, as if that he were wood,
And the spoile of the countrey conquered
Emongst his young ones shall diuide with bountyhed.

XLVIII

Tho when the terme is full accomplishid,
There shall a sparke of fire, which hath long-while
Bene in his ashes raked vp, and hid,
Be freshly kindled in the fruitfull Ile
Of *Mona*, where it lurked in exile;
Which shall breake forth into bright burning flame,
And reach into the house, that beares the stile
Of royall maiesty and soueraigne name;
So shall the Briton bloud their crowne againe reclame.

XLIX

Thenceforth eternall vnion shall be made
Betweene the nations different afore,
And sacred Peace shall louingly perswade
The warlike minds, to learne her goodly lore,
And ciuile armes to exercise no more:
Then shall a royall virgin raine, which shall
Stretch her white rod ouer the *Belgicke* shore,
And the great Castle smite so sore with all,
That it shall make him shake, and shortly learne to fall.

L

But yet the end is not. There *Merlin* stayd,
As ouercomen of the spirites powre,
Or other ghastly spectacle dismayd,
That secretly he saw, yet note discoure:
Which suddein fit, and halfe extatick stoure
When the two fearefull women saw, they grew
Greatly confused in behauioure;
At last the fury past, to former hew
Hee turnd againe, and chearefull looks as earst did shew.

LI

Then, when them selues they well instructed had
Of all, that needed them to be inquird,
They both conceiuing hope of comfort glad,
With lighter hearts vnto their home retird;
Where they in secret counsell close conspird,
How to effect so hard an enterprize,
And to possesse the purpose they desird:
Now this, now that twixt them they did deuise,
And diuerse plots did frame, to maske in strange disguise.

LII

At last the Nourse in her foolhardy wit
Conceiu'd a bold deuise, and thus bespake;
Daughter, I deeme that counsell aye most fit,
That of the time doth dew aduauntage take;
Ye see that good king *Vther* now doth make
Strong warre vpon the Paynim brethren, hight
Octa and *Oza*, whom he lately brake
Beside *Cayr Verolame*, in victorious fight,
That now all *Britanie* doth burne in armes bright.

LIII

That therefore nought our passage may empeach,
Let vs in feigned armes our selues disguize,
And our weake hands (whom need new strength shall teach)
The dreadfull speare and shield to exercize:
Ne certes daughter that same warlike wize
I weene, would you misseeme; for ye bene tall,
And large of limbe, t'atchieue an hard emprize,
Ne ought ye want, but skill, which practize small
Will bring, and shortly make you a mayd Martiall.

LIV

And sooth, it ought your courage much inflame,
To heare so often, in that royall hous,
From whence to none inferiour ye came:
Bards tell of many women valorous
Which haue full many feats aduenturous
Performd, in paragone of proudest men:
The bold *Bunduca*, whose victorious
Exploits made *Rome* to quake, stout *Guendolen*,
Renowmed *Martia*, and redoubted *Emmilen*.

LV

And that, which more then all the rest may sway,
Late dayes ensample, which these eyes beheld,
In the last field before *Meneuia*
Which *Vther* with those forrein Pagans held,
I saw a *Saxon* Virgin, the which feld
Great *Vlfin* thrise vpon the bloudy plaine,
And had not *Carados* her hand withheld
From rash reuenge, she had him surely slaine,
Yet *Carados* himselfe from her escapt with paine.

LVI

Ah read, (quoth *Britomart*) how is she hight?
Faire *Angela* (quoth she) men do her call,
No whit lesse faire, then terrible in fight:
She hath the leading of a Martiall
And mighty people, dreaded more then all
The other *Saxons*, which do for her sake
And loue, themselues of her name *Angles* call.
Therefore faire Infant her ensample make
Vnto thy selfe, and equall courage to thee take.

LVII

Her harty words so deepe into the mynd
Of the young Damzell sunke, that great desire
Of warlike armes in her forthwith they tynd,
And generous stout courage did inspire,
That she resolu'd, vnweeting to her Sire,
Aduent'rous knighthood on her selfe to don,
And counseld with her Nourse, her Maides attire
To turne into a massy habergeon,
And bad her all things put in readinesse anon.

LVIII

Th' old woman nought, that needed, did omit;
But all things did conueniently puruay:
It fortuned (so time their turne did fit)
A band of Britons ryding on forray
Few dayes before, had gotten a great pray
Of Saxon goods, emongst the which was seene
A goodly Armour, and full rich aray,
Which long'd to *Angela*, the Saxon Queene,
All fretted round with gold, and goodly well beseene.

LIX

The same, with all the other ornaments,
King *Ryence* caused to be hanged hy
In his chiefe Church, for endlesse moniments
Of his successe and gladfull victory:
Of which her selfe auising readily,
In th'euening late old *Glauce* thither led
Faire *Britomart*, and that same Armory
Downe taking, her therein appareled,
Well as she might, and with braue bauldrick garnished.

LX

Beside those armes there stood a mighty speare,
Which *Bladud* made by Magick art of yore,
And vsd the same in battell aye to beare;
Sith which it had bin here preseru'd in store,
For his great vertues proued long afore:
For neuer wight so fast in sell could sit,
But him perforce vnto the ground it bore:
Both speare she tooke, and shield, which hong by it:
Both speare and shield of great powre, for her purpose fit.

LXI

Thus when she had the virgin all arayd,
Another harnesse, which did hang thereby,
About her selfe she dight, that the young Mayd
She might in equall armes accompany,
And as her Squire attend her carefully:
Tho to their ready Steeds they clombe full light,
And through back wayes, that none might them espy,
Couered with secret cloud of silent night,
Themselues they forth conuayd, and passed forward right.

LXII

Ne rested they, till that to Faery lond
They came, as *Merlin* them directed late:
Where meeting with this *Redcrosse* knight, she fond
Of diuerse things discourses to dilate,
But most of *Arthegall*, and his estate.
At last their wayes so fell, that they mote part:
Then each to other well affectionate,
Friendship professed with vnfained hart,
The *Redcrosse* knight diuerst, but forth rode *Britomart*.

Canto IV

Bold Marinell of Britomart,
Is throwne on the Rich strond:
Faire Florimell of Arthur is
Long followed, but not fond.

I

WHere is the Antique glory now become,
That whilome wont in women to appeare?
Where be the braue atchieuements doen by some?
Where be the battels, where the shield and speare,
And all the conquests, which them high did reare,
That matter made for famous Poets verse,
And boastfull men so oft abasht to heare?
Bene they all dead, and laid in dolefull herse?
Or doen they onely sleepe, and shall againe reuerse?

II

If they be dead, then woe is me therefore:
But if they sleepe, O let them soone awake:
For all too long I burne with enuy sore,
To heare the warlike feates, which *Homere* spake
Of bold *Pænthesilee*, which made a lake
Of *Greekish* bloud so oft in *Troian* plaine;
But when I read, how stout *Debora* strake
Proud *Sisera*, and how *Camill'* hath slaine
The huge *Orsilochus*, I swell with great disdaine.

III

Yet these, and all that else had puissaunce,
Cannot with noble *Britomart* compare,
Aswell for glory of great valiaunce,
As for pure chastitie and vertue rare,
That all her goodly deeds do well declare.
Well worthy stock, from which the branches sprong,
That in late yeares so faire a blossome bare,
As thee, O Queene, the matter of my song,
Whose lignage from this Lady I deriue along.

IV

Who when through speaches with the *Redcrosse* knight,
She learned had th'estate of *Arthegall*,
And in each point her selfe informd aright,

A friendly league of loue perpetuall
She with him bound, and *Congé* tooke withall.
Then he forth on his iourney did proceede,
To seeke aduentures, which mote him befall,
And win him worship through his warlike deed,
Which alwayes of his paines he made the chiefest meed.

V

But *Britomart* kept on her former course,
Ne euer dofte her armes, but all the way
Grew pensiue through that amorous discourse,
By which the *Redcrosse* knight did earst display
Her louers shape, and cheualrous aray;
A thousand thoughts she fashioned in her mind,
And in her feigning fancie did pourtray
Him such, as fittest she for loue could find,
Wise, warlike, personable, curteous, and kind.

VI

With such selfe-pleasing thoughts her wound she fed,
And thought so to beguile her grieuous smart;
But so her smart was much more grieuous bred,
And the deepe wound more deepe engord her hart,
That nought but death her dolour mote depart.
So forth she rode without repose or rest,
Searching all lands and each remotest part,
Following the guidaunce of her blinded guest,
Till that to the sea-coast at length she her addrest.

VII

There she alighted from her light-foot beast,
And sitting downe vpon the rocky shore,
Bad her old Squire vnlace her lofty creast;
Tho hauing vewd a while the surges hore,
That gainst the craggy clifts did loudly rore,
And in their raging surquedry disdaynd,
That the fast earth affronted them so sore,
And their deuouring couetize restraynd,
Thereat she sighed deepe, and after thus complaynd.

VIII

Huge sea of sorrow, and tempestuous griefe,
Wherein my feeble barke is tossed long,

Far from the hoped hauen of reliefe,
Why do thy cruell billowes beat so strong,
And thy moyst mountaines each on others throng,
Threatning to swallow vp my fearefull life?
O do thy cruell wrath and spightfull wrong
At length allay, and stint thy stormy strife,
Which in these troubled bowels raignes, and rageth rife.

IX

For else my feeble vessell crazd, and crackt
Through thy strong buffets and outrageous blowes,
Cannot endure, but needs it must be wrackt
On the rough rocks, or on the sandy shallowes,
The whiles that loue it steres, and fortune rowes;
Loue my lewd Pilot hath a restlesse mind
And fortune Boteswaine no assuraunce knowes,
But saile withouten starres, gainst tide and wind:
How can they other do, sith both are bold and blind?

X

Thou God of winds, that raignest in the seas,
That raignest also in the Continent,
At last blow vp some gentle gale of ease,
The which may bring my ship, ere it be rent,
Vnto the gladsome port of her intent:
Then when I shall my selfe in safety see,
A table for eternall moniment
Of thy great grace, and my great ieopardee,
Great *Neptune*, I auow to hallow vnto thee.

XI

Then sighing softly sore, and inly deepe,
She shut vp all her plaint in priuy griefe;
For her great courage would not let her weepe,
Till that old *Glauce* gan with sharpe repriefe,
Her to restraine, and giue her good reliefe,
Through hope of those, which *Merlin* had her told
Should of her name and nation be chiefe,
And fetch their being from the sacred mould
Of her immortall wombe, to be in heauen enrold.

XII

Thus as she her recomforted, she spyde,
Where farre away one all in armour bright,
With hastie gallop towards her did ryde;
Her dolour soone she ceast, and on her dight
Her Helmet, to her Courser mounting light:
Her former sorrow into suddein wrath,
Both coosen passions of distroubled spright,
Conuerting, forth she beates the dustie path;
Loue and despight attonce her courage kindled hath.

XIII

As when a foggy mist hath ouercast
The face of heauen, and the cleare aire engrost,
The world in darkenesse dwels, till that at last
The watry Southwinde from the seabord cost
Vpblowing, doth disperse the vapour lo'st,
And poures it selfe forth in a stormy showre;
So the faire *Britomart* hauing disclo'st
Her clowdy care into a wrathfull stowre,
The mist of griefe dissolu'd, did into vengeance powre.

XIV

Eftsoones her goodly shield addressing faire,
That mortall speare she in her hand did take,
And vnto battell did her selfe prepaire.
The knight approching, sternely her bespake;
Sir knight, that doest thy voyage rashly make
By this forbidden way in my despight,
Ne doest by others death ensample take,
I read thee soone retyre, whiles thou hast might,
Least afterwards it be too late to take thy flight.

XV

Ythrild with deepe disdaine of his proud threat,
She shortly thus; Fly they, that need to fly;
Words fearen babes. I meane not thee entreat
To passe; but maugre thee will passe or dy.
Ne lenger stayd for th'other to reply,
But with sharpe speare the rest made dearly knowne.
Strongly the straunge knight ran, and sturdily
Strooke her full on the brest, that made her downe
Decline her head, and touch her crouper with her crowne.

XVI

But she againe him in the shield did smite
With so fierce furie and great puissaunce,
That through his threesquare scuchin percing quite,
And through his mayled hauberque, by mischaunce
The wicked steele through his left side did glaunce;
Him so transfixed she before her bore
Beyond his croupe, the length of all her launce,
Till sadly soucing on the sandie shore,
He tombled on an heape, and wallowd in his gore.

XVII

Like as the sacred Oxe, that carelesse stands,
With gilden hornes, and flowry girlonds crownd,
Proud of his dying honor and deare bands,
Whiles th'altars fume with frankincense arownd,
All suddenly with mortall stroke astownd,
Doth groueling fall, and with his streaming gore
Distaines the pillours, and the holy grownd,
And the faire flowres, that decked him afore;
So fell proud *Marinell* vpon the pretious shore.

XVIII

The martiall Mayd stayd not him to lament,
But forward rode, and kept her readie way
Along the strond, which as she ouer-went,
She saw bestrowed all with rich aray
Of pearles and pretious stones of great assay,
And all the grauell mixt with golden owre;
Whereat she wondred much, but would not stay
For gold, or perles, or pretious stones an howre,
But them despised all; for all was in her powre.

XIX

Whiles thus he lay in deadly stonishment,
Tydings hereof came to his mothers eare;
His mother was the blacke-browd *Cymoent*,
The daughter of great *Nereus*, which did beare
This warlike sonne vnto an earthly peare,
The famous *Dumarin*; who on a day
Finding the Nymph a sleepe in secret wheare,
As he by chaunce did wander that same way,
Was taken with her loue, and by her closely lay.

XX

There he this knight of her begot, whom borne
She of his father *Marinell* did name,
And in a rocky caue as wight forlorne,
Long time she fostred vp, till he became
A mightie man at armes, and mickle fame
Did get through great aduentures by him donne:
For neuer man he suffred by that same
 Rich strond to trauell, whereas he did wonne,
But that he must do battell with the Sea-nymphes sonne.

XXI

An hundred knights of honorable name
He had subdew'd, and them his vassals made,
That through all Farie lond his noble fame
Now blazed was, and feare did all inuade,
That none durst passen through that perilous glade.
And to aduance his name and glorie more,
Her Sea-god syre she dearely did perswade,
T'endow her sonne with threasure and rich store,
Boue all the sonnes, that were of earthly wombes ybore.

XXII

The God did graunt his daughters deare demaund,
To doen his Nephew in all riches flow;
Eftsoones his heaped waues he did commaund,
Out of their hollow bosome forth to throw
All the huge threasure, which the sea below
Had in his greedie gulfe deuoured deepe,
And him enriched through the ouerthrow
And wreckes of many wretches, which did weepe,
And often waile their wealth, which he from them did keepe.

XXIII

Shortly vpon that shore there heaped was,
Exceeding riches and all pretious things,
The spoyle of all the world, that it did pas
The wealth of th'East, and pompe of *Persian* kings;
Gold, amber, yuorie, perles, owches, rings,
And all that else was pretious and deare,
The sea vnto him voluntary brings,
That shortly he a great Lord did appeare,
As was in all the lond of Faery, or elsewheare.

XXIV

Thereto he was a doughtie dreaded knight,
Tryde often to the scath of many deare,
That none in equall armes him matchen might,
The which his mother seeing, gan to feare
Least his too haughtie hardines might reare
Some hard mishap, in hazard of his life:
For thy she oft him counseld to forbeare
The bloudie battell, and to stirre vp strife,
But after all his warre, to rest his wearie knife.

XXV

And for his more assurance, she inquir'd
One day of *Proteus* by his mightie spell,
(For *Proteus* was with prophecie inspir'd)
Her deare sonnes destinie to her to tell,
And the sad end of her sweet *Marinell*.
Who through foresight of his eternall skill,
Bad her from womankind to keepe him well:
For of a woman he should haue much ill,
A virgin strange and stout him should dismay, or kill.

XXVI

For thy she gaue him warning euery day,
The loue of women not to entertaine;
A lesson too too hard for liuing clay,
From loue in course of nature to refraine:
Yet he his mothers lore did well retaine,
And euer from faire Ladies loue did fly;
Yet many Ladies faire did oft complaine,
That they for loue of him would algates dy:
Dy, who so list for him, he was loues enimy.

XXVII

But ah, who can deceiue his destiny,
Or weene by warning to auoyd his fate?
That when he sleepes in most security,
And safest seemes, him soonest doth amate,
And findeth dew effect or soone or late.
So feeble is the powre of fleshly arme.
His mother bad him womens loue to hate,
For she of womans force did feare no harme;
So weening to haue arm'd him, she did quite disarme.

XXVIII

This was that woman, this that deadly wound,
That *Proteus* prophecide should him dismay,
The which his mother vainely did expound,
To be hart-wounding loue, which should assay
To bring her sonne vnto his last decay.
So tickle be the termes of mortall state,
And full of subtile sophismes, which do play
With double senses, and with false debate,
T'approue the vnknowen purpose of eternall fate.

XXIX

Too true the famous *Marinell* it fownd,
Who through late triall, on that wealthy Strond
Inglorious now lies in senselesse swownd,
Through heauy stroke of *Britomartis* hond.
Which when his mother deare did vnderstond,
And heauy tydings heard, whereas she playd
Amongst her watry sisters by a pond,
Gathering sweet daffadillyes, to haue made
Gay girlonds, from the Sun their forheads faire to shade.

XXX

Eftsoones both flowres and girlonds farre away
She flong, and her faire deawy lockes yrent,
To sorrow huge she turnd her former play,
And gamesom merth to grieuous dreriment:
She threw her selfe downe on the Continent,
Ne word did speake, but lay as in a swowne,
Whiles all her sisters did for her lament,
With yelling outcries, and with shrieking sowne;
And euery one did teare her girlond from her crowne.

XXXI

Soone as she vp out of her deadly fit
Arose, she bad her charet to be brought,
And all her sisters, that with her did sit,
Bad eke attonce their charets to be sought;
Tho full of bitter griefe and pensiue thought,
She to her wagon clombe; clombe all the rest,
And forth together went, with sorrow fraught.
The waues obedient to their beheast,
Them yielded readie passage, and their rage surceast.

XXXII

Great *Neptune* stood amazed at their sight,
Whiles on his broad round backe they softly slid
And eke himselfe mournd at their mournfull plight,
Yet wist not what their wailing ment, yet did
For great compassion of their sorrow, bid
His mightie waters to them buxome bee:
Eftsoones the roaring billowes still abid,
And all the griesly Monsters of the See
Stood gaping at their gate, and wondred them to see.

XXXIII

A teme of Dolphins raunged in aray,
Drew the smooth charet of sad *Cymoent*;
They were all taught by *Triton*, to obay
To the long raynes, at her commaundement:
As swift as swallowes, on the waues they went,
That their broad flaggie finnes no fome did reare,
Ne bubbling roundell they behind them sent;
The rest of other fishes drawen weare,
Which with their finny oars the swelling sea did sheare.

XXXIV

Soone as they bene arriu'd vpon the brim
Of the *Rich strond*, their charets they forlore,
And let their temed fishes softly swim
Along the margent of the fomy shore,
Least they their finnes should bruze, and surbate sore
Their tender feet vpon the stony ground:
And comming to the place, where all in gore
And cruddy bloud enwallowed they found
The lucklesse *Marinell*, lying in deadly swound;

XXXV

His mother swowned thrise, and the third time
Could scarce recouered be out of her paine;
Had she not bene deuoyd of mortall slime,
She should not then haue bene reliu'd againe,
But soone as life recouered had the raine,
She made so piteous mone and deare wayment,
That the hard rocks could scarse from teares refraine,
And all her sister Nymphes with one consent
Supplide her sobbing breaches with sad complement.

XXXVI

Deare image of my selfe (she said) that is,
The wretched sonne of wretched mother borne,
Is this thine high aduauncement, O is this
Th'immortall name, with which thee yet vnborne
Thy Gransire *Nereus* promist to adorne?
Now lyest thou of life and honor reft;
Now lyest thou a lumpe of earth forlorne,
Ne of thy late life memory is left,
Ne can thy irreuocable destiny be weft?

XXXVII

Fond *Proteus*, father of false prophecis,
And they more fond, that credit to thee giue,
Not this the worke of womans hand ywis,
That so deepe wound through these deare members driue.
I feared loue: but they that loue do liue,
But they that die, doe neither loue nor hate.
Nath'lesse to thee thy folly I forgiue,
And to my selfe, and to accursed fate
The guilt I doe ascribe: deare wisedome bought too late.

XXXVIII

O what auailes it of immortall seed
To beene ybred and neuer borne to die?
Farre better I it deeme to die with speed,
Then waste in woe and wailefull miserie.
Who dyes the vtmost dolour doth abye,
But who that liues, is left to waile his losse:
So life is losse, and death felicitie.
Sad life worse then glad death: and greater crosse
To see friends graue, then dead the graue selfe to engrosse.

XXXIX

But if the heauens did his dayes enuie,
And my short blisse maligne, yet mote they well
Thus much afford me, ere that he did die
That the dim eyes of my deare *Marinell*
I mote haue closed, and him bed farewell,
Sith other offices for mother meet
They would not graunt.
Yet maulgre them farewell, my sweetest sweet;
Farewell my sweetest sonne, sith we no more shall meet.

XL

Thus when they all had sorrowed their fill,
They softly gan to search his griesly wound:
And that they might him handle more at will,
They him disarm'd, and spredding on the ground
Their watchet mantles frindgd with siluer round,
They softly wipt away the gelly blood
From th'orifice; which hauing well vpbound,
They pourd in soueraine balme, and Nectar good,
Good both for earthly med'cine, and for heauenly food.

XLI

Tho when the lilly handed *Liagore*,
(This *Liagore* whylome had learned skill
In leaches craft, by great *Appolloes* lore,
Sith her whylome vpon the high *Pindus* hill,
He loued, and at last her wombe did fill
With heauenly seed, whereof wise *Paeon* sprong)
Did feele his pulse, she knew there staied still
Some litle life his feeble sprites emong;
Which to his mother told, despeire she from her flong.

XLII

Tho vp him taking in their tender hands,
They easily vnto her charet beare:
Her teme at her commaundement quiet stands,
Whiles they the corse into her wagon reare,
And strow with flowres the lamentable beare:
Then all the rest into their coches clim,
And through the brackish waues their passage sheare;
Vpon great *Neptunes* necke they softly swim,
And to her watry chamber swiftly carry him.

XLIII

Deepe in the bottome of the sea, her bowre
Is built of hollow billowes heaped hye,
Like to thicke cloudes, that threat a stormy showre,
And vauted all within, like to the sky,
In which the Gods do dwell eternally:
There they him laid in easie couch well dight;
And sent in haste for *Tryphon*, to apply
Salues to his wounds, and medicines of might:
For *Tryphon* of sea gods the soueraine leach is hight.

XLIV

The whiles the *Nymphes* sit all about him round,
Lamenting his mishap and heauy plight;
And oft his mother vewing his wide wound,
Cursed the hand, that did so deadly smight
Her dearest sonne, her dearest harts delight.
But none of all those curses ouertooke
The warlike Maid, th'ensample of that might,
But fairely well she thriu'd, and well did brooke
Her noble deeds, ne her right course for ought forsooke.

XLV

Yet did false *Archimage* her still pursew,
To bring to passe his mischieuous intent,
Now that he had her singled from the crew
Of courteous knights, the Prince, and Faery gent,
Whom late in chace of beautie excellent
She left, pursewing that same foster strong;
Of whose foule outrage they impatient,
And full of fiery zeale, him followed long,
To reskew her from shame, and to reuenge her wrong.

XLVI

Through thick and thin, through mountaines and through plains,
Those two great champions did attonce pursew
The fearefull damzell, with incessant paines:
Who from them fled, as light-foot hare from vew
Of hunter swift, and sent of houndes trew.
At last they came vnto a double way,
Where, doubtfull which to take, her to reskew,
Themselues they did dispart, each to assay,
Whether more happie were, to win so goodly pray.

XLVII

But *Timias*, the Princes gentle Squire,
That Ladies loue vnto his Lord forlent,
And with proud enuy, and indignant ire,
After that wicked foster fiercely went.
So beene they three three sundry wayes ybent.
But fairest fortune to the Prince befell,
Whose chaunce it was, that soone he did repent,
To take that way, in which that Damozell
Was fled afore, affraid of him, as feend of hell.

XLVIII

At last of her farre off he gained vew:
Then gan he freshly pricke his fomy steed,
And euer as he nigher to her drew,
So euermore he did increase his speed,
And of each turning still kept warie heed:
Aloud to her he oftentimes did call,
To doe away vaine doubt, and needlesse dreed:
Full myld to her he spake, and oft let fall
Many meeke wordes, to stay and comfort her withall.

XLIX

But nothing might relent her hastie flight;
So deepe the deadly feare of that foule swaine
Was earst impressed in her gentle spright:
Like as a fearefull Doue, which through the raine,
Of the wide aire her way does cut amaine,
Hauing farre off espyde a Tassell gent,
Which after her his nimble wings doth straine,
Doubleth her haste for feare to be for-hent,
And with her pineons cleaues the liquid firmament.

L

With no lesse haste, and eke with no lesse dreed,
That fearefull Ladie fled from him, that ment
To her no euill thought, nor euill deed;
Yet former feare of being fowly shent,
Carried her forward with her first intent:
And though oft looking backward, well she vewd,
Her selfe freed from that foster insolent,
And that it was a knight, which now her sewd,
Yet she no lesse the knight feard, then that villein rude.

LI

His vncouth shield and straunge armes her dismayd,
Whose like in Faery lond were seldome seene,
That fast she from him fled, no lesse affrayd,
Then of wild beastes if she had chased beene:
Yet he her followd still with courage keene,
So long that now the golden *Hesperus*
Was mounted high in top of heauen sheene,
And warnd his other brethren ioyeous,
To light their blessed lamps in *Ioues* eternall hous.

LII

All suddenly dim woxe the dampish ayre,
And griesly shadowes couered heauen bright,
That now with thousand starres was decked fayre;
Which when the Prince beheld, a lothfull sight,
And that perforce, for want of lenger light,
He mote surcease his suit, and lose the hope
Of his long labour, he gan fowly wyte
His wicked fortune, that had turnd aslope,
And cursed night, that reft from him so goodly scope.

LIII

Tho when her wayes he could no more descry,
But to and fro at disauenture strayd;
Like as a ship, whose Lodestarre suddenly
Couered with cloudes, her Pilot hath dismayd;
His wearisome pursuit perforce he stayd,
And from his loftie steed dismounting low,
Did let him forage. Downe himselfe he layd
Vpon the grassie ground, to sleepe a throw;
The cold earth was his couch, the hard steele his pillow.

LIV

But gentle Sleepe enuyde him any rest;
In stead thereof sad sorrow, and disdaine
Of his hard hap did vexe his noble brest,
And thousand fancies bet his idle braine
With their light wings, the sights of semblants vaine:
Oft did he wish, that Lady faire mote bee
His Faery Queene, for whom he did complaine:
Or that his Faery Queene were such, as shee:
And euer hastie Night he blamed bitterlie.

LV

Night thou foule Mother of annoyance sad,
Sister of heauie death, and nourse of woe,
Which wast begot in heauen, but for thy bad
And brutish shape thrust downe to hell below,
Where by the grim floud of *Cocytus* slow
Thy dwelling is, in *Herebus* blacke hous,
(Blacke *Herebus* thy husband is the foe
Of all the Gods) where thou vngratious,
Halfe of thy dayes doest lead in horrour hideous.

LVI

What had th'eternall Maker need of thee,
The world in his continuall course to keepe,
That doest all things deface, ne lettest see
The beautie of his worke? Indeed in sleepe
The slouthfull bodie, that doth loue to steepe
His lustlesse limbes, and drowne his baser mind,
Doth praise thee oft, and oft from *Stygian* deepe
Calles thee, his goddesse in his error blind,
And great Dame Natures handmaide, chearing euery kind.

LVII

But well I wote, that to an heauy hart
Thou art the root and nurse of bitter cares,
Breeder of new, renewer of old smarts:
In stead of rest thou lendest rayling teares,
In stead of sleepe thou sendest troublous feares,
And dreadfull visions, in the which aliue
The drearie image of sad death appeares:
So from the wearie spirit thou doest driue
Desired rest, and men of happinesse depriue.

LVIII

Vnder thy mantle blacke there hidden lye,
Light-shonning theft, and traiterous intent,
Abhorred bloudshed, and vile felony,
Shamefull deceipt, and daunger imminent;
Foule horror, and eke hellish dreriment:
All these I wote in thy protection bee,
And light doe shonne, for feare of being shent:
For light ylike is loth'd of them and thee,
And all that lewdnesse loue, doe hate the light to see.

LIX

For day discouers all dishonest wayes,
And sheweth each thing, as it is indeed:
The prayses of high God he faire displayes,
And his large bountie rightly doth areed.
Dayes dearest children be the blessed seed,
Which darknesse shall subdew, and heauen win:
Truth is his daughter; he her first did breed,
Most sacred virgin, without spot of sin.
Our life is day, but death with darknesse doth begin.

LX

O when will day then turne to me againe,
And bring with him his long expected light?
O *Titan*, haste to reare thy ioyous waine:
Speed thee to spred abroad thy beames bright,
And chase away this too long lingring night,
Chase her away, from whence she came, to hell.
She, she it is, that hath me done despight:
There let her with the damned spirits dwell,
And yeeld her roome to day, that can it gouerne well.

LXI

Thus did the Prince that wearie night outweare,
In restlesse anguish and vnquiet paine:
And earely, ere the morrow did vpreare
His deawy head out of the *Ocean* maine,
He vp arose, as halfe in great disdaine,
And clombe vnto his steed. So forth he went,
With heauie looke and lumpish pace, that plaine
In him bewraid great grudge and maltalent:
His steed eke seem'd t'apply his steps to his intent.

Canto V

> *Prince Arthur heares of Florimell:*
> *three fosters Timias wound,*
> *Belphebe finds him almost dead,*
> *and reareth out of sownd.*

I

Wonder it is to see, in diuerse minds,
How diuersly loue doth his pageants play,
And shewes his powre in variable kinds:
The baser wit, whose idle thoughts alway
Are wont to cleaue vnto the lowly clay,
It stirreth vp to sensuall desire,
And in lewd slouth to wast his carelesse day:
But in braue sprite it kindles goodly fire,
That to all high desert and honour doth aspire.

II

Ne suffereth it vncomely idlenesse,
In his free thought to build her sluggish nest:
Ne suffereth it thought of vngentlenesse,

Euer to creepe into his noble brest,
But to the highest and the worthiest
Lifteth it vp, that else would lowly fall:
It lets not fall, it lets it not to rest:
It lets not scarse this Prince to breath at all,
But to his first poursuit him forward still doth call.

III

Who long time wandred through the forrest wyde,
To finde some issue thence, till that at last
He met a Dwarfe, that seemed terrifyde
With some late perill, which he hardly past,
Or other accident, which him aghast;
Of whom he asked, whence he lately came,
And whither now he trauelled so fast:
For sore he swat, and running through that same
Thicke forest, was bescratcht, and both his feet nigh lame.

IV

Panting for breath, and almost out of hart,
The Dwarfe him answerd, Sir, ill mote I stay
To tell the same. I lately did depart
From Faery court, where I haue many a day
Serued a gentle Lady of great sway,
And high accompt though out all Elfin land,
Who lately left the same, and tooke this way:
Her now I seeke, and if ye vnderstand
Which way she fared hath, good Sir tell out of hand.

V

What mister wight (said he) and how arayd?
Royally clad (quoth he) in cloth of gold,
As meetest may beseeme a noble mayd;
Her faire lockes in rich circlet be enrold,
A fairer wight did neuer Sunne behold,
And on a Palfrey rides more white then snow,
Yet she her selfe is whiter manifold:
The surest signe, whereby ye may her know,
Is, that she is the fairest wight aliue, I trow.

VI

Now certes swaine (said he) such one I weene,
Fast flying through this forest from her fo,

A foule ill fauoured foster, I haue seene;
Her selfe, well as I might, I reskewd tho,
But could not stay; so fast she did foregoe,
Carried away with wings of speedy feare.
Ah dearest God (quoth he) that is great woe,
And wondrous ruth to all, that shall it heare.
But can ye read Sir, how I may her find, or where?

VII

Perdy me leuer were to weeten that,
(Said he) then ransome of the richest knight,
Or all the good that euer yet I gat:
But froward fortune, and too forward Night
Such happinesse did, maulgre, to me spight,
And fro me reft both life and light attone.
But Dwarfe aread, what is that Lady bright,
That through this forest wandreth thus alone;
For of her errour straunge I haue great ruth and mone.

VIII

That Lady is (quoth he) where so she bee,
The bountiest virgin, and most debonaire,
That euer liuing eye I weene did see;
Liues none this day, that may with her compare
In stedfast chastitie and vertue rare,
The goodly ornaments of beautie bright;
And is ycleped *Florimell* the faire,
Faire *Florimell* belou'd of many a knight,
Yet she loues none but one, that *Marinell* is hight.

IX

A Sea-nymphes sonne, that *Marinell* is hight,
Of my deare Dame is loued dearely well;
In other none, but him, she sets delight,
All her delight is set on *Marinell*;
But he sets nought at all by *Florimell*:
For Ladies loue his mother long ygoe
Did him, they say, forwarne through sacred spell.
But fame now flies, that of a forreine foe
He is yslaine, which is the ground of all our woe.

X

Fiue dayes there be, since he (they say) was slaine,
And foure, since *Florimell* the Court for-went,
And vowed neuer to returne againe,
Till him aliue or dead she did inuent.
Therefore, faire Sir, for loue of knighthood gent,
And honour of trew Ladies, if ye may
By your good counsell, or bold hardiment,
Or succour her, or me direct the way;
Do one, or other good, I you most humbly pray.

XI

So may you gaine to you full great renowme,
Of all good Ladies through the world so wide,
And haply in her hart find highest rowme,
Of whom ye seeke to be most magnifide:
At least eternall meede shall you abide.
To whom the Prince; Dwarfe, comfort to thee take,
For till thou tidings learne, what her betide,
I here auow thee neuer to forsake.
Ill weares he armes, that nill them vse for Ladies sake.

XII

So with the Dwarfe he backe return'd againe,
To seeke his Lady, where he mote her find;
But by the way he greatly gan complaine
The want of his good Squire late left behind,
For whom he wondrous pensiue grew in mind,
For doubt of daunger, which mote him betide;
For him he loued aboue all mankind,
Hauing him trew and faithfull euer tride,
And bold, as euer Squire that waited by knights side.

XIII

Who all this while full hardly was assayd
Of deadly daunger, which to him betid;
For whiles his Lord pursewd that noble Mayd,
After that foster fowle he fiercely rid,
To bene auenged of the shame, he did
To that faire Damzell: Him he chaced long
Through the thicke woods, wherein he would haue hid
His shamefull head from his auengement strong,
And oft him threatned death for his outrageous wrong.

XIV

Nathlesse the villen sped himselfe so well,
Whether through swiftnesse of his speedy beast;
Or knowledge of those woods, where he did dwell,
That shortly he from daunger was releast,
And out of sight escaped at the least;
Yet not escaped from the dew reward
Of his bad deeds, which dayly he increast,
Ne ceased not, till him oppressed hard
The heauy plague, that for such leachours is prepard.

XV

For soone as he was vanisht out of sight,
His coward courage gan emboldned bee,
And cast t'auenge him of that fowle despight,
Which he had borne of his bold enimee.
Tho to his brethren came: for they were three
Vngratious children of one gracelesse sire,
And vnto them complained, how that he
Had vsed bene of that foolehardy Squire;
So them with bitter words he stird to bloudy ire.

XVI

Forthwith themselues with their sad instruments
Of spoyle and murder they gan arme byliue,
And with him forth into the forest went,
To wreake the wrath, which he did earst reuiue
In their sterne brests, on him which late did driue
Their brother to reproch and shamefull flight:
For they had vow'd, that neuer he aliue
Out of that forest should escape their might;
Vile rancour their rude harts had fild with such despight.

XVII

Within that wood there was a couert glade,
Foreby a narrow foord, to them well knowne,
Through which it was vneath for wight to wade;
And now by fortune it was ouerflowne:
By that same way they knew that Squire vnknowne
Mote algates passe; for thy themselues they set
There in await, with thicke woods ouer growne,
And all the while their malice they did whet
With cruell threats, his passage through the ford to let.

XVIII

It fortuned, as they deuized had,
The gentle Squire came ryding that same way,
Vnweeting of their wile and treason bad,
And through the ford to passen did assay;
But that fierce foster, which late fled away,
Stoutly forth stepping on the further shore,
Him boldly bad his passage there to stay,
Till he had made amends, and full restore
For all the damage, which he had him doen afore.

XIX

With that at him a quiu'ring dart he threw,
With so fell force and villeinous despighte,
That through his haberieon the forkehead flew,
And through the linked mayles empierced quite,
But had no powre in his soft flesh to bite:
That stroke the hardy Squire did sore displease,
But more that him he could not come to smite;
For by no meanes the high banke he could sease,
But labour'd long in that deepe ford with vaine disease.

XX

And still the foster with his long bore-speare
Him kept from landing at his wished will;
Anone one sent out of the thicket neare
A cruell shaft, headed with deadly ill,
And fethered with an vnlucky quill;
The wicked steele stayd not, till it did light
In his left thigh, and deepely did it thrill:
Exceeding griefe that wound in him empight,
But more that with his foes he could not come to fight.

XXI

At last through wrath and vengeaunce making way,
He on the bancke arriu'd with mickle paine,
Where the third brother did him sore assay,
And droue at him with all his might and maine
A forrest bill, which both his hands did straine;
But warily he did auoide the blow,
And with his speare requited him againe,
That both his sides were thrilled with the throw,
And a large streame of bloud out of the wound did flow.

XXII

He tombling downe, with gnashing teeth did bite
The bitter earth, and bad to let him in
Into the balefull house of endlesse night,
Where wicked ghosts do waile their former sin.
Tho gan the battell freshly to begin;
For nathemore for that spectacle bad,
Did th'other two their cruell vengeaunce blin,
But both attonce on both sides him bestad,
And load vpon him layd, his life for to haue had.

XXIII

Tho when that villain he auiz'd, which late
Affrighted had the fairest *Florimell,*
Full of fiers fury, and indignant hate,
To him he turned, and with rigour fell
Smote him so rudely on the Pannikell,
That to the chin he cleft his head in twaine:
Downe on the ground his carkas groueling fell;
His sinfull soule with desperate disdaine,
Out of her fleshly ferme fled to the place of paine.

XXIV

That seeing now the onely last of three,
Who with that wicked shaft him wounded had,
Trembling with horrour, as that did foresee
The fearefull end of his auengement sad,
Through which he follow should his brethren bad,
His bootelesse bow in feeble hand vpcaught,
And therewith shot an arrow at the lad;
Which faintly fluttring, scarce his helmet raught,
And glauncing fell to ground, but him annoyed naught.

XXV

With that he would haue fled into the wood;
But *Timias* him lightly ouerhent,
Right as he entring was into the flood,
And strooke at him with force so violent,
That headlesse him into the foord he sent:
The carkas with the streame was carried downe,
But th'head fell backeward on the Continent.
So mischief fel vpon the meaners crowne;
They three be dead with shame, the Squire liues with renowne.

XXVI

He liues, but takes small ioy of his renowne;
For of that cruell wound he bled so sore,
That from his steed he fell in deadly swowne;
Yet still the bloud forth gusht in so great store,
That he lay wallowd all in his owne gore.
Now God thee keepe, thou gentlest Squire aliue,
Else shall thy louing Lord thee see no more,
But both of comfort him thou shalt depriue,
And eke thy selfe of honour, which thou didst atchiue.

XXVII

Prouidence heauenly passeth liuing thought,
And doth for wretched mens reliefe make way;
For loe great grace or fortune thither brought
Comfort to him, that comfortlesse now lay.
In those same woods, ye well remember may,
How that a noble hunteresse did wonne,
She, that base *Braggadochio* did affray,
And made him fast out of the forrest runne;
Belphoebe was her name, as faire as *Phoebus* sunne.

XXVIII

She on a day, as she pursewd the chace
Of some wild beast, which with her arrowes keene
She wounded had, the same along did trace
By tract of bloud, which she had freshly seene,
To haue besprinckled all the grassy greene;
By the great persue, which she there perceau'd,
Well hoped she the beast engor'd had beene,
And made more hast, the life to haue bereau'd:
But ah, her expectation greatly was deceau'd.

XXIX

Shortly she came, whereas that woefull Squire
With bloud deformed, lay in deadly swownd:
In whose faire eyes, like lamps of quenched fire,
The Christall humour stood congealed rownd;
His locks, like faded leaues fallen to grownd,
Knotted with bloud, in bounches rudely ran,
And his sweete lips, on which before that stownd
The bud of youth to blossome faire began,
Spoild of their rosie red, were woxen pale and wan.

XXX

Saw neuer liuing eye more heauy sight,
That could haue made a rocke of stone to rew,
Or riue in twaine: which when that Lady bright
Besides all hope with melting eyes did vew,
All suddeinly abasht she chaunged hew,
And with sterne horrour backward gan to start:
But when she better him beheld, she grew
Full of soft passion and vnwonted smart:
The point of pitty perced through her tender hart.

XXXI

Meekely she bowed downe, to weete if life
Yet in his frosen members did remaine,
And feeling by his pulses beating rife,
That the weake soule her seat did yet retaine,
She cast to comfort him with busie paine:
His double folded necke she reard vpright,
And rubd his temples, and each trembling vaine;
His mayled haberieon she did vndight,
And from his head his heauy burganet did light.

XXXII

Into the woods thenceforth in hast she went,
To seeke for hearbes, that mote him remedy;
For she of hearbes had great intendiment,
Taught of the Nymphe, which from her infancy
Her nourced had in trew Nobility:
There, whether it diuine *Tobacco* were,
Or *Panachaea*, or *Polygony*,
She found, and brought it to her patient deare
Who al this while lay bleeding out his hart-bloud neare.

XXXIII

The soueraigne weede betwixt two marbles plaine
She pownded small, and did in peeces bruze,
And then atweene her lilly handes twaine,
Into his wound the iuyce thereof did scruze,
And round about, as she could well it vze,
The flesh therewith she suppled and did steepe,
T'abate all spasme, and soke the swelling bruze,
And after hauing searcht the intuse deepe,
She with her scarfe did bind the wound from cold to keepe.

XXXIV

By this he had sweet life recur'd againe,
And groning inly deepe, at last his eyes,
His watry eyes, drizling like deawy raine,
He vp gan lift toward the azure skies,
From whence descend all hopelesse remedies:
Therewith he sigh'd, and turning him aside,
The goodly Mayd full of diuinities,
And gifts of heauenly grace he by him spide,
Her bow and gilden quiuer lying him beside.

XXXV

Mercy deare Lord (said he) what grace is this,
That thou hast shewed to me sinfull wight,
To send thine Angell from her bowre of blis,
To comfort me in my distressed plight?
Angell, or Goddesse do I call thee right?
What seruice may I do vnto thee meete,
That hast from darkenesse me returnd to light,
And with thy heauenly salues and med'cines sweete,
Hast drest my sinfull wounds? I kisse thy blessed feete.

XXXVI

Thereat she blushing said, Ah gentle Squire,
Nor Goddesse I, nor Angell, but the Mayd,
And daughter of a woody Nymphe, desire
No seruice, but thy safety and ayd;
Which if thou gaine, I shalbe well apayd.
We mortall wights, whose liues and fortunes bee
To commun accidents still open layd,
Are bound with commun bond of frailtee,
To succour wretched wights, whom we captiued see.

XXXVII

By this her Damzels, which the former chace
Had vndertaken after her, arriu'd,
As did *Belphœbe*, in the bloudy place,
And thereby deemd the beast had bene depriu'd
Of life, whom late their Ladies arrow ryu'd:
For thy the bloudy tract they followd fast,
And euery one to runne the swiftest stryu'd;
But two of them the rest far ouerpast,
And where their Lady was, arriued at the last.

XXXVIII

Where when they saw that goodly boy, with blood
Defowled, and their Lady dresse his wownd,
They wondred much, and shortly vnderstood,
How him in deadly case their Lady fownd,
And reskewed out of the heauy stownd.
Eftsoones his warlike courser, which was strayd
Farre in the woods, whiles that he lay in swownd,
She made those Damzels search, which being stayd,
They did him set thereon, and forth with them conuayd.

XXXIX

Into that forest farre they thence him led,
Where was their dwelling, in a pleasant glade,
With mountaines round about enuironed,
And mighty woods, which did the valley shade,
And like a stately Theatre it made,
Spreading it selfe into a spatious plaine.
And in the midst a little riuer plaide
Emongst the pumy stones, which seemd to plaine
With gentle murmure, that his course they did restraine.

XL

Beside the same a dainty place there lay,
Planted with mirtle trees and laurels greene,
In which the birds song many a louely lay
Of gods high prayse, and of their loues sweet teene,
As it an earthly Paradize had beene:
In whose enclosed shadow there was pight
A faire Pauilion, scarcely to be seene,
The which was all within most richly dight,
That greatest Princes liuing it mote well delight.

XLI

Thither they brought that wounded Squire, and layd
In easie couch his feeble limbes to rest,
He rested him a while, and then the Mayd
His ready wound with better salues new drest;
Dayly she dressed him, and did the best
His grieuous hurt to garish, that she might,
That shortly she his dolour hath redrest,
And his foule sore reduced to faire plight:
It she reduced, but himselfe destroyed quight.

XLII

O foolish Physick, and vnfruitfull paine,
That heales vp one and makes another wound:
She his hurt thigh to him recur'd againe,
But hurt his hart, the which before was sound,
Through an vnwary dart, which did rebound
From her faire eyes and gracious countenaunce.
What bootes it him from death to be vnbound,
To be captiued in endlesse duraunce
Of sorrow and despaire without aleggeaunce?

XLIII

Still as his wound did gather, and grow hole,
So still his hart woxe sore, and health decayd:
Madnesse to saue a part, and lose the whole.
Still whenas he beheld the heauenly Mayd,
Whiles dayly plaisters to his wound she layd,
So still his Malady the more increast,
The whiles her matchlesse beautie him dismayd.
Ah God, what other could he do at least,
But loue so faire a Lady, that his life releast?

XLIV

Long while he stroue in his courageous brest,
With reason dew the passion to subdew,
And loue for to dislodge out of his nest:
Still when her excellencies he did vew,
Her soueraigne bounty, and celestiall hew,
The same to loue he strongly was constraind:
But when his meane estate he did reuew,
He from such hardy boldnesse was restraind,
And of his lucklesse lot and cruell loue thus plaind.

XLV

Vnthankfull wretch (said he) is this the meed,
With which her soueraigne mercy thou doest quight?
Thy life she saued by her gracious deed,
But thou doest weene with villeinous despight,
To blot her honour, and her heauenly light.
Dye rather, dye, then so disloyally
Deeme of her high desert, or seeme so light:
Faire death it is to shonne more shame, to dy:
Dye rather, dy, then euer loue disloyally.

XLVI

But if to loue disloyalty it bee,
Shall I then hate her, that from deathes dore
Me brought? ah farre be such reproch fro mee.
What can I lesse do, then her loue therefore,
Sith I her dew reward cannot restore:
Dye rather, dye, and dying do her serue,
Dying her serue, and liuing her adore;
Thy life she gaue, thy life she doth deserue:
Dye rather, dye, then euer from her seruice swerue.

XLVII

But foolish boy, what bootes thy seruice bace
To her, to whom the heauens do serue and sew?
Thou a meane Squire, of meeke and lowly place,
She heauenly borne, and of celestiall hew.
How then? of all loue taketh equall vew:
And doth not highest God vouchsafe to take
The loue and seruice of the basest crew?
If she will not, dye meekly for her sake;
Dye rather, dye, then euer so faire loue forsake.

XLVIII

Thus warreid he long time against his will,
Till that through weaknesse he was forst at last,
To yield himselfe vnto the mighty ill:
Which as a victour proud, gan ransack fast
His inward parts, and all his entrayles wast,
That neither bloud in face, nor life in hart
It left, but both did quite drye vp, and blast;
As percing leuin, which the inner part
Of euery thing consumes, and calcineth by art.

XLIX

Which seeing faire *Belphœbe*, gan to feare,
Least that his wound were inly well not healed,
Or that the wicked steele empoysned were:
Litle she weend, that loue he close concealed;
Yet still he wasted, as the snow congealed,
When the bright sunne his beams thereon doth beat;
Yet neuer he his hart to her reuealed,
But rather chose to dye for sorrow great,
Then with dishonorable termes her to entreat.

L

She gracious Lady, yet no paines did spare,
To do him ease, or do him remedy:
Many Restoratiues of vertues rare,
And costly Cordialles she did apply,
To mitigate his stubborne mallady:
But that sweet Cordiall, which can restore
A loue-sick hart, she did to him enuy;
To him, and to all th'vnworthy world forlore
She did enuy that soueraigne salue, in secret store.

LI

That dainty Rose, the daughter of her Morne,
More deare then life she tendered, whose flowre
The girlond of her honour did adorne:
Ne suffred she the Middayes scorching powre,
Ne the sharp Northerne wind thereon to showre,
But lapped vp her silken leaues most chaire,
When so the froward skye began to lowre:
But soone as calmed was the Christall aire,
She did it faire dispred, and let to florish faire.

LII

Eternall God in his almighty powre,
To make ensample of his heauenly grace,
In Paradize whilome did plant this flowre,
Whence he it fetcht out of her natiue place,
And did in stocke of earthly flesh enrace,
That mortall men her glory should admire:
In gentle Ladies brest, and bounteous race
Of woman kind it fairest flowre doth spire,
And beareth fruit of honour and all chast desire.

LIII

Faire ympes of beautie, whose bright shining beames
Adorne the world with like to heauenly light,
And to your willes both royalties and Realmes
Subdew, through conquest of your wondrous might,
With this faire flowre your goodly girlonds dight,
Of chastity and vertue virginall,
That shall embellish more your beautie bright,
And crowne your heades with heauenly coronall,
Such as the Angels weare before Gods tribunall.

LIV

To your faire selues a faire ensample frame,
Of this faire virgin, this *Belphœbe* faire,
To whom in perfect loue, and spotlesse fame
Of chastitie, none liuing may compaire:
Ne poysnous Enuy iustly can empaire
The prayse of her fresh flowring Maidenhead;
For thy she standeth on the highest staire
Of th'honorable stage of womanhead,
That Ladies all may follow her ensample dead.

LV

In so great prayse of stedfast chastity,
Nathlesse she was so curteous and kind,
Tempred with grace, and goodly modesty,
That seemed those two vertues stroue to find
The higher place in her Heroick mind:
So striuing each did other more augment,
And both encreast the prayse of woman kind,
And both encreast her beautie excellent;
So all did make in her a perfect complement.

Canto VI

> *The birth of faire Belphœbe and*
> *Of Amoret is told.*
> *The Gardins of Adonis fraught*
> *With pleasures manifold.*

I

WEll may I weene, faire Ladies, all this while
Ye wonder, how this noble Damozell
So great perfections did in her compile,
Sith that in saluage forests she did dwell,
So farre from court and royall Citadell,
The great schoolmistresse of all curtesy:
Seemeth that such wild woods should far expell
All ciuill vsage and gentility,
And gentle sprite deforme with rude rusticity.

II

But to this faire *Belphœbe* in her berth
The heauens so fauourable were and free,
Looking with myld aspect vpon the earth,

In th'*Horoscope* of her natiuitee,
That all the gifts of grace and chastitee
On her they poured forth of plenteous horne;
Ioue laught on *Venus* from his soueraigne see,
And *Phœbus* with faire beames did her adorne,
And all the *Graces* rockt her cradle being borne.

III

Her berth was of the wombe of Morning dew,
And her conception of the ioyous Prime,
And all her whole creation did her shew
Pure and vnspotted from all loathly crime,
That is ingenerate in fleshly slime.
So was this virgin borne, so was she bred,
So was she trayned vp from time to time,
In all chast vertue, and true bounti-hed
Till to her dew perfection she was ripened.

IV

Her mother was the faire *Chrysogonee*,
The daughter of *Amphisa*, who by race
A Faerie was, yborne of high degree,
She bore *Belphaebe*, she bore in like cace
Faire *Amoretta* in the second place:
These two were twinnes, and twixt them two did share
The heritage of all celestiall grace.
That all the rest it seem'd they robbed bare
Of bountie, and of beautie, and all vertues rare.

V

It were a goodly storie, to declare,
By what straunge accident faire *Chrysogone*
Conceiu'd these infants, and how she them bare,
In this wild forrest wandring all alone,
After she had nine moneths fulfild and gone:
For not as other wemens commune brood,
They were enwombed in the sacred throne
Of her chaste bodie, nor with commune food,
As other wemens babes, they sucked vitall blood.

VI

But wondrously they were begot, and bred
Through influence of th'heauens fruitfull ray,

Page | 955

As it in antique bookes is mentioned.
It was vpon a Sommers shynie day,
When *Titan* faire his beames did display,
In a fresh fountaine, farre from all mens vew,
She bath'd her brest, the boyling heat t'allay;
She bath'd with roses red, and violets blew,
And all the sweetest flowres, that in the forrest grew.

VII

Till faint through irkesome wearinesse, adowne
Vpon the grassie ground her selfe she layd
To sleepe, the whiles a gentle slombring swowne
Vpon her fell all naked bare displayd;
The sunne-beames bright vpon her body playd,
Being through former bathing mollifide,
And pierst into her wombe, where they embayd
With so sweet sence and secret power vnspide,
That in her pregnant flesh they shortly fructifide.

VIII

Miraculous may seeme to him, that reades
So straunge ensample of conception;
But reason teacheth that the fruitfull seades
Of all things liuing, through impression
Of the sunbeames in moyst complexion,
Doe life conceiue and quickned are by kynd:
So after *Nilus* invndation,
Infinite shapes of creatures men do fynd,
Informed in the mud, on which the Sunne hath shynd.

IX

Miraculous may seeme to him, that reades
So straunge ensample of conception;
But reason teacheth that the fruitfull seades
Of all things liuing, through impression
Of the sunbeames in moyst complexion,
Doe life conceiue and quickned are by kynd:
So after *Nilus* invndation,
Infinite shapes of creatures men do fynd,
Informed in the mud, on which the Sunne hath shynd.

X

Whereof conceiuing shame and foule disgrace,
Albe her guiltlesse conscience her cleard,
She fled into the wildernesse a space,
Till that vnweeldy burden she had reard,
And shund dishonor, which as death she feard:
Where wearie of long trauell, downe to rest
Her selfe she set, and comfortably cheard;
There a sad cloud of sleepe her ouerkest,
And seized euery sense with sorrow sore opprest.

XI

It fortuned, faire *Venus* hauing lost
Her little sonne, the winged god of loue,
Who for some light displeasure, which him crost,
Was from her fled, as flit as ayerie Doue,
And left her blisfull bowre of ioy aboue,
(So from her often he had fled away,
When she for ought him sharpely did reproue,
And wandred in the world in strange aray,
Disguiz'd in thousand shapes, that none might him bewray.)

XII

Him for to seeke, she left her heauenly hous,
The house of goodly formes and faire aspects,
Whence all the world deriues the glorious
Features of beautie, and all shapes select,
With which high God his workmanship hath deckt;
And searched euery way, through which his wings
Had borne him, or his tract she mote detect:
She promist kisses sweet, and sweeter things
Vnto the man, that of him tydings to her brings.

XIII

First she him sought in Court, where most he vsed
Whylome to haunt, but there she found him not;
But many there she found, which sore accused
His falsehood, and with foule infamous blot
His cruell deedes and wicked wyles did spot:
Ladies and Lords she euery where mote heare
Complayning, how with his empoysned shot
Their wofull harts he wounded had whyleare,
And so had left them languishing twixt hope and feare.

XIV

She then the Citties sought from gate to gate,
And euery one did aske, did he him see;
And euery one her answerd, that too late
He had him seene, and felt the crueltie
Of his sharpe darts and whot artillerie;
And euery one threw forth reproches rife
Of his mischieuous deedes, and said, That hee
Was the disturber of all ciuill life,
The enimy of peace, and author of all strife.

XV

Then in the countrey she abroad him sought,
And in the rurall cottages inquired,
Where also many plaints to her were brought,
How he their heedlesse harts with loue had fyred,
And his false venim through their veines inspyred;
And eke the gentle shepheard swaynes, which sat
Keeping their fleecie flockes, as they were hyred,
She sweetly heard complaine, both how and what
Her sonne had to them doen; yet she did smile thereat.

XVI

But when in none of all these she him got,
She gan auize, where else he mote him hyde:
At last she her bethought, that she had not
Yet sought the saluage woods and forrests wyde,
In which full many louely Nymphes abyde,
Mongst whom might be, that he did closely lye,
Or that the loue of some of them him tyde:
For thy she thither cast her course t'apply,
To search the secret haunts of *Dianes* company.

XVII

Shortly vnto the wastefull woods she came,
Whereas she found the Goddesse with her crew,
After late chace of their embrewed game,
Sitting beside a fountaine in a rew,
Some of them washing with the liquid dew
From off their dainty limbes the dustie sweat,
And soyle which did deforme their liuely hew;
Others lay shaded from the scorching heat;
The rest vpon her person gaue attendance great.

XVIII

She hauing hong vpon a bough on high
Her bow and painted quiuer, had vnlaste
Her siluer buskins from her nimble thigh,
And her lancke loynes vngirt, and brests vnbraste,
After her heat the breathing cold to taste;
Her golden lockes, that late in tresses bright
Embreaded were for hindring of her haste,
Now loose about her shoulders hong vndight,
And were with sweet *Ambrosia* all besprinckled light.

XIX

Soone as she *Venus* saw behind her backe,
She was asham'd to be so loose surprized
And woxe halfe wroth against her damzels slacke,
That had not her thereof before auized,
But suffred her so carelesly disguized
Be ouertaken. Soone her garments loose
Vpgath'ring, in her bosome she comprized,
Well as she might, and to the Goddesse rose,
Whiles all her Nymphes did like a girlond her enclose.

XX

Goodly she gan faire *Cytherea* greet,
And shortly asked her, what cause her brought
Into that wildernesse for her vnmeet,
From her sweet bowres, and beds with pleasures fraught:
That suddein change she strange aduenture thought.
To whom halfe weeping, she thus answered,
That she her dearest sonne *Cupido* sought,
Who in his frowardnesse from her was fled;
That she repented sore, to haue him angered.

XXI

Thereat *Diana* gan to smile, in scorne
Of her vaine plaint, and to her scoffing sayd;
Great pittie sure, that ye be so forlorne
Of your gay sonne, that giues ye so good ayd
To your disports: ill mote ye bene apayd.
But she was more engrieued, and replide;
Faire sister, ill beseemes it to vpbrayd
A dolefull heart with so disdainfull pride;
The like that mine, may be your paine another tide.

XXII

As you in woods and wanton wildernesse
Your glory set, to chace the saluage beasts,
So my delight is all in ioyfulnesse,
In beds, in bowres, in banckets, and in feasts:
And ill becomes you with your loftie creasts,
To scorne the ioy, that *Ioue* is glad to seeke;
We both are bound to follow heauens beheasts,
And tend our charges with obeisance meeke:
Spare, gentle sister, with reproch my paine to eeke.

XXIII

And tell me, if that ye my sonne haue heard,
To lurke emongst your Nymphes in secret wize;
Or keepe their cabins: much I am affeard,
Least he like one of them him selfe disguize,
And turne his arrowes to their exercize:
So may he long himselfe full easie hide:
For he is faire and fresh in face and guize,
As any Nymph (let not it be enuyde.)
So saying euery Nymph full narrowly she eyde.

XXIV

But *Phœbe* therewith sore was angered,
And sharply said; Goe Dame, goe seeke your boy,
Where you him lately left, in *Mars* his bed;
He comes not here, we scorne his foolish ioy,
Ne lend we leisure to his idle toy:
But if I catch him in this company,
By *Stygian* lake I vow, whose sad annoy
The Gods doe dread, he dearely shall abye:
Ile clip his wanton wings, that he no more shall fly.

XXV

Whom when as *Venus* saw so sore displeased,
She inly sory was, and gan relent,
What she had said: so her she soone appeased,
With sugred words and gentle blandishment,
Which as a fountaine from her sweet lips went,
And welled goodly forth, that in short space
She was well pleasd, and forth her damzels sent,
Through all the woods, to search from place to place,
If any tract of him or tydings they mote trace.

XXVI

To search the God of loue, her Nymphes she sent
Throughout the wandring forrest euery where:
And after them her selfe eke with her went
To seeke the fugitiue, both farre and nere,
So long they sought, till they arriued were
In that same shadie couert, whereas lay
Faire *Crysogone* in slombry traunce whilere:
Who in her sleepe (a wondrous thing to say)
Vnwares had borne two babes, as faire as springing day.

XXVII

Vnwares she them conceiu'd, vnwares she bore:
She bore withouten paine, that she conceiued
Withouten pleasure: ne her need implore
Lucinaes aide: which when they both perceiued,
They were through wonder nigh of sense bereaued,
And gazing each on other, nought bespake:
At last they both agreed, her seeming grieued
Out of her heauy swowne not to awake,
But from her louing side the tender babes to take.

XXVIII

Vp they them tooke, each one a babe vptooke,
And with them carried, to be fostered;
Dame *Phaebe* to a Nymph her babe betooke,
To be vpbrought in perfect Maydenhed,
And of her selfe her name *Belphœbe* red:
But *Venus* hers thence farre away conuayd,
To be vpbrought in goodly womanhed,
And in her litle loues stead, which was strayd,
Her *Amoretta* cald, to comfort her dismayd.

XXIX

She brought her to her ioyous Paradize,
Where most she wonnes, when she on earth does dwel.
So faire a place, as Nature can deuize:
Whether in *Paphos*, or *Cytheron* hill,
Or it in *Gnidus* be, I wote not well;
But well I wote by tryall, that this same
All other pleasant places doth excell,
And called is by her lost louers name,
The *Gardin* of *Adonis*, farre renowmd by fame.

XXX

In that same Gardin all the goodly flowres,
Wherewith dame Nature doth her beautifie,
And decks the girlonds of her paramoures,
Are fetcht: there is the first seminarie
Of all things, that are borne to liue and die,
According to their kindes. Long worke it were,
Here to account the endlesse progenie
Of all the weedes, that bud and blossome there;
But so much as doth need, must needs be counted here.

XXXI

It sited was in fruitfull soyle of old,
And girt in with two walles on either side;
The one of yron, the other of bright gold,
That none might thorough breake, nor ouer-stride:
And double gates it had, which opened wide,
By which both in and out men moten pas;
Th'one faire and fresh, the other old and dride:
Old *Genius* the porter of them was,
Old *Genius*, the which a double nature has.

XXXII

He letteth in, he letteth out to wend,
All that to come into the world desire;
A thousand thousand naked babes attend
About him day and night, which doe require,
That he with fleshly weedes would them attire:
Such as him list, such as eternall fate
Ordained hath, he clothes with sinfull mire,
And sendeth forth to liue in mortall state,
Till they againe returne backe by the hinder gate.

XXXIII

After that they againe returned beene,
They in that Gardin planted be againe;
And grow afresh, as they had neuer seene
Fleshly corruption, nor mortall paine.
Some thousand yeares so doen they there remaine;
And then of him are clad with other hew,
Or sent into the chaungefull world againe,
Till thither they returne, where first they grew:
So like a wheele around they runne from old to new.

XXXIV

Ne needs there Gardiner to set, or sow,
To plant or prune: for of their owne accord
All things, as they created were, doe grow,
And yet remember well the mightie word,
Which first was spoken by th'Almightie lord,
That bad them to increase and multiply:
Ne doe they need with water of the ford,
Or of the clouds to moysten their roots dry;
For in themselues eternall moisture they imply.

XXXV

Infinite shapes of creatures there are bred,
And vncouth formes, which none yet euer knew,
And euery sort is in a sundry bed
Set by it selfe, andranckt in comely rew:
Some fit for reasonable soules t'indew,
Some made for beasts, some made for birds to weare,
And all the fruitfull spawne of fishes hew
In endlesse rancks along enraunged were,
That seem'd the *Ocean* could not containe them there.

XXXVI

Daily they grow, and daily forth are sent
Into the world, it to replenish more;
Yet is the stocke not lessened, nor spent,
But still remaines in euerlasting store,
As it at first created was of yore.
For in the wide wombe of the world there lyes,
In hatefull darkenesse and in deepe horrore,
An huge eternall *Chaos*, which supplyes
The substances of natures fruitfull progenyes.

XXXVII

All things from thence doe their first being fetch,
And borrow matter, whereof they are made,
Which when as forme and feature it does ketch,
Becomes a bodie, and doth then inuade
The state of life, out of the griesly shade.
That substance is eterne, and bideth so,
Ne when the life decayes, and forme does fade,
Doth it consume, and into nothing go,
But chaunged is, and often altred to and fro.

XXXVIII

The substance is not chaunged, nor altered,
But th'only forme and outward fashion;
For euery substance is conditioned
To change her hew, and sundry formes to don,
Meet for her temper and complexion:
For formes are variable and decay,
By course of kind, and by occasion;
And that faire flowre of beautie fades away,
As doth the lilly fresh before the sunny ray.

XXXIX

Great enimy to it, and to all the rest,
That in the *Gardin* of *Adonis* springs,
Is wicked *Time*, who with his scyth addrest,
Does mow the flowring herbes and goodly things,
And all their glory to the ground downe flings,
Where they doe wither, and are fowly mard:
He flyes about, and with his flaggy wings
Beates downe both leaues and buds without regard,
Ne euer pittie may relent his malice hard.

XL

Yet pittie often did the gods relent,
To see so faire things mard, and spoyled quight:
And their great mother *Venus* did lament
The losse of her deare brood, her deare delight;
Her hart was pierst with pittie at the sight,
When walking through the Gardin, them she spyde,
Yet no'te she find redresse for such despight.
For all that liues, is subiect to that law:
All things decay in time, and to their end do draw.

XLI

But were it not, that *Time* their troubler is,
All that in this delightfull Gardin growes,
Should happie be, and haue immortall blis:
For here all plentie, and all pleasure flowes,
And sweet loue gentle fits emongst them throwes,
Without fell rancor, or fond gealosie;
Franckly each paramour his leman knowes,
Each bird his mate, ne any does enuie
Their goodly meriment, and gay felicitie.

XLII

There is continuall spring, and haruest there
Continuall, both meeting at one time:
For both the boughes doe laughing blossomes beare,
And with fresh colours decke the wanton Prime,
And eke attonce the heauy trees they clime,
Which seeme to labour vnder their fruits lode:
The whiles the ioyous birdes make their pastime
Emongst the shadie leaues, their sweet abode,
And their true loues without suspition tell abrode.

XLIII

Right in the middest of that Paradise,
There stood a stately Mount, on whose round top
A gloomy groue of mirtle trees did rise,
Whose shadie boughes sharpe steele did neuer lop,
Nor wicked beasts their tender buds did crop,
But like a girlond compassed the hight,
And from their fruitfull sides sweet gum did drop,
That all the ground with precious deaw bedight,
Threw forth most dainty odours, and most sweet delight.

XLIV

And in the thickest couert of that shade,
There was a pleasant arbour, not by art,
But of the trees owne inclination made,
Which knitting their rancke braunches part to part,
With wanton yuie twyne entrayld athwart,
And Eglantine, and Caprifole emong,
Fashiond aboue within their inmost part,
That nether *Phœbus* beams could through them throng,
Nor *Aeolus* sharp blast could worke them any wrong.

XLV

And all about grew euery sort of flowre,
To which sad louers were transformd of yore;
Fresh *Hyacinthus*, *Phœbus* paramoure,
Foolish *Narcisse*, that likes the watry shore,
Sad *Amaranthus*, made a flowre but late,
Sad *Amaranthus*, in whose purple gore
Me seemes I see *Amintas* wretched fate,
To whom sweet Poets verse hath giuen endlesse date.

XLVI

There wont faire *Venus* often to enioy
Her deare *Adonis* ioyous company,
And reape sweet pleasure of the wanton boy;
There yet, some say, in secret he does ly,
Lapped in flowres and pretious spycery,
By her hid from the world, and from the skill
Of *Stygian* Gods, which doe her loue enuy;
But she her selfe, when euer that she will,
Possesseth him, and of his sweetnesse takes her fill.

XLVII

And sooth it seemes they say: for he may not
For euer die, and euer buried bee
In balefull night, where all things are forgot;
All be he subiect to mortalitie,
Yet is eterne in mutabilitie,
And by succession made perpetuall,
Transformed oft, and chaunged diuerslie:
For him the Father of all formes they call;
Therefore needs mote he liue, that liuing giues to all.

XLVIII

There now he liueth in eternall blis,
Ioying his goddesse, and of her enioyd:
Ne feareth he henceforth that foe of his,
Which with his cruell tuske him deadly cloyd:
For that wilde Bore, the which him once annoyd,
She firmely hath emprisoned for ay,
That her sweet loue his malice mote auoyd,
In a strong rocky Caue, which is they say,
Hewen vnderneath that Mount, that none him losen may.

XLIX

There now he liues in euerlasting ioy,
With many of the Gods in company,
Which thither haunt, and with the winged boy
Sporting himselfe in safe felicity:
Who when he hath with spoiles and cruelty
Ransackt the world, and in the wofull harts
Of many wretches set his triumphes hye,
Thither resorts, and laying his sad darts
Aside, with faire *Adonis* playes his wanton parts.

L

And his true loue faire *Psyche* with him playes,
Faire *Psyche* to him lately reconcyld,
After long troubles and vnmeet vpbrayes,
With which his mother *Venus* her reuyld,
And eke himselfe her cruelly exyld:
But now in stedfast loue and happy state
She with him liues, and hath him borne a chyld,
Pleasure, that doth both gods and men aggrate,
Pleasure, the daughter of *Cupid* and *Psyche* late.

LI

Hither great *Venus* brought this infant faire,
The younger daughter of *Chrysogonee*,
And vnto *Psyche* with great trust and care
Committed her, yfostered to bee,
And trained vp in true feminitee:
Who no lesse carefully her tendered,
Then her owne daughter *Pleasure*, to whom shee
Made her companion, and her lessoned
In all the lore of loue, and goodly womanhead.

LII

In which when she to perfect ripenesse grew,
Of grace and beautie noble Paragone,
She brought her forth into the worldes vew,
To be th'ensample of true loue alone,
And Lodestarre of all chaste affectione,
To all faire Ladies, that doe liue on ground.
To Faery court she came, where many one
Admyrd her goodly haueour, and found
His feeble hart wide launched with loues cruell wound.

LIII

But she to none of them her loue did cast,
Saue to the noble knight Sir *Scudamore*,
To whom her louing hart she linked fast
In faithfull loue, t'abide for euermore,
And for his dearest sake endured sore,
Sore trouble of an hainous enimy;
Who her would forced haue to haue forlore
Her former loue, and stedfast loialty,
As ye may elsewhere read that ruefull history.

LIV

But well I weene, ye first desire to learne,
What end vnto that fearefull Damozell,
Which fled so fast from that same foster stearne,
Whom with his brethren *Timias* slew, befell:
That was to weet, the goodly *Florimell*;
Who wandring for to seeke her louer deare,
Her louer deare, her dearest *Marinell*,
Into misfortune fell, as ye did heare,
And from Prince *Arthur* fled with wings of idle feare.

Canto VII

The witches sonne loues Florimell:
she flyes, he faines to die.
Satyrane saues the Squire of Dames
from Gyants tyrannie.

I

LIke as an Hynd forth singled from the heard,
That hath escaped from a rauenous beast,
Yet flyes away of her owne feet affeard,
And euery leafe, that shaketh with the least
Murmure of winde, her terror hath encreast;
So fled faire *Florimell* from her vaine feare,
Long after she from perill was releast:
Each shade she saw, and each noyse she did heare,
Did seeme to be the same, which she escapt whyleare.

II

All that same euening she in flying spent,
And all that night her course continewed:
Ne did she let dull sleepe once to relent,
Nor wearinesse to slacke her hast, but fled
Euer alike, as if her former dred
Were hard behind, her readie to arrest:
And her white Palfrey hauing conquered
The maistring raines out of her weary wrest,
Perforce her carried, where euer he thought best.

III

So long as breath, and hable puissance
Did natiue courage vnto him supply,
His pace he freshly forward did aduaunce,

And carried her beyond all ieopardy,
But nought that wanteth rest, can long aby.
He hauing through incessant trauell spent
His force, at last perforce a downe did ly,
Ne foot could further moue: The Lady gent
Thereat was suddein strooke with great astonishment.

IV

And forst t'alight, on foot mote algates fare,
A traueller vnwonted to such way:
Need teacheth her this lesson hard and rare,
That fortune all in equall launce doth sway,
And mortall miseries doth make her play.
So long she trauelled, till at length she came
To an hilles side, which did to her bewray
A little valley, subiect to the same,
All couerd with thick woods, that quite it ouercame.

V

Through the tops of the high trees she did descry
A litle smoke, whose vapour thin and light,
Reeking aloft, vprolled to the sky:
Which, chearefull signe did send vnto her sight,
That in the same did wonne some liuing wight.
Eftsoones her steps she thereunto applyde,
And came at last in weary wretched plight
Vnto the place, to which her hope did guyde,
To find some refuge there, and rest her weary syde.

VI

There in a gloomy hollow glen she found
A little cottage, built of stickes and reedes
In homely wize, and wald with sods around,
In which a witch did dwell, in loathly weedes,
And wilfull want, all carelesse of her needes;
So choosing solitarie to abide,
Far from all neighbours, that her deuilish deedes
And hellish arts from people she might hide,
And hurt far off vnknowne, whom euer she enuide.

VII

The Damzell there arriuing entred in;
Where sitting on the flore the Hag she found,

Busie (as seem'd) about some wicked gin:
Who soone as she beheld that suddein stound,
Lightly vpstarted from the dustie ground,
And with fell looke and hollow deadly gaze
Stared on her awhile, as one astound,
Ne had one word to speake, for great amaze,
But shewd by outward signes, that dread her sence did daze.

VIII

At last turning her feare to foolish wrath,
She askt, what deuill had her thither brought,
And who she was, and what vnwonted path
Had guided her, vnwelcomed, vnsought?
To which the Damzell full of doubtfull thought,
Her mildly answer'd; Beldame be not wroth
With silly Virgin by aduenture brought
Vnto your dwelling, ignorant and loth,
That craue but rowme to rest, while tempest ouerblo'th.

IX

With that adowne out of her Christall eyne
Few trickling teares she softly forth let fall,
That like two Orient pearles, did purely shyne
Vpon her snowy cheeke; and therewithall
She sighed soft, that none so bestiall,
Nor saluage hart, but ruth of her sad plight
Would make to melt, or pitteously appall;
And that vile Hag, all were her whole delight
In mischiefe, was much moued at so pitteous sight.

X

And gan recomfort her in her rude wyse,
With womanish compassion of her plaint,
Wiping the teares from her suffused eyes,
And bidding her sit downe, to rest her faint
And wearie limbes a while. She nothing quaint
Nor s'deignfull of so homely fashion,
Sith brought she was now to so hard constraint,
Sate downe vpon the dusty ground anon,
As glad of that small rest, as Bird of tempest gon.

XI

Tho gan she gather vp her garments rent,
And her loose lockes to dight in order dew,
With golden wreath and gorgeous ornament;
Whom such whenas the wicked Hag did vew,
She was astonisht at her heauenly hew,
And doubted her to deeme an earthly wight,
But or some Goddesse, or of *Dianes* crew,
And thought her to adore with humble spright;
T'adore thing so diuine as beauty, were but right.

XII

This wicked woman had a wicked sonne,
The comfort of her age and weary dayes,
A laesie loord, for nothing good to donne,
But stretched forth in idlenesse alwayes,
Ne euer cast his mind to couet prayse,
Or ply him selfe to any honest trade,
But all the day before the sunny rayes
He vs'd to slug, or sleepe in slothfull shade:
Such laesinesse both lewd and poore attonce him made.

XIII

He comming home at vndertime, there found
The fairest creature, that he euer saw,
Sitting beside his mother on the ground;
The sight whereof did greatly him adaw,
And his base thought with terrour and with aw
So inly smot, that as one, which had gazed
On the bright Sunne vnwares, doth soone withdraw
His feeble eyne, with too much brightnesse dazed;
So stared he on her, and stood long while amazed.

XIV

Softly at last he gan his mother aske,
What mister wight that was, and whence deriued,
That in so straunge disguizement there did maske,
And by what accident she there arriued:
But she, as one nigh of her wits depriued,
With nought but ghastly lookes him answered,
Like to a ghost, that lately is reuiued
From *Stygian* shores, where late it wandered;
So both at her, and each at other wondered.

XV

But the faire Virgin was so meeke and mild,
That she to them vouchsafed to embace
Her goodly port, and to their senses vild,
Her gentle speach applide, that in short space
She grew familiare in that desert place.
During which time, the Chorle through her so kind
And curteise vse conceiu'd affection bace,
And cast to loue her in his brutish mind;
No loue, but brutish lust, that was so beastly tind.

XVI

Closely the wicked flame his bowels brent,
And shortly grew into outrageous fire;
Yet had he not the hart, nor hardiment,
As vnto her to vtter his desire;
His caytiue thought durst not so high aspire,
But with soft sighes, and louely semblaunces,
He ween'd that his affection entire
She should aread; many resemblaunces
To her he made, and many kind remembraunces.

XVII

Oft from the forrest wildings he did bring,
Whose sides empurpled were with smiling red,
And oft young birds, which he had taught to sing
His mistresse prayses, sweetly caroled,
Girlonds of flowres sometimes for her faire hed
He fine would dight; sometimes the squirell wild
He brought to her in bands, as conquered
To be her thrall, his fellow seruant vild;
All which, she of him tooke with countenance meeke and mild.

XVIII

But past awhile, when she fit season saw
To leaue that desert mansion, she cast
In secret wize her selfe thence to withdraw,
For feare of mischiefe, which she did forecast
Might by the witch or by her sonne compast:
Her wearie Palfrey closely, as she might,
Now well recouered after long repast,
In his proud furnitures she freshly dight,
His late miswandred wayes now to remeasure right.

XIX

And earely ere the dawning day appeard,
She forth issewed, and on her iourney went;
She went in perill, of each noyse affeard,
And of each shade, that did it selfe present;
For still she feared to be ouerhent,
Of that vile hag, or her vnciuile sonne:
Who when too late awaking, well they kent,
That their faire guest was gone, they both begonne
To make exceeding mone, as they had bene vndonne.

XX

But that lewd louer did the most lament
For her depart, that euer man did heare;
He knockt his brest with desperate intent,
And scratcht his face, and with his teeth did teare
His rugged flesh, and rent his ragged heare:
That his sad mother seeing his sore plight,
Was greatly woe begon, and gan to feare,
Least his fraile senses were emperisht quight,
And loue to frenzy turnd, sith loue is franticke hight.

XXI

All wayes she sought, him to restore to plight,
With herbs, with charms, with counsell, and with teares,
But tears, nor charms, nor herbs, nor counsell might
Asswage the fury, which his entrails teares:
So strong is passion, that no reason heares.
Tho when all other helpes she saw to faile,
She turnd her selfe backe to her wicked leares
And by her deuilish arts thought to preuaile,
To bring her backe againe, or worke her finall bale.

XXII

Eftsoones out of her hidden caue she cald
An hideous beast, of horrible aspect,
That could the stoutest courage haue appald;
Monstrous mishapt, and his backe was spect
With thousand spots of colours queint elect,
Thereto so swift, that it all beasts did pas:
Like neuer yet did liuing eye detect;
But likest it to an *Hyena* was,
That feeds on womens flesh, as others feede on gras.

XXIII

It forth she cald, and gaue it streight in charge,
Through thicke and thin her to pursew apace,
Ne once to stay to rest, or breath at large,
Till her he had attaind, and brought in place,
Or quite deuourd her beauties scornefull grace.
The Monster swift as word, that from her went,
Went forth in hast, and did her footing trace
So sure and swiftly, through his perfect sent,
And passing speede, that shortly he her ouerhent.

XXIV

Whom when the fearefull Damzell nigh espide,
No need to bid her fast away to flie;
That vgly shape so sore her terrifide,
That it she shund no lesse, then dread to die,
And her flit Palfrey did so well apply
His nimble feet to her conceiued feare,
That whilest his breath did strength to him supply,
From perill free he her away did beare:
But when his force gan faile, his pace gan wex areare.

XXV

Which whenas she perceiu'd, she was dismayd
At that same last extremitie full sore,
And of her safetie greatly grew afrayd;
And now she gan approch to the sea shore,
As it befell, that she could flie no more,
But yield her selfe to spoile of greedinesse.
Lightly she leaped, as a wight forlore,
From her dull horse, in desperate distresse,
And to her feet betooke her doubtfull sickernesse.

XXVI

Not halfe so fast the wicked *Myrrha* fled
From dread of her reuenging fathers hond:
Nor halfe so fast to saue her maidenhed,
Fled fearefull *Daphne* on th'*AEgaean* strond,
As *Florimell* fled from that Monster yond,
To reach the sea, ere she of him were raught:
For in the sea to drowne her selfe she fond,
Rather then of the tyrant to be caught:
Thereto feare gaue her wings, and neede her courage taught.

XXVII

It fortuned (high God did so ordaine)
As she arriued on the roring shore,
In minde to leape into the mighty maine,
A little boate lay houing her before,
In which there slept a fisher old and pore,
The whiles his nets were drying on the sand:
Into the same she leapt, and with the ore
Did thrust the shallop from the floting strand:
So safetie found at sea, which she found not at land.

XXVIII

The Monster ready on the pray to sease,
Was of his forward hope deceiued quight;
Ne durst assay to wade the perlous seas,
But greedily long gaping at the sight,
At last in vaine was forst to turne his flight,
And tell the idle tidings to his Dame:
Yet to auenge his deuilish despight,
He set vpon her Palfrey tired lame,
And slew him cruelly, ere any reskew came.

XXIX

And after hauing him embowelled,
To fill his hellish gorge, it chaunst a knight
To passe that way, as forth he trauelled;
It was a goodly Swaine, and of great might,
As euer man that bloudy field did fight;
But in vaine sheows, that wont yong knights bewitch,
And courtly seruices tooke no delight,
But rather ioyd to be, then seemen sich:
For both to be and seeme to him was labour lich.

XXX

It was to weete the good Sir *Satyrane,*
That raungd abroad to seeke aduentures wilde,
As was his wont in forrest, and in plaine;
He was all armd in rugged steele vnfilde,
As in the smoky forge it was compilde,
And in his Scutchin bore a Satyres hed:
He comming present, where the Monster vilde
Vpon that milke-white Palfreyes carkas fed,
Vnto his reskew ran, and greedily him sped.

XXXI

There well perceiu'd he, that it was the horse,
Whereon faire *Florimell* was wont to ride,
That of that feend was rent without remorse:
Much feared he, least ought did ill betide
To that faire Mayd, the flowre of womens pride;
For her he dearely loued, and in all
His famous conquests highly magnifide:
Besides her golden girdle, which did fall
From her in flight, he found, that did him sore apall.

XXXII

Full of sad feare, and doubtfull agony,
Fiercely he flew vpon that wicked feend,
And with huge strokes, and cruell battery
Him forst to leaue his pray, for to attend
Him selfe from deadly daunger to defend:
Full many wounds in his corrupted flesh
He did engraue, and muchell bloud did spend,
Yet might not do him dye, but aye more fresh
And fierce he still appeard, the more he did him thresh.

XXXIII

He wist not, how him to despoile of life,
Ne how to win the wished victory,
Sith him he saw still stronger grow through strife,
And him selfe weaker through infirmity;
Greatly he grew enrag'd, and furiously
Hurling his sword away, he lightly lept
Vpon the beast, that with great cruelty
Rored, and raged to be vnder-kept:
Yet he perforce him held, and strokes vpon him hept.

XXXIV

As he that striues to stop a suddein flood,
And in strong banckes his violence enclose,
Forceth it swell aboue his wonted mood,
And largely ouerflow the fruitfull plaine,
That all the countrey seemes to be a Maine,
And the rich furrowes flote, all quite fordonne:
The wofull husbandman doth lowd complaine,
To see his whole yeares labour lost so soone,
For which to God he made so many an idle boone.

XXXV

So him he held, and did through might amate:
So long he held him, and him bet so long,
That at the last his fiercenesse gan abate,
And meekely stoup vnto the victour strong:
Who to auenge the implacable wrong,
Which he supposed donne to *Florimell*,
Sought by all meanes his dolour to prolong,
Sith dint of steele his carcas could not quell:
His maker with her charmes had framed him so well.

XXXVI

The golden ribband, which that virgin wore
About her sclender wast, he tooke in hand,
And with it bound the beast, that lowd did rore
For great despight of that vnwonted band,
Yet dared not his victour to withstand,
But trembled like a lambe, fled from the pray,
And all the way him followd on the strand,
As he had long bene learned to obay;
Yet neuer learned he such seruice, till that day.

XXXVII

Thus as he led the Beast along the way,
He spide far off a mighty Giauntesse,
Fast flying on a Courser dapled gray,
From a bold knight, that with great hardinesse
Her hard pursewd, and sought for to suppresse;
She bore before her lap a dolefull Squire,
Lying athwart her horse in great distresse,
Fast bounden hand and foote with cords of wire,
Whom she did meane to make the thrall of her desire.

XXXVIII

Which whenas *Satyrane* beheld, in hast
He left his captiue Beast at liberty,
And crost the nearest way, by which he cast
Her to encounter, ere she passed by:
But she the way shund nathemore for thy,
But forward gallopt fast; which when he spyde,
His mighty speare he couched warily,
And at her ran: she hauing him descryde,
Her selfe to fight addrest, and threw her lode aside.

XXXIX

Like as a Goshauke, that in foote doth beare
A trembling Culuer, hauing spied on hight
An Egle, that with plumy wings doth sheare
The subtile ayre, stouping with all his might,
The quarrey throwes to ground with fell despight,
And to the battell doth her selfe prepare:
So ran the Geauntesse vnto the fight;
Her firie eyes with furious sparkes did stare,
And with blasphemous bannes high God in peeces tare.

XL

She caught in hand an huge great yron mace,
Wherewith she many had of life depriued,
But ere the stroke could seize his aymed place,
His speare amids her sun-broad shield arriued;
Yet nathemore the steele a sunder riued,
All were the beame in bignesse like a mast,
Ne her out of the stedfast sadle driued,
But glauncing on the tempred mettall, brast
In thousand shiuers, and so forth beside her past.

XLI

Her Steed did stagger with that puissaunt strooke;
But she no more was moued with that might,
Then it had lighted on an aged Oke;
Or on the marble Pillour, that is pight
Vpon the top of Mount *Olympus* hight,
For the braue youthly Champions to assay,
With burning charet wheeles it nigh to smite:
But who that smites it, mars his ioyous play,
And is the spectacle of ruinous decay.

XLII

Yet therewith sore enrag'd, with sterne regard
Her dreadfull weapon she to him addrest,
Which on his helmet martelled so hard,
That made him low incline his lofty crest,
And bowd his battred visour to his brest:
Wherewith he was so stund, that he n'ote ryde,
But reeled to and fro from East to West:
Which when his cruell enimy espyde,
She lightly vnto him adioyned side to syde;

XLIII

And on his collar laying puissant hand,
Out of his wauering seat him pluckt perforse,
Perforse him pluckt, vnable to withstand,
Or helpe himselfe, and laying thwart her horse,
In loathly wise like to a carion corse,
She bore him fast away. Which when the knight,
That her pursewed, saw with great remorse,
He neare was touched in his noble spright,
And gan encrease his speed, as she encreast her flight.

XLIV

Whom when as nigh approching she espyde,
She threw away her burden angrily;
For she list not the battell to abide,
But made her selfe more light, away to fly:
Yet her the hardy knight pursewd so nye,
That almost in the backe he oft her strake:
But still when him at hand she did espy,
She turnd, and semblaunce of faire fight did make;
But when he stayd, to flight againe she did her take.

XLV

By this the good Sir *Satyrane* gan wake
Out of his dreame, that did him long entraunce,
And seeing none in place, he gan to make
Exceeding mone, and curst that cruell chaunce,
Which reft from him so faire a cheuisaunce:
At length he spide, whereas that wofull Squire,
Whom he had reskewed from captiuaunce
Of his strong foe, lay tombled in the myre,
Vnable to arise, or foot or hand to styre.

XLVI

To whom approching, well he mote perceiue
In that foule plight a comely personage,
And louely face, made fit for to deceiue
Fraile Ladies hart with loues consuming rage,
Now in the blossome of his freshest age:
He reard him vp, and loosd his yron bands,
And after gan inquire his parentage,
And how he fell into that Gyaunts hands,
And who that was, which chaced her along the lands.

XLVII

Then trembling yet through feare, the Squire bespake,
That Geauntesse *Argante* is behight,
A daughter of the *Titans* which did make
Warre against heauen, and heaped hils on hight,
To scale the skyes, and put *Ioue* from his right:
Her sire *Typhœus* was, who mad through merth,
And drunke with bloud of men, slaine by his might,
Through incest, her of his owne mother Earth
Whilome begot, being but halfe twin of that berth.

XLVIII

For at that berth another Babe she bore,
To weet the mighty *Ollyphant*, that wrought
Great wreake to many errant knights of yore,
And many hath to foule confusion brought.
These twinnes, men say, (a thing far passing thought)
Whiles in their mothers wombe enclosd they were,
Ere they into the lightsome world were brought,
In fleshly lust were mingled both yfere,
And in that monstrous wise did to the world appere.

XLIX

So liu'd they euer after in like sin,
Gainst natures law, and good behauioure:
But greatest shame was to that maiden twin,
Who not content so fowly to deuoure
Her natiue flesh, and staine her brothers bowre,
Did wallow in all other fleshly myre,
And suffred beasts her body to deflowre:
So whot she burned in that lustfull fyre,
Yet all that might not slake her sensuall desyre.

L

But ouer all the countrey she did raunge,
To seeke young men, to quench her flaming thurst,
And feed her fancy with delightfull chaunge:
Whom so she fittest finds to serue her lust,
Through her maine strength, in which she most doth trust,
She with her brings into a secret Ile,
Where in eternall bondage dye he must,
Or be the vassall of her pleasures vile,
And in all shamefull sort him selfe with her defile.

LI

Me seely wretch she so at vauntage caught,
After she long in waite for me did lye,
And meant vnto her prison to haue brought,
Her lothsome pleasure there to satisfye;
That thousand deathes me leuer were to dye,
Then breake the vow, that to faire *Columbell*
I plighted haue, and yet keepe stedfastly:
As for my name, it mistreth not to tell;
Call me the *Squyre of Dames* that me beseemeth well.

LII

But that bold knight, whom ye pursuing saw
That Geauntesse, is not such, as she seemed,
But a faire virgin, that in martiall law,
And deedes of armes aboue all Dames is deemed,
And aboue many knights is eke esteemed,
For her great worth; She *Palladine* is hight:
She you from death, you me from dread redeemed.
Ne any may that Monster match in fight,
But she, or such as she, that is so chaste a wight.

LIII

Her well beseemes that Quest (quoth *Satyrane*)
But read, thou *Squyre of Dames*, what vow is this,
Which thou vpon thy selfe hast lately ta'ne?
That shall I you recount (quoth he) ywis,
So be ye pleasd to pardon all amis.
That gentle Lady, whom I loue and serue,
After long suit and weary seruicis,
Did aske me, how I could her loue deserue,
And how she might be sure, that I would neuer swerue.

LIV

I glad by any meanes her grace to gaine,
Bad her commaund my life to saue, or spill.
Eftsoones she bad me, with incessaunt paine
To wander through the world abroad at will,
And euery where, where with my power or skill
I might do seruice vnto gentle Dames,
That I the same should faithfully fulfill,
And at the twelue monethes end should bring their names
And pledges; as the spoiles of my victorious games.

LV

So well I to faire Ladies seruice did,
And found such fauour in their louing hartes,
That ere the yeare his course had compassid,
Three hundred pledges for my good desartes,
And thrise three hundred thanks for my good partes
I with me brought, and did to her present:
Which when she saw, more bent to eke my smartes,
Then to reward my trusty true intent,
She gan for me deuise a grieuous punishment.

LVI

To weet, that I my trauell should resume,
And with like labour walke the world around,
Ne euer to her presence should presume,
Till I so many other Dames had found,
The which, for all the suit I could propound,
Would me refuse their pledges to afford,
But did abide for euer chast and sound.
Ah gentle Squire (quoth he) tell at one word,
How many foundst thou such to put in thy record?

LVII

In deed Sir knight (said he) one word may tell
All, that I euer found so wisely stayd;
For onely three they were disposd so well,
And yet three yeares I now abroad haue strayd,
To find them out. Mote I (then laughing sayd
The knight) inquire of thee, what were those three,
The which thy proffred curtesie denayd?
Or ill they seemed sure auizd to bee,
Or brutishly brought vp, that neu'r did fashions see.

LVIII

The first which then refused me (said hee)
Certes was but a common Courtisane,
Yet flat refusd to haue a do with mee,
Because I could not giue her many a Iane.
(Thereat full hartely laughed *Satyrane*)
The second was an holy Nunne to chose,
Which would not let me be her Chappellane,
Because she knew, she said, I would disclose
Her counsell, if she should her trust in me repose.

LIX

The third a Damzell was of low degree,
Whom I in countrey cottage found by chaunce;
Full little weened I, that chastitee
Had lodging in so meane a maintenaunce,
Yet was she faire, and in her countenance
Dwelt simple truth in seemely fashion.
Long thus I woo'd her with dew obseruance,
In hope vnto my pleasure to haue won;
But was as farre at last, as when I first begon.

LX

Safe her, I neuer any woman found,
That chastity did for it selfe embrace,
But were for other causes firme and sound;
Either for want of handsome time and place,
Or else for feare of shame and fowle disgrace.
Thus am I hopelesse euer to attaine
My Ladies loue, in such a desperate case,
But all my dayes am like to wast in vaine,
Seeking to match the chaste with th'vnchaste Ladies traine.

LXI

Perdy, (said *Satyrane*) thou *Squire of Dames*,
Great labour fondly hast thou hent in hand,
To get small thankes, and therewith many blames,
That may emongst *Alcides* labours stand.
Thence backe returning to the former land,
Where late he left the Beast, he ouercame,
He found him not; for he had broke his band,
And was return'd againe vnto his Dame,
To tell what tydings of faire *Florimell* became.

Canto VIII

The Witch creates a snowy Lady,
like to Florimell,
Who wrongd by Carle by Proteus sau'd,
is sought by Paridell.

I

SO oft as I this history record,
My hart doth melt with meere compassion,
To thinke, how causelesse of her owne accord

This gentle Damzell, whom I write vpon,
Should plonged be in such affliction,
Without all hope of comfort or reliefe,
That sure I weene, the hardest hart of stone,
Would hardly find to aggrauate her griefe;
For misery craues rather mercie, then repriefe.

II

But that accursed Hag, her hostesse late,
Had so enranckled her malitious hart,
That she desyrd th'abridgement of her fate,
Or long enlargement of her painefull smart.
Now when the Beast, which by her wicked art
Late forth she sent, she backe returning spyde,
Tyde with her broken girdle, it a part
Of her rich spoyles, whom he had earst destroyd,
She weend, and wondrous gladnesse to her hart applyde.

III

And with it running hast'ly to her sonne,
Thought with that sight him much to haue reliued;
Who thereby deeming sure the thing as donne,
His former griefe with furie fresh reuiued,
Much more then earst, and would haue algates riued
The hart out of his brest: for sith her ded
He surely dempt, himselfe he thought depriued
Quite of all hope, wherewith he long had fed
His foolish maladie, and long time had misled.

IV

With thought whereof, exceeding mad he grew,
And in his rage his mother would haue slaine,
Had she not fled into a secret mew,
Where she was wont her Sprights to entertaine
The maisters of her art: there was she faine
To call them all in order to her ayde,
And them coniure vpon eternall paine,
To counsell her so carefully dismayd,
How she might heale her sonne, whose senses were decayd.

V

By their aduise, and her owne wicked wit,
She there deuiz'd a wondrous worke to frame,

Whose like on earth was neuer framed yit,
That euen Nature selfe enuide the same,
And grudg'd to see the counterfet should shame
The thing it selfe. In hand she boldly tooke
To make another like the former Dame,
Another *Florimell*, in shape and looke
So liuely and so like, that many it mistooke.

VI

The substance, whereof she the bodie made,
Was purest snow in massie mould congeald,
Which she had gathered in a shadie glade
Of the *Riphœan* hils, to her reueald
By errant Sprights, but from all men conceald:
The same she tempred with fine Mercury,
And virgin wex, that neuer yet was seald,
And mingled them with perfect vermily,
That like a liuely sanguine it seem'd to the eye.

VII

In stead of eyes two burning lampes she set
In siluer sockets, shyning like the skyes,
And a quicke mouing Spirit did arret
To stirre and roll them, like a womans eyes;
In stead of yellow lockes she did deuise,
With golden wyre to weaue her curled head;
Yet golden wyre was not so yellow thrise
As *Florimells* faire haire: and in the stead
Of life, she put a Spright to rule the carkasse dead.

VIII

A wicked Spright yfraught with fawning guile,
And faire resemblance aboue all the rest,
Which with the Prince of Darknesse fell somewhile,
From heauens blisse and euerlasting rest;
Him needed not instruct, which way were best
Himselfe to fashion likest *Florimell*,
Ne how to speake, ne how to vse his gest,
For he in counterfeisance did excell,
And all the wyles of wemens wits knew passing well.

IX

Him shaped thus, she deckt in garments gay,
Which *Florimell* had left behind her late,
That who so then her saw, would surely say,
It was her selfe, whom it did imitate,
Or fairer then her selfe, if ought algate
Might fairer be. And then she forth her brought
Vnto her sonne, that lay in feeble state;
Who seeing her gan streight vpstart, and thought
She was the Lady selfe, whom he so long had sought.

X

Tho fast her clipping twixt his armes twaine,
Extremely ioyed in so happie sight,
And soone forgot his former sickly paine;
But she, the more to seeme such as she hight,
Coyly rebutted his embracement light;
Yet still with gentle countenaunce retained,
Enough to hold a foole in vaine delight:
Him long she so with shadowes entertained,
As her Creatresse had in charge to her ordained.

XI

Till on a day, as he disposed was
To walke the woods with that his Idole faire,
Her to disport, and idle time to pas,
In th'open freshnesse of the gentle aire,
A knight that way there chaunced to repaire;
Yet knight he was not, but a boastfull swaine,
That deedes of armes had euer in despaire,
Proud *Braggadocchio*, that in vaunting vaine
His glory did repose, and credit did maintaine.

XII

He seeing with that Chorle so faire a wight,
Decked with many a costly ornament,
Much merueiled thereat, as well he might,
And thought that match a fowle disparagement:
His bloudie speare eftsoones he boldly bent
Against the silly clowne, who dead through feare,
Fell streight to ground in great astonishment;
Villein (said he) this Ladie is my deare,
Dy, if thou it gainesay: I will away her beare.

XIII

The fearefull Chorle durst not gainesay, nor dooe,
But trembling stood, and yielded him the pray;
Who finding litle leasure her to wooe,
On *Tromparts* steed her mounted without stay,
And without reskew led her quite away.
Proud man himselfe then *Braggadocchio* deemed,
And next to none, after that happie day,
Being possessed of that spoyle, which seemed
The fairest wight on ground, and most of men esteemed.

XIV

But when he saw himselfe free from poursute,
He gan make gentle purpose to his Dame,
With termes of loue and lewdnesse dissolute;
For he could well his glozing speaches frame
To such vaine vses, that him best became:
But she thereto would lend but light regard,
As seeming sory, that she euer came
Into his powre, that vsed her so hard,
To reaue her honor, which she more then life prefard.

XV

Thus as they two of kindnesse treated long,
There them by chaunce encountred on the way
An armed knight, vpon a courser strong,
Whose trampling feet vpon the hollow lay
Seemed to thunder, and did nigh affray
That Capons courage: yet he looked grim,
And fain'd to cheare his Ladie in dismay;
Who seem'd for feare to quake in euery lim,
And her to saue from outrage, meekely prayed him.

XVI

Fiercely that stranger forward came, and nigh
Approching, with bold words and bitter threat,
Bad that same boaster, as he mote, on high
To leaue to him that Lady for excheat,
Or bide him battell without further treat.
That challenge did too peremptory seeme,
And fild his senses with abashment great;
Yet seeing nigh him ieopardy extreme,
He it dissembled well, and light seem'd to esteeme.

XVII

Saying, Thou foolish knight, that weenst with words
To steale away, that I with blowes haue wonne,
And brought throgh points of many perilous swords:
But if thee list to see thy Courser ronne,
Or proue thy selfe, this sad encounter shonne,
And seeke else without hazard of thy hed.
At those proud words that other knight begonne
To wexe exceeding wroth, and him ared
To turne his steede about, or sure he should be ded.

XVIII

Sith then (said *Braggadocchio*) needes thou wilt
Thy dayes abridge, through proofe of puissance,
Turne we our steedes, that both in equall tilt
May meet againe, and each take happie chance.
This said, they both a furlongs mountenance
Retyrd their steeds, to ronne in euen race:
But *Braggadocchio* with his bloudie lance
Once hauing turnd, no more returnd his face,
But left his loue to losse, and fled himselfe apace.

XIX

The knight him seeing fly, had no regard
Him to poursew, but to the Ladie rode,
And hauing her from *Trompart* lightly reard,
Vpon his Courser set the louely lode,
And with her fled away without abode.
Well weened he, that fairest *Florimell*
It was, with whom in company he yode,
And so her selfe did alwaies to him tell;
So made him thinke him selfe in heauen, that was in hell.

XX

But *Florimell* her selfe was farre away,
Driuen to great distresse by Fortune straunge,
And taught the carefull Mariner to play,
Sith late mischaunce had her compeld to chaunge
The land for sea, at randon there to raunge:
Yet there that cruell Queene auengeresse,
Not satisfide so farre her to estraunge
From courtly blisse and wonted happinesse,
Did heape on her new waues of weary wretchednesse.

XXI

For being fled into the fishers bote,
For refuge from the Monsters crueltie,
Long so she on the mightie maine did flote,
And with the tide droue forward careleslie;
For th'aire was milde, and cleared was the skie,
And all his windes *Dan Aeolus* did keepe,
From stirring vp their stormy enmitie,
As pittying to see her waile and weepe;
But all the while the fisher did securely sleepe.

XXII

At last when droncke with drowsinesse, he woke,
And saw his drouer driue along the streame,
He was dismayd, and thrise his breast he stroke,
For maruell of that accident extreame;
But when he saw that blazing beauties beame,
Which with rare light his bote did beautifie,
He marueild more, and thought he yet did dreame
Not well awakt, or that some extasie
Assotted had his sense, or dazed was his eie.

XXIII

But when her well auizing, he perceiued
To be no vision, nor fantasticke sight,
Great comfort of her presence he conceiued,
And felt in his old courage new delight
To gin awake, and stirre his frozen spright:
Tho rudely askt her, how she thither came.
Ah (said she) father, I note read aright,
What hard misfortune brought me to the same;
Yet am I glad that here I now in safety am.

XXIV

But thou good man, sith farre in sea we bee,
And the great waters gin apace to swell,
That now no more we can the maine-land see,
Haue care, I pray, to guide the cock-bote well,
Least worse on sea then vs on land befell.
Thereat th'old man did nought but fondly grin,
And said, his boat the way could wisely tell:
But his deceiptfull eyes did neuer lin,
To looke on her faire face, and marke her snowy skin.

XXV

The sight whereof in his congealed flesh,
Infixt such secret sting of greedy lust,
That the drie withered stocke it gan refresh,
And kindled heat, that soone in flame forth brust:
The driest wood is soonest burnt to dust.
Rudely to her he lept, and his rough hand
Where ill became him, rashly would haue thrust,
But she with angry scorne him did withstond,
And shamefully reproued for his rudenesse fond.

XXVI

But he, that neuer good nor maners knew,
Her sharpe rebuke full litle did esteeme;
Hard is to teach an old horse amble trew.
The inward smoke, that did before but steeme,
Broke into open fire and rage extreme,
And now he strength gan adde vnto his will,
Forcing to doe, that did him fowle misseeme:
Beastly he threw her downe, ne car'd to spill
Her garments gay with scales of fish, that all did fill.

XXVII

The silly virgin stroue him to withstand,
All that she might, and him in vaine reuild:
She struggled strongly both with foot and hand,
To saue her honor from that villaine vild,
And cride to heauen, from humane helpe exild.
O ye braue knights, that boast this Ladies loue,
Where be ye now, when she is nigh defild
Of filthy wretch? well may shee you reproue
Of falshood or of slouth, when most it may behoue.

XXVIII

But if that thou, Sir *Satyran*, didst weete,
Or thou, Sir *Peridure*, her sorie state,
How soone would yee assemble many a fleete,
To fetch from sea, that ye at land lost late;
Towres, Cities, Kingdomes ye would ruinate,
In your auengement and dispiteous rage,
Ne ought your burning fury mote abate;
But if Sir *Calidore* could it presage,
No liuing creature could his cruelty asswage.

XXIX

But sith that none of all her knights is nye,
See how the heauens of voluntary grace,
And soueraine fauour towards chastity,
Doe succour send to her distressed cace:
So much high God doth innocence embrace.
It fortuned, whilest thus she stifly stroue,
And the wide sea importuned long space
With shrilling shriekes, *Proteus* abrode did roue,
Along the fomy waues driuing his finny droue.

XXX

Proteus is Shepheard of the seas of yore,
And hath the charge of *Neptunes* mightie heard;
An aged sire with head all frory hore,
And sprinckled frost vpon his deawy beard:
Who when those pittifull outcries he heard,
Through all the seas so ruefully resound,
His charet swift in haste he thither steard,
Which with a teeme of scaly *Phocas* bound
Was drawne vpon the waues, that fomed him around.

XXXI

And comming to that Fishers wandring bote,
That went at will, withouten carde or sayle,
He therein saw that yrkesome sight, which smote
Deepe indignation and compassion frayle
Into his hart attonce: streight did he hayle
The greedy villein from his hoped pray,
Of which he now did very litle fayle,
And with his staffe, that driues his Heard astray,
Him bet so sore, that life and sense did much dismay.

XXXII

The whiles the pitteous Ladie vp did ryse,
Ruffled and fowly raid with filthy soyle,
And blubbred face with teares of her faire eyes:
Her heart nigh broken was with weary toyle,
To saue her selfe from that outrageous spoyle,
But when she looked vp, to weet, what wight
Had her from so infamous fact assoyld,
For shame, but more for feare of his grim sight,
Downe in her lap she hid her face, and loudly shright.

XXXIII

Her selfe not saued yet from daunger dred
She thought, but chaung'd from one to other feare;
Like as a fearefull Partridge, that is fled
From the sharpe Hauke, which her attached neare,
And fals to ground, to seeke for succour theare,
Whereas the hungry Spaniels she does spy,
With greedy iawes her readie for to teare;
In such distresse and sad perplexity
Was *Florimell*, when *Proteus* she did see thereby.

XXXIV

But he endeuoured with speeches milde
Her to recomfort, and accourage bold,
Bidding her feare no more her foeman vilde,
Nor doubt himselfe; and who he was, her told.
Yet all that could not from affright her hold,
Ne to recomfort her at all preuayld;
For her faint heart was with the frozen cold
Benumbd so inly, that her wits nigh fayld,
And all her senses with abashment quite were quayld.

XXXV

Her vp betwixt his rugged hands he reard,
And with his frory lips full softly kist,
Whiles the cold ysickles from his rough beard,
Dropped adowne vpon her yuorie brest:
Yet he himselfe so busily addrest,
That her out of astonishment he wrought,
And out of that same fishers filthy nest
Remouing her, into his charet brought,
And there with many gentle termes her faire besought.

XXXVI

But that old leachour, which with bold assault
That beautie durst presume to violate,
He cast to punish for his hainous fault;
Then tooke he him yet trembling sith of late,
And tyde behind his charet, to aggrate
The virgin, whom he had abusde so sore:
So drag'd him through the waues in scornefull state,
And after cast him vp, vpon the shore;
But *Florimell* with him vnto his bowre he bore.

XXXVII

His bowre is in the bottome of the maine,
Vnder a mightie rocke, gainst which do raue
The roaring billowes in their proud disdaine,
That with the angry working of the waue,
Therein is eaten out an hollow caue,
That seemes rough Masons hand with engines keene
Had long while laboured it to engraue:
There was his wonne, ne liuing wight was seene,
Saue one old *Nymph*, hight *Panope* to keepe it cleane.

XXXVIII

Thither he brought the sory *Florimell*,
And entertained her the best he might
And *Panope* her entertaind eke well,
As an immortall mote a mortall wight,
To winne her liking vnto his delight:
With flattering words he sweetly wooed her,
And offered faire gifts t'allure her sight,
But she both offers and the offerer
Despysde, and all the fawning of the flatterer.

XXXIX

Daily he tempted her with this or that,
And neuer suffred her to be at rest:
But euermore she him refused flat,
And all his fained kindnesse did detest,
So firmely she had sealed vp her brest.
Sometimes he boasted, that a God he hight:
But she a mortall creature loued best:
Then he would make himselfe a mortall wight;
But then she said she lou'd none, but a Faerie knight.

XL

Then like a Faerie knight himselfe he drest;
For euery shape on him he could endew:
Then like a king he was to her exprest,
And offred kingdomes vnto her in vew,
To be his Leman and his Ladie trew:
But when all this he nothing saw preuaile,
With harder meanes he cast her to subdew,
And with sharpe threates her often did assaile,
So thinking for to make her stubborne courage quaile.

XLI

To dreadfull shapes he did himselfe transforme,
Now like a Gyant, now like to a feend,
Then like a Centaure, then like to a storme,
Raging within the waues: thereby he weend
Her will to win vnto his wished end.
But when with feare, nor fauour, nor with all
He else could doe, he saw himselfe esteemd,
Downe in a Dongeon deepe he let her fall,
And threatned there to make her his eternall thrall.

XLII

Eternall thraldome was to her more liefe,
Then losse of chastitie, or chaunge of loue:
Die had she rather in tormenting griefe,
Then any should of falsenesse her reproue,
Or loosenesse, that she lightly did remoue.
Most vertuous virgin, glory be thy meed,
And crowne of heauenly praise with Saints aboue,
Where most sweet hymmes of this thy famous deed
Are still emongst them song, that far my rymes exceed.

XLIII

Fit song of Angels caroled to bee;
But yet what so my feeble Muse can frame,
Shall be t'aduance thy goodly chastitee,
And to enroll thy memorable name,
In th'heart of euery honourable Dame,
That they thy vertuous deedes may imitate,
And be partakers of thy endlesse fame.
It yrkes me, leaue thee in this wofull state,
To tell of *Satyrane*, where I him left of late.

XLIV

Who hauing ended with that *Squire of Dames*
A long discourse of his aduentures vaine,
The which himselfe, then Ladies more defames,
And finding not th'*Hyena* to be slaine,
With that same *Squire*, returned backe againe
To his first way. And as they forward went,
They spyde a knight faire pricking on the plaine,
As if he were on some aduenture bent,
And in his port appeared manly hardiment.

XLV

Sir *Satyrane* him towards did addresse,
To weet, what wight he was, and what his quest:
And comming nigh, eftsoones he gan to gesse
Both by the burning hart, which on his brest
He bare, and by the colours in his crest,
That *Paridell* it was. Tho to him yode,
And him saluting, as beseemed best,
Gan first inquire of tydings farre abrode;
And afterwardes, on what aduenture now he rode.

XLVI

Who thereto answering, said; The tydings bad,
Which now in Faerie court all men do tell,
Which turned hath great mirth, to mourning sad,
Is the late ruine of proud *Marinell*,
And suddein parture of faire *Florimell*,
To find him forth: and after her are gone
All the braue knights, that doen in armes excell,
To sauegard her, ywandred all alone;
Emongst the rest my lot (vnworthy) is to be one.

XLVII

Ah gentle knight (said then Sir *Satyrane*)
Thy labour all is lost, I greatly dread,
That hast a thanklesse seruice on thee ta'ne,
And offrest sacrifice vnto the dead:
For dead, I surely doubt, thou maist aread
Henceforth for euer *Florimell* to be,
That all the noble knights of *Maydenhead*,
Which her ador'd, may sore repent with me,
And all faire Ladies may for euer sory be.

XLVIII

Which words when *Paridell* had heard, his hew
Gan greatly chaunge, and seem'd dismayd to bee;
Then said, Faire Sir, how may I weene it trew,
That ye doe tell in such vncertaintee?
Or speake ye of report, or did ye see
Iust cause of dread, that makes ye doubt so sore?
For perdie else how mote it euer bee,
That euer hand should dare for to engore
Her noble bloud? the heauens such crueltie abhore.

XLIX

These eyes did see, that they will euer rew
T'haue seene, (quoth he) when as a monstrous beast
The Palfrey, whereon she did trauell, slew,
And of his bowels made his bloudie feast:
Which speaking token sheweth at the least
Her certaine losse, if not her sure decay:
Besides, that more suspition encreast,
I found her golden girdle cast astray,
Distaynd with durt and bloud, as relique of the pray.

L

Aye me, (said *Paridell*) the signes be sad,
And but God turne the same to good soothsay,
That Ladies safetie is sore to be drad:
Yet will I not forsake my forward way,
Till triall doe more certaine truth bewray.
Faire Sir (quoth he) well may it you succeed,
Ne long shall *Satyrane* behind you stay,
But to the rest, which in this Quest proceed
My labour adde, and be partaker of their speed.

LI

Ye noble knights (said then the *Squire of Dames*)
Well may ye speed in so praiseworthy paine:
But sith the Sunne now ginnes to slake his beames,
In deawy vapours of the westerne maine,
And lose the teme out of his weary waine,
Mote not mislike you also to abate
Your zealous hast, till morrow next againe
Both light of heauen, and strength of men relate:
Which if ye please, to yonder castle turne your gate.

LII

That counsell pleased well; so all yfere
Forth marched to a Castle them before,
Where soone arriuing, they restrained were
Of readie entrance, which ought euermore
To errant knights be commun: wondrous sore
Thereat displeasd they were, till that young Squire
Gan them informe the cause, why that same dore
Was shut to all, which lodging did desire:
The which to let you weet, will further time require.

Canto IX

Malbecco will no straunge knights host,
For peeuish gealosie:
Paridell giusts with Britomart:
Both shew their auncestrie.

I

REdoubted knights, and honorable Dames,
To whom I leuell all my labours end,
Right sore I feare, least with vnworthy blames
This odious argument my rimes should shend,
Or ought your goodly patience offend,
Whiles of a wanton Lady I do write,
Which with her loose incontinence doth blend
The shyning glory of your soueraigne light,
And knighthood fowle defaced by a faithlesse knight.

II

But neuer let th'ensample of the bad
Offend the good: for good by paragone
Of euill, may more notably be rad,
As white seemes fairer, macht with blacke attone;
Ne all are shamed by the fault of one:
For lo in heauen, whereas all goodnesse is,
Emongst the Angels, a whole legione
Of wicked Sprights did fall from happy blis;
What wonder then, if one of women all did mis?

III

Then listen Lordings, if ye list to weet
The cause, why *Satyrane* and *Paridell*
Mote not be entertaynd, as seemed meet,
Into that Castle (as that Squire does tell.)
Therein a cancred crabbed Carle does dwell,
That has no skill of Court nor courtesie,
Ne cares, what men say of him ill or well;
For all his dayes he drownes in priuitie,
Yet has full large to liue, and spend at libertie.

IV

But all his mind is set on mucky pelfe,
To hoord vp heapes of euill gotten masse,
For which he others wrongs, and wreckes himselfe;

Yet he is lincked to a louely lasse,
Whose beauty doth her bounty far surpasse,
The which to him both far vnequall yeares,
And also far vnlike conditions has;
For she does ioy to play emongst her peares,
And to be free from hard restraint and gealous feares.

                                        V

But he is old, and withered like hay,
Vnfit faire Ladies seruice to supply;
The priuie guilt whereof makes him alway
Suspect her truth, and keepe continuall spy
Vpon her with his other blincked eye;
Ne suffreth he resort of liuing wight
Approch to her, ne keepe her company,
But in close bowre her mewes from all mens sight,
Depriu'd of kindly ioy and naturall delight.

                                        VI

Malbecco he, and *Hellenore* she hight,
Vnfitly yokt together in one teeme,
That is the cause, why neuer any knight
Is suffred here to enter, but he seeme
Such, as no doubt of him he neede misdeeme.
Thereat Sir *Satyrane* gan smile, and say;
Extremely mad the man I surely deeme,
That weenes with watch and hard restraint to stay
A womans will, which is disposd to go astray.

                                        VII

In vaine he feares that, which he cannot shonne:
For who wotes not, that womans subtiltyes
Can guilen *Argus*, when she list misdonne?
It is not yron bandes, nor hundred eyes,
Nor brasen walls, nor many wakefull spyes,
That can withhold her wilfull wandring feet;
But fast good will with gentle curtesyes,
And timely seruice to her pleasures meet
May her perhaps containe, that else would algates fleet.

                                        VIII

Then is he not more mad (said *Paridell*)
That hath himselfe vnto such seruice sold,

In dolefull thraldome all his dayes to dwell?
For sure a foole I do him firmely hold,
That loues his fetters, though they were of gold.
But why do we deuise of others ill,
Whiles thus we suffer this same dotard old,
To keepe vs out, in scorne of his owne will,
And rather do not ransack all, and him selfe kill?

IX

Nay let vs first (said *Satyrane*) entreat
The man by gentle meanes, to let vs in,
And afterwardes affray with cruell threat,
Ere that we to efforce it do begin:
Then if all fayle, we will by force it win,
And eke reward the wretch for his mesprise,
As may be worthy of his haynous sin.
That counsell pleasd: then *Paridell* did rise,
And to the Castle gate approcht in quiet wise.

X

Whereat soft knocking, entrance he desyrd.
The good man selfe, which then the Porter playd,
Him answered, that all were now retyrd
Vnto their rest, and all the keyes conuayd
Vnto their maister, who in bed was layd,
That none him durst awake out of his dreme;
And therefore them of patience gently prayd.
Then *Paridell* began to chaunge his theme,
And threatned him with force and punishment extreme.

XI

But all in vaine; for nought mote him relent,
And now so long before the wicket fast
They wayted, that the night was forward spent,
And the faire welkin fowly ouercast,
Gan blowen vp a bitter stormy blast,
With shoure and hayle so horrible and dred,
That this faire many were compeld at last,
To fly for succour to a little shed,
The which beside the gate for swine was ordered.

XII

It fortuned, soone after they were gone,
Another knight, whom the tempest thither brought,
Came to that Castle, and with earnest mone,
Like as the rest, late entrance deare besought;
But like so as the rest he prayd for nought,
For flatly he of entrance was refusd,
Sorely thereat he was displeasd, and thought
How to auenge himselfe so sore abusd,
And euermore the Carle of curtesie accusd.

XIII

But to auoyde th'intollerable stowre,
He was compeld to seeke some refuge neare,
And to that shed, to shrowd him from the showre,
He came, which full of guests he found whyleare,
So as he was not let to enter there:
Whereat he gan to wex exceeding wroth,
And swore, that he would lodge with them yfere,
Or them dislodge, all were they liefe or loth;
And so defide them each, and so defide them both.

XIV

Both were full loth to leaue that needfull tent,
And both full loth in darkenesse to debate;
Yet both full liefe him lodging to haue lent,
And both full liefe his boasting to abate;
But chiefly *Paridell* his hart did grate,
To heare him threaten so despightfully,
As if he did a dogge to kenell rate,
That durst not barke; and rather had he dy,
Then when he was defide, in coward corner ly.

XV

Tho hastily remounting to his steed,
He forth issew'd; like as a boistrous wind,
Which in th'earthes hollow caues hath long bin hid,
And shut vp fast within her prisons blind,
Makes the huge element against her kind
To moue, and tremble as it were agast,
Vntill that it an issew forth may find;
Then forth it breakes, and with his furious blast
Confounds both land and seas, and skyes doth ouercast.

XVI

Their steel-hed speares they strongly coucht, and met
Together with impetuous rage and forse,
That with the terrour of their fierce affret,
They rudely droue to ground both man and horse,
That each awhile lay like a sencelesse corse.
But *Paridell* sore brused with the blow,
Could not arise, the counterchaunge to scorse,
Till that young Squire him reared from below;
Then drew he his bright sword, and gan about him throw.

XVII

But *Satyrane* forth stepping, did them stay
And with faire treatie pacifide their ire,
Then when they were accorded from the fray,
Against that Castles Lord they gan conspire,
To heape on him dew vengeaunce for his hire.
They bene agreed, and to the gates they goe
To burne the same with vnquenchable fire,
And that vncurteous Carle their commune foe
To do fowle death to dye, or wrap in grieuous woe.

XVIII

Malbecco seeing them resolu'd in deed
To flame the gates, and hearing them to call
For fire in earnest, ran with fearefull speed,
And to them calling from the castle wall,
Besought them humbly, him to beare with all,
As ignoraunt of seruants bad abuse,
And slacke attendaunce vnto straungers call.
The knights were willing all things to excuse,
Though nought beleu'd, and entraunce late did not refuse.

XIX

They bene ybrought into a comely bowre,
And seru'd of all things that mote needfull bee;
Yet secretly their hoste did on them lowre,
And welcomde more for feare, then charitee;
But they dissembled, what they did not see,
And welcomed themselues. Each gan vndight
Their garments wet, and weary armour free,
To dry them selues by *Vulcanes* **flaming light,**
And eke their lately bruzed parts to bring in plight.

XX

And eke that straunger knight emongst the rest,
Was for like need enforst to disaray:
Tho whenas vailed was her loftie crest,
Her golden locks, that were in tramels gay
Vpbounden, did them selues adowne display,
And raught vnto her heeles; like sunny beames,
That in a cloud their light did long time stay,
Their vapour vaded, shew their golden gleames,
And through the persant aire shoote forth their azure streames.

XXI

She also dofte her heauy haberieon,
Which the faire feature of her limbs did hyde,
And her well plighted frock, which she did won
To tucke about her short, when she did ryde,
She low let fall, that flowd from her lanck syde
Downe to her foot, with carelesse modestee.
Then of them all she plainly was espyde,
To be a woman wight, vnwist to bee,
The fairest woman wight, that euer eye did see.

XXII

Like as *Minerua*, being late returnd
From slaughter of the Giaunts conquered;
Where proud *Encelade*, whose wide nosethrils burnd
With breathed flames, like to a furnace red,
Transfixed with the speare, downe tombled ded
From top of *Hemus*, by him heaped hye;
Hath loosd her helmet from her lofty hed,
And her *Gorgonian* shield gins to vntye
From her left arme, to rest in glorious victorye.

XXIII

Which whenas they beheld, they smitten were
With great amazement of so wondrous sight,
And each on other, and they all on her
Stood gazing, as if suddein great affright
Had them surprised. At last auizing right,
Her goodly personage and glorious hew,
Which they so much mistooke, they tooke delight
In their first errour, and yet still anew
With wonder of her beauty fed their hungry vew.

XXIV

Yet note their hungry vew be satisfide,
But seeing still the more desir'd to see,
And euer firmely fixed did abide
In contemplation of diuinitie:
But most they meruaild at her cheualree,
And noble prowesse, which they had approued,
That much they faynd to know, who she mote bee;
Yet none of all them her thereof amoued,
Yet euery one her likte, and euery one her loued.

XXV

And *Paridell* though partly discontent
With his late fall, and fowle indignity,
Yet was soone wonne his malice to relent,
Through gracious regard of her faire eye,
And knightly worth, which he too late did try,
Yet tried did adore. Supper was dight;
Then they *Malbecco* prayd of curtesy,
That of his Lady they might haue the sight,
And company at meat, to do them more delight.

XXVI

But he to shift their curious request,
Gan causen, why she could not come in place;
Her crased health, her late recourse to rest,
And humid euening ill for sicke folkes cace:
But none of those excuses could take place;
Ne would they eate, till she in presence came.
She came in presence with right comely grace,
And fairely them saluted, as became,
And shewd her selfe in all a gentle curteous Dame.

XXVII

They sate to meat, and *Satyrane* his chaunce
Was her before, and *Paridell* besyde;
But he him selfe sate looking still askaunce,
Gainst *Britomart*, and euer closely eyde
Sir *Satyrane*, that glaunces might not glyde:
But his blind eye, that syded *Paridell*,
All his demeasnure from his sight did hyde:
On her faire face so did he feede his fill,
And sent close messages of loue to her at will.

Page | 1003

XXVIII

And euer and anone, when none was ware,
With speaking lookes, that close embassage bore,
He rou'd at her, and told his secret care:
For all that art he learned had of yore.
Ne was she ignoraunt of that lewd lore,
But in his eye his meaning wisely red,
And with the like him answerd euermore:
She sent at him one firie dart, whose hed
Empoisned was with priuy lust, and gealous dred.

XXIX

He from that deadly throw made no defence,
But to the wound his weake hart opened wyde;
The wicked engine through false influence,
Past through his eyes, and secretly did glyde
Into his hart, which it did sorely gryde.
But nothing new to him was that same paine,
Ne paine at all; for he so oft had tryde
The powre thereof, and lou'd so oft in vaine,
That thing of course he counted, loue to entertaine.

XXX

Thenceforth to her he sought to intimate
His inward griefe, by meanes to him well knowne,
Now *Bacchus* fruit out of the siluer plate
He on the table dasht, as ouerthrowne,
Or of the fruitfull liquor ouerflowne,
And by the dauncing bubbles did diuine,
Or therein write to let his loue be showne;
Which well she red out of the learned line,
A sacrament prophane in mistery of wine.

XXXI

And when so of his hand the pledge she raught,
The guilty cup she fained to mistake,
And in her lap did shed her idle draught,
Shewing desire her inward flame to slake:
By such close signes they secret way did make
Vnto their wils, and one eyes watch escape;
Two eyes him needeth, for to watch and wake,
Who louers will deceiue. Thus was the ape,
By their faire handling, put into *Malbeccoes* cape.

XXXII

Now when of meats and drinks they had their fill,
Purpose was moued by that gentle Dame,
Vnto those knights aduenturous, to tell
Of deeds of armes, which vnto them became,
And euery one his kindred, and his name.
Then *Paridell*, in whom a kindly pryde
Of gracious speach, and skill his words to frame
Abounded, being glad of so fit tyde
Him to commend to her, thus spake, of all well eyde.

XXXIII

Troy, that art now nought, but an idle name,
And in thine ashes buried low dost lie,
Though whilome far much greater then thy fame,
Before that angry Gods, and cruell skye
Vpon thee heapt a direfull destinie,
What boots it boast thy glorious descent,
And fetch from heauen thy great Genealogie,
Sith all thy worthy prayses being blent,
Their of-spring hath embaste, and later glory shent.

XXXIV

Most famous Worthy of the world, by whome
That warre was kindled, which did *Troy* inflame,
And stately towres of *Ilion* whilome
Brought vnto balefull ruine, was by name
Sir *Paris* far renowmd through noble fame,
Who through great prowesse and bold hardinesse,
From *Lacedaemon* fetcht the fairest Dame,
That euer *Greece* did boast, or knight possesse,
Whom *Venus* to him gaue for meed of worthinesse.

XXXV

Faire *Helene*, flowre of beautie excellent,
And girlond of the mighty Conquerours,
That madest many Ladies deare lament
The heauie losse of their braue Paramours,
Which they far off beheld from *Troian* toures,
And saw the fieldes of faire *Scamander* strowne
With carcases of noble warrioures,
Whose fruitlesse liues were vnder furrow sowne,
And *Xanthus* sandy bankes with bloud all ouerflowne.

XXXVI

From him my linage I deriue aright,
Who long before the ten yeares siege of *Troy*,
Whiles yet on *Ida* he a shepheard hight,
On faire *Oenone* got a louely boy,
Whom for remembraunce of her passed ioy,
She of his Father *Parius* did name;
Who, after *Greekes* did *Priams* realme destroy,
Gathred the *Troian* reliques sau'd from flame,
And with them sayling thence, to th'Isle of *Paros* came.

XXXVII

That was by him cald *Paros*, which before
Hight *Nausa*, there he many yeares did raine,
And built *Nausicle* by the *Pontick* shore,
The which he dying left next in remaine
To *Paridas* his sonne.
From whom I *Paridell* by kin descend;
But for faire Ladies loue, and glories gaine,
My natiue soile haue left, my dayes to spend
In sewing deeds of armes, my liues and labours end.

XXXVIII

Whenas the noble *Britomart* heard tell
Of *Troian* warres, and *Priams* Citie sackt,
The ruefull story of Sir *Paridell*,
She was empassiond at that piteous act,
With zelous enuy of Greekes cruell fact,
Against that nation, from whose race of old
She heard, that she was lineally extract:
For noble *Britons* sprong from *Troians* bold,
And *Troynouant* was built of old *Troyes* ashes cold.

XXXIX

Then sighing soft awhile, at last she thus:
O lamentable fall of famous towne,
Which raignd so many yeares victorious,
And of all *Asie* bore the soueraigne crowne,
In one sad night consumd, and throwen downe:
What stony hart, that heares thy haplesse fate,
Is not empierst with deepe compassiowne,
And makes ensample of mans wretched state,
That floures so fresh at morne, and fades at euening late?

XL

Behold, Sir, how your pitifull complaint
Hath found another partner of your payne:
For nothing may impresse so deare constraint,
As countries cause, and commune foes disdayne.
But if it should not grieue you, backe agayne
To turne your course, I would to heare desyre,
What to *Aeneas* fell; sith that men sayne
He was not in the Cities wofull fyre
Consum'd, but did him selfe to safetie retyre.

XLI

Anchyses sonne begot of *Venus* faire,
(Said he,) out of the flames for safegard fled,
And with a remnant did to sea repaire,
Where he through fatall errour long was led
Full many yeares, and weetlesse wandered
From shore to shore, emongst the Lybicke sands,
Ere rest he found. Much there he suffered,
And many perils past in forreine lands,
To saue his people sad from victours vengefull hands.

XLII

At last in *Latium* he did arriue,
Where he with cruell warre was entertaind
Of th'inland folke, which sought him backe to driue,
Till he with old *Latinus* was constraind,
To contract wedlock: (so the fates ordaind.)
Wedlock contract in bloud, and eke in blood
Accomplished, that many deare complaind:
The riuall slaine, the victour through the flood
Escaped hardly, hardly praisd his wedlock good.

XLIII

Yet after all, he victour did suruiue,
And with *Latinus* did the kingdome part.
But after, when both nations gan to striue,
Into their names the title to conuart,
His sonne *Iu"lus* did from thence depart,
With all the warlike youth of *Troians* bloud,
And in long *Alba* plast his throne apart,
Where faire it florished, and long time stoud,
Till *Romulus* renewing it, to *Rome* remoud.

XLIV

There there (said *Britomart*) a fresh appeard
The glory of the later world to spring,
And *Troy* againe out of her dust was reard,
To sit in second seat of soueraigne king,
Of all the world vnder her gouerning.
But a third kingdome yet is to arise,
Out of the *Troians* scattered of-spring,
That in all glory and great enterprise,
Both first and second *Troy* shall dare to equalise.

XLV

It *Troynouant* is hight, that with the waues
Of wealthy *Thamis* washed is along,
Vpon whose stubborne neck, whereat he raues
With roring rage, and sore him selfe does throng,
That all men feare to tempt his billowes strong,
She fastned hath her foot, which standes so hy,
That it a wonder of the world is song
In forreine landes, and all which passen by,
Beholding it from far, do thinke it threates the skye.

XLVI

The *Troian Brute* did first that Citie found,
And Hygate made the meare thereof by West,
And *Ouert* gate by North: that is the bound
Toward the land; two riuers bound the rest.
So huge a scope at first him seemed best,
To be the compasse of his kingdomes seat:
So huge a mind could not in lesser rest,
Ne in small meares containe his glory great,
That *Albion* had conquered first by warlike feat.

XLVII

Ah fairest Lady knight, (said *Paridell*)
Pardon I pray my heedlesse ouersight,
Who had forgot, that whilome I heard tell
From aged *Mnemon*; for my wits bene light.
Indeed he said (if I remember right,)
That of the antique *Troian* stocke, there grew
Another plant, that raught to wondrous hight,
And far abroad his mighty branches threw,
Into the vtmost Angle of the world he knew.

XLVIII

For that same *Brute*, whom much he did aduaunce
In all his speach, was *Syluius* his sonne,
Whom hauing slaine, through luckles arrowes glaunce
He fled for feare of that he had misdonne,
Or else for shame, so fowle reproch to shonne,
And with him led to sea an youthly trayne,
Where wearie wandring they long time did wonne,
And many fortunes prou'd in th'*Ocean* mayne,
And great aduentures found, that now were long to sayne.

XLIX

At last by fatall course they driuen were
Into an Island spatious and brode,
The furthest North, that did to them appeare:
Which after rest they seeking far abrode,
Found it the fittest soyle for their abode,
Fruitfull of all things fit for liuing foode,
But wholy wast, and void of peoples trode,
Saue an huge nation of the Geaunts broode,
That fed on liuing flesh, and druncke mens vitall blood.

L

Whom he through wearie wars and labours long,
Subdewd with losse of many *Britons* bold:
In which the great *Goemagot* of strong
 Corineus, and *Coulin* of *Debon* old
Were ouerthrowne, and layd on th'earth full cold,
Which quaked vnder their so hideous masse,
A famous history to be enrold
In euerlasting moniments of brasse,
That all the antique Worthies merits far did passe.

LI

His worke great *Troynouant*, his worke is eke
Faire *Lincolne*, both renowmed far away,
That who from East to West will endlong seeke,
Cannot two fairer Cities find this day,
Except *Cleopolis*: so heard I say
Old *Mnemon*. Therefore Sir, I greet you well
Your countrey kin, and you entirely pray
Of pardon for the strife, which late befell
Betwixt vs both vnknowne. So ended *Paridell*.

LII

But all the while, that he these speaches spent,
Vpon his lips hong faire Dame *Hellenore*,
With vigilant regard, and dew attent,
Fashioning worlds of fancies euermore
In her fraile wit, that now her quite forlore:
The whiles vnwares away her wondring eye,
And greedy eares her weake hart from her bore:
Which he perceiuing, euer priuily
In speaking, many false belgardes at her let fly.

LIII

So long these knights discoursed diuersly,
Of straunge affaires, and noble hardiment,
Which they had past with mickle ieopardy,
That now the humid night was farforth spent,
And heauenly lampes were halfendeale ybrent:
Which th'old man seeing well, who too long thought
Euery discourse and euery argument,
Which by the houres he measured, besought
Them go to rest. So all vnto their bowres were brought.

Canto X

Paridell rapeth Hellenore:
Malbecco her pursewes:
Findes emongst Satyres, whence with him
To turne she doth refuse.

I

THe morow next, so soone as *Phœbus* Lamp
Bewrayed had the world with early light,
And fresh *Aurora* had the shady damp
Out of the goodly heauen amoued quight,
Faire *Britomart* and that same *Faerie* knight
Vprose, forth on their iourney for to wend:
But *Paridell* complaynd, that his late fight
With *Britomart*, so sore did him offend,
That ryde he could not, till his hurts he did amend.

II

So forth they far'd, but he behind them stayd,
Maulgre his host, who grudged grieuously,
To house a guest, that would be needes obayd,

And of his owne him left not liberty:
Might wanting measure moueth surquedry.
Two things he feared, but the third was death;
That fierce youngmans vnruly maistery;
His money, which he lou'd as liuing breath;
And his faire wife, whom honest long he kept vneath.

III

But patience perforce he must abie,
What fortune and his fate on him will lay,
Fond is the feare, that findes no remedie;
Yet warily he watcheth euery way,
By which he feareth euill happen may:
So th'euill thinkes by watching to preuent;
Ne doth he suffer her, nor night, nor day,
Out of his sight her selfe once to absent.
So doth he punish her and eke himselfe torment.

IV

But *Paridell* kept better watch, then hee,
A fit occasion for his turne to find:
False loue, why do men say, thou canst not see,
And in their foolish fancie feigne thee blind,
That with thy charmes the sharpest sight doest bind,
And to thy will abuse? Thou walkest free,
And seest euery secret of the mind;
Thou seest all, yet none at all sees thee;
All that is by the working of thy Deitee.

V

So perfect in that art was *Paridell*,
That he *Melbeccoes* halfen eye did wyle,
His halfen eye he wiled wondrous well,
And *Hellenors* both eyes did eke beguyle,
Both eyes and hart attonce, during the whyle
That he there soiourned his wounds to heale;
That *Cupid* selfe it seeing, close did smyle,
To weet how he her loue away did steale,
And bad, that none their ioyous treason should reueale.

VI

The learned louer lost no time nor tyde,
That least auantage mote to him afford,

Yet bore so faire a saile, that none espyde
His secret drift, till he her layd abord.
When so in open place, and commune bord,
He fortun'd her to meet, with commune speach
Her courted her, yet bayted euery word,
That his vngentle hoste n'ote him appeach
Of vile vngentlenesse, or hospitages breach.

VII

But when apart (if euer her apart)
He found, then his false engins fast he plyde,
And all the sleights vnbosomd in his hart;
He sigh'd, he sobd, he swownd, he perdy dyde,
And cast himselfe on ground her fast besyde:
Tho when againe he him bethought to liue,
He wept, and wayld, and false laments belyde,
Saying, but if she Mercie would him giue
That he mote algates dye, yet did his death forgiue.

VIII

And otherwhiles with amorous delights,
And pleasing toyes he would her entertaine,
Now singing sweetly, to surprise her sprights,
Now making layes of loue and louers paine,
Bransles, Ballads, virelayes, and verses vaine;
Oft purposes, oft riddles he deuysd,
And thousands like, which flowed in his braine,
With which he fed her fancie, and entysd
To take to his new loue, and leaue her old despysd.

IX

And euery where he might, and euery while
He did her seruice dewtifull, and sewed
At hand with humble pride, and pleasing guile,
So closely yet, that none but she it vewed,
Who well perceiued all, and all indewed.
Thus finely did he his false nets dispred,
With which he many weake harts had subdewed
Of yore, and many had ylike misled:
What wonder then, if she were likewise carried?

X

No fort so fensible, no wals so strong,
But that continuall battery will riue,
Or daily siege through dispuruayance long,
And lacke of reskewes will to parley driue;
And Peece, that vnto parley eare will giue,
Will shortly yeeld it selfe, and will be made
The vassall of the victors will byliue:
That stratageme had oftentimes assayd
This crafty Paramoure, and now it plaine displayd.

XI

For through his traines he her intrapped hath,
That she her loue and hart hath wholy sold
To him, without regard of gaine, or scath,
Or care of credite, or of husband old,
Whom she hath vow'd to dub a faire Cucquold.
Nought wants but time and place, which shortly shee
Deuized hath, and to her louer told.
It pleased well. So well they both agree;
So readie rype to ill, ill wemens counsels bee.

XII

Darke was the Euening, fit for louers stealth,
When chaunst *Melbecco* busie be elsewhere,
She to his closet went, where all his wealth
Lay hid: thereof she countlesse summes did reare,
The which she meant away with her to beare;
The rest she fyr'd for sport, or for despight;
As *Hellene*, when she saw aloft appeare
The *Troiane* flames, and reach to heauens hight
Did clap her hands, and ioyed at that dolefull sight.

XIII

This second *Hellene*, faire Dame *Hellenore*,
The whiles her husband ranne with sory haste,
To quench the flames which she had tyn'd before,
Laught at his foolish labour spent in waste;
And ranne into her louers armes right fast;
Where streight embraced, she to him did cry,
And call aloud for helpe, ere helpe were past;
For loe that Guest would beare her forcibly,
And meant to rauish her, that rather had to dy.

XIV

The wretched man hearing her call for ayd,
And readie seeing him with her to fly,
In his disquiet mind was much dismayd:
But when againe he backward cast his eye,
And saw the wicked fire so furiously
Consume his hart, and scorch his Idoles face,
He was therewith distressed diuersly,
Ne wist he how to turne, nor to what place;
Was neuer wretched man in such a wofull cace.

XV

Ay when to him she cryde, to her he turnd,
And left the fire; loue money ouercame:
But when he marked, how his money burnd,
He left his wife; money did loue disclame:
Both was he loth to loose his loued Dame,
And loth to leaue his liefest pelfe behind,
Yet sith he n'ote saue both, he sau'd that same,
Which was the dearest to his donghill mind,
The God of his desire, the ioy of misers blind.

XVI

Thus whilest all things in troublous vprore were,
And all men busie to suppresse the flame,
The louing couple need no reskew feare,
But leasure had, and libertie to frame
Their purpost flight, free from all mens reclame;
And Night, the patronesse of loue-stealth faire,
Gaue them safe conduct, till to end they came:
So bene they gone yfeare, a wanton paire
Of louers loosely knit, where list them to repaire.

XVII

Soone as the cruell flames yslaked were,
 Malbecco seeing, how his losse did lye,
Out of the flames, which he had quencht whylere
Into huge waues of griefe and gealosye
Full deepe emplonged was, and drowned nye,
Twixt inward doole and felonous despight;
He rau'd, he wept, he stampt, he lowd did cry,
And all the passions, that in man may light,
Did him attonce oppresse, and vex his caytiue spright.

XVIII

Long thus he chawd the cud of inward griefe,
And did consume his gall with anguish sore,
Still when he mused on his late mischiefe,
Then still the smart thereof increased more,
And seem'd more grieuous, then it was before:
At last when sorrow he saw booted nought,
Ne griefe might not his loue to him restore,
He gan deuise, how her he reskew mought,
Ten thousand wayes he cast in his confused thought.

XIX

At last resoluing, like a pilgrim pore,
To search her forth, where so she might be fond,
And bearing with him treasure in close store,
The rest he leaues in ground: So takes in hond
To seeke her endlong, both by sea and lond.
Long he her sought, he sought her farre and nere,
And euery where that he mote vnderstond,
Of knights and ladies any meetings were,
And of eachone he met, he tydings did inquere.

XX

But all in vaine, his woman was too wise,
Euer to come into his clouch againe,
And he too simple euer to surprise
The iolly *Paridell*, for all his paine.
One day, as he forpassed by the plaine
With weary pace, he farre away espide
A couple, seeming well to be his twaine,
Which houed close vnder a forrest side,
As if they lay in wait, or else themselues did hide.

XXI

Well weened he, that those the same mote bee,
And as he better did their shape auize,
Him seemed more their manner did agree;
For th'one was armed all in warlike wize,
Whom, to be *Paridell* he did deuize;
And th'other all yclad in garments light,
Discolour'd like to womanish disguise,
He did resemble to his Ladie bright;
And euer his faint hart much earned at the sight.

XXII

And euer faine he towards them would goe,
But yet durst not for dread approchen nie,
But stood aloofe, vnweeting what to doe;
Till that prickt forth with loues extremitie,
That is the father of foule gealosy,
He closely nearer crept, the truth to weet:
But, as he nigher drew, he easily
Might scerne, that it was not his sweetest sweet,
Ne yet her Belamour, the partner of his sheet.

XXIII

But it was scornefull *Braggadocchio*,
That with his seruant *Trompart* houerd there,
Sith late he fled from his too earnest foe:
Whom such when as *Malbecco* spyed clere,
He turned backe, and would haue fled arere;
Till *Trompart* ronning hastily, him did stay,
And bad before his soueraine Lord appere:
That was him loth, yet durst he not gainesay,
And comming him before, low louted on the lay.

XXIV

The Boaster at him sternely bent his browe,
As if he could haue kild him with his looke,
That to the ground him meekely made to bowe,
And awfull terror deepe into him strooke,
That euery member of his bodie quooke.
Said he, thou man of nought, what doest thou here,
Vnfitly furnisht with thy bag and booke,
Where I expected one with shield and spere,
To proue some deedes of armes vpon an equall pere.

XXV

The wretched man at his imperious speach,
Was all abasht, and low prostrating, said;
Good Sir, let not my rudenesse be no breach
Vnto your patience, ne be ill ypaid;
For I vnwares this way by fortune straid,
A silly Pilgrim driuen to distresse,
That seeke a Lady, There he suddein staid,
And did the rest with grieuous sighes suppresse,
While teares stood in his eies, few drops of bitternesse.

XXVI

What Ladie, man? (said *Trompart*) take good hart,
And tell thy griefe, if any hidden lye;
Was neuer better time to shew thy smart,
Then now, that noble succour is thee by,
That is the whole worlds commune remedy.
That chearefull word his weake hart much did cheare,
And with vaine hope his spirits faint supply,
That bold he said; O most redoubted Pere,
Vouchsafe with mild regard a wretches cace to heare.

XXVII

Then sighing sore, It is not long (said hee)
Sith I enioyd the gentlest Dame aliue;
Of whom a knight, no knight at all perdee,
But shame of all, that doe for honor striue,
By treacherous deceipt did me depriue;
Through open outrage he her bore away,
And with fowle force vnto his will did driue,
Which all good knights, that armes do beare this day,
Are bound for to reuenge, and punish if they may.

XXVIII

And you most noble Lord, that can and dare
Redresse the wrong of miserable wight,
Cannot employ your most victorious speare
In better quarrell, then defence of right,
And for a Ladie gainst a faithlesse knight;
So shall your glory be aduaunced much,
And all faire Ladies magnifie your might,
And eke my selfe, albe I simple such,
Your worthy paine shall well reward with guerdon rich.

XXIX

With that out of his bouget forth he drew
Great store of treasure, therewith him to tempt;
But he on it lookt scornefully askew,
As much disdeigning to be so misdempt,
Or a war-monger to be basely nempt;
And said; thy offers base I greatly loth,
And eke thy words vncourteous and vnkempt;
I tread in dust thee and thy money both,
That, were it not for shame, So turned from him wroth.

XXX

But *Trompart*, that his maisters humor knew,
In lofty lookes to hide an humble mind,
Was inly tickled with that golden vew,
And in his eare him rounded close behind:
Yet stoupt he not, but lay still in the wind,
Waiting aduauntage on the pray to sease;
Till *Trompart* lowly to the ground inclind,
Besought him his great courage to appease,
And pardon simple man, that rash did him displease.

XXXI

Bigge looking like a doughtie Doucepere,
At last he thus; Thou clod of vilest clay,
I pardon yield, and with thy rudenesse beare;
But weete henceforth, that all that golden pray,
And all that else the vaine world vaunten may,
I loath as doung, ne deeme my dew reward:
Fame is my meed, and glory vertues pray.
But minds of mortall men are muchell mard,
And mou'd amisse with massie mucks vnmeet regard.

XXXII

And more, I graunt to thy great miserie
Gratious respect, thy wife shall backe be sent,
And that vile knight, who euer that he bee,
Which hath thy Lady reft, and knighthood shent,
By *Sanglamort* my sword, whose deadly dent
The bloud hath of so many thousands shed,
I sweare, ere long shall dearely it repent;
Ne he twixt heauen and earth shall hide his hed,
But soone he shall be found, and shortly doen be ded.

XXXIII

The foolish man thereat woxe wondrous blith,
As if the word so spoken, were halfe donne,
And humbly thanked him a thousand sith,
That had from death to life him newly wonne.
Tho forth the Boaster marching, braue begonne
His stolen steed to thunder furiously,
As if he heauen and hell would ouerronne,
And all the world confound with cruelty,
That much *Malbecco* ioyed in his iollity.

XXXIV

Thus long they three together traueiled,
Through many a wood, and many an vncouth way,
To seeke his wife, that was farre wandered:
But those two sought nought, but the present pray,
To weete the treasure, which he did bewray,
On which their eies and harts were wholly set,
With purpose, how they might it best betray;
For sith the houre, that first he did them let
The same behold, therewith their keene desires were whet.

XXXV

It fortuned as they together far'd,
They spide, where *Paridell* came pricking fast
Vpon the plaine, the which himselfe prepar'd
To giust with that braue straunger knight a cast,
As on aduenture by the way he past:
Alone he rode without his Paragone;
For hauing filcht her bels, her vp he cast
To the wide world, and let her fly alone,
He nould be clogd. So had he serued many one.

XXXVI

The gentle Lady, loose at randon left,
The greene-wood long did walke, and wander wide
At wilde aduenture, like a forlorne weft,
Till on a day the *Satyres* her espide
Straying alone withouten groome or guide;
Her vp they tooke, and with them home her led,
With them as housewife euer to abide,
To milke their gotes, and make them cheese and bred,
And euery one as commune good her handeled.

XXXVII

That shortly she *Malbecco* has forgot,
And eke Sir *Paridell*, all were he deare;
Who from her went to seeke another lot,
And now by fortune was arriued here,
Where those two guilers with *Malbecco* were:
Soone as the oldman saw Sir *Paridell*,
He fainted, and was almost dead with feare,
Ne word he had to speake, his griefe to tell,
But to him louted low, and greeted goodly well.

XXXVIII

And after asked him for *Hellenore*,
I take no keepe of her (said *Paridell*)
She wonneth in the forrest there before.
So forth he rode, as his aduenture fell;
The whiles the Boaster from his loftie sell
Faynd to alight, something amisse to mend;
But the fresh Swayne would not his leasure dwell,
But went his way; whom when he passed kend,
He vp remounted light, and after faind to wend.

XXXIX

Perdy nay (said *Malbecco*) shall ye not:
But let him passe as lightly, as he came:
For litle good of him is to be got,
And mickle perill to be put to shame.
But let vs go to seeke my dearest Dame,
Whom he hath left in yonder forrest wyld:
For of her safety in great doubt I am,
Least saluage beastes her person haue despoyld:
Then all the world is lost, and we in vaine haue toyld.

XL

They all agree, and forward them addrest:
Ah but (said craftie *Trompart*) weete ye well,
That yonder in that wastefull wildernesse
Huge monsters haunt, and many dangers dwell;
Dragons, and Minotaures, and feendes of hell,
And many wilde woodmen, which robbe and rend
All trauellers; therefore aduise ye well,
Before ye enterprise that way to wend:
One may his iourney bring too soone to euill end.

XLI

Malbecco stopt in great astonishment,
And with pale eyes fast fixed on the rest,
Their counsell crau'd, in daunger imminent.
Said *Trompart*, you that are the most opprest
With burden of great treasure, I thinke best
Here for to stay in safetie behind;
My Lord and I will search the wide forrest.
That counsell pleased not *Malbeccoes* mind;
For he was much affraid, himselfe alone to find.

XLII

Then is it best (said he) that ye doe leaue
Your treasure here in some securitie,
Either fast closed in some hollow greaue,
Or buried in the ground from ieopardie,
Till we returne againe in safetie:
As for vs two, least doubt of vs ye haue,
Hence farre away we will blindfolded lie,
Ne priuie be vnto your treasures graue.
It pleased: so he did. Then they march forward braue.

XLIII

Now when amid the thickest woods they were,
They heard a noyse of many bagpipes shrill,
And shrieking Hububs them approching nere,
Which all the forrest did with horror fill:
That dreadfull sound the boasters hart did thrill,
With such amazement, that in haste he fled,
Ne euer looked backe for good or ill,
And after him eke fearefull *Trompart* sped;
The old man could not fly, but fell to ground halfe ded.

XLIV

Yet afterwards close creeping, as he might,
He in a bush did hide his fearefull hed,
The iolly *Satyres* full of fresh delight,
Came dauncing forth, and with them nimbly led
Faire *Helenore*, with girlonds all bespred,
Whom their May-lady they had newly made:
She proud of that new honour, which they red,
And of their louely fellowship full glade,
Daunst liuely, and her face did with a Lawrell shade.

XLV

The silly man that in the thicket lay
Saw all this goodly sport, and grieued sore,
Yet durst he not against it doe or say,
But did his hart with bitter thoughts engore,
To see th'vnkindnesse of his *Hellenore*.
All day they daunced with great lustihed,
And with their horned feet the greene grasse wore,
The whiles their Gotes vpon the brouzes fed,
Till drouping *Phœbus* gan to hide his golden hed.

XLVI

Tho vp they gan their merry pypes to trusse,
And all their goodly heards did gather round,
But euery *Satyre* first did giue a busse
To *Hellenore*: so busses did abound.
Now gan the humid vapour shed the ground
With perly deaw, and th'Earthes gloomy shade
Did dim the brightnesse of the welkin round,
That euery bird and beast awarned made,
To shrowd themselues, whiles sleepe their senses did inuade.

XLVII

Which when *Melbecco* saw, out of his bush
Vpon his hands and feete he crept full light,
And like a Gote emongst the Gotes did rush,
That through the helpe of his faire hornes on hight,
And misty dampe of misconceiuing night,
And eke through likenesse of his gotish beard,
He did the better counterfeite aright:
So home he marcht emongst the horned heard,
That none of all the *Satyres* him espyde or heard.

XLVIII

At night, when all they went to sleepe, he vewd,
Whereas his louely wife emongst them lay,
Embraced of a *Satyre* rough and rude,
Who all the night did minde his ioyous play:
Nine times he heard him come aloft ere day,
That all his hart with gealosie did swell;
But yet that nights ensample did bewray,
That not for nought his wife them loued so well,
When one so oft a night did ring his matins bell.

XLIX

So closely as he could, he to them crept,
When wearie of their sport to sleepe they fell,
And to his wife, that now full soundly slept,
He whispered in her eare, and did her tell,
That it was he, which by her side did dwell,
And therefore prayd her wake, to heare him plaine.
As one out of a dreame not waked well,
She turned her, and returned backe againe:
Yet her for to awake he did the more constraine.

L

At last with irkesome trouble she abrayd;
And then perceiuing, that it was indeed
Her old *Malbecco*, which did her vpbrayd,
With loosenesse of her loue, and loathly deed,
She was astonisht with exceeding dreed,
And would haue wakt the *Satyre* by her syde;
But he her prayd, for mercy, or for meed,
To saue his life, ne let him be descryde,
But hearken to his lore, and all his counsell hyde.

LI

Tho gan he her perswade, to leaue that lewd
And loathsome life, of God and man abhord,
And home returne, where all should be renewd
With perfect peace, and bandes of fresh accord,
And she receiu'd againe to bed and bord,
As if no trespasse euer had bene donne:
But she it all refused at one word,
And by no meanes would to his will be wonne,
But chose emongst the iolly *Satyres* still to wonne.

LII

He wooed her, till day spring he espyde;
But all in vaine: and then turnd to the heard,
Who butted him with hornes on euery syde,
And trode downe in the durt, where his hore beard
Was fowly dight, and he of death afeard.
Early before the heauens fairest light
Out of the ruddy East was fully reard,
The heardes out of their foldes were loosed quight,
And he emongst the rest crept forth in sory plight.

LIII

So soone as he the Prison dore did pas,
He ran as fast, as both his feete could beare,
And neuer looked, who behind him was,
Ne scarsely who before: like as a Beare
That creeping close, amongst the hiues to reare
An hony combe, the wakefull dogs espy,
And him assayling, sore his carkasse teare,
That hardly he with life away does fly,
Ne stayes, till safe himselfe he see from ieopardy.

LIV

Ne stayd he, till he came vnto the place,
Where late his treasure he entombed had,
Where when he found it not (for *Trompart* bace
Had it purloyned for his maister bad:)
With extreme fury he became quite mad,
And ran away, ran with himselfe away:
That who so straungely had him seene bestad,
With vpstart haire, and staring eyes dismay,
From Limbo lake him late escaped sure would say.

LV

High ouer hilles and ouer dales he fled,
As if the wind him on his winges had borne,
Ne banck nor bush could stay him, when he sped
His nimble feet, as treading still on thorne:
Griefe, and despight, and gealosie, and scorne
Did all the way him follow hard behind,
And he himselfe himselfe loath'd so forlorne,
So shamefully forlorne of womankind;
That as a Snake, still lurked in his wounded mind.

LVI

Still fled he forward, looking backward still,
Ne stayd his flight, nor fearefull agony,
Till that he came vnto a rockie hill,
Ouer the sea, suspended dreadfully,
That liuing creature it would terrify,
To looke adowne, or vpward to the hight:
From thence he threw himselfe dispiteously,
All desperate of his fore-damned spright,
That seem'd no helpe for him was left in liuing sight.

LVII

But through long anguish, and selfe-murdring thought
He was so wasted and forpined quight,
That all his substance was consum'd to nought,
And nothing left, but like an aery Spright,
That on the rockes he fell so flit and light,
That he thereby receiu'd no hurt at all,
But chaunced on a craggy cliff to light;
Whence he with crooked clawes so long did crall,
That at the last he found a caue with entrance small.

LVIII

Into the same he creepes, and thenceforth there
Resolu'd to build his balefull mansion,
In drery darkenesse, and continuall feare
Of that rockes fall, which euer and anon
Threates with huge ruine him to fall vpon,
That he dare neuer sleepe, but that one eye
Still ope he keepes for that occasion;
Ne euer rests he in tranquillity,
The roring billowes beat his bowre so boystrously.

LIX

Ne euer is he wont on ought to feed,
But toades and frogs, his pasture poysonous,
Which in his cold complexion do breed
A filthy bloud, or humour rancorous,
Matter of doubt and dread suspitious,
That doth with curelesse care consume the hart,
Corrupts the stomacke with gall vitious,
Croscuts the liuer with internall smart,
And doth transfixe the soule with deathes eternall dart.

LX

Yet can he neuer dye, but dying liues,
And doth himselfe with sorrow new sustaine,
That death and life attonce vnto him giues.
And painefull pleasure turnes to pleasing paine.
There dwels he euer, miserable swaine,
Hatefull both to him selfe, and euery wight;
Where he through priuy griefe, and horrour vaine,
Is woxen so deform'd, that he has quight
Forgot he was a man, and *Gealosie* is hight.

Canto XI

> *Britomart chaceth Ollyphant,*
> *findes Scudamour distrest:*
> *Assayes the house of Busyrane,*
> *where Loues spoyles are exprest.*

I

O Hatefull hellish Snake, what furie furst
Brought thee from balefull house of *Proserpine*,
Where in her bosome she thee long had nurst,

And fostred vp with bitter milke of tine,
Fowle Gealosie, that turnest loue diuine
To ioylesse dread, and mak'st the louing hart
With hatefull thoughts to languish and to pine,
And feed it selfe with selfe-consuming smart?
Of all the passions in the mind thou vilest art.

II

O let him far be banished away,
And in his stead let Loue for euer dwell,
Sweet Loue, that doth his golden wings embay
In blessed Nectar, and pure Pleasures well,
Vntroubled of vile feare, or bitter fell.
And ye faire Ladies, that your kingdomes make
In th'harts of men, them gouerne wisely well,
And of faire *Britomart* ensample take,
That was as trew in loue, as Turtle to her make.

III

Who with Sir *Satyrane*, as earst ye red,
Forth ryding from *Malbeccoes* hostlesse hous,
Farr off aspyde a young man, the which fled
From an huge Geaunt, that with hideous
And hatefull outrage long him chaced thus;
It was that *Ollyphant*, the brother deare
Of that *Argante* vile and vitious,
From whom the *Squire of Dames* was reft whylere;
This all as bad as she, and worse, if worse ought were.

IV

For as the sister did in feminine
And filthy lust exceede all woman kind,
So he surpassed his sex masculine,
In beastly vse that I did euer find;
Whom when as *Britomart* beheld behind
The fearefull boy so greedily pursew,
She was emmoued in her noble mind,
T'employ her puissaunce to his reskew,
And pricked fiercely forward, where she him did vew.

V

Ne was Sir *Satyrane* her far behinde,
But with like fiercenesse did ensew the chace:

Whom when the Gyaunt saw, he soone resinde
His former suit, and from them fled apace;
They after both, and boldly bad him bace,
And each did striue the other to out-goe,
But he them both outran a wondrous space,
For he was long, and swift as any Roe,
And now made better speed, t'escape his feared foe.

VI

It was not *Satyrane*, whom he did feare,
But *Britomart* the flowre of chastity;
For he the powre of chast hands might not beare,
But alwayes did their dread encounter fly:
And now so fast his feet he did apply,
That he has gotten to a forrest neare,
Where he is shrowded in security.
The wood they enter, and search euery where,
They searched diuersely, so both diuided were.

VII

Faire *Britomart* so long him followed,
That she at last came to a fountaine sheare,
By which there lay a knight all wallowed
Vpon the grassy ground, and by him neare
His haberieon, his helmet, and his speare;
A little off, his shield was rudely throwne,
On which the winged boy in colours cleare
Depeincted was, full easie to be knowne,
And he thereby, where euer it in field was showne.

VIII

His face vpon the ground did groueling ly,
As if he had bene slombring in the shade,
That the braue Mayd would not for courtesy,
Out of his quiet slomber him abrade,
Nor seeme too suddeinly him to inuade:
Still as she stood, she heard with grieuous throb
Him grone, as if his hart were peeces made,
And with most painefull pangs to sigh and sob,
That pitty did the Virgins hart of patience rob.

IX

At last forth breaking into bitter plaintes
He said; O soueraigne Lord that sit'st on hye,
And raignst in blis emongst thy blessed Saintes,
How suffrest thou such shamefull cruelty,
So long vnwreaked of thine enimy?
Or hast thou, Lord, of good mens cause no heed?
Or doth thy iustice sleepe, and silent ly?
What booteth then the good and righteous deed,
If goodnesse find no grace, nor righteousnesse no meed?

X

If good find grace, and righteousnesse reward,
Why then is *Amoret* in caytiue band,
Sith that more bounteous creature neuer far'd
On foot, vpon the face of liuing land?
Or if that heauenly iustice may withstand
The wrongfull outrage of vnrighteous men,
Why then is *Busirane* with wicked hand
Suffred, these seuen monethes day in secret den
My Lady and my loue so cruelly to pen?

XI

My Lady and my loue is cruelly pend
In dolefull darkenesse from the vew of day,
Whilest deadly torments do her chast brest rend,
And the sharpe steele doth riue her hart in tway,
All for she *Scudamore* will not denay.
Yet thou vile man, vile *Scudamore* art sound,
Ne canst her ayde, ne canst her foe dismay;
Vnworthy wretch to tread vpon the ground,
For whom so faire a Lady feeles so sore a wound.

XII

There an huge heape of singults did oppresse
His strugling soule, and swelling throbs empeach
His foltring toung with pangs of drerinesse,
Choking the remnant of his plaintife speach,
As if his dayes were come to their last reach.
Which when she heard, and saw the ghastly fit,
Threatning into his life to make a breach,
Both with great ruth and terrour she was smit,
Fearing least from her cage the wearie soule would flit.

XIII

Tho stooping downe she him amoued light;
Who therewith somewhat starting, vp gan looke,
And seeing him behind a straunger knight,
Whereas no liuing creature he mistooke,
With great indignaunce he that sight forsooke,
And downe againe himselfe disdainefully
Abiecting, th'earth with his faire forhead strooke:
Which the bold Virgin seeing, gan apply
Fit medcine to his griefe, and spake thus courtesly.

XIV

Ah gentle knight, whose deepe conceiued griefe
Well seemes t'exceede the powre of patience,
Yet if that heauenly grace some good reliefe
You send, submit you to high prouidence,
And euer in your noble hart prepense,
That all the sorrow in the world is lesse,
Then vertues might, and values confidence,
For who nill bide the burden of distresse,
Must not here thinke to liue: for life is wretchednesse.

XV

Therefore, faire Sir, do comfort to you take,
And freely read, what wicked felon so
Hath outrag'd you, and thrald your gentle make.
Perhaps this hand may helpe to ease your woe,
And wreake your sorrow on your cruell foe,
At least it faire endeuour will apply.
Those feeling wordes so neare the quicke did goe,
That vp his head he reared easily,
And leaning on his elbow, these few wordes let fly.

XVI

What boots it plaine, that cannot be redrest,
And sow vaine sorrow in a fruitlesse eare,
Sith powre of hand, nor skill of learned brest,
Ne worldly price cannot redeeme my deare,
Out of her thraldome and continuall feare?
For he the tyraunt, which her hath in ward
By strong enchauntments and blacke Magicke leare,
Hath in a dungeon deepe her close embard,
And many dreadfull feends hath pointed to her gard.

XVII

There he tormenteth her most terribly,
And day and night afflicts with mortall paine,
Because to yield him loue she doth deny,
Once to me yold, not to be yold againe:
But yet by torture he would her constraine
Loue to conceiue in her disdainfull brest,
Till so she do, she must in doole remaine,
Ne may by liuing meanes be thence relest:
What boots it then to plaine, that cannot be redrest?

XVIII

With this sad hersall of his heauy stresse,
The warlike Damzell was empassiond sore,
And said; Sir knight, your cause is nothing lesse,
Then is your sorrow, certes if not more;
For nothing so much pitty doth implore,
As gentle Ladies helplesse misery.
But yet, if please ye listen to my lore,
I will with proofe of last extremity,
Deliuer her fro thence, or with her for you dy.

XIX

Ah gentlest knight aliue, (said *Scudamore*)
What huge heroicke magnanimity
Dwels in thy bounteous brest? what couldst thou more,
If she were thine, and thou as now am I?
O spare thy happy dayes, and them apply
To better boot, but let me dye, that ought;
More is more losse: one is enough to dy.
Life is not lost, (said she) for which is bought
Endlesse renowm, that more then death is to be sought.

XX

Thus she at length perswaded him to rise,
And with her wend, to see what new successe
Mote him befall vpon new enterprise;
His armes, which he had vowed to disprofesse,
She gathered vp and did about him dresse,
And his forwandred steed vnto him got:
So forth they both yfere make their progresse,
And march not past the mountenaunce of a shot,
Till they arriu'd, whereas their purpose they did plot.

XXI

There they dismounting, drew their weapons bold
And stoutly came vnto the Castle gate;
Whereas no gate they found, them to withhold,
Nor ward to wait at morne and euening late,
But in the Porch, that did them sore amate,
A flaming fire, ymixt with smouldry smoke,
And stinking Sulphure, that with griesly hate
And dreadfull horrour did all entraunce choke,
Enforced them their forward footing to reuoke.

XXII

Greatly thereat was *Britomart* dismayd,
Ne in that stownd wist, how her selfe to beare;
For daunger vaine it were, to haue assayd
That cruell element, which all things feare,
Ne none can suffer to approchen neare:
And turning backe to *Scudamour*, thus sayd;
What monstrous enmity prouoke we heare,
Foolhardy as th'Earthes children, the which made
Battell against the Gods? so we a God inuade.

XXIII

Daunger without discretion to attempt,
Inglorious and beastlike is: therefore Sir knight,
Aread what course of you is safest dempt,
And how we with our foe may come to fight.
This is (quoth he) the dolorous despight,
Which earst to you I playnd: for neither may
This fire be quencht by any wit or might,
Ne yet by any meanes remou'd away,
So mighty be th'enchauntments, which the same do stay.

XXIV

What is there else, but cease these fruitlesse paines,
And leaue me to my former languishing?
Faire *Amoret* must dwell in wicked chaines,
And *Scudamore* here dye with sorrowing.
Perdy not so; (said she) for shamefull thing
It were t'abandon noble cheuisaunce,
For shew of perill, without venturing:
Rather let try extremities of chaunce,
Then enterprised prayse for dread to disauaunce.

XXV

Therewith resolu'd to proue her vtmost might,
Her ample shield she threw before her face,
And her swords point directing forward right,
Assayld the flame, the which eftsoones gaue place,
And did it selfe diuide with equall space,
That through she passed; as a thunder bolt
Perceth the yielding ayre, and doth displace
The soring cloudes into sad showres ymolt;
So to her yold the flames, and did their force reuolt.

XXVI

Whom whenas *Scudamour* saw past the fire,
Safe and vntoucht, he likewise gan assay,
With greedy will, and enuious desire,
And bad the stubborne flames to yield him way:
But cruell *Mulciber* would not obay
His threatfull pride, but did the more augment
His mighty rage, and with imperious sway
Him forst (maulgre) his fiercenesse to relent,
And backe retire, all scorcht and pitifully brent.

XXVII

With huge impatience he inly swelt,
More for great sorrow, that he could not pas,
Then for the burning torment, which he felt,
That with fell woodnesse he effierced was,
And wilfully him throwing on the gras,
Did beat and bounse his head and brest full sore;
The whiles the Championesse now entred has
The vtmost rowme, and past the formest dore,
The vtmost rowme, abounding with all precious store.

XXVIII

For round about, the wals yclothed were
With goodly arras of great maiesty,
Wouen with gold and silke so close and nere,
That the rich metall lurked priuily,
As faining to be hid from enuious eye;
Yet here, and there, and euery where vnwares
It shewd it selfe, and shone vnwillingly;
Like a discolourd Snake, whose hidden snares
Through the greene gras his long bright burnisht backe declares.

XXIX

And in those Tapets weren fashioned
Many faire pourtraicts, and many a faire feate,
And all of loue, and all of lusty-hed,
As seemed by their semblaunt did entreat;
And eke all *Cupids* warres they did repeate,
And cruell battels, which he whilome fought
Gainst all the Gods, to make his empire great;
Besides the huge massacres, which he wrought
On mighty kings and kesars, into thraldome brought.

XXX

Therein was writ, how often thundring *Ioue*
Had felt the point of his hart-percing dart,
And leauing heauens kingdome, here did roue
In straunge disguize, to slake his scalding smart;
Now like a Ram, faire *Helle* to peruart,
Now like a Bull, *Europa* to withdraw:
Ah, how the fearefull Ladies tender hart
Did liuely seeme to tremble, when she saw
The huge seas vnder her t'obay her seruaunts law.

XXXI

Soone after that into a golden showre
Him selfe he chaung'd faire *Danae* to vew,
And through the roofe of her strong brasen towre
Did raine into her lap an hony dew,
The whiles her foolish garde, that little knew
Of such deceipt, kept th'yron dore fast bard,
And watcht, that none should enter nor issew;
Vaine was the watch, and bootlesse all the ward,
Whenas the God to golden hew him selfe transfard.

XXXII

Then was he turnd into a snowy Swan,
To win faire *Leda* to his louely trade:
O wondrous skill, and sweet wit of the man,
That her in daffadillies sleeping made,
From scorching heat her daintie limbes to shade:
Whiles the proud Bird ruffing his fethers wyde,
And brushing his faire brest, did her inuade;
She slept, yet twixt her eyelids closely spyde,
How towards her he rusht, and smiled at his pryde.

XXXIII

Then shewd it, how the *Thebane Semelee*
Deceiu'd of gealous *Iuno*, did require
To see him in his soueraigne maiestee,
Armd with his thunderbolts and lightning fire,
Whence dearely she with death bought her desire.
But faire *Alcmena* better match did make,
Ioying his loue in likenesse more entire;
Three nights in one, they say, that for her sake
He then did put, her pleasures lenger to partake.

XXXIV

Twise was he seene in soaring Eagles shape,
And with wide wings to beat the buxome ayre,
Once, when he with *Asterie* did scape,
Againe, when as the *Troiane* boy so faire
He snatcht from *Ida* hill, and with him bare:
Wondrous delight it was, there to behould,
How the rude Shepheards after him did stare,
Trembling through feare, least down he fallen should
And often to him calling, to take surer hould.

XXXV

In *Satyres* shape *Antiopa* he snatcht:
And like a fire, when he *Aegin'* assayd:
A shepheard, when *Mnemosyne* he catcht:
And like a Serpent to the *Thracian* mayd.
Whiles thus on earth great *Ioue* these pageaunts playd,
The winged boy did thrust into his throne,
And scoffing, thus vnto his mother sayd,
Lo now the heauens obey to me alone,
And take me for their *Ioue*, whiles *Ioue* to earth is gone.

XXXVI

And thou, faire *Phœbus*, in thy colours bright
Wast there enwouen, and the sad distresse,
In which that boy thee plonged, for despight,
That thou bewray'dst his mothers wantonnesse,
When she with *Mars* was meynt in ioyfulnesse:
For thy he thrild thee with a leaden dart,
To loue faire *Daphne*, which thee loued lesse:
Lesse she thee lou'd, then was thy iust desart,
Yet was thy loue her death, and her death was thy smart.

XXXVII

So louedst thou the lusty *Hyacinct*,
So louedst thou the faire *Coronis* deare:
Yet both are of thy haplesse hand extinct,
Yet both in flowres do liue, and loue thee beare,
The one a Paunce, the other a sweet breare:
For griefe whereof, ye mote haue liuely seene
The God himselfe rending his golden heare,
And breaking quite his gyrlond euer greene,
With other signes of sorrow and impatient teene.

XXXVIII

Both for those two, and for his owne deare sonne,
The sonne of *Climene* he did repent,
Who bold to guide the charet of the Sunne,
Himselfe in thousand peeces fondly rent,
And all the world with flashing fier brent,
So like, that all the walles did seeme to flame.
Yet cruell *Cupid*, not herewith content,
Forst him eftsoones to follow other game,
And loue a Shepheards daughter for his dearest Dame.

XXXIX

He loued *Isse* for his dearest Dame,
And for her sake her cattell fed a while,
And for her sake a cowheard vile became,
The seruant of *Admetus* cowheard vile,
Whiles that from heauen he suffered exile.
Long were to tell each other louely fit,
Now like a Lyon, hunting after spoile,
Now like a Hag, now like a faulcon flit:
All which in that faire arras was most liuely writ.

XL

Next vnto him was *Neptune* pictured,
In his diuine resemblance wondrous lyke:
His face was rugged, and his hoarie hed
Dropped with brackish deaw; his three-forkt Pyke
He stearnly shooke, and therewith fierce did stryke
The raging billowes, that on euery syde
They trembling stood, and made a long broad dyke,
That his swift charet might haue passage wyde,
Which foure great *Hippodames* did draw in temewise tyde.

XLI

His sea-horses did seeme to snort amayne,
And from their nosethrilles blow the brynie streame,
That made the sparckling waues to smoke agayne,
And flame with gold, but the white fomy creame,
Did shine with siluer, and shoot forth his beame.
The God himselfe did pensiue seeme and sad,
And hong adowne his head, as he did dreame:
For priuy loue his brest empierced had,
Ne ought but deare *Bisaltis* ay could make him glad.

XLII

He loued eke *Iphimedia* deare,
And *Aeolus* faire daughter *Arne* hight,
For whom he turnd him selfe into a Steare,
And fed on fodder, to beguile her sight.
Also to win *Deucalions* daughter bright,
He turnd him selfe into a Dolphin fayre;
And like a winged horse he tooke his flight,
To snaky-locke *Medusa* to repayre,
On whom he got faire *Pegasus*, **that flitteth in the ayre.**

XLIII

Next *Saturne* was, **(but who would euer weene,**
That sullein *Saturne* euer weend to loue?
Yet loue is sullein, and *Saturnlike* seene,
As he did for *Erigone* it proue,)
That to a *Centaure* did him selfe transmoue.
So proou'd it eke that gracious God of wine,
When for to compasse *Philliras* hard loue,
He turnd himselfe into a fruitfull vine,
And into her faire bosome made his grapes decline.

XLIV

Long were to tell the amorous assayes,
And gentle pangues, with which he maked meeke
The mighty *Mars*, to learne his wanton playes:
How oft for *Venus*, and how often eek
For many other Nymphes he sore did shreek,
With womanish teares, and with vnwarlike smarts,
Priuily moystening his horrid cheek.
There was he painted full of burning darts,
And many wide woundes launched through his inner parts.

XLV

Ne did he spare (so cruell was the Elfe)
His owne deare mother, (ah why should he so?)
Ne did he spare sometime to pricke himselfe,
That he might tast the sweet consuming woe,
Which he had wrought to many others moe.
But to declare the mournfull Tragedyes,
And spoiles, wherewith he all the ground did strow,
More eath to number, with how many eyes
High heauen beholds sad louers nightly theeueryes.

XLVI

Kings Queenes, Lords Ladies, Knights and Damzels gent
Were heap'd together with the vulgar sort,
And mingled with the raskall rablement,
Without respect of person or of port,
To shew Dan *Cupids* powre and great effort:
And round about a border was entrayld,
Of broken bowes and arrowes shiuered short,
And a long bloudy riuer through them rayld,
So liuely and so like, that liuing sence it fayld.

XLVII

And at the vpper end of that faire rowme,
There was an Altar built of pretious stone,
Of passing valew, and of great renowme,
On which there stood an Image all alone,
Of massy gold, which with his owne light shone;
And wings it had with sundry colours dight,
More sundry colours, then the proud *Pauone*
Beares in his boasted fan, or *Iris* bright,
When her discolourd bow she spreds through heauen bright.

XLVIII

Blindfold he was, and in his cruell fist
A mortall bow and arrowes keene did hold,
With which he shot at randon, when him list,
Some headed with sad lead, some with pure gold;
(Ah man beware, how thou those darts behold)
A wounded Dragon vnder him did ly,
Whose hideous tayle his left foot did enfold,
And with a shaft was shot through either eye,
That no man forth might draw, ne no man remedye.

XLIX

And vnderneath his feet was written thus,
Vnto the Victor of the Gods this bee:
And all the people in that ample hous
Did to that image bow their humble knee,
And oft committed fowle Idolatree.
That wondrous sight faire *Britomart* amazed,
Ne seeing could her wonder satisfie,
But euermore and more vpon it gazed,
The whiles the passing brightnes her fraile sences dazed.

L

Tho as she backward cast her busie eye,
To search each secret of that goodly sted
Ouer the dore thus written she did spye
Be bold: she oft and oft it ouer-red,
Yet could not find what sence it figured:
But what so were therein or writ or ment,
She was no whit thereby discouraged
From prosecuting of her first intent,
But forward with bold steps into the next roome went.

LI

Much fairer, then the former, was that roome,
And richlier by many partes arayd:
For not with arras made in painefull loome,
But with pure gold it all was ouerlayd,
Wrought with wilde Antickes, which their follies playd,
In the rich metall, as they liuing were:
A thousand monstrous formes therein were made,
Such as false loue doth oft vpon him weare,
For loue in thousand monstrous formes doth oft appeare.

LII

And all about, the glistring walles were hong
With warlike spoiles, and with victorious prayes,
Of mighty Conquerours and Captaines strong,
Which were whilome captiued in their dayes
To cruell loue, and wrought their owne decayes:
Their swerds and speres were broke, and hauberques rent;
And their proud girlonds of tryumphant bayes
Troden in dust with fury insolent,
To shew the victors might and mercilesse intent.

LIII

The warlike Mayde beholding earnestly
The goodly ordinance of this rich place,
Did greatly wonder, ne could satisfie
Her greedy eyes with gazing a long space,
But more she meruaild that no footings trace,
Nor wight appear'd, but wastefull emptinesse,
And solemne silence ouer all that place:
Straunge thing it seem'd, that none was to possesse
So rich purueyance, ne them keepe with carefulnesse.

LIV

And as she lookt about, she did behold,
How ouer that same dore was likewise writ,
Be bold, be bold, and euery where *Be bold*,
That much she muz'd, yet could not construe it
By any ridling skill, or commune wit.
At last she spyde at that roomes vpper end,
Another yron dore, on which was writ,
Be not too bold; whereto though she did bend
Her earnest mind, yet wist not what it might intend.

LV

Thus she there waited vntill euentyde,
Yet liuing creature none she saw appeare:
And now sad shadowes gan the world to hyde,
From mortall vew, and wrap in darkenesse dreare;
Yet nould she d'off her weary armes, for feare
Of secret daunger, ne let sleepe oppresse
Her heauy eyes with natures burdein deare,
But drew her selfe aside in sickernesse,
And her welpointed weapons did about her dresse.

Canto XII

The maske of Cupid, and th'enchaunted
Chamber are displayd,
Whence Britomart redeemes faire
Amoret, through charmes decayd.

I

THo when as chearlesse Night ycouered had
Faire heauen with an vniuersall cloud,
That euery wight dismayd with darknesse sad,

In silence and in sleepe themselues did shroud,
She heard a shrilling Trompet sound aloud,
Signe of nigh battell, or got victory;
Nought therewith daunted was her courage proud,
But rather stird to cruell enmity,
Expecting euer, when some foe she might descry.

II

With that, an hideous storme of winde arose,
With dreadfull thunder and lightning atwixt,
And an earth-quake, as if it streight would lose
The worlds foundations from his centre fixt;
A direfull stench of smoke and sulphure mixt
Ensewd, whose noyance fild the fearefull sted,
From the fourth houre of night vntill the sixt;
Yet the bold *Britonesse* was nought ydred,
Though much emmou'd, but stedfast still perseuered.

III

All suddenly a stormy whirlwind blew
Throughout the house, that clapped euery dore,
With which that yron wicket open flew,
As it with mightie leuers had bene tore:
And forth issewd, as on the ready flore
Of some Theatre, a graue personage,
That in his hand a branch of laurell bore,
With comely haueour and count'nance sage,
Yclad in costly garments, fit for tragicke Stage.

IV

Proceeding to the midst, he still did stand,
As if in mind he somewhat had to say,
And to the vulgar beckning with his hand,
In signe of silence, as to heare a play,
By liuely actions he gan bewray
Some argument of matter passioned;
Which doen, he backe retyred soft away,
And passing by, his name discouered,
Ease, on his robe in golden letters cyphered.

V

The noble Mayd, still standing all this vewd,
And merueild at his strange intendiment;

With that a ioyous fellowship issewd
Of Minstrals, making goodly meriment,
With wanton Bardes, and Rymers impudent,
All which together sung full chearefully
A lay of loues delight, with sweet concent:
After whom marcht a iolly company,
In manner of a maske, enranged orderly.

VI

The whiles a most delitious harmony,
In full straunge notes was sweetly heard to sound,
That the rare sweetnesse of the melody
The feeble senses wholly did confound,
And the fraile soule in deepe delight nigh dround:
And when it ceast, shrill trompets loud did bray,
That their report did farre away rebound,
And when they ceast, it gan againe to play,
The whiles the maskers marched forth in trim aray.

VII

The first was *Fancy*, like a louely boy,
Of rare aspect, and beautie without peare;
Matchable either to that ympe of *Troy*,
Whom *Ioue* did loue, and chose his cup to beare,
Or that same daintie lad, which was so deare
To great *Alcides*, that when as he dyde,
He wailed womanlike with many a teare,
And euery wood, and euery valley wyde
He fild with *Hylas* name; the Nymphes eke *Hylas* cryde.

VIII

His garment neither was of silke nor say,
But painted plumes, in goodly order dight,
Like as the sunburnt *Indians* do aray
Their tawney bodies, in their proudest plight:
As those same plumes, so seemd he vaine and light,
That by his gate might easily appeare;
For still he far'd as dauncing in delight,
And in his hand a windy fan did beare,
That in the idle aire he mou'd still here and there.

IX

And him beside marcht amorous *Desyre*,
Who seemd of riper yeares, then th'other Swaine,
Yet was that other swayne this elders syre,
And gaue him being, commune to them twaine:
His garment was disguised very vaine,
And his embrodered Bonet sat awry;
Twixt both his hands few sparkes he close did straine,
Which still he blew, and kindled busily,
That soone they life conceiu'd, and forth in flames did fly.

X

Next after him went *Doubt*, who was yclad
In a discolour'd cote, of straunge disguyse,
That at his backe a brode Capuccio had,
And sleeues dependant *Albanese*-wyse:
He lookt askew with his mistrustfull eyes,
And nicely trode, as thornes lay in his way,
Or that the flore to shrinke he did auyse,
And on a broken reed he still did stay
His feeble steps, which shrunke, when hard theron he lay.

XI

With him went *Daunger*, cloth'd in ragged weed,
Made of Beares skin, that him more dreadfull made,
Yet his owne face was dreadfull, ne did need
Straunge horrour, to deforme his griesly shade;
A net in th'one hand, and rustie blade
In th'other was, this Mischiefe, that Mishap;
With th'one his foes he threatned to inuade,
With th'other he his friends ment to enwrap:
For whom he could not kill, he practizd to entrap.

XII

Next him was *Feare*, all arm'd from top to toe,
Yet thought himselfe not safe enough thereby,
But feard each shadow mouing to and fro,
And his owne armes when glittering he did spy,
Or clashing heard, he fast away did fly,
As ashes pale of hew, and wingyheeld;
And euermore on daunger fixt his eye,
Gainst whom he alwaies bent a brasen shield,
Which his right hand vnarmed fearefully did wield.

XIII

With him went *Hope* in rancke, a handsome Mayd,
Of chearefull looke and louely to behold;
In silken samite she was light arayd,
And her faire lockes were wouen vp in gold;
She alway smyld, and in her hand did hold
An holy water Sprinckle, dipt in deowe,
With which she sprinckled fauours manifold,
On whom she list, and did great liking sheowe,
Great liking vnto many, but true loue to feowe.

XIV

And after them *Dissemblance*, and *Suspect*
Marcht in one rancke, yet an vnequall paire:
For she was gentle, and of milde aspect,
Courteous to all, and seeming debonaire,
Goodly adorned, and exceeding faire:
Yet was that all but painted, and purloynd,
And her bright browes were deckt with borrowed haire:
Her deedes were forged, and her words false coynd,
And alwaies in her hand two clewes of silke she twynd.

XV

But he was foule, ill fauoured, and grim,
Vnder his eyebrowes looking still askaunce;
And euer as *Dissemblance* laught on him,
He lowrd on her with daungerous eyeglaunce;
Shewing his nature in his countenance;
His rolling eyes did neuer rest in place,
But walkt each where, for feare of hid mischaunce,
Holding a lattice still before his face,
Through which he still did peepe, as forward he did pace.

XVI

Next him went *Griefe*, and *Fury* matched yfere;
Griefe all in sable sorrowfully clad,
Downe hanging his dull head, with heauy chere,
Yet inly being more, then seeming sad:
A paire of Pincers in his hand he had,
With which he pinched people to the hart,
That from thenceforth a wretched life they lad,
In wilfull languor and consuming smart,
Dying each day with inward wounds of dolours dart.

XVII

But *Fury* was full ill appareiled
In rags, that naked nigh she did appeare,
With ghastly lookes and dreadfull drerihed;
For from her backe her garments she did teare,
And from her head oft rent her snarled heare:
In her right hand a firebrand she did tosse
About her head, still roming here and there;
As a dismayed Deare in chace embost,
Forgetfull of his safety, hath his right way lost.

XVIII

After them went *Displeasure* and *Pleasance*,
He looking lompish and full sullein sad,
And hanging downe his heauy countenance;
She chearefull fresh and full of ioyance glad,
As if no sorrow she ne felt ne drad;
That euill matched paire they seemd to bee:
An angry Waspe th'one in a viall had
Th'other in hers an hony-lady Bee;
Thus marched these six couples forth in faire degree.

XIX

After all these there marcht a most faire Dame,
Led of two grysie villeins, th'one *Despight*,
The other cleped *Cruelty* by name:
She dolefull Lady, like a dreary Spright,
Cald by strong charmes out of eternall night,
Had deathes owne image figurd in her face,
Full of sad signes, fearefull to liuing sight;
Yet in that horror shewd a seemely grace,
And with her feeble feet did moue a comely pace.

XX

Her brest all naked, as net iuory,
Without adorne of gold or siluer bright,
Wherewith the Craftesman wonts it beautify,
Of her dew honour was despoyled quight,
And a wide wound therein (O ruefull sight)
Entrenched deepe with knife accursed keene,
Yet freshly bleeding forth her fainting spright,
(The worke of cruell hand) was to be seene,
That dyde in sanguine red her skin all snowy cleene.

XXI

At that wide orifice her trembling hart
Was drawne forth, and in siluer basin layd,
Quite through transfixed with a deadly dart,
And in her bloud yet steeming fresh embayd:
And those two villeins, which her steps vpstayd,
When her weake feete could scarcely her sustaine,
And fading vitall powers gan to fade,
Her forward still with torture did constraine,
And euermore encreased her consuming paine.

XXII

Next after her the winged God himselfe
Came riding on a Lion rauenous,
Taught to obay the menage of that Elfe,
That man and beast with powre imperious
Subdeweth to his kingdome tyrannous:
His blindfold eyes he bad a while vnbind,
That his proud spoyle of that same dolorous
Faire Dame he might behold in perfect kind;
Which seene, he much reioyced in his cruell mind.

XXIII

Of which full proud, himselfe vp rearing hye,
He looked round about with sterne disdaine;
And did suruay his goodly company:
And marshalling the euill ordered traine,
With that the darts which his right hand did straine,
Full dreadfully he shooke that all did quake,
And clapt on hie his coulourd winges twaine,
That all his many it affraide did make:
Tho blinding him againe, his way he forth did take.

XXIV

Behinde him was *Reproch, Repentance, Shame*;
Reproch the first, *Shame* next, *Repent* behind:
Repentance feeble, sorrowfull, and lame:
Reproch despightfull, carelesse, and vnkind;
Shame most ill fauourd, bestiall, and blind:
Shame lowrd, *Repentance* sigh'd, *Reproch* did scould;
Reproch sharpe stings, *Repentance* whips entwind,
Shame burning brond-yrons in her hand did hold:
All three to each vnlike, yet all made in one mould.

XXV

And after them a rude confused rout
Of persons flockt, whose name is hard to read:
Emongst them was sterne *Strife*, and *Anger* stout,
Vnquiet *Care*, and fond *Vnthriftihead*,
Lewd *Losse of Time*, and *Sorrow* seeming dead,
Inconstant *Chaunge*, and false *Disloyaltie*,
Consuming *Riotise*, and guilty *Dread*
Of heauenly vengeance, faint *Infirmitie*,
Vile *Pouertie*, and lastly *Death* with infamie.

XXVI

There were full many moe like maladies,
Whose names and natures I note readen well;
So many moe, as there be phantasies
In wauering wemens wit, that none can tell,
Or paines in loue, or punishments in hell;
All which disguized marcht in masking wise,
About the chamber with that Damozell,
And then returned, hauing marched thrise,
Into the inner roome, from whence they first did rise.

XXVII

So soone as they were in, the dore streight way
Fast locked, driuen with that stormy blast,
Which first it opened; and bore all away.
Then the braue Maid, which all this while was plast,
In secret shade, and saw both first and last,
Issewed forth, and went vnto the dore,
To enter in, but found it locked fast:
It vaine she thought with rigorous vprore
For to efforce, when charmes had closed it afore.

XXVIII

Where force might not auaile, there sleights and art
She cast to vse, both fit for hard emprize;
For thy from that same roome not to depart
Till morrow next, she did her selfe auize,
When that same Maske againe should forth arize.
The morrow next appeard with ioyous cheare,
Calling men to their daily exercize,
Then she, as morrow fresh, her selfe did reare
Out of her secret stand, that day for to out weare.

XXIX

All that day she outwore in wandering,
And gazing on that Chambers ornament,
Till that againe the second euening
Her couered with her sable vestiment,
Wherewith the worlds faire beautie she hath blent:
Then when the second watch was almost past,
That brasen dore flew open, and in went
Bold *Britomart*, as she had late forecast,
Neither of idle shewes, nor of false charmes aghast.

XXX

So soone as she was entred, round about
She cast her eies, to see what was become
Of all those persons, which she saw without:
But lo, they streight were vanisht all and some,
Ne liuing wight she saw in all that roome,
Saue that same woefull Ladie, both whose hands
Were bounden fast, that did her ill become,
And her small wast girt round with yron bands,
Vnto a brasen pillour, by the which she stands.

XXXI

And her before the vile Enchaunter sate,
Figuring straunge characters of his art,
With liuing bloud he those characters wrate,
Dreadfully dropping from her dying hart,
Seeming transfixed with a cruell dart,
And all perforce to make her him to loue.
Ah who can loue the worker of her smart?
A thousand charmes he formerly did proue;
Yet thousand charmes could not her stedfast heart remoue.

XXXII

Soone as that virgin knight he saw in place,
His wicked bookes in hast he ouerthrew,
Not caring his long labours to deface,
And fiercely ronning to that Lady trew,
A murdrous knife out of his pocket drew,
The which he thought, for villeinous despight,
In her tormented bodie to embrew:
But the stout Damzell to him leaping light,
His cursed hand withheld, and maistered his might.

XXXIII

From her, to whom his fury first he ment,
The wicked weapon rashly he did wrest,
And turning to her selfe his fell intent,
Vnwares it strooke into her snowie chest,
That little drops empurpled her faire brest.
Exceeding wroth therewith the virgin grew,
Albe the wound were nothing deepe imprest,
And fiercely forth her mortall blade she drew,
To giue him the reward for such vile outrage dew.

XXXIV

So mightily she smote him, that to ground
He fell halfe dead; next stroke him should haue slaine,
Had not the Lady, which by him stood bound,
Dernely vnto her called to abstaine,
From doing him to dy. For else her paine
Should be remedilesse, sith none but hee,
Which wrought it, could the same recure againe.
Therewith she stayd her hand, loth stayd to bee;
For life she him enuyde, and long'd reuenge to see.

XXXV

And to him said, Thou wicked man, whose meed
For so huge mischiefe, and vile villany
Is death, or if that ought do death exceed,
Be sure, that nought may saue thee from to dy,
But if that thou this Dame doe presently
Restore vnto her health, and former state;
This doe and liue, else die vndoubtedly.
He glad of life, that lookt for death but late,
Did yield himselfe right willing to prolong his date.

XXXVI

And rising vp, gan streight to ouerlooke
Those cursed leaues, his charmes backe to reuerse;
Full dreadfull things out of that balefull booke
He red, and measur'd many a sad verse,
That horror gan the virgins hart to perse,
And her faire lockes vp stared stiffe on end,
Hearing him those same bloudy lines reherse;
And all the while he red, she did extend
Her sword high ouer him, if ought he did offend.

XXXVII

Anon she gan perceiue the house to quake,
And all the dores to rattle round about;
Yet all that did not her dismaied make,
Nor slacke her threatfull hand for daungers dout,
But still with stedfast eye and courage stout
Abode, to weet what end would come of all.
At last that mightie chaine, which round about
Her tender waste was wound, adowne gan fall,
And that great brasen pillour broke in peeces small.

XXXVIII

The cruell steele, which thrild her dying hart,
Fell softly forth, as of his owne accord,
And the wyde wound, which lately did dispart
Her bleeding brest, and riuen bowels gor'd,
Was closed vp, as it had not bene bor'd,
And euery part to safety full sound,
As she were neuer hurt, was soone restor'd:
Tho when she felt her selfe to be vnbound,
And perfect hole, prostrate she fell vnto the ground.

XXXIX

Before faire *Britomart*, she fell prostrate,
Saying, Ah noble knight, what worthy meed
Can wretched Lady, quit from wofull state,
Yield you in liew of this your gratious deed?
Your vertue selfe her owne reward shall breed,
Euen immortall praise, and glory wyde,
Which I your vassall, by your prowesse freed,
Shall through the world make to be notifyde,
And goodly well aduance, that goodly well was tryde.

XL

But *Britomart* vprearing her from ground,
Said, Gentle Dame, reward enough I weene
For many labours more, then I haue found,
This, that in safety now I haue you seene,
And meane of your deliuerance haue beene:
Henceforth faire Lady comfort to you take,
And put away remembrance of late teene;
In stead thereof know, that your louing Make,
Hath no lesse griefe endured for your gentle sake.

XLI

She was much cheard to heare him mentiond,
Whom of all liuing wights she loued best.
Then laid the noble Championesse strong hond
Vpon th'enchaunter, which had her distrest
So sore, and with foule outrages opprest:
With that great chaine, wherewith not long ygo
He bound that pitteous Lady prisoner, now relest,
Himselfe she bound, more worthy to be so,
And captiue with her led to wretchednesse and wo.

XLII

Returning backe, those goodly roomes, which erst
She saw so rich and royally arayd,
Now vanisht vtterly, and cleane subuerst
She found, and all their glory quite decayd,
That sight of such a chaunge her much dismayd.
Thence forth descending to that perlous Porch,
Those dreadfull flames she also found delayd,
And quenched quite, like a consumed torch,
That erst all entrers wont so cruelly to scorch.

XLIII

More easie issew now, then entrance late
She found: for now that fained dreadfull flame,
Which chokt the porch of that enchaunted gate,
And passage bard to all, that thither came,
Was vanisht quite, as it were not the same,
And gaue her leaue at pleasure forth to passe.
Th'Enchaunter selfe, which all that fraud did frame,
To haue efforst the loue of that faire lasse,
Seeing his worke now wasted deepe engrieued was.

XLIV

But when the victoresse arriued there,
Where late she left the pensife *Scudamore*,
With her owne trusty Squire, both full of feare,
Neither of them she found where she them lore:
Thereat her noble hart was stonisht sore;
But most faire *Amoret*, whose gentle spright
Now gan to feede on hope, which she before
Conceiued had, to see her owne deare knight,
Being thereof beguyld was fild with new affright.

XLV

But he sad man, when he had long in drede
Awayted there for *Britomarts* returne,
Yet saw her not nor signe of her good speed,
His expectation to despaire did turne,
Misdeeming sure that her those flames did burne;
And therefore gan aduize with her old Squire,
Who her deare nourslings losse no lesse did mourne,
Thence to depart for further aide t'enquire:
Where let them wend at will, whilest here I doe respire.

XLVI

At last she came vnto the place, where late
She left Sir *Scudamour* in great distresse,
Twixt dolour and despight halfe desperate,
Of his loues succour, of his owne redresse,
And of the hardie *Britomarts* successe:
There on the cold earth him now throwne she found,
In wilfull anguish, and dead heauinesse,
And to him cald; whose voices knowen sound
Soone as he heard, himself he reared light from ground.

2.8.2 Reading and Review Questions

1. How, in what ways, and why does Spenser identify the Redcrosse Knight with/as St. George?

2. Archimago seems to act as an artist figure, as representing the imagination's power to recreate images. What does he suggest about art, about the power of art? How does Spenser's comments on the uses and abuses of art compare with Chaucer's?

3. How does the House of Pride hearken back to medieval allegory, and why? How does it compare with that of *Everyman* or *Gawain and the Green Knight*, for example?

4. Unlike holiness, temperance is a physical virtue. How does the landscape in Book II reflect this physicality?

5. Britomart, a female, is the Knight of Chastity. Yet her story is seminal, genealogical, in that she figures as a mother (of Elizabeth I) of a multitude through the dynasty that leads from Brutus to Arthur to Artegall (Arthur's brother by Igrain) to Elizabeth. What does Spenser's art suggest about sexuality here? Why does sex and subterfuge go so often together? How does sexuality become a virtue?

2.9 SIR WALTER RALEIGH

(1552-1618)

A soldier, explorer, scholar, and courtier, Walter Raleigh fought on the side of the French Protestants, the Huguenots, possibly in the Battle of Jarnac during the French Wars of Religion (1562–1598). He also participated in the massacre at Smerwick, brutally suppressing Irish rebels and slaughtering papal troops. He was tutored by the vicar John Ford, enrolled at Oriel College, Oxford University, and studied at one of the Inns of Court, the Middle Temple. Family connections probably won him a place in Elizabeth I's court, as Esquire of the Body Extraordinary.

Image 2.9 | Sir Walter Raleigh
Artist | Nicholas Hilliard
Source | Wikimedia Commons
License | Public Domain

His own charisma won him many favors from Elizabeth I, including a license to tax vintners for retailing wine in England, Durham House, a knighthood, the title of Lord and Governor of Virginia, thousands of acres of land in Ireland, and an appointment as Captain of the Guard. He also was elected to Parliament and appointed Lord Warden of the Stanneries, Lord Lieutenant of Cornwall, and Vice-Admiral of Cornwall and Devon. He used his wealth to fund voyages to Roanoke Island in hopes of settling a colony there and instead mysteriously losing the colonists. Although he did not introduce the potato and tobacco in Virginia, as he is often credited for doing, he did popularize smoking at Court.

He lost Elizabeth I's favor when he secretly married one of her maids of honor, Elizabeth Throckmorton (1565–1647), who as a royal attendant could only marry with the Queen's permission. She briefly imprisoned them both in the Tower of London. He soon continued his colonizing efforts by exploring Guiana in South America and futilely searching for El Dorado, the so-called Lost City of Gold.

Much of what he gained from Elizabeth Raleigh lost when she was succeeded by James I. Raleigh was implicated in two conspiracies against James I, the Bye and the Main Plots, for which he was condemned of treason and imprisoned for over ten years in the Tower. Upon his release, he courted James I's favor by again voyaging to Guiana in search of gold. He failed in this intention and, worse, disobeyed James I's injunction not to violate Spanish rights when his men destroyed the village of Santo Tome de Guyana. For endangering England's peace with Spain, Raleigh was beheaded.

Raleigh's writing records the fierce, cynical, plausible voice of the man and his many exploits. His love poetry wooed and "won" Elizabeth I; his book *The*

Discoverie of the large and bewtiful Empire of Guiana mythologized El Dorado; and his *History of the World* educated James I's son, whom Raleigh befriended during his imprisonment. His pastoral poetry both repeats and renews that classical genre, with his reply to Marlowe's *Passionate Shepherd* gaining much attention. His poem *The Lie*, with its all-encompassing attacks on the Court, Church, Men of High Condition, faith, wit, and learning, provoked several answering, often defensive, poems. His travelogue, like many that follow, blends fiction with "fact." And his History recovers the past in an attempt to shape the future.

2.9.1 "Farewell, False Love"

(1588)

Farewell, false love, the oracle of lies,
A mortal foe and enemy to rest,
An envious boy, from whom all cares arise,
A bastard vile, a beast with rage possessed,
A way of error, a temple full of treason,
In all effects contrary unto reason.

A poisoned serpent covered all with flowers,
Mother of sighs, and murderer of repose,
A sea of sorrows whence are drawn such showers
As moisture lend to every grief that grows;
A school of guile, a net of deep deceit,
A gilded hook that holds a poisoned bait.

A fortress foiled, which reason did defend,
A siren song, a fever of the mind,
A maze wherein affection finds no end,
A raging cloud that runs before the wind,
A substance like the shadow of the sun,
A goal of grief for which the wisest run.

A quenchless fire, a nurse of trembling fear,
A path that leads to peril and mishap,
A true retreat of sorrow and despair,
An idle boy that sleeps in pleasure's lap,
A deep mistrust of that which certain seems,
A hope of that which reason doubtful deems.

Sith then thy trains my younger years betrayed,
And for my faith ingratitude I find;
And sith repentance hath my wrongs bewrayed,

Whose course was ever contrary to kind:
False love, desire, and beauty frail, adieu!
Dead is the root whence all these fancies grew.

2.9.2 "If Cynthia Be a Queen, a Princess, and Supreme"

(1604/1618?)

If Cynthia be a queen, a princess, and supreme,
Keep these among the rest, or say it was a dream,
For those that like, expound, and those that loathe express
Meanings according as their minds are moved more or less;
For writing what thou art, or showing what thou were,
Adds to the one disdain, to the other but despair,
Thy mind of neither needs, in both seeing it exceeds.

2.9.3 "The Nymph's Reply to the Shepherd"

(1600)

If all the world and love were young,
And truth in every Shepherd's tongue,
These pretty pleasures might me move,
To live with thee, and be thy love.

Time drives the flocks from field to fold,
When Rivers rage and Rocks grow cold,
And *Philomel* becometh dumb,
The rest complains of cares to come.

The flowers do fade, and wanton fields,
To wayward winter reckoning yields,
A honey tongue, a heart of gall,
Is fancy's spring, but sorrow's fall.

Thy gowns, thy shoes, thy beds of Roses,
Thy cap, thy kirtle, and thy posies
Soon break, soon wither, soon forgotten:
In folly ripe, in reason rotten.

Thy belt of straw and Ivy buds,
The Coral clasps and amber studs,
All these in me no means can move
To come to thee and be thy love.

But could youth last, and love still breed,
Had joys no date, nor age no need,
Then these delights my mind might move
To live with thee, and be thy love.

2.9.4 "The Lie"

(1608)

Go, soul, the body's guest,
Upon a thankless errand;
Fear not to touch the best;
The truth shall be thy warrant.
Go, since I needs must die,
And give the world the lie.

Say to the court, it glows
And shines like rotten wood;
Say to the church, it shows
What's good, and doth no good.
If church and court reply,
Then give them both the lie.

Tell potentates, they live
Acting by others' action;
Not loved unless they give,
Not strong but by a faction.
If potentates reply,
Give potentates the lie.

Tell men of high condition,
That manage the estate,
Their purpose is ambition,
Their practice only hate.
And if they once reply,
Then give them all the lie.

Tell them that brave it most,
They beg for more by spending,
Who, in their greatest cost,
Seek nothing but commending.
And if they make reply,
Then give them all the lie.

Tell zeal it wants devotion;
Tell love it is but lust;
Tell time it is but motion;
Tell flesh it is but dust.
And wish them not reply,
For thou must give the lie.

Tell age it daily wasteth;
Tell honor how it alters;
Tell beauty how she blasteth;
Tell favor how it falters.
And as they shall reply,
Give every one the lie.

Tell wit how much it wrangles
In tickle points of niceness;
Tell wisdom she entangles
Herself in overwiseness.
And when they do reply,
Straight give them both the lie.

Tell physic of her boldness;
Tell skill it is pretension;
Tell charity of coldness;
Tell law it is contention.
And as they do reply,
So give them still the lie.

Tell fortune of her blindness;
Tell nature of decay;
Tell friendship of unkindness;
Tell justice of delay.
And if they will reply,
Then give them all the lie.

Tell arts they have no soundness,
But vary by esteeming;
Tell schools they want profoundness,
And stand too much on seeming.
If arts and schools reply,
Give arts and schools the lie.

Tell faith it's fled the city;
Tell how the country erreth;
Tell manhood shakes off pity;
Tell virtue least preferreth.
And if they do reply,
Spare not to give the lie.

So when thou hast, as I
Commanded thee, done blabbing—
Although to give the lie
Deserves no less than stabbing—
Stab at thee he that will,
No stab the soul can kill.

2.9.5 "Nature, That Washed Her Hands in Milk"

(Published in 1902)

Nature, that washed her hands in milk,
And had forgot to dry them,
Instead of earth took snow and silk,
At love's request to try them,
If she a mistress could compose
To please love's fancy out of those.

Her eyes he would should be of light,
A violet breath, and lips of jelly;
Her hair not black, nor overbright,
And of the softest down her belly;
As for her inside he'd have it
Only of wantonness and wit.

At love's entreaty such a one
Nature made, but with her beauty
She hath framed a heart of stone;
So as love, by ill destiny,
Must die for her whom nature gave him,
Because her darling would not save him.

But time (which nature doth despise,
And rudely gives her love the lie,
Makes hope a fool, and sorrow wise)
His hands do neither wash nor dry;

But being made of steel and rust,
Turns snow and silk and milk to dust.

The light, the belly, lips, and breath,
He dims, discolors, and destroys;
With those he feeds but fills not death,
Which sometimes were the food of joys.
Yea, time doth dull each lively wit,
And dries all wantonness with it.

Oh, cruel time! which takes in trust
Our youth, our joys, and all we have,
And pays us but with age and dust;
Who in the dark and silent grave
When we have wandered all our ways
Shuts up the story of our days.

2.9.6 From *The Discovery of the Large, Rich, and Beautiful Empire of Guiana*

(1599)

The next morning we also left the port, and sailed westward up to the river, to view the famous river called Caroli, as well because it was marvelous of itself, as also for that I understood it led to the strongest nations of all the frontiers, that were enemies to the Epuremei, which are subjects to Inga, emperor of Guiana and Manoa. And that night we anchored at another island called Caiama, of some five or six miles in length; and the next day arrived at the mouth of Caroli. When we were short of it as low or further down as the port of Morequito, we heard the great roar and fall of the river. But when we came to enter with our barge and wherries, thinking to have gone up some forty miles to the nations of the Cassipagotos, we were not able with a barge of eight oars to row one stone's cast in an hour; and yet the river is as broad as the Thames at Woolwich, and we tried both sides, and the middle, and every part of the river. So as we encamped upon the banks adjoining, and sent off our Orenoquepone which came with us from Morequito to give knowledge to the nations upon the river of our being there, and that we desired to see the lords of Canuria, which dwelt within the province upon that river, making them know that we were enemies to the Spaniards; for it was on this river side that Morequito slew the friar, and those nine Spaniards which came from Manoa, the city of Inga, and took from them 14,000 pesos of gold. So as the next day there came down a lord or cacique, called Wanuretona, with many people with him, and brought all store of provisions to entertain us, as the rest had done. And as I had before made my coming known to Topiawari, so did I acquaint this cacique therewith, and how I was sent by her Majesty for the purpose aforesaid, and gathered also what I could of him touching the estate of Guiana. And I found that those also of Caroli were not only enemies to the Spaniards, but most of all to the Epuremei, which abound in gold. And by this Wanuretona I had knowledge that on the head of this river were three mighty nations, which were seated on a great lake, from whence this river descended, and were called Cassipagotos, Eparegotos, and Arawagotos; and that all those either against the Spaniards or the Epuremei would join with us, and that if we entered the land over the mountains of Curaa we should satisfy ourselves with gold and all other good things. He told us farther of a nation called Iwarawaqueri, before spoken of, that held daily war with the Epuremei that inhabited Macureguarai, and first civil town of Guiana, of the subjects of Inga, the emperor.

Upon this river one Captain George, that I took with Berreo, told me that there was a great silver mine, and that it was near the banks of the said river. But by this time as well Orenoque, Caroli, as all the rest of the rivers were risen four or five feet in height, so as it was not possible by the strength of any men, or with any boat whatsoever, to row into the river against the stream. I therefore sent Captain Thyn, Captain Greenvile, my nephew John Gilbert, my cousin Butshead Gorges, Captain Clarke, and some thirty shot more to coast the river by land, and to go to a town some twenty miles over the valley called Amnatapoi; and they found guides there to go farther towards the mountain foot to another great town called Capurepana, belonging to a cacique called Haharacoa, that was a nephew to old Topiawari, king of Aromaia, our chiefest friend, because this town and province of Capurepana adjoined to Macureguarai, which was a frontier town of the empire. And the meanwhile myself with Captain Gifford, Captain Caulfield, Edward Hancock, and some half-a-dozen shot marched overland to view the strange overfalls of the river of Caroli, which roared so far off; and also to see the plains adjoining, and the rest of the province of Canuri. I sent also Captain Whiddon, William Connock, and some eight shot with them, to see if they could find any mineral stone alongst the river's side. When we were come to the tops of the first hills of the plains adjoining to the river, we beheld that wonderful breach of waters which ran down Caroli; and might from that mountain see the river how it ran in three parts, above twenty miles off, and there appeared some ten or twelve overfalls in sight, every one as high over the other as a church tower, which fell with that fury, that the rebound of water made it seem as if it had been all covered over with a great shower of rain; and in some places we took it at the first for a smoke that had risen over some great town. For mine own part I was well persuaded from thence to have returned, being a very ill footman; but the rest were all so desirous to go near the said strange thunder of waters, as they drew me on by little and little, till we came into the next valley, where we might better discern the same. I never saw a more beautiful country, nor more lively prospects; hills so raised here and there over the valley; the river winding into divers branches; the plains adjoining without bush or stubble, all fair green grass; the ground of hard sand, easy to march on, either for horse or foot; the deer crossing in every path; the birds towards the evening singing on every tree with a thousand several tunes; cranes and herons of white, crimson, and carnation, perching in the river's side; the air fresh with a gentle easterly wind; and every stone that we stooped to take up promised either gold or silver by his complexion. Your Lordship shall see of many sorts, and I hope some of them cannot be bettered under the sun; and yet we had no means but with our daggers and fingers to tear them out here and there, the rocks being most hard of that mineral spar aforesaid, which is like a flint, and is altogether as hard or harder, and besides the veins lie a fathom or two deep in the rocks. But we wanted all things requisite save only our desires and good will to have performed more if it had pleased God. To be short, when both our companies returned, each of them brought also several sorts of stones that appeared very fair, but were such as they found loose on the ground, and were for the most part but coloured, and had not any gold fixed in them. Yet such as had no judgment or experience kept all that glistered, and would not be persuaded but it was rich because of the lustre; and brought of those, and of marcasite withal, from Trinidad, and have delivered of those stones to be tried in many places, and have thereby bred an opinion that all the rest is of the same. Yet some of these stones I shewed afterward to a Spaniard of the Caracas, who told me that it was El Madre del Oro, that is, the mother of gold, and that the mine was farther in the ground. . . .

For the rest, which myself have seen, I will promise these things that follow, which I know to be true. Those that are desirous to discover and to see many nations may be satisfied within this river, which bringeth forth so many arms and branches leading to several countries and provinces, above 2,000 miles east and west and 800 miles south and north, and of these the most either rich in gold or in other merchandises. The common soldier shall here fight for gold, and pay himself, instead of pence, with plates of half-a-foot broad, whereas he breaketh his bones in other wars for provant and penury. Those commanders and chieftains that shoot at honour and abundance shall find there more rich and beautiful cities, more temples adorned with golden images, more sepulchres filled with treasure, than either Cortes found in Mexico or Pizarro in Peru. And the shining glory of this conquest will eclipse all those so far-extended beams of the Spanish nation. There is no country which yieldeth more pleasure to the inhabitants, either for those common delights of hunting, hawking, fishing, fowling, and the rest, than Guiana doth; it hath so many plains, clear rivers, and abundance of pheasants, partridges, quails, rails, cranes, herons, and all other fowl; deer of all sorts, porks, hares, lions, tigers, leopards, and divers other sorts of beasts, either for chase or food. It hath a kind of beast called cama or anta, as big as an English beef, and in great plenty. To speak of the several sorts of every kind I fear would be troublesome to the reader, and therefore I will omit them, and conclude that both for health, good air, pleasure, and riches, I am resolved it cannot be equalled by any region either in the east or west. Moreover the country is so healthful, as of an hundred persons and more, which lay without shift most sluttishly, and were every day almost melted with heat in rowing and marching, and suddenly wet again with great showers, and did eat of all sorts of corrupt fruits, and made meals of fresh fish without seasoning, of tortugas, of lagartos or crocodiles, and of all sorts good and bad, without either order or measure, and besides lodged in the open air every night, we lost not any one, nor had one ill-disposed to my knowledge; nor found any calentura or other of those pestilent diseases which dwell in all hot regions, and so near the equinoctial line. . . .

To conclude, Guiana is a country that hath yet her maidenhead, never sacked, turned, nor wrought; the face of the earth hath not been torn, nor the virtue and salt of the soil spent by manurance. The graves have not been opened for gold, the mines not broken with sledges, nor their images pulled down out of their temples. It hath never been entered by any army of strength, and never conquered or possessed by any Christian prince. It is besides so defensible, that if two forts be builded in one of the provinces which I have seen, the flood setteth in so near the bank, where the channel also lieth, that no ship can pass up but within a pike's length of the artillery, first of the one, and afterwards of the other. Which two forts will be a sufficient guard both to the empire of Inga, and to an hundred other several kingdoms, lying within the said river, even to the city of Quito in Peru.

There is therefore great difference between the easiness of the conquest of Guiana, and the defence of it being conquered, and the West or East Indies. Guiana hath but one entrance by the sea, if it hath that, for any vessels of burden. So as whosoever shall first possess it, it shall be found unaccessible for any enemy, except he come in wherries, barges, or canoas, or else in flat-bottomed boats; and if he do offer to enter it in that manner, the woods are so thick 200 miles together upon the rivers of such entrance, as a mouse cannot sit in a boat unhit from the bank. By land it is more impossible to approach; for it hath the strongest situation of any region under the sun, and it is so environed with impassable mountains on every side, as it is impossible to victual any company in the passage. Which hath been well proved by the Spanish nation, who since the conquest of Peru have never left five years free from attempting this empire, or discovering some way into it; and yet of three-and-twenty several gentlemen, knights, and noblemen, there was never any that knew which way to lead an army by land, or to conduct ships by sea, anything near the said country. Orellana, of whom the river of Amazons taketh name, was the first, and Don Antonio de Berreo, whom we displanted, the last: and I doubt much whether he himself or any of his yet know the best way into the said empire. It can therefore hardly be regained, if any strength be formerly set down, but in one or two places, and but two or three crumsters or galleys built and furnished upon the river within. The West Indies have many ports, watering places, and landings; and nearer than 300 miles to Guiana, no man can harbour a ship, except he know one only place, which is not learned in haste, and which I will undertake there is not any one of my companies that knoweth, whosoever hearkened most after it.

Besides, by keeping one good fort, or building one town of strength, the whole empire is guarded; and whatsoever companies shall be afterwards planted within the land, although in twenty several provinces, those shall be able all to reunite themselves upon any occasion either by the way of one river, or be able to march by land without either wood, bog, or mountain. Whereas in the West Indies there are few towns or provinces that can succour or relieve one the other by land or sea. By land the countries are either desert, mountainous, or strong enemies. By sea, if any man invade to the eastward, those to the west cannot in many months turn against the breeze and eastern wind. Besides, the Spaniards are therein so dispersed as they are nowhere strong, but in Nueva Espana only; the sharp mountains, the thorns, and poisoned prickles, the sandy and deep ways in the valleys, the smothering heat and air, and want of water in other places are their only and best defence; which, because those nations that invade them are not victualled or provided to stay, neither have any place to friend adjoining, do serve them instead of good arms and great multitudes.

The West Indies were first offered her Majesty's grandfather by Columbus, a stranger, in whom there might be doubt of deceit; and besides it was then thought incredible that there were such and so many lands and regions never written of before. This Empire is made known to her Majesty by her own vassal, and by him that oweth to her more duty than an ordinary subject; so that it shall ill sort with the many graces and benefits which I have received to abuse her Highness, either with fables or imaginations. The country is already discovered, many nations won to her Majesty's love and obedience, and those Spaniards which have latest and longest laboured about the conquest, beaten out, discouraged, and disgraced, which among these nations were thought invincible. Her Majesty may in this enterprise employ all those soldiers and gentlemen that are younger brethren, and all captains and chieftains that want employment, and the charge will be only the first setting out in victualling and arming them; for after the first or second year I doubt not but to see in London a Contractation-House of more receipt for Guiana than there is now in Seville for the West Indies.

And I am resolved that if there were but a small army afoot in Guiana, marching towards Manoa, the chief city of Inga, he would yield to her Majesty by composition so many hundred thousand pounds yearly as should both defend all enemies abroad, and defray all expenses at home; and that he would besides pay a garrison of three or four thousand soldiers very royally to defend him against other nations. For he cannot but know how his predecessors, yea, how his own great uncles, Guascar and Atabalipa, sons to Guiana-Capac, emperor of Peru, were, while they contended for the empire, beaten out by the Spaniards, and that both of late years and ever since the said conquest, the Spaniards have sought the passages and entry of his country; and of their cruelties used to the borderers he cannot be ignorant. In which respects no doubt but he will be brought to tribute with great gladness; if not, he hath neither shot nor iron weapon in all his empire, and therefore may easily be conquered.

And I further remember that Berreo confessed to me and others, which I protest before the Majesty of God to be true, that there was found among the prophecies in Peru, at such time as the empire was reduced to the Spanish obedience, in their chiefest temples, amongst divers others which foreshadowed the loss of the said empire, that from Inglatierra those Ingas should be again in time to come restored, and delivered from the servitude of the said conquerors. And I hope, as we with these few hands have displanted the first garrison, and driven them out of the said country, so her Majesty will give order for the rest, and either defend it, and hold it as tributary, or conquer and keep it as empress of the same. For whatsoever prince shall possess it, shall be greatest; and if the king of Spain enjoy it, he will become unresistible. Her Majesty hereby shall confirm and strengthen the opinions of all nations as touching her great and princely actions. And where the south border of Guiana reacheth to the dominion and empire of the Amazons, those women shall hereby hear the name of a virgin, which is not only able to defend her own territories and her neighbours, but also to invade and conquer so great empires and so far removed.

To speak more at this time I fear would be but troublesome: I trust in God, this being true, will suffice, and that he which is King of all Kings, and Lord of Lords, will put it into her heart which is Lady of Ladies to possess it. If not, I will judge those men worthy to be kings thereof, that by her grace and leave will undertake it of themselves.

2.9.7 Reading and Review Questions

1. To what degree, if any, do you see Raleigh expressing his society's values in his poetry and prose, and how? To what degree, if any, do you see Raleigh expressing personal values in his poetry and prose, and how? How do these expressions compare to More's or Spenser's?

2. What attitude towards the pastoral tradition in literature does "The Nymph's Reply" convey, and how?

3. Considering Raleigh's determined pursuit of glory, fame, courtly influence, and wealth, how seriously, if at all, do you think he intends his readers to take the condemnations in "The Lie?"

4. In "To Cynthia," how, if at all, does Raleigh obliquely refer to Elizabeth I, and why? What relationship, if any, between the two might we infer from this poem, and why? How does his reference to Elizabeth I compare to Spenser's?

5. In "The Discoverie," how, if at all, does Raleigh persuade his readers of the truth of what he is describing? What rhetorical devices, if any, does he use? What appeals to logic, if any, does he use? With what detail does Raleigh describe the native peoples, and why?

2.10 SIR PHILIP SIDNEY

(1554-1586)

From his early youth, Sir Philip Sidney, whose parents were companions to monarchs, demonstrated remarkable erudition and intellect. He was enrolled in Shrewsbury School where he studied under Thomas Ashton before entering Christ Church, Oxford. He perfected his knowledge of modern languages and rhetoric through two years of travel on the Continent, particularly Germany, Italy, and France. While in Paris, he witnessed the events culminating in the St. Bartholomew's Day Massacre, the slaughter of French Protestants, or Huguenots, that ensued after the attempted assassination of Gaspard de Coligny (1519-1572), advisor to the Huguenot King Henry III of Navarre (1553-1610).

Upon his return to England, Sidney sought to use his knowledge of the Continent to good effect through

Image 2.10 | Sir Philip Sidney
Artist | Unknown
Source | Wikimedia Commons
License | Public Domain

political appointments by Elizabeth I. He eventually was chosen to lead an embassy ostensibly of condolence to the family of Maximilian II of Austria (1527-1576) but actually of political intent to create a Protestant League in Europe. This intent continued upon his return to England during negotiations with William I of Orange (1533-1584). These political aspirations were frustrated by Elizabeth I's defensive strategies of playing Spain off against France, a strategy that a Protestant League might upset. His estrangement from Elizabeth I and her court was further exacerbated by his publicly discouraging her possible marriage to the Catholic Duke of Anjou.

Turning away from politics, Sidney then turned his considerable talents to writing. As a poet, Sidney experimented in new metrics in his pastoral romances *Old Arcadia* (1581) and *New Arcadia* (1590) and the Petrarchan sonnet cycle in *Astrophil and Stella* (1591). This sonnet sequence is particularly Petrarchan in its conventional depiction of unrequited love, in its aloof Stella and suffering Astrophil. Sidney wrote his important work of literary criticism, *The Defense of Poesy*, probably in response to *The School of Abuse* (1579), a work by Stephen Gosson (1554-1624) that deplored the immorality fostered by poetry that was dedicated to Sidney. The *Defense* demonstrates Sidney's extraordinary knowledge of the classics as well as modern authors, including Dante (c. 1265-1321), Jacopo Sannazaro (1458-1530)—whose humanist *Arcadia* (1504) directly influenced Sidney's versions—Ludovico Ariosto (1474-1533), and Petrarch. And countering Gosson's allegations against poetry, Sidney's *Defense* takes up the gauntlet that Plato (c. 428-c. 348 BCE) threw down when he banished poets from the ideal Republic for their potential to lead citizens into immorality. Sidney shapes his *Defense* according to the seven-part classical structure: an introduction, proposition, division, examination, refutation, peroration, and digression. Thus, he not only demonstrates but also lauds poetry's ability to teach, to give light to darkness through its beauty and sweet delight.

THE

DEFENCE OF

Poelie.

By Sir Phillip Sidney,
Knight.

LONDON

Printed for *rrilliam Penfonby.*

1595.

Image 2.11 | *The Defence of Poesie*
Artist | Sir Phillip Sidney
Source | Luminarium
License | Public Domain

As the *Defense* asserts, right thought leads to right action. Sidney turned to action when Elizabeth I appointed him as governor of Vlissengen in the Netherlands, still in the throes of its rebellion against Catholic Spain. Sidney's uncle Robert Dudley, Earl of Leicester, the Governor-General of the Netherlands, supported the Dutch rebels. With an English army that included Sidney, Leicester besieged the town of Zutphen. During battle, Sidney received a leg wound that later turned gangrenous. Legend has it that when close to death Sidney—always the consummate courtly gentleman—refused a cup of water in favor of another wounded soldier, saying "Thy necessity is yet greater than mine." After his death, Mary (Sidney) Herbert, Countess of Pembroke, became Sidney's literary executor and the many elegies for Sidney she encouraged, including Spenser's and her own, give some sense of Sidney's impact from his era up to our own.

2.10.1 *The Defence of Poesy*

(1595)

When the right virtuous Edward Wotton and I were at the Emperor's [Maximilian II] court together, we gave ourselves to learn horsemanship of John Pietro Pugliano, one that with great commendation had the place of an esquire in his stable; and he, according to the fertileness of the Italian wit, did not only afford us the demonstration of his practice, but sought to enrich our minds with the contemplations therein which he thought most precious. But with none I remember mine ears were at any time more loaded, than when—either angered with slow payment, or moved with our learner-like admiration—he exercised his speech in the praise of his faculty. He said soldiers were the noblest estate of mankind, and horsemen the noblest of soldiers. He said they were the masters of war and ornaments of peace, speedy goers and strong abiders, triumphers both in camps and courts. Nay, to so unbelieved a point he proceeded, as that no earthly thing bred such wonder to a prince as to be a good horseman; skill of government was but a *pedanteria* [pedantry—ed.] in comparison. Then would he add certain praises, by telling what a peerless beast the horse was, the only serviceable courtier without flattery, the beast of most beauty, faithfulness, courage, and such more, that if I had not been a piece of a logician before I came to him, I think he would have persuaded me to have wished myself a horse. But thus much at least with his no few words he drove into me, that self-love is better than any gilding to make that seem gorgeous wherein ourselves be parties.

Wherein if Pugliano's strong affection and weak arguments will not satisfy you, I will give you a nearer example of myself, who, I know not by what mischance, in these my not old years and idlest times, having slipped into the title of a poet, am provoked to say something unto you in the defense of that my unelected vocation, which if I handle with more good will than good reasons, bear with me, since the scholar is to be pardoned that follows the steps of his master. And yet I must say that, as I have just cause to make a pitiful defense of poor poetry, which from almost the highest estimation of learning is fallen to be the laughing-stock of children, so have I need to bring some more available proofs, since the former is by no man barred of his deserved credit, the silly [weak—ed] latter has had even the names of philosophers used to the defacing of it, with great danger of civil war among the Muses.

And first, truly, to all them that, professing learning, inveigh against poetry, may justly be objected that they go very near to ungratefulness, to seek to deface that which, in the noblest nations and languages that are known, has been the first light-giver to ignorance, and first nurse, whose milk by little and little enabled them to feed afterwards of tougher knowledges. And will they now play the hedgehog, that, being received into the den, drove out his host? Or rather the vipers, that with their birth kill their parents? Let learned Greece in any of her manifold sciences be able to show me one book before Musæus, Homer, and Hesiod, all three nothing else but poets. Nay, let any history be brought that can say any writers were there before them, if they were not men of the same skill, as Orpheus, Linus, and some other are named, who, having been the first of that country that made pens deliver of their knowledge to their posterity, may justly challenge to be called their fathers in learning. For not only in time they had this priority—although in itself antiquity be venerable—but went before them as causes, to draw with their charming sweetness the wild untamed wits to an admiration of knowledge. So as Amphion was said to move stones with his poetry to build Thebes, and Orpheus to be listened to by beasts,—indeed stony and beastly people. So among the Romans were Livius Andronicus and Ennius; so in the Italian language the first that made it aspire to be a treasure-house of science were the poets Dante, Boccace, and Petrarch; so in our English were Gower and Chaucer, after whom, encouraged and delighted with their excellent foregoing, others have followed to beautify our mother-tongue, as well in the same kind as in other arts.

This did so notably show itself, that the philosophers of Greece durst not a long time appear to the world but under the masks of poets. So Thales, Empedocles, and Parmenides sang their natural philosophy in verses; so did Pythagoras and Phocylides their moral counsels; so did Tyrtæus in war matters, and Solon in matters of policy; or rather they, being poets; did exercise their delightful vein in those points of highest knowledge which before them lay hidden to the world. For that wise Solon was directly a poet it is manifest, having written in verse the notable fable of the Atlantic Island which was continued by Plato. And truly even Plato whosoever well considers, shall find that in the body of his work though the inside and strength were philosophy, the skin as it were and beauty depended most of poetry. For all stands upon dialogues; wherein he feigns many honest burgesses of Athens to speak of such matters that, if they had been set on the rack, they would never have confessed them; besides his poetical describing the circumstances of their meetings, as the well-ordering of a banquet, the delicacy of a walk, with interlacing mere tales, as Gyges' Ring and others, which who knows not to be flowers of poetry did never walk into Apollo's garden.

And even historiographers, although their lips sound of things done, and verity be written in their foreheads, have been glad to borrow both fashion and perchance weight of the poets. So Herodotus entitled [the various books of—ed.] his history by the name of the nine Muses; and both he and all the rest that followed him either stole or usurped of poetry their passionate describing of passions, the many particularities of battles which no man could affirm, or, if that be denied me, long orations put in the mouths of great kings and captains, which it is certain they never pronounced.

So that truly neither philosopher nor historiographer could at the first have entered into the gates of popular judgments, if they had not taken a great passport of poetry, which in all nations at this day, where learning flourishes not, is plain to be seen; in all which they have some feeling of poetry. In Turkey, besides their lawgiving divines they have no other writers but poets. In our neighbor country Ireland, where truly learning goes very bare, yet are their poets held in a devout reverence. Even among the most barbarous and simple Indians, where no writing is, yet have they their poets, who make and sing songs (which they call *areytos*), both of their ancestors' deeds and praises of their gods,—a sufficient probability that, if ever learning come among them, it must be by having their hard dull wits softened and sharpened with the sweet delights of poetry; for until they find a pleasure in the exercise of the mind, great promises of much knowledge will little persuade them that know not the fruits of knowledge. In Wales, the true remnant of the ancient Britons, as there are good authorities to show the long time they had poets which they called bards, so through all the conquests of Romans, Saxons, Danes, and Normans, some of whom did seek to ruin all memory of learning from among them, yet do their poets even to this day last; so as it is not more notable in soon beginning, than in long continuing.

But since the authors of most of our sciences were the Romans, and before them the Greeks, let us a little stand upon their authorities, but even [only—ed.] so far as to see what names they have given unto this now scorned skill. Among the Romans a poet was called *vates*, which is as much as a diviner, foreseer, or prophet, as by his conjoined words, *vaticinium* and *vaticinari*, is manifest; so heavenly a title did that excellent people bestow upon this heart-ravishing knowledge. And so far were they carried into the admiration thereof, that they thought in the chanceable hitting upon any such verses great fore-tokens of their following fortunes were placed; whereupon grew the word of *Sortes Virgilianæ*, when by sudden opening Virgil's book they lighted upon some verse of his making. Whereof the histories of the Emperors' lives are full: as of Albinus, the governor of our island, who in his childhood met with this verse,

Arma amens capio, nec sat rationis in armis,
[Angered, I take up arms, but reason does not lie in arms—ed.]

and in his age performed it. Although it were a very vain and godless superstition, as also it was to think that spirits were commanded by such verses—whereupon this word charms, derived of *carmina*, comes—so yet serves it to show the great reverence those wits were held in, and altogether not [not altogether—ed] without ground, since both the oracles of Delphos and Sibylla's prophecies were wholly delivered in verses; for that same exquisite observing of number and measure in words, and that high-flying liberty of conceit [concept, invention—ed.], proper to the poet, did seem to have some divine force in it.

And may not I presume a little further to show the reasonableness of this word *Vates*, and say that the holy David's Psalms are a divine poem? If I do, I shall not do it without the testimony of great learned men, both ancient and modern. But even the name of Psalms will speak for me, which, being interpreted, is nothing but Songs; then, that it is fully written in metre, as all learned Hebricians agree, although the rules be not yet fully found; lastly and principally, his handling his prophecy, which is merely poetical. For what else is the awaking his musical instruments, the often and free changing of persons, his notable prosopopoeias, when he makes you, as it were, see God coming in His majesty, his telling of the beasts' joyfulness and hills' leaping, but a heavenly poesy, wherein almost he shows himself a passionate lover of that unspeakable and everlasting beauty to be seen by the eyes of the mind, only cleared by faith? But truly now having named him, I fear

I seem to profane that holy name, applying it to poetry, which is among us thrown down to so ridiculous an estimation. But they that with quiet judgments will look a little deeper into it, shall find the end and working of it such as, being rightly applied, deserves not to be scourged out of the church of God.

But now let us see how the Greeks named it and how they deemed of it. The Greeks called him "a poet," which name has, as the most excellent, gone through other languages. It comes of this word *poiein*, which is "to make"; wherein I know not whether by luck or wisdom we Englishmen have met with the Greeks in calling him "a maker." Which name how high and incomparable a title it is, I had rather were known by marking the scope of other sciences than by any partial allegation. There is no art delivered unto mankind that has not the works of nature for his principal object, without which they could not consist, and on which they so depend as they become actors and players, as it were, of what nature will have set forth. So doth the astronomer look upon the stars, and, by that he sees, set down what order nature has taken therein. So do the geometrician and arithmetician in their divers sorts of quantities. So doth the musician in times tell you which by nature agree, which not. The natural philosopher thereon has his name, and the moral philosopher stands upon the natural virtues, vices, and passions of man; and "follow nature," says he, "therein, and thou shalt not err." The lawyer says what men have determined, the historian what men have done. The grammarian speaks only of the rules of speech, and the rhetorician and logician, considering what in nature will soonest prove and persuade, thereon give artificial rules, which still are compassed within the circle of a question, according to the proposed matter. The physician weighs the nature of man's body, and the nature of things helpful or hurtful unto it. And the metaphysic, though it be in the second and abstract notions, and therefore be counted supernatural, yet doth he, indeed, build upon the depth of nature.

Only the poet, disdaining to be tied to any such subjection, lifted up with the vigor of his own invention, doth grow, in effect, into another nature, in making things either better than nature brings forth, or, quite anew, forms such as never were in nature, as the heroes, demi-gods, cyclops, chimeras, furies, and such like; so as he goes hand in hand with nature, not enclosed within the narrow warrant of her gifts, but freely ranging within the zodiac of his own wit. Nature never set forth the earth in so rich tapestry as divers poets have done; neither with pleasant rivers, fruitful trees, sweet-smelling flowers, nor whatsoever else may make the too-much-loved earth more lovely; her world is brazen, the poets only deliver a golden.

But let those things alone, and go to man—for whom as the other things are, so it seems in him her uttermost cunning is employed—and know whether she have brought forth so true a lover as Theagenes; so constant a friend as Pylades; so valiant a man as Orlando; so right a prince as Xenophon's Cyrus; so excellent a man every way as Virgil's Æneas? Neither let this be jestingly conceived, because the works of the one be essential, the other in imitation or fiction; for any understanding knows the skill of each artificer stands in that idea, or fore-conceit of the work, and not in the work itself. And that the poet has that idea is manifest, by delivering them forth in such excellency as he has imagined them. Which delivering forth, also, is not wholly imaginative, as we are wont to say by them that build castles in the air; but so far substantially it works, not only to make a Cyrus, which had been but a particular excellency, as nature might have done, but to bestow a Cyrus upon the world to make many Cyruses, if they will learn aright why and how that maker made him. Neither let it be deemed too saucy a comparison to balance the highest point of man's wit with the efficacy of nature; but rather give right honor to the Heavenly Maker of that maker, who, having made man to His own likeness, set him beyond and over all the works of that second nature. Which in nothing he shows so much as in poetry, when with the force of a divine breath he brings things forth far surpassing her doings, with no small argument to the incredulous of that first accursed fall of Adam,—since our erected wit makes us know what perfection is, and yet our infected will keeps us from reaching unto it. But these arguments will by few be understood, and by fewer granted; thus much I hope will be given me, that the Greeks with some probability of reason gave him the name above all names of learning.

Now let us go to a more ordinary opening of him, that the truth may be the more palpable; and so, I hope, though we get not so unmatched a praise as the etymology of his names will grant, yet his very description, which no man will deny, shall not justly be barred from a principal commendation.

Poesy, therefore, is an art of imitation, for so Aristotle terms it in his word *mimēsis*, that is to say, a representing, counterfeiting, or figuring forth; to speak metaphorically, a speaking picture, with this end,—to teach and delight.

Of this have been three general kinds. The chief, both in antiquity and excellency, were they that did imitate the inconceivable excellencies of God. Such were David in his Psalms; Solomon in his Song of Songs, in his Ecclesiastes and Proverbs; Moses and Deborah in their Hymns; and the writer of Job; which, beside other, the learned Emanuel Tremellius and Franciscus Junius do entitle the poetical part of the Scripture. Against these none will speak that has the Holy Ghost in due holy reverence. In this kind, though in a full wrong divinity, were Orpheus, Amphion, Homer in his Hymns, and many other, both Greeks and Romans. And this poesy must be used by whosoever will follow St. James' counsel in singing psalms when they are merry; and I know is used with the fruit of comfort by some, when, in sorrowful pangs of their death-bringing sins, they find the consolation of the never-leaving goodness.

The second kind is of them that deal with matters philosophical, either moral, as Tyrtæus, Phocylides, and Cato; or natural, as Lucretius and Virgil's Georgics; or astronomical, as Manilius and Pontanus; or historical, as Lucan; which who mislike, the fault is in their judgment quite out of taste, and not in the sweet food of sweetly uttered knowledge.

But because this second sort is wrapped within the fold of the proposed subject, and takes not the free course of his own invention, whether they properly be poets or no, let grammarians dispute, and go to the third, indeed right poets, of whom chiefly this question arises. Betwixt whom and these second is such a kind of difference as betwixt the meaner sort of painters, who counterfeit only such faces as are set before them, and the more excellent, who having no law but wit, bestow that in colors upon you which is fittest for the eye to see,—as the constant though lamenting look of Lucretia, when she punished in herself another's fault; wherein he paints not Lucretia, whom he never saw, but paints the outward beauty of such a virtue. For these third be they which most properly do imitate to teach and delight; and to imitate borrow nothing of what is, has been, or shall be; but range, only reined with learned discretion, into the divine consideration of what may be and should be. These be they that, as the first and most noble sort may justly be termed vates, so these are waited on in the excellentest languages and best understandings with the fore-described name of poets. For these, indeed, do merely make to imitate, and imitate both to delight and teach, and delight to move men to take that goodness in hand, which without delight they would fly as from a stranger; and teach to make them know that goodness whereunto they are moved:—which being the noblest scope to which ever any learning was directed, yet want there not idle tongues to bark at them.

These be subdivided into sundry more special denominations. The most notable be the heroic, lyric, tragic, comic, satiric, iambic, elegiac, pastoral, and certain others, some of these being termed according to the matter they deal with, some by the sort of verse they liked best to write in,—for indeed the greatest part of poets have appareled their poetical inventions in that numberous kind of writing which is called verse. Indeed but appareled, verse being but an ornament and no cause to poetry, since there have been many most excellent poets that never versified, and now swarm many versifiers that need never answer to the name of poets. For Xenophon, who did imitate so excellently as to give us *effigiem justi imperii*—the portraiture of a just empire under the name of Cyrus (as Cicero says of him)—made therein an absolute heroical poem; so did Heliodorus in his sugared invention of that picture of love in Theagenes and Chariclea; and yet both these wrote in prose. Which I speak to show that it is not riming and versing that makes a poet—no more than a long gown makes an advocate, who, though he pleaded in armor, should be an advocate and no soldier—but it is that feigning notable images of virtues, vices, or what else, with that delightful teaching, which must be the right describing note to know a poet by. Although indeed the senate of poets has chosen verse as their fittest raiment, meaning, as in matter they passed all in all, so in manner to go beyond them; not speaking, table-talk fashion, or like men in a dream, words as they chanceably fall from the mouth, but peizing [weighing—ed.] each syllable of each word by just proportion, according to the dignity of the subject.

Now, therefore, it shall not be amiss, first to weigh this latter sort of poetry by his works, and then by his parts; and if in neither of these anatomies he be condemnable, I hope we shall obtain a more favorable sentence. This purifying of wit, this enriching of memory, enabling of judgment, and enlarging of conceit, which commonly we call learning, under what name soever it come forth or to what immediate end soever it be directed, the final end is to lead and draw us to as high a perfection as our degenerate souls, made worse by their clay lodgings, can be capable of. This, according to the inclination of man, bred many-formed impressions. For some that thought this felicity principally to be gotten by knowledge, and no knowledge to be so high or heavenly as acquaintance with the stars, gave themselves to astronomy; others, persuading themselves to be demi-gods if they knew the causes of things, became natural and supernatural philosophers. Some an admirable delight drew to music, and some the certainty of demonstration to the mathematics; but all, one and other, having this scope:—to know, and by knowledge to lift up the mind from the dungeon of the body to the enjoying his own divine essence. But when by the balance of experience it was found that the astronomer, looking to the stars, might fall into a ditch, that the inquiring philosopher might be blind in himself, and the mathematician might draw forth a straight line with a crooked heart; then lo! did proof, the overruler of opinions, make manifest, that all these are but serving sciences, which, as they have each a private end in themselves, so yet are they all directed to the highest end of the mistress knowledge, by the Greeks called *architektonikē*, which stands, as I think, in the knowledge of a man's self, in the ethic and politic consideration, with the end of well-doing, and not of well-knowing only:—even as the saddler's next end is to make a good saddle, but his further end to serve a nobler faculty, which is horsemanship; so the horseman's to soldiery; and the soldier not only to have the skill, but to perform the practice of a soldier. So that the ending end of all earthly learning being virtuous action, those skills that most serve to bring forth that have a most just title to be princes over all the rest; wherein, if we can show, the poet is worthy to have it before any other competitors.

Among whom as principal challengers step forth the moral philosophers; whom, me thinks, I see coming toward me with a sullen gravity, as though they could not abide vice by daylight; rudely clothed, for to witness outwardly their contempt of outward things; with books in their hands against glory, whereto they set their names; sophistically speaking against subtlety; and angry with any man in whom they see the foul fault of anger. These men, casting largess as they go of definitions, divisions, and distinctions, with a scornful interrogative do soberly ask whether it be possible to find any path so ready to lead a man to virtue, as that which teaches what virtue is, and teaches it not only by delivering forth his very being, his causes and effects, but also by making known his enemy, vice, which must be destroyed, and his cumbersome servant, passion, which must be mastered; by showing the generalities that contain it, and the specialities that are derived from it; lastly, by plain setting down how it extends itself out of the limits of a man's own little world, to the government of families, and maintaining of public societies?

The historian scarcely gives leisure to the moralist to say so much, but that he, loaded with old mouse-eaten records, authorizing himself for the most part upon other histories, whose greatest authorities are built upon the notable foundation of hearsay; having much ado to accord differing writers, and to pick truth out of partiality; better acquainted with a thousand years ago than with the present age, and yet better knowing how this world goes than how his own wit runs; curious for antiquities and inquisitive of novelties, a wonder to young folks and a tyrant in table-talk; denies, in a great chafe [agitation—ed.], that any man for teaching of virtue and virtuous actions is comparable to him "I am *testis temporum, lux veritatis, vita memoriæ, magistra vitæ, nuntia vetustatis* [the witness of the times, the light of truth, the life of memory, the directress of life, the messenger of antiquity—ed.]. The philosopher," says he, "teaches a disputative virtue, but I do an active. His virtue is excellent in the dangerless Academy of Plato, but mine shows forth her honorable face in the battles of Marathon, Pharsalia, Poitiers, and Agincourt. He teaches virtue by certain abstract considerations, but I only bid you follow the footing of them that have gone before you Old-aged experience goes beyond the fine-witted philosopher; but I give the experience of many ages. Lastly, if he make the songbook, I put the learner's hand to the lute; and if he be the guide, I am the light." Then would he allege you innumerable examples, confirming story by story, how much the wisest senators and princes have been directed by the credit of history, as Brutus, Alphonsus of Aragon—and who not, if need be? At length the long line of their disputation makes [comes to—ed] a point in this,—that the one gives the precept, and the other the example.

Now whom shall we find, since the question stands for the highest form in the school of learning, to be moderator? Truly, as me seems, the poet; and if not a moderator, even the man that ought to carry the title from them both, and much more from all other serving sciences. Therefore compare we the poet with the historian and with the moral philosopher; and if he go beyond them both, no other human skill can match him. For as for the divine, with all reverence it is ever to be excepted, not only for having his scope as far beyond any of these as eternity exceeds a moment, but even for passing each of these in themselves. And for the lawyer, though *Jus* be the daughter of Justice, and Justice the chief of virtues, yet because he seeks to make men good rather *formidine poeœnæ* [fear of punishment] than *virtutis amore* [love of virtue—ed.] or, to say righter, doth not endeavor to make men good, but that their evil hurt not others; having no care, so he be a good citizen, how bad a man he be; therefore, as our wickedness makes him necessary, and necessity makes him honorable, so is he not in the deepest truth to stand in rank with these, who all endeavor to take naughtiness away, and plant goodness even in the secretest cabinet of our souls. And these four are all that any way deal in that consideration of men's manners, which being the supreme knowledge, they that best breed it deserve the best commendation.

The philosopher therefore and the historian are they which would win the goal, the one by precept, the other by example; but both not having both, do both halt. For the philosopher, setting down with thorny arguments the bare rule, is so hard of utterance and so misty to be conceived, that one that has no other guide but him shall wade in him till he be old, before he shall find sufficient cause to be honest. For his knowledge stands so upon the abstract and general that happy is that man who may understand him, and more happy that can apply what he doth understand. On the other side, the historian, wanting the precept, is so tied, not to what should be but to what is, to the particular truth of things, and not to the general reason of things, that his example draws no necessary consequence, and therefore a less fruitful doctrine.

Now doth the peerless poet perform both; for whatsoever the philosopher says should be done, he gives a perfect picture of it in some one by whom he presupposes it was done, he gives a perfect picture of it in in some one by whom he presupposes it was done, so as he couples the general notion with the particular example. A perfect picture, I say; for he yields to the powers of the mind an image of that whereof the philosopher bestows but a wordish description, which doth neither strike, pierce, nor possess the sight of the soul so much as that other doth. For as, in outward things, to a man that had never seen an elephant or a rhinoceros, who should tell him most exquisitely all their shapes, color, bigness, and particular marks; or of a gorgeous palace, an architector, with declaring the full beauties, might well make the hearer able to repeat, as it were by rote, all he had heard, yet should never satisfy his inward conceit with being witness to itself of a true lively [vital—ed.] knowledge; but the same man, as soon as he might see those beasts well painted, or that house well in model, should straightway grow, without need of any description, to a judicial comprehending of them; so no doubt the philosopher, with his learned definitions, be it of virtues or vices, matters of public policy or private government, replenishes the memory with many infallible grounds of wisdom, which notwithstanding lie dark before the imaginative and judging power, if they be not illuminated or figured forth by the speaking picture of poesy.

Tully takes much pains, and many times not without poetical helps, to make us know the force love of our country has in us. Let us but hear old Anchises speaking in the midst of Troy's flames, or see Ulysses, in the fullness of all Calypso's delights, bewail his absence from barren and beggarly Ithaca. Anger, the Stoics said, was a short madness. Let but Sophocles bring you Ajax on a stage, killing and whipping sheep and oxen, thinking them the army of Greeks, with their chieftains Agamemnon and Menelaus, and tell me if you have not a more familiar insight into anger, than finding in the schoolmen his genus and difference. See whether wisdom and temperance in Ulysses and Diomedes, valor in Achilles, friendship in Nisus and Euryalus, even to an ignorant man carry not an apparent shining. And, contrarily, the remorse of conscience, in Oedipus; the soon-repenting pride of Agamemnon; the self-devouring cruelty in his father Atreus; the violence of ambition in the two Theban brothers; the sour sweetness of revenge in Medea; and, to fall lower, the Terentian Gnatho and our Chaucer's Pandar so expressed that we now use their names to signify their trades; and finally, all virtues, vices, and passions so in their own natural states laid to the view, that we seem not to hear of them, but clearly to see through them.

But even in the most excellent determination of goodness, what philosopher's counsel can so readily direct a prince, as the feigned Cyrus in Xenophon? Or a virtuous man in all fortunes, as Æneas in Virgil? Or a whole commonwealth, as the way of Sir Thomas More's Utopia? I say the way, because where Sir Thomas More erred, it was the fault of the man, and not of the poet; for that way of patterning a commonwealth was most absolute, though he, perchance, has not so absolutely performed it. For the question is, whether the feigned image of poesy, or the regular instruction of philosophy, has the more force in teaching. Wherein if the philosophers have more rightly showed themselves philosophers than the poets have attained to the high top of their profession,—as in truth,

> Mediocribus esse poetis
>   Non Dii, non homines, non concessere columnæ—
> [Not gods nor men nor booksellers allow poets to be mediocre—ed.]

it is, I say again, not the fault of the art, but that by few men that art can be accomplished.

Certainly, even our Savior Christ could as well have given the moral commonplaces of uncharitableness and humbleness as the divine narration of Dives and Lazarus; or of disobedience and mercy, as that heavenly discourse of the lost child and the gracious father; but that his thorough-searching wisdom knew the estate of Dives burning in hell, and of Lazarus in Abraham's bosom, would more constantly, as it were, inhabit both the memory and judgment. Truly, for myself, me seems I see before mine eyes the lost child's disdainful prodigality, turned to envy a swine's dinner; which by the learned divines are thought not historical acts, but instructing parables.

For conclusion, I say the philosopher teaches, but he teaches obscurely, so as the learned only can understand him; that is to say, he teaches them that are already taught. But the poet is the food for the tenderest stomachs; the poet is indeed the right popular philosopher. Whereof Æsop's tales give good proof; whose pretty allegories, stealing under the formal tales of beasts, make many, more beastly than beasts, begin to hear the sound of virtue from those dumb speakers.

But now it may be alleged that if this imagining of matters be so fit for the imagination, then must the historian needs surpass, who brings you images of true matters, such as indeed were done, and not such as fantastically [fancifully—ed.] or falsely may be suggested to have been done. Truly, Aristotle himself, in his Discourse of Poesy, plainly determines this question, saying that poetry is *philosophoteron* and *spoudaioteron*, that is to say, it is more philosophical and more studiously serious than history. His reason is, because poesy deals with *katholou*, that is to say with the universal consideration, and the history with *kathekaston*, the particular.

"Now," says he, "the universal weighs what is fit to be said or done, either in likelihood or necessity—which the poesy considers in his imposed names; and the particular only marks whether Alcibiades did, or suffered, this or that." Thus far Aristotle. Which reason of his, as all his, is most full of reason.

For, indeed, if the question were whether it were better to have a particular act truly or falsely set down, there is no doubt which is to be chosen, no more than whether you had rather have Vespasian's picture right as he was, or, at the painter's pleasure, nothing resembling. But if the question be for your own use and learning, whether it be better to have it set down as it should be or as it was, then certainly is more doctrinable [instructive—ed.] the feigned Cyrus in Xenophon than the true Cyrus in Justin; and the feigned Æneas in Virgil than the right Æneas in Dares Phrygius; as to a lady that desired to fashion her countenance to the best grace, a painter should more benefit her to portrait a most sweet face, writing Canidia upon it, than to paint Canidia as she was, who, Horace swears, was foul and ill-favored.

If the poet do his part aright, he will show you in Tantalus, Atreus, and such like, nothing that is not to be shunned; in Cyrus, Æneas, Ulysses, each thing to be followed. Where the historian, bound to tell things as things were, cannot be liberal—without he will be poetical—of a perfect pattern; but, as in Alexander, or Scipio himself, show doings, some to be liked, some to be misliked; and then how will you discern what to follow but by your own discretion, which you had without reading Quintus Curtius? And whereas a man may say, though in universal consideration of doctrine the poet prevails, yet that the history, in his saying such a thing was done, doth warrant a man more in that he shall follow,—the answer is manifest: that if he stand upon that *was*, as if he should argue, because it rained yesterday therefore it should rain to-day, then indeed it has some advantage to a gross conceit. But if he know an example only informs a conjectured likelihood, and so go by reason, the poet doth so far exceed him as he is to frame his example to that which is most reasonable, be it in warlike, politic, or private matters; where the historian in his bare *was* has many times that which we call fortune to overrule the best wisdom. Many times he must tell events whereof he can yield no cause; or if he do, it must be poetically.

For, that a feigned example has as much force to teach as a true example—for as for to move, it is clear, since the feigned may be tuned to the highest key of passion— let us take one example wherein a poet and a historian do concur Herodotus and Justin do both testify that Zopyrus, king Darius' faithful servant, seeing his master long resisted by the rebellious Babylonians, feigned himself in extreme disgrace of his king; for verifying of which he caused his own nose and ears to be cut off, and so flying to the Babylonians, was received, and for his known valor so far credited, that he did find means to deliver them over to Darius. Muchlike matter doth Livy record of Tarquinius and his son. Xenophon excellently feigns such another stratagem, performed by Abradatas in Cyrus' behalf. Now would I fain know, if occasion be presented unto you to serve your prince by such an honest dissimulation, why do you not as well learn it of Xenophon's fiction as of the other's verity? and, truly, so much the better, as you shall save your nose by the bargain; for Abradatas did not counterfeit so far.

So, then, the best of the historian is subject to the poet; for whatsoever action or faction, whatsoever counsel, policy, or war-stratagem the historian is bound to recite, that may the poet, if he list, with his imitation make his own, beautifying it both for further teaching and more delighting, as it pleases him; having all, from

Dante's Heaven to his Hell, under the authority of his pen. Which if I be asked what poets have done? so as I might well name some, yet say I, and say again, I speak of the art, and not of the artificer.

Now, to that which is commonly attributed to the praise of history, in respect of the notable learning is gotten by marking the success, as though therein a man should see virtue exalted and vice punished,—truly that commendation is peculiar to poetry and far off from history. For, indeed, poetry ever sets virtue so out in her best colors, making Fortune her well-waiting handmaid, that one must needs be enamored of her. Well may you see. Ulysses in a storm, and in other hard plights; but they are but exercises of patience and magnanimity, to make them shine the more in the near following prosperity. And, of the contrary part, if evil men come to the stage, they ever go out—as the tragedy writer answered to one that misliked the show of such persons—so manacled as they little animate folks to follow them. But the historian, being captived to the truth of a foolish world, is many times a terror from well-doing, and an encouragement to unbridled wickedness. For see we not valiant Miltiades rot in his fetters? The just Phocion and the accomplished Socrates put to death like traitors? The cruel Severus live prosperously? The excellent Severus miserably murdered? Sylla and Marius dying in their beds? Pompey and Cicero slain then, when they would have thought exile a happiness? See we not virtuous Cato driven to kill himself, and rebel Cæsar so advanced that his name yet, after sixteen hundred years, lasts in the highest honor? And mark but even Cæsar's own words of the forenamed Sylla—who in that only did honestly, to put down his dishonest tyranny—*literas nescivit*, [he was without learning—ed.] as if want of learning caused him to do well. He meant it not by poetry, which, not content with earthly plagues, devises new punishments in hell for tyrants; nor yet by philosophy, which teaches *occidendos esse* [that they are to be killed—ed.] but, no doubt, by skill in history, for that indeed can afford you Cypselus, Periander, Phalaris, Dionysius, and I know not how many more of the same kennel, that speed well enough in their abominable injustice or usurpation.

I conclude, therefore, that he excels history, not only in furnishing the mind with knowledge, but in setting it forward to that which deserves to be called and accounted good; which setting forward, and moving to well-doing, indeed sets the laurel crown upon the poet as victorious, not only of the historian, but over the philosopher, howsoever in teaching it may be questionable. For suppose it be granted—that which I suppose with great reason may be denied—that the philosopher, in respect of his methodical proceeding, teach more perfectly than the poet, yet do I think that no man is so much *Philophilosophos*[a friend to the philosopher—ed.] as to compare the philosopher in moving with the poet. And that moving is of a higher degree than teaching, it may by this appear, that it is well nigh both the cause and the effect of teaching; for who will be taught, if he be not moved with desire to be taught? And what so much good doth that teaching bring forth—I speak still of moral doctrine—as that it moves one to do that which it doth teach? For, as Aristotle says, it is not *Gnosis* [knowing] but *Praxis* [doing—ed.] must be the fruit; and how *Praxis* cannot be, without being moved to practice, it is no hard matter to consider. The philosopher shows you the way, he informs you of the particularities, as well of the tediousness of the way, as of the pleasant lodging you shall have when your journey is ended, as of the many by-turnings that may divert you from your way; but this is to no man but to him that will read him, and read him with attentive, studious painfulness; which constant desire whosoever has in him, has already passed half the hardness of the way, and therefore is beholding to the philosopher but for the other half. Nay, truly, learned men have learnedly thought, that where once reason has so much overmastered passion as that the mind has a free desire to do well, the inward light each mind has in itself is as good as a philosopher's book; since in nature we know it is well to do well, and what is well and what is evil, although not in the words of art which philosophers bestow upon us; for out of natural conceit the philosophers drew it. But to be moved to do that which we know, or to be moved with desire to know, *hoc opus, hic labor est* [this is the work, this is the labor—ed.]

Now therein of all sciences—I speak still of human, and according to the human conceit—is our poet the monarch. For he doth not only show the way, but gives so sweet a prospect into the way as will entice any man to enter into it. Nay, he doth, as **if your journey should lie through a fair vineyard, at the very first give you a cluster of** grapes, that full of that taste you may long to pass further. He begins not with obscure **definitions, which must blur the margent [margin—ed.] with interpretations, and** load the memory with doubtfulness. But he comes to you with words set in delightful proportion, either accompanied with, or prepared for, the well-enchanting skill of music; and with a tale, forsooth, he comes unto you, with a tale which holds children from play, and old men from the chimney-corner, and, pretending no more, doth intend the winning of the mind from wickedness to virtue; even as the child is often brought to take most wholesome things, by hiding them in such other as to have a pleasant taste,—which, if one should begin to tell them the nature of the aloes or rhubarb they should receive, would sooner take their physic at their ears than at their mouth. So is it in men, most of which are childish in the best things, till they be cradled in their graves,—glad they will be to hear the tales of Hercules, Achilles, Cyrus, Æneas; and, hearing them, must needs hear the right description of wisdom, valor, and justice; which, if they had been barely, that is to say philosophically, set out, they would swear they be brought to school again.

That imitation whereof poetry is, has the most conveniency to nature of all other; insomuch that, as Aristotle says, those things which in themselves are horrible, as cruel battles, unnatural monsters, are made in poetical imitation delightful. Truly, I have known men, that even with reading *Amadis de Gaule*, which, God knows, wants much of a perfect poesy, have found their hearts moved to the exercise of courtesy, liberality, and especially courage. Who reads Æneas carrying old Anchises on his back, that wishes not it were his fortune to perform so excellent an act? Whom do not those words of Turnus move, the tale of Turnus having planted his image in the imagination?

Fugientem haec terra videbit?
  Usque adeone mori miserum est?
[Shall this land see him in flight? Is it so wretched to die?—ed.]

Where the philosophers, as they scorn to delight, so must they be content little to move—saving wrangling whether virtue be the chief or the only good, whether the contemplative or the active life do excel—which Plato and Boethius well knew, and therefore made Mistress Philosophy very often borrow the masking raiment of Poesy. For even those hard-hearted evil men who think virtue a school-name, and know no other good but *indulgere genio* [indulge one's inclination—ed.], and therefore despise the austere admonitions of the philosopher, and feel not the inward reason they stand upon, yet will be content to be delighted, which is all the good-fellow poet seems to promise; and so steal to see the form of goodness—which seen, they cannot but love—ere themselves be aware, as if they took a medicine of cherries.

Infinite proofs of the strange effects of this poetical invention might be alleged; only two shall serve, which are so often remembered as I think all men know them. The one of Menenius Agrippa, who, when the whole people of Rome had resolutely divided themselves from the senate, with apparent show of utter ruin, though he were, for that time, an excellent orator, came not among them upon trust either of figurative speeches or cunning insinuations, and much less with far-fetched maxims of philosophy, which, especially if they were Platonic, they must have learned geometry before they could well have conceived; but, forsooth, he behaves himself like a homely and familiar poet. He tells them a tale, that there was a time when all parts of the body made a mutinous conspiracy against the belly, which they thought devoured the fruits of each other's labor; they concluded they would let so unprofitable a spender starve. In the end, to be short—for the tale is notorious, and as notorious that it was a tale—with punishing the belly they plagued themselves. This, applied by him, wrought such effect in the people, as I never read that ever words brought forth but then so sudden and so good an alteration; for upon reasonable conditions a perfect reconcilement ensued.

The other is of Nathan the prophet, who, when the holy David had so far forsaken God as to confirm adultery with murder, when he was to do the tenderest office of a friend, in laying his own shame before his eyes,—sent by God to call again so chosen a servant, how doth he it but by telling of a man whose beloved lamb was ungratefully taken from his bosom? The application most divinely true, but the discourse itself feigned; which made David (I speak of the second and instrumental cause) as in a glass to see his own filthiness, as that heavenly Psalm of Mercy well testifies.

By these, therefore, examples and reasons, I think it may be manifest that the poet, with that same hand of delight, doth draw the mind more effectually than any other art doth. And so a conclusion not unfitly ensues: that as virtue is the most excellent resting-place for all worldly learning to make his end of, so poetry, being the most familiar to teach it, and most princely to move towards it, in the most excellent work is the most excellent workman.

But I am content not only to decipher him by his works—although works in commendation or dispraise must ever hold a high authority—but more narrowly will examine his parts; so that, as in a man, though all together may carry a presence full of majesty and beauty, perchance in some one defectious piece we may find a blemish.

Now in his parts, kinds, or species, as you list to term them, it is to be noted that some poesies have coupled together two or three kinds,—as tragical and comical, whereupon is risen the tragi-comical; some, in the like manner, have mingled prose and verse, as Sannazzaro and Boethius; some have mingled matters heroical and pastoral; but that comes all to one in this question, for, if severed they be good, the conjunction cannot be hurtful. Therefore, perchance forgetting some, and leaving some as needless to be remembered, it shall not be amiss in a word to cite the special kinds, to see what faults may be found in the right use of them.

Is it then the pastoral poem which is misliked?—for perchance where the hedge is lowest they will soonest leap over. Is the poor pipe disdained, which sometimes out of Meliboeoeus' mouth can show the misery of people under hard lords and ravening soldiers, and again, by Tityrus, what blessedness is derived to them that lie lowest from the goodness of them that sit highest? sometimes, under the pretty tales of wolves and sheep, can include the whole considerations of wrong-doing and patience; sometimes show that contention for trifles can get but a trifling victory; where perchance a man may see that even Alexander and Darius, when they strove who should be cock of this world's dunghill, the benefit they got was that the after-livers may say:

> *Hœc memini et victum frustra contendere Thyrsim;*
> *Ex illo Corydon, Corydon est tempore nobis*
> [I remember such things, and that the defeated Thyrsis struggled vainly; From that time, with us Corydon is the Corydon—ed.]

Or is it the lamenting elegiac, which in a kind heart would move rather pity than blame; who bewails, with the great philosopher Heraclitus, the weakness of mankind and the wretchedness of the world; who surely is to be praised, either for compassionate accompanying just causes of lamentation, or for rightly painting out how weak be the passions of woefulness?

Is it the bitter and wholesome iambic, who rubs the galled mind, in making shame the trumpet of villainy with bold and open crying out against naughtiness? Or the satiric? who

> *Omne vafer vitium ridenti tangit amico;*
> [The sly fellow touches every vice while making his friend laugh—ed.]

who sportingly never leaves till he make a man laugh at folly, and at length ashamed to laugh at himself, which he cannot avoid without avoiding the folly;

who, while *circum præcordia ludit* [he plays around his heartstrings], gives us to feel how many headaches a passionate life brings us to,—how, when all is done,

Est Ulubris, animus si nos non deficit æquus.
[If we do not lack the equable temperament, it is in Ulubrae (noted for desolation)—ed.]

No, perchance it is the comic; whom naughty play-makers and stage-keepers have justly made odious. To the argument of abuse I will answer after. Only thus much now is to be said, that the comedy in an imitation of the common errors of our life, which he represents in the most ridiculous and scornful sort that may be, so as it is impossible that any beholder can be content to be such a one. Now, as in geometry the oblique must be known as well as the right, and in arithmetic the odd as well as the even; so in the actions of our life who sees not the filthiness of evil, wants a great foil to perceive the beauty of virtue. This doth the comedy handle so, in our private and domestic matters, as with hearing it we get, as it were, an experience what is to be looked for of a niggardly Demea, of a crafty Davus, of a flattering Gnatho, of a vain-glorious Thraso; and not only to know what effects are to be expected, but to know who be such, by the signifying badge given them by the comedian. And little reason has any man to say that men learn evil by seeing it so set out; since, as I said before, there is no man living, but by the force truth has in nature, no sooner sees these men play their parts, but wishes them *in pistrinum* [in the mill (place of punishment)—ed.], although perchance the sack of his own faults lie so behind his back, that he sees not himself to dance the same measure,—whereto yet nothing can more open his eyes than to find his own actions contemptibly set forth.

So that the right use of comedy will, I think, by nobody be blamed, and much less of the high and excellent tragedy, that opens the greatest wounds, and shows forth the ulcers that are covered with tissue; that makes kings fear to be tyrants, and tyrants manifest their tyrannical humors; that with stirring the effects of admiration and commiseration teaches the uncertainty of this world, and upon how weak foundations gilded roofs are builded; that makes us know:

Qui sceptra sævus duro imperio regit,
Timet timentes, metus in auctorem redit
[The savage king who wields the scepter with cruel sway Fears those who fear him; dread comes back to the head of the originator—ed.]

But how much it can move, Plutarch yields a notable testimony of the abominable tyrant Alexander Pheræus; from whose eyes a tragedy, well made and represented, drew abundance of tears, who without all pity had murdered infinite numbers, and some of his own blood; so as he that was not ashamed to make matters for tragedies, yet could not resist the sweet violence of a tragedy. And if it wrought no further good in him, it was that he, in despite of himself, withdrew himself from

Page | 1081

hearkening to that which might mollify his hardened heart. But it is not the tragedy they do mislike, for it were too absurd to cast out so excellent a representation of whatsoever is most worthy to be learned.

Is it the lyric that most displeases, who with his tuned lyre and well accorded voice, gives praise, the reward of virtue, to virtuous acts; who gives moral precepts and natural problems; who sometimes raises up his voice to the height of the heavens, in singing the lauds of the immortal God? Certainly I must confess mine own barbarousness; I never heard the old song of Percy and Douglas that I found not my heart moved more than with a trumpet; and yet it is sung but by some blind crowder [a public entertainer, singing for a crowd—ed.], with no rougher voice than rude style; which being so evil appareled in the dust and cobwebs of that uncivil age, what would it work, trimmed in the gorgeous eloquence of Pindar? In Hungary I have seen it the manner of all feasts, and other such meetings, to have songs of their ancestors' valor, which that right soldierlike nation think the chiefest kindlers of brave courage. The incomparable Lacedæmonians did not only carry that kind of music ever with them to the field, but even at home, as such songs were made, so were they all content to be singers of them; when the lusty men were to tell what they did, the old men what they had done, and the young men what they would do. And where a man may say that Pindar many times praises highly victories of small moment, matters rather of sport than virtue; as it may be answered, it was the fault of the poet, and not of the poetry, so indeed the chief fault was in the time and custom of the Greeks, who set those toys at so high a price that Philip of Macedon reckoned a horserace won at Olympus among his three fearful felicities. But as the unimitable Pindar often did, so is that kind most capable and most fit to awake the thoughts from the sleep of idleness, to embrace honorable enterprises.

There rests the heroical, whose very name, I think, should daunt all backbiters. For by what conceit can a tongue be directed to speak evil of that which draws with it no less champions than Achilles, Cyrus, Æneas, Turnus Tydeus, Rinaldo? who doth not only teach and move to a truth, but teaches and moves to the most high and excellent truth; who makes magnanimity and justice shine through all misty fearfulness and foggy desires; who, if the saying of Plato and Tully be true, that who could see virtue would be wonderfully ravished with the love of her beauty, this man sets her out to make her more lovely, in her holiday apparel, to the eye of any that will deign not to disdain until they understand. But if anything be already said in the defense of sweet poetry, all concurs to the maintaining the heroical, which is not only a kind, but the best and most accomplished kind of poetry. For, as the image of each action stirs and instructs the mind, so the lofty image of such worthies most inflames the mind with desire to be worthy, and informs with counsel how to be worthy. Only let Æneas be worn in the tablet of your memory, how he governs himself in the ruin of his country; in the preserving his old father, and carrying away his religious ceremonies; in obeying the god's commandment to leave Dido, though not only all passionate kindness, but even the human consideration of virtuous gratefulness, would have craved other of him; how in storms, how in storms, how in sports, how in war, how in peace, how a fugitive, how victorious, how besieged, how besieging, how to strangers, how to allies, how to enemies, how to his own; lastly, how in his inward self, and how in his outward government; and I think, in a mind most prejudiced with a prejudicating humor, he will be found in excellency fruitful,—yea, even as Horace says, *melius Chrysippo et Crantore* [better than Chrysippus and Crantor (famous philosophers)—ed.]. But truly I imagine it falls out with these poet-whippers as with some good women who often are sick, but in faith they cannot tell where. So the name of poetry is odious to them, but neither his cause nor effects, neither the sum that contains him nor the particularities descending from him, give any fast handle to their carping dispraise.

Since, then, poetry is of all human learnings the most ancient and of most fatherly antiquity, as from whence other learnings have taken their beginnings, since it is so universal that no learned nation doth despise it, nor barbarous nation is without it; since both Roman and Greek gave divine names unto it, the one of "prophesying," the other of "making," and that indeed that name of "making" is fit for him, considering that whereas other arts retain themselves within their subjects, and receive, as it were, their being from it, the poet only brings his own stuff, and doth not learn a conceit out of a matter, but makes matter for a conceit; since neither his description nor his end contains any evil, the thing described cannot be evil; since his effects be so good as to teach goodness, and delight the learners of it; since therein—namely in moral doctrine, the chief of all knowledges—he doth not only far pass the historian, but for instructing is well nigh comparable to the philosopher, and for moving leaves him behind him; since the Holy Scripture, wherein there is no uncleanness, has whole parts in it poetical, and that even our Savior Christ vouchsafed to use the flowers of it; since all his kinds are not only in their united forms, but in their several dissections fully commendable; I think, and think I think rightly, the laurel crown appointed for triumphant captains doth worthily, of all other learnings, honor the poet's triumph.

But because we have ears as well as tongues, and that the lightest reasons that may be will seem to weigh greatly, if nothing be put in the counter-balance, let us hear, and, as well as we can, ponder, what objections be made against this art, which may be worthy either of yielding or answering.

First, truly, I note not only in these *misomousoi*, poet-haters, but in all that kind of people who seek a praise by dispraising others, that they do prodigally spend a great many wandering words in quips and scoffs, carping and taunting at each thing which, by stirring the spleen, may stay the brain from a through-beholding the worthiness of the subject. Those kind of objections, as they are full of a very idle easiness—since there is nothing of so sacred a majesty but that an itching tongue may rub itself upon it—so deserve they no other answer, but, instead of laughing at the jest, to laugh at the jester. We know a playing wit can praise the discretion of an ass, the comfortableness of being in debt, and the jolly commodity of being sick of the plague. So of the contrary side, if we will turn Ovid's verse,

Ut lateat virtus proximitate mali,
[that good lie hid in nearness of the evil,—ed.]

Agrippa will be as merry in showing the vanity of science, as Erasmus was in commending of folly; neither shall any man or matter escape some touch of these smiling railers. But for Erasmus and Agrippa, they had another foundation than the superficial part would promise Marry, these other pleasant fault-finders, who will correct the verb before they understand the noun, and confute others' knowledge before they confirm their own, I would have them only remember that scoffing comes not of wisdom; so as the best title in true English they get with their merriments is to be called good fools,—for so have our grave forefathers ever termed that humorous kind of jesters.

But that which gives greatest scope to their scorning humor is riming and versing. It is already said, and as I think truly said, it is not riming and versing that makes poesy. One may be a poet without versing, and a versifier without poetry. But yet presuppose it were inseparable—as indeed it seems Scaliger judges—truly it were an inseparable commendation. For if *oratio* next to *ratio*, speech next to reason, be the greatest gift bestowed upon mortality, that cannot be praiseless which doth most polish that blessing of speech; which considers each word, not only as a man may say by his forcible quality, but by his best-measured quantity; carrying even in themselves a harmony,—without, perchance, number, measure, order, proportion be in our time grown odious.

But lay aside the just praise it has by being the only fit speech for music—music, I say, the most divine striker of the senses—thus much is undoubtedly true, that if reading be foolish without remembering, memory being the only treasurer of knowledge, those words which are fittest for memory are likewise most convenient for knowledge. Now that verse far exceeds prose in the knitting up of the memory, the reason is manifest; the words, besides their delight, which has a great affinity to memory, being so set, as one cannot be lost but the whole work fails; which, accusing itself, calls the remembrance back to itself, and so most strongly confirms it. Besides, one word so, as it were, begetting another, as, be it in rime or measured verse, by the former a man shall have a near guess to the follower. Lastly, even they that have taught the art of memory have showed nothing so apt for it as a certain room divided into many places, well and thoroughly known; now that has the verse in effect perfectly, every word having his natural seat, which seat must needs make the word remembered. But what needs more in a thing so known to all men? Who is it that ever was a scholar that doth not carry away some verses of Virgil, Horace, or Cato, which in his youth he learned, and even to his old age serve him for hourly lessons? as:

Percontatorem fugito, nam garrulus idem est
[Stay away from an inquisitive man: he is sure to be garrulous—ed.]
[and] *Dum sibi quisque placet, credula turba sumus*
[While each pleases himself, we are a credulous mob—ed]

But the fitness it has for memory is notably proved by all delivery of arts, wherein, for the most part, from grammar to logic, mathematic, physic, and the rest, the rules chiefly necessary to be borne away are compiled in verses. So that verse being in itself sweet and orderly, and being best for memory, the only handle of knowledge; it must be in jest that any man can speak against it.

Now then go we to the most important imputations laid to the poor poets; for aught I can yet learn they are these.

First, that there being many other more fruitful knowledges, a man might better spend his time in them than in this.

Secondly, that it is the mother of lies.

Thirdly, that it is the nurse of abuse, infecting us with many pestilent desires, with a siren's sweetness drawing the mind to the serpent's tail of sinful fancies,— and herein especially comedies give the largest field to ear [plough—ed] as Chaucer says; how, both in other nations and in ours, before poets did soften us, we were full of courage, given to martial exercises, the pillars of manlike liberty, and not lulled asleep in shady idleness with poets' pastimes.

And, lastly and chiefly, they cry out with an open mouth, as if they had overshot Robin Hood, that Plato banished them out of his Commonwealth. Truly this is much, if there be much truth in it.

First, to the first, that a man might better spend his time is a reason indeed; but it doth, as they say, but *petere principium* [to return or revert to the beginning— ed.] For if it be, as I affirm, that no learning is so good as that which teaches and moves to virtue, and that none can both teach and move thereto so much as poesy, then is the conclusion manifest that ink and paper cannot be to a more profitable purpose employed. And certainly, though a man should grant their first assumption, it should follow, methinks, very unwillingly, that good is not good because better is better. But I still and utterly deny that there is sprung out of earth a more fruitful knowledge.

To the second, therefore, that they should be the principal liars, I answer paradoxically, but truly, I think truly, that of all writers under the sun the poet is the least liar; and though he would, as a poet can scarcely be a liar. The astronomer, with his cousin the geometrician, can hardly escape when they take upon them to measure the height of the stars. How often, think you, do the physicians lie, when they aver things good for sicknesses, which afterwards send Charon a great number of souls drowned in a potion before they come to his ferry? And no less of the rest which take upon them to affirm. Now for the poet, he nothing affirms, and therefore never lies. For, as I take it, to lie is to affirm that to be true which is false; so as the other artists, and especially the historian, affirming many things, can, in the cloudy knowledge of mankind, hardly escape from many lies. But the poet, as I said before, never affirms. The poet never makes any circles about your imagination, to conjure you to believe for true what he writes. He cites not authorities of other histories, but even for his entry calls the sweet Muses to inspire into him a good invention; in troth, not laboring to tell you what is or is not, but what should or should not be. And therefore though he recount things not true, yet because he tells them not for true he lies not; without we will say that Nathan lied in his speech, before alleged, to David; which, as a wicked man durst scarce say, so think I none so simple would say that Æsop lied in the tales of his beasts; for who thinks that Æsop wrote it for actually true, were well worthy to have his name chronicled among the beasts he writes of. What child is there that, coming to a play, and seeing. Thebes written in great letters upon an old door, doth believe that it is Thebes? If then a man can arrive at that child's age, to know that the poet's persons and doings are but pictures what should be, and not stories what have been, they will never give the lie to things not affirmatively but allegorically and figuratively written. And therefore, as in history looking for truth, they may go away full-fraught with falsehood, so in poesy looking but for fiction, they shall use the narration but as an imaginative ground—plot of a profitable invention. But hereto is replied that the poets give names to men they write of, which argues a conceit of an actual truth, and so, not being true, proves a falsehood. And doth the lawyer lie then, when, under the names of John of the Stile, and John of the Nokes, he puts his case? But that is easily answered: their naming of men is but to make their picture the more lively, and not to build any history. Painting men, they cannot leave men nameless. We see we cannot play at chess but that we must give names to our chess-men; and yet, me thinks, he were a very partial champion of truth that would say we lied for giving a piece of wood the reverend title of a bishop. The poet names Cyrus and Æneas no other way than to show what men of their fames, fortunes, and estates should do.

Their third is, how much it abuses men's wit, training it to wanton sinfulness and lustful love. For indeed that is the principal, if not the only, abuse I can hear alleged. They say the comedies rather teach than reprehend amorous conceits. They say the lyric is larded with passionate sonnets, the elegiac weeps the want of his mistress, and that even to the heroical Cupid has ambitiously climbed Alas! Love, I would thou couldst as well defend thyself as thou canst offend others! I would those on whom thou dost attend could either put thee away, or yield good reason why they keep thee! But grant love of beauty to be a beastly fault, although it be very hard, since only man, and no beast, has that gift to discern beauty; grant that lovely name of Love to deserve all hateful reproaches, although even some of my masters the philosophers spent a good deal of their lamp-oil in setting forth the excellency of it; grant, I say, whatsoever they will have granted that not only love, but lust, but vanity, but, if they list, scurrility possesses many leaves of the poets' books; yet think I when this is granted, they will find their sentence may with good manners put the last words foremost, and not say that poetry abuses man's wit, but that man's wit abuses poetry.

For I will not deny, but that man's wit may make poesy, which should be *eikastike*, which some learned have defined "figuring forth good things," to be *phantastike*, which doth contrariwise infect the fancy with unworthy objects; as the painter that should give to the eye either some excellent perspective, or some fine picture fit for building or fortification, or containing in it some no table example, as Abraham sacrificing his son Isaac, Judith killing Holofernes, David fighting with Goliath, may leave those, and please an ill pleased eye with wanton shows of better-hidden matters. But what! shall the abuse of a thing make the right use odious? Nay, truly, though I yield that poesy may not only be abused, but that being abused, by the reason of his sweet charming force, it can do more hurt than any other army of words, yet shall it be so far from concluding that the abuse should give reproach to the abused, that contrariwise it is a good reason, that whatsoever, being abused, doth most harm, being rightly used—and upon the right use each thing receives his title—doth most good. Do we not see the skill of physic, the best rampire [rampart—ed] to our often-assaulted bodies, being abused, teach poison, the most violent destroyer? Doth not knowledge of law, whose end is to even and right all things, being abused, grow the crooked fosterer of horrible injuries? Doth not, to go in the highest, God's word abused breed heresy, and his name abused become blasphemy? Truly a needle cannot do much hurt, and as truly—with leave of ladies be it spoken—it cannot do much good. With a sword thou may kill thy father, and with a sword thou may defend thy prince and country. So that, as in their calling poets the fathers of lies they say nothing, so in this their argument of abuse they prove the commendation.

They allege herewith, that before poets began to be in price our nation has set their hearts' delight upon action, and not upon imagination; rather doing things worthy to be written, than writing things fit to be done. What that before-time was. I think scarcely Sphinx can tell; since no memory is so ancient that has the precedence of poetry. And certain it is that, in our plainest homeliness, yet never was the Albion nation without poetry. Marry, this argument, though it be leveled against poetry, yet is it indeed a chainshot against all learning,—or bookishness, as they commonly term it. Of such mind were certain Goths, of whom it is written that, having in the spoil of a famous city taken a fair library, one hangman—belike fit to execute the fruits of their wits—who had murdered a great number of bodies, would have set fire in it "No," said another very gravely, "take heed what you do; for while they are busy about these toys, we shall with more leisure conquer their countries." This, indeed, is the ordinary doctrine of ignorance, and many words sometimes I have heard spent in it; but because this reason is generally against all learning, as well as poetry, or rather all learning but poetry; because it were too large a digression to handle, or at least too superfluous, since it is manifest that all government of action is to be gotten by knowledge, and knowledge best by gathering many knowledges, which is reading; I only, with Horace, to him that is of that opinion

Jubeo stultum esse libenter
[I gladly bid him to be a fool—ed.]

for as for poetry itself, it is the freest from this objection, for poetry is the companion of the camps. I dare undertake, Orlando Furioso or honest King Arthur will never displease a soldier; but the quiddity of *ens*, and *prima materia*, will hardly agree with a corselet. And therefore, as I said in the beginning, even Turks and Tartars are delighted with poets. Homer, a Greek, flourished before Greece flourished; and if to a slight conjecture a conjecture may be opposed, truly it may seem, that as by him their learned men took almost their first light of knowledge, so their active men received their first motions of courage. Only Alexander's example may serve, who by Plutarch is accounted of such virtue, that Fortune was not his guide but his footstool; whose acts speak for him, though Plutarch did not; indeed the phoenix of warlike princes. This Alexander left his schoolmaster, living Aristotle, behind him, but took dead Homer with him. He put the philosopher Callistheries to death for his seeming philosophical, indeed mutinous, stubbornness; but the chief thing he was ever heard to wish for was that Homer had been alive. He well found he received more bravery of mind by the pattern of Achilles, than by hearing the definition of fortitude. And therefore if Cato misliked Fulvius for carrying Ennius with him to the field, it may be answered that if Cato misliked it, the noble Fulvius liked it, or else he had not done it. For it was not the excellent Cato Uticensis, whose authority. I would much more have reverenced; but it was the former, in truth a bitter punisher of faults, but else a man that had never sacrificed to the Graces. He misliked and cried out upon all Greek learning; and yet, being fourscore years old, began to learn it, belike fearing that Pluto understood not Latin Indeed, the Roman laws allowed no person to be carried to the wars but he that was in the soldiers' roll. And therefore though Cato misliked his unmustered person, he misliked not his work. And if he had, Scipio Nasica, judged by common consent the best Roman, loved him. Both the other Scipio brothers, who had by their virtues no less surnames than of Asia and Afric, so loved him that they caused his body to be buried in their sepulcher. So as Cato's authority being but against his person, and that answered with so far greater than himself, is herein of no validity.

But now, indeed, my burthen is great, that Plato's name is laid upon me, whom I must confess, of all philosophers I have ever esteemed most worthy of reverence; and with great reason, since of all philosophers he is the most poetical; yet if he will defile the fountain out of which his flowing streams have proceeded, let us boldly examine with what reasons he did it.

First, truly, a man might maliciously object that Plato, being a philosopher, was a natural enemy of poets. For, indeed, after the philosophers had picked out of the sweet mysteries of poetry the right discerning true points of knowledge, they forthwith, putting it in method, and making a school-art of that which the poets did only teach by a divine delightfulness, beginning to spurn at their guides, like ungrateful prentices were not content to set up shops for themselves, but sought by all means to discredit their masters; which by the force of delight being barred them, the less they could overthrow them the more they hated them. For, indeed, they found for Homer seven cities strove who should have him for their citizen; where many cities banished philosophers, as not fit members to live among them. For only repeating certain of Euripides' verses, many Athenians had their lives saved of the Syracusans, where the Athenians themselves thought many philosophers unworthy to live. Certain poets as Simonides and Pindar, had so prevailed with Heiro the First, that of a tyrant they made him a just king; where Plato could do so little with Dionysius, that he himself of a philosopher was made a slave. But who should do thus, I confess, should requite the objections made against poets with like cavillations against philosophers; as likewise one should do that should bid one read Phædrus or Symposium in Plato, or the Discourse of Love in Plutarch, and see whether any poet do authorize abominable filthiness, as they do.

Again, a man might ask out of what commonwealth Plato doth banish them. In sooth, thence where he himself allows community of women. So as belike this banishment grew not for effeminate wantonness, since little should poetical sonnets be hurtful when a man might have what woman he listed. But I honor philosophical instructions, and bless the wits which bred them, so as they be not abused, which is likewise stretched to poetry. Saint Paul himself, who yet, for the credit of poets, alleges twice two poets, and one of them by the name of a prophet, sets a watchword upon philosophy,—indeed upon the abuse. So doth Plato upon the abuse, not upon poetry. Plato found fault that the poets of his time filled the world with wrong opinions of the gods, making light tales of that unspotted essence, and therefore would not have the youth depraved with such opinions. Herein may much be said; let this suffice: the poets did not induce such opinions, but did imitate those opinions already induced. For all the Greek stories can well testify that the very religion of that time stood upon many and many-fashioned gods; not taught so by the poets, but followed according to their nature of imitation. Who list may read in Plutarch the discourses of Isis and Osiris, of the Cause why Oracles ceased, of the Divine Providence, and see whether the theology of that nation stood not upon such dreams,—which the poets indeed superstitiously observed; and truly, since they had not the light of Christ, did much better in it than the philosophers, who, shaking off superstition, brought in atheism.

Plato therefore, whose authority I had much rather justly construe than unjustly resist, meant not in general of poets, in those words of which Julius Scaliger says, *Qua authoritate barbari quidam atque hispidi, abuti velint ad poetas e republica exigendos* [which authority (Plato's) some barbarians want to abuse, in order to banish poets from the state—ed] but only meant to drive out those wrong opinions of the Deity, whereof now, without further law, Christianity has taken away all the hurtful belief, perchance, as he thought, nourished by the then esteemed poets. And a man need go no further than to Plato himself to know his meaning; who, in his dialogue called *Ion*, gives high and rightly divine commendation unto poetry. So as Plato, banishing the abuse, not the thing, not banishing it, but giving due honor unto it, shall be our patron and not our adversary. For, indeed, I had much rather, since truly I may do it, show their mistaking of Plato, under whose lion's skin they would make an ass—like braying against poesy, than go about to overthrow his authority; whom, the wiser a man is, the more just cause he shall find to have in admiration; especially since he attributes unto poesy more than myself do, namely to be a very inspiring of a divine force, far above man's wit, as in the forenamed dialogue is apparent.

Of the other side, who would show the honors have been by the best sort of judgments granted them, a whole sea of examples would present themselves: Alexanders, Cæsars, Scipios, all favorers of poets; Lælius, called the Roman Socrates, himself a poet, so as part of *Heautontimoroumenos* in Terence was supposed to be made by him. And even the Greek Socrates, whom Apollo confirmed to be the only wise man, is said to have spent part of his old time in putting Æsop's Fables into verses; and therefore full evil should it become his scholar, Plato, to put such words in his master's mouth against poets. But what needs more? Aristotle writes the Art of Poesy; and why, if it should not be written? Plutarch teaches the use to be gathered of them; and how, if they should not be read? And who reads Plutarch's either history or philosophy, shall find he trims both their garments with guards [ornaments—ed.] of poesy. But I list not to defend poesy with the help of his underling historiography. Let it suffice that it is a fit soil for praise to dwell upon; and what dispraise may set upon it, is either easily overcome, or transformed into just commendation.

So that since the excellencies of it may be so easily and so justly confirmed, and the low-creeping objections so soon trodden down: it not being an art of lies, but of true doctrine; not of effeminateness, but of notable stirring of courage; not of abusing man's wit, but of strengthening man's wit; not banished, but honored by Plato; let us rather plant more laurels for to engarland our poets' heads—which honor of being laureate, as besides them only triumphant captains were, is a sufficient authority to show the price they ought to be held in—than suffer the ill-savored breath of such wrong speakers once to blow upon the clear springs of poesy.

But since I have run so long a career in this matter, methinks, before I give my pen a full stop, it shall be but a little more lost time to inquire why England, the mother of excellent minds, should be grown so hard a stepmother to poets; who certainly in wit ought to pass all others, since all only proceeds from their wit, being indeed makers of themselves, not takers of others. How can I but exclaim,

Musa, mihi causas memora, quo numine læso?
[O Muse, recall to me the causes by which her divine will had been slighted—ed.]

Sweet poesy! that has anciently had kings, emperors, senators, great captains, such as, besides a thousand others, David, Adrian, Sophocles, Germanicus, not only to favor poets, but to be poets; and of our nearer times can present for her patrons a Robert, King of Sicily; the great King Francis of France; King James of Scotland; such cardinals as Bembus and Bibbiena; such famous preachers and teachers as Beza and Melancthon; so learned philosophers as Fracastorius and Scaliger; so great orators as Pontanus and Muretus; so piercing wits as George Buchanan; so grave counselors as—besides many, but before all—that Hospital of France, than whom, I think, that realm never brought forth a more accomplished judgment more firmly builded upon virtue; I say these, with numbers of others, not only to read others' poesies but to poetize for others' reading. That poesy, thus embraced in all other places, should only find in our time a hard welcome in England, I think the very earth laments it, and therefore decks our soil with fewer laurels than it was accustomed. For heretofore poets have in England also flourished; and, which is to be noted, even in those time when the trumpet of Mars did sound loudest. And now that an over-faint quietness should seem to strew the house for poets, they are almost in as good reputation as the mountebanks at Venice. Truly even that, as of the one side it gives great praise to poesy, which, like Venus—but to better purpose—has rather be troubled in the net with Mars, than enjoy the homely quiet of Vulcan; so serves it for a piece of a reason why they are less grateful to idle England, which now can scarce endure the pain of a pen. Upon this necessarily follows, that base men with servile wits undertake it, who think it enough if they can be rewarded of the printer. And so as Epaminondas is said, with the honor of his virtue to have made an office, by his exercising it, which before was contemptible, to become highly respected; so these men, no more but setting their names to it, by their own disgracefulness disgrace the most graceful poesy. For now, as if all the Muses were got with child to bring forth bastard poets, without any commission they do post over the banks of Helicon, till they make their readers more weary than posthorses; while, in the meantime, they,

> Queis meliore luto finxit præcordia Titan,
> [On hearts the Titan has formed better clay—ed.]

are better content to suppress the outflowings of their wit, than by publishing them to be accounted knights of the same order.

But I that, before ever I dust aspire unto the dignity, am admitted into the company of the paper-blurrers, do find the very true cause of our wanting estimation is want of desert, taking upon us to be poets in despite of Pallas [though lacking inspiration—ed.]. Now wherein we want desert were a thank-worthy labor to express; but if I knew, I should have mended myself. But as I never desired the title, so have I neglected the means to come by it; only, overmastered by some thoughts, I yielded an inky tribute unto them Marry, they that delight in poesy itself should seek to know what they do and how they do; and especially look themselves in an unflattering glass of reason, if they be inclinable unto it. For poesy must not be drawn by the ears, it must be gently led, or rather it must lead; which was partly the cause that made the ancient learned affirm it was a divine gift, and no human skill, since all other knowledges lie ready for any that has strength of wit, a poet no industry can make if his own genius be not carried into it. And therefore is it an old proverb: Orator fit, poeta nascitur [the orator is made, the poet is born—ed.]. Yet confess I always that, as the fertilest ground must be manured [cultivated—ed.], so must the highest-flying wit have a Dædalus to guide him. That Dædalus, they say, both in this and in other, has three wings to bear itself up into the air of due commendation: that is, art, imitation, and exercise. But these neither artificial rules nor imitative patterns, we much cumber ourselves withal. Exercise indeed we do, but that very fore-backwardly, for where we should exercise to know, we exercise as having known; and so is our brain delivered of much matter which never was begotten by knowledge. For there being two principal parts, matter to be expressed by words, and words to express the matter, in neither we use art or imitation rightly. Our matter is *quodlibet* indeed, though wrongly performing Ovid's verse,

> *Quicquid conabar dicere, versus erat;*
> [Whatever I tried to say was poetry—ed.]

never marshalling it into any assured rank, that almost the readers cannot tell where to find themselves.

Chaucer, undoubtedly, did excellently in his *Troilus and Cressida*; of whom, truly, I know not whether to marvel more, either that he in that misty time could see so clearly, or that we in this clear age walk so stumblingly after him. Yet had he great wants, fit to be forgiven in so revered antiquity. I account the *Mirror of Magistrates* meetly furnished of beautiful parts; and in the Earl of Surrey's lyrics many things tasting of a noble birth, and worthy of a noble mind. The *Shepherd's Calendar* has much poetry in his eclogues, indeed worthy the reading, if I be not deceived. That same framing of his style to an old rustic language I dare not allow, since neither Theocritus in Greek, Virgil in Latin, nor Sannazzaro in Italian did affect it. Besides these, I do not remember to have seen but few (to speak boldly) printed, that have poetical sinews in them. For proof whereof, let but most of the verses be put in prose, and then ask the meaning, and it will be found that one verse did but beget another, without ordering at the first what should be at the last; which becomes a confused mass of words, with a tinkling sound of rime, barely accompanied with reason.

Our tragedies and comedies not without cause cried out against, observing rules neither of honest civility nor of skilful poetry, excepting *Gorboduc,*—again I say of those that I have seen. Which notwithstanding as it is full of stately speeches and well-sounding phrases, climbing to the height of Seneca's style, and as full of notable morality, which it doth most delightfully teach, and so obtain the very end of poesy; yet in truth it is very defectious in the circumstances, which grieves me, because it might not remain as an exact model of all tragedies. For it is faulty both in place and time, the two necessary companions of all corporal actions. For where the stage should always represent but one place, and the uttermost time presupposed in it should be, both by Aristotle's precept and common reason, but one day; there is both many days and many places inartificially imagined.

But if it be so in *Gorboduc,* how much more in all the rest? where you shall have Asia of the one side, and Afric of the other, and so many other under-kingdoms, that the player, when he comes in, must ever begin with telling where he is, or else the tale will not be conceived. Now ye shall have three ladies walk to gather flowers, and then we must believe the stage to be a garden. By and by we hear news of shipwreck in the same place, and then we are to blame if we accept it not for a rock.

Upon the back of that comes out a hideous monster with fire and smoke, and then the miserable beholders are bound to take it for a cave. While in the mean time two armies fly in, represented with four swords and bucklers, and then what hard heart will not receive it for a pitched field?

Now of time they are much more liberal. For ordinary it is that two young princes fall in love; after many traverses she is got with child, delivered of a fair boy, he is lost, grows a man, falls in love, and is ready to get another child,—and all this in two hours' space; which how absurd it is in sense even sense may imagine, and art has taught, and all ancient examples justified, and at this day the ordinary players in Italy will not err in. Yet will some bring in an example of *Eunuchus* in Terence, that contains matter of two days, yet far short of twenty years. True it is, and so was it to be played in two days, yet far short of twenty years. True it is, and so was it to be played in two days, and so fitted to the time it set forth. And though Plautus have in one place done amiss, let us hit with him, and not miss with him. But they will say, How then shall we set forth a story which contains both many places and many times? And do they not know that a tragedy is tied to the laws of poesy, and not of history; not bound to follow the story, but having liberty either to feign a quite new matter, or to frame the history to the most tragical convenience? Again, many things may be told which cannot be showed,—if they know the difference betwixt reporting and representing. As for example I may speak, though I am here, of Peru, and in speech digress from that to the description of Calicut; but in action I cannot represent it without Pacolet's horse. And so was the manner the ancients took, by some Nuntius [messenger—ed] to recount things done in former time or other place.

Lastly, if they will represent a history, they must not, as Horace says, begin *ab ovo* [from the egg—ed] but they must come to the principal point of that one action which they will represent. By example this will be best expressed. I have a story of young Polydorus, delivered for safety's sake, with great riches, by his father Priamus to Polymnestor, King of Thrace, in the Trojan war time. He, after some years, hearing the overthrow of Priamus, for to make the treasure his own murders the child; the body of the child is taken up by Hecuba; she, the same day, finds a sleight to be revenged most cruelly of the tyrant. Where now would one of our tragedy writers begin, but with the delivery of the child? Then should he sail over into Thrace, and so spend I know not how many years, and travel numbers of places. But where doth Euripides? Even with the finding of the body, leaving the rest to be told by the spirit of Polydorus. This needs no further to be enlarged; the dullest wit may conceive it.

But, besides these gross absurdities, how all their plays be neither right tragedies nor right comedies, mingling kings and clowns, not because the matter so carries it, but thrust in the clown by head and shoulders to play a part in majestical matters, with neither decency nor discretion; so as neither the admiration and commiseration, nor the right sportfulness, is by their mongrel tragi-comedy obtained. I know Apuleius did somewhat so, but that is a thing recounted with space of time, not represented in one moment; and I know the ancients have one or two examples of tragi-comedies, as Plautus has *Amphytrio*. But, if we mark them well, we shall find that they never, or very daintily, match hornpipes and funerals. So falls it out that, having indeed no right comedy in that comical part of our tragedy, we have nothing but scurrility, unworthy of any chaste ears, or some extreme show of doltishness, indeed fit to lift up a loud laughter, and nothing else; where the whole tract of a comedy should be full of delight, as the tragedy should be still maintained in a well-raised admiration.

But our comedians think there is no delight without laughter, which is very wrong; for though laughter may come with delight, yet comes it not of delight, as though delight should be the cause of laughter; but well may one thing breed both together. Nay, rather in themselves they have, as it were, a kind of contrariety. For delight we scarcely do, but in things that have a convenience to ourselves, or to the general nature; laughter almost ever comes of things most disproportioned to ourselves and nature. Delight has a joy in it either permanent or present; laughter has only a scornful tickling. For example, we are ravished with delight to see a fair woman, and yet are far from being moved to laughter. We laugh at deformed creatures, wherein certainly we cannot delight. We delight in good chances, we laugh at mischances. We delight to hear the happiness of our friends and country, at which he were worthy to be laughed at that would laugh. We shall, contrarily, laugh sometimes to find a matter quite mistaken and go down the hill against the bias, in the mouth of some such men, as for the respect of them one shall be heartily sorry he cannot choose but laugh, and so is rather pained than delighted with laughter. Yet deny I not but that they may go well together. For as in Alexander's picture well set out we delight without laughter, and in twenty mad antics we laugh without delight; so in Hercules, painted with his great beard and furious countenance, in woman's attire, spinning at Omphale's commandment, it breeds both delight and laughter; for the representing of so strange a power in love, procures delight, and the scornfulness of the action stirs laughter.

But I speak to this purpose, that all the end of the comical part be not upon such scornful matters as stir laughter only, but mixed with it that delightful teaching which is the end of poesy. And the great fault, even in that point of laughter, and forbidden plainly by Aristotle, is that they stir laughter in sinful things, which are rather execrable than ridiculous; or in miserable, which are rather to be pitied than scorned. For what is it to make folks gape at a wretched beggar or a beggarly clown, or, against law of hospitality, to jest at strangers because they speak not English so well as we do? what do we learn? since it is certain:

Nil habet infelix paupertas durius in se,
Quam quod ridiculos homines facit.
[Unhappy poverty has nothing in it harder than this: It makes men ridiculous—ed.]

But rather a busy loving courtier; a heartless threatening Thraso; a self-wise-seeming schoolmaster; a wry transformed traveler: these if we saw walk in stage-names, which we play naturally, therein were delightful laughter and teaching delightfulness,—as in the other, the tragedies of Buchanan do justly bring forth a divine admiration.

But I have lavished out too many words of this playmatter. I do it, because as they are excelling parts of poesy, so is there none so much used in England, and none can be more pitifully abused; which, like an unmannerly daughter, showing a bad education, causes her mother Poesy's honesty to be called in question.

Other sorts of poetry almost have we none, but that lyrical kind of songs and sonnets, which, Lord if he gave us so good minds, how well it might be employed, and with how heavenly fruits both private and public, in singing the praises of the immortal beauty, the immortal goodness of that God who gives us hands to write, and wits to conceive!—of which we might well want words, but never matter; of which we could turn our eyes to nothing, but we should ever have new-budding occasions.

But truly, many of such writings as come under the banner of unresistible love, if I were a mistress would never persuade me they were in love; so coldly they apply fiery speeches, as men that had rather read lovers' writings, and so caught up certain swelling phrases—which hang together like a man which once told me the wind was at north-west and by south, because he would be sure to name winds enough—than that in truth they feel those passions, which easily, as I think, may be bewrayed by that same forcibleness, or *energia* (as the Greeks call it) of the writer. But let this be a sufficient, though short note, that we miss the right use of the material point of poesy.

Now for the outside of it, which is words, or (as I may term it) diction, it is even well worse, so is that honey-flowing matron eloquence appareled or rather disguised, in a courtesan-like painted affectation: one time with so farfetched words, that many seem monsters—but must seem strangers—to any poor Englishman; another time with coursing of a letter [alliteration—ed.] as if they were bound to follow the method of a dictionary; another time with figures and flowers extremely winter-starved.

But I would this fault were only peculiar to versifiers, and had not as large possession among prose-printers, and, which is to be marveled, among many scholars, and, which is to be pitied, among some preachers. Truly I could wish—if at least I might be so bold to wish in a thing beyond the reach of my capacity—the diligent imitators of Tully and Demosthenes (most worthy to be imitated) did not so much keep. Nizolian paper-books of their figures and phrases, as by attentive translation, as it were devour them whole, and make them wholly theirs. For now they cast sugar and spice upon every dish that is served to the table; like those Indians, not content to wear ear-rings at the fit and natural place of the ears, but they will thrust jewels through their nose and lips, because they will be sure to be fine. Tully, when he was to drive out Catiline as it were with a thunderbolt of eloquence, often used that figure of repetition, as *Vivit Vivit? Immo vero etiam in senatum venit, etc.* [He lives Does he live? In truth, he even comes to the Senate—ed.]. Indeed, inflamed with a well-grounded rage, he would have his words, as it were, double out of his mouth; and so do that artificially, which we see men in choler do naturally. And we, having noted the grace of those words, hale them in sometime to a familiar epistle, when it were too much choler to be choleric. How well store of *similiter* cadences [rhymes—ed.] doth sound with the gravity of the pulpit, I would but invoke Demosthenes' soul to tell, who with a rare daintiness uses them. Truly they have made me think of the sophister that with too much subtlety would prove two eggs three, and though he might be counted a sophister, had none for his labor. So these men bringing in such a kind of eloquence, well may they obtain an opinion of a seeming fineness, but persuade few,—which should be the end of their fineness.

Now for similitudes in certain printed discourses, I think all herbarists, all stories of beasts, fowls, and fishes are rifled up, that they may come in multitudes to wait upon any of our conceits, which certainly is as absurd a surfeit to the ears as is possible. For the force of a similitude not being to prove any thing to a contrary disputer, but only to explain to a willing hearer; when that is done, the rest is a most tedious prattling, rather overswaying the memory from the purpose whereto they were applied, then any whit informing the judgment, already either satisfied of by similitudes not to be satisfied.

For my part, I do not doubt, when Antonius and Crassus, the great forefathers of Cicero in eloquence, the one (as Cicero testifies of them) pretended not to know art, the other not to set by it, because [so that—ed.] with a plain sensibleness they might win credit of popular ears, which credit is the nearest step to persuasion, which persuasion is the chief mark of oratory,—I do not doubt, I say, but that they used these knacks, very sparingly; which who doth generally use any man may see doth dance to his own music, and so be noted by the audience more careful to speak curiously than truly. Undoubtedly (at least to my opinion undoubtedly) I have found in divers small-learned courtiers a more sound style than in some professors of learning; of which I can guess no other cause, but that the courtier following that which by practice he finds fittest to nature, therein, though he know it not, doth according to art—though not by art; where the other, using art to show art and not to hide art as in these cases he should do—flies from nature, and indeed abuses art.

But what! me thinks I deserve to be pounded for straying from poetry to oratory. But both have such an affinity in the wordish consideration, that I think this digression will make my meaning receive the fuller understanding:—which is not to take upon me to teach poets how they should do, but only, finding myself sick among the rest, to show some one or two spots of the common infection grown among the most part of writers; that, acknowledging ourselves somewhat awry, we may bend to the right use both of matter and manner: whereto our language gives us great occasion, being, indeed, capable of any excellent exercising of it.

I know some will say it is a mingled language. And why not so much the better, taking the best of both the other? Another will say it wants grammar. Nay, truly, it has that praise that it wants not grammar. For grammar it might have, but it needs it not; being so easy in itself, and so void of those cumbersome differences of cases, genders, moods, and tenses, which, I think, was a piece of the Tower of Babylon's curse, that a man should be put to school to learn his mother-tongue. But for the uttering sweetly and properly the conceits of the mind, which is the end of speech, that has it equally with any other tongue in the world; and is particularly happy in compositions of two or three words together, near the Greek, far beyond the Latin,—which is one of the greatest beauties that can be in a language.

Now of versifying there are two sorts, the one ancient, the other modern. The ancient marked the quantity of each syllable, and according to that framed his verse, the modern observing only number, with some regard of the accent, the chief life of it stands in that like sounding of the words, which we call rime. Whether of these be the more excellent would bear many speeches; the ancient no doubt more fit for music, both words and tune observing quantity; and more fit lively to express divers passions, by the low or lofty sound of the well-weighed syllable. The latter likewise with his rime strikes a certain music to the ear; and, in fine, since it doth delight, though by another way, it obtains the same purpose; there being in either, sweetness, and wanting in neither, majesty. Truly the English, before any other vulgar language I know, is fit for both sorts. For, for the ancient, the Italian is so full of vowels that it must ever be cumbered with elisions; the Dutch so, of the other side, with consonants, that they cannot yield the sweet sliding fit for a verse. The French in his whole language has not one word that has his accent in the last syllable saving two, called antepenultima, and little more has the Spanish; and therefore very gracelessly may they use dactyls. The English is subject to none of these defects. Now for rime [rhythm—ed.], though we do not observe quantity, yet we observe the accent very precisely, which other languages either cannot do, or will not do so absolutely. That cæsura, or breathing-place in the midst of the verse, neither Italian nor Spanish have, the French and we never almost fail of.

Lastly, even the very rime itself the Italian cannot put in the last syllable, by the French named the masculine rime, but still in the next to the last, which the French call the female, or the next before that, which the Italians term *sdrucciola*. The example of the former is *buono: suono*; of the *sdrucciola* is *femina: semina*. The French, of the other side, has both the male, as *bon: son*, and the female, as *plaise: taise*; but the *sdrucciola* he has not. Where the English has all three, as *due: true, father: rather, motion: potion*; with much more which might be said, but that already I find the triflingness of this discourse is much too much enlarged.

So that since the ever praiseworthy poesy is full of virtue-breeding delightfulness, and void of no gift that ought to be in the noble name of learning; since the blames laid against it are either false or feeble; since the cause why it is not esteemed in England is the fault of poet-apes, not poets; since, lastly, our tongue is most fit to honor poesy, and to be honored by poesy; I conjure you all that have had the evil luck to read this ink-wasting toy of mine, even in the name of the Nine Muses, no more to scorn the sacred mysteries of poesy; no more to laugh at the name of poets, as though they were next inheritors to fools; no more to jest at the reverend title of "a rhymer"; but to believe, with Aristotle, that they were the ancient treasurers of the Grecians' divinity; to believe, with Bembus, that they were first bringers—in of all civility; to believe, with Scaliger, that no philosopher's precepts can sooner make you an honest man than the reading of Virgil; to believe, with Clauserus, the translator of Cornutus, that it pleased the Heavenly Deity by Hesiod and Homer, under the veil of fables, to give us all knowledge, logic, rhetoric, philosophy natural and moral, and *quid non?* to believe, with me, that there are many mysteries contained in poetry which of purpose were written darkly, lest by profane wits it should be abused; to believe, with Landino, that they are so beloved of the gods, that whatsoever they write proceeds of a divine fury; lastly, to believe themselves, when they tell you they will make you immortal by their verses.

Thus doing, your name shall flourish in the printers' shops. Thus doing, you shall be of kin to many a poetical preface. Thus doing, you shall be most fair, most rich, most wise, most all; you shall dwell upon superlatives. Thus doing, though you be *libertino patre natus* [the son of a freedman], you shall suddenly grow *Herculean proles* [Herculean offspring—ed]:

Si quid mea carmina possunt.
[If my verses can do anything—ed.]

Thus doing, your soul shall be placed with Dante's Beatrice or Virgil's Anchises.

But if—fie of such a but!—you be born so near the dull-making cataract of Nilus, that you cannot hear the planet-like music of poetry; if you have so earth-creeping a mind that it cannot lift itself up to look to the sky of poetry, or rather, by a certain rustical disdain, will become such a mome [blockhead—ed.], as to be a Momus of poetry; then, though I will not wish unto you the ass' ears of Midas, nor to be driven by a poet's verses, as Bubonax was, to hang himself; nor to be rimed to death, as is said to be done in Ireland; yet thus much curse. I must send you in the behalf of all poets:—that while you live in love, and never get favor for lacking skill of a sonnet; and when you die, your memory die from the earth for want of an epitaph.

The text used here is from *An Apologie for Poetrie*, ed Edward Arber (London, 1858), with additional material from *Sidney's Apologie for Poetrie*, ed. J. Churton Collins (Oxford, 1907) and *The Defense of Poesy*, ed A. S. Cook (Boston, 1890).

2.10.2 Reading and Review Questions

1. How is learning synonymous with poetry, do you think? What does Sidney mean by delightful teaching?

2. Why does Sidney believe that poetry has a moral purpose? What are his arguments? What relation, if any, does poetry have to action, do you

think, and why? How does his representation of the uses of art compare with Chaucer's or Spenser's?

3. To what degree, if any, does Sidney's Protestantism factor into his reasons for defending poetry, and how?

4. The Defense includes amongst its characters Edward Wotton, a friend of Sidney; John Pietro Pugliano, the Italian riding master to the Emperor; and himself in his historical persona as Sir Philip Sidney, poet and courtier. How does he construct his role of poet in the Defense? How does he construct his role of courtier in the Defense? How are the two roles related, if at all, in the Defense? How does his self-depiction compare with Chaucer's or More's?

5. How does poetry build national identity, according to Sidney? What are his arguments? Do his views validate Spenser's poetry in *The Faerie Queene*, for instance?

2.11 MARY (SIDNEY) HERBERT, COUNTESS OF PEMBROKE

(1562-1621)

Unlike her brother Sir Philip Sidney, Mary Sidney Herbert, Countess of Pembroke, did not attend a public school or university; instead, she was tutored at home in Latin, French, and Italian languages and literature. And at the age of fifteen, her family arranged her marriage to the wealthy Henry Herbert, 2nd Earl of Pembroke (1538-1601), thus cementing their families' already strong alliance. While she served her family's political goals, Mary Sidney Herbert managed to develop her own interests within her private realms, the Pembroke estate at Wilton and Baynards Castle in London, where she shaped literary and scientific coteries. She further supported her family by sponsoring elegies to her brother Sir Philip Sidney who died in 1586 from wounds suffered at the Battle

Image 2.12 | Mary Sidney Herbert, Countess of Pembroke
Artist | Unknown
Source | Wikimedia Commons
License | Public Domain

of Zutphen. "The Doleful Lay of Clorinda," Mary Sidney Herbert's first published work, appeared in a collection of elegies that included "Astrophil," Spenser's tribute to Sir Philip Sidney.

The genres in which she wrote revealed Elizabethan attitudes towards women, their scope and purpose within society. In the accepted role of "conduit," she translated works by Petrarch, Robert Garnier (1544-1590), and Phillippe Duplessis Mornay (1549-1623), dedicated works and encomia to her sovereign (first Elizabeth I) and Queen Anne (wife of James I), and elegized Sir Philip Sidney. She took on the accepted role of relative being to Sir Philip Sidney, gaining fame and acceptance as his sister, by completing his unfinished works, and advocating his literary legacy. Her elegies to her brother were done in the pastoral tradition. Her translations from the French and Italian demonstrate the importance of Continental traditions to English literature. Her metric translations of Psalms 44-150, translations that introduced an astonishing array of metrical verse forms, demonstrate the Protestant influence on both sacred and secular expressions of faith. All her publications reveal Mary Sidney Herbert's attitude toward herself as a writer in her own right, as she published her works under her own name.

2.11.1 "The Doleful Lay of Clorinda"

(1595)

Ay me, to whom shall I my case complain,
That may compassion my impatient grief?
Or where shall I unfold my inward pain,
That my enriven heart may find relief?
    Shall I unto the heavenly pow'rs it show,
    Or unto earthly men that dwell below?

To heavens? Ah, they, alas, the authors were,
And workers of my unremedied woe:
For they foresee what to us happens here,
And they foresaw, yet suffered this be so.
    From them comes good, from them comes also ill,
    That which they made, who can them warn to spill.

To men? Ah, they, alas, like wretched be,
And subject to the heavens' ordinance:
Bound to abide whatever they decree.
Their best redress is their best sufferance.
    How then can they, like wretched, comfort me,
    The which no less need comforted to be?

Then to myself will I my sorrow mourn,
Sith none alive like sorrowful remains:
And to myself my plaints shall back return,
To pay their usury with doubled pains.

The woods, the hills, the rivers shall resound
The mournful accent of my sorrow's ground.

Woods, hills, and rivers now are desolate,
Sith he is gone the which them all did grace:
And all the fields do wail their widow state,
Sith death their fairest flow'r did late deface.
    The fairest flow'r in field that ever grew,
    Was Astrophel; that was, we all may rue.

What cruel hand of cursed foe unknown,
Hath cropped the stalk which bore so fair a flow'r?
Untimely cropped, before it well were grown,
And clean defaced in untimely hour.
    Great loss to all that ever him did see,
    Great loss to all, but greatest loss to me.

Break now your garlands, O ye shepherds' lasses,
Sith the fair flow'r, which them adorned, is gone:
The flow'r, which them adorned, is gone to ashes,
Never again let lass put garland on.
    Instead of garland, wear sad cypress now,
    And bitter elder, broken from the bough.

Ne ever sing the love-lays which he made:
Who ever made such lays of love as he?
Ne ever read the riddles, which he said
Unto yourselves, to make you merry glee.
    Your merry glee is now laid all abed,
    Your merry maker now, alas, is dead.

Death, the devourer of all the world's delight,
Hath robbed you and reft from me my joy:
Both you and me and all the world he quite
Hath robbed of joyance, and left sad annoy.
    Joy of the world, and shepherds' pride was he,
    Shepherds' hope never like again to see.

O Death, that hast us of such riches reft,
Tell us at least, what hast thou with it done?
What is become of him whose flow'r here left
Is but the shadow of his likeness gone:

Scarce like the shadow of that which he was,
Naught like, but that he like a shade did pass.

But that immortal spirit, which was decked
With all the dowries of celestial grace:
By sovereign choice from th'heavenly choirs select,
And lineally derived from angels' race,
    Oh, what is now of it become, aread.
    Ay me, can so divine a thing be dead?

Ah no: it is not dead, ne can it die,
But lives for aye, in blissful Paradise:
Where like a new-born babe it soft doth lie,
In bed of lilies wrapped in tender wise,
    And compassed all about with roses sweet,
    And dainty violets from head to feet.

There thousand birds all of celestial brood,
To him do sweetly carol day and night:
And with strange notes, of him well understood,
Lull him asleep in angel-like delight;
    Whilst in sweet dream to him presented be
    Immortal beauties, which no eye may see.

But he them sees and takes exceeding pleasure
Of their divine aspects, appearing plain,
And kindling love in him above all measure,
Sweet love still joyous, never feeling pain.
    For what so goodly form he there doth see,
    He may enjoy from jealous rancor free.

There liveth he in everlasting bliss,
Sweet spirit never fearing more to die:
Ne dreading harm from any foes of his,
Ne fearing savage beasts' more cruelty.
    Whilst we here, wretches, wail his private lack,
    And with vain vows do often call him back.

But live thou there still happy, happy spirit,
And give us leave thee here thus to lament:
Not thee that dost thy heaven's joy inherit,
But our own selves that here in dole are drent.
    Thus do we weep and wail, and wear our eyes,
    Mourning in other's, our own miseries.

2.11.2 "To the Angel Spirit of the Most Excellent Sir Philip Sidney"

(1623)
(Variant printed in Samuel Daniel's 1623 Works)

To thee, pure spirit, to thee alone addressed
Is this joint work, by double interest thine,
Thine by his own, and what is done of mine
Inspired by thee, thy secret power impressed.
My Muse with thine, itself dared to combine
As mortal stuff with that which is divine:
Let thy fair beams give luster to the rest

That Israel's King may deign his own, transformed
In substance no, but superficial 'tire;
And English guised in some sort may aspire
To better grace thee what the vulgar formed:
His sacred tones, age after age admire;
Nations grow great in pride and pure desire
So to excel in holy rites performed.

Oh, had that soul which honor brought to rest
Too soon not left and reft the world of all
What man could show, which we perfection call,
This precious piece had sorted with the best.
But ah, wide festered wounds that never shall
Nor must be closed, unto fresh bleeding fall:
Ah, memory, what needs this new arrest?

Yet blessed grief, that sweetness can impart
Since thou art blest! Wrongly do I complain:
Whatever weights my heavy thoughts sustain
Dear feels my soul for thee. I know my part
Nor be my weakness to thy rites a stain,
Rites to aright, life-blood would not refrain:
Assist me, then, that life what thine did part.

Time may bring forth what time hath yet suppressed
In whom thy loss hath laid to utter waste;
The wrack of time, untimely all defaced,
Remaining as the tomb of life deceased,
Where, in my heart the highest room thou hast;

There, truly there, thy earthly being is placed,
Triumph of death: in life how more than blest.

Behold, oh, that thou were now to behold
This finished long perfection's part begun,
The rest but pieced, as left by thee undone.
Pardon blest soul, presumption overbold,
If love and zeal hath to this error run:
'Tis zealous love, love that hath never done,
Nor can enough, though justly here controlled.

But since it hath no other scope to go,
Nor other purpose but to honor thee,
That thine may shine, where all the Graces be;
And that my thoughts (like smallest streams that flow,
Pay to their sea, their tributary fee)
Do strive, yet have no means to quit nor free
That mighty debt of infinities I owe

To thy great worth which time to times enroll,
Wonder of men, sole born, sole of thy kind
Complete in all, but heavenly was thy mind,
For wisdom, goodness, sweetness, fairest soul:
Too good to wish, too fair for earth, refined
For heaven, where all true glory rests confined;
And where but there no life without control?

Oh, when from this account, this cast-up sum,
This reck'ning made the audit of my woe,
Sometime of rase my swelling passions know
How work my thoughts, my sense is stricken dumb
That would thee more than words could ever show,
Which all fall short. Who knew thee best do know
There lives no wit that may thy praise become.

And rest fair monuments of thy fair fame,
Though not complete. Nor can we reach, in thought,
What on that goodly piece time would have wrought
Had divers so spared that life (but life) to frame
The rest. Alas, such loss! The world hath naught
Can equal it, nor, oh, more grievance brought,
Yet what remains must ever crown thy name.

Receive these hymns, these obsequies receive,
(If any mark of thy secret spirit thou bear)
Made only thine, and no name else must wear.
I can no more: Dear Soul, I take my leave;
My sorrow strives to mount the highest sphere.

2.11.3 "Psalm 51"

(1599)

O Lord, whose grace no limits comprehend;
    Sweet Lord, whose mercies stand from measure free;
To me that grace, to me that mercy send,
      And wipe, O Lord, my sins from sinful me.
      Oh, cleanse, oh, wash, my foul iniquity;
          Cleanse still my spots, still wash away my stainings,
          Till stains and spots in me leave no remainings.

For I, alas, acknowledging do know
    My filthy fault, my faulty filthiness
To my soul's eye incessantly doth show,
      Which done to thee, to thee I do confess,
      Just judge, true witness, that for righteousness
          Thy doom may pass against my guilt awarded,
          Thy evidence for truth may be regarded.

My mother, lo, when I began to be,
    Conceiving me, with me did sin conceive:
And as with living heat she cherished me,
      Corruption did like cherishing receive.
      But, lo, thy love to purest good doth cleave,
          And inward truth: which, hardly else discerned,
          My truant soul in thy hid school hath learned.

Then as thyself to lepers hast assigned,
    With hyssop, Lord, thy hyssop, purge me so:
And that shall cleanse the lepry of my mind.
    Make over me thy mercy's streams to flow,
    So shall my whiteness scorn the whitest snow.
        To ear and heart send sounds and thoughts of gladness,
        That bruised bones may dance away their sadness.

Thy ill-pleased eye from my misdeeds avert:
    Cancel the registers my sins contain:

Create in me a pure, clean, spotless heart;
    Inspire a sprite where love of right may reign
    Ah, cast me not from thee; take not again
        Thy breathing grace; again thy comfort send me,
        And let the guard of thy free sprite attend me.

So I to them a guiding hand will be,
    Whose faulty feet have wandered from thy way,
And turned from sin will make return to thee,
    Whom turned from thee sin erst had led astray.
    O God, God of my health, oh, do away
        My bloody crime: so shall my tongue be raised
        To praise thy truth, enough cannot be praised.

Unlock my lips, shut up with sinful shame:
    Then shall my mouth, O Lord, thy honor sing.
For bleeding fuel for thy altar's flame,
    To gain thy grace what boots it me to bring?
    Burnt-off'rings are to thee no pleasant thing.
        The sacrifice that God will hold respected,
        Is the heart-broken soul, the sprite dejected.

Lastly, O Lord, how so I stand or fall,
    Leave not thy loved Zion to embrace;
But with thy favor build up Salem's wall,
    And still in peace, maintain that peaceful place.
    Then shalt thou turn a well-accepting face
        To sacred fires with offered gifts perfumed:
        Till ev'n whole calves on altars be consumed.

2.11.4 "Psalm 55"

(1599)

My God, most glad to look, most prone to hear,
    An open ear, oh, let my prayer find,
        And from my plaint turn not thy face away.
        Behold my gestures, hearken what I say,
    While uttering moans with most tormented mind,
My body I no less torment and tear.
For, lo, their fearful threat'nings would mine ear,
    Who griefs on griefs on me still heaping lay,
        A mark to wrath and hate and wrong assigned;
        Therefore, my heart hath all his force resigned

To trembling pants; death terrors on me pray;
I fear, nay, shake, nay, quiv'ring quake with fear.

Then say I, oh, might I but cut the wind,
    Borne on the wing the fearful dove doth bear:
        Stay would I not, till I in rest might stay.
        Far hence, oh, far, then would I take my way
    Unto the desert, and repose me there,
These storms of woe, these tempests left behind.
But swallow them, O Lord, in darkness blind,
    Confound their counsels, lead their tongues astray,
        That what they mean by words may not appear.
        For mother Wrong within their town each where,
    And daughter Strife their ensigns so display,
As if they only thither were confined.

These walk their city walls both night and day;
    Oppressions, tumults, guiles of every kind
        Are burgesses and dwell the middle near;
        About their streets his masking robes doth wear
    Mischief clothed in deceit, with treason lined,
Where only he, he only bears the sway.
But not my foe with me this prank did play,
    For then I would have borne with patient cheer
        An unkind part from whom I know unkind,
        Nor he whose forehead Envy's mark had signed,
    His trophies on my ruins sought to rear,
From whom to fly I might have made assay.

But this to thee, to thee impute I may,
    My fellow, my companion, held most dear,
        My soul, my other self, my inward friend:
        Whom unto me, me unto whom did bind
    Exchanged secrets, who together were
God's temple wont to visit, there to pray.
Oh, let a sudden death work their decay,
    Who speaking fair such cankered malice mind,
        Let them be buried breathing in their bier;
        But purple morn, black ev'n, and midday clear
    Shall see my praying voice to God inclined,
Rousing him up, and naught shall me dismay.

He ransomed me; he for my safety fined
    In fight where many sought my soul to slay;
        He, still himself to no succeeding heir
        Leaving his empire shall no more forbear
    But at my motion, all these atheists pay,
By whom, still one, such mischiefs are designed.
Who but such caitiffs would have undermined,
    Nay, overthrown, from whom but kindness mere
        They never found? Who would such trust betray?
        What buttered words! Yet war their hearts bewray.
    Their speech more sharp than sharpest sword or spear
Yet softer flows than balm from wounded rind.

But my o'erloaden soul, thyself upcheer,
    Cast on God's shoulders what thee down doth weigh
        Long borne by thee with bearing pained and pined:
        To care for thee he shall be ever kind;
    By him the just in safety held away
Changeless shall enter, live, and leave the year:
But, Lord, how long shall these men tarry here?
    Fling them in pit of death where never shined
        The light of life, and while I make my stay
        On thee, let who their thirst with blood allay
    Have their life-holding thread so weakly twined
That it, half-spun, death may in sunder shear.

2.11.5 "Psalm 57"

(1599)

Thy mercy, Lord, Lord, now thy mercy show:
        On thee I lie;
        To thee I fly.
    Hide me, hive me, as thine own,
    Till these blasts be overblown,
Which now do fiercely blow.

To highest God I will erect my cry,
        Who quickly shall
        Dispatch this all.
    He shall down from heaven send
    From disgrace me to defend
His love and verity.

My soul encaged lies with lions' brood,
        Villains whose hands
        Are fiery brands,
    Teeth more sharp than shaft or spear,
    Tongues far better edge do bear
Than swords to shed my blood.

As high as highest heav'n can give thee place,
        O Lord, ascend,
        And thence extend
    With most bright, most glorious show
    Over all the earth below,
The sunbeams of thy face.

Me to entangle every way I go
        Their trap and net
        Is ready set.
    Holes they dig but their own holes
    Pitfalls make for their own souls:
So, Lord, oh, serve them so.

My heart prepared, prepared is my heart
        To spread thy praise
        With tuned lays:
    Wake my tongue, my lute awake,
    Thou my harp the consort make,
Myself will bear a part.

Myself when first the morning shall appear,
        With voice and string
        So will thee sing:
    That this earthly globe, and all
    Treading on this earthly ball,
My praising notes shall hear.

For god, my only God, thy gracious love
        Is mounted far
        Above each star,
    Thy unchanged verity
    Heav'nly wings do lift as high
As clouds have room to move.

As high as highest heav'n can give thee place,
O Lord, ascend
And thence extend
With most bright, most glorious show
Over all the earth below,
The sunbeams of thy face.

2.11.6 "Psalm 84"

(1599)

How lovely is thy dwelling,
Great god, to whom all greatness is belonging!
To view thy courts far, far from any telling
My soul doth long and pine with longing
Unto the God that liveth,
The God that all life giveth,
My heart and body both aspire,
Above delight, beyond desire.

Alas, the sparrow knoweth
The house where free and fearless she resideth;
Directly to the nest the swallow goeth,
Where with her sons she safe abideth.
Oh, altars thine, most mighty
In war, yea, most almighty:
Thy altars, Lord, ah, why should I
From altars thine excluded lie?

Oh, happy who remaineth
Thy household-man and still thy praise unfoldeth!
Oh, happy who himself on thee sustaineth,
Who to thy house his journey holdeth!
Me seems I see them going
Where mulberries are growing:
How wells they dig in thirsty plain,
And cisterns make for falling rain.

Me seems I see augmented
Still troop with troop, till all at length discover
Zion, where to their sight is represented
The Lord of hosts, the Zion lover.
O Lord, O God, most mighty
In war, yea, most almighty:

Hear what I beg; hearken, I say,
O Jacob's God, to what I pray.

Thou art the shield us shieldeth:
Then, Lord, behold the face of thine anointed
  One day spent in thy courts more comfort yieldeth
Than thousands otherwise appointed.
    I count it clearer pleasure
    To spend my age's treasure
  Waiting a porter at thy gates
Than dwell a lord with wicked mates.

Thou art the sun that shineth;
Thou art the buckler, Lord that us defendeth:
  Glory and grace Jehovah's hand assigneth
And good without refusal sendeth
    To him who truly treadeth
    The path to pureness leadeth.
  O Lord of might, thrice blessed he
Whose confidence is built on thee.

2.11.7 "Psalm 102"

(1599)

  O Lord, my praying hear;
    Lord, let my cry come to thine ear.
Hide not thy face away,
  But haste, and answer me,
In this my most, most miserable day,
  Wherein I pray and cry to thee.

  My days as smoke are past;
  My bones as flaming fuel waste,
Mown down in me, alas.
  With scythe of sharpest pain.
My heart is withered like the wounded grass;
  My stomach doth all food disdain.

  So lean my woes me leave,
  That to my flesh my bones do cleave;
And so I bray and howl,
  As use to howl and bray

The lonely pelican and desert owl,
 Like whom I languish long the day.

  I languish so the day,
   The night in watch I waste away;
Right as the sparrow sits,
 Bereft of spouse, or son,
Which irked alone with dolor's deadly fits
 To company will not be won.

  As day to day succeeds,
   So shame on shame to me proceeds
From them that do me hate,
 Who of my wrack so boast,
That wishing ill, they wish but my estate,
 Yet think they wish of ills the most.

  Therefore my bread is clay;
   Therefore my tears my wine allay.
For how else should it be,
 Sith thou still angry art,
And seem'st for naught to have advanced me,
 But me advanced to subvert?

  The sun of my life-days
   Inclines to west with falling rays,
And I as hay am dried,
 While yet in steadfast seat
Eternal thou eternally dost bide,
 Thy memory no years can fret.

  Oh, then at length arise;
   On Zion cast thy mercy's eyes.
Now is the time that thou
 To mercy shouldst incline
Concerning her: O Lord, the time is now
 Thyself for mercy didst assign.

  Thy servants wait the day
   When she, who like a carcass lay
Stretched forth in ruin's bier,
 Shall so arise and live,

The nations all Jehova's name shall fear,
   All kings to thee shall glory give.

     Because thou hast anew
     Made Zion stand, restored to view
Thy glorious presence there,
     Because thou hast, I say,
Beheld our woes and not refused to hear
     What wretched we did plaining pray,

     This of record shall bide
     To this and every age beside.
And they commend thee shall
     Whom thou anew shall make,
That from the prospect of thy heav'nly hall
     Thy eye of earth survey did take,

     Heark'ning to prisoners' groans,
     And setting free condemned ones,
That they, when nations come,
     And realms to serve the Lord,
In Zion and in Salem might become
     Fit means his honor to record.

     But what is this if I
     In the mid way should fall and die?
My God, to thee I pray,
     Who canst my prayer give.
Turn not to night the noontide of my day,
     Since endless thou dost ageless live.

     The earth, the heaven stands
     Once founded, formed by thy hands:
They perish, thou shalt bide;
     They old, as clothes shall wear,
Till changing still, full change shall them betide,
     Unclothed of all the clothes they bear.

     But thou art one, still one:
     Time interest in thee hath none.
Then hope, who godly be,
     Or come of godly race:

Endless your bliss, as never ending he,
    His presence your unchanged place.

2.11.8 "Psalm 150"

(1599)

Oh, laud the Lord, the God of hosts commend,
    Exalt his pow'r, advance his holiness:
    With all your might lift his almightiness;
Your greatest praise upon his greatness spend.

Make trumpet's noise in shrillest notes ascend;
    Make lute and lyre his loved fame express;
    Him let the pipe, him let the tabret bless,
Him organ's breath, that winds or waters lend

Let ringing timbrels so his honor sound,
    Let sounding cymbals so his glory ring,
    That in their tunes such melody be found
As fits the pomp of most triumphant king.

Conclude: by all that air or life enfold,
    Let high Jehovah highly be extolled.

2.11.9 Reading and Review Questions

1. In "Doleful Lay," Mary Herbert Spenser names the speaker who is clearly a woman. How does she give Clorinda a distinctly and distinctively female-gendered voice?

2. How does Mary Herbert Spenser use nature imagery in "Doleful Lay?" To what degree, if any, is it idealized and/or allegorized?

3. Mary Herbert Spenser dedicates her translations of the Psalms to her brother with the elegy "To the Angel Spirit of the Most Excellent Sir Philip Sidney." In this poem, she attributes the translations' heavenly power to her brother, an expressed humility and subordination she repeats in various ways, including deploring her own weakness and presumption. To what degree, if any, is Mary Herbert Spenser in these ways fulfilling elegiac versus gender conventions? How does her representation of gender compare with Elizabeth I's?

4. How, if at all, does Mary Herbert Spenser reveal her Protestant faith in her translations of the Psalms?

5. Considering the restrictions that her era placed upon females taking any public role in religious practices, to what degree, if at all, does Mary Herbert Spenser distinguish between private or personal versus public and universal expressions of faith in her translations of the Psalms? How, if at all, does her prowess and versatility in metrical verse play into this distinction?

2.12 CHRISTOPHER MARLOWE

(1564-1593)

Christopher Marlowe was the son of a shoemaker. He attended King's School in Canterbury and then, by winning an Archbishop Parker scholarship, he studied at Corpus Christi College, Cambridge. He earned his Bachelor of Arts degree which should have been followed three years later by a Master's degree. To earn a Master's, Marlowe was expected to take orders. That he didn't, and that the university only awarded Marlowe the Masters after receiving a letter from the Privy Council, speaks to mysteries and uncertainties in Marlowe's activities while at Cambridge. During the time when he was ostensibly studying for his Master's, Marlowe left Cambridge for extended lengths of time. His destinations and actions during these frequent absences

Image 2.13 | Christopher Marlowe
Artist | Unknown
Source | Wikimedia Commons
License | Public Domain

remain unknown. However, the Privy Council reassured the university by letter in which it declared that Marlowe was working for England's benefit and for the Queen's good service. Some scholars believe that this service involved spying against expatriate Roman Catholics (and their conspiracies against Elizabeth) in Rheims. That Marlowe's work remains a mystery suggests that it was deliberately kept secret by the government.

His post-graduate public career began when he left Cambridge for London. There, he may have continued his work for the government, but he certainly began writing plays. His *Tamburlaine the Great* (1590) proved a great success and heralded the new age of great Elizabethan Theater, directly influencing its flowering. Marlowe was one of the first playwrights to use blank verse; Thomas Kyd (1558-1594) imitated it in *The Spanish Tragedy* (c. 1585). Marlowe's style was astounding; his title characters and his plays' actions are larger than life—almost incomprehensively so. Edward II was a powerful monarch who was also flawed and ultimately deposed (though it is unclear whether or not Marlowe wrote a play called *Edward II*); the Jew of Malta was phenomenally wealthy yet morally bankrupt; Dr. Faustus is a demigod in his magical powers who heedlessly diminishes and damns himself. Faustus aspires to a dominion that stretches "as far as doth the mind of man" (I.i.61) but ultimately wishes to be changed to a dumb beast.

Marlowe's own character may have been as compelling and ambiguous as those in his plays. Suspicion surrounded him, and friends and acquaintances denounced him for atheism or leanings toward the Roman Catholic faith. In 1593, Thomas Kyd, with whom Marlowe at one time shared lodgings, testified that Marlowe read atheistical texts, upon which testimony Marlowe was arrested for heresy, or atheism (which was then a crime). He was not brought to trial, nor even imprisoned. Instead, he was released on the condition that he report to an officer of the court. Within days of his release, Marlowe was killed by Ingram Frizer (d. 1627). Apparently, the two fought over a lodging house bill, and Frizer fatally stabbed Marlowe in the forehead. Frizer served Sir Francis Walsingham (c. 1532-1590) who ran an intelligence service. Some scholars believe Frizer assassinated Marlowe for being a spy, or counter-spy. But no evidence has proven such conjectures.

We do know that Marlowe was an extraordinary artist and playwright, one who certainly influenced his contemporaries, including William Shakespeare—who also created a famously-divided character (like Dr. Faustus) in his Hamlet and an avaricious, vengeful Jew in his Shylock. And in his Sonnet 29, when Shakespeare acknowledges envy for "this man's art," it does not take much stretch of the imagination to wonder if he may have had Marlowe in mind.

Image 2.14 | *The Tragical History of Doctor Faustus* Title Page
Artist | Christopher Marlowe
Source | Wikimedia Commons
License | Public Domain

2.12.1 *The Tragical History of Doctor Faustus*

(1604)

DRAMATIS PERSONAE.
THE POPE.
CARDINAL OF LORRAIN.

THE EMPEROR OF GERMANY.
DUKE OF VANHOLT.
FAUSTUS.
VALDES, friend to FAUSTUS.
CORNELIUS, friend to FAUSTUS.
WAGNER, servant to FAUSTUS.
Clown.
ROBIN.
RALPH.
Vintner.
Horse-courser.
A KNIGHT.
An Old Man.
Scholars, Friars, and Attendants.
DUCHESS OF VANHOLT
LUCIFER.
BELZEBUB.
MEPHISTOPHILIS.
Good Angel.
Evil Angel.
The Seven Deadly Sins.
Devils.
Spirits in the shapes of ALEXANDER THE GREAT, of his Paramour
and of HELEN.
Chorus.

[Enter CHORUS.]

                              CHORUS.
Not marching now in fields of Thrasymene,
Where Mars did mate the Carthaginians;
Nor sporting in the dalliance of love,
In courts of kings where state is overturn'd;
Nor in the pomp of proud audacious deeds,
Intends our Muse to vaunt her heavenly verse:
Only this, gentlemen,—we must perform
The form of Faustus' fortunes, good or bad:
To patient judgments we appeal our plaud,
And speak for Faustus in his infancy.
Now is he born, his parents base of stock,
In Germany, within a town call'd Rhodes:
Of riper years, to Wertenberg he went,
Whereas his kinsmen chiefly brought him up.
So soon he profits in divinity,

The fruitful plot of scholarism grac'd,
That shortly he was grac'd with doctor's name,
Excelling all whose sweet delight disputes
In heavenly matters of theology;
Till swoln with cunning, of a self-conceit,
His waxen wings did mount above his reach,
And, melting, heavens conspir'd his overthrow;
For, falling to a devilish exercise,
And glutted now with learning's golden gifts,
He surfeits upon cursed necromancy;
Nothing so sweet as magic is to him,
Which he prefers before his chiefest bliss:
And this the man that in his study sits.
[Exit.]

[FAUSTUS discovered in his study.]

                              FAUSTUS.
Settle thy studies, Faustus, and begin
To sound the depth of that thou wilt profess:
Having commenc'd, be a divine in shew,
Yet level at the end of every art,
And live and die in Aristotle's works.
Sweet Analytics, 'tis thou hast ravish'd me!
Bene disserere est finis logices.
Is, to dispute well, logic's chiefest end?
Affords this art no greater miracle?
Then read no more; thou hast attain'd that end:
A greater subject fitteth Faustus' wit:
Bid Economy farewell, and Galen come,
Seeing, *Ubi desinit philosophus, ibi incipit medicus*:
Be a physician, Faustus; heap up gold,
And be eterniz'd for some wondrous cure:
Summum bonum medicinae sanitas,
The end of physic is our body's health.
Why, Faustus, hast thou not attain'd that end?
Is not thy common talk found aphorisms?
Are not thy bills hung up as monuments,
Whereby whole cities have escap'd the plague,
And thousand desperate maladies been eas'd?
Yet art thou still but Faustus, and a man.
Couldst thou make men to live eternally,
Or, being dead, raise them to life again,

Then this profession were to be esteem'd.
Physic, farewell! Where is Justinian?

[Reads.]
Si una eademque res legatur duobus, alter rem,
alter valorem rei, &c.
A pretty case of paltry legacies!

[Reads.]
Exhoereditare filium non potest pater, nisi, &c.
Such is the subject of the institute,
And universal body of the law:
This study fits a mercenary drudge,
Who aims at nothing but external trash;
Too servile and illiberal for me.
When all is done, divinity is best:
Jerome's Bible, Faustus; view it well.

[Reads.]
Stipendium peccati mors est.
Ha!
Stipendium, &c.
The reward of sin is death: that's hard.

[Reads.]
Si peccasse negamus, fallimur, et nulla est in nobis veritas;
If we say that we have no sin, we deceive ourselves, and
there's no truth in us. Why, then, belike we must sin, and so
consequently die:
Ay, we must die an everlasting death.
What doctrine call you this, *Che sera, sera,*
What will be, shall be? Divinity, adieu!
These metaphysics of magicians,
And necromantic books are heavenly;
Lines, circles, scenes, letters, and characters;
Ay, these are those that Faustus most desires.
O, what a world of profit and delight,
Of power, of honour, of omnipotence,
Is promis'd to the studious artizan!
All things that move between the quiet poles
Shall be at my command: emperors and kings
Are but obeyed in their several provinces,
Nor can they raise the wind, or rend the clouds;
But his dominion that exceeds in this,

Stretcheth as far as doth the mind of man;
A sound magician is a mighty god:
Here, Faustus, tire thy brains to gain a deity.

[Enter WAGNER.]

Wagner, commend me to my dearest friends,
The German Valdes and Cornelius;
Request them earnestly to visit me.

WAGNER.

I will, sir.
[Exit.]

FAUSTUS.

Their conference will be a greater help to me
Than all my labours, plod I ne'er so fast.

[Enter GOOD ANGEL and EVIL ANGEL.]

GOOD ANGEL.

O, Faustus, lay that damned book aside,
And gaze not on it, lest it tempt thy soul,
And heap God's heavy wrath upon thy head!
Read, read the Scriptures:—that is blasphemy.

EVIL ANGEL.

Go forward, Faustus, in that famous art
Wherein all Nature's treasure is contain'd:
Be thou on earth as Jove is in the sky,
Lord and commander of these elements.
[Exeunt Angels.]

FAUSTUS.

How am I glutted with conceit of this!
Shall I make spirits fetch me what I please,
Resolve me of all ambiguities,
Perform what desperate enterprise I will?
I'll have them fly to India for gold,
Ransack the ocean for orient pearl,
And search all corners of the new-found world
For pleasant fruits and princely delicates;
I'll have them read me strange philosophy,
And tell the secrets of all foreign kings;

I'll have them wall all Germany with brass,
And make swift Rhine circle fair Wertenberg;
I'll have them fill the public schools with silk,
Wherewith the students shall be bravely clad;
I'll levy soldiers with the coin they bring,
And chase the Prince of Parma from our land,
And reign sole king of all the provinces;
Yea, stranger engines for the brunt of war,
Than was the fiery keel at Antwerp's bridge,
I'll make my servile spirits to invent.

[Enter VALDES and CORNELIUS.]

Come, German Valdes, and Cornelius,
And make me blest with your sage conference.
Valdes, sweet Valdes, and Cornelius,
Know that your words have won me at the last
To practice magic and concealed arts:
Yet not your words only, but mine own fantasy,
That will receive no object; for my head
But ruminates on necromantic skill.
Philosophy is odious and obscure;
Both law and physic are for petty wits;
Divinity is basest of the three,
Unpleasant, harsh, contemptible, and vile:
'Tis magic, magic, that hath ravish'd me.
Then, gentle friends, aid me in this attempt;
And I, that have with concise syllogisms
Gravell'd the pastors of the German church,
And made the flowering pride of Wertenberg
Swarm to my problems, as the infernal spirits
On sweet Musaeus when he came to hell,
Will be as cunning as Agrippa was,
Whose shadow made all Europe honour him.

                    VALDES.
Faustus, these books, thy wit, and our experience,
Shall make all nations to canonize us.
As Indian Moors obey their Spanish lords,
So shall the spirits of every element
Be always serviceable to us three;
Like lions shall they guard us when we please;
Like Almain rutters with their horsemen's staves,
Or Lapland giants, trotting by our sides;

Sometimes like women, or unwedded maids,
Shadowing more beauty in their airy brows
Than have the white breasts of the queen of love:
From Venice shall they drag huge argosies,
And from America the golden fleece
That yearly stuffs old Philip's treasury;
If learned Faustus will be resolute.

FAUSTUS.

Valdes, as resolute am I in this
As thou to live: therefore object it not.

CORNELIUS.

The miracles that magic will perform
Will make thee vow to study nothing else.
He that is grounded in astrology,
Enrich'd with tongues, well seen in minerals,
Hath all the principles magic doth require:
Then doubt not, Faustus, but to be renowm'd,
And more frequented for this mystery
Than heretofore the Delphian oracle.
The spirits tell me they can dry the sea,
And fetch the treasure of all foreign wrecks,
Ay, all the wealth that our forefathers hid
Within the massy entrails of the earth:
Then tell me, Faustus, what shall we three want?

FAUSTUS.

Nothing, Cornelius. O, this cheers my soul!
Come, shew me some demonstrations magical,
That I may conjure in some lusty grove,
And have these joys in full possession.

VALDES.

Then haste thee to some solitary grove,
And bear wise Bacon's and Albertus' works,
The Hebrew Psalter, and New Testament;
And whatsoever else is requisite
We will inform thee ere our conference cease.

CORNELIUS.

Valdes, first let him know the words of art;
And then, all other ceremonies learn'd,
Faustus may try his cunning by himself.

VALDES.

First I'll instruct thee in the rudiments,
And then wilt thou be perfecter than I.

FAUSTUS.

Then come and dine with me, and, after meat,
We'll canvass every quiddity thereof;
For, ere I sleep, I'll try what I can do:
This night I'll conjure, though I die therefore.
[Exeunt.]

[Enter two SCHOLARS.]

FIRST SCHOLAR.

I wonder what's become of Faustus, that was wont
to make our schools ring with *sic probo.*

SECOND SCHOLAR.

That shall we know, for see, here comes his boy.

Enter WAGNER.

FIRST SCHOLAR.

How now, sirrah! where's thy master?

WAGNER.

God in heaven knows.

SECOND SCHOLAR.

Why, dost not thou know?

WAGNER.

Yes, I know; but that follows not.

FIRST SCHOLAR.

Go to, sirrah! leave your jesting, and tell us
where he is.

WAGNER.

That follows not necessary by force of argument, that you,
being licentiates, should stand upon: therefore acknowledge
your error, and be attentive.

SECOND SCHOLAR.

Why, didst thou not say thou knewest?

WAGNER.

Have you any witness on't?

FIRST SCHOLAR.

Yes, sirrah, I heard you.

WAGNER.

Ask my fellow if I be a thief.

SECOND SCHOLAR.

Well, you will not tell us?

WAGNER.

Yes, sir, I will tell you: yet, if you were not dunces,
you would never ask me such a question; for is not he corpus
naturale? and is not that mobile? then wherefore should you
ask me such a question? But that I am by nature phlegmatic,
slow to wrath, and prone to lechery (to love, I would say),
it were not for you to come within forty foot of the place
of execution, although I do not doubt to see you both hanged
the next sessions. Thus having triumphed over you, I will set
my countenance like a precisian, and begin to speak thus:—
Truly, my dear brethren, my master is within at dinner,
with Valdes and Cornelius, as this wine, if it could speak,
would inform your worships: and so, the Lord bless you,
preserve you, and keep you, my dear brethren, my dear brethren!
[Exit.]

FIRST SCHOLAR.

Nay, then, I fear he is fallen into that damned art
for which they two are infamous through the world.

SECOND SCHOLAR.

Were he a stranger, and not allied to me, yet should
I grieve for him. But, come, let us go and inform the Rector,
and see if he by his grave counsel can reclaim him.

FIRST SCHOLAR.

O, but I fear me nothing can reclaim him!

SECOND SCHOLAR.

Yet let us try what we can do.
[Exeunt.]

[Enter FAUSTUS to conjure.]

FAUSTUS.

Now that the gloomy shadow of the earth,
Longing to view Orion's drizzling look,
Leaps from th' antartic world unto the sky,
And dims the welkin with her pitchy breath,
Faustus, begin thine incantations,
And try if devils will obey thy hest,
Seeing thou hast pray'd and sacrific'd to them.
Within this circle is Jehovah's name,
Forward and backward anagrammatiz'd,
Th' abbreviated names of holy saints,
Figures of every adjunct to the heavens,
And characters of signs and erring stars,
By which the spirits are enforc'd to rise:
Then fear not, Faustus, but be resolute,
And try the uttermost magic can perform.—
Sint mihi dei Acherontis propitii! Valeat numen triplex Jehovoe!
Ignei, aerii, aquatani spiritus, salvete! Orientis princeps
Belzebub, inferni ardentis monarcha, et Demogorgon, propitiamus
vos, ut appareat et surgat Mephistophilis, quod tumeraris:
per Jehovam, Gehennam, et consecratam aquam quam nunc spargo,
signumque crucis quod nunc facio, et per vota nostra, ipse nunc
surgat nobis dicatus Mephistophilis!

[Enter MEPHISTOPHILIS.]

I charge thee to return, and change thy shape;
Thou art too ugly to attend on me:
Go, and return an old Franciscan friar;
That holy shape becomes a devil best.

[Exit MEPHISTOPHILIS.]

I see there's virtue in my heavenly words:
Who would not be proficient in this art?
How pliant is this Mephistophilis,
Full of obedience and humility!

Such is the force of magic and my spells:
No, Faustus, thou art conjuror laureat,
That canst command great Mephistophilis:
Quin regis Mephistophilis fratris imagine.

[Re-enter MEPHISTOPHILIS like a Franciscan friar.]

MEPHIST.
Now, Faustus, what wouldst thou have me do?

FAUSTUS.
I charge thee wait upon me whilst I live,
To do whatever Faustus shall command,
Be it to make the moon drop from her sphere,
Or the ocean to overwhelm the world.

MEPHIST.
I am a servant to great Lucifer,
And may not follow thee without his leave:
No more than he commands must we perform.

FAUSTUS.
Did not he charge thee to appear to me?

MEPHIST.
No, I came hither of mine own accord.

FAUSTUS.
Did not my conjuring speeches raise thee? speak.

MEPHIST.
That was the cause, but yet per accidens;
For, when we hear one rack the name of God,
Abjure the Scriptures and his Saviour Christ,
We fly, in hope to get his glorious soul;
Nor will we come, unless he use such means
Whereby he is in danger to be damn'd.
Therefore the shortest cut for conjuring
Is stoutly to abjure the Trinity,
And pray devoutly to the prince of hell.

FAUSTUS.
So Faustus hath
Already done; and holds this principle,

There is no chief but only Belzebub;
To whom Faustus doth dedicate himself.
This word "damnation" terrifies not him,
For he confounds hell in Elysium:
His ghost be with the old philosophers!
But, leaving these vain trifles of men's souls,
Tell me what is that Lucifer thy lord?

MEPHIST.
Arch-regent and commander of all spirits.

FAUSTUS.
Was not that Lucifer an angel once?

MEPHIST.
Yes, Faustus, and most dearly lov'd of God.

FAUSTUS.
How comes it, then, that he is prince of devils?

MEPHIST.
O, by aspiring pride and insolence;
For which God threw him from the face of heaven.

FAUSTUS.
And what are you that live with Lucifer?

MEPHIST.
Unhappy spirits that fell with Lucifer,
Conspir'd against our God with Lucifer,
And are for ever damn'd with Lucifer.
FAUSTUS.
Where are you damn'd?

MEPHIST.
In hell.

FAUSTUS.
How comes it, then, that thou art out of hell?

MEPHIST.
Why, this is hell, nor am I out of it:
Think'st thou that I, who saw the face of God,

And tasted the eternal joys of heaven,
Am not tormented with ten thousand hells,
In being depriv'd of everlasting bliss?
O, Faustus, leave these frivolous demands,
Which strike a terror to my fainting soul!

                                    FAUSTUS.
What, is great Mephistophilis so passionate
For being deprived of the joys of heaven?
Learn thou of Faustus manly fortitude,
And scorn those joys thou never shalt possess.
Go bear these tidings to great Lucifer:
Seeing Faustus hath incurr'd eternal death
By desperate thoughts against Jove's deity,
Say, he surrenders up to him his soul,
So he will spare him four and twenty years,
Letting him live in all voluptuousness;
Having thee ever to attend on me,
To give me whatsoever I shall ask,
To tell me whatsoever I demand,
To slay mine enemies, and aid my friends,
And always be obedient to my will.
Go and return to mighty Lucifer,
And meet me in my study at midnight,
And then resolve me of thy master's mind.

                                    MEPHIST.
I will, Faustus.
[Exit.]

                                    FAUSTUS.
Had I as many souls as there be stars,
I'd give them all for Mephistophilis.
By him I'll be great emperor of the world,
And make a bridge thorough the moving air,
To pass the ocean with a band of men;
I'll join the hills that bind the Afric shore,
And make that country continent to Spain,
And both contributory to my crown:
The Emperor shall not live but by my leave,
Nor any potentate of Germany.
Now that I have obtain'd what I desir'd,
I'll live in speculation of this art,

Till Mephistophilis return again.
[Exit.]

[Enter WAGNER and CLOWN.]

WAGNER.

Sirrah boy, come hither.

CLOWN.

How, boy! swowns, boy! I hope you have seen many boys
with such pickadevaunts as I have: boy, quotha!

WAGNER.

Tell me, sirrah, hast thou any comings in?

CLOWN.

Ay, and goings out too; you may see else.

WAGNER.

Alas, poor slave! see how poverty jesteth in his nakedness!
the villain is bare and out of service, and so hungry, that I know
he would give his soul to the devil for a shoulder of mutton,
though it were blood-raw.

CLOWN.

How! my soul to the devil for a shoulder of mutton, though
'twere blood-raw! not so, good friend: by'r lady, I had need
have it well roasted, and good sauce to it, if I pay so dear.

WAGNER.

Well, wilt thou serve me, and I'll make thee go like
Qui mihi discipulus?

CLOWN.

How, in verse?

WAGNER.

No, sirrah; in beaten silk and staves-acre.

CLOWN.

How, how, knaves-acre! ay, I thought that was all the land
his father left him. Do you hear? I would be sorry to rob you of
your living.

WAGNER.

Sirrah, I say in staves-acre.

CLOWN.

Oho, oho, staves-acre! why, then, belike, if I were your
man, I should be full of vermin.

WAGNER.

So thou shalt, whether thou beest with me or no. But,
sirrah, leave your jesting, and bind yourself presently unto me
for seven years, or I'll turn all the lice about thee into
familiars, and they shall tear thee in pieces.

CLOWN.

Do you hear, sir? you may save that labour; they are too
familiar with me already: swowns, they are as bold with my flesh
as if they had paid for their meat and drink.

WAGNER.

Well, do you hear, sirrah? hold, take these guilders.

[Gives money.]

CLOWN.

Gridirons! what be they?

WAGNER.

Why, French crowns.

CLOWN.

Mass, but for the name of French crowns, a man were as good
have as many English counters. And what should I do with these?

WAGNER.

Why, now, sirrah, thou art at an hour's warning, whensoever
or wheresoever the devil shall fetch thee.

CLOWN.

No, no; here, take your gridirons again.

WAGNER.

Truly, I'll none of them.

CLOWN.

Truly, but you shall.

WAGNER.

Bear witness I gave them him.

CLOWN.

Bear witness I give them you again.

WAGNER.

Well, I will cause two devils presently to fetch thee
away.—Baliol and Belcher!

CLOWN.

Let your Baliol and your Belcher come here, and I'll
knock them, they were never so knocked since they were devils:
say I should kill one of them, what would folks say? "Do ye see
yonder tall fellow in the round slop? he has killed the devil."
So I should be called Kill-devil all the parish over.

[Enter two DEVILS; and the CLOWN runs up and down crying.]

WAGNER.

Baliol and Belcher,—spirits, away!

Exeunt DEVILS.

CLOWN.

What, are they gone? a vengeance on them! they have vile
long nails. There was a he-devil and a she-devil: I'll tell you
how you shall know them; all he-devils has horns, and all
she-devils has clifts and cloven feet.

WAGNER.

Well, sirrah, follow me.

CLOWN.

But, do you hear? if I should serve you, would you teach
me to raise up Banios and Belcheos?

WAGNER.

I will teach thee to turn thyself to any thing, to a dog,
or a cat, or a mouse, or a rat, or any thing.

CLOWN.

How! a Christian fellow to a dog, or a cat, a mouse,
or a rat! no, no, sir; if you turn me into any thing, let it be
in the likeness of a little pretty frisking flea, that I may be
here and there and every where: O, I'll tickle the pretty wenches'
plackets! I'll be amongst them, i'faith.

WAGNER.

Well, sirrah, come.

CLOWN.

But, do you hear, Wagner?

WAGNER.

How!—Baliol and Belcher!

CLOWN.

O Lord! I pray, sir, let Banio and Belcher go sleep.

WAGNER.

Villain, call me Master Wagner, and let thy left eye be
diametarily fixed upon my right heel, with *quasi vestigiis
nostris insistere.*
[Exit.]

CLOWN.

God forgive me, he speaks Dutch fustian. Well, I'll follow
him; I'll serve him, that's flat.
[Exit.]

[FAUSTUS discovered in his study.]

FAUSTUS.

Now, Faustus, must
Thou needs be damn'd, and canst thou not be sav'd:
What boots it, then, to think of God or heaven?
Away with such vain fancies, and despair;
Despair in God, and trust in Belzebub:
Now go not backward; no, Faustus, be resolute:
Why waver'st thou? O, something soundeth in mine ears,
"Abjure this magic, turn to God again!"
Ay, and Faustus will turn to God again.
To God? he loves thee not;
The god thou serv'st is thine own appetite,

Wherein is fix'd the love of Belzebub:
To him I'll build an altar and a church,
And offer lukewarm blood of new-born babes.

[Enter GOOD ANGEL and EVIL ANGEL.]

GOOD ANGEL.
Sweet Faustus, leave that execrable art.

FAUSTUS.
Contrition, prayer, repentance—what of them?

GOOD ANGEL.
O, they are means to bring thee unto heaven!

EVIL ANGEL.
Rather illusions, fruits of lunacy,
That make men foolish that do trust them most.

GOOD ANGEL.
Sweet Faustus, think of heaven and heavenly things.

EVIL ANGEL.
No, Faustus; think of honour and of wealth.

[Exeunt ANGELS.]

FAUSTUS.
Of wealth!
Why, the signiory of Embden shall be mine.
When Mephistophilis shall stand by me,
What god can hurt thee, Faustus? thou art safe
Cast no more doubts.—Come, Mephistophilis,
And bring glad tidings from great Lucifer;—
Is't not midnight?—come, Mephistophilis,
Veni, veni, Mephistophile!

[Enter MEPHISTOPHILIS.]

Now tell me what says Lucifer, thy lord?

MEPHIST.
That I shall wait on Faustus whilst he lives,
So he will buy my service with his soul.

FAUSTUS.
Already Faustus hath hazarded that for thee.

MEPHIST.
But, Faustus, thou must bequeath it solemnly,
And write a deed of gift with thine own blood;
For that security craves great Lucifer.
If thou deny it, I will back to hell.

FAUSTUS.
Stay, Mephistophilis, and tell me, what good will my soul
do thy lord?

MEPHIST.
Enlarge his kingdom.

FAUSTUS.
Is that the reason why he tempts us thus?

MEPHIST.
Solamen miseris socios habuisse doloris.

FAUSTUS.
Why, have you any pain that torture others!

MEPHIST.
As great as have the human souls of men.
But, tell me, Faustus, shall I have thy soul?
And I will be thy slave, and wait on thee,
And give thee more than thou hast wit to ask.

FAUSTUS.
Ay, Mephistophilis, I give it thee.

MEPHIST.
Then, Faustus, stab thine arm courageously,
And bind thy soul, that at some certain day
Great Lucifer may claim it as his own;
And then be thou as great as Lucifer.

FAUSTUS.
[Stabbing his arm] Lo, Mephistophilis, for love of thee,
I cut mine arm, and with my proper blood

Assure my soul to be great Lucifer's,
Chief lord and regent of perpetual night!
View here the blood that trickles from mine arm,
And let it be propitious for my wish.

                         MEPHIST.
But, Faustus, thou must
Write it in manner of a deed of gift.

                         FAUSTUS.
Ay, so I will [Writes]. But, Mephistophilis,
My blood congeals, and I can write no more.

                         MEPHIST.
I'll fetch thee fire to dissolve it straight.
[Exit.]
                         FAUSTUS.
What might the staying of my blood portend?
Is it unwilling I should write this bill?
Why streams it not, that I may write afresh?
FAUSTUS GIVES TO THEE HIS SOUL: ah, there it stay'd!
Why shouldst thou not? is not thy soul shine own?
Then write again, FAUSTUS GIVES TO THEE HIS SOUL.

[Re-enter MEPHISTOPHILIS with a chafer of coals.]

                         MEPHIST.
Here's fire; come, Faustus, set it on.

                         FAUSTUS.
 So, now the blood begins to clear again;
Now will I make an end immediately.
[Writes.]

                         MEPHIST.
O, what will not I do to obtain his soul?
[Aside.]

                         FAUSTUS.
Consummatum est; this bill is ended,
And Faustus hath bequeath'd his soul to Lucifer.
But what is this inscription on mine arm?
Homo, fuge: whither should I fly?

If unto God, he'll throw me down to hell.
My senses are deceiv'd; here's nothing writ:—
I see it plain; here in this place is writ,
Homo, fuge: yet shall not Faustus fly.

MEPHIST.
I'll fetch him somewhat to delight his mind.
[Aside, and then exit.]

[Re-enter MEPHISTOPHILIS with DEVILS, who give crowns and rich apparel to
FAUSTUS, dance, and then depart.]

FAUSTUS.
Speak, Mephistophilis, what means this show?

MEPHIST.
Nothing, Faustus, but to delight thy mind withal,
And to shew thee what magic can perform.

FAUSTUS.
But may I raise up spirits when I please?

MEPHIST.
Ay, Faustus, and do greater things than these.

FAUSTUS.
Then there's enough for a thousand souls.
Here, Mephistophilis, receive this scroll,
A deed of gift of body and of soul:
But yet conditionally that thou perform
All articles prescrib'd between us both.

MEPHIST.
Faustus, I swear by hell and Lucifer
To effect all promises between us made!

FAUSTUS.
Then hear me read them. [Reads] *On these conditions*
Following. First, that Faustus may be a spirit in form and
Substance. Secondly, that Mephistophilis shall be his servant,
And at his command. Thirdly, that Mephistophilis do for him,
And bring him whatsoever he desires. Fourthly, that he shall
Be in his chamber or house invisible. Lastly, that he shall appear
To the said John Faustus, at all times, in what form or shape

Soever he please. I, John Faustus, of Wertenberg, Doctor, by
These presents, do give both body and soul to Lucifer Prince of
The East, and his minister Mephistophilis; and futhermore grant
Unto them, that, twenty-four years being expired, the articles
Above-written inviolate, full power to fetch or carry the said
John Faustus, body and soul, flesh, blood, or goods, into their
Habitation wheresoever. By me, John Faustus.

MEPHIST.

Speak, Faustus, do you deliver this as your deed?

FAUSTUS.

Ay, take it, and the devil give thee good on't!

MEPHIST.

Now, Faustus, ask what thou wilt.

FAUSTUS.

First will I question with thee about hell.
Tell me, where is the place that men call hell?

MEPHIST.

Under the heavens.

FAUSTUS.

Ay, but whereabout?

MEPHIST.

Within the bowels of these elements,
Where we are tortur'd and remain for ever:
Hell hath no limits, nor is circumscrib'd
In one self place; for where we are is hell,
And where hell is, there must we ever be:
And, to conclude, when all the world dissolves,
And every creature shall be purified,
All places shall be hell that are not heaven.

FAUSTUS.

Come, I think hell's a fable.

MEPHIST.

Ay, think so still, till experience change thy mind.

FAUSTUS.

Why, think'st thou, then, that Faustus shall be damn'd?

MEPHIST.

Ay, of necessity, for here's the scroll
Wherein thou hast given thy soul to Lucifer.

FAUSTUS.

Ay, and body too: but what of that?
Think'st thou that Faustus is so fond to imagine
That, after this life, there is any pain?
Tush, these are trifles and mere old wives' tales.

MEPHIST.

But, Faustus, I am an instance to prove the contrary,
For I am damn'd, and am now in hell.

FAUSTUS.

How! now in hell!
Nay, an this be hell, I'll willingly be damn'd here:
What! walking, disputing, &c.
But, leaving off this, let me have a wife,
The fairest maid in Germany;
For I am wanton and lascivious,
And cannot live without a wife.

MEPHIST.

How! a wife!
I prithee, Faustus, talk not of a wife.

FAUSTUS.

Nay, sweet Mephistophilis, fetch me one, for I will have
one.

MEPHIST.

Well, thou wilt have one? Sit there till I come: I'll
fetch thee a wife in the devil's name.
[Exit.]

[Re-enter MEPHISTOPHILIS with a DEVIL drest like a WOMAN, with fire-works.]

MEPHIST.

Tell me, Faustus, how dost thou like thy wife?

FAUSTUS.

A plague on her for a hot whore!

MEPHIST.

Tut, Faustus,
Marriage is but a ceremonial toy;
If thou lovest me, think no more of it.
I'll cull thee out the fairest courtezans,
And bring them every morning to thy bed:
She whom thine eye shall like, thy heart shall have,
Be she as chaste as was Penelope,
As wise as Saba, or as beautiful
As was bright Lucifer before his fall.
Hold, take this book, peruse it thoroughly:
[Gives book.]
The iterating of these lines brings gold;
The framing of this circle on the ground
Brings whirlwinds, tempests, thunder, and lightning;
Pronounce this thrice devoutly to thyself,
And men in armour shall appear to thee,
Ready to execute what thou desir'st.

FAUSTUS.

Thanks, Mephistophilis: yet fain would I have a book
wherein I might behold all spells and incantations, that I
might raise up spirits when I please.

MEPHIST.

Here they are in this book.
[Turns to them.]

FAUSTUS.

Now would I have a book where I might see all characters
and planets of the heavens, that I might know their motions and
dispositions.

MEPHIST.

Here they are too.
[Turns to them.]

FAUSTUS.

Nay, let me have one book more,—and then I have done,—
wherein I might see all plants, herbs, and trees, that grow upon
the earth.

MEPHIST.
Here they be.

FAUSTUS.
O, thou art deceived.

MEPHIST.
Tut, I warrant thee.
[Turns to them.]

FAUSTUS.
When I behold the heavens, then I repent,
And curse thee, wicked Mephistophilis,
Because thou hast depriv'd me of those joys.

MEPHIST.
Why, Faustus,
Thinkest thou heaven is such a glorious thing?
I tell thee, 'tis not half so fair as thou,
Or any man that breathes on earth.

FAUSTUS.
How prov'st thou that?

MEPHIST.
'Twas made for man, therefore is man more excellent.

FAUSTUS.
If it were made for man, 'twas made for me:
I will renounce this magic and repent.

[Enter GOOD ANGEL and EVIL ANGEL.]

GOOD ANGEL.
Faustus, repent; yet God will pity thee.

EVIL ANGEL.
Thou art a spirit; God cannot pity thee.

FAUSTUS.
Who buzzeth in mine ears I am a spirit?
Be I a devil, yet God may pity me;
Ay, God will pity me, if I repent.

EVIL ANGEL.

Ay, but Faustus never shall repent.

[Exeunt ANGELS.]

FAUSTUS.

My heart's so harden'd, I cannot repent:
Scarce can I name salvation, faith, or heaven,
But fearful echoes thunder in mine ears,
"Faustus, thou art damn'd!" then swords, and knives,
Poison, guns, halters, and envenom'd steel
Are laid before me to despatch myself;
And long ere this I should have slain myself,
Had not sweet pleasure conquer'd deep despair.
Have not I made blind Homer sing to me
Of Alexander's love and Oenon's death?
And hath not he, that built the walls of Thebes
With ravishing sound of his melodious harp,
Made music with my Mephistophilis?
Why should I die, then, or basely despair?
I am resolv'd; Faustus shall ne'er repent.—
Come, Mephistophilis, let us dispute again,
And argue of divine astrology.
Tell me, are there many heavens above the moon
Are all celestial bodies but one globe,
As is the substance of this centric earth?

MEPHIST.

As are the elements, such are the spheres,
Mutually folded in each other's orb,
And, Faustus,
All jointly move upon one axletree,
Whose terminine is term'd the world's wide pole;
Nor are the names of Saturn, Mars, or Jupiter
Feign'd, but are erring stars.

FAUSTUS.

But, tell me, have they all one motion, both situ et
tempore?

MEPHIST.

All jointly move from east to west in twenty-four hours
upon the poles of the world; but differ in their motion upon
the poles of the zodiac.

FAUSTUS.

Tush,
These slender trifles Wagner can decide:
Hath Mephistophilis no greater skill?
Who knows not the double motion of the planets?
The first is finish'd in a natural day;
The second thus; as Saturn in thirty years; Jupiter in twelve;
Mars in four; the Sun, Venus, and Mercury in a year; the Moon in
twenty-eight days. Tush, these are freshmen's suppositions.
But, tell me, hath every sphere a dominion or intelligentia?

MEPHIST.

Ay.

FAUSTUS.

How many heavens or spheres are there?

MEPHIST.

Nine; the seven planets, the firmament, and the empyreal
heaven.

FAUSTUS.

Well, resolve me in this question; why have we not
conjunctions, oppositions, aspects, eclipses, all at one time,
but in some years we have more, in some less?

MEPHIST.

Per inoequalem motum respectu totius.

FAUSTUS.

Well, I am answered. Tell me who made the world?

MEPHIST.

I will not.

FAUSTUS.

Sweet Mephistophilis, tell me.

MEPHIST.

Move me not, for I will not tell thee.

FAUSTUS.

Villain, have I not bound thee to tell me any thing?

MEPHIST.
Ay, that is not against our kingdom; but this is. Think
thou on hell, Faustus, for thou art damned.

FAUSTUS.
Think, Faustus, upon God that made the world.

MEPHIST.
Remember this.
[Exit.]

FAUSTUS.
Ay, go, accursed spirit, to ugly hell!
'Tis thou hast damn'd distressed Faustus' soul.
Is't not too late?

[Re-enter GOOD ANGEL and EVIL ANGEL.]

EVIL ANGEL.
Too late.

GOOD ANGEL.
Never too late, if Faustus can repent.

EVIL ANGEL.
If thou repent, devils shall tear thee in pieces.

GOOD ANGEL.
Repent, and they shall never raze thy skin.

[Exeunt ANGELS.]

FAUSTUS.
Ah, Christ, my Saviour,
Seek to save distressed Faustus' soul!

[Enter LUCIFER, BELZEBUB, and MEPHISTOPHILIS.]

LUCIFER.
Christ cannot save thy soul, for he is just:
There's none but I have interest in the same.

FAUSTUS.

O, who art thou that look'st so terrible?

LUCIFER.

I am Lucifer,
And this is my companion-prince in hell.

FAUSTUS.

O, Faustus, they are come to fetch away thy soul!

LUCIFER.

We come to tell thee thou dost injure us;
Thou talk'st of Christ, contrary to thy promise:
Thou shouldst not think of God: think of the devil,
And of his dam too.

FAUSTUS.

Nor will I henceforth: pardon me in this,
And Faustus vows never to look to heaven,
Never to name God, or to pray to him,
To burn his Scriptures, slay his ministers,
And make my spirits pull his churches down.

LUCIFER.

Do so, and we will highly gratify thee. Faustus, we are
come from hell to shew thee some pastime: sit down, and thou
shalt see all the Seven Deadly Sins appear in their proper shapes.

FAUSTUS.

That sight will be as pleasing unto me,
As Paradise was to Adam, the first day
Of his creation.

LUCIFER.

Talk not of Paradise nor creation; but mark this show:
talk of the devil, and nothing else.—Come away!

[Enter the SEVEN DEADLY SINS.]

Now, Faustus, examine them of their several names and dispositions.

FAUSTUS.

What art thou, the first?

PRIDE.

I am Pride. I disdain to have any parents. I am like to
Ovid's flea; I can creep into every corner of a wench; sometimes,
like a perriwig, I sit upon her brow; or, like a fan of feathers,
I kiss her lips; indeed, I do—what do I not? But, fie, what a
scent is here! I'll not speak another word, except the ground
were perfumed, and covered with cloth of arras.

FAUSTUS.

What art thou, the second?

COVETOUSNESS.

I am Covetousness, begotten of an old churl, in an
old leathern bag: and, might I have my wish, I would desire that
this house and all the people in it were turned to gold, that I
might lock you up in my good chest: O, my sweet gold!

FAUSTUS.

What art thou, the third?

WRATH.

I am Wrath. I had neither father nor mother: I leapt out
of a lion's mouth when I was scarce half-an-hour old; and ever
since I have run up and down the world with this case
of rapiers, wounding myself when I had nobody to fight withal.
I was born in hell; and look to it, for some of you shall be
my father.

FAUSTUS.

What art thou, the fourth?

ENVY.

I am Envy, begotten of a chimney-sweeper and an oyster-wife.
I cannot read, and therefore wish all books were burnt. I am lean
with seeing others eat. O, that there would come a famine through
all the world, that all might die, and I live alone! then thou
shouldst see how fat I would be. But must thou sit, and I stand?
come down, with a vengeance!

FAUSTUS.

Away, envious rascal!—What art thou, the fifth?

GLUTTONY.

Who I, sir? I am Gluttony. My parents are all dead,
and the devil a penny they have left me, but a bare pension, and
that is thirty meals a-day and ten bevers,—a small trifle
to suffice nature. O, I come of a royal parentage! my grandfather
was a Gammon of Bacon, my grandmother a Hogshead of Claret-wine;
my godfathers were these, Peter Pickle-herring and Martin
Martlemas-beef; O, but my godmother, she was a jolly gentlewoman,
and well-beloved in every good town and city; her name was Mistress
Margery March-beer. Now, Faustus, thou hast heard all my progeny;
wilt thou bid me to supper?

FAUSTUS.

No, I'll see thee hanged: thou wilt eat up all my victuals.

GLUTTONY.

Then the devil choke thee!

FAUSTUS.

Choke thyself, glutton!—What art thou, the sixth?

SLOTH.

I am Sloth. I was begotten on a sunny bank, where I have
lain ever since; and you have done me great injury to bring me
from thence: let me be carried thither again by Gluttony and
Lechery. I'll not speak another word for a king's ransom.

FAUSTUS.

What are you, Mistress Minx, the seventh and last?

LECHERY.

Who I, sir? I am one that loves an inch of raw mutton
better than an ell of fried stock-fish; and the first letter
of my name begins with L.

FAUSTUS.

Away, to hell, to hell!

[Exeunt the SINS.]

LUCIFER.

Now, Faustus, how dost thou like this?

FAUSTUS.

O, this feeds my soul!

LUCIFER.

Tut, Faustus, in hell is all manner of delight.

FAUSTUS.

O, might I see hell, and return again,
How happy were I then!

LUCIFER.

Thou shalt; I will send for thee at midnight.
In meantime take this book; peruse it throughly,
And thou shalt turn thyself into what shape thou wilt.

FAUSTUS.

Great thanks, mighty Lucifer!
This will I keep as chary as my life.

LUCIFER.

Farewell, Faustus, and think on the devil.

FAUSTUS.

Farewell, great Lucifer.

[Exeunt LUCIFER and BELZEBUB.]

Come, Mephistophilis.

[Exeunt.]
[Enter CHORUS.]

CHORUS.

Learned Faustus,
To know the secrets of astronomy
Graven in the book of Jove's high firmament,
Did mount himself to scale Olympus' top,
Being seated in a chariot burning bright,
Drawn by the strength of yoky dragons' necks.
He now is gone to prove cosmography,
And, as I guess, will first arrive at Rome,
To see the Pope and manner of his court,
And take some part of holy Peter's feast,
That to this day is highly solemniz'd.
[Exit.]

[Enter FAUSTUS and MEPHISTOPHILIS.]

FAUSTUS.

Having now, my good Mephistophilis,
Pass'd with delight the stately town of Trier,
Environ'd round with airy mountain-tops,
With walls of flint, and deep-entrenched lakes,
Not to be won by any conquering prince;
From Paris next, coasting the realm of France,
We saw the river Maine fall into Rhine,
Whose banks are set with groves of fruitful vines;
Then up to Naples, rich Campania,
Whose buildings fair and gorgeous to the eye,
The streets straight forth, and pav'd with finest brick,
Quarter the town in four equivalents:
There saw we learned Maro's golden tomb,
The way he cut, an English mile in length,
Thorough a rock of stone, in one night's space;
From thence to Venice, Padua, and the rest,
In one of which a sumptuous temple stands,
That threats the stars with her aspiring top.
Thus hitherto hath Faustus spent his time:
But tell me now what resting-place is this?
Hast thou, as erst I did command,
Conducted me within the walls of Rome?

MEPHIST.

Faustus, I have; and, because we will not be unprovided,
I have taken up his Holiness' privy-chamber for our use.

FAUSTUS.

I hope his Holiness will bid us welcome.

MEPHIST.

Tut, 'tis no matter; man; we'll be bold with his good cheer.
And now, my Faustus, that thou mayst perceive
What Rome containeth to delight thee with,
Know that this city stands upon seven hills
That underprop the groundwork of the same:
Just through the midst runs flowing Tiber's stream
With winding banks that cut it in two parts;
Over the which four stately bridges lean,
That make safe passage to each part of Rome:

Upon the bridge call'd Ponte Angelo
Erected is a castle passing strong,
Within whose walls such store of ordnance are,
And double cannons fram'd of carved brass,
As match the days within one complete year;
Besides the gates, and high pyramides,
Which Julius Caesar brought from Africa.

FAUSTUS.

Now, by the kingdoms of infernal rule,
Of Styx, of Acheron, and the fiery lake
Of ever-burning Phlegethon, I swear
That I do long to see the monuments
And situation of bright-splendent Rome:
Come, therefore, let's away.

MEPHIST.

Nay, Faustus, stay: I know you'd fain see the Pope,
And take some part of holy Peter's feast,
Where thou shalt see a troop of bald-pate friars,
Whose *summum bonum* is in belly-cheer.

FAUSTUS.

Well, I'm content to compass then some sport,
And by their folly make us merriment.
Then charm me, that I
May be invisible, to do what I please,
Unseen of any whilst I stay in Rome.
[Mephistophilis charms him.]

MEPHIST.

So, Faustus; now
Do what thou wilt, thou shalt not be discern'd.

[Sound a Sonnet. Enter the POPE and the CARDINAL OF LORRAIN to the
banquet, with FRIARS attending.]

POPE.
My Lord of Lorrain, will't please you draw near?

FAUSTUS.
Fall to, and the devil choke you, an you spare!

POPE.

How now! who's that which spake?—Friars, look about.

FIRST FRIAR.

Here's nobody, if it like your Holiness.

POPE.

My lord, here is a dainty dish was sent me from the Bishop
of Milan.

FAUSTUS.

I thank you, sir.
[Snatches the dish.]

POPE.

How now! who's that which snatched the meat from me? will
no man look?—My lord, this dish was sent me from the Cardinal
of Florence.

FAUSTUS.

You say true; I'll ha't.
[Snatches the dish.]

POPE.

What, again!—My lord, I'll drink to your grace.

FAUSTUS.

I'll pledge your grace.
[Snatches the cup.]

C. OF LOR.

My lord, it may be some ghost, newly crept out of
Purgatory, come to beg a pardon of your Holiness.

POPE.

It may be so.—Friars, prepare a dirge to lay the fury
of this ghost.—Once again, my lord, fall to.
[The POPE crosses himself.]

FAUSTUS.

What, are you crossing of yourself?
Well, use that trick no more, I would advise you.
[The POPE crosses himself again.]

Well, there's the second time. Aware the third;
I give you fair warning.
[The POPE crosses himself again, and FAUSTUS hits him a box
of the ear; and they all run away.]
Come on, Mephistophilis; what shall we do?

MEPHIST.
Nay, I know not: we shall be cursed with bell, book,
and candle.

FAUSTUS.
How! bell, book, and candle,—candle, book, and bell,—
Forward and backward, to curse Faustus to hell!
Anon you shall hear a hog grunt, a calf bleat, and an ass bray,
Because it is Saint Peter's holiday.

[Re-enter all the FRIARS to sing the Dirge.]

FIRST FRIAR.
Come, brethren, let's about our business with good devotion.
They sing.
Cursed be he that stole away his holiness' meat from the table! maledicat Dominus!
Cursed be he that struck his holiness a blown on the face!
maledicat Dominus!
Cursed be he that took Friar Sandelo a blow on the pate!
maledicat Dominus!
Cursed be he that disturbeth our holy dirge! maledicat
Dominus!
Cursed be he that took away his holiness' wine! maledicat
Dominus? ['?' sic]
Et omnes Sancti! Amen!
[MEPHISTOPHILIS and FAUSTUS beat the FRIARS, and fling
fire-works among them; and so exeunt.]

[Enter CHORUS.]

CHORUS.
When Faustus had with pleasure ta'en the view
Of rarest things, and royal courts of kings,
He stay'd his course, and so returned home;
Where such as bear his absence but with grief,
I mean his friends and near'st companions,
Did gratulate his safety with kind words,

And in their conference of what befell,
Touching his journey through the world and air,
They put forth questions of astrology,
Which Faustus answer'd with such learned skill
As they admir'd and wonder'd at his wit.
Now is his fame spread forth in every land:
Amongst the rest the Emperor is one,
Carolus the Fifth, at whose palace now
Faustus is feasted 'mongst his noblemen.
What there he did, in trial of his art,
I leave untold; your eyes shall see['t] perform'd.
[Exit.]

[Enter ROBIN the Ostler, with a book in his hand.]

                    ROBIN.
O, this is admirable! here I ha' stolen one of Doctor
Faustus' conjuring-books, and, i'faith, I mean to search some
circles for my own use. Now will I make all the maidens in our
parish dance at my pleasure, stark naked, before me; and so
by that means I shall see more than e'er I felt or saw yet.

[Enter RALPH, calling ROBIN.]

                    RALPH.
Robin, prithee, come away; there's a gentleman tarries
to have his horse, and he would have his things rubbed and made
clean: he keeps such a chafing with my mistress about it; and
she has sent me to look thee out; prithee, come away.

                    ROBIN.
Keep out, keep out, or else you are blown up, you are
dismembered, Ralph: keep out, for I am about a roaring piece
of work.

                    RALPH.
Come, what doest thou with that same book? thou canst
not read?

                    ROBIN.
Yes, my master and mistress shall find that I can read,
he for his forehead, she for her private study; she's born to
bear with me, or else my art fails.

RALPH.

Why, Robin, what book is that?

ROBIN.

What book! why, the most intolerable book for conjuring
that e'er was invented by any brimstone devil.

RALPH.

Canst thou conjure with it?

ROBIN.

I can do all these things easily with it; first, I can
make thee drunk with ippocras at any tabern in Europe
for nothing; that's one of my conjuring works.

RALPH.

Our Master Parson says that's nothing.

ROBIN.

True, Ralph: and more, Ralph, if thou hast any mind to
Nan Spit, our kitchen-maid, then turn her and wind her to thy own
use, as often as thou wilt, and at midnight.

RALPH.

O, brave, Robin! shall I have Nan Spit, and to mine own
use? On that condition I'll feed thy devil with horse-bread as
long as he lives, of free cost.

ROBIN.

No more, sweet Ralph: let's go and make clean our boots,
which lie foul upon our hands, and then to our conjuring in the
devil's name.
[Exeunt.]

[Enter ROBIN and RALPH with a silver goblet.]

ROBIN.

Come, Ralph: did not I tell thee, we were for ever made
by this Doctor Faustus' book? ecce, signum! here's a simple
purchase for horse-keepers: our horses shall eat no hay as
long as this lasts.

RALPH.

But, Robin, here comes the Vintner.

ROBIN.

Hush! I'll gull him supernaturally.

[Enter VINTNER.]

Drawer, I hope all is paid; God be with you!—Come, Ralph.

VINTNER.

Soft, sir; a word with you. I must yet have a goblet paid
from you, ere you go.

ROBIN.

I a goblet, Ralph, I a goblet!—I scorn you; and you are
but a, &c. I a goblet! search me.

VINTNER.

I mean so, sir, with your favour.
[Searches ROBIN.]

ROBIN.

How say you now?

VINTNER.

I must say somewhat to your fellow.—You, sir!

RALPH.

Me, sir! me, sir! search your fill. [VINTNER searches him.]
Now, sir, you may be ashamed to burden honest men with a matter
of truth.

VINTNER.

Well, tone of you hath this goblet about you.

ROBIN.

You lie, drawer, 'tis afore me [Aside].—Sirrah you, I'll
teach you to impeach honest men;—stand by;—I'll scour you for
a goblet;—stand aside you had best, I charge you in the name of
Belzebub.—Look to the goblet, Ralph [Aside to RALPH].

VINTNER.

What mean you, sirrah?

ROBIN.

I'll tell you what I mean. [Reads from a book] Sanctobulorum
Periphrasticon—nay, I'll tickle you, Vintner.—Look to the goblet,
Ralph [Aside to RALPH].—[Reads] Polypragmos Belseborams framanto
pacostiphos tostu, Mephistophilis, &c.

[Enter MEPHISTOPHILIS, sets squibs at their backs, and then exit. They run
about.]

VINTNER.

O, *nomine Domini*! what meanest thou, Robin? thou hast no
goblet.

RALPH.

Peccatum peccatorum!—Here's thy goblet, good Vintner.
[Gives the goblet to VINTNER, who exit.]

ROBIN.

Misericordia pro nobis! what shall I do? Good devil, forgive
me now, and I'll never rob thy library more.

[Re-enter MEPHISTOPHILIS.]

MEPHIST.

Monarch of Hell, under whose black survey
Great potentates do kneel with awful fear,
Upon whose altars thousand souls do lie,
How am I vexed with these villains' charms?
From Constantinople am I hither come,
Only for pleasure of these damned slaves.

ROBIN.

How, from Constantinople! you have had a great journey:
will you take sixpence in your purse to pay for your supper, and
be gone?

MEPHIST.

Well, villains, for your presumption, I transform thee
into an ape, and thee into a dog; and so be gone!
[Exit.]

ROBIN.

How, into an ape! that's brave: I'll have fine sport with
the boys; I'll get nuts and apples enow.

RALPH.
And I must be a dog.

ROBIN.
I'faith, thy head will never be out of the pottage-pot.
[Exeunt.]

[Enter EMPEROR, FAUSTUS, and a KNIGHT, with ATTENDANTS.]

EMPEROR.
Master Doctor Faustus, I have heard strange report
of thy knowledge in the black art, how that none in my empire
nor in the whole world can compare with thee for the rare effects
of magic: they say thou hast a familiar spirit, by whom thou canst
accomplish what thou list. This, therefore, is my request, that
thou let me see some proof of thy skill, that mine eyes may be
witnesses to confirm what mine ears have heard reported: and here
I swear to thee, by the honour of mine imperial crown, that,
whatever thou doest, thou shalt be no ways prejudiced or endamaged.

KNIGHT.
I'faith, he looks much like a conjurer.
[Aside.]

FAUSTUS.
My gracious sovereign, though I must confess myself far
inferior to the report men have published, and nothing answerable
to the honour of your imperial majesty, yet, for that love and duty
binds me thereunto, I am content to do whatsoever your majesty
shall command me.

EMPEROR.
Then, Doctor Faustus, mark what I shall say.
As I was sometime solitary set
Within my closet, sundry thoughts arose
About the honour of mine ancestors,
How they had won by prowess such exploits,
Got such riches, subdu'd so many kingdoms,
As we that do succeed, or they that shall
Hereafter possess our throne, shall
(I fear me) ne'er attain to that degree
Of high renown and great authority:
Amongst which kings is Alexander the Great,

Chief spectacle of the world's pre-eminence,
The bright shining of whose glorious acts
Lightens the world with his reflecting beams,
As when I hear but motion made of him,
It grieves my soul I never saw the man:
If, therefore, thou, by cunning of thine art,
Canst raise this man from hollow vaults below,
Where lies entomb'd this famous conqueror,
And bring with him his beauteous paramour,
Both in their right shapes, gesture, and attire
They us'd to wear during their time of life,
Thou shalt both satisfy my just desire,
And give me cause to praise thee whilst I live.

FAUSTUS.

My gracious lord, I am ready to accomplish your request,
so far forth as by art and power of my spirit I am able to perform.

KNIGHT.

I'faith, that's just nothing at all.
[Aside.]

FAUSTUS.

But, if it like your grace, it is not in my ability
to present before your eyes the true substantial bodies of those
two deceased princes, which long since are consumed to dust.

KNIGHT.

Ay, marry, Master Doctor, now there's a sign of grace in
you, when you will confess the truth.
[Aside.]

FAUSTUS.

But such spirits as can lively resemble Alexander and
his paramour shall appear before your grace, in that manner that
they both lived in, in their most flourishing estate; which
I doubt not shall sufficiently content your imperial majesty.

EMPEROR.

Go to, Master Doctor; let me see them presently.

KNIGHT.

Do you hear, Master Doctor? you bring Alexander and his
paramour before the Emperor!

FAUSTUS.

How then, sir?

KNIGHT.

I'faith, that's as true as Diana turned me to a stag.

FAUSTUS.

No, sir; but, when Actaeon died, he left the horns for
you.—Mephistophilis, be gone.
[Exit MEPHISTOPHILIS.]

KNIGHT.

Nay, an you go to conjuring, I'll be gone.
[Exit.]

FAUSTUS.

I'll meet with you anon for interrupting me so.
—Here they are, my gracious lord.

[Re-enter MEPHISTOPHILIS with SPIRITS in the shapes of ALEXANDER and his
PARAMOUR.]

EMPEROR.

Master Doctor, I heard this lady, while she lived, had a
wart or mole in her neck: how shall I know whether it be so or no?

FAUSTUS.

Your highness may boldly go and see.

EMPEROR.

Sure, these are no spirits, but the true substantial
bodies of those two deceased princes.

Exeunt Spirits.

FAUSTUS.

Wilt please your highness now to send for the knight
that was so pleasant with me here of late?

EMPEROR.

One of you call him forth.
[Exit ATTENDANT.]

[Re-enter the KNIGHT with a pair of horns on his head.]

How now, sir knight! why, I had thought thou hadst been a bachelor,
but now I see thou hast a wife, that not only gives thee horns,
but makes thee wear them. Feel on thy head.

KNIGHT.
Thou damned wretch and execrable dog,
Bred in the concave of some monstrous rock,
How dar'st thou thus abuse a gentleman?
Villain, I say, undo what thou hast done!

FAUSTUS.
O, not so fast, sir! there's no haste: but, good, are
you remembered how you crossed me in my conference with the
Emperor? I think I have met with you for it.

EMPEROR.
Good Master Doctor, at my entreaty release him: he hath
done penance sufficient.

FAUSTUS.
My gracious lord, not so much for the injury he offered
me here in your presence, as to delight you with some mirth, hath
Faustus worthily requited this injurious knight; which being all
I desire, I am content to release him of his horns:—and,
sir knight, hereafter speak well of scholars.—Mephistophilis,
transform him straight. [MEPHISTOPHILIS removes the horns.]
—Now, my good lord, having done my duty, I humbly take my leave.

EMPEROR.
Farewell, Master Doctor: yet, ere you go,
Expect from me a bounteous reward.

[Exeunt EMPEROR, KNIGHT, and ATTENDANTS.]

FAUSTUS.
Now, Mephistophilis, the restless course
That time doth run with calm and silent foot,
Shortening my days and thread of vital life,
Calls for the payment of my latest years:
Therefore, sweet Mephistophilis, let us
Make haste to Wertenberg.

MEPHIST.
What, will you go on horse-back or on foot[?]

FAUSTUS.
Nay, till I'm past this fair and pleasant green,
I'll walk on foot.

[Enter a HORSE-COURSER.]

HORSE-COURSER.
I have been all this day seeking one Master Fustian:
mass, see where he is!—God save you, Master Doctor!

FAUSTUS.
What, horse-courser! you are well met.

HORSE-COURSER.
Do you hear, sir? I have brought you forty dollars
for your horse.

FAUSTUS.
I cannot sell him so: if thou likest him for fifty, take
him.

HORSE-COURSER.
Alas, sir, I have no more!—I pray you, speak for
me.

MEPHIST.
I pray you, let him have him: he is an honest fellow,
and he has a great charge, neither wife nor child.

FAUSTUS.
Well, come, give me your money [HORSE-COURSER gives
FAUSTUS the money]: my boy will deliver him to you. But I must
tell you one thing before you have him; ride him not into the
water, at any hand.

HORSE-COURSER.
Why, sir, will he not drink of all waters?

FAUSTUS.

O, yes, he will drink of all waters; but ride him not
into the water: ride him over hedge or ditch, or where thou wilt,
but not into the water.

HORSE-COURSER.

Well, sir.—Now am I made man for ever: I'll not
leave my horse for forty: if he had but the quality of
hey-ding-ding, hey-ding-ding, I'd make a brave living on him:
he has a buttock as slick as an eel [Aside].—Well, God b'wi'ye,
sir: your boy will deliver him me: but, hark you, sir; if my horse
be sick or ill at ease, if I bring his water to you, you'll tell
me what it is?

FAUSTUS.

Away, you villain! what, dost think I am a horse-doctor?
[Exit HORSE-COURSER.]
What art thou, Faustus, but a man condemn'd to die?
Thy fatal time doth draw to final end;
Despair doth drive distrust into my thoughts:
Confound these passions with a quiet sleep:
Tush, Christ did call the thief upon the Cross;
Then rest thee, Faustus, quiet in conceit.
[Sleeps in his chair.]

[Re-enter HORSE-COURSER, all wet, crying.]

HORSE-COURSER.

Alas, alas! Doctor Fustian, quoth a mass, Doctor
Lopus was never such a doctor: has given me a purgation, has
purged me of forty dollars; I shall never see them more. But yet,
like an ass as I was, I would not be ruled by him, for he bade me
I should ride him into no water: now I, thinking my horse had had
some rare quality that he would not have had me know of, I,
like a venturous youth, rid him into the deep pond at the town's
end. I was no sooner in the middle of the pond, but my horse
vanished away, and I sat upon a bottle of hay, never so near
drowning in my life. But I'll seek out my doctor, and have my
forty dollars again, or I'll make it the dearest horse!—O,
yonder is his snipper-snapper.—Do you hear? you, hey-pass,
where's your master?

MEPHIST.

Why, sir, what would you? you cannot speak with him.

HORSE-COURSER.

But I will speak with him.

MEPHIST.

Why, he's fast asleep: come some other time.

HORSE-COURSER.

I'll speak with him now, or I'll break his
glass-windows about his ears.

MEPHIST.

I tell thee, he has not slept this eight nights.

HORSE-COURSER.

An he have not slept this eight weeks, I'll
speak with him.

MEPHIST.

See, where he is, fast asleep.

HORSE-COURSER.

Ay, this is he.—God save you, Master Doctor,
Master Doctor, Master Doctor Fustian! forty dollars, forty dollars
for a bottle of hay!

MEPHIST.

Why, thou seest he hears thee not.

HORSE-COURSER.

So-ho, ho! so-ho, ho! [Hollows in his ear.] No,
will you not wake? I'll make you wake ere I go. [Pulls FAUSTUS
by the leg, and pulls it away.] Alas, I am undone! what shall
I do?

FAUSTUS.

O, my leg, my leg!—Help, Mephistophilis! call the
officers.—My leg, my leg!

MEPHIST.

Come, villain, to the constable.

HORSE-COURSER.

O Lord, sir, let me go, and I'll give you forty
dollars more!

MEPHIST.

Where be they?

HORSE-COURSER.

I have none about me: come to my ostry,
and I'll give them you.

MEPHIST.

Be gone quickly.
[HORSE-COURSER runs away.]

FAUSTUS.

What, is he gone? farewell he! Faustus has his leg again,
and the Horse-courser, I take it, a bottle of hay for his labour:
well, this trick shall cost him forty dollars more.

Enter WAGNER.

How now, Wagner! what's the news with thee?

WAGNER.

Sir, the Duke of Vanholt doth earnestly entreat your
company.

FAUSTUS.

The Duke of Vanholt! an honourable gentleman, to whom
I must be no niggard of my cunning.—Come, Mephistophilis,
let's away to him.
[Exeunt.]

[Enter the DUKE OF VANHOLT, the DUCHESS, and FAUSTUS.]

DUKE.

Believe me, Master Doctor, this merriment hath much pleased
me.

FAUSTUS.

My gracious lord, I am glad it contents you so well.
—But it may be, madam, you take no delight in this. I have heard

that great-bellied women do long for some dainties or other: what
is it, madam? tell me, and you shall have it.

DUCHESS.
Thanks, good Master Doctor: and, for I see your courteous
intent to pleasure me, I will not hide from you the thing my heart
desires; and, were it now summer, as it is January and the dead
time of the winter, I would desire no better meat than a dish
of ripe grapes.

FAUSTUS.
Alas, madam, that's nothing!—Mephistophilis, be gone.
[Exit MEPHISTOPHILIS.] Were it a greater thing than this, so it
would content you, you should have it.

[Re-enter MEPHISTOPHILIS with grapes.]

Here they be, madam: wilt please you taste on them?

DUKE.
Believe me, Master Doctor, this makes me wonder above the
rest, that being in the dead time of winter and in the month of
January, how you should come by these grapes.

FAUSTUS.
If it like your grace, the year is divided into two
circles over the whole world, that, when it is here winter with
us, in the contrary circle it is summer with them, as in India,
Saba, and farther countries in the east; and by means of a
swift spirit that I have, I had them brought hither, as you see.
—How do you like them, madam? be they good?

DUCHESS.
Believe me, Master Doctor, they be the best grapes that
e'er I tasted in my life before.

FAUSTUS.
I am glad they content you so, madam.

DUKE.
Come, madam, let us in, where you must well reward this
learned man for the great kindness he hath shewed to you.

DUCHESS.

And so I will, my lord; and, whilst I live, rest
beholding for this courtesy.

FAUSTUS.

I humbly thank your grace.

DUKE.

Come, Master Doctor, follow us, and receive your reward.
[Exeunt.]

[Enter WAGNER.]

WAGNER.

I think my master means to die shortly,
For he hath given to me all his goods:
And yet, methinks, if that death were near,
He would not banquet, and carouse, and swill
Amongst the students, as even now he doth,
Who are at supper with such belly-cheer
As Wagner ne'er beheld in all his life.
See, where they come! belike the feast is ended.
[Exit.]

[Enter FAUSTUS with two or three SCHOLARS, and MEPHISTOPHILIS.]

FIRST SCHOLAR.

Master Doctor Faustus, since our conference about
fair ladies, which was the beautifulest in all the world, we have
determined with ourselves that Helen of Greece was the admirablest
lady that ever lived: therefore, Master Doctor, if you will do us
that favour, as to let us see that peerless dame of Greece, whom
all the world admires for majesty, we should think ourselves much
beholding unto you.

FAUSTUS.

Gentlemen,
For that I know your friendship is unfeign'd,
And Faustus' custom is not to deny
The just requests of those that wish him well,
You shall behold that peerless dame of Greece,
No otherways for pomp and majesty
Than when Sir Paris cross'd the seas with her,

And brought the spoils to rich Dardania.
Be silent, then, for danger is in words.
[Music sounds, and HELEN passeth over the stage.]

SECOND SCHOLAR.
Too simple is my wit to tell her praise,
Whom all the world admires for majesty.

THIRD SCHOLAR.
No marvel though the angry Greeks pursu'd
With ten years' war the rape of such a queen,
Whose heavenly beauty passeth all compare.

FIRST SCHOLAR.
Since we have seen the pride of Nature's works,
And only paragon of excellence,
Let us depart; and for this glorious deed
Happy and blest be Faustus evermore!

FAUSTUS.
Gentlemen, farewell: the same I wish to you.

[Exeunt SCHOLARS.]
[Enter an OLD MAN.]

OLD MAN.
Ah, Doctor Faustus, that I might prevail
To guide thy steps unto the way of life,
By which sweet path thou mayst attain the goal
That shall conduct thee to celestial rest!
Break heart, drop blood, and mingle it with tears,
Tears falling from repentant heaviness
Of thy most vile and loathsome filthiness,
The stench whereof corrupts the inward soul
With such flagitious crimes of heinous sin
As no commiseration may expel,
But mercy, Faustus, of thy Saviour sweet,
Whose blood alone must wash away thy guilt.

FAUSTUS.
Where art thou, Faustus? wretch, what hast thou done?
Damn'd art thou, Faustus, damn'd; despair and die!
Hell calls for right, and with a roaring voice

Says, "Faustus, come; thine hour is almost come;"
And Faustus now will come to do thee right.
[MEPHISTOPHILIS gives him a dagger.]

OLD MAN.

Ah, stay, good Faustus, stay thy desperate steps!
I see an angel hovers o'er thy head,
And, with a vial full of precious grace,
Offers to pour the same into thy soul:
Then call for mercy, and avoid despair.

FAUSTUS.

Ah, my sweet friend, I feel
Thy words to comfort my distressed soul!
Leave me a while to ponder on my sins.

OLD MAN.

I go, sweet Faustus; but with heavy cheer,
Fearing the ruin of thy hopeless soul.
[Exit.]

FAUSTUS.

Accursed Faustus, where is mercy now?
I do repent; and yet I do despair:
Hell strives with grace for conquest in my breast:
What shall I do to shun the snares of death?

MEPHIST.

Thou traitor, Faustus, I arrest thy soul
For disobedience to my sovereign lord:
Revolt, or I'll in piece-meal tear thy flesh.

FAUSTUS.

Sweet Mephistophilis, entreat thy lord
To pardon my unjust presumption,
And with my blood again I will confirm
My former vow I made to Lucifer.

MEPHIST.

Do it, then, quickly, with unfeigned heart,
Lest greater danger do attend thy drift.

FAUSTUS.

Torment, sweet friend, that base and crooked age,
That durst dissuade me from thy Lucifer,
With greatest torments that our hell affords.

MEPHIST.

His faith is great; I cannot touch his soul;
But what I may afflict his body with
I will attempt, which is but little worth.

FAUSTUS.

One thing, good servant, let me crave of thee,
To glut the longing of my heart's desire,—
That I might have unto my paramour
That heavenly Helen which I saw of late,
Whose sweet embracings may extinguish clean
Those thoughts that do dissuade me from my vow,
And keep mine oath I made to Lucifer.

MEPHIST.

Faustus, this, or what else thou shalt desire,
Shall be perform'd in twinkling of an eye.

Re-enter HELEN.

FAUSTUS.

Was this the face that launch'd a thousand ships,
And burnt the topless towers of Ilium—
Sweet Helen, make me immortal with a kiss.—
[Kisses her.]
Her lips suck forth my soul: see, where it flies!—
Come, Helen, come, give me my soul again.
Here will I dwell, for heaven is in these lips,
And all is dross that is not Helena.
I will be Paris, and for love of thee,
Instead of Troy, shall Wertenberg be sack'd;
And I will combat with weak Menelaus,
And wear thy colours on my plumed crest;
Yea, I will wound Achilles in the heel,
And then return to Helen for a kiss.
O, thou art fairer than the evening air
Clad in the beauty of a thousand stars;
Brighter art thou than flaming Jupiter

When he appear'd to hapless Semele;
More lovely than the monarch of the sky
In wanton Arethusa's azur'd arms;
And none but thou shalt be my paramour!
[Exeunt.]

[Enter the OLD MAN.]

OLD MAN.

Accursed Faustus, miserable man,
That from thy soul exclud'st the grace of heaven,
And fly'st the throne of his tribunal-seat!

[Enter DEVILS.]

Satan begins to sift me with his pride:
As in this furnace God shall try my faith,
My faith, vile hell, shall triumph over thee.
Ambitious fiends, see how the heavens smile
At your repulse, and laugh your state to scorn!
Hence, hell! for hence I fly unto my God.
[Exeunt,—on one side, DEVILS, on the other, OLD MAN.]

[Enter FAUSTUS, with SCHOLARS.]

FAUSTUS.

Ah, gentlemen!

FIRST SCHOLAR.

What ails Faustus?

FAUSTUS.

Ah, my sweet chamber-fellow, had I lived with thee,
then had I lived still! but now I die eternally. Look, comes
he not? comes he not?

SECOND SCHOLAR.

What means Faustus?

THIRD SCHOLAR.

Belike he is grown into some sickness by being
over-solitary.

FIRST SCHOLAR.

If it be so, we'll have physicians to cure him.
—'Tis but a surfeit; never fear, man.

FAUSTUS.

A surfeit of deadly sin, that hath damned both body
and soul.

SECOND SCHOLAR.

Yet, Faustus, look up to heaven; remember God's
mercies are infinite.

FAUSTUS.

But Faustus' offence can ne'er be pardoned: the serpent
that tempted Eve may be saved, but not Faustus. Ah, gentlemen,
hear me with patience, and tremble not at my speeches! Though
my heart pants and quivers to remember that I have been a student
here these thirty years, O, would I had never seen Wertenberg,
never read book! and what wonders I have done, all Germany can
witness, yea, all the world; for which Faustus hath lost both
Germany and the world, yea, heaven itself, heaven, the seat of
God, the throne of the blessed, the kingdom of joy; and must
remain in hell for ever, hell, ah, hell, for ever! Sweet friends,
what shall become of Faustus, being in hell for ever?

THIRD SCHOLAR.

Yet, Faustus, call on God.

FAUSTUS.

On God, whom Faustus hath abjured! on God, whom Faustus
hath blasphemed! Ah, my God, I would weep! but the devil draws in
my tears. Gush forth blood, instead of tears! yea, life and soul!
O, he stays my tongue! I would lift up my hands; but see, they
hold them, they hold them!

ALL.

Who, Faustus?

FAUSTUS.

Lucifer and Mephistophilis. Ah, gentlemen, I gave them
my soul for my cunning!

ALL.

God forbid!

FAUSTUS.

God forbade it, indeed; but Faustus hath done it: for
vain pleasure of twenty-four years hath Faustus lost eternal joy
and felicity. I writ them a bill with mine own blood: the date
is expired; the time will come, and he will fetch me.

FIRST SCHOLAR.

Why did not Faustus tell us of this before,
that divines might have prayed for thee?

FAUSTUS.

Oft have I thought to have done so; but the devil
threatened to tear me in pieces, if I named God, to fetch both
body and soul, if I once gave ear to divinity: and now 'tis too
late. Gentlemen, away, lest you perish with me.

SECOND SCHOLAR.

O, what shall we do to save Faustus?

FAUSTUS.

Talk not of me, but save yourselves, and depart.

THIRD SCHOLAR.

God will strengthen me; I will stay with Faustus.

FIRST SCHOLAR.

Tempt not God, sweet friend; but let us into the
next room, and there pray for him.

FAUSTUS.

Ay, pray for me, pray for me; and what noise soever
ye hear, come not unto me, for nothing can rescue me.

SECOND SCHOLAR.

Pray thou, and we will pray that God may have
mercy upon thee.

FAUSTUS.

Gentlemen, farewell: if I live till morning, I'll visit
you; if not, Faustus is gone to hell.

ALL.

Faustus, farewell.
[Exeunt SCHOLARS.—The clock strikes eleven.]

FAUSTUS.

Ah, Faustus,
Now hast thou but one bare hour to live,
And then thou must be damn'd perpetually!
Stand still, you ever-moving spheres of heaven,
That time may cease, and midnight never come;
Fair Nature's eye, rise, rise again, and make
Perpetual day; or let this hour be but
A year, a month, a week, a natural day,
That Faustus may repent and save his soul!
O lente, lente currite, noctis equi!
The stars move still, time runs, the clock will strike,
The devil will come, and Faustus must be damn'd.
O, I'll leap up to my God!—Who pulls me down?—
See, see, where Christ's blood streams in the firmament!
One drop would save my soul, half a drop: ah, my Christ!—
Ah, rend not my heart for naming of my Christ!
Yet will I call on him: O, spare me, Lucifer!—
Where is it now? 'tis gone: and see, where God
Stretcheth out his arm, and bends his ireful brows!
Mountains and hills, come, come, and fall on me,
And hide me from the heavy wrath of God!
No, no!
Then will I headlong run into the earth:
Earth, gape! O, no, it will not harbour me!
You stars that reign'd at my nativity,
Whose influence hath allotted death and hell,
Now draw up Faustus, like a foggy mist.
Into the entrails of yon labouring cloud[s],
That, when you vomit forth into the air,
My limbs may issue from your smoky mouths,
So that my soul may but ascend to heaven!
[The clock strikes the half-hour.]
Ah, half the hour is past! 'twill all be past anon
O God,
If thou wilt not have mercy on my soul,
Yet for Christ's sake, whose blood hath ransom'd me,
Impose some end to my incessant pain;
Let Faustus live in hell a thousand years,

A hundred thousand, and at last be sav'd!
O, no end is limited to damned souls!
Why wert thou not a creature wanting soul?
Or why is this immortal that thou hast?
Ah, Pythagoras' metempsychosis, were that true,
This soul should fly from me, and I be chang'd
Unto some brutish beast! all beasts are happy,
For, when they die,
Their souls are soon dissolv'd in elements;
But mine must live still to be plagu'd in hell.
Curs'd be the parents that engender'd me!
No, Faustus, curse thyself, curse Lucifer
That hath depriv'd thee of the joys of heaven.
[The clock strikes twelve.]
O, it strikes, it strikes! Now, body, turn to air,
Or Lucifer will bear thee quick to hell!
[Thunder and lightning.]
O soul, be chang'd into little water-drops,
And fall into the ocean, ne'er be found!

[Enter DEVILS.]

My God, my god, look not so fierce on me!
Adders and serpents, let me breathe a while!
Ugly hell, gape not! come not, Lucifer!
I'll burn my books!—Ah, Mephistophilis!

[Exeunt DEVILS with FAUSTUS.]
[Enter CHORUS.]

CHORUS.
Cut is the branch that might have grown full straight,
And burned is Apollo's laurel-bough,
That sometime grew within this learned man.
Faustus is gone: regard his hellish fall,
Whose fiendful fortune may exhort the wise,
Only to wonder at unlawful things,
Whose deepness doth entice such forward wits
To practice more than heavenly power permits.
[Exit.]

2.12.2 Reading and Review Questions

1. What is Faustus's true ambition? Why is it that he turns to magic and to Mephistophilis, against whom he has been particularly warned? What relationship, if any, does he seem to have with the Christian God? What is his attitude towards the Christian God? How does Faustus's character compare with the Redcrosse Knight's, for example?

2. How do Faustus's ambitions for his magic compare with what he achieves with his magic? If you see a discrepancy between the two, then what accounts for this discrepancy, do you think?

3. Why do you think that Faustus has several opportunities to repent? Why does he reaffirm his pact with Lucifer? What keeps him from repenting, even to the very end of the play?

4. The Old Man appears near the end of Faustus's term of contract. Who is the Old Man, do you think? Why does he appear so suddenly at this point in the play? What purpose, if any, does he serve? What might he represent?

5. How, if at all, does the character of Faustus and his actions reflect the religious conflicts and concerns that occurred during Marlowe's lifetime?

2.13 WILLIAM SHAKESPEARE

(1564-1616)

Shakespeare was born on April 23, and he died on April 23. He was born in Stratford-upon-Avon, and he died in Stratford-upon-Avon. These facts frame many additional facts and many conjectures. He probably received an education in Latin studies at the town's grammar school, as his father was a municipal officer (mayor and justice of the peace) so could send his son to the school for free. At the age of eighteen, Shakespeare married Anne Hathaway (1556-1623), a woman who was eight years his senior and who lived in nearby Shottery. Their child Susanna (1583-1649) was born five months later. Two years after that, their twins Hamnet and Judith were born, with Hamnet dying at the age of eleven and Judith surviving to the age of seventy-seven. Anne outlived

Image 2.15 | William Shakespeare
Artist | John Taylor
Source | Wikimedia Commons
License | Public Domain

Shakespeare by seven years, receiving in his will his second-best bed and being buried next to him in the Church of the Holy Trinity, Stratford-upon-Avon.

Seven years after the birth of the twins, Robert Greene (1558-1592) writes of Shakespeare as an actor and playwright in London, describing him in *Greenes Groatsworth of Wit* (1592) as "an upstart crow, beautified with our feathers, that with his Tiger's heart wrapt in a player's hide, supposes he is as well able to bombast out a blank verse as the best of you: and being an absolute Johannes Factotum, is in his own conceit the only Shake-scene in a country." Green was a member of the "University Wits," a group of Cambridge and Oxford young men—including Christopher Marlowe—that sought to bring their classical learning to the stage. Although Shakespeare attended neither Cambridge nor Oxford, his early plays echo Marlowe's blank verse; indeed, Shakespeare's *Henry VI Parts I, II,* and *III*, according to the Oxford University Press, may have been co-written by Marlowe, so Marlowe's influence may have been direct. Shakespeare also demonstrated classical learning on the stage with his Plautean *Comedy of Errors* (performed in 1594) and his Senecan tragedy *Titus Andronicus* (performed in 1594).

He dedicated two classically-themed poems to his patron Henry Wriothesley, third earl of Southampton. Both *Venus and Adonis* (1593) and *The Rape of Lucrece* (1594) were published as quarto pamphlets, with *Venus and Adonis* running through eighteen editions and *The Rape of Lucrece*, eight editions by 1655. In 1594, Shakespeare was a partner in the Lord Chamberlain's Men, a theater company from which he derived profits for such plays as *Romeo and Juliet* (performed around 1595-1596), *The Merchant of Venice* (performed around 15996-97), *Henry IV Parts I* and *II* (performed around 1597-1598), and *Twelfth Night: Or, What You Will* (performed around 1600-1602).

From 1595, he also probably worked on his sonnet sequence that was not published until 1609. These sonnets employ numerous conventions, such as the idealized and aloof woman. He also used the already-extant rhyme scheme of ABAB CDCD EFEF GG. Yet he used it so deftly and naturally that the form is now known as the Shakespearean sonnet. His sonnets reflect on the power of poetry and the matters of poetic art, such as romantic love, in language that compels belief in their truth and authenticity—even though their possibly autobiographical elements have not been proven. For example, they trace a friendship with a beautiful young man and a romance with a dark lady. The identity of either of these figures is unknown, though early conjectures identify the young man as Shakespeare's patron Wriothesley and the dark lady as a sonnet convention along the lines of Petrarch's Laura. When published, the sequence was dedicated to an unknown Mr. W. H., described as the sonnets' only begetter.

In 1599, Shakespeare's company built the Globe Theater, with Shakespeare being one of six shareholders; the others included the great actor Richard Burbage (1567-1619) and John Heminges (1566-1630) who, with Henry Condell (1576-1627), edited the *First Folio* (1623) collection of Shakespeare's plays. In 1613, during a performance of Shakespeare's Henry VIII, the Globe was destroyed by fire but was

Image 2.16 | Cordelia and King Lear
Artist | William Shakespeare
Source | Wikimedia Commons
License | Public Domain

rebuilt the next year. Upon the accession of James I (1603), the Lord Chamberlain's Men was renamed the King's Men, and Shakespeare began writing his greatest tragedies, including *Othello* (performed around 1604), *King Lear* (performed around 1605-1606), and *Macbeth* (performed around 1606). With his profits, Shakespeare built New Place, the second largest house in Stratford-upon-Avon.

In 1606, the King's Men acquired a private theater, Blackfriars, along with its playwrights Francis Beaumont (1584-1616) and John Fletcher (1579-1625), whose style may have influenced Shakespeare's final romances, including *Cymbeline* (performed around 1609-1610), *The Winter's Tale* (performed around 1610-1611), and *The Tempest* (performed in 1611). Shakespeare collaborated with Fletcher on *Henry VIII* (performed around 1612-1613), *The Two Noble Kinsmen* (performed around 1612-1613), and *Cardenio* (performed around 1612-1613). In 1613, Shakespeare retired to Stratford-upon-Avon. He died in 1616, a little over two months after his daughter Judith married Thomas Quiney (1589-1663).

Although these facts seem sparse, they are more in number than facts known about other playwrights of Shakespeare's time. Yet, they still offer too little knowledge to those around the world who have loved Shakespeare's works over the course of four hundred years—a man whose invented words enrich the English language; whose characters fill imaginations; and whose range of style, sheer beauty of expression, and depth and breadth of insight authenticate the most profound of human emotions.

The interpretation of Shakespeare over time provides a mirror to the history of interpretation itself. In 1693, Thomas Rymer attacked *Othello* as not a tragedy but a farce due to its offering, in his opinion, neither meaning nor moral. In 1699, James Drake similarly demonstrated the expectation for moral lessons in art when he admired the poetic justice of *Hamlet* (first performed around 1609). The eighteenth century evinced interest in the particularities of Shakespeare's characters; for example, in 1777, Maurice Morgann wrote an essay on the character of Falstaff describing him as not a coward but a sensible man.

Shakespeare's *King Lear* suggests a way to interpret or gain meaning from this play (and perhaps his others). This extraordinarily dynamic work, with wheels within wheels of meaning, depicts extreme betrayal, cruelty, and suffering of such intensity that an audience may wish to turn away from it. The character Edgar serves as a type of audience, as almost a pure observer of a painful scene between the mad King Lear and the blinded Duke of Gloucester, Edgar's own father. But Edgar will not turn away, saying in an aside—presumably to the actual audience—that he would not take this scene from report. And he offers a possible explanation for the purpose and effect of art when he describes himself as one who has gained compassion through suffering, as one who "by the art of known and feeling sorrows,/ Am pregnant to good pity" (220-21).

2.13.1 Selected Sonnets

(1598)

2

When forty winters shall besiege thy brow,
And dig deep trenches in thy beauty's field,
Thy youth's proud livery, so gaz'd on now,
Will be a tatter'd weed, of small worth held;
Then being ask'd where all thy beauty lies,
Where all the treasure of thy lusty days,
To say, within thine own deep-sunken eyes,
Were an all-eating shame and thriftless praise.
How much more praise deserv'd thy beauty's use,
If thou couldst answer 'This fair child of mine
Shall sum my count, and make my old excuse,'
Proving his beauty by succession thine!
    This were to be new made when thou art old,
    And see thy blood warm when thou feel'st it cold.

12

When I do count the clock that tells the time,
And see the brave day sunk in hideous night;
When I behold the violet past prime,
And sable curls, all silvered o'er with white;
When lofty trees I see barren of leaves,
Which erst from heat did canopy the herd,
And summer's green all girded up in sheaves,
Borne on the bier with white and bristly beard,
Then of thy beauty do I question make,
That thou among the wastes of time must go,
Since sweets and beauties do themselves forsake
And die as fast as they see others grow;
    And nothing 'gainst Time's scythe can make defence
    Save breed, to brave him when he takes thee hence

13

O! that you were your self; but, love you are
No longer yours, than you your self here live:
Against this coming end you should prepare,
And your sweet semblance to some other give:
So should that beauty which you hold in lease
Find no determination; then you were
Yourself again, after yourself's decease,
When your sweet issue your sweet form should bear.
Who lets so fair a house fall to decay,
Which husbandry in honour might uphold,
Against the stormy gusts of winter's day
And barren rage of death's eternal cold?
　　O! none but unthrifts. Dear my love, you know,
　　You had a father: let your son say so.

15

When I consider every thing that grows
Holds in perfection but a little moment,
That this huge stage presenteth nought but shows
Whereon the stars in secret influence comment;
When I perceive that men as plants increase,
Cheered and checked even by the self-same sky,
Vaunt in their youthful sap, at height decrease,
And wear their brave state out of memory;
Then the conceit of this inconstant stay
Sets you most rich in youth before my sight,
Where wasteful Time debateth with decay
To change your day of youth to sullied night,
　　And all in war with Time for love of you,
　　As he takes from you, I engraft you new.

18

Shall I compare thee to a summer's day?
Thou art more lovely and more temperate:
Rough winds do shake the darling buds of May,
And summer's lease hath all too short a date:
Sometime too hot the eye of heaven shines,
And often is his gold complexion dimm'd,
And every fair from fair sometime declines,
By chance, or nature's changing course untrimm'd:
But thy eternal summer shall not fade,

Nor lose possession of that fair thou ow'st,
Nor shall death brag thou wander'st in his shade,
When in eternal lines to time thou grow'st,
    So long as men can breathe, or eyes can see,
    So long lives this, and this gives life to thee.

22

My glass shall not persuade me I am old,
So long as youth and thou are of one date;
But when in thee time's furrows I behold,
Then look I death my days should expiate.
For all that beauty that doth cover thee,
Is but the seemly raiment of my heart,
Which in thy breast doth live, as thine in me:
How can I then be elder than thou art?
O! therefore love, be of thyself so wary
As I, not for myself, but for thee will;
Bearing thy heart, which I will keep so chary
As tender nurse her babe from faring ill.
    Presume not on th' heart when mine is slain,
    Thou gav'st me thine not to give back again.

23

As an unperfect actor on the stage,
Who with his fear is put beside his part,
Or some fierce thing replete with too much rage,
Whose strength's abundance weakens his own heart;
So I, for fear of trust, forget to say
The perfect ceremony of love's rite,
And in mine own love's strength seem to decay,
O'ercharg'd with burthen of mine own love's might.
O! let my looks be then the eloquence
And dumb presagers of my speaking breast,
Who plead for love, and look for recompense,
More than that tongue that more hath more express'd.
    O! learn to read what silent love hath writ:
    To hear with eyes belongs to love's fine wit.

29

When in disgrace with fortune and men's eyes
I all alone beweep my outcast state,
And trouble deaf heaven with my bootless cries,

And look upon myself, and curse my fate,
Wishing me like to one more rich in hope,
Featur'd like him, like him with friends possess'd,
Desiring this man's art, and that man's scope,
With what I most enjoy contented least;
Yet in these thoughts my self almost despising,
Haply I think on thee,—and then my state,
Like to the lark at break of day arising
From sullen earth, sings hymns at heaven's gate;
    For thy sweet love remember'd such wealth brings
    That then I scorn to change my state with kings.

40

Take all my loves, my love, yea take them all;
What hast thou then more than thou hadst before?
No love, my love, that thou mayst true love call;
All mine was thine, before thou hadst this more.
Then if for my love thou my love receivest,
I cannot blame thee, for my love thou usest;
But yet be blam'd, if thou thyself deceivest
By wilful taste of what thyself refusest.
I do forgive thy robbery, gentle thief,
Although thou steal thee all my poverty;
And yet, love knows, it is a greater grief
To bear love's wrong, than hate's known injury.
    Lascivious grace, in whom all ill well shows,
    Kill me with spites, yet we must not be foes.

55

Not marble, nor the gilded monuments
Of princes, shall outlive this powerful rhyme;
But you shall shine more bright in these contents
Than unswept stone, besmear'd with sluttish time.
When wasteful war shall statues overturn,
And broils root out the work of masonry,
Nor Mars his sword, nor war's quick fire shall burn
The living record of your memory.
'Gainst death, and all-oblivious enmity
Shall you pace forth; your praise shall still find room
Even in the eyes of all posterity
That wear this world out to the ending doom.
    So, till the judgment that yourself arise,
    You live in this, and dwell in lovers' eyes.

71

No longer mourn for me when I am dead
Than you shall hear the surly sullen bell
Give warning to the world that I am fled
From this vile world with vilest worms to dwell:
Nay, if you read this line, remember not
The hand that writ it, for I love you so,
That I in your sweet thoughts would be forgot,
If thinking on me then should make you woe.
O! if,—I say you look upon this verse,
When I perhaps compounded am with clay,
Do not so much as my poor name rehearse;
But let your love even with my life decay;
    Lest the wise world should look into your moan,
    And mock you with me after I am gone.

78

So oft have I invoked thee for my Muse,
And found such fair assistance in my verse
As every alien pen hath got my use
And under thee their poesy disperse.
Thine eyes, that taught the dumb on high to sing
And heavy ignorance aloft to fly,
Have added feathers to the learned's wing
And given grace a double majesty.
Yet be most proud of that which I compile,
Whose influence is thine, and born of thee:
In others' works thou dost but mend the style,
And arts with thy sweet graces graced be;
    But thou art all my art, and dost advance
    As high as learning, my rude ignorance.

87

Farewell! thou art too dear for my possessing,
And like enough thou know'st thy estimate,
The charter of thy worth gives thee releasing:
My bonds in thee are all determinate.
For how do I hold thee but by thy granting,
And for that riches where is my deserving?
The cause of this fair gift in me is wanting,
And so my patent back again is swerving.
Thy self thou gav'st, thy own worth then not knowing,

Or me to whom thou gav'st it, else mistaking,
So thy great gift, upon misprision growing,
Comes home again, on better judgement making.
    Thus have I had thee as a dream doth flatter,
    In sleep a King, but waking no such matter.

96

Some say thy fault is youth, some wantonness;
Some say thy grace is youth and gentle sport;
Both grace and faults are lov'd of more and less:
Thou mak'st faults graces that to thee resort.
As on the finger of a throned queen
The basest jewel will be well esteem'd,
So are those errors that in thee are seen
To truths translated, and for true things deem'd.
How many lambs might the stern wolf betray,
If like a lamb he could his looks translate!
How many gazers mightst thou lead away,
If thou wouldst use the strength of all thy state!
    But do not so; I love thee in such sort,
    As, thou being mine, mine is thy good report.

106

When in the chronicle of wasted time
I see descriptions of the fairest wights,
And beauty making beautiful old rime,
In praise of ladies dead and lovely knights,
Then, in the blazon of sweet beauty's best,
Of hand, of foot, of lip, of eye, of brow,
I see their antique pen would have express'd
Even such a beauty as you master now.
So all their praises are but prophecies
Of this our time, all you prefiguring;
And for they looked but with divining eyes,
They had not skill enough your worth to sing:
    For we, which now behold these present days,
    Have eyes to wonder, but lack tongues to praise.

127

In the old age black was not counted fair,
Or if it were, it bore not beauty's name;
But now is black beauty's successive heir,

And beauty slander'd with a bastard shame:
For since each hand hath put on Nature's power,
Fairing the foul with Art's false borrowed face,
Sweet beauty hath no name, no holy bower,
But is profan'd, if not lives in disgrace.
Therefore my mistress' eyes are raven black,
Her eyes so suited, and they mourners seem
At such who, not born fair, no beauty lack,
Sland'ring creation with a false esteem:
    Yet so they mourn becoming of their woe,
    That every tongue says beauty should look so.

130

My mistress' eyes are nothing like the sun;
Coral is far more red, than her lips red:
If snow be white, why then her breasts are dun;
If hairs be wires, black wires grow on her head.
I have seen roses damask'd, red and white,
But no such roses see I in her cheeks;
And in some perfumes is there more delight
Than in the breath that from my mistress reeks.
I love to hear her speak, yet well I know
That music hath a far more pleasing sound:
I grant I never saw a goddess go,—
My mistress, when she walks, treads on the ground:
    And yet by heaven, I think my love as rare,
    As any she belied with false compare.

135

Whoever hath her wish, thou hast thy 'Will,'
And 'Will' to boot, and 'Will' in over-plus;
More than enough am I that vex'd thee still,
To thy sweet will making addition thus.
Wilt thou, whose will is large and spacious,
Not once vouchsafe to hide my will in thine?
Shall will in others seem right gracious,
And in my will no fair acceptance shine?
The sea, all water, yet receives rain still,
And in abundance addeth to his store;
So thou, being rich in 'Will,' add to thy 'Will'
One will of mine, to make thy large will more.
    Let no unkind 'No' fair beseechers kill;
    Think all but one, and me in that one 'Will.'

138

When my love swears that she is made of truth,
I do believe her though I know she lies,
That she might think me some untutor'd youth,
Unlearned in the world's false subtleties.
Thus vainly thinking that she thinks me young,
Although she knows my days are past the best,
Simply I credit her false-speaking tongue;
On both sides thus is simple truth suppressed.
But wherefore says she not she is unjust?
And wherefore say not I that I am old?
O! love's best habit is in seeming trust,
And age in love loves not to have years told:
    Therefore I lie with her, and she with me,
    And in our faults by lies we flatter'd be.

144

Two loves I have of comfort and despair,
Which like two spirits do suggest me still:
The better angel is a man right fair,
The worser spirit a woman colour'd ill.
To win me soon to hell, my female evil,
Tempteth my better angel from my side,
And would corrupt my saint to be a devil,
Wooing his purity with her foul pride.
And whether that my angel be turn'd fiend,
Suspect I may, yet not directly tell;
But being both from me, both to each friend,
I guess one angel in another's hell:
    Yet this shall I ne'er know, but live in doubt,
    Till my bad angel fire my good one out.

2.13.2 *Much Ado About Nothing*

Act I

Scene I. Before LEONATO'S House.
[Enter LEONATO, HERO, BEATRICE and others, with a Messenger.]

LEONATO.
I learn in this letter that Don Pedro of Arragon comes this night to Messina.

MESSENGER.
He is very near by this: he was not three leagues off when I left him.

LEONATO.

How many gentlemen have you lost in this action?

MESSENGER.

But few of any sort, and none of name.

LEONATO.

A victory is twice itself when the achiever brings home full numbers. I find here that Don Pedro hath bestowed much honour on a young Florentine called Claudio.

MESSENGER.

Much deserved on his part, and equally remembered by Don Pedro. He hath borne himself beyond the promise of his age, doing in the figure of a lamb the feats of a lion: he hath indeed better bettered expectation than you must expect of me to tell you how.

LEONATO.

He hath an uncle here in Messina will be very much glad of it.

MESSENGER.

I have already delivered him letters, and there appears much joy in him; even so much that joy could not show itself modest enough without a badge of bitterness.

LEONATO.

Did he break out into tears?

MESSENGER.

In great measure.

LEONATO.

A kind overflow of kindness. There are no faces truer than those that are so washed; how much better is it to weep at joy than to joy at weeping!

BEATRICE.

I pray you, is Signior Mountanto returned from the wars or no?

MESSENGER.

I know none of that name, lady: there was none such in the army of any sort.

LEONATO.

What is he that you ask for, niece?

HERO.

My cousin means Signior Benedick of Padua.

MESSENGER.

O! he is returned, and as pleasant as ever he was.

BEATRICE.

He set up his bills here in Messina and challenged Cupid at the flight; and my uncle's fool, reading the challenge, subscribed for Cupid, and challenged him at the bird-bolt. I pray you, how many hath he killed and eaten in these wars? But how many hath he killed? for, indeed, I promised to eat all of his killing.

LEONATO.

Faith, niece, you tax Signior Benedick too much; but he'll be meet with you, I doubt it not.

MESSENGER.

He hath done good service, lady, in these wars.

BEATRICE.

You had musty victual, and he hath holp to eat it; he is a very valiant trencher-man; he hath an excellent stomach.

MESSENGER.

And a good soldier too, lady.

BEATRICE.

And a good soldier to a lady; but what is he to a lord?

MESSENGER.

A lord to a lord, a man to a man; stuffed with all honourable virtues.

BEATRICE.

It is so indeed; he is no less than a stuffed man; but for the stuffing,—well, we are all mortal.

LEONATO.

You must not, sir, mistake my niece. There is a kind of merry war betwixt Signior Benedick and her; they never meet but there's a skirmish of wit between them.

BEATRICE.

Alas! he gets nothing by that. In our last conflict four of his five wits went halting off, and now is the whole man governed with one! so that if he have wit enough to keep himself warm, let him bear it for a difference between himself and his horse; for it is all the wealth that he hath left to be known a reasonable creature. Who is his companion now? He hath every month a new sworn brother.

MESSENGER.

Is't possible?

BEATRICE.

Very easily possible: he wears his faith but as the fashion of his hat; it ever changes with the next block.

MESSENGER.

I see, lady, the gentleman is not in your books.

BEATRICE.

No; an he were, I would burn my study. But, I pray you, who is his companion? Is there no young squarer now that will make a voyage with him to the devil?

MESSENGER.

He is most in the company of the right noble Claudio.

BEATRICE.

O Lord, he will hang upon him like a disease: he is sooner caught than the pestilence, and the taker runs presently mad. God help the noble Claudio! If he have caught the Benedick, it will cost him a thousand pound ere a' be cured.

MESSENGER.

I will hold friends with you, lady.

BEATRICE.

Do, good friend.

LEONATO.

You will never run mad, niece.

BEATRICE.

No, not till a hot January.

MESSENGER.

Don Pedro is approached.

[Enter DON PEDRO, DON JOHN, CLAUDIO, BENEDICK, BALTHAZAR, and Others.]

DON PEDRO.

Good Signior Leonato, you are come to meet your trouble: the fashion of the world is to avoid cost, and you encounter it.

LEONATO.

Never came trouble to my house in the likeness of your Grace, for trouble being gone, comfort should remain; but when you depart from me, sorrow abides and happiness takes his leave.

DON PEDRO.

You embrace your charge too willingly. I think this is your daughter.

LEONATO.

Her mother hath many times told me so.

BENEDICK.

Were you in doubt, sir, that you asked her?

LEONATO.

Signior Benedick, no; for then were you a child.

DON PEDRO.

You have it full, Benedick: we may guess by this what you are, being a man. Truly the lady fathers herself. Be happy, lady, for you are like an honourable father.

BENEDICK.

If Signior Leonato be her father, she would not have his head on her shoulders for all Messina, as like him as she is.

BEATRICE.

I wonder that you will still be talking, Signior Benedick: nobody marks you.

BENEDICK.

What! my dear Lady Disdain, are you yet living?

BEATRICE.

Is it possible Disdain should die while she hath such meet food to feed it as Signior Benedick? Courtesy itself must convert to disdain if you come in her presence.

BENEDICK.

Then is courtesy a turncoat. But it is certain I am loved of all ladies, only you excepted; and I would I could find in my heart that I had not a hard heart; for, truly, I love none.

BEATRICE.

A dear happiness to women: they would else have been troubled with a pernicious suitor. I thank God and my cold blood, I am of your humour for that. I had rather hear my dog bark at a crow than a man swear he loves me.

BENEDICK.

God keep your ladyship still in that mind; so some gentleman or other shall 'scape a predestinate scratched face.

BEATRICE.

Scratching could not make it worse, an 'twere such a face as yours were.

BENEDICK.

Well, you are a rare parrot-teacher.

BEATRICE.

A bird of my tongue is better than a beast of yours.

BENEDICK.

I would my horse had the speed of your tongue, and so good a continuer. But keep your way, i' God's name; I have done.

BEATRICE.

You always end with a jade's trick: I know you of old.

DON PEDRO.

That is the sum of all, Leonato: Signior Claudio, and Signior Benedick, my dear friend Leonato hath invited you all. I tell him we shall stay here at the least a month, and he heartily prays some occasion may detain us longer: I dare swear he is no hypocrite, but prays from his heart.

LEONATO.

If you swear, my lord, you shall not be forsworn. [To DON JOHN] Let me bid you welcome, my lord: being reconciled to the prince your brother, I owe you all duty.

DON JOHN.

I thank you: I am not of many words, but I thank you.

LEONATO.

Please it your Grace lead on?

DON PEDRO.

Your hand, Leonato; we will go together.
[Exeunt all but BENEDICK and CLAUDIO.]

CLAUDIO.

Benedick, didst thou note the daughter of Signior Leonato?

BENEDICK.

I noted her not; but I looked on her.

CLAUDIO.

Is she not a modest young lady?

BENEDICK.

Do you question me, as an honest man should do, for my simple true judgment; or would you have me speak after my custom, as being a professed tyrant to their sex?

CLAUDIO.

No; I pray thee speak in sober judgment.

BENEDICK.

Why, i' faith, methinks she's too low for a high praise, too brown for a fair praise, and too little for a great praise; only this commendation I can afford her, that were she other than she is, she were unhandsome, and being no other but as she is, I do not like her.

CLAUDIO.

Thou thinkest I am in sport: I pray thee tell me truly how thou likest her.

BENEDICK.

Would you buy her, that you enquire after her?

CLAUDIO.

Can the world buy such a jewel?

BENEDICK.

Yea, and a case to put it into. But speak you this with a sad brow, or do you play the flouting Jack, to tell us Cupid is a good hare-finder, and Vulcan a rare carpenter? Come, in what key shall a man take you, to go in the song?

CLAUDIO.

In mine eye she is the sweetest lady that ever I looked on.

BENEDICK.

I can see yet without spectacles and I see no such matter: there's her cousin an she were not possessed with a fury, exceeds her as much in beauty as the first of May doth the last of December. But I hope you have no intent to turn husband, have you?

CLAUDIO.

I would scarce trust myself, though I had sworn to the contrary, if Hero would be my wife.

BENEDICK.

Is't come to this, i' faith? Hath not the world one man but he will wear his cap with suspicion? Shall I never see a bachelor of threescore again? Go to, i' faith; an thou wilt needs thrust thy neck into a yoke, wear the print of it and sigh away Sundays. Look! Don Pedro is returned to seek you.
[Re-enter DON PEDRO.]

DON PEDRO.

What secret hath held you here, that you followed not to Leonato's?

BENEDICK.

I would your Grace would constrain me to tell.

DON PEDRO.

I charge thee on thy allegiance.

BENEDICK.

You hear, Count Claudio: I can be secret as a dumb man; I would have you think so; but on my allegiance mark you this, on my allegiance: he is in love. With who? now that is your Grace's part. Mark how short his answer is: with Hero, Leonato's short daughter.

CLAUDIO.

If this were so, so were it uttered.

BENEDICK.

Like the old tale, my lord: 'it is not so, nor 'twas not so; but indeed, God forbid it should be so.'

CLAUDIO.

If my passion change not shortly. God forbid it should be otherwise.

DON PEDRO.

Amen, if you love her; for the lady is very well worthy.

CLAUDIO.

You speak this to fetch me in, my lord.

DON PEDRO.

By my troth, I speak my thought.

CLAUDIO.

And in faith, my lord, I spoke mine.

BENEDICK.

And by my two faiths and troths, my lord, I spoke mine.

CLAUDIO.

That I love her, I feel.

DON PEDRO.

That she is worthy, I know.

BENEDICK.

That I neither feel how she should be loved nor know how she should be worthy, is the opinion that fire cannot melt out of me: I will die in it at the stake.

DON PEDRO.

Thou wast ever an obstinate heretic in the despite of beauty.

CLAUDIO.

And never could maintain his part but in the force of his will.

BENEDICK.

That a woman conceived me, I thank her; that she brought me up, I likewise give her most humble thanks; but that I will have a recheat winded in my forehead, or hang my bugle in an invisible baldrick, all women shall pardon me. Because I will not do them the wrong to mistrust any, I will do myself the right to trust none; and the fine is,—for the which I may go the finer,—I will live a bachelor.

DON PEDRO.

I shall see thee, ere I die, look pale with love.

BENEDICK.

With anger, with sickness, or with hunger, my lord; not with love: prove that ever I lose more blood with love than I will get again with drinking, pick out mine eyes with a ballad-maker's pen and hang me up at the door of a brothel-house for the sign of blind Cupid.

DON PEDRO.

Well, if ever thou dost fall from this faith, thou wilt prove a notable argument.

BENEDICK.

If I do, hang me in a bottle like a cat and shoot at me; and he that hits me, let him be clapped on the shoulder and called Adam.

DON PEDRO.

Well, as time shall try: 'In time the savage bull doth bear the yoke.'

BENEDICK.

The savage bull may; but if ever the sensible Benedick bear it, pluck off the bull's horns and set them in my forehead; and let me be vilely painted, and in such great letters as they write, 'Here is good horse to hire,' let them signify under my sign 'Here you may see Benedick the married man.'

CLAUDIO.

If this should ever happen, thou wouldst be horn-mad.

DON PEDRO.

Nay, if Cupid have not spent all his quiver in Venice, thou wilt quake for this shortly.

BENEDICK.

I look for an earthquake too then.

DON PEDRO.

Well, you will temporize with the hours. In the meantime, good Signior Benedick, repair to Leonato's: commend me to him and tell him I will not fail him at supper; for indeed he hath made great preparation.

BENEDICK.

I have almost matter enough in me for such an embassage; and so I commit you—

CLAUDIO.

To the tuition of God: from my house, if I had it,—

DON PEDRO.

The sixth of July: your loving friend, Benedick.

BENEDICK.

Nay, mock not, mock not. The body of your discourse is sometime guarded with fragments, and the guards are but slightly basted on neither: ere you flout old ends any further, examine your conscience: and so I leave you.
[Exit.]

CLAUDIO.

My liege, your highness now may do me good.

DON PEDRO.

My love is thine to teach: teach it but how,
And thou shalt see how apt it is to learn
hard lesson that may do thee good.

CLAUDIO.

Hath Leonato any son, my lord?

DON PEDRO.

No child but Hero's he's his only heir.
Dost thou affect her, Claudio?

CLAUDIO.

O! my lord,
When you went onward on this ended action,
I looked upon her with a soldier's eye,
That lik'd, but had a rougher task in hand
Than to drive liking to the name of love;
But now I am return'd, and that war-thoughts
Have left their places vacant, in their rooms
Come thronging soft and delicate desires,
All prompting me how fair young Hero is,
Saying, I lik'd her ere I went to wars.

DON PEDRO.

Thou wilt be like a lover presently,
And tire the hearer with a book of words.
If thou dost love fair Hero, cherish it,
And I will break with her, and with her father,
And thou shalt have her. Was't not to this end
That thou began'st to twist so fine a story?

CLAUDIO.

How sweetly you do minister to love,
That know love's grief by his complexion!
But lest my liking might too sudden seem,
I would have salv'd it with a longer treatise.

DON PEDRO.

What need the bridge much broader than the flood?
The fairest grant is the necessity.
Look, what will serve is fit: 'tis once, thou lov'st,
And I will fit thee with the remedy.
I know we shall have revelling to-night:
I will assume thy part in some disguise,
And tell fair Hero I am Claudio;
And in her bosom I'll unclasp my heart,
And take her hearing prisoner with the force

And strong encounter of my amorous tale:
Then, after to her father will I break;
And the conclusion is, she shall be thine.
In practice let us put it presently.
[Exeunt.]

Scene II. A room in LEONATO'S house.
[Enter LEONATO and ANTONIO, meeting.]

LEONATO.

How now, brother! Where is my cousin your son? Hath he provided this music?

ANTONIO.

He is very busy about it. But, brother, I can tell you strange news that you yet
dreamt not of.

LEONATO.

Are they good?

ANTONIO.

As the event stamps them: but they have a good cover; they show well outward.
The prince and Count Claudio, walking in a thick-pleached alley in my orchard,
were thus much overheard by a man of mine: the prince discovered to Claudio that
he loved my niece your daughter and meant to acknowledge it this night in a dance;
and if he found her accordant, he meant to take the present time by the top and
instantly break with you of it.

LEONATO.

Hath the fellow any wit that told you this?

ANTONIO.

A good sharp fellow: I will send for him; and question him yourself.

LEONATO.

No, no; we will hold it as a dream till it appear itself: but I will acquaint my daughter
withal, that she may be the better prepared for an answer, if peradventure this be
true. Go you, and tell her of it.
[Several persons cross the stage.]
Cousins, you know what you have to do. O!I cry you mercy, friend; go you with me,
and I will use your skill. Good cousin, have a care this busy time.
[Exeunt.]

Scene III. Another room in LEONATO'S house.
[Enter DON JOHN and CONRADE.]

CONRADE.

What the good-year, my lord! why are you thus out of measure sad?

DON JOHN.

There is no measure in the occasion that breeds; therefore the sadness is without limit.

CONRADE.

You should hear reason.

DON JOHN.

And when I have heard it, what blessings brings it?

CONRADE.

If not a present remedy, at least a patient sufferance.

DON JOHN.

I wonder that thou, being,—as thou say'st thou art,—born under Saturn, goest about to apply a moral medicine to a mortifying mischief. I cannot hide what I am: I must be sad when I have cause, and smile at no man's jests; eat when I have stomach, and wait for no man's leisure; sleep when I am drowsy, and tend on no man's business; laugh when I am merry, and claw no man in his humour.

CONRADE.

Yea; but you must not make the full show of this till you may do it without controlment. You have of late stood out against your brother, and he hath ta'en you newly into his grace; where it is impossible you should take true root but by the fair weather that you make yourself: it is needful that you frame the season for your own harvest.

DON JOHN.

I had rather be a canker in a hedge than a rose in his grace; and it better fits my blood to be disdained of all than to fashion a carriage to rob love from any: in this, though I cannot be said to be a flattering honest man, it must not be denied but I am a plain-dealing villain. I am trusted with a muzzle and enfranchised with a clog; therefore I have decreed not to sing in my cage. If I had my mouth, I would bite; if I had my liberty, I would do my liking: in the meantime, let me be that I am, and seek not to alter me.

CONRADE.

Can you make no use of your discontent?

DON JOHN.

I make all use of it, for I use it only. Who comes here?
[Enter Borachio.]
What news, Borachio?

BORACHIO.

I came yonder from a great supper: the prince your brother is royally entertained
by Leonato; and I can give you intelligence of an intended marriage.

DON JOHN.

Will it serve for any model to build mischief on? What is he for a fool that betroths
himself to unquietness?

BORACHIO.

Marry, it is your brother's right hand.

DON JOHN.

Who? the most exquisite Claudio?

BORACHIO.

Even he.

DON JOHN.

A proper squire! And who, and who? which way looks he?

BORACHIO.

Marry, on Hero, the daughter and heir of Leonato.

DON JOHN.

A very forward March-chick! How came you to this?

BORACHIO.

Being entertained for a perfumer, as I was smoking a musty room, comes me the
prince and Claudio, hand in hand, in sad conference: I whipt me behind the arras,
and there heard it agreed upon that the prince should woo Hero for himself, and
having obtained her, give her to Count Claudio.

DON JOHN.

Come, come; let us thither: this may prove food to my displeasure. That young
start-up hath all the glory of my overthrow: if I can cross him any way, I bless
myself every way. You are both sure, and will assist me?

CONRADE.

To the death, my lord.

DON JOHN.

Let us to the great supper: their cheer is the greater that I am subdued. Would the cook were of my mind! Shall we go to prove what's to be done?

BORACHIO.

We'll wait upon your lordship.
[Exeunt.]

Act II

Scene I. A hall in LEONATO'S house.
[Enter LEONATO, ANTONIO, HERO, BEATRICE, and Others.]

LEONATO.

Was not Count John here at supper?

ANTONIO.

I saw him not.

BEATRICE.

How tartly that gentleman looks! I never can see him but I am heart-burned an hour after.

HERO.

He is of a very melancholy disposition.

BEATRICE.

He were an excellent man that were made just in the mid-way between him and Benedick: the one is too like an image, and says nothing; and the other too like my lady's eldest son, evermore tattling.

LEONATO.

Then half Signior Benedick's tongue in Count John's mouth, and half Count John's melancholy in Signior Benedick's face,—

BEATRICE.

With a good leg and a good foot, uncle, and money enough in his purse, such a man would win any woman in the world if he could get her good will.

LEONATO.

By my troth, niece, thou wilt never get thee a husband, if thou be so shrewd of thy tongue.

ANTONIO.

In faith, she's too curst.

BEATRICE.

Too curst is more than curst: I shall lessen God's sending that way; for it is said, 'God sends a curst cow short horns;' but to a cow too curst he sends none.

LEONATO.

So, by being too curst, God will send you no horns?

BEATRICE.

Just, if he send me no husband; for the which blessing I am at him upon my knees every morning and evening. Lord! I could not endure a husband with a beard on his face: I had rather lie in the woollen.

LEONATO.

You may light on a husband that hath no beard.

BEATRICE.

What should I do with him? dress him in my apparel and make him my waiting-gentlewoman? He that hath a beard is more than a youth, and he that hath no beard is less than a man; and he that is more than a youth is not for me; and he that is less than a man, I am not for him: therefore I will even take sixpence in earnest of the bear-ward, and lead his apes into hell.

LEONATO.

Well then, go you into hell?

BEATRICE.

No; but to the gate; and there will the devil meet me, like an old cuckold, with horns on his head, and say, 'Get you to heaven, Beatrice, get you to heaven; here's no place for you maids.' So deliver I up my apes, and away to Saint Peter for the heavens; he shows me where the bachelors sit, and there live we as merry as the day is long.

ANTONIO.

[To Hero.] Well, niece, I trust you will be ruled by your father.

BEATRICE.

Yes, faith; it is my cousin's duty to make curtsy, and say, 'Father, as it please you:'— but yet for all that, cousin, let him be a handsome fellow, or else make another curtsy, and say, 'Father, as it please me.'

LEONATO.

Well, niece, I hope to see you one day fitted with a husband.

BEATRICE.

Not till God make men of some other metal than earth. Would it not grieve a woman to be over-mastered with a piece of valiant dust? to make an account of her life to a clod of wayward marl? No, uncle, I'll none: Adam's sons are my brethren; and truly, I hold it a sin to match in my kinred.

LEONATO.

Daughter, remember what I told you: if the prince do solicit you in that kind, you know your answer.

BEATRICE.

The fault will be in the music, cousin, if you be not wooed in good time: if the prince be too important, tell him there is measure in everything, and so dance out the answer. For, hear me, Hero: wooing, wedding, and repenting is as a Scotch jig, a measure, and a cinque- pace: the first suit is hot and hasty, like a Scotch jig, and full as fantastical; the wedding, mannerly-modest, as a measure, full of state and ancientry; and then comes Repentance, and with his bad legs, falls into the cinque-pace faster and faster, till he sink into his grave.

LEONATO.

Cousin, you apprehend passing shrewdly.

BEATRICE.

I have a good eye, uncle: I can see a church by daylight.

LEONATO.

The revellers are entering, brother: make good room.
[Enter, DON PEDRO, CLAUDIO, BENEDICK, BALTHASAR, DON JOHN, BORACHIO, MARGARET, URSULA, and Others, masked.]

DON PEDRO.

Lady, will you walk about with your friend?

HERO.

So you walk softly and look sweetly and say nothing, I am yours for the walk; and especially when I walk away.

DON PEDRO.

With me in your company?

HERO.

I may say so, when I please.

DON PEDRO.

And when please you to say so?

HERO.

When I like your favour; for God defend the lute should be like the case!

DON PEDRO.

My visor is Philemon's roof; within the house is Jove.

HERO.

Why, then, your visor should be thatch'd.

DON PEDRO.

Speak low, if you speak love.
[Takes her aside.]

BALTHAZAR.

Well, I would you did like me.

MARGARET.

So would not I, for your own sake; for I have many ill qualities.

BALTHAZAR.

Which is one?

MARGARET.

I say my prayers aloud.

BALTHAZAR.

I love you the better; the hearers may cry Amen.

MARGARET.

God match me with a good dancer!

BALTHAZAR.

Amen.

MARGARET.

And God keep him out of my sight when the dance is done! Answer, clerk.

BALTHAZAR.

No more words: the clerk is answered.

URSULA.

I know you well enough: you are Signior Antonio.

ANTONIO.

At a word, I am not.

URSULA.

I know you by the waggling of your head.

ANTONIO.

To tell you true, I counterfeit him.

URSULA.

You could never do him so ill-well, unless you were the very man.
Here's his dry hand up and down: you are he, you are he.

ANTONIO.

At a word, I am not.

URSULA.

Come, come; do you think I do not know you by your excellent wit?
Can virtue hide itself? Go to, mum, you are he: graces will appear, and there's an
end.

BEATRICE.

Will you not tell me who told you so?

BENEDICK.

No, you shall pardon me.

BEATRICE.

Nor will you not tell me who you are?

BENEDICK.

Not now.

BEATRICE.

That I was disdainful, and that I had my good wit out of the 'Hundred Merry Tales.'
Well, this was Signior Benedick that said so.

BENEDICK.

What's he?

BEATRICE.

I am sure you know him well enough.

BENEDICK.

Not I, believe me.

BEATRICE.

Did he never make you laugh?

BENEDICK.

I pray you, what is he?

BEATRICE.

Why, he is the prince's jester: a very dull fool; only his gift is in devising impossible slanders: none but libertines delight in him; and the commendation is not in his wit, but in his villany; for he both pleases men and angers them, and then they laugh at him and beat him. I am sure he is in the fleet: I would he had boarded me!

BENEDICK.

When I know the gentleman, I'll tell him what you say.

BEATRICE.

Do, do: he'll but break a comparison or two on me; which, peradventure not marked or not laughed at, strikes him into melancholy; and then there's a partridge wing saved, for the fool will eat no supper that night. [Music within.] We must follow the leaders.

BENEDICK.

In every good thing.

BEATRICE.

Nay, if they lead to any ill, I will leave them at the next turning.
[Dance. Then exeunt all but DON JOHN, BORACHIO, and CLAUDIO.]

DON JOHN.

Sure my brother is amorous on Hero, and hath withdrawn her father to break with him about it. The ladies follow her and but one visor remains.

BORACHIO.

And that is Claudio: I know him by his bearing.

DON JOHN.

Are you not Signior Benedick?

CLAUDIO.

You know me well; I am he.

DON JOHN.

Signior, you are very near my brother in his love: he is enamoured on Hero; I pray you, dissuade him from her; she is no equal for his birth: you may do the part of an honest man in it.

CLAUDIO.

How know you he loves her?

DON JOHN.

I heard him swear his affection.

BORACHIO.

So did I too; and he swore he would marry her to-night.

DON JOHN.

Come, let us to the banquet.
[Exeunt DON JOHN and BORACHIO.]

CLAUDIO.

Thus answer I in name of Benedick,
But hear these ill news with the ears of Claudio.
'Tis certain so; the prince wooes for himself.
Friendship is constant in all other things
Save in the office and affairs of love:
herefore all hearts in love use their own tongues;
Let every eye negotiate for itself
And trust no agent; for beauty is a witch
Against whose charms faith melteth into blood.
This is an accident of hourly proof,
Which I mistrusted not. Farewell, therefore, Hero!
[Re-enter Benedick.]

BENEDICK.

Count Claudio?

CLAUDIO.

Yea, the same.

BENEDICK.

Come, will you go with me?

CLAUDIO.

Whither?

BENEDICK.

Even to the next willow, about your own business, count. What fashion will you wear the garland of? About your neck, like a usurer's chain? or under your arm, like a lieutenant's scarf? You must wear it one way, for the prince hath got your Hero.

CLAUDIO.

I wish him joy of her.

BENEDICK.

Why, that's spoken like an honest drovier: so they sell bullocks. But did you think the prince would have served you thus?

CLAUDIO.

I pray you, leave me.

BENEDICK.

Ho! now you strike like the blind man: 'twas the boy that stole your meat, and you'll beat the post.

CLAUDIO.

If it will not be, I'll leave you.
[Exit.]

BENEDICK.

Alas! poor hurt fowl. Now will he creep into sedges. But, that my Lady Beatrice should know me, and not know me! The prince's fool! Ha! it may be I go under that title because I am merry. Yea, but so I am apt to do myself wrong; I am not so reputed: it is the base though bitter disposition of Beatrice that puts the world into her person, and so gives me out. Well, I'll be revenged as I may.
[Re-enter Don Pedro.]

DON PEDRO.

Now, signior, where's the count? Did you see him?

BENEDICK.

Troth, my lord, I have played the part of Lady Fame. I found him here as melancholy as a lodge in a warren. I told him, and I think I told him true, that your Grace had got the good will of this young lady; and I offered him my company to a willow tree, either to make him a garland, as being forsaken, or to bind him up a rod, as being worthy to be whipped.

DON PEDRO.

To be whipped! What's his fault?

BENEDICK.

The flat transgression of a school-boy, who, being overjoy'd with finding a bird's nest, shows it his companion, and he steals it.

DON PEDRO.

Wilt thou make a trust a transgression? The transgression is in the stealer.

BENEDICK.

Yet it had not been amiss the rod had been made, and the garland too; for the garland he might have worn himself, and the rod he might have bestowed on you, who, as I take it, have stolen his bird's nest.

DON PEDRO.

I will but teach them to sing, and restore them to the owner.

BENEDICK.

If their singing answer your saying, by my faith, you say honestly.

DON PEDRO.

The Lady Beatrice hath a quarrel to you: the gentleman that danced with her told her she is much wronged by you.

BENEDICK.

O! she misused me past the endurance of a block: an oak but with one green leaf on it, would have answered her: my very visor began to assume life and scold with her. She told me, not thinking I had been myself, that I was the prince's jester, that I was duller than a great thaw; huddling jest upon jest with such impossible conveyance upon me, that I stood like a man at a mark, with a whole army shooting at me. She speaks poniards, and every word stabs: if her breath were as terrible as her terminations, there were no living near her; she would infect to the north star. I would not marry her, though she were endowed with all that Adam had left him before he transgressed: she would have made Hercules have turned spit, yea, and have cleft his club to make the fire too. Come, talk not of her; you shall find her the infernal Ate in good apparel. I would to God some scholar would conjure her, for certainly, while she is here, a man may live as quiet in hell as in a sanctuary; and people sin upon purpose because they would go thither; so indeed, all disquiet, horror and perturbation follow her.

[Re-enter CLAUDIO, BEATRICE, HERO, and LEONATO.]

DON PEDRO.

Look! here she comes.

BENEDICK.

Will your Grace command me any service to the world's end? I will go on the slightest errand now to the Antipodes that you can devise to send me on; I will fetch you a toothpicker now from the furthest inch of Asia; bring you the length of Prester John's foot; fetch you a hair off the Great Cham's beard; do you any embassage to the Pygmies, rather than hold three words' conference with this harpy. You have no employment for me?

DON PEDRO.

None, but to desire your good company.

BENEDICK.

O God, sir, here's a dish I love not: I cannot endure my Lady Tongue.
[Exit.]

DON PEDRO.

Come, lady, come; you have lost the heart of Signior Benedick.

BEATRICE.

Indeed, my lord, he lent it me awhile; and I gave him use for it, a double heart for a single one: marry, once before he won it of me with false dice, therefore your Grace may well say I have lost it.

DON PEDRO.

You have put him down, lady, you have put him down.

BEATRICE.

So I would not he should do me, my lord, lest I should prove the mother of fools. I have brought Count Claudio, whom you sent me to seek.

DON PEDRO.

Why, how now, count! wherefore are you sad?

CLAUDIO.

Not sad, my lord.

DON PEDRO.

How then? Sick?

CLAUDIO.

Neither, my lord.

BEATRICE.

The count is neither sad, nor sick, nor merry, nor well; but civil count, civil as an orange, and something of that jealous complexion.

DON PEDRO.

I' faith, lady, I think your blazon to be true; though, I'll be sworn, if he be so, his conceit is false. Here, Claudio, I have wooed in thy name, and fair Hero is won; I have broke with her father, and, his good will obtained; name the day of marriage, and God give thee joy!

LEONATO.

Count, take of me my daughter, and with her my fortunes: his Grace hath made the match, and all grace say Amen to it!

BEATRICE.

Speak, Count, 'tis your cue.

CLAUDIO.

Silence is the perfectest herald of joy: I were but little happy, if I could say how much. Lady, as you are mine, I am yours: I give away myself for you and dote upon the exchange.

BEATRICE.

Speak, cousin; or, if you cannot, stop his mouth with a kiss, and let not him speak neither.

DON PEDRO.

In faith, lady, you have a merry heart.

BEATRICE.

Yea, my lord; I thank it, poor fool, it keeps on the windy side of care. My cousin tells him in his ear that he is in her heart.

CLAUDIO.

And so she doth, cousin.

BEATRICE.

Good Lord, for alliance! Thus goes every one to the world but I, and I am sunburnt. I may sit in a corner and cry heigh-ho for a husband!

DON PEDRO.

Lady Beatrice, I will get you one.

BEATRICE.

I would rather have one of your father's getting. Hath your Grace ne'er a brother like you? Your father got excellent husbands, if a maid could come by them.

DON PEDRO.

Will you have me, lady?

BEATRICE.

No, my lord, unless I might have another for working days: your Grace is too costly to wear every day. But, I beseech your Grace, pardon me; I was born to speak all mirth and no matter.

DON PEDRO.

Your silence most offends me, and to be merry best becomes you; for out of question, you were born in a merry hour.

BEATRICE.

No, sure, my lord, my mother cried; but then there was a star danced, and under that was I born. Cousins, God give you joy!

LEONATO.

Niece, will you look to those things I told you of?

BEATRICE.

I cry you mercy, uncle. By your Grace's pardon.
[Exit.]

DON PEDRO.

By my troth, a pleasant spirited lady.

LEONATO.

There's little of the melancholy element in her, my lord: she is never sad but when she sleeps; and not ever sad then, for I have heard my daughter say, she hath often dreamed of unhappiness and waked herself with laughing.

DON PEDRO.

She cannot endure to hear tell of a husband.

LEONATO.

O! by no means: she mocks all her wooers out of suit.

DON PEDRO.

She were an excellent wife for Benedick.

LEONATO.

O Lord! my lord, if they were but a week married, they would talk themselves mad.

DON PEDRO.

Count Claudio, when mean you to go to church?

CLAUDIO.

To-morrow, my lord. Time goes on crutches till love have all his rites.

LEONATO.

Not till Monday, my dear son, which is hence a just seven-night; and a time too brief too, to have all things answer my mind.

DON PEDRO.

Come, you shake the head at so long a breathing; but, I warrant thee, Claudio, the time shall not go dully by us. I will in the interim undertake one of Hercules' labours, which is, to bring Signior Benedick and the Lady Beatrice into a mountain of affection the one with the other. I would fain have it a match; and I doubt not but to fashion it, if you three will but minister such assistance as I shall give you direction.

LEONATO.

My lord, I am for you, though it cost me ten nights' watchings.

CLAUDIO.

And I, my lord.

DON PEDRO.

And you too, gentle Hero?

HERO.

I will do any modest office, my lord, to help my cousin to a good husband.

DON PEDRO.

And Benedick is not the unhopefullest husband that I know. Thus far can I praise him; he is of a noble strain, of approved valour, and confirmed honesty. I will teach you how to humour your cousin, that she shall fall in love with Benedick; and I, with your two helps, will so practise on Benedick that, in despite of his quick wit and his queasy stomach, he shall fall in love with Beatrice. If we can do this, Cupid

is no longer an archer: his glory shall be ours, for we are the only love-gods. Go in
with me, and I will tell you my drift.
[Exeunt.]

Scene II. Another room in LEONATO'S house.
[Enter DON JOHN and BORACHIO.]

DON JOHN.

It is so; the Count Claudio shall marry the daughter of Leonato.

BORACHIO.

Yea, my lord; but I can cross it.

DON JOHN.

Any bar, any cross, any impediment will be medicinable to me: I am sick in
displeasure to him, and whatsoever comes athwart his affection ranges evenly with
mine. How canst thou cross this marriage?

BORACHIO.

Not honestly, my lord; but so covertly that no dishonesty shall appear in me.

DON JOHN.

Show me briefly how.

BORACHIO.

I think I told your lordship, a year since, how much I am in the favour of Margaret,
the waiting-gentlewoman to Hero.

DON JOHN.

I remember.

BORACHIO.

I can, at any unseasonable instant of the night, appoint her to look out at her lady's
chamber window.

DON JOHN.

What life is in that, to be the death of this marriage?

BORACHIO.

The poison of that lies in you to temper. Go you to the prince your brother; spare not
to tell him, that he hath wronged his honour in marrying the renowned Claudio,—
whose estimation do you mightily hold up,—to a contaminated stale, such a one as
Hero.

DON JOHN.
What proof shall I make of that?

BORACHIO.
Proof enough to misuse the prince, to vex Claudio, to undo Hero, and kill
LEONATO.
Look you for any other issue?

DON JOHN.
Only to despite them, I will endeavour anything.

BORACHIO.
Go then; find me a meet hour to draw Don Pedro and the Count Claudio alone: tell
them that you know that Hero loves me; intend a kind of zeal both to the prince and
Claudio, as—in love of your brother's honour, who hath made this match, and his
friend's reputation, who is thus like to be cozened with the semblance of a maid,—
that you have discovered thus. They will scarcely believe this without trial: offer
them instances, which shall bear no less likelihood than to see me at her chamber-
window, hear me call Margaret Hero, hear Margaret term me Claudio; and bring
them to see this the very night before the intended wedding: for in the meantime
I will so fashion the matter that Hero shall be absent; and there shall appear such
seeming truth of Hero's disloyalty, that jealousy shall be called assurance, and all
the preparation overthrown.

DON JOHN.
Grow this to what adverse issue it can, I will put it in practice. Be cunning in the
working this, and thy fee is a thousand ducats.

BORACHIO.
Be you constant in the accusation, and my cunning shall not shame me.

DON JOHN.
I will presently go learn their day of marriage.
[Exeunt.]

Scene III. LEONATO'S Garden.
[Enter Benedick.]

BENEDICK.
Boy!
[Enter a Boy.]

BOY.
Signior?

BENEDICK.

In my chamber-window lies a book; bring it hither to me in the orchard.

BOY.

I am here already, sir.

BENEDICK.

I know that; but I would have thee hence, and here again. [Exit Boy.] I do much wonder that one man, seeing how much another man is a fool when he dedicates his behaviours to love, will, after he hath laughed at such shallow follies in others, become the argument of his own scorn by falling in love: and such a man is Claudio. I have known, when there was no music with him but the drum and the fife; and now had he rather hear the tabor and the pipe: I have known when he would have walked ten mile afoot to see a good armour; and now will he lie ten nights awake, carving the fashion of a new doublet. He was wont to speak plain and to the purpose, like an honest man and a soldier; and now is he turned orthography; his words are a very fantastical banquet, just so many strange dishes. May I be so converted, and see with these eyes? I cannot tell; I think not: I will not be sworn but love may transform me to an oyster; but I'll take my oath on it, till he have made an oyster of me, he shall never make me such a fool. One woman is fair, yet I am well; another is wise, yet I am well; another virtuous, yet I am well; but till all graces be in one woman, one woman shall not come in my grace. Rich she shall be, that's certain; wise, or I'll none; virtuous, or I'll never cheapen her; fair, or I'll never look on her; mild, or come not near me; noble, or not I for an angel; of good discourse, an excellent musician, and her hair shall be of what colour it please God. Ha! the prince and Monsieur Love! I will hide me in the arbour.
[Withdraws.]
[Enter DON PEDRO, LEONATO, and CLAUDIO, followed by BALTHAZAR and Musicians.]

DON PEDRO.

Come, shall we hear this music?

CLAUDIO.

Yea, my good lord. How still the evening is, As hush'd on purpose to grace harmony!

DON PEDRO.

See you where Benedick hath hid himself?

CLAUDIO.

O! very well, my lord: the music ended, We'll fit the kid-fox with a penny-worth.

DON PEDRO.

Come, Balthazar, we'll hear that song again.

BALTHAZAR.
O! good my lord, tax not so bad a voice To slander music any more than once.

DON PEDRO.
It is the witness still of excellency, To put a strange face on his own perfection. I pray thee, sing, and let me woo no more.

BALTHAZAR.
Because you talk of wooing, I will sing; Since many a wooer doth commence his suit To her he thinks not worthy; yet he wooes; Yet will he swear he loves.

DON PEDRO.
Nay, pray thee come; Or if thou wilt hold longer argument, Do it in notes.

BALTHAZAR.
Note this before my notes; There's not a note of mine that's worth the noting.

DON PEDRO.
Why these are very crotchets that he speaks; Notes, notes, forsooth, and nothing!
[Music.]

BENEDICK.
Now, divine air! now is his soul ravished! Is it not strange that sheep's guts should hale souls out of men's bodies? Well, a horn for my money, when all's done.
[Balthasar sings.]
Sigh no more, ladies, sigh no more,
Men were deceivers ever;
One foot in sea, and one on shore,
To one thing constant never.
Then sigh not so,
But let them go,
And be you blithe and bonny,
Converting all your sounds of woe
Into Hey nonny, nonny.
Sing no more ditties, sing no mo
Of dumps so dull and heavy;
The fraud of men was ever so,
Since summer first was leavy.
Then sigh not so,
But let them go,
And be you blithe and bonny,
Converting all your sounds of woe
Into Hey nonny, nonny.

DON PEDRO.

By my troth, a good song.

BALTHAZAR.

And an ill singer, my lord.

DON PEDRO.

Ha, no, no, faith; thou singest well enough for a shift.

BENEDICK.

[Aside.] An he had been a dog that should have howled thus, thcy would have hanged him; and I pray God his bad voice bode no mischief. I had as lief have heard the night-raven, come what plague could have come after it.

DON PEDRO.

Yea, marry; dost thou hear, Balthazar? I pray thee, get us some excellent music, for to-morrow night we would have it at the Lady Hero's chamber-window.

BALTHAZAR.

The best I can, my lord.

DON PEDRO.

Do so: farewell.
[Exeunt BALTHAZAR and Musicians.]
Come hither, Leonato: what was it you told me of to-day, that your niece Beatrice was in love with Signior Benedick?

CLAUDIO.

O! ay:— [Aside to DON PEDRO] Stalk on, stalk on; the fowl sits. I did never think that lady would have loved any man.

LEONATO.

No, nor I neither; but most wonderful that she should so dote on Signior Benedick, whom she hath in all outward behaviours seemed ever to abhor.

BENEDICK.

[Aside.] Is't possible? Sits the wind in that corner?

LEONATO.

By my troth, my lord, I cannot tell what to think of it but that she loves him with an enraged affection: it is past the infinite of thought.

DON PEDRO.

May be she doth but counterfeit.

CLAUDIO.

Faith, like enough.

LEONATO.

O God! counterfeit! There was never counterfeit of passion came so near the life of passion as she discovers it.

DON PEDRO.

Why, what effects of passion shows she?

CLAUDIO.

[Aside.] Bait the hook well: this fish will bite.

LEONATO.

What effects, my lord? She will sit you; [To Claudio.] You heard my daughter tell you how.

CLAUDIO.

She did, indeed.

DON PEDRO.

How, how, I pray you? You amaze me: I would have thought her spirit had been invincible against all assaults of affection.

LEONATO.

I would have sworn it had, my lord; especially against Benedick.

BENEDICK.

[Aside] I should think this a gull, but that the white-bearded fellow speaks it: knavery cannot, sure, hide itself in such reverence.

CLAUDIO.

[Aside.] He hath ta'en the infection: hold it up.

DON PEDRO.

Hath she made her affection known to Benedick?

LEONATO.

No; and swears she never will: that's her torment.

CLAUDIO.

Tis true, indeed;so your daughter says: 'Shall I,' says she, 'that have so oft encountered him with scorn, write to him that I love him?'

LEONATO.

This says she now when she is beginning to write to him; for she'll be up twenty times a night, and there will she sit in her smock till she have writ a sheet of paper: my daughter tells us all.

CLAUDIO.

Now you talk of a sheet of paper, I remember a pretty jest your daughter told us of.

LEONATO.

O! when she had writ it, and was reading it over, she found Benedick and Beatrice between the sheet?

CLAUDIO.

That.

LEONATO.

O! she tore the letter into a thousand halfpence; railed at herself, that she should be so immodest to write to one that she knew would flout her: 'I measure him,' says she, 'by my own spirit; for I should flout him, if he writ to me; yea, though I love him, I should.'

CLAUDIO.

Then down upon her knees she falls, weeps, sobs, beats her heart, tears her hair, prays, curses; 'O sweet Benedick! God give me patience!'

LEONATO.

She doth indeed; my daughter says so; and the ecstasy hath so much overborne her, that my daughter is sometimes afeard she will do a desperate outrage to herself. It is very true.

DON PEDRO.

It were good that Benedick knew of it by some other, if she will not discover it.

CLAUDIO.

To what end? he would make but a sport of it and torment the poor lady worse.

DON PEDRO.

An he should, it were an alms to hang him. She's an excellent sweet lady, and, out of all suspicion, she is virtuous.

CLAUDIO.

And she is exceeding wise.

DON PEDRO.
In everything but in loving Benedick.

LEONATO.
O! my lord, wisdom and blood combating in so tender a body, we have ten proofs to one that blood hath the victory. I am sorry for her, as I have just cause, being her uncle and her guardian.

DON PEDRO.
I would she had bestowed this dotage on me; I would have daffed all other respects and made her half myself. I pray you, tell Benedick of it, and hear what a' will say.

LEONATO.
Were it good, think you?

CLAUDIO.
Hero thinks surely she will die; for she says she will die if he love her not, and she will die ere she make her love known, and she will die if he woo her, rather than she will bate one breath of her accustomed crossness.

DON PEDRO.
She doth well: if she should make tender of her love, 'tis very possible he'll scorn it; for the man,—as you know all,—hath a contemptible spirit.

CLAUDIO.
He is a very proper man.

DON PEDRO.
He hath indeed a good outward happiness.

CLAUDIO.
Fore God, and in my mind, very wise.

DON PEDRO.
He doth indeed show some sparks that are like wit.

CLAUDIO.
And I take him to be valiant.

DON PEDRO.
As Hector, I assure you: and in the managing of quarrels you may say he is wise; for either he avoids them with great discretion, or undertakes them with a most Christian-like fear.

LEONATO.

If he do fear God, a' must necessarily keep peace: if he break the peace, he ought to enter into a quarrel with fear and trembling.

DON PEDRO.

And so will he do; for the man doth fear God, howsoever it seems not in him by some large jests he will make. Well, I am sorry for your niece. Shall we go seek Benedick and tell him of her love?

CLAUDIO.

Never tell him, my lord: let her wear it out with good counsel.

LEONATO.

Nay, that's impossible: she may wear her heart out first.

DON PEDRO.

Well, we will hear further of it by your daughter: let it cool the while. I love Benedick well, and I could wish he would modestly examine himself, to see how much he is unworthy so good a lady.

LEONATO.

My lord, will you walk? dinner is ready.

CLAUDIO.

[Aside.] If he do not dote on her upon this, I will never trust my expectation.

DON PEDRO.

[Aside.] Let there be the same net spread for her; and that must your daughter and her gentle-woman carry. The sport will be, when they hold one an opinion of another's dotage, and no such matter: that's the scene that I would see, which will be merely a dumb-show. Let us send her to call him in to dinner.
[Exeunt DON PEDRO, CLAUDIO, and LEONATO.]

BENEDICK.

[Advancing from the arbour.] This can be no trick: the conference was sadly borne. They have the truth of this from Hero. They seem to pity the lady: it seems her affections have their full bent. Love me! why, it must be requited. I hear how I am censured: they say I will bear myself proudly, if I perceive the love come from her;they say too that she will rather die than give any sign of affection. I did never think to marry: I must not seem proud: happy are they that hear their detractions, and can put them to mending. They say the lady is fair: 'tis a truth, I can bear them witness; and virtuous: 'tis so, I cannot reprove it; and wise, but for loving me: by my troth, it is no addition to her wit, nor no great argument of her folly, for I will

be horribly in love with her. I may chance have some odd quirks and remnants of wit broken on me, because I have railed so long against marriage; but doth not the appetite alter? A man loves the meat in his youth that he cannot endure in his age. Shall quips and sentences and these paper bullets of the brain awe a man from the career of his humour? No; the world must be peopled. When I said I would die a bachelor, I did not think I should live till I were married. Here comes Beatrice. By this day! she's a fair lady: I do spy some marks of love in her.
[Enter BEATRICE.]

BEATRICE.
Against my will I am sent to bid you come in to dinner.

BENEDICK.
Fair Beatrice, I thank you for your pains.

BEATRICE.
I took no more pains for those thanks than you take pains to thank me: if it had been painful, I would not have come.

BENEDICK.
You take pleasure then in the message?

BEATRICE.
Yea, just so much as you may take upon a knife's point, and choke a daw withal. You have no stomach, signior: fare you well.
[Exit.]

BENEDICK.
Ha! 'Against my will I am sent to bid you come in to dinner,' there's a double meaning in that. 'I took no more pains for those thanks than you took pains to thank me,' that's as much as to say, Any pains that I take for you is as easy as thanks. If I do not take pity of her, I am a villain; if I do not love her, I am a Jew. I will go get her picture.
[Exit.]

Act III

Scene I. Leonato's Garden
[Enter HERO, MARGARET, and URSULA.]

HERO.
Good Margaret, run thee to the parlour;
There shalt thou find my cousin Beatrice
Proposing with the prince and Claudio:

Whisper her ear, and tell her, I and Ursala
Walk in the orchard, and our whole discourse
Is all of her; say that thou overheard'st us,
And bid her steal into the pleached bower,
Where honey-suckles, ripen'd by the sun,
Forbid the sun to enter; like favourites,
Made proud by princes, that advance their pride
Against that power that bred it. There will she hide her,
To listen our propose. This is thy office;
Bear thee well in it and leave us alone.

MARGARET.

I'll make her come, I warrant you, presently.
[Exit.]

HERO.

Now, Ursula, when Beatrice doth come,
As we do trace this alley up and down,
Our talk must only be of Benedick:
When I do name him, let it be thy part
To praise him more than ever man did merit.
My talk to thee must be how Benedick
Is sick in love with Beatrice: of this matter
Is little Cupid's crafty arrow made,
That only wounds by hearsay.
[Enter BEATRICE, behind.]
Now begin; For look where Beatrice, like a lapwing, runs
Close by the ground, to hear our conference.

URSULA.

The pleasant'st angling is to see the fish
Cut with her golden oars the silver stream,
And greedily devour the treacherous bait:
So angle we for Beatrice; who even now
Is couched in the woodbine coverture.
Fear you not my part of the dialogue.

HERO.

Then go we near her, that her ear lose nothing
Of the false sweet bait that we lay for it.
[They advance to the bower.]
No, truly, Ursula, she is too disdainful;
I know her spirits are as coy and wild
As haggards of the rock.

URSULA.

But are you sure
That Benedick loves Beatrice so entirely?

HERO.

So says the prince, and my new-trothed lord.

URSULA.

And did they bid you tell her of it, madam?

HERO.

They did entreat me to acquaint her of it;
But I persuaded them, if they lov'd Benedick,
To wish him wrestle with affection,
And never to let Beatrice know of it.

URSULA.

Why did you so? Doth not the gentleman
Deserve as full as fortunate a bed
As ever Beatrice shall couch upon?

HERO.

O god of love! I know he doth deserve
As much as may be yielded to a man;
But nature never fram'd a woman's heart
Of prouder stuff than that of Beatrice;
Disdain and scorn ride sparkling in her eyes,
Misprising what they look on, and her wit
Values itself so highly, that to her
All matter else seems weak. She cannot love,
Nor take no shape nor project of affection,
She is so self-endear'd.

URSULA.

Sure I think so; And therefore certainly it were not good
She knew his love, lest she make sport at it.

HERO.

Why, you speak truth. I never yet saw man,
How wise, how noble, young, how rarely featur'd,
But she would spell him backward: if fair-fac'd,
She would swear the gentleman should be her sister;
If black, why, Nature, drawing of an antick,

Made a foul blot; if tall, a lance ill-headed;
If low, an agate very vilely cut;
If speaking, why, a vane blown with all winds;
If silent, why, a block moved with none.
So turns she every man the wrong side out,
And never gives to truth and virtue that
Which simpleness and merit purchaseth.

                        URSULA.
Sure, sure, such carping is not commendable.

                        HERO.
No; not to be so odd, and from all fashions,
As Beatrice is, cannot be commendable.
But who dare tell her so? If I should speak,
She would mock me into air: O! she would laugh me
Out of myself, press me to death with wit.
Therefore let Benedick, like cover'd fire,
Consume away in sighs, waste inwardly:
It were a better death than die with mocks,
Which is as bad as die with tickling.

                        URSULA.
Yet tell her of it: hear what she will say.

                        HERO.
No; rather I will go to Benedick,
And counsel him to fight against his passion.
And, truly, I'll devise some honest slanders
To stain my cousin with. One doth not know
How much an ill word may empoison liking.

                        URSULA.
O! do not do your cousin such a wrong.
She cannot be so much without true judgment,—
Having so swift and excellent a wit
As she is priz'd to have,—as to refuse
So rare a gentleman as Signior Benedick.

                        HERO.
He is the only man of Italy,
Always excepted my dear Claudio.

URSULA.

I pray you, be not angry with me, madam,
Speaking my fancy: Signior Benedick,
For shape, for bearing, argument and valour,
Goes foremost in report through Italy.

HERO.

Indeed, he hath an excellent good name.

URSULA.

His excellence did earn it, ere he had it.
When are you married, madam?

HERO.

Why, every day, to-morrow. Come, go in:
I'll show thee some attires, and have thy counsel
Which is the best to furnish me to-morrow.

URSULA.

She's lim'd, I warrant you: we have caught her, madam.

HERO.

If it prove so, then loving goes by haps:
Some Cupid kills with arrows, some with traps.
[Exeunt HERO and URSULA.]

BEATRICE.

[Advancing.] What fire is in mine ears? Can this be true?
Stand I condemn'd for pride and scorn so much?
Contempt, farewell! and maiden pride, adieu!
No glory lives behind the back of such.
And, Benedick, love on; I will requite thee,
Taming my wild heart to thy loving hand:
If thou dost love, my kindness shall incite thee
To bind our loves up in a holy band;
For others say thou dost deserve, and I
Believe it better than reportingly.
[Exit.]

Scene II. A Room in LEONATO'S House
[Enter DON PEDRO, CLAUDIO, BENEDICK, and LEONATO.]

DON PEDRO.

I do but stay till your marriage be consummate, and then go I toward Arragon.

CLAUDIO.

I'll bring you thither, my lord, if you'll vouchsafe me.

DON PEDRO.

Nay, that would be as great a soil in the new gloss of your marriage, as to show a child his new coat and forbid him to wear it. I will only be bold with Benedick for his company; for, from the crown of his head to the sole of his foot, he is all mirth; he hath twice or thrice cut Cupid's bowstring, and the little hangman dare not shoot at him. He hath a heart as sound as a bell, and his tongue is the clapper; for what his heart thinks his tongue speaks.

BENEDICK.

Gallants, I am not as I have been.

LEONATO.

So say I: methinks you are sadder.

CLAUDIO.

I hope he be in love.

DON PEDRO.

Hang him, truant! there's no true drop of blood in him, to be truly touched with love. If he be sad, he wants money.

BENEDICK.

I have the tooth-ache.

DON PEDRO.

Draw it.

BENEDICK.

Hang it.

CLAUDIO.

You must hang it first, and draw it afterwards.

DON PEDRO.

What! sigh for the tooth-ache?

LEONATO.

Where is but a humour or a worm?

BENEDICK.

Well, every one can master a grief but he that has it.

CLAUDIO.

Yet say I, he is in love.

DON PEDRO.

There is no appearance of fancy in him, unless it be a fancy that he hath to strange disguises; as to be a Dutchman to-day, a Frenchman to-morrow; or in the shape of two countries at once, as a German from the waist downward, all slops, and a Spaniard from the hip upward, no doublet. Unless he have a fancy to this foolery, as it appears he hath, he is no fool for fancy, as you would have it appear he is.

CLAUDIO.

If he be not in love with some woman, there is no believing old signs: a' brushes his hat a mornings; what should that bode?

DON PEDRO.

Hath any man seen him at the barber's?

CLAUDIO.

No, but the barber's man hath been seen with him; and the old ornament of his cheek hath already stuffed tennis-balls.

LEONATO.

Indeed he looks younger than he did, by the loss of a beard.

DON PEDRO.

Nay, a' rubs himself with civet: can you smell him out by that?

CLAUDIO.

That's as much as to say the sweet youth's in love.

DON PEDRO.

The greatest note of it is his melancholy.

CLAUDIO.

And when was he wont to wash his face?

DON PEDRO.

Yea, or to paint himself? for the which, I hear what they say of him.

CLAUDIO.

Nay, but his jesting spirit; which is now crept into a lute-string, and new-governed by stops.

DON PEDRO.

Indeed, that tells a heavy tale for him. Conclude, conclude he is in love.

CLAUDIO.

Nay, but I know who loves him.

DON PEDRO.

That would I know too: I warrant, one that knows him not.

CLAUDIO.

Yes, and his ill conditions; and in despite of all, dies for him.

DON PEDRO.

She shall be buried with her face upwards.

BENEDICK.

Yet is this no charm for the tooth-ache. Old signior, walk aside with me: I have studied eight or nine wise words to speak to you, which these hobby-horses must not hear.
[Exeunt BENEDICK and LEONATO.]

DON PEDRO.

For my life, to break with him about Beatrice.

CLAUDIO.

'Tis even so. Hero and Margaret have by this played their parts with Beatrice, and then the two bears will not bite one another when they meet.
[Enter DON JOHN.]

DON JOHN.

My lord and brother, God save you!

DON PEDRO.

Good den, brother.

DON JOHN.

If your leisure served, I would speak with you.

DON PEDRO.

In private?

DON JOHN.

If it please you; yet Count Claudio may hear, for what I would speak of concerns him.

DON PEDRO.

What's the matter?

DON JOHN.

[To CLAUDIO.] Means your lordship to be married to-morrow?

DON PEDRO.

You know he does.

DON JOHN.

I know not that, when he knows what I know.

CLAUDIO.

If there be any impediment, I pray you discover it.

DON JOHN.

You may think I love you not: let that appear hereafter, and aim better at me by that I now will manifest. For my brother, I think he holds you well, and in dearness of heart hath holp to effect your ensuing marriage; surely suit ill-spent and labour ill bestowed!

DON PEDRO.

Why, what's the matter?

DON JOHN.

I came hither to tell you; and circumstances shortened,—for she has been too long a talking of,—the lady is disloyal.

CLAUDIO.

Who, Hero?

DON JOHN.

Even she: Leonato's Hero, your Hero, every man's Hero.

CLAUDIO.

Disloyal?

DON JOHN.

The word's too good to paint out her wickedness; I could say, she were worse: think you of a worse title, and I will fit her to it. Wonder not till further warrant: go but with me to-night, you shall see her chamber-window entered, even the night before her wedding-day: if you love her then, to-morrow wed her; but it would better fit your honour to change your mind.

CLAUDIO.

May this be so?

DON PEDRO.

I will not think it.

DON JOHN.

If you dare not trust that you see, confess not that you know. If you will follow me, I will show you enough; and when you have seen more and heard more, proceed accordingly.

CLAUDIO.

If I see anything to-night why I should not marry her to-morrow, in the congregation, where I should wed, there will I shame her.

DON PEDRO.

And, as I wooed for thee to obtain her, I will join with thee to disgrace her.

DON JOHN.

I will disparage her no farther till you are my witnesses: bear it coldly but till midnight, and let the issue show itself.

DON PEDRO.

O day untowardly turned!

CLAUDIO.

O mischief strangely thwarting!

DON JOHN.

O plague right well prevented! So will you say when you have seen the sequel. [Exeunt.]

Scene III. A Street
[Enter DOGBERRY and VERGES, with the Watch.]

DOGBERRY.

Are you good men and true?

VERGES.

Yea, or else it were pity but they should suffer salvation, body and soul.

DOGBERRY.

Nay, that were a punishment too good for them, if they should have any allegiance in them, being chosen for the prince's watch.

VERGES.

Well, give them their charge, neighbour Dogberry.

DOGBERRY.

First, who think you the most desartless man to be constable?

FIRST WATCH.

Hugh Oatcake, sir, or George Seacoal; for they can write and read.

DOGBERRY.

Come hither, neighbour Seacoal. God hath blessed you with a good name: to be a well-favoured man is the gift of fortune; but to write and read comes by nature.

SECOND WATCH.

Both which, Master Constable,—

DOGBERRY.

You have: I knew it would be your answer. Well, for your favour, sir, why, give God thanks, and make no boast of it; and for your writing and reading, let that appear when there is no need of such vanity. You are thought here to be the most senseless and fit man for the constable of the watch; therefore bear you the lanthorn. This is your charge: you shall comprehend all vagrom men; you are to bid any man stand, in the prince's name.

SECOND WATCH.

How, if a' will not stand?

DOGBERRY.

Why, then, take no note of him, but let him go; and presently call the rest of the watch together, and thank God you are rid of a knave.

VERGES.

If he will not stand when he is bidden, he is none of the prince's subjects.

DOGBERRY.

True, and they are to meddle with none but the prince's subjects. You shall also make no noise in the streets: for, for the watch to babble and to talk is most tolerable and not to be endured.

SECOND WATCH.

We will rather sleep than talk: we know what belongs to a watch.

DOGBERRY.

Why, you speak like an ancient and most quiet watchman, for I cannot see how sleeping should offend; only have a care that your bills be not stolen. Well, you are to call at all the alehouses, and bid those that are drunk get them to bed.

SECOND WATCH.

How if they will not?

DOGBERRY.

Why then, let them alone till they are sober: if they make you not then the better answer, you may say they are not the men you took them for.

SECOND WATCH.

Well, sir.

DOGBERRY.

If you meet a thief, you may suspect him, by virtue of your office, to be no true man; and, for such kind of men, the less you meddle or make with them, why, the more is for your honesty.

SECOND WATCH.

If we know him to be a thief, shall we not lay hands on him?

DOGBERRY.

Truly, by your office, you may; but I think they that touch pitch will be defiled. The most peaceable way for you, if you do take a thief, is to let him show himself what he is and steal out of your company.

VERGES.

You have been always called a merciful man, partner.

DOGBERRY.

Truly, I would not hang a dog by my will, much more a man who hath any honesty in him.

VERGES.

If you hear a child cry in the night, you must call to the nurse and bid her still it.

SECOND WATCH.

How if the nurse be asleep and will not hear us?

DOGBERRY.

Why then, depart in peace, and let the child wake her with crying; for the ewe that will not hear her lamb when it baes, will never answer a calf when he bleats.

VERGES.
'Tis very true.

DOGBERRY.
This is the end of the charge. You constable, are to present the prince's own person: if you meet the prince in the night, you may stay him.

VERGES.
Nay, by'r lady, that I think, a' cannot.

DOGBERRY.
Five shillings to one on't, with any man that knows the statutes, he may stay him: marry, not without the prince be willing; for, indeed, the watch ought to offend no man, and it is an offence to stay a man against his will.

VERGES.
By'r lady, I think it be so.

DOGBERRY.
Ha, ah, ha! Well, masters, good night: an there be any matter of weight chances, call up me: keep your fellows' counsels and your own, and good night. Come, neighbour.

SECOND WATCH.
Well, masters, we hear our charge: let us go sit here upon the church-bench till two, and then all to bed.

DOGBERRY.
One word more, honest neighbours. I pray you, watch about Signior Leonato's door; for the wedding being there to-morrow, there is a great coil to-night. Adieu; be vigitant, I beseech you.
[Exeunt DOGBERRY and VERGES.]
[Enter BORACHIO and CONRADE.]

BORACHIO.
What, Conrade!

WATCH.
[Aside.] Peace! stir not.

BORACHIO.
Conrade, I say!

CONRADE.

Here, man. I am at thy elbow.

BORACHIO.

Mass, and my elbow itched; I thought there would a scab follow.

CONRADE.

I will owe thee an answer for that; and now forward with thy tale.

BORACHIO.

Stand thee close then under this penthouse, for it drizzles rain, and I will, like a true drunkard, utter all to thee.

WATCH.

[Aside.] Some treason, masters; yet stand close.

BORACHIO.

Therefore know, I have earned of Don John a thousand ducats.

CONRADE.

Is it possible that any villany should be so dear?

BORACHIO.

Thou shouldst rather ask if it were possible any villany should be so rich; for when rich villains have need of poor ones, poor ones may make what price they will.

CONRADE.

I wonder at it.

BORACHIO.

That shows thou art unconfirmed. Thou knowest that the fashion of a doublet, or a hat, or a cloak, is nothing to a man.

CONRADE.

Yes, it is apparel.

BORACHIO.

I mean, the fashion.

CONRADE.

Yes, the fashion is the fashion.

BORACHIO.

Tush! I may as well say the fool's the fool. But seest thou not what a deformed thief
this fashion is?

WATCH.

[Aside.] I know that Deformed; a' has been a vile thief this seven years; a' goes up
and down like a gentleman: I remember his name.

BORACHIO.

Didst thou not hear somebody?

CONRADE.

No: 'twas the vane on the house.

BORACHIO.

Seest thou not, I say, what a deformed thief this fashion is? how giddily he turns
about all the hot bloods between fourteen and five-and-thirty? sometime fashioning
them like Pharaoh's soldiers in the reechy painting; sometime like god Bel's priests
in the old church-window; sometime like the shaven Hercules in the smirched
worm-eaten tapestry, where his codpiece seems as massy as his club?

CONRADE.

All this I see, and I see that the fashion wears out more apparel than the man. But
art not thou thyself giddy with the fashion too, that thou hast shifted out of thy tale
into telling me of the fashion?

BORACHIO.

Not so neither; but know, that I have to-night wooed Margaret, the Lady Hero's
gentlewoman, by the name of Hero: she leans me out at her mistress' chamber-
window, bids me a thousand times good night,—I tell this tale vilely:—I should first
tell thee how the prince, Claudio, and my master, planted and placed and possessed
by my master Don John, saw afar off in the orchard this amiable encounter.

CONRADE.

And thought they Margaret was Hero?

BORACHIO.

Two of them did, the prince and Claudio; but the devil my master, knew she was
Margaret; and partly by his oaths, which first possessed them, partly by the dark
night, which did deceive them, but chiefly by my villany, which did confirm any
slander that Don John had made, away went Claudio enraged; swore he would
meet her, as he was appointed, next morning at the temple, and there, before the
whole congregation, shame her with what he saw o'er night, and send her home
again without a husband.

FIRST WATCH.

We charge you in the prince's name, stand!

SECOND WATCH.

Call up the right Master Constable. We have here recovered the most dangerous piece of lechery that ever was known in the commonwealth.

FIRST WATCH.

And one Deformed is one of them: I know him, a' wears a lock.

CONRADE.

Masters, masters!

SECOND WATCH.

You'll be made bring Deformed forth, I warrant you.

CONRADE.

Masters,—

FIRST WATCH.

Never speak: we charge you let us obey you to go with us.

BORACHIO.

We are like to prove a goodly commodity, being taken up of these men's bills.

CONRADE.

A commodity in question, I warrant you. Come, we'll obey you.
[Exeunt.]

Scene IV. A Room in LEONATO'S House.
[Enter HERO, MARGARET, and URSULA.]

HERO.

Good Ursula, wake my cousin Beatrice, and desire her to rise.

URSULA.

I will, lady.

HERO.

And bid her come hither.

URSULA.

Well.
[Exit.]

MARGARET.

Troth, I think your other rabato were better.

HERO.

No, pray thee, good Meg, I'll wear this.

MARGARET.

By my troth's not so good; and I warrant your cousin will say so.

HERO.

My cousin's a fool, and thou art another: I'll wear none but this.

MARGARET.

I like the new tire within excellently, if the hair were a thought browner; and your gown's a most rare fashion, i' faith. I saw the Duchess of Milan's gown that they praise so.

HERO.

O! that exceeds, they say.

MARGARET.

By my troth's but a night-gown in respect of yours: cloth o' gold, and cuts, and laced with silver, set with pearls, down sleeves, side sleeves, and skirts round, **underborne with a blush tinsel; but for a fine, quaint, graceful, and excellent** fashion, yours is worth ten on 't.

HERO.

God give me joy to wear it! for my heart is exceeding heavy.

MARGARET.

'Twill be heavier soon by the weight of a man.

HERO.

Fie upon thee! art not ashamed?

MARGARET.

Of what, lady? of speaking honourably? is not marriage honourable in a beggar? Is not your lord honourable without marriage? I think you would have me say, 'saving your reverence, a husband.' An bad thinking do not wrest true speaking, I'll **offend nobody. Is there any harm in 'the heavier for a husband'? None, I think, an** it be the right husband and the right wife; otherwise 'tis light, and not heavy: ask my Lady Beatrice else; here she comes.

[Enter BEATRICE.]

HERO.

Good morrow, coz.

BEATRICE.

Good morrow, sweet Hero.

HERO.

Why, how now? do you speak in the sick tune?

BEATRICE.

I am out of all other tune, methinks.

MARGARET.

Clap's into 'Light o' love'; that goes without a burden: do you sing it, and I'll dance
it.

BEATRICE.

Ye, light o' love with your heels! then, if your husband have stables enough, you'll
see he shall lack no barnes.

MARGARET.

O illegitimate construction! I scorn that with my heels.

BEATRICE.

'Tis almost five o'clock, cousin; 'tis time you were ready. By my troth, I am exceeding
ill. Heigh-ho!

MARGARET.

For a hawk, a horse, or a husband?

BEATRICE.

For the letter that begins them all, H.

MARGARET.

Well, an you be not turned Turk, there's no more sailing by the star.

BEATRICE.

What means the fool, trow?

MARGARET.

Nothing I; but God send every one their heart's desire!

HERO.

These gloves the Count sent me; they are an excellent perfume.

BEATRICE.

I am stuffed, cousin, I cannot smell.

MARGARET.

A maid, and stuffed! there's goodly catching of cold.

BEATRICE.

O, God help me! God help me! how long have you professed apprehension?

MARGARET.

Ever since you left it. Doth not my wit become me rarely!

BEATRICE.

It is not seen enough, you should wear it in your cap. By my troth, I am sick.

MARGARET.

Get you some of this distilled Carduus Benedictus, and lay it to your heart: it is the only thing for a qualm.

HERO.

There thou prick'st her with a thistle.

BEATRICE.

Benedictus! why benedictus? you have some moral in this Benedictus.

MARGARET.

Moral! no, by my troth, I have no moral meaning; I meant, plain holy-thistle. You may think, perchance, that I think you are in love: nay, by'r lady, I am not such a fool to think what I list; nor I list not to think what I can; nor, indeed, I cannot think, if I would think my heart out of thinking, that you are in love, or that you will be in love, or that you can be in love. Yet Benedick was such another, and now is he become a man: he swore he would never marry; and yet now, in despite of his heart, he eats his meat without grudging: and how you may be converted, I know not; but methinks you look with your eyes as other women do.

BEATRICE.

What pace is this that thy tongue keeps?

MARGARET.

Not a false gallop.

[Re-enter URSULA.]

URSULA.
Madam, withdraw: the prince, the count, Signior Benedick, Don John, and all the gallants of the town, are come to fetch you to church.

HERO.
Help to dress me, good coz, good Meg, good Ursula.
[Exeunt.]

Scene V. Another Room in LEONATO'S House
[Enter LEONATO and DOGBERRY and VERGES.]

LEONATO.
What would you with me, honest neighbour?

DOGBERRY.
Marry, sir, I would have some confidence with you, that decerns you nearly.

LEONATO.
Brief, I pray you; for you see it is a busy time with me.

DOGBERRY.
Marry, this it is, sir.

VERGES.
Yes, in truth it is, sir.

LEONATO.
What is it, my good friends?

DOGBERRY.
Goodman Verges, sir, speaks a little off the matter: an old man, sir, and his wits are not so blunt as, God help, I would desire they were; but, in faith, honest as the skin between his brows.

VERGES.
Yes, I thank God, I am as honest as any man living, that is an old man and no honester than I.

DOGBERRY.
Comparisons are odorous: palabras, neighbour Verges.

LEONATO.

Neighbours, you are tedious.

DOGBERRY.

It pleases your worship to say so, but we are the poor duke's officers; but truly, for mine own part, if I were as tedious as a king, I could find in my heart to bestow it all of your worship.

LEONATO.

All thy tediousness on me! ha?

DOGBERRY.

Yea, an't were a thousand pound more than 'tis; for I hear as good exclamation on your worship, as of any man in the city, and though I be but a poor man, I am glad to hear it.

VERGES.

And so am I.

LEONATO.

I would fain know what you have to say.

VERGES.

Marry, sir, our watch to-night, excepting your worship's presence, ha' ta'en a couple of as arrant knaves as any in Messina.

DOGBERRY.

A good old man, sir; he will be talking; as they say, 'when the age is in, the wit is out.' God help us! it is a world to see! Well said, i' faith, neighbour Verges: well, God's a good man; an two men ride of a horse, one must ride behind. An honest soul, i' faith, sir; by my troth he is, as ever broke bread; but God is to be worshipped: all men are not alike; alas! good neighbour.

LEONATO.

Indeed, neighbour, he comes too short of you.

DOGBERRY.

Gifts that God gives.

LEONATO.

I must leave you.

DOGBERRY.

One word, sir: our watch, sir, hath indeed comprehended two aspicious persons, and we would have them this morning examined before your worship.

LEONATO.

Take their examination yourself, and bring it me: I am now in great haste, as may appear unto you.

DOGBERRY.

It shall be suffigance.

LEONATO.

Drink some wine ere you go: fare you well.
[Enter a Messenger.]

MESSENGER.

My lord, they stay for you to give your daughter to her husband.

LEONATO.

I'll wait upon them: I am ready.
[Exeunt LEONATO and Messenger.]

DOGBERRY.

Go, good partner, go, get you to Francis Seacoal; bid him bring his pen and inkhorn to the gaol: we are now to examination these men.

VERGES.

And we must do it wisely.

DOGBERRY.

We will spare for no wit, I warrant you; here's that shall drive some of them to a non-come: only get the learned writer to set down our excommunication, and meet me at the gaol.
[Exeunt.]

Act IV

Scene I. The Inside of a Church.
[Enter DON PEDRO, DON JOHN, LEONATO, FRIAR FRANCIS, CLAUDIO, BENEDICK, HERO, BEATRICE, &c.]

LEONATO.

Come, Friar Francis, be brief: only to the plain form of marriage, and you shall recount their particular duties afterwards.

FRIAR.

You come hither, my lord, to marry this lady?

CLAUDIO.

No.

LEONATO.

To be married to her, friar; you come to marry her.

FRIAR.

Lady, you come hither to be married to this count?

HERO.

I do.

FRIAR.

If either of you know any inward impediment, why you should not be conjoined, I charge you, on your souls, to utter it.

CLAUDIO.

Know you any, Hero?

HERO.

None, my lord.

FRIAR.

Know you any, count?

LEONATO.

I dare make his answer; none.

CLAUDIO.

O! what men dare do! what men may do! what men daily do, not knowing what they do!

BENEDICK.

How now! Interjections? Why then, some be of laughing, as ah! ha! he!

CLAUDIO.

Stand thee by, friar. Father, by your leave: Will you with free and unconstrained soul Give me this maid, your daughter?

LEONATO.

As freely, son, as God did give her me.

CLAUDIO.

And what have I to give you back whose worth
May counterpoise this rich and precious gift?

DON PEDRO.

Nothing, unless you render her again.

CLAUDIO.

Sweet prince, you learn me noble thankfulness.
There, Leonato, take her back again:
Give not this rotten orange to your friend;
She's but the sign and semblance of her honour.
Behold! how like a maid she blushes here.
O! what authority and show of truth
Can cunning sin cover itself withal.
Comes not that blood as modest evidence
To witness simple virtue? Would you not swear,
All you that see her, that she were a maid,
By these exterior shows? But she is none:
She knows the heat of a luxurious bed;
Her blush is guiltiness, not modesty.

LEONATO.

What do you mean, my lord?

CLAUDIO.

Not to be married,
Not to knit my soul to an approved wanton.

LEONATO.

Dear my lord, if you, in your own proof,
Have vanquish'd the resistance of her youth,
And made defeat of her virginity,—

CLAUDIO.

I know what you would say: if I have known her,
You'll say she did embrace me as a husband,
And so extenuate the 'forehand sin: No, Leonato,
I never tempted her with word too large;
But, as a brother to his sister, show'd
Bashful sincerity and comely love.

HERO.

And seem'd I ever otherwise to you?

CLAUDIO.

Out on thee! Seeming! I will write against it:
You seem to me as Dian in her orb,
As chaste as is the bud ere it be blown;
But you are more intemperate in your blood
Than Venus, or those pamper'd animals
That rage in savage sensuality.

HERO.

Is my lord well, that he doth speak so wide?

LEONATO.

Sweet prince, why speak not you?

DON PEDRO.

What should I speak?
I stand dishonour'd, that have gone about
To link my dear friend to a common stale.

LEONATO.

Are these things spoken, or do I but dream?

DON JOHN.

Sir, they are spoken, and these things are true.

BENEDICK.

This looks not like a nuptial.

HERO.

True! O God!

CLAUDIO.

Leonato, stand I here? Is this the prince?
Is this the prince's brother?
Is this face Hero's? Are our eyes our own?

LEONATO.

All this is so; but what of this, my lord?

CLAUDIO.

Let me but move one question to your daughter,
And by that fatherly and kindly power
That you have in her, bid her answer truly.

LEONATO.

I charge thee do so, as thou art my child.

HERO.

O, God defend me! how am I beset!
What kind of catechizing call you this?

CLAUDIO.

To make you answer truly to your name.

HERO.

Is it not Hero? Who can blot that name
With any just reproach?

CLAUDIO.

Marry, that can Hero:
Hero itself can blot out Hero's virtue.
What man was he talk'd with you yesternight
Out at your window, betwixt twelve and one?
Now, if you are a maid, answer to this.

HERO.

I talk'd with no man at that hour, my lord.

DON PEDRO.

Why, then are you no maiden.
Leonato, I am sorry you must hear: upon my honour,
Myself, my brother, and this grieved count,
Did see her, hear her, at that hour last night,
Talk with a ruffian at her chamber-window;
Who hath indeed, most like a liberal villain,
Confess'd the vile encounters they have had
A thousand times in secret.

DON JOHN.

Fie, fie! they are not to be nam'd, my lord,
Not to be spoke of;
There is not chastity enough in language
Without offence to utter them. Thus, pretty lady,
I am sorry for thy much misgovernment.

CLAUDIO.

O Hero! what a Hero hadst thou been,
If half thy outward graces had been plac'd

About thy thoughts and counsels of thy heart!
But fare thee well, most foul, most fair! farewell,
Thou pure impiety, and impious purity!
For thee I'll lock up all the gates of love,
And on my eyelids shall conjecture hang,
To turn all beauty into thoughts of harm,
And never shall it more be gracious.

LEONATO.
Hath no man's dagger here a point for me?
[HERO swoons.]

BEATRICE.
Why, how now, cousin! wherefore sink you down?

DON JOHN.
Come, let us go. These things, come thus to light,
Smother her spirits up.
[Exeunt DON PEDRO, DON JOHN and CLAUDIO.]

BENEDICK.
How doth the lady?

BEATRICE.
Dead, I think! help, uncle! Hero! why, Hero! Uncle! Signior Benedick! Friar!

LEONATO.
O Fate! take not away thy heavy hand:
Death is the fairest cover for her shame
That may be wish'd for.

BEATRICE.
How now, cousin Hero?

FRIAR.
Have comfort, lady.

LEONATO.
Dost thou look up?

FRIAR.
Yea; wherefore should she not?

LEONATO.

Wherefore! Why, doth not every earthly thing
Cry shame upon her? Could she here deny
The story that is printed in her blood?
Do not live, Hero; do not ope thine eyes;
For, did I think thou wouldst not quickly die,
Thought I thy spirits were stronger than thy shames,
Myself would, on the rearward of reproaches,
Strike at thy life. Griev'd I, I had but one?
Chid I for that at frugal nature's frame?
O! one too much by thee. Why had I one?
Why ever wast thou lovely in mine eyes?
Why had I not with charitable hand
Took up a beggar's issue at my gates,
Who smirched thus, and mir'd with infamy,
I might have said, 'No part of it is mine;
This shame derives itself from unknown loins?'
But mine, and mine I lov'd, and mine I prais'd,
And mine that I was proud on, mine so much
That I myself was to myself not mine,
Valuing of her; why, she—O! she is fallen
Into a pit of ink, that the wide sea
Hath drops too few to wash her clean again,
And salt too little which may season give
To her foul-tainted flesh.

BENEDICK.

Sir, sir, be patient.
For my part, I am so attir'd in wonder,
I know not what to say.

BEATRICE.

O! on my soul, my cousin is belied!

BENEDICK.

Lady, were you her bedfellow last night?

BEATRICE.

No, truly, not; although, until last night I have this twelvemonth been her bedfellow.

LEONATO.

Confirm'd, confirm'd! O! that is stronger made,
Which was before barr'd up with ribs of iron.

Would the two princes lie? and Claudio lie,
Who lov'd her so, that, speaking of her foulness,
Wash'd it with tears? Hence from her! let her die.

FRIAR.

Hear me a little;
For I have only been silent so long,
And given way unto this course of fortune,
By noting of the lady: I have mark'd
A thousand blushing apparitions
To start into her face; a thousand innocent shames
In angel whiteness bear away those blushes;
And in her eye there hath appear'd a fire,
To burn the errors that these princes hold
Against her maiden truth. Call me a fool;
Trust not my reading nor my observations,
Which with experimental seal doth warrant
The tenure of my book; trust not my age,
My reverence, calling, nor divinity,
If this sweet lady lie not guiltless here
Under some biting error.

LEONATO.

Friar, it cannot be.
Thou seest that all the grace that she hath left
Is that she will not add to her damnation
A sin of perjury: she not denies it.
Why seek'st thou then to cover with excuse
That which appears in proper nakedness?

FRIAR.

Lady, what man is he you are accus'd of?

HERO.

They know that do accuse me, I know none;
If I know more of any man alive
Than that which maiden modesty doth warrant,
Let all my sins lack mercy! O, my father!
Prove you that any man with me convers'd
At hours unmeet, or that I yesternight
Maintain'd the change of words with any creature,
Refuse me, hate me, torture me to death.

FRIAR.

There is some strange misprision in the princes.

BENEDICK.

Two of them have the very bent of honour;
And if their wisdoms be misled in this,
The practice of it lives in John the bastard,
Whose spirits toil in frame of villanies.

LEONATO.

I know not. If they speak but truth of her,
These hands shall tear her;if they wrong her honour,
The proudest of them shall well hear of it.
Time hath not yet so dried this blood of mine,
Nor age so eat up my invention,
Nor fortune made such havoc of my means,
Nor my bad life reft me so much of friends,
But they shall find, awak'd in such a kind,
Both strength of limb and policy of mind,
Ability in means and choice of friends,
To quit me of them throughly.

FRIAR.

Pause awhile, And let my counsel sway you in this case.
Your daughter here the princes left for dead;
Let her awhile be secretly kept in,
And publish it that she is dead indeed:
Maintain a mourning ostentation;
And on your family's old monument
Hang mournful epitaphs and do all rites
That appertain unto a burial.

LEONATO.

What shall become of this? What will this do?

FRIAR.

Marry, this well carried shall on her behalf
Change slander to remorse; that is some good.
But not for that dream I on this strange course,
But on this travail look for greater birth.
She dying, as it must be so maintain'd,
Upon the instant that she was accus'd,
Shall be lamented, pitied and excus'd

Of every hearer; for it so falls out
That what we have we prize not to the worth
Whiles we enjoy it, but being lack'd and lost,
Why, then we rack the value, then we find
The virtue that possession would not show us
Whiles it was ours. So will it fare with Claudio:
When he shall hear she died upon his words,
The idea of her life shall sweetly creep
Into his study of imagination,
And every lovely organ of her life
Shall come apparell'd in more precious habit,
More moving-delicate, and full of life
Into the eye and prospect of his soul,
Than when she liv'd indeed: then shall he mourn,—
If ever love had interest in his liver,—
And wish he had not so accused her,
No, though be thought his accusation true.
Let this be so, and doubt not but success
Will fashion the event in better shape
Than I can lay it down in likelihood.
But if all aim but this be levell'd false,
The supposition of the lady's death
Will quench the wonder of her infamy:
And if it sort not well, you may conceal her,—
As best befits her wounded reputation,—
In some reclusive and religious life,
Out of all eyes, tongues, minds, and injuries.

                    BENEDICK.
Signior Leonato, let the friar advise you:
And though you know my inwardness and love
Is very much unto the prince and Claudio,
Yet, by mine honour, I will deal in this
As secretly and justly as your soul
Should with your body.

                    LEONATO.
Being that I flow in grief, The smallest twine may lead me.

                    FRIAR.
'Tis well consented: presently away;
For to strange sores strangely they strain the cure.
Come, lady, die to live: this wedding day

Perhaps is but prolong'd: have patience and endure.
[Exeunt FRIAR, HERO, and LEONATO.]

BENEDICK.
Lady Beatrice, have you wept all this while?

BEATRICE.
Yea, and I will weep a while longer.

BENEDICK.
I will not desire that.

BEATRICE.
You have no reason; I do it freely.

BENEDICK.
Surely I do believe your fair cousin is wronged.

BEATRICE.
Ah! how much might the man deserve of me that would right her.

BENEDICK.
Is there any way to show such friendship?

BEATRICE.
A very even way, but no such friend.

BENEDICK.
May a man do it?

BEATRICE.
It is a man's office, but not yours.

BENEDICK.
I do love nothing in the world so well as you: is not that strange?

BEATRICE.
As strange as the thing I know not. It were as possible for me to say
I loved nothing so well as you; but believe me not, and yet I lie not;
I confess nothing, nor I deny nothing. I am sorry for my cousin.

BENEDICK.
By my sword, Beatrice, thou lovest me.

BEATRICE.

Do not swear by it, and eat it.

BENEDICK.

I will swear by it that you love me; and I will make him eat it that says I love not you.

BEATRICE.

Will you not eat your word?

BENEDICK.

With no sauce that can be devised to it. I protest I love thee.

BEATRICE.

Why then, God forgive me!

BENEDICK.

What offence, sweet Beatrice?

BEATRICE.

You have stayed me in a happy hour: I was about to protest I loved you.

BENEDICK.

And do it with all thy heart.

BEATRICE.

I love you with so much of my heart that none is left to protest.

BENEDICK.

Come, bid me do anything for thee.

BEATRICE.

Kill Claudio.

BENEDICK.

Ha! not for the wide world.

BEATRICE.

You kill me to deny it. Farewell.

BENEDICK.

Tarry, sweet Beatrice.

BEATRICE.

I am gone, though I am here: there is no love in you: nay, I pray you, let me go.

BENEDICK.

Beatrice,—

BEATRICE.

In faith, I will go.

BENEDICK.

We'll be friends first.

BEATRICE.

You dare easier be friends with me than fight with mine enemy.

BENEDICK.

Is Claudio thine enemy?

BEATRICE.

Is he not approved in the height a villain, that hath slandered, scorned, dishonoured my kinswoman? O! that I were a man. What! bear her in hand until they come to take hands, and then, with public accusation, uncovered slander, unmitigated rancour,—O God, that I were a man! I would eat his heart in the market-place.

BENEDICK.

Hear me, Beatrice,—

BEATRICE.

Talk with a man out at a window! a proper saying!

BENEDICK.

Nay, but Beatrice,—

BEATRICE.

Sweet Hero! she is wronged, she is slandered, she is undone.

BENEDICK.

Beat—-

BEATRICE.

Princes and counties! Surely, a princely testimony, a goodly Count Comfect; a sweet gallant, surely! O! that I were a man for his sake, or that I had any friend would be a man for my sake! But manhood is melted into cursies, valour into compliment, and men are only turned into tongue, and trim ones too: he is now as valiant as Hercules, that only tells a lie and swears it. I cannot be a man with wishing, therefore I will die a woman with grieving.

BENEDICK.
Tarry, good Beatrice. By this hand, I love thee.

BEATRICE.
Use it for my love some other way than swearing by it.

BENEDICK.
Think you in your soul the Count Claudio hath wronged Hero?

BEATRICE.
Yea, as sure is I have a thought or a soul.

BENEDICK.
Enough! I am engaged, I will challenge him. I will kiss your hand, and so leave you. By this hand, Claudio shall render me a dear account. As you hear of me, so think of me. Go, comfort your cousin: I must say she is dead; and so, farewell. [Exeunt.]

Scene II. A Prison
[Enter DOGBERRY, VERGES, and SEXTON, in gowns; and the Watch, with CONRADE and BORACHIO.]

DOGBERRY.
Is our whole dissembly appeared?

VERGES.
O! a stool and a cushion for the sexton.

SEXTON.
Which be the malefactors?

DOGBERRY.
Marry, that am I and my partner.

VERGES.
Nay, that's certain: we have the exhibition to examine.

SEXTON.
But which are the offenders that are to be examined? let them come before Master constable.

DOGBERRY.

Yea, marry, let them come before me. What is your name, friend?

BORACHIO.

Borachio.

DOGBERRY.

Pray write down Borachio. Yours, sirrah?

CONRADE.

I am a gentleman, sir, and my name is Conrade.

DOGBERRY.

Write down Master gentleman Conrade. Masters, do you serve God?

BOTH.

Yea, sir, we hope.

DOGBERRY.

Write down that they hope they serve God: and write God first; for God defend but God should go before such villains! Masters, it is proved already that you are little better than false knaves, and it will go near to be thought so shortly. How answer you for yourselves?

CONRADE.

Marry, sir, we say we are none.

DOGBERRY.

A marvellous witty fellow, I assure you; but I will go about with him. Come you hither, sirrah; a word in your ear: sir, I say to you, it is thought you are false knaves.

BORACHIO.

Sir, I say to you we are none.

DOGBERRY.

Well, stand aside. Fore God, they are both in a tale. Have you writ down, that they are none?

SEXTON.

Master constable, you go not the way to examine: you must call forth the watch that are their accusers.

DOGBERRY.

Yea, marry, that's the eftest way. Let the watch come forth. Masters, I charge you, in the prince's name, accuse these men.

FIRST WATCH.

This man said, sir, that Don John, the prince's brother, was a villain.

DOGBERRY.

Write down Prince John a villain. Why, this is flat perjury, to call a prince's brother villain.

BORACHIO.

Master Constable,—

DOGBERRY.

Pray thee, fellow, peace: I do not like thy look, I promise thee.

SEXTON.

What heard you him say else?

SECOND WATCH.

Marry, that he had received a thousand ducats of Don John for accusing the Lady Hero wrongfully.

DOGBERRY.

Flat burglary as ever was committed.

VERGES.

Yea, by the mass, that it is.

SEXTON.

What else, fellow?

FIRST WATCH.

And that Count Claudio did mean, upon his words, to disgrace Hero before the whole assembly, and not marry her.

DOGBERRY.

O villain! thou wilt be condemned into everlasting redemption for this.

SEXTON.

What else?

SECOND WATCH.

This is all.

SEXTON.

And this is more, masters, than you can deny. Prince John is this morning secretly
stolen away: Hero was in this manner accused, in this manner refused, and, upon
the grief of this, suddenly died. Master Constable, let these men be bound, and
brought to Leonato's: I will go before and show him their examination.
[Exit.]

DOGBERRY.

Come, let them be opinioned.

VERGES.

Let them be in the hands—

CONRADE.

Off, coxcomb!

DOGBERRY.

God's my life! where's the sexton? let him write down the prince's officer coxcomb.
Come, bind them. Thou naughty varlet!

CONRADE.

Away! you are an ass; you are an ass.

DOGBERRY.

Dost thou not suspect my place? Dost thou not suspect my years? O that he were
here to write me down an ass! but, masters, remember that I am an ass; though
it be not written down, yet forget not that I am an ass. No, thou villain, thou art
full of piety, as shall be proved upon thee by good witness. I am a wise fellow; and,
which is more, an officer; and, which is more, a householder; and, which is more,
as pretty a piece of flesh as any in Messina; and one that knows the law, go to; and
a rich fellow enough, go to; and a fellow that hath had losses; and one that hath two
gowns, and everything handsome about him. Bring him away. O that I had been
writ down an ass!
[Exeunt.]

Act V

Scene I. Before LEONATO'S House.
[Enter LEONATO and ANTONIO.]

ANTONIO.

If you go on thus, you will kill yourself
And 'tis not wisdom thus to second grief
Against yourself.

LEONATO.

I pray thee, cease thy counsel,
Which falls into mine ears as profitless
As water in a sieve: give not me counsel;
Nor let no comforter delight mine ear
But such a one whose wrongs do suit with mine:
Bring me a father that so lov'd his child,
Whose joy of her is overwhelm'd like mine,
And bid him speak to me of patience;
Measure his woe the length and breadth of mine,
And let it answer every strain for strain,
As thus for thus and such a grief for such,
In every lineament, branch, shape, and form:
If such a one will smile, and stroke his beard;
Bid sorrow wag, cry 'hem' when he should groan,
Patch grief with proverbs; make misfortune drunk
With candle-wasters; bring him yet to me,
And I of him will gather patience.
But there is no such man; for, brother, men
Can counsel and speak comfort to that grief
Which they themselves not feel; but, tasting it,
Their counsel turns to passion, which before
Would give preceptial medicine to rage,
Fetter strong madness in a silken thread,
Charm ache with air and agony with words.
No, no; 'tis all men's office to speak patience
To those that wring under the load of sorrow,
But no man's virtue nor sufficiency
To be so moral when he shall endure
The like himself. Therefore give me no counsel:
My griefs cry louder than advertisement.

ANTONIO.

Therein do men from children nothing differ.

LEONATO.

I pray thee peace! I will be flesh and blood;
For there was never yet philosopher

That could endure the toothache patiently,
However they have writ the style of gods
And made a push at chance and sufferance.

ANTONIO.
Yet bend not all the harm upon yourself;
Make those that do offend you suffer too.

LEONATO.
There thou speak'st reason: nay, I will do so.
My soul doth tell me Hero is belied;
And that shall Claudio know; so shall the prince,
And all of them that thus dishonour her.

ANTONIO.
Here comes the prince and Claudio hastily.
[Enter DON PEDRO and CLAUDIO.]

DON PEDRO.
Good den, good den.

CLAUDIO.
Good day to both of you.

LEONATO.
Hear you, my lords,—

DON PEDRO.
We have some haste, Leonato.

LEONATO.
Some haste, my lord! well, fare you well, my lord:
Are you so hasty now?—well, all is one.

DON PEDRO.
Nay, do not quarrel with us, good old man.

ANTONIO.
If he could right himself with quarrelling,
Some of us would lie low.

CLAUDIO.
Who wrongs him?

LEONATO.

Marry, thou dost wrong me; thou dissembler, thou.
Nay, never lay thy hand upon thy sword; I fear thee not.

CLAUDIO.

Marry, beshrew my hand,
If it should give your age such cause of fear.
In faith, my hand meant nothing to my sword.

LEONATO.

Tush, tush, man! never fleer and jest at me:
I speak not like a dotard nor a fool,
As, under privilege of age, to brag
What I have done being young, or what would do,
Were I not old. Know, Claudio, to thy head,
Thou hast so wrong'd mine innocent child and me
That I am forc'd to lay my reverence by,
And, with grey hairs and bruise of many days,
Do challenge thee to trial of a man.
I say thou hast belied mine innocent child:
Thy slander hath gone through and through her heart,
And she lied buried with her ancestors;
O! in a tomb where never scandal slept,
Save this of hers, fram'd by thy villany!

CLAUDIO.

My villany?

LEONATO.

Thine, Claudio; thine, I say.

DON PEDRO.

You say not right, old man,

LEONATO.

My lord, my lord,
I'll prove it on his body, if he dare,
Despite his nice fence and his active practice,
His May of youth and bloom of lustihood.

CLAUDIO.

Away! I will not have to do with you.

LEONATO.

Canst thou so daff me? Thou hast kill'd my child;
If thou kill'st me, boy, thou shalt kill a man.

ANTONIO.

He shall kill two of us, and men indeed:
But that's no matter; let him kill one first:
Win me and wear me; let him answer me.
Come, follow me, boy; come, sir boy, come, follow me.
Sir boy, I'll whip you from your foining fence;
Nay, as I am a gentleman, I will.

LEONATO.

Brother,—

ANTONIO.

Content yourself. God knows I lov'd my niece;
And she is dead, slander'd to death by villains,
That dare as well answer a man indeed
As I dare take a serpent by the tongue.
Boys, apes, braggarts, Jacks, milksops!

LEONATO.

Brother Antony,—

ANTONIO.

Hold your content. What, man! I know them, yea,
And what they weigh, even to the utmost scruple,
Scambling, out-facing, fashion-monging boys,
That lie and cog and flout, deprave and slander,
Go antickly, show outward hideousness,
And speak off half a dozen dangerous words,
How they might hurt their enemies, if they durst;
And this is all!

LEONATO.

But, brother Antony,—

ANTONIO.

Come, 'tis no matter:
Do not you meddle, let me deal in this.

DON PEDRO.

Gentlemen both, we will not wake your patience.
My heart is sorry for your daughter's death;
But, on my honour, she was charg'd with nothing
But what was true and very full of proof.

LEONATO.

My lord, my lord—

DON PEDRO.

I will not hear you.

LEONATO.

No? Come, brother, away. I will be heard.—

ANTONIO.

And shall, or some of us will smart for it.
[Exeunt LEONATO and ANTONIO.]
[Enter BENEDICK.]

DON PEDRO.

See, see; here comes the man we went to seek.

CLAUDIO.

Now, signior, what news?

BENEDICK.

Good day, my lord.

DON PEDRO.

Welcome, signior: you are almost come to part almost a fray.

CLAUDIO.

We had like to have had our two noses snapped off with two old men without teeth.

DON PEDRO.

Leonato and his brother. What think'st thou? Had we fought, I doubt we should
have been too young for them.

BENEDICK.

In a false quarrel there is no true valour. I came to seek you both.

CLAUDIO.

We have been up and down to seek thee; for we are high-proof melancholy, and would fain have it beaten away. Wilt thou use thy wit?

BENEDICK.

It is in my scabbard; shall I draw it?

DON PEDRO.

Dost thou wear thy wit by thy side?

CLAUDIO.

Never any did so, though very many have been beside their wit. I will bid thee draw, as we do the minstrels; draw, to pleasure us.

DON PEDRO.

As I am an honest man, he looks pale. Art thou sick, or angry?

CLAUDIO.

What, courage, man! What though care killed a cat, thou hast mettle enough in thee to kill care.

BENEDICK.

Sir, I shall meet your wit in the career, an you charge it against me. I pray you choose another subject.

CLAUDIO.

Nay then, give him another staff: this last was broke cross.

DON PEDRO.

By this light, he changes more and more: I think he be angry indeed.

CLAUDIO.

If he be, he knows how to turn his girdle.

BENEDICK.

Shall I speak a word in your ear?

CLAUDIO.

God bless me from a challenge!

BENEDICK.

[Aside to CLAUDIO.]
] You are a villain, I jest not: I will make it good how you dare, with what you dare,

and when you dare. Do me right, or I will protest your cowardice. You have killed a sweet lady, and her death shall fall heavy on you. Let me hear from you.

CLAUDIO.

Well I will meet you, so I may have good cheer.

DON PEDRO.

What, a feast, a feast?

CLAUDIO.

I' faith, I thank him; he hath bid me to a calf's-head and a capon, the which if I do not carve most curiously, say my knife's naught. Shall I not find a woodcock too?

BENEDICK.

Sir, your wit ambles well; it goes easily.

DON PEDRO.

I'll tell thee how Beatrice praised thy wit the other day. I said, thou hadst a fine wit.
'True,' says she, 'a fine little one.'
'No,' said I, 'a great wit.'
'Right,' said she, 'a great gross one.'
'Nay,' said I, 'a good wit.'
'Just,' said she, 'it hurts nobody.'
'Nay,' said I, 'the gentleman is wise.'
'Certain,' said she,a wise gentleman.'
'Nay,' said I, 'he hath the tongues.'
'That I believe' said she, 'for he swore a thing to me on Monday
night, which he forswore on Tuesday morning: there's a double tongue;
there's two tongues.'
Thus did she, an hour together, trans-shape thy particular virtues;
yet at last she concluded with a sigh, thou wast the properest man in Italy.

CLAUDIO.

For the which she wept heartily and said she cared not.

DON PEDRO.

Yea, that she did; but yet, for all that, an if she did not hate him deadly, she would love him dearly. The old man's daughter told us all.

CLAUDIO.

All, all; and moreover, God saw him when he was hid in the garden.

DON PEDRO.

But when shall we set the savage bull's horns on the sensible Benedick's head?

CLAUDIO.

Yea, and text underneath, 'Here dwells Benedick the married man!'

BENEDICK.

Fare you well, boy: you know my mind. I will leave you now to your gossip-like humour; you break jests as braggarts do their blades, which, God be thanked, hurt not. My lord, for your many courtesies I thank you: I must discontinue your company. Your brother the bastard is fled from Messina: you have, among you, killed a sweet and innocent lady. For my Lord Lack-beard there, he and I shall meet; and till then, peace be with him.
[Exit.]

DON PEDRO.

He is in earnest.

CLAUDIO.

In most profound earnest; and, I'll warrant you, for the love of Beatrice.

DON PEDRO.

And hath challenged thee?

CLAUDIO.

Most sincerely.

DON PEDRO.

What a pretty thing man is when he goes in his doublet and hose and leaves off his wit!

CLAUDIO.

He is then a giant to an ape; but then is an ape a doctor to such a man.

DON PEDRO.

But, soft you; let me be: pluck up, my heart, and be sad! Did he not say my brother was fled?
[Enter DOGBERRY, VERGES, and the Watch, with CONRADE and BORACHIO.]

DOGBERRY.

Come you, sir: if justice cannot tame you, she shall ne'er weigh more reasons in her balance. Nay, an you be a cursing hypocrite once, you must be looked to.

DON PEDRO.

How now! two of my brother's men bound! Borachio, one!

CLAUDIO.

Hearken after their offence, my lord.

DON PEDRO.

Officers, what offence have these men done?

DOGBERRY.

Marry, sir, they have committed false report; moreover, they have spoken untruths; secondarily, they are slanders; sixth and lastly, they have belied a lady; thirdly, they have verified unjust things; and to conclude, they are lying knaves.

DON PEDRO.

First, I ask thee what they have done; thirdly, I ask thee what's their offence; sixth and lastly, why they are committed; and, to conclude, what you lay to their charge?

CLAUDIO.

Rightly reasoned, and in his own division; and, by my troth, there's one meaning well suited.

DON PEDRO.

Who have you offended, masters, that you are thus bound to your answer? this learned constable is too cunning to be understood. What's your offence?

BORACHIO.

Sweet prince, let me go no further to mine answer: do you hear me, and let this count kill me. I have deceived even your very eyes: what your wisdoms could not discover, these shallow fools have brought to light; who, in the night overheard me confessing to this man how Don John your brother incensed me to slander the Lady Hero; how you were brought into the orchard and saw me court Margaret in Hero's garments; how you disgraced her, when you should marry her. My villany they have upon record; which I had rather seal with my death than repeat over to my shame. The lady is dead upon mine and my master's false accusation; and, briefly, I desire nothing but the reward of a villain.

DON PEDRO.

Runs not this speech like iron through your blood?

CLAUDIO.

I have drunk poison whiles he utter'd it.

DON PEDRO.

But did my brother set thee on to this?

BORACHIO.
Yea; and paid me richly for the practice of it.

DON PEDRO.
He is compos'd and fram'd of treachery: And fled he is upon this villany.

CLAUDIO.
Sweet Hero! now thy image doth appear In the rare semblance that I lov'd it first.

DOGBERRY.
Come, bring away the plaintiffs: by this time our sexton hath reformed Signior Leonato of the matter. And masters, do not forget to specify, when time and place shall serve, that I am an ass.

VERGES.
Here, here comes Master Signior Leonato, and the sexton too.
[Re-enter LEONATO, ANTONIO, and the Sexton.]

LEONATO.
Which is the villain? Let me see his eyes,
That, when I note another man like him,
I may avoid him. Which of these is he?

BORACHIO.
If you would know your wronger, look on me.

LEONATO.
Art thou the slave that with thy breath hast kill'd
Mine innocent child?

BORACHIO.
Yea, even I alone.

LEONATO.
No, not so, villain; thou beliest thyself:
Here stand a pair of honourable men;
A third is fled, that had a hand in it.
I thank you, princes, for my daughter's death:
Record it with your high and worthy deeds.
'Twas bravely done, if you bethink you of it.

CLAUDIO.
I know not how to pray your patience;
Yet I must speak. Choose your revenge yourself;

Impose me to what penance your invention
Can lay upon my sin: yet sinn'd I not
But in mistaking.

DON PEDRO.

By my soul, nor I:
And yet, to satisfy this good old man,
I would bend under any heavy weight
That he'll enjoin me to.

LEONATO.

I cannot bid you bid my daughter live;
That were impossible; but, I pray you both,
Possess the people in Messina here
How innocent she died; and if your love
Can labour aught in sad invention,
Hang her an epitaph upon her tomb,
And sing it to her bones: sing it to-night.
To-morrow morning come you to my house,
And since you could not be my son-in-law,
Be yet my nephew. My brother hath a daughter,
Almost the copy of my child that's dead,
And she alone is heir to both of us:
Give her the right you should have given her cousin,
And so dies my revenge.

CLAUDIO.

O noble sir,
Your over-kindness doth wring tears from me!
I do embrace your offer; and dispose
For henceforth of poor Claudio.

LEONATO.

To-morrow then I will expect your coming;
To-night I take my leave. This naughty man
Shall face to face be brought to Margaret,
Who, I believe, was pack'd in all this wrong,
Hir'd to it by your brother.

BORACHIO.

No, by my soul she was not;
Nor knew not what she did when she spoke to me;
But always hath been just and virtuous
In anything that I do know by her.

DOGBERRY.

Moreover, sir,—which, indeed, is not under white and black,— this plaintiff here, the offender, did call me ass: I beseech you, let it be remembered in his punishment. And also, the watch heard them talk of one Deformed: they say he wears a key in his ear and a lock hanging by it, and borrows money in God's name, the which he hath used so long and never paid, that now men grow hard-hearted, and will lend nothing for God's sake. Pray you, examine him upon that point.

LEONATO.

I thank thee for thy care and honest pains.

DOGBERRY.

Your worship speaks like a most thankful and reverent youth, and I praise God for you.

LEONATO.

There's for thy pains.

DOGBERRY.

God save the foundation!

LEONATO.

Go, I discharge thee of thy prisoner, and I thank thee.

DOGBERRY.

I leave an arrant knave with your worship; which I beseech your worship to correct yourself, for the example of others. God keep your worship! I wish your worship well; God restore you to health! I humbly give you leave to depart, and if a merry meeting may be wished, God prohibit it! Come, neighbour.
[Exeunt DOGBERRY and VERGES.]

LEONATO.

Until to-morrow morning, lords, farewell.

ANTONIO.

Farewell, my lords: we look for you to-morrow.

DON PEDRO.

We will not fail.

CLAUDIO.

To-night I'll mourn with Hero.
[Exeunt DON PEDRO and CLAUDIO.]

LEONATO.

[To the Watch.] Bring you these fellows on. We'll talk with Margaret, How her acquaintance grew with this lewd fellow.
[Exeunt.]

Scene 2. LEONATO'S Garden
[Enter BENEDICK and MARGARET, meeting.]

BENEDICK.

Pray thee, sweet Mistress Margaret, deserve well at my hands by helping me to the speech of Beatrice.

MARGARET.

Will you then write me a sonnet in praise of my beauty?

BENEDICK.

In so high a style, Margaret, that no man living shall come over it; for, in most comely truth, thou deservest it.

MARGARET.

To have no man come over me! why, shall I always keep below stairs?

BENEDICK.

Thy wit is as quick as the greyhound's mouth; it catches.

MARGARET.

And yours as blunt as the fencer's foils, which hit, but hurt not.

BENEDICK.

A most manly wit, Margaret; it will not hurt a woman: and so, I pray thee, call Beatrice. I give thee the bucklers.

MARGARET.

Give us the swords, we have bucklers of our own.

BENEDICK.

If you use them, Margaret, you must put in the pikes with a vice; and they are dangerous weapons for maids.

MARGARET.

Well, I will call Beatrice to you, who I think hath legs.

BENEDICK.

And therefore will come.
[Exit MARGARET.]
The god of love,
That sits above,
And knows me, and knows me,
How pitiful I deserve,—
I mean, in singing: but in loving, Leander the good swimmer, Troilus the first
employer of panders, and a whole book full of these quondam carpet-mongers,
whose names yet run smoothly in the even road of a blank verse, why, they were
never so truly turned over and over as my poor self in love. Marry, I cannot show it
in rime; I have tried: I can find out no rime to 'lady' but 'baby', an innocent rhyme;
for 'scorn,' 'horn', a hard rime; for 'school', 'fool', a babbling rhyme; very ominous
endings: no, I was not born under a riming planet, nor I cannot woo in festival
terms.
[Enter BEATRICE.]
Sweet Beatrice, wouldst thou come when I called thee?

BEATRICE.

Yea, signior; and depart when you bid me.

BENEDICK.

O, stay but till then!

BEATRICE.

'Then' is spoken; fare you well now: and yet, ere I go, let me go with that I came for;
which is, with knowing what hath passed between you and Claudio.

BENEDICK.

Only foul words; and thereupon I will kiss thee.

BEATRICE.

Foul words is but foul wind, and foul wind is but foul breath, and foul breath is
noisome; therefore I will depart unkissed.

BENEDICK.

Thou hast frighted the word out of his right sense, so forcible is thy wit. But I must
tell thee plainly, Claudio undergoes my challenge, and either I must shortly hear
from him, or I will subscribe him a coward. And, I pray thee now, tell me, for which
of my bad parts didst thou first fall in love with me?

BEATRICE.

For them all together; which maintained so politic a state of evil that they will not admit any good part to intermingle with them. But for which of my good parts did you first suffer love for me?

BENEDICK.

'Suffer love,' a good epithet! I do suffer love indeed, for I love thee against my will.

BEATRICE.

In spite of your heart, I think. Alas, poor heart! If you spite it for my sake, I will spite it for yours; for I will never love that which my friend hates.

BENEDICK.

Thou and I are too wise to woo peaceably.

BEATRICE.

It appears not in this confession: there's not one wise man among twenty that will praise himself.

BENEDICK.

An old, an old instance, Beatrice, that lived in the time of good neighbours. If a man do not erect in this age his own tomb ere he dies, he shall live no longer in monument than the bell rings and the widow weeps.

BEATRICE.

And how long is that think you?

BENEDICK.

Question: why, an hour in clamour and a quarter in rheum: therefore is it most expedient for the wise,—if Don Worm, his conscience, find no impediment to the contrary,—to be the trumpet of his own virtues, as I am to myself. So much for praising myself, who, I myself will bear witness, is praiseworthy. And now tell me, how doth your cousin?

BEATRICE.

Very ill.

BENEDICK.

And how do you?

BEATRICE.

Very ill too.

BENEDICK.

Serve God, love me, and mend. There will I leave you too, for here comes one in haste.

[Enter URSULA.]

URSULA.

Madam, you must come to your uncle. Yonder's old coil at home: it is proved, my Lady Hero hath been falsely accused, the prince and Claudio mightily abused; and Don John is the author of all, who is fled and gone. Will you come presently?

BEATRICE.

Will you go hear this news, signior?

BENEDICK.

I will live in thy heart, die in thy lap, and be buried in thy eyes; and moreover I will go with thee to thy uncle's.
[Exeunt.]

Scene III. The Inside of a Church
[Enter DON PEDRO, CLAUDIO, and Attendants, with music and tapers]

CLAUDIO.

Is this the monument of Leonato?

A LORD.

It is, my lord.

CLAUDIO.

[Reads from a scroll.]
Done to death by slanderous tongues
Was the Hero that here lies:
Death, in guerdon of her wrongs,
Gives her fame which never dies.
So the life that died with shame
Lives in death with glorious fame.
Hang thou there upon the tomb,
Praising her when I am dumb.
Now, music, sound, and sing your solemn hymn.
SONG.
Pardon, goddess of the night,
Those that slew thy virgin knight;
For the which, with songs of woe,
Round about her tomb they go.
Midnight, assist our moan;
Help us to sigh and groan,
Heavily, heavily:

Graves, yawn and yield your dead,
Till death be uttered,
Heavily, heavily.

CLAUDIO.

Now, unto thy bones good night!
Yearly will I do this rite.

DON PEDRO.

Good morrow, masters: put your torches out.
The wolves have prey'd; and look, the gentle day,
Before the wheels of Phoebus, round about
Dapples the drowsy east with spots of grey.
Thanks to you all, and leave us: fare you well.

CLAUDIO.

Good morrow, masters: each his several way.

DON PEDRO.

Come, let us hence, and put on other weeds; And then to Leonato's we will go.

CLAUDIO.

And Hymen now with luckier issue speed's,
Than this for whom we rend'red up this woe!
[Exeunt.]

Scene IV. A Room in LEONATO'S House.
[Enter LEONATO, ANTONIO, BENEDICK, BEATRICE, MARGARET, URSULA, FRIAR FRANCIS, and HERO.]

FRIAR.

Did I not tell you she was innocent?

LEONATO.

So are the prince and Claudio, who accus'd her
Upon the error that you heard debated:
But Margaret was in some fault for this,
Although against her will, as it appears
In the true course of all the question.

ANTONIO.

Well, I am glad that all things sort so well.

BENEDICK.
And so am I, being else by faith enforc'd
To call young Claudio to a reckoning for it.

LEONATO.
Well, daughter, and you gentlewomen all,
Withdraw into a chamber by yourselves,
And when I send for you, come hither mask'd:
The prince and Claudio promis'd by this hour
To visit me.
[Exeunt Ladies.]
You know your office, brother;
You must be father to your brother's daughter,
And give her to young Claudio.

ANTONIO.
Which I will do with confirm'd countenance.

BENEDICK.
Friar, I must entreat your pains, I think.

FRIAR.
To do what, signior?

BENEDICK.
To bind me, or undo me; one of them.
Signior Leonato, truth it is, good signior,
Your niece regards me with an eye of favour.

LEONATO.
That eye my daughter lent her: 'tis most true.

BENEDICK.
And I do with an eye of love requite her.

LEONATO.
The sight whereof I think, you had from me,
From Claudio, and the prince. But what's your will?

BENEDICK.
Your answer, sir, is enigmatical:
But, for my will, my will is your good will
May stand with ours, this day to be conjoin'd

In the state of honourable marriage:
In which, good friar, I shall desire your help.

LEONATO.
My heart is with your liking.

FRIAR.
And my help. Here comes the prince and Claudio.
[Enter DON PEDRO and CLAUDIO, with Attendants.]

DON PEDRO.
Good morrow to this fair assembly.

LEONATO.
Good morrow, prince; good morrow, Claudio:
We here attend you. Are you yet determin'd
To-day to marry with my brother's daughter?

CLAUDIO.
I'll hold my mind, were she an Ethiope.

LEONATO.
Call her forth, brother: here's the friar ready.
[Exit ANTONIO.]

DON PEDRO.
Good morrow, Benedick. Why, what's the matter,
That you have such a February face,
So full of frost, of storm and cloudiness?

CLAUDIO.
I think he thinks upon the savage bull.
Tush! fear not, man, we'll tip thy horns with gold,
And all Europa shall rejoice at thee,
As once Europa did at lusty Jove,
When he would play the noble beast in love.

BENEDICK.
Bull Jove, sir, had an amiable low:
And some such strange bull leap'd your father's cow,
And got a calf in that same noble feat,
Much like to you, for you have just his bleat.

CLAUDIO.

For this I owe you: here comes other reckonings.
[Re-enter ANTONIO, with the ladies masked.]
Which is the lady I must seize upon?

ANTONIO.

This same is she, and I do give you her.

CLAUDIO.

Why then, she's mine. Sweet, let me see your face.

LEONATO.

No, that you shall not, till you take her hand
Before this friar, and swear to marry her.

CLAUDIO.

Give me your hand: before this holy friar,
I am your husband, if you like of me.

HERO.

And when I liv'd, I was your other wife:
[Unmasking.] And when you lov'd, you were my other husband.

CLAUDIO.

Another Hero!

HERO.

Nothing certainer:
One Hero died defil'd, but I do live,
And surely as I live, I am a maid.

DON PEDRO.

The former Hero! Hero that is dead!

LEONATO.

She died, my lord, but whiles her slander liv'd.

FRIAR.

All this amazement can I qualify:
When after that the holy rites are ended,
I'll tell you largely of fair Hero's death:
Meantime, let wonder seem familiar,
And to the chapel let us presently.

BENEDICK.
Soft and fair, friar. Which is Beatrice?

BEATRICE.
[Unmasking.] I answer to that name. What is your will?

BENEDICK.
Do not you love me?

BEATRICE.
Why, no; no more than reason.

BENEDICK.
Why, then, your uncle and the prince and Claudio
Have been deceived; for they swore you did.

BEATRICE.
Do not you love me?

BENEDICK.
Troth, no; no more than reason.

BEATRICE.
Why, then my cousin, Margaret, and Ursula,
Are much deceiv'd; for they did swear you did.

BENEDICK.
They swore that you were almost sick for me.

BEATRICE.
They swore that you were well-nigh dead for me.

BENEDICK.
Tis no such matter. Then you do not love me?

BEATRICE.
No, truly, but in friendly recompense.

LEONATO.
Come, cousin, I am sure you love the gentleman.

CLAUDIO.
And I'll be sworn upon't that he loves her;
For here's a paper written in his hand,

A halting sonnet of his own pure brain,
Fashion'd to Beatrice.

HERO.

And here's another,
Writ in my cousin's hand, stolen from her pocket,
Containing her affection unto Benedick.

BENEDICK.

A miracle! here's our own hands against our hearts. Come, I will have thee; but, by
this light, I take thee for pity.

BEATRICE.

I would not deny you; but, by this good day, I yield upon great persuasion, and
partly to save your life, for I was told you were in a consumption.

BENEDICK.

Peace! I will stop your mouth. [Kisses her.]

DON PEDRO.

How dost thou, Benedick, the married man?

BENEDICK.

I'll tell thee what, prince; a college of witcrackers cannout flout me out of my
humour. Dost thou think I care for a satire or an epigram? No; if man will be beaten
with brains, a' shall wear nothing handsome about him. In brief, since I do purpose
to marry, I will think nothing to any purpose that the world can say against it; and
therefore never flout at me for what I have said against it, for man is a giddy thing,
and this is my conclusion. For thy part, Claudio, I did think to have beaten thee;
but, in that thou art like to be my kinsman, live unbruised, and love my cousin.

CLAUDIO.

I had well hoped thou wouldst have denied Beatrice, that I might have cudgelled
thee out of thy single life, to make thee a double-dealer; which, out of question,
thou wilt be, if my cousin do not look exceeding narrowly to thee.

BENEDICK.

Come, come, we are friends. Let's have a dance ere we are married, that we may
lighten our own hearts and our wives' heels.

LEONATO.

We'll have dancing afterward.

BENEDICK.

First, of my word; therefore play, music! Prince, thou art sad; get thee a wife, get thee a wife: there is no staff more reverent than one tipped with horn.
[Enter Messenger.]

MESSENGER.

My lord, your brother John is ta'en in flight, And brought with armed men back to Messina.

BENEDICK.

Think not on him till to-morrow: I'll devise thee brave punishments for him. Strike up, pipers!
[Dance. Exeunt.]

2.13.3 King Lear

Act I

Scene I. A Room of State in King Lear's Palace
[Enter KENT, GLOUCESTER, and EDMUND]

KENT.

I thought the King had more affected the Duke of Albany than Cornwall.

GLOU.

It did always seem so to us; but now, in the division of the kingdom, it appears not which of the Dukes he values most, for equalities are so weighed that curiosity in neither can make choice of either's moiety.

KENT.

Is not this your son, my lord?

GLOU.

His breeding, sir, hath been at my charge: I have so often blush'd to acknowledge him that now I am braz'd to't.

KENT.

I cannot conceive you.

GLOU.

Sir, this young fellow's mother could: whereupon she grew round-wombed, and had indeed, sir, a son for her cradle ere she had a husband for her bed. Do you smell a fault?

KENT.
I cannot wish the fault undone, the issue of it being so proper.

GLOU.
But I have, sir, a son by order of law, some year elder than
this, who yet is no dearer in my account: though this knave came
something saucily into the world before he was sent for, yet was
his mother fair; there was good sport at his making, and the
whoreson must be acknowledged.—Do you know this noble gentleman,
Edmund?

EDM.
No, my lord.

GLOU.
My Lord of Kent: remember him hereafter as my honourable friend.

EDM.
My services to your lordship.

KENT.
I must love you, and sue to know you better.

EDM.
Sir, I shall study deserving.

GLOU.
He hath been out nine years, and away he shall again.—The king
is coming.
[Sennet within.]
[Enter LEAR, CORNWALL, ALBANY, GONERIL, REGAN, CORDELIA, and
ATTENDANTS.]

LEAR.
Attend the lords of France and Burgundy,
Gloucester.

GLOU.
I shall, my liege.
[Exeunt GLOUCESTER and EDMUND.]

LEAR.
Meantime we shall express our darker purpose.—
Give me the map there.—Know that we have divided

In three our kingdom: and 'tis our fast intent
To shake all cares and business from our age;
Conferring them on younger strengths, while we
Unburden'd crawl toward death.—Our son of Cornwall,
And you, our no less loving son of Albany,
We have this hour a constant will to publish
Our daughters' several dowers, that future strife
May be prevented now. The princes, France and Burgundy,
Great rivals in our youngest daughter's love,
Long in our court have made their amorous sojourn,
And here are to be answer'd.—Tell me, my daughters,—
Since now we will divest us both of rule,
Interest of territory, cares of state,—
Which of you shall we say doth love us most?
That we our largest bounty may extend
Where nature doth with merit challenge.—Goneril,
Our eldest-born, speak first.

GON.

Sir, I love you more than words can wield the matter;
Dearer than eyesight, space, and liberty;
Beyond what can be valu'd, rich or rare;
No less than life, with grace, health, beauty, honour;
As much as child e'er lov'd, or father found;
A love that makes breath poor and speech unable;
Beyond all manner of so much I love you.

COR.

[Aside.] What shall Cordelia speak? Love, and be silent.

LEAR.

Of all these bounds, even from this line to this,
With shadowy forests and with champains rich'd,
With plenteous rivers and wide-skirted meads,
We make thee lady: to thine and Albany's issue
Be this perpetual.—What says our second daughter,
Our dearest Regan, wife to Cornwall? Speak.

REG.

Sir, I am made of the selfsame metal that my sister is,
And prize me at her worth. In my true heart
I find she names my very deed of love;
Only she comes too short,—that I profess

Myself an enemy to all other joys
Which the most precious square of sense possesses,
And find I am alone felicitate
In your dear highness' love.

COR.

[Aside.] Then poor Cordelia!
And yet not so; since, I am sure, my love's
More richer than my tongue.

LEAR.

To thee and thine hereditary ever
Remain this ample third of our fair kingdom;
No less in space, validity, and pleasure
Than that conferr'd on Goneril.—Now, our joy,
Although the last, not least; to whose young love
The vines of France and milk of Burgundy
Strive to be interess'd; what can you say to draw
A third more opulent than your sisters? Speak.

COR.

Nothing, my lord.

LEAR.

Nothing!

COR.

Nothing.

LEAR.

Nothing can come of nothing: speak again.

COR.

Unhappy that I am, I cannot heave
My heart into my mouth: I love your majesty
According to my bond; no more nor less.

LEAR.

How, how, Cordelia! mend your speech a little,
Lest you may mar your fortunes.

COR.

Good my lord,
You have begot me, bred me, lov'd me: I

Return those duties back as are right fit,
Obey you, love you, and most honour you.
Why have my sisters husbands if they say
They love you all? Haply, when I shall wed,
That lord whose hand must take my plight shall carry
Half my love with him, half my care and duty:
Sure I shall never marry like my sisters,
To love my father all.

LEAR.

But goes thy heart with this?

COR.

Ay, good my lord.

LEAR.

So young, and so untender?

COR.

So young, my lord, and true.

LEAR.

Let it be so,—thy truth then be thy dower:
For, by the sacred radiance of the sun,
The mysteries of Hecate, and the night;
By all the operation of the orbs,
From whom we do exist and cease to be;
Here I disclaim all my paternal care,
Propinquity, and property of blood,
And as a stranger to my heart and me
Hold thee, from this for ever. The barbarous Scythian,
Or he that makes his generation messes
To gorge his appetite, shall to my bosom
Be as well neighbour'd, pitied, and reliev'd,
As thou my sometime daughter.

KENT.

Good my liege,—

LEAR.

Peace, Kent!
Come not between the dragon and his wrath.
I lov'd her most, and thought to set my rest

On her kind nursery.—Hence, and avoid my sight!—[To Cordelia.]
So be my grave my peace, as here I give
Her father's heart from her!—Call France;—who stirs?
Call Burgundy!—Cornwall and Albany,
With my two daughters' dowers digest this third:
Let pride, which she calls plainness, marry her.
I do invest you jointly in my power,
Pre-eminence, and all the large effects
That troop with majesty.—Ourself, by monthly course,
With reservation of an hundred knights,
By you to be sustain'd, shall our abode
Make with you by due turns. Only we still retain
The name, and all the additions to a king;
The sway,
Revenue, execution of the rest,
Beloved sons, be yours; which to confirm,
This coronet part betwixt you.
[Giving the crown.]

KENT.

Royal Lear,
Whom I have ever honour'd as my king,
Lov'd as my father, as my master follow'd,
As my great patron thought on in my prayers.—

LEAR.

The bow is bent and drawn; make from the shaft.

KENT.

Let it fall rather, though the fork invade
The region of my heart: be Kent unmannerly
When Lear is mad. What wouldst thou do, old man?
Think'st thou that duty shall have dread to speak
When power to flattery bows? To plainness honour's bound
When majesty falls to folly. Reverse thy state;
And in thy best consideration check
This hideous rashness: answer my life my judgment,
Thy youngest daughter does not love thee least;
Nor are those empty-hearted whose low sound
Reverbs no hollowness.

LEAR.

Kent, on thy life, no more.

KENT.

My life I never held but as a pawn
To wage against thine enemies; nor fear to lose it,
Thy safety being the motive.

LEAR.

Out of my sight!

KENT.

See better, Lear; and let me still remain
The true blank of thine eye.

LEAR.

Now, by Apollo,—

KENT.

Now by Apollo, king,
Thou swear'st thy gods in vain.

LEAR.

O vassal! miscreant!
[Laying his hand on his sword.]
ALB. and CORN.
Dear sir, forbear!

KENT.

Do;
Kill thy physician, and the fee bestow
Upon the foul disease. Revoke thy gift,
Or, whilst I can vent clamour from my throat,
I'll tell thee thou dost evil.

LEAR.

Hear me, recreant!
On thine allegiance, hear me!—
Since thou hast sought to make us break our vow,—
Which we durst never yet,—and with strain'd pride
To come between our sentence and our power,—
Which nor our nature nor our place can bear,—
Our potency made good, take thy reward.
Five days we do allot thee for provision
To shield thee from diseases of the world;
And on the sixth to turn thy hated back

Upon our kingdom: if, on the tenth day following,
Thy banish'd trunk be found in our dominions,
The moment is thy death. Away! by Jupiter,
This shall not be revok'd.

KENT.

Fare thee well, king: sith thus thou wilt appear,
Freedom lives hence, and banishment is here.—
[To CORDELIA.] The gods to their dear shelter take thee, maid,
That justly think'st and hast most rightly said!
[To REGAN and GONERIL.]
And your large speeches may your deeds approve,
That good effects may spring from words of love.—
Thus Kent, O princes, bids you all adieu;
He'll shape his old course in a country new.
[Exit.]
[Flourish. Re-enter GLOUCESTER, with FRANCE, BURGUNDY, and
ATTENDANTS.]

GLOU.

Here's France and Burgundy, my noble lord.

LEAR.

My Lord of Burgundy,
We first address toward you, who with this king
Hath rivall'd for our daughter: what in the least
Will you require in present dower with her,
Or cease your quest of love?

BUR.

Most royal majesty,
I crave no more than hath your highness offer'd,
Nor will you tender less.

LEAR.

Right noble Burgundy,
When she was dear to us, we did hold her so;
But now her price is fall'n. Sir, there she stands:
If aught within that little seeming substance,
Or all of it, with our displeasure piec'd,
And nothing more, may fitly like your grace,
She's there, and she is yours.

BUR.

I know no answer.

LEAR.

Will you, with those infirmities she owes,
Unfriended, new-adopted to our hate,
Dower'd with our curse, and stranger'd with our oath,
Take her, or leave her?

BUR.

Pardon me, royal sir;
Election makes not up on such conditions.

LEAR.

Then leave her, sir; for, by the power that made me,
I tell you all her wealth.—[To France] For you, great king,
I would not from your love make such a stray
To match you where I hate; therefore beseech you
To avert your liking a more worthier way
Than on a wretch whom nature is asham'd
Almost to acknowledge hers.

FRANCE.

This is most strange,
That she, who even but now was your best object,
The argument of your praise, balm of your age,
Most best, most dearest, should in this trice of time
Commit a thing so monstrous, to dismantle
So many folds of favour. Sure her offence
Must be of such unnatural degree
That monsters it, or your fore-vouch'd affection
Fall'n into taint; which to believe of her
Must be a faith that reason without miracle
Should never plant in me.

COR.

I yet beseech your majesty,—
If for I want that glib and oily art
To speak and purpose not; since what I well intend,
I'll do't before I speak,—that you make known
It is no vicious blot, murder, or foulness,
No unchaste action or dishonour'd step,
That hath depriv'd me of your grace and favour;

But even for want of that for which I am richer,—
A still-soliciting eye, and such a tongue
As I am glad I have not, though not to have it
Hath lost me in your liking.

LEAR.

Better thou
Hadst not been born than not to have pleas'd me better.

FRANCE.

Is it but this,—a tardiness in nature
Which often leaves the history unspoke
That it intends to do?—My lord of Burgundy,
What say you to the lady? Love's not love
When it is mingled with regards that stands
Aloof from the entire point. Will you have her?
She is herself a dowry.

BUR.

Royal king,
Give but that portion which yourself propos'd,
And here I take Cordelia by the hand,
Duchess of Burgundy.

LEAR.

Nothing: I have sworn; I am firm.

BUR.

I am sorry, then, you have so lost a father
That you must lose a husband.

COR.

Peace be with Burgundy!
Since that respects of fortune are his love,
I shall not be his wife.

FRANCE.

Fairest Cordelia, that art most rich, being poor;
Most choice, forsaken; and most lov'd, despis'd!
Thee and thy virtues here I seize upon:
Be it lawful, I take up what's cast away.
Gods, gods! 'tis strange that from their cold'st neglect
My love should kindle to inflam'd respect.—

Thy dowerless daughter, king, thrown to my chance,
Is queen of us, of ours, and our fair France:
Not all the dukes of waterish Burgundy
Can buy this unpriz'd precious maid of me.—
Bid them farewell, Cordelia, though unkind:
Thou losest here, a better where to find.

LEAR.

Thou hast her, France: let her be thine; for we
Have no such daughter, nor shall ever see
That face of hers again.—Therefore be gone
Without our grace, our love, our benison.—
Come, noble Burgundy.
[Flourish. Exeunt LEAR, BURGUNDY, CORNWALL, ALBANY, GLOUCESTER,
and ATTENDANTS.]

FRANCE.

Bid farewell to your sisters.

COR.

The jewels of our father, with wash'd eyes
Cordelia leaves you: I know you what you are;
And, like a sister, am most loath to call
Your faults as they are nam'd. Love well our father:
To your professed bosoms I commit him:
But yet, alas, stood I within his grace,
I would prefer him to a better place.
So, farewell to you both.

REG.

Prescribe not us our duties.

GON.

Let your study
Be to content your lord, who hath receiv'd you
At fortune's alms. You have obedience scanted,
And well are worth the want that you have wanted.

COR.

Time shall unfold what plighted cunning hides:
Who cover faults, at last shame them derides.
Well may you prosper!

FRANCE.

Come, my fair Cordelia.
[Exeunt FRANCE and CORDELIA.]

GON.

Sister, it is not little I have to say of what most nearly
appertains to us both. I think our father will hence to-night.

REG.

That's most certain, and with you; next month with us.

GON.

You see how full of changes his age is; the observation we
have made of it hath not been little: he always loved our
sister most; and with what poor judgment he hath now cast her
off appears too grossly.

REG.

'Tis the infirmity of his age: yet he hath ever but slenderly
known himself.

GON.

The best and soundest of his time hath been but rash; then must
we look to receive from his age, not alone the imperfections of
long-ingraffed condition, but therewithal the unruly waywardness
that infirm and choleric years bring with them.

REG.

Such unconstant starts are we like to have from him as this of
Kent's banishment.

GON.

There is further compliment of leave-taking between France and
him. Pray you let us hit together: if our father carry authority
with such dispositions as he bears, this last surrender of his
will but offend us.

REG.

We shall further think of it.

GON.

We must do something, and i' th' heat.
[Exeunt.]

Scene II. A Hall in the Earl of Gloucester's Castle.
[Enter Edmund with a letter.]

EDM.

Thou, nature, art my goddess; to thy law
My services are bound. Wherefore should I
Stand in the plague of custom, and permit
The curiosity of nations to deprive me,
For that I am some twelve or fourteen moonshines
Lag of a brother? Why bastard? wherefore base?
When my dimensions are as well compact,
My mind as generous, and my shape as true
As honest madam's issue? Why brand they us
With base? with baseness? bastardy? base, base?
Who, in the lusty stealth of nature, take
More composition and fierce quality
Than doth, within a dull, stale, tired bed,
Go to the creating a whole tribe of fops
Got 'tween asleep and wake?—Well then,
Legitimate Edgar, I must have your land:
Our father's love is to the bastard Edmund
As to the legitimate: fine word—legitimate!
Well, my legitimate, if this letter speed,
And my invention thrive, Edmund the base
Shall top the legitimate. I grow; I prosper.—
Now, gods, stand up for bastards!
[Enter Gloucester.]

GLOU.

Kent banish'd thus! and France in choler parted!
And the king gone to-night! subscrib'd his pow'r!
Confin'd to exhibition! All this done
Upon the gad!—Edmund, how now! What news?

EDM.

So please your lordship, none.
[Putting up the letter.]

GLOU.

Why so earnestly seek you to put up that letter?

EDM.

I know no news, my lord.

GLOU.

What paper were you reading?

EDM.

Nothing, my lord.

GLOU.

No? What needed, then, that terrible dispatch of it into your
pocket? the quality of nothing hath not such need to hide itself.
Let's see.
Come, if it be nothing, I shall not need spectacles.

EDM.

I beseech you, sir, pardon me. It is a letter from my brother
that I have not all o'er-read; and for so much as I have perus'd,
I find it not fit for your o'erlooking.

GLOU.

Give me the letter, sir.

EDM.

I shall offend, either to detain or give it. The contents, as in
part I understand them, are to blame.

GLOU.

Let's see, let's see!

EDM.

I hope, for my brother's justification, he wrote this but as an
essay or taste of my virtue.

GLOU.

[Reads.] 'This policy and reverence of age makes the world
bitter to the best of our times; keeps our fortunes from us
till our oldness cannot relish them. I begin to find an idle
and fond bondage in the oppression of aged tyranny; who sways,
not as it hath power, but as it is suffered. Come to me, that
of this I may speak more. If our father would sleep till I
waked him, you should enjoy half his revenue for ever, and live
the beloved of your brother,
EDGAR.'
Hum! Conspiracy?—'Sleep till I waked him,—you should enjoy half
his revenue.'—My son Edgar! Had he a hand to write this? a heart
and brain to breed it in? When came this to you? who brought it?

EDM.

It was not brought me, my lord, there's the cunning of it; I
found it thrown in at the casement of my closet.

GLOU.

You know the character to be your brother's?

EDM.

If the matter were good, my lord, I durst swear it were his; but
in respect of that, I would fain think it were not.

GLOU.

It is his.

EDM.

It is his hand, my lord; but I hope his heart is not in the
contents.

GLOU.

Hath he never before sounded you in this business?

EDM.

Never, my lord: but I have heard him oft maintain it to be fit
that, sons at perfect age, and fathers declined, the father
should be as ward to the son, and the son manage his revenue.

GLOU.

O villain, villain!—His very opinion in the letter! Abhorred
villain!—Unnatural, detested, brutish villain! worse than
brutish!—Go, sirrah, seek him; I'll apprehend him. Abominable
villain!—Where is he?

EDM.

I do not well know, my lord. If it shall please you to suspend
your indignation against my brother till you can derive from him
better testimony of his intent, you should run a certain course;
where, if you violently proceed against him, mistaking his
purpose, it would make a great gap in your own honour, and shake
in pieces the heart of his obedience. I dare pawn down my life
for him that he hath writ this to feel my affection to your
honour, and to no other pretence of danger.

GLOU.

Think you so?

EDM.

If your honour judge it meet, I will place you where you shall
hear us confer of this, and by an auricular assurance have your
satisfaction; and that without any further delay than this very evening.

GLOU.

He cannot be such a monster.

EDM.

Nor is not, sure.

GLOU.

To his father, that so tenderly and entirely loves him.—Heaven
and earth!—Edmund, seek him out; wind me into him, I pray you:
frame the business after your own wisdom. I would unstate myself
to be in a due resolution.

EDM.

I will seek him, sir, presently; convey the business as I shall
find means, and acquaint you withal.

GLOU.

These late eclipses in the sun and moon portend no good to us:
though the wisdom of nature can reason it thus and thus, yet
nature finds itself scourged by the sequent effects: love cools,
friendship falls off, brothers divide: in cities, mutinies; in
countries, discord; in palaces, treason; and the bond cracked
'twixt son and father. This villain of mine comes under the
prediction; there's son against father: the king falls from
bias of nature; there's father against child. We have seen the
best of our time: machinations, hollowness, treachery, and all
ruinous disorders follow us disquietly to our graves.—Find out
this villain, Edmund; it shall lose thee nothing; do it
carefully.—And the noble and true-hearted Kent banished! his
offence, honesty!—'Tis strange.
[Exit.]

EDM.

This is the excellent foppery of the world, that, when we are
sick in fortune,—often the surfeit of our own behaviour,—we
make guilty of our disasters the sun, the moon, and the stars; as
if we were villains on necessity; fools by heavenly compulsion;
knaves, thieves, and treachers by spherical pre-dominance;

drunkards, liars, and adulterers by an enforced obedience of
planetary influence; and all that we are evil in, by a divine
thrusting on: an admirable evasion of whoremaster man, to lay his
goatish disposition to the charge of a star! My father compounded
with my mother under the dragon's tail, and my nativity was under
ursa major; so that it follows I am rough and lecherous.—Tut! I
should have been that I am, had the maidenliest star in the
firmament twinkled on my bastardizing.
[Enter Edgar.]
Pat!—he comes, like the catastrophe of the old comedy: my cue
is villainous melancholy, with a sigh like Tom o' Bedlam.—O,
these eclipses do portend these divisions! fa, sol, la, mi.

EDG.

How now, brother Edmund! what serious contemplation are you in?

EDM.

I am thinking, brother, of a prediction I read this other day,
what should follow these eclipses.

EDG.

Do you busy yourself with that?

EDM.

I promise you, the effects he writes of succeed unhappily: as of
unnaturalness between the child and the parent; death, dearth,
dissolutions of ancient amities; divisions in state, menaces and
maledictions against king and nobles; needless diffidences,
banishment of friends, dissipation of cohorts, nuptial breaches,
and I know not what.

EDG.

How long have you been a sectary astronomical?

EDM.

Come, come! when saw you my father last?

EDG.

The night gone by.

EDM.

Spake you with him?

EDG.

Ay, two hours together.

EDM.

Parted you in good terms? Found you no displeasure in him by word
or countenance?

EDG.

None at all.

EDM.

Bethink yourself wherein you may have offended him: and at my
entreaty forbear his presence until some little time hath
qualified the heat of his displeasure; which at this instant so
rageth in him that with the mischief of your person it would
scarcely allay.

EDG.

Some villain hath done me wrong.

EDM.

That's my fear. I pray you have a continent forbearance till the
speed of his rage goes slower; and, as I say, retire with me to
my lodging, from whence I will fitly bring you to hear my lord
speak: pray you, go; there's my key.—If you do stir abroad, go
armed.

EDG.

Armed, brother!

EDM.

Brother, I advise you to the best; I am no honest man
if there be any good meaning toward you: I have told you what I
have seen and heard but faintly; nothing like the image and
horror of it: pray you, away!

EDG.

Shall I hear from you anon?

EDM.

I do serve you in this business.
[Exit Edgar.]
A credulous father! and a brother noble,

Whose nature is so far from doing harms
That he suspects none; on whose foolish honesty
My practices ride easy!—I see the business.
Let me, if not by birth, have lands by wit:
All with me's meet that I can fashion fit.
[Exit.]

Scene III. A Room in the Duke of Albany's Palace.
[Enter Goneril and Oswald.]

GON.

Did my father strike my gentleman for chiding of his fool?

OSW.

Ay, madam.

GON.

By day and night, he wrongs me; every hour
He flashes into one gross crime or other,
That sets us all at odds; I'll not endure it:
His knights grow riotous, and himself upbraids us
On every trifle.—When he returns from hunting,
I will not speak with him; say I am sick.—
If you come slack of former services,
You shall do well; the fault of it I'll answer.

OSW.

He's coming, madam; I hear him.
[Horns within.]

GON.

Put on what weary negligence you please,
You and your fellows; I'd have it come to question:
If he distaste it, let him to our sister,
Whose mind and mine, I know, in that are one,
Not to be overruled. Idle old man,
That still would manage those authorities
That he hath given away!—Now, by my life,
Old fools are babes again; and must be us'd
With checks as flatteries,—when they are seen abus'd.
Remember what I have said.

OSW.

Very well, madam.

GON.

And let his knights have colder looks among you;
What grows of it, no matter; advise your fellows so;
I would breed from hence occasions, and I shall,
That I may speak.—I'll write straight to my sister
To hold my very course.—Prepare for dinner.
[Exeunt.]

Scene IV. A Hall in Albany's Palace.
[Enter Kent, disguised.]

KENT.

If but as well I other accents borrow,
That can my speech defuse, my good intent
May carry through itself to that full issue
For which I rais'd my likeness.—Now, banish'd Kent,
If thou canst serve where thou dost stand condemn'd,
So may it come, thy master, whom thou lov'st,
Shall find thee full of labours.
[Horns within. Enter King Lear, Knights, and Attendants.]

LEAR.

Let me not stay a jot for dinner; go get it ready.
[Exit an Attendant.]
How now! what art thou?

KENT.

A man, sir.

LEAR.

What dost thou profess? What wouldst thou with us?

KENT.

I do profess to be no less than I seem; to serve him truly that
will put me in trust; to love him that is honest; to converse
with him that is wise and says little; to fear judgment; to fight
when I cannot choose; and to eat no fish.

LEAR.

What art thou?

KENT.

A very honest-hearted fellow, and as poor as the king.

LEAR.

If thou be'st as poor for a subject as he's for a king, thou art
poor enough. What wouldst thou?

KENT.

Service.

LEAR.

Who wouldst thou serve?

KENT.

You.

LEAR.

Dost thou know me, fellow?

KENT.

No, sir; but you have that in your countenance which I would fain
call master.

LEAR.

What's that?

KENT.

Authority.

LEAR.

What services canst thou do?

KENT.

I can keep honest counsel, ride, run, mar a curious tale in
telling it and deliver a plain message bluntly. That which
ordinary men are fit for, I am qualified in, and the best of
me is diligence.

LEAR.

How old art thou?

KENT.

Not so young, sir, to love a woman for singing; nor so old to
dote on her for anything: I have years on my back forty-eight.

LEAR.

Follow me; thou shalt serve me. If I like thee no worse after
dinner, I will not part from thee yet.—Dinner, ho, dinner!—
Where's my knave? my fool?—Go you and call my fool hither.
[Exit an attendant.]
[Enter Oswald.]
You, you, sirrah, where's my daughter?

OSW.

So please you,—
[Exit.]

LEAR.

What says the fellow there? Call the clotpoll back.—
[Exit a KNIGHT.]
Where's my fool, ho?—I think the world's asleep.
[Re-enter KNIGHT.]
How now! where's that mongrel?

KNIGHT.

He says, my lord, your daughter is not well.

LEAR.

Why came not the slave back to me when I called him?

KNIGHT.

Sir, he answered me in the roundest manner, he would not.

LEAR.

He would not!

KNIGHT.

My lord, I know not what the matter is; but to my judgment your
highness is not entertained with that ceremonious affection as
you were wont; there's a great abatement of kindness appears as
well in the general dependants as in the duke himself also and
your daughter.

LEAR.

Ha! say'st thou so?

KNIGHT.

I beseech you pardon me, my lord, if I be mistaken; for my duty
cannot be silent when I think your highness wronged.

LEAR.

Thou but rememberest me of mine own conception: I have perceived
a most faint neglect of late; which I have rather blamed as mine
own jealous curiosity than as a very pretence and purpose of
unkindness: I will look further into't.—But where's my fool? I
have not seen him this two days.

KNIGHT.

Since my young lady's going into France, sir, the fool hath much
pined away.

LEAR.

No more of that; I have noted it well.—Go you and tell my
daughter I would speak with her.—
[Exit Attendant.]
Go you, call hither my fool.
[Exit another Attendant.]
[Re-enter Oswald.]
O, you, sir, you, come you hither, sir: who am I, sir?

OSW.

My lady's father.

LEAR.

My lady's father! my lord's knave: you whoreson dog! you slave!
you cur!

OSW.

I am none of these, my lord; I beseech your pardon.

LEAR.

Do you bandy looks with me, you rascal?
[Striking him.]

OSW.

I'll not be struck, my lord.

KENT.

Nor tripp'd neither, you base football player.
[Tripping up his heels.]

LEAR.

I thank thee, fellow; thou servest me, and I'll love thee.

KENT.

Come, sir, arise, away! I'll teach you differences: away, away!
If you will measure your lubber's length again, tarry; but away!
go to; have you wisdom? so.
[Pushes Oswald out.]

LEAR.

Now, my friendly knave, I thank thee: there's earnest of thy
service.
[Giving Kent money.]
[Enter FOOL.]

FOOL.

Let me hire him too; here's my coxcomb.
[Giving Kent his cap.]

LEAR.

How now, my pretty knave! how dost thou?

FOOL.

Sirrah, you were best take my coxcomb.

KENT.

Why, fool?

FOOL.

Why, for taking one's part that's out of favour. Nay, an thou
canst not smile as the wind sits, thou'lt catch cold shortly:
there, take my coxcomb: why, this fellow hath banish'd two on's
daughters, and did the third a blessing against his will; if
thou follow him, thou must needs wear my coxcomb.—How now,
nuncle! Would I had two coxcombs and two daughters!

LEAR.

Why, my boy?

FOOL.

If I gave them all my living, I'd keep my coxcombs myself.
There's mine; beg another of thy daughters.

LEAR.

Take heed, sirrah,—the whip.

FOOL.

Truth's a dog must to kennel; he must be whipped out, when
the lady brach may stand by the fire and stink.

LEAR.

A pestilent gall to me!

FOOL.

Sirrah, I'll teach thee a speech.

LEAR.

Do.

FOOL.

Mark it, nuncle:—
Have more than thou showest,
Speak less than thou knowest,
Lend less than thou owest,
Ride more than thou goest,
Learn more than thou trowest,
Set less than thou throwest;
Leave thy drink and thy whore,
And keep in-a-door,
And thou shalt have more
Than two tens to a score.

KENT.

This is nothing, fool.

FOOL.

Then 'tis like the breath of an unfee'd lawyer,—you gave me
nothing for't.—Can you make no use of nothing, nuncle?

LEAR.

Why, no, boy; nothing can be made out of nothing.

FOOL.

[to Kent] Pr'ythee tell him, so much the rent of his land
comes to: he will not believe a fool.

LEAR.

A bitter fool!

FOOL.

Dost thou know the difference, my boy, between a bitter fool and
a sweet one?

LEAR.

No, lad; teach me.

FOOL.

That lord that counsell'd thee
To give away thy land,
Come place him here by me,—
Do thou for him stand:
The sweet and bitter fool
Will presently appear;
The one in motley here,
The other found out there.

LEAR.

Dost thou call me fool, boy?

FOOL.

All thy other titles thou hast given away; that thou wast born
with.

KENT.

This is not altogether fool, my lord.

FOOL.

No, faith; lords and great men will not let me: if I had a
monopoly out, they would have part on't and loads too: they
will not let me have all the fool to myself; they'll be
snatching.—Nuncle, give me an egg, and I'll give thee two
crowns.

LEAR.

What two crowns shall they be?

FOOL.

Why, after I have cut the egg i' the middle and eat up the
meat, the two crowns of the egg. When thou clovest thy crown i'
the middle and gav'st away both parts, thou borest thine ass on
thy back o'er the dirt: thou hadst little wit in thy bald crown
when thou gavest thy golden one away. If I speak like myself in

this, let him be whipped that first finds it so.
[Singing.]
Fools had ne'er less wit in a year;
For wise men are grown foppish,
And know not how their wits to wear,
Their manners are so apish.

LEAR.

When were you wont to be so full of songs, sirrah?

FOOL.

I have used it, nuncle, e'er since thou mad'st thy daughters thy
mothers; for when thou gav'st them the rod, and puttest down
thine own breeches,
[Singing.]
Then they for sudden joy did weep,
And I for sorrow sung,
That such a king should play bo-peep
And go the fools among.
Pr'ythee, nuncle, keep a schoolmaster that can teach thy fool to
lie; I would fain learn to lie.

LEAR.

An you lie, sirrah, we'll have you whipped.

FOOL.

I marvel what kin thou and thy daughters are: they'll have me
whipped for speaking true; thou'lt have me whipped for lying;
and sometimes I am whipped for holding my peace. I had rather be
any kind o' thing than a fool: and yet I would not be thee,
nuncle: thou hast pared thy wit o' both sides, and left nothing
i' the middle:—here comes one o' the parings.
[Enter Goneril.]

LEAR.

How now, daughter? What makes that frontlet on? Methinks you
are too much of late i' the frown.

FOOL.

Thou wast a pretty fellow when thou hadst no need to care for
her frowning. Now thou art an O without a figure: I am better
than thou art; I am a fool, thou art nothing.—Yes, forsooth, I
will hold my tongue. So your face [To Goneril.] bids me, though

you say nothing. Mum, mum,
He that keeps nor crust nor crum,
Weary of all, shall want some.—
[Pointing to LEAR.] That's a shealed peascod.

                              GON.

Not only, sir, this your all-licens'd fool,
But other of your insolent retinue
Do hourly carp and quarrel; breaking forth
In rank and not-to-be-endured riots. Sir,
I had thought, by making this well known unto you,
To have found a safe redress; but now grow fearful,
By what yourself too late have spoke and done,
That you protect this course, and put it on
By your allowance; which if you should, the fault
Would not scape censure, nor the redresses sleep,
Which, in the tender of a wholesome weal,
Might in their working do you that offence
Which else were shame, that then necessity
Will call discreet proceeding.

                              FOOL.

For you know, nuncle,
The hedge-sparrow fed the cuckoo so long
That it had it head bit off by it young.
So out went the candle, and we were left darkling.

                              LEAR.

Are you our daughter?

                              GON.

Come, sir,
I would you would make use of that good wisdom,
Whereof I know you are fraught; and put away
These dispositions, that of late transform you
From what you rightly are.

                              FOOL.

May not an ass know when the cart draws the horse?—Whoop, Jug! I
love thee!

                              LEAR.

Doth any here know me?—This is not Lear;
Doth Lear walk thus? speak thus? Where are his eyes?

Either his notion weakens, his discernings
Are lethargied.—Ha! waking? 'Tis not so!—
Who is it that can tell me who I am?

FOOL.

Lear's shadow.

LEAR.

I would learn that; for, by the marks of sovereignty,
Knowledge, and reason,
I should be false persuaded I had daughters.

FOOL.

Which they will make an obedient father.

LEAR.

Your name, fair gentlewoman?

GON.

This admiration, sir, is much o' the favour
Of other your new pranks. I do beseech you
To understand my purposes aright:
As you are old and reverend, you should be wise.
Here do you keep a hundred knights and squires;
Men so disorder'd, so debosh'd, and bold
That this our court, infected with their manners,
Shows like a riotous inn: epicurism and lust
Make it more like a tavern or a brothel
Than a grac'd palace. The shame itself doth speak
For instant remedy: be, then, desir'd
By her that else will take the thing she begs
A little to disquantity your train;
And the remainder, that shall still depend,
To be such men as may besort your age,
Which know themselves, and you.

LEAR.

Darkness and devils!—
Saddle my horses; call my train together.—
Degenerate bastard! I'll not trouble thee:
Yet have I left a daughter.

GON.

You strike my people; and your disorder'd rabble
Make servants of their betters.
[Enter Albany.]

LEAR.

Woe that too late repents!—
[To Albany.] O, sir, are you come?
Is it your will? Speak, sir.—Prepare my horses.—
Ingratitude, thou marble-hearted fiend,
More hideous when thou show'st thee in a child
Than the sea-monster!

ALB.

Pray, sir, be patient.

LEAR.

[to Goneril] Detested kite, thou liest!:
My train are men of choice and rarest parts,
That all particulars of duty know;
And in the most exact regard support
The worships of their name.—O most small fault,
How ugly didst thou in Cordelia show!
Which, like an engine, wrench'd my frame of nature
From the fix'd place; drew from my heart all love,
And added to the gall. O Lear, Lear, Lear!
Beat at this gate that let thy folly in [Striking his head.]
And thy dear judgment out!—Go, go, my people.

ALB.

My lord, I am guiltless, as I am ignorant
Of what hath mov'd you.

LEAR.

It may be so, my lord.
Hear, nature, hear; dear goddess, hear
Suspend thy purpose, if thou didst intend
To make this creature fruitful!
Into her womb convey sterility!
Dry up in her the organs of increase;
And from her derogate body never spring
A babe to honour her! If she must teem,
Create her child of spleen, that it may live

And be a thwart disnatur'd torment to her!
Let it stamp wrinkles in her brow of youth;
With cadent tears fret channels in her cheeks;
Turn all her mother's pains and benefits
To laughter and contempt; that she may feel
How sharper than a serpent's tooth it is
To have a thankless child!—Away, away!
[Exit.]

ALB.

Now, gods that we adore, whereof comes this?

GON.

Never afflict yourself to know more of it;
But let his disposition have that scope
That dotage gives it.
[Re-enter LEAR.]

LEAR.

What, fifty of my followers at a clap!
Within a fortnight!

ALB.

What's the matter, sir?

LEAR.

I'll tell thee.—Life and death!—[To Goneril] I am asham'd
That thou hast power to shake my manhood thus;
That these hot tears, which break from me perforce,
Should make thee worth them.—Blasts and fogs upon thee!
Th' untented woundings of a father's curse
Pierce every sense about thee!—Old fond eyes,
Beweep this cause again, I'll pluck you out,
And cast you, with the waters that you lose,
To temper clay. Ha!
Let it be so: I have another daughter,
Who, I am sure, is kind and comfortable:
When she shall hear this of thee, with her nails
She'll flay thy wolvish visage. Thou shalt find
That I'll resume the shape which thou dost think
I have cast off for ever.
[Exeunt Lear, Kent, and Attendants.]

GON.

Do you mark that?

ALB.

I cannot be so partial, Goneril,
To the great love I bear you,—

GON.

Pray you, content.—What, Oswald, ho!
[To the Fool] You, sir, more knave than fool, after your master.

FOOL.

Nuncle Lear, nuncle Lear, tarry,—take the fool with thee.—
A fox when one has caught her,
And such a daughter,
Should sure to the slaughter,
If my cap would buy a halter;
So the fool follows after.
[Exit.]

GON.

This man hath had good counsel.—A hundred knights!
'Tis politic and safe to let him keep
At point a hundred knights: yes, that on every dream,
Each buzz, each fancy, each complaint, dislike,
He may enguard his dotage with their powers,
And hold our lives in mercy.—Oswald, I say!—

ALB.

Well, you may fear too far.

GON.

Safer than trust too far:
Let me still take away the harms I fear,
Not fear still to be taken: I know his heart.
What he hath utter'd I have writ my sister:
If she sustain him and his hundred knights,
When I have show'd th' unfitness,—
[Re-enter Oswald.]
How now, Oswald!
What, have you writ that letter to my sister?

OSW.

Ay, madam.

GON.

Take you some company, and away to horse:
Inform her full of my particular fear;
And thereto add such reasons of your own
As may compact it more. Get you gone;
And hasten your return.
[Exit Oswald.]
No, no, my lord!
This milky gentleness and course of yours,
Though I condemn it not, yet, under pardon,
You are much more attask'd for want of wisdom
Than prais'd for harmful mildness.

ALB.

How far your eyes may pierce I cannot tell:
Striving to better, oft we mar what's well.

GON.

Nay then,—

ALB.

Well, well; the event.
[Exeunt.]

Scene V. Court before the Duke of Albany's Palace.
[Enter Lear, Kent, and FOOL.]

LEAR.

Go you before to Gloucester with these letters: acquaint my
daughter no further with anything you know than comes from her
demand out of the letter. If your diligence be not speedy, I
shall be there afore you.

KENT.

I will not sleep, my lord, till I have delivered your letter.
[Exit.]

FOOL.

If a man's brains were in's heels, were't not in danger of kibes?

LEAR.

Ay, boy.

FOOL.

Then I pr'ythee be merry; thy wit shall not go slipshod.

LEAR.

Ha, ha, ha!

FOOL.

Shalt see thy other daughter will use thee kindly; for though
she's as like this as a crab's like an apple, yet I can tell
what I can tell.

LEAR.

What canst tell, boy?

FOOL.

She'll taste as like this as a crab does to a crab. Thou
canst tell why one's nose stands i' the middle on's face?

LEAR.

No.

FOOL.

Why, to keep one's eyes of either side's nose, that what a man
cannot smell out, he may spy into.

LEAR.

I did her wrong,—

FOOL.

Canst tell how an oyster makes his shell?

LEAR.

No.

FOOL.

Nor I neither; but I can tell why a snail has a house.

LEAR.

Why?

FOOL.

Why, to put's head in; not to give it away to his daughters, and
leave his horns without a case.

LEAR.

I will forget my nature. So kind a father!—Be my horses ready?

FOOL.

Thy asses are gone about 'em. The reason why the seven stars are
no more than seven is a pretty reason.

LEAR.

Because they are not eight?

FOOL.

Yes indeed: thou wouldst make a good fool.

LEAR.

To tak't again perforce!—Monster ingratitude!

FOOL.

If thou wert my fool, nuncle, I'ld have thee beaten for being
old before thy time.

LEAR.

How's that?

FOOL.

Thou shouldst not have been old till thou hadst been wise.

LEAR.

O, let me not be mad, not mad, sweet heaven!
Keep me in temper; I would not be mad!—
[Enter Gentleman.]
How now? are the horses ready?

GENT.

Ready, my lord.

LEAR.

Come, boy.

FOOL.

She that's a maid now, and laughs at my departure,
Shall not be a maid long, unless things be cut shorter.
[Exeunt.]

Act II

Scene I. A court within the Castle of the Earl of Gloucester.
[Enter Edmund and Curan, meeting.]

EDM.

Save thee, Curan.

CUR.

And you, sir. I have been with your father, and given him
notice that the Duke of Cornwall and Regan his duchess will be
here with him this night.

EDM.

How comes that?

CUR.

Nay, I know not.—You have heard of the news abroad; I mean the
whispered ones, for they are yet but ear-kissing arguments?

EDM.

Not I: pray you, what are they?

CUR.

Have you heard of no likely wars toward, 'twixt the two dukes
of Cornwall and Albany?

EDM.

Not a word.

CUR.

You may do, then, in time. Fare you well, sir.
[Exit.]

EDM.

The Duke be here to-night? The better! best!
This weaves itself perforce into my business.
My father hath set guard to take my brother;
And I have one thing, of a queasy question,
Which I must act:—briefness and fortune work!—
Brother, a word!—descend:—brother, I say!
[Enter Edgar.]
My father watches:—sir, fly this place;
Intelligence is given where you are hid;

You have now the good advantage of the night.—
Have you not spoken 'gainst the Duke of Cornwall?
He's coming hither; now, i' the night, i' the haste,
And Regan with him: have you nothing said
Upon his party 'gainst the Duke of Albany?
Advise yourself.

EDG.

I am sure on't, not a word.

EDM.

I hear my father coming:—pardon me;
In cunning I must draw my sword upon you:—
Draw: seem to defend yourself: now quit you well.—
Yield:—come before my father.—Light, ho, here!
Fly, brother.—Torches, torches!—So farewell.
[Exit Edgar.]
Some blood drawn on me would beget opinion
Of my more fierce endeavour: [Wounds his arm.]
I have seen drunkards
Do more than this in sport.—Father, father!
Stop, stop! No help?
[Enter Gloucester, and Servants with torches.]

GLOU.

Now, Edmund, where's the villain?

EDM.

Here stood he in the dark, his sharp sword out,
Mumbling of wicked charms, conjuring the moon
To stand auspicious mistress,—

GLOU.

But where is he?

EDM.

Look, sir, I bleed.

GLOU.

Where is the villain, Edmund?

EDM.

Fled this way, sir. When by no means he could,—

GLOU.

Pursue him, ho!—Go after.
[Exeunt Servants.]
—By no means what?

EDM.

Persuade me to the murder of your lordship;
But that I told him the revenging gods
'Gainst parricides did all their thunders bend;
Spoke with how manifold and strong a bond
The child was bound to the father;—sir, in fine,
Seeing how loathly opposite I stood
To his unnatural purpose, in fell motion
With his prepared sword, he charges home
My unprovided body, lanc'd mine arm;
But when he saw my best alarum'd spirits,
Bold in the quarrel's right, rous'd to the encounter,
Or whether gasted by the noise I made,
Full suddenly he fled.

GLOU.

Let him fly far;
Not in this land shall he remain uncaught;
And found—dispatch'd.—The noble duke my master,
My worthy arch and patron, comes to-night:
By his authority I will proclaim it,
That he which finds him shall deserve our thanks,
Bringing the murderous coward to the stake;
He that conceals him, death.

EDM.

When I dissuaded him from his intent,
And found him pight to do it, with curst speech
I threaten'd to discover him: he replied,
'Thou unpossessing bastard! dost thou think,
If I would stand against thee, would the reposal
Of any trust, virtue, or worth in thee
Make thy words faith'd? No: what I should deny
As this I would; ay, though thou didst produce
My very character, I'd turn it all
To thy suggestion, plot, and damned practice:
And thou must make a dullard of the world,
If they not thought the profits of my death

Were very pregnant and potential spurs
To make thee seek it.'

GLOU.

Strong and fast'ned villain!
Would he deny his letter?—I never got him.
[Trumpets within.]
Hark, the duke's trumpets! I know not why he comes.—
All ports I'll bar; the villain shall not scape;
The duke must grant me that: besides, his picture
I will send far and near, that all the kingdom
May have due note of him; and of my land,
Loyal and natural boy, I'll work the means
To make thee capable.
[Enter Cornwall, Regan, and Attendants.]

CORN.

How now, my noble friend! since I came hither,—
Which I can call but now,—I have heard strange news.

REG.

If it be true, all vengeance comes too short
Which can pursue the offender. How dost, my lord?

GLOU.

O madam, my old heart is crack'd,—it's crack'd!

REG.

What, did my father's godson seek your life?
He whom my father nam'd? your Edgar?

GLOU.

O lady, lady, shame would have it hid!

REG.

Was he not companion with the riotous knights
That tend upon my father?

GLOU.

I know not, madam:—
It is too bad, too bad.

EDM.

Yes, madam, he was of that consort.

REG.

No marvel then though he were ill affected:
'Tis they have put him on the old man's death,
To have the expense and waste of his revenues.
I have this present evening from my sister
Been well inform'd of them; and with such cautions
That if they come to sojourn at my house,
I'll not be there.

CORN.

Nor I, assure thee, Regan.—
Edmund, I hear that you have shown your father
A childlike office.

EDM.

'Twas my duty, sir.

GLOU.

He did bewray his practice; and receiv'd
This hurt you see, striving to apprehend him.

CORN.

Is he pursu'd?

GLOU.

Ay, my good lord.

CORN.

If he be taken, he shall never more
Be fear'd of doing harm: make your own purpose,
How in my strength you please.—For you, Edmund,
Whose virtue and obedience doth this instant
So much commend itself, you shall be ours:
Natures of such deep trust we shall much need;
You we first seize on.

EDM.

I shall serve you, sir,
Truly, however else.

GLOU.

For him I thank your grace.

CORN.

You know not why we came to visit you,—

REG.

Thus out of season, threading dark-ey'd night:
Occasions, noble Gloucester, of some poise,
Wherein we must have use of your advice:—
Our father he hath writ, so hath our sister,
Of differences, which I best thought it fit
To answer from our home; the several messengers
From hence attend despatch. Our good old friend,
Lay comforts to your bosom; and bestow
Your needful counsel to our business,
Which craves the instant use.

GLOU.

I serve you, madam:
Your graces are right welcome.
[Exeunt.]

Scene II. Before Gloucester's Castle.
[Enter Kent and Oswald, severally.]

OSW.

Good dawning to thee, friend: art of this house?

KENT.

Ay.

OSW.

Where may we set our horses?

KENT.

I' the mire.

OSW.

Pr'ythee, if thou lov'st me, tell me.

KENT.

I love thee not.

OSW.

Why then, I care not for thee.

KENT.

If I had thee in Lipsbury pinfold, I would make thee care for me.

OSW.

Why dost thou use me thus? I know thee not.

KENT.

Fellow, I know thee.

OSW.

What dost thou know me for?

KENT.

A knave; a rascal; an eater of broken meats; a base, proud,
shallow, beggarly, three-suited, hundred-pound, filthy,
worsted-stocking knave; a lily-livered, action-taking, whoreson,
glass-gazing, superserviceable, finical rogue;
one-trunk-inheriting slave; one that wouldst be a bawd in way of
good service, and art nothing but the composition of a
knave, beggar, coward, pander, and the son and heir of a mongrel
bitch: one whom I will beat into clamorous whining, if thou
denyest the least syllable of thy addition.

OSW.

Why, what a monstrous fellow art thou, thus to rail on one that's
neither known of thee nor knows thee?

KENT.

What a brazen-faced varlet art thou, to deny thou knowest me! Is
it two days ago since I beat thee and tripped up thy heels before
the king? Draw, you rogue: for, though it be night, yet the moon
shines; I'll make a sop o' the moonshine of you: draw, you
whoreson cullionly barbermonger, draw!
[Drawing his sword.]

OSW.

Away! I have nothing to do with thee.

KENT.

Draw, you rascal: you come with letters against the king; and
take vanity the puppet's part against the royalty of her father:
draw, you rogue, or I'll so carbonado your shanks:—
draw, you rascal; come your ways!

OSW.

Help, ho! murder! help!

KENT.

Strike, you slave; stand, rogue, stand; you neat slave, strike!
[Beating him.]

OSW.

Help, ho! murder! murder!
[Enter Edmund, Cornwall, Regan, Gloucester, and Servants.]

EDM.

How now! What's the matter?

KENT.

With you, goodman boy, an you please: come, I'll flesh you; come
on, young master.

GLOU.

Weapons! arms! What's the matter here?

CORN.

Keep peace, upon your lives;
He dies that strikes again. What is the matter?

REG.

The messengers from our sister and the king.

CORN.

What is your difference? speak.

OSW.

I am scarce in breath, my lord.

KENT.

No marvel, you have so bestirr'd your valour. You cowardly
rascal, nature disclaims in thee; a tailor made thee.

CORN.

Thou art a strange fellow: a tailor make a man?

KENT.

Ay, a tailor, sir: a stonecutter or a painter could not have
made him so ill, though he had been but two hours at the trade.

CORN.

Speak yet, how grew your quarrel?

OSW.

This ancient ruffian, sir, whose life I have spared at suit of
his grey beard,—

KENT.

Thou whoreson zed! thou unnecessary letter!—My lord, if you'll
give me leave, I will tread this unbolted villain into mortar and
daub the walls of a jakes with him.—Spare my grey beard, you
wagtail?

CORN.

Peace, sirrah!
You beastly knave, know you no reverence?

KENT.

Yes, sir; but anger hath a privilege.

CORN.

Why art thou angry?

KENT.

That such a slave as this should wear a sword,
Who wears no honesty. Such smiling rogues as these,
Like rats, oft bite the holy cords a-twain
Which are too intrinse t' unloose; smooth every passion
That in the natures of their lords rebel;
Bring oil to fire, snow to their colder moods;
Renege, affirm, and turn their halcyon beaks
With every gale and vary of their masters,
Knowing naught, like dogs, but following.—
A plague upon your epileptic visage!
Smile you my speeches, as I were a fool?
Goose, an I had you upon Sarum plain,
I'd drive ye cackling home to Camelot.

CORN.

What, art thou mad, old fellow?

GLOU.

How fell you out?
Say that.

KENT.

No contraries hold more antipathy
Than I and such a knave.

CORN.

Why dost thou call him knave? What is his fault?

KENT.

His countenance likes me not.

CORN.

No more perchance does mine, or his, or hers.

KENT.

Sir, 'tis my occupation to be plain:
I have seen better faces in my time
Than stands on any shoulder that I see
Before me at this instant.

CORN.

This is some fellow
Who, having been prais'd for bluntness, doth affect
A saucy roughness, and constrains the garb
Quite from his nature: he cannot flatter, he,—
An honest mind and plain,—he must speak truth!
An they will take it, so; if not, he's plain.
These kind of knaves I know which in this plainness
Harbour more craft and more corrupter ends
Than twenty silly-ducking observants
That stretch their duties nicely.

KENT.

Sir, in good faith, in sincere verity,
Under the allowance of your great aspect,
Whose influence, like the wreath of radiant fire
On flickering Phoebus' front,—

CORN.

What mean'st by this?

KENT.

To go out of my dialect, which you discommend so much. I know,
sir, I am no flatterer: he that beguiled you in a plain accent

was a plain knave; which, for my part, I will not be, though I
should win your displeasure to entreat me to't.

CORN.

What was the offence you gave him?

OSW.

I never gave him any:
It pleas'd the king his master very late
To strike at me, upon his misconstruction;
When he, compact, and flattering his displeasure,
Tripp'd me behind; being down, insulted, rail'd
And put upon him such a deal of man,
That worthied him, got praises of the king
For him attempting who was self-subdu'd;
And, in the fleshment of this dread exploit,
Drew on me here again.

KENT.

None of these rogues and cowards
But Ajax is their fool.

CORN.

Fetch forth the stocks!—
You stubborn ancient knave, you reverent braggart,
We'll teach you,—

KENT.

Sir, I am too old to learn:
Call not your stocks for me: I serve the king;
On whose employment I was sent to you:
You shall do small respect, show too bold malice
Against the grace and person of my master,
Stocking his messenger.

CORN.

Fetch forth the stocks!—As I have life and honour,
there shall he sit till noon.

REG.

Till noon! Till night, my lord; and all night too!

KENT.

Why, madam, if I were your father's dog,
You should not use me so.

REG.

Sir, being his knave, I will.

CORN.

This is a fellow of the self-same colour
Our sister speaks of.—Come, bring away the stocks!
[Stocks brought out.]

GLOU.

Let me beseech your grace not to do so:
His fault is much, and the good king his master
Will check him for't: your purpos'd low correction
Is such as basest and contemned'st wretches
For pilferings and most common trespasses,
Are punish'd with: the king must take it ill
That he, so slightly valu'd in his messenger,
Should have him thus restrain'd.

CORN.

I'll answer that.

REG.

My sister may receive it much more worse,
To have her gentleman abus'd, assaulted,
For following her affairs.—Put in his legs.—
[Kent is put in the stocks.]
Come, my good lord, away.
[Exeunt all but Gloucester and KENT.]

GLOU.

I am sorry for thee, friend; 'tis the duke's pleasure,
Whose disposition, all the world well knows,
Will not be rubb'd nor stopp'd; I'll entreat for thee.

KENT.

Pray do not, sir: I have watch'd, and travell'd hard;
Some time I shall sleep out, the rest I'll whistle.
A good man's fortune may grow out at heels:
Give you good morrow!

GLOU.

The duke's to blame in this: 'twill be ill taken.
[Exit.]

KENT.

Good king, that must approve the common saw,—
Thou out of heaven's benediction com'st
To the warm sun!
Approach, thou beacon to this under globe,
That by thy comfortable beams I may
Peruse this letter.—Nothing almost sees miracles
But misery:—I know 'tis from Cordelia,
Who hath most fortunately been inform'd
Of my obscured course; and shall find time
From this enormous state,—seeking to give
Losses their remedies,—All weary and o'erwatch'd,
Take vantage, heavy eyes, not to behold
This shameful lodging.
Fortune, good night: smile once more, turn thy wheel!
[He sleeps.]

Scene III. The open Country.
[Enter Edgar.]

EDG.

I heard myself proclaim'd;
And by the happy hollow of a tree
Escap'd the hunt. No port is free; no place
That guard and most unusual vigilance
Does not attend my taking. While I may scape,
I will preserve myself: and am bethought
To take the basest and most poorest shape
That ever penury, in contempt of man,
Brought near to beast: my face I'll grime with filth;
Blanket my loins; elf all my hair in knots;
And with presented nakedness outface
The winds and persecutions of the sky.
The country gives me proof and precedent
Of Bedlam beggars, who, with roaring voices,
Strike in their numb'd and mortified bare arms
Pins, wooden pricks, nails, sprigs of rosemary;
And with this horrible object, from low farms,
Poor pelting villages, sheep-cotes, and mills,

Sometime with lunatic bans, sometime with prayers,
Enforce their charity.—Poor Turlygod! poor Tom!
That's something yet:—Edgar I nothing am.
[Exit.]

Scene IV. Before Gloucester's Castle; Kent in the stocks.
[Enter Lear, Fool, and Gentleman.]

LEAR.

'Tis strange that they should so depart from home,
And not send back my messenger.

GENT.

As I learn'd,
The night before there was no purpose in them
Of this remove.

KENT.

Hail to thee, noble master!

LEAR.

Ha!
Mak'st thou this shame thy pastime?

KENT.

No, my lord.

FOOL.

Ha, ha! he wears cruel garters. Horses are tied by the
head; dogs and bears by the neck, monkeys by the loins, and
men by the legs: when a man is over-lusty at legs, then he
wears wooden nether-stocks.

LEAR.

What's he that hath so much thy place mistook
To set thee here?

KENT.

It is both he and she,
Your son and daughter.

LEAR.

No.

KENT.

Yes.

LEAR.

No, I say.

KENT.

I say, yea.

LEAR.

By Jupiter, I swear no.

KENT.

By Juno, I swear ay.

LEAR.

They durst not do't.
They would not, could not do't; 'tis worse than murder,
To do upon respect such violent outrage:
Resolve me, with all modest haste, which way
Thou mightst deserve or they impose this usage,
Coming from us.

KENT.

My lord, when at their home
I did commend your highness' letters to them,
Ere I was risen from the place that show'd
My duty kneeling, came there a reeking post,
Stew'd in his haste, half breathless, panting forth
From Goneril his mistress salutations;
Deliver'd letters, spite of intermission,
Which presently they read: on whose contents,
They summon'd up their meiny, straight took horse;
Commanded me to follow and attend
The leisure of their answer; gave me cold looks:
And meeting here the other messenger,
Whose welcome I perceiv'd had poison'd mine,—
Being the very fellow which of late
Display'd so saucily against your highness,—
Having more man than wit about me, drew:
He rais'd the house with loud and coward cries.
Your son and daughter found this trespass worth
The shame which here it suffers.

FOOL.

Winter's not gone yet, if the wild geese fly that way.
Fathers that wear rags
Do make their children blind;
But fathers that bear bags
Shall see their children kind.
Fortune, that arrant whore,
Ne'er turns the key to th' poor.
But for all this, thou shalt have as many dolours for thy
daughters as thou canst tell in a year.

LEAR.

O, how this mother swells up toward my heart!
Hysterica passio,—down, thou climbing sorrow,
Thy element's below!—Where is this daughter?

KENT.

With the earl, sir, here within.

LEAR.

Follow me not;
Stay here.
[Exit.]

GENT.

Made you no more offence but what you speak of?

KENT.

None.
How chance the king comes with so small a number?

FOOL.

An thou hadst been set i' the stocks for that question,
thou hadst well deserved it.

KENT.

Why, fool?

FOOL.

We'll set thee to school to an ant, to teach thee there's no
labouring in the winter. All that follow their noses are led by
their eyes but blind men; and there's not a nose among twenty
but can smell him that's stinking. Let go thy hold when a great

wheel runs down a hill, lest it break thy neck with following
it; but the great one that goes up the hill, let him draw thee
after.
When a wise man gives thee better counsel, give me mine again: I
would have none but knaves follow it, since a fool gives it.
That sir which serves and seeks for gain,
And follows but for form,
Will pack when it begins to rain,
And leave thee in the storm.
But I will tarry; the fool will stay,
And let the wise man fly:
The knave turns fool that runs away;
The fool no knave, perdy.

                            KENT.

Where learn'd you this, fool?

                            FOOL.

Not i' the stocks, fool.
[Re-enter Lear, with Gloucester.]

                            LEAR.

Deny to speak with me? They are sick? they are weary?
They have travell'd all the night? Mere fetches;
The images of revolt and flying off.
Fetch me a better answer.

                            GLOU.

My dear lord,
You know the fiery quality of the duke;
How unremovable and fix'd he is
In his own course.

                            LEAR.

Vengeance! plague! death! confusion!—
Fiery? What quality? why, Gloucester, Gloucester,
I'd speak with the Duke of Cornwall and his wife.

                            GLOU.

Well, my good lord, I have inform'd them so.

                            LEAR.

Inform'd them! Dost thou understand me, man?

GLOU.

Ay, my good lord.

LEAR.

The King would speak with Cornwall; the dear father
Would with his daughter speak, commands her service:
Are they inform'd of this?—My breath and blood!—
Fiery? the fiery duke?—Tell the hot duke that—
No, but not yet: may be he is not well:
Infirmity doth still neglect all office
Whereto our health is bound: we are not ourselves
When nature, being oppress'd, commands the mind
To suffer with the body: I'll forbear;
And am fallen out with my more headier will,
To take the indispos'd and sickly fit
For the sound man.—Death on my state! Wherefore
[Looking on KENT.]
Should he sit here? This act persuades me
That this remotion of the duke and her
Is practice only. Give me my servant forth.
Go tell the duke and's wife I'd speak with them,
Now, presently: bid them come forth and hear me,
Or at their chamber door I'll beat the drum
Till it cry 'Sleep to death.'

GLOU.

I would have all well betwixt you.
[Exit.]

LEAR.

O me, my heart, my rising heart!—but down!

FOOL.

Cry to it, nuncle, as the cockney did to the eels when she
put 'em i' the paste alive; she knapped 'em o' the coxcombs with
a stick and cried 'Down, wantons, down!' 'Twas her brother that,
in pure kindness to his horse, buttered his hay.
[Enter Cornwall, Regan, Gloucester, and Servants.]

LEAR.

Good-morrow to you both.

CORN.

Hail to your grace!
[Kent is set at liberty.]

REG.

I am glad to see your highness.

LEAR.

Regan, I think you are; I know what reason
I have to think so: if thou shouldst not be glad,
I would divorce me from thy mother's tomb,
Sepulchring an adultress.—[To Kent] O, are you free?
Some other time for that.—Beloved Regan,
Thy sister's naught: O Regan, she hath tied
Sharp-tooth'd unkindness, like a vulture, here,—
[Points to his heart.]
I can scarce speak to thee; thou'lt not believe
With how deprav'd a quality—O Regan!

REG.

I pray you, sir, take patience: I have hope
You less know how to value her desert
Than she to scant her duty.

LEAR.

Say, how is that?

REG.

I cannot think my sister in the least
Would fail her obligation: if, sir, perchance
She have restrain'd the riots of your followers,
'Tis on such ground, and to such wholesome end,
As clears her from all blame.

LEAR.

My curses on her!

REG.

O, sir, you are old;
Nature in you stands on the very verge
Of her confine: you should be rul'd and led
By some discretion, that discerns your state
Better than you yourself. Therefore, I pray you,

That to our sister you do make return;
Say you have wrong'd her, sir.

LEAR.

Ask her forgiveness?
Do you but mark how this becomes the house:
'Dear daughter, I confess that I am old;
[Kneeling.]
Age is unnecessary: on my knees I beg
That you'll vouchsafe me raiment, bed, and food.'

REG.

Good sir, no more! These are unsightly tricks:
Return you to my sister.

LEAR.

[Rising.] Never, Regan:
She hath abated me of half my train;
Look'd black upon me; struck me with her tongue,
Most serpent-like, upon the very heart:—
All the stor'd vengeances of heaven fall
On her ingrateful top! Strike her young bones,
You taking airs, with lameness!

CORN.

Fie, sir, fie!

LEAR.

You nimble lightnings, dart your blinding flames
Into her scornful eyes! Infect her beauty,
You fen-suck'd fogs, drawn by the powerful sun,
To fall and blast her pride!

REG.

O the blest gods!
So will you wish on me when the rash mood is on.

LEAR.

No, Regan, thou shalt never have my curse:
Thy tender-hefted nature shall not give
Thee o'er to harshness: her eyes are fierce; but thine
Do comfort, and not burn. 'Tis not in thee
To grudge my pleasures, to cut off my train,

To bandy hasty words, to scant my sizes,
And, in conclusion, to oppose the bolt
Against my coming in: thou better know'st
The offices of nature, bond of childhood,
Effects of courtesy, dues of gratitude;
Thy half o' the kingdom hast thou not forgot,
Wherein I thee endow'd.

REG.

Good sir, to the purpose.

LEAR.

Who put my man i' the stocks?
[Tucket within.]

CORN.

What trumpet's that?

REG.

I know't—my sister's: this approves her letter,
That she would soon be here.
[Enter Oswald.]
Is your lady come?

LEAR.

This is a slave, whose easy-borrowed pride
Dwells in the fickle grace of her he follows.—
Out, varlet, from my sight!

CORN.

What means your grace?

LEAR.

Who stock'd my servant? Regan, I have good hope
Thou didst not know on't.—Who comes here? O heavens!
[Enter Goneril.]
If you do love old men, if your sweet sway
Allow obedience, if yourselves are old,
Make it your cause; send down, and take my part!—
[To Goneril.] Art not asham'd to look upon this beard?—
O Regan, wilt thou take her by the hand?

GON.

Why not by the hand, sir? How have I offended?
All's not offence that indiscretion finds
And dotage terms so.

LEAR.

O sides, you are too tough!
Will you yet hold?—How came my man i' the stocks?

CORN.

I set him there, sir: but his own disorders
Deserv'd much less advancement.

LEAR.

You? did you?

REG.

I pray you, father, being weak, seem so.
If, till the expiration of your month,
You will return and sojourn with my sister,
Dismissing half your train, come then to me:
I am now from home, and out of that provision
Which shall be needful for your entertainment.

LEAR.

Return to her, and fifty men dismiss'd?
No, rather I abjure all roofs, and choose
To wage against the enmity o' the air;
To be a comrade with the wolf and owl,—
Necessity's sharp pinch!—Return with her?
Why, the hot-blooded France, that dowerless took
Our youngest born, I could as well be brought
To knee his throne, and, squire-like, pension beg
To keep base life afoot.—Return with her?
Persuade me rather to be slave and sumpter
To this detested groom.
[Pointing to Oswald.]

GON.

At your choice, sir.

LEAR.

I pr'ythee, daughter, do not make me mad:
I will not trouble thee, my child; farewell:

We'll no more meet, no more see one another:—
But yet thou art my flesh, my blood, my daughter;
Or rather a disease that's in my flesh,
Which I must needs call mine: thou art a boil,
A plague sore, an embossed carbuncle
In my corrupted blood. But I'll not chide thee;
Let shame come when it will, I do not call it:
I do not bid the thunder-bearer shoot
Nor tell tales of thee to high-judging Jove:
Mend when thou canst; be better at thy leisure:
I can be patient; I can stay with Regan,
I and my hundred knights.

REG.

Not altogether so:
I look'd not for you yet, nor am provided
For your fit welcome. Give ear, sir, to my sister;
For those that mingle reason with your passion
Must be content to think you old, and so—
But she knows what she does.

LEAR.

Is this well spoken?

REG.

I dare avouch it, sir: what, fifty followers?
Is it not well? What should you need of more?
Yea, or so many, sith that both charge and danger
Speak 'gainst so great a number? How in one house
Should many people, under two commands,
Hold amity? 'Tis hard; almost impossible.

GON.

Why might not you, my lord, receive attendance
From those that she calls servants, or from mine?

REG.

Why not, my lord? If then they chanc'd to slack you,
We could control them. If you will come to me,—
For now I spy a danger,—I entreat you
To bring but five-and-twenty: to no more
Will I give place or notice.

LEAR.

I gave you all,—

REG.

And in good time you gave it.

LEAR.

Made you my guardians, my depositaries;
But kept a reservation to be follow'd
With such a number. What, must I come to you
With five-and-twenty, Regan? said you so?

REG.

And speak't again my lord; no more with me.

LEAR.

Those wicked creatures yet do look well-favour'd
When others are more wicked; not being the worst
Stands in some rank of praise.—
[To Goneril.] I'll go with thee:
Thy fifty yet doth double five-and-twenty,
And thou art twice her love.

GON.

Hear, me, my lord:
What need you five-and-twenty, ten, or five,
To follow in a house where twice so many
Have a command to tend you?

REG.

What need one?

LEAR.

O, reason not the need: our basest beggars
Are in the poorest thing superfluous:
Allow not nature more than nature needs,
Man's life is cheap as beast's: thou art a lady;
If only to go warm were gorgeous,
Why, nature needs not what thou gorgeous wear'st
Which scarcely keeps thee warm.—But, for true need,—
You heavens, give me that patience, patience I need!
You see me here, you gods, a poor old man,
As full of grief as age; wretched in both!

If it be you that stirs these daughters' hearts
Against their father, fool me not so much
To bear it tamely; touch me with noble anger,
And let not women's weapons, water-drops,
Stain my man's cheeks!—No, you unnatural hags,
I will have such revenges on you both
That all the world shall,—I will do such things,—
What they are yet, I know not; but they shall be
The terrors of the earth. You think I'll weep;
No, I'll not weep:—
I have full cause of weeping; but this heart
Shall break into a hundred thousand flaws
Or ere I'll weep.—O fool, I shall go mad!
[Exeunt Lear, Gloucester, Kent, and FOOL. Storm heard at a distance.]

CORN.

Let us withdraw; 'twill be a storm.

REG.

This house is little: the old man and his people
Cannot be well bestow'd.

GON.

'Tis his own blame; hath put himself from rest
And must needs taste his folly.

REG.

For his particular, I'll receive him gladly,
But not one follower.

GON.

So am I purpos'd.
Where is my lord of Gloucester?

CORN.

Followed the old man forth:—he is return'd.
[Re-enter Gloucester.]

GLOU.

The king is in high rage.

CORN.

Whither is he going?

GLOU.
He calls to horse; but will I know not whither.

CORN.
'Tis best to give him way; he leads himself.

GON.
My lord, entreat him by no means to stay.

GLOU.
Alack, the night comes on, and the high winds
Do sorely ruffle; for many miles about
There's scarce a bush.

REG.
O, sir, to wilful men
The injuries that they themselves procure
Must be their schoolmasters. Shut up your doors:
He is attended with a desperate train;
And what they may incense him to, being apt
To have his ear abus'd, wisdom bids fear.

CORN.
Shut up your doors, my lord; 'tis a wild night:
My Regan counsels well: come out o' the storm.
[Exeunt.]

Act III

Scene I. A Heath.
[A storm with thunder and lightning. Enter Kent and a Gentleman, meeting.]

KENT.
Who's there, besides foul weather?

GENT.
One minded like the weather, most unquietly.

KENT.
I know you. Where's the king?

GENT.

Contending with the fretful elements;
Bids the wind blow the earth into the sea,
Or swell the curled waters 'bove the main,
That things might change or cease; tears his white hair,
Which the impetuous blasts, with eyeless rage,
Catch in their fury and make nothing of;
Strives in his little world of man to outscorn
The to-and-fro-conflicting wind and rain.
This night, wherein the cub-drawn bear would couch,
The lion and the belly-pinched wolf
Keep their fur dry, unbonneted he runs,
And bids what will take all.

KENT.

But who is with him?

GENT.

None but the fool, who labours to out-jest
His heart-struck injuries.

KENT.

Sir, I do know you;
And dare, upon the warrant of my note,
Commend a dear thing to you. There is division,
Although as yet the face of it be cover'd
With mutual cunning, 'twixt Albany and Cornwall;
Who have,—as who have not, that their great stars
Throne and set high?—servants, who seem no less,
Which are to France the spies and speculations
Intelligent of our state; what hath been seen,
Either in snuffs and packings of the dukes;
Or the hard rein which both of them have borne
Against the old kind king; or something deeper,
Whereof, perchance, these are but furnishings;—
But, true it is, from France there comes a power
Into this scatter'd kingdom; who already,
Wise in our negligence, have secret feet
In some of our best ports, and are at point
To show their open banner.—Now to you:
If on my credit you dare build so far
To make your speed to Dover, you shall find
Some that will thank you making just report

Of how unnatural and bemadding sorrow
The king hath cause to plain.
I am a gentleman of blood and breeding;
And from some knowledge and assurance offer
This office to you.

GENT.

I will talk further with you.

KENT.

No, do not.
For confirmation that I am much more
Than my out wall, open this purse, and take
What it contains. If you shall see Cordelia,—
As fear not but you shall,—show her this ring;
And she will tell you who your fellow is
That yet you do not know. Fie on this storm!
I will go seek the king.

GENT.

Give me your hand: have you no more to say?

KENT.

Few words, but, to effect, more than all yet,—
That, when we have found the king,—in which your pain
That way, I'll this,—he that first lights on him
Holla the other.
[Exeunt severally.]

Scene II. Another part of the heath. Storm continues.
[Enter Lear and FOOL.]

LEAR.

Blow, winds, and crack your cheeks! rage! blow!
You cataracts and hurricanoes, spout
Till you have drench'd our steeples, drown'd the cocks!
You sulphurous and thought-executing fires,
Vaunt couriers to oak-cleaving thunderbolts,
Singe my white head! And thou, all-shaking thunder,
Strike flat the thick rotundity o' the world!
Crack nature's moulds, all germens spill at once,
That make ingrateful man!

FOOL.

O nuncle, court holy water in a dry house is better than this
rain water out o' door. Good nuncle, in; and ask thy daughters
blessing: here's a night pities nether wise men nor fools.

LEAR.

Rumble thy bellyful! Spit, fire! spout, rain!
Nor rain, wind, thunder, fire are my daughters:
I tax not you, you elements, with unkindness;
I never gave you kingdom, call'd you children;
You owe me no subscription: then let fall
Your horrible pleasure; here I stand, your slave,
A poor, infirm, weak, and despis'd old man:—
But yet I call you servile ministers,
That will with two pernicious daughters join
Your high-engender'd battles 'gainst a head
So old and white as this! O! O! 'tis foul!

FOOL.

He that has a house to put's head in has a good head-piece.
The codpiece that will house
Before the head has any,
The head and he shall louse:
So beggars marry many.
The man that makes his toe
What he his heart should make
Shall of a corn cry woe,
And turn his sleep to wake.
—for there was never yet fair woman but she made mouths in a
glass.

LEAR.

No, I will be the pattern of all patience;
I will say nothing.
[Enter KENT.]

KENT.

Who's there?

FOOL.

Marry, here's grace and a codpiece; that's a wise man and a fool.

KENT.

Alas, sir, are you here? Things that love night
Love not such nights as these; the wrathful skies
Gallow the very wanderers of the dark,
And make them keep their caves; since I was man,
Such sheets of fire, such bursts of horrid thunder,
Such groans of roaring wind and rain I never
Remember to have heard: man's nature cannot carry
Th' affliction nor the fear.

LEAR.

Let the great gods,
That keep this dreadful pother o'er our heads,
Find out their enemies now. Tremble, thou wretch,
That hast within thee undivulged crimes
Unwhipp'd of justice: hide thee, thou bloody hand;
Thou perjur'd, and thou simular man of virtue
That art incestuous: caitiff, to pieces shake
That under covert and convenient seeming
Hast practis'd on man's life: close pent-up guilts,
Rive your concealing continents, and cry
These dreadful summoners grace.—I am a man
More sinn'd against than sinning.

KENT.

Alack, bareheaded!
Gracious my lord, hard by here is a hovel;
Some friendship will it lend you 'gainst the tempest:
Repose you there, whilst I to this hard house,—
More harder than the stones whereof 'tis rais'd;
Which even but now, demanding after you,
Denied me to come in,—return, and force
Their scanted courtesy.

LEAR.

My wits begin to turn.—
Come on, my boy. how dost, my boy? art cold?
I am cold myself.—Where is this straw, my fellow?
The art of our necessities is strange,
That can make vile things precious. Come, your hovel.—
Poor fool and knave, I have one part in my heart
That's sorry yet for thee.

FOOL.

[Singing.]
He that has and a little tiny wit—
With hey, ho, the wind and the rain,—
Must make content with his fortunes fit,
For the rain it raineth every day.

LEAR.

True, boy.—Come, bring us to this hovel.
[Exeunt Lear and KENT.]

FOOL.

This is a brave night to cool a courtezan.—
I'll speak a prophecy ere I go:—
When priests are more in word than matter;
When brewers mar their malt with water;
When nobles are their tailors' tutors;
No heretics burn'd, but wenches' suitors;
When every case in law is right;
No squire in debt nor no poor knight;
When slanders do not live in tongues;
Nor cutpurses come not to throngs;
When usurers tell their gold i' the field;
And bawds and whores do churches build;—
Then shall the realm of Albion
Come to great confusion:
Then comes the time, who lives to see't,
That going shall be us'd with feet.
This prophecy Merlin shall make; for I live before his time.
[Exit.]

Scene III. A Room in Gloucester's Castle.
[Enter Gloucester and Edmund.]

GLOU.

Alack, alack, Edmund, I like not this unnatural dealing. When I
desired their leave that I might pity him, they took from me the
use of mine own house; charged me on pain of perpetual displeasure,
neither to speak of him, entreat for him, nor any way sustain him.

EDM.

Most savage and unnatural!

GLOU.

Go to; say you nothing. There is division betwixt the dukes,
and a worse matter than that: I have received a letter this
night;—'tis dangerous to be spoken;—I have locked the letter in
my closet: these injuries the king now bears will be revenged
home; there's part of a power already footed: we must incline to
the king. I will seek him, and privily relieve him: go you and
maintain talk with the duke, that my charity be not of him
perceived: if he ask for me, I am ill, and gone to bed. If I
die for it, as no less is threatened me, the king my old master
must be relieved. There is some strange thing toward, Edmund;
pray you be careful.
[Exit.]

EDM.

This courtesy, forbid thee, shall the duke
Instantly know; and of that letter too:—
This seems a fair deserving, and must draw me
That which my father loses,—no less than all:
The younger rises when the old doth fall.
[Exit.]

Scene IV. A part of the Heath with a Hovel. Storm continues.
[Enter Lear, Kent, and FOOL.]

KENT.

Here is the place, my lord; good my lord, enter:
The tyranny of the open night's too rough
For nature to endure.

LEAR.

Let me alone.

KENT.

Good my lord, enter here.

LEAR.

Wilt break my heart?

KENT.

I had rather break mine own. Good my lord, enter.

LEAR.

Thou think'st 'tis much that this contentious storm
Invades us to the skin: so 'tis to thee
But where the greater malady is fix'd,
The lesser is scarce felt. Thou'dst shun a bear;
But if thy flight lay toward the raging sea,
Thou'dst meet the bear i' the mouth. When the mind's free,
The body's delicate: the tempest in my mind
Doth from my senses take all feeling else
Save what beats there.—Filial ingratitude!
Is it not as this mouth should tear this hand
For lifting food to't?—But I will punish home:—
No, I will weep no more.—In such a night
To shut me out!—Pour on; I will endure:—
In such a night as this! O Regan, Goneril!—
Your old kind father, whose frank heart gave all,—
O, that way madness lies; let me shun that;
No more of that.

KENT.

Good my lord, enter here.

LEAR.

Pr'ythee go in thyself; seek thine own ease:
This tempest will not give me leave to ponder
On things would hurt me more.—But I'll go in.—
[To the FOOL.] In, boy; go first.—You houseless poverty,—
Nay, get thee in. I'll pray, and then I'll sleep.—
[Fool goes in.]
Poor naked wretches, wheresoe'er you are,
That bide the pelting of this pitiless storm,
How shall your houseless heads and unfed sides,
Your loop'd and window'd raggedness, defend you
From seasons such as these? O, I have ta'en
Too little care of this! Take physic, pomp;
Expose thyself to feel what wretches feel,
That thou mayst shake the superflux to them
And show the heavens more just.

EDG.

[Within.] Fathom and half, fathom and half! Poor Tom!
[The Fool runs out from the hovel.]

FOOL.

Come not in here, nuncle, here's a spirit.
Help me, help me!

KENT.

Give me thy hand.—Who's there?

FOOL.

A spirit, a spirit: he says his name's poor Tom.

KENT.

What art thou that dost grumble there i' the straw?
Come forth.
[Enter Edgar, disguised as a madman.]

EDG.

Away! the foul fiend follows me!—
Through the sharp hawthorn blows the cold wind.—
Hum! go to thy cold bed, and warm thee.

LEAR.

Didst thou give all to thy two daughters?
And art thou come to this?

EDG.

Who gives anything to poor Tom? whom the foul fiend hath led
through fire and through flame, through ford and whirlpool, o'er
bog and quagmire; that hath laid knives under his pillow and
halters in his pew, set ratsbane by his porridge; made him proud
of heart, to ride on a bay trotting horse over four-inched
bridges, to course his own shadow for a traitor.—Bless thy five
wits!—Tom's a-cold.—O, do de, do de, do de.—Bless thee from
whirlwinds, star-blasting, and taking! Do poor Tom some charity,
whom the foul fiend vexes:—there could I have him now,—and
there,—and there again, and there.
[Storm continues.]

LEAR.

What, have his daughters brought him to this pass?—
Couldst thou save nothing? Didst thou give 'em all?

FOOL.

Nay, he reserv'd a blanket, else we had been all shamed.

LEAR.

Now all the plagues that in the pendulous air
Hang fated o'er men's faults light on thy daughters!

KENT.

He hath no daughters, sir.

LEAR.

Death, traitor! nothing could have subdu'd nature
To such a lowness but his unkind daughters.—
Is it the fashion that discarded fathers
Should have thus little mercy on their flesh?
Judicious punishment! 'twas this flesh begot
Those pelican daughters.

EDG.

Pillicock sat on Pillicock-hill:—
Halloo, halloo, loo loo!

FOOL.

This cold night will turn us all to fools and madmen.

EDG.

Take heed o' th' foul fiend: obey thy parents; keep thy word
justly; swear not; commit not with man's sworn spouse; set not
thy sweet heart on proud array. Tom's a-cold.

LEAR.

What hast thou been?

EDG.

A serving-man, proud in heart and mind; that curled my hair;
wore gloves in my cap; served the lust of my mistress' heart, and
did the act of darkness with her; swore as many oaths as I spake
words, and broke them in the sweet face of heaven: one that
slept in the contriving of lust, and waked to do it: wine loved
I deeply, dice dearly; and in woman out-paramour'd the Turk;
false of heart, light of ear, bloody of hand; hog in sloth, fox
in stealth, wolf in greediness, dog in madness, lion in prey.
Let not the creaking of shoes nor the rustling of silks betray
thy poor heart to woman: keep thy foot out of brothel, thy hand
out of placket, thy pen from lender's book, and defy the foul
fiend.—Still through the hawthorn blows the cold wind: says

suum, mun, nonny. Dolphin my boy, boy, sessa! let him trot by.
[Storm still continues.]

LEAR.

Why, thou wert better in thy grave than to answer with thy
uncovered body this extremity of the skies.—Is man no more than
this? Consider him well. Thou owest the worm no silk, the beast
no hide, the sheep no wool, the cat no perfume.—Ha! here's three
on's are sophisticated! Thou art the thing itself:
unaccommodated man is no more but such a poor, bare, forked
animal as thou art.—Off, off, you lendings!—Come, unbutton
here.
[Tears off his clothes.]

FOOL.

Pr'ythee, nuncle, be contented; 'tis a naughty night to swim
in.—Now a little fire in a wild field were like an old lecher's
heart,—a small spark, all the rest on's body cold.—Look, here
comes a walking fire.

EDG.

This is the foul fiend Flibbertigibbet: he begins at curfew,
and walks till the first cock; he gives the web and the pin,
squints the eye, and makes the harelip; mildews the white wheat,
and hurts the poor creature of earth.
Swithold footed thrice the old;
He met the nightmare, and her nine-fold;
Bid her alight
And her troth plight,
And aroint thee, witch, aroint thee!

KENT.

How fares your grace?
[Enter Gloucester with a torch.]

LEAR.

What's he?

KENT.

Who's there? What is't you seek?

GLOU.

What are you there? Your names?

EDG.

Poor Tom; that eats the swimming frog, the toad, the todpole, the
wall-newt and the water; that in the fury of his heart, when the
foul fiend rages, eats cow-dung for sallets; swallows the old rat
and the ditch-dog; drinks the green mantle of the standing pool;
who is whipped from tithing to tithing, and stocked, punished,
and imprisoned; who hath had three suits to his back, six shirts
to his body, horse to ride, and weapons to wear;—
But mice and rats, and such small deer,
Have been Tom's food for seven long year.
Beware my follower.—Peace, Smulkin; peace, thou fiend!

GLOU.

What, hath your grace no better company?

EDG.

The prince of darkness is a gentleman:
Modo he's call'd, and Mahu.

GLOU.

Our flesh and blood, my lord, is grown so vile
That it doth hate what gets it.

EDG.

Poor Tom's a-cold.

GLOU.

Go in with me: my duty cannot suffer
To obey in all your daughters' hard commands;
Though their injunction be to bar my doors,
And let this tyrannous night take hold upon you,
Yet have I ventur'd to come seek you out
And bring you where both fire and food is ready.

LEAR.

First let me talk with this philosopher.—
What is the cause of thunder?

KENT.

Good my lord, take his offer; go into the house.

LEAR.

I'll talk a word with this same learned Theban.—
What is your study?

EDG.

How to prevent the fiend and to kill vermin.

LEAR.

Let me ask you one word in private.

KENT.

Importune him once more to go, my lord;
His wits begin to unsettle.

GLOU.

Canst thou blame him?
His daughters seek his death:—ah, that good Kent!—
He said it would be thus,—poor banish'd man!—
Thou say'st the king grows mad; I'll tell thee, friend,
I am almost mad myself: I had a son,
Now outlaw'd from my blood; he sought my life
But lately, very late: I lov'd him, friend,—
No father his son dearer: true to tell thee,
[Storm continues.]
The grief hath craz'd my wits.—What a night's this!—
I do beseech your grace,—

LEAR.

O, cry you mercy, sir.—
Noble philosopher, your company.

EDG.

Tom's a-cold.

GLOU.

In, fellow, there, into the hovel; keep thee warm.

LEAR.

Come, let's in all.

KENT.

This way, my lord.

LEAR.

With him;
I will keep still with my philosopher.

KENT.

Good my lord, soothe him; let him take the fellow.

GLOU.

Take him you on.

KENT.

Sirrah, come on; go along with us.

LEAR.

Come, good Athenian.

GLOU.

No words, no words: hush.

EDG.

Child Rowland to the dark tower came,
His word was still—Fie, foh, and fum,
I smell the blood of a British man.
[Exeunt.]

Scene V. A Room in Gloucester's Castle.
[Enter Cornwall and Edmund.]

CORN.

I will have my revenge ere I depart his house.

EDM.

How, my lord, I may be censured, that nature thus gives way to
loyalty, something fears me to think of.

CORN.

I now perceive it was not altogether your brother's evil
disposition made him seek his death; but a provoking merit, set
a-work by a reproveable badness in himself.

EDM.

How malicious is my fortune, that I must repent to be just! This
is the letter he spoke of, which approves him an intelligent
party to the advantages of France. O heavens! that this treason
were not—or not I the detector!

CORN.

Go with me to the duchess.

EDM.

If the matter of this paper be certain, you have mighty business
in hand.

CORN.

True or false, it hath made thee earl of Gloucester. Seek out
where thy father is, that he may be ready for our apprehension.

EDM.

[Aside.] If I find him comforting the king, it will stuff his
suspicion more fully.—I will persever in my course of loyalty,
though the conflict be sore between that and my blood.

CORN.

I will lay trust upon thee; and thou shalt find a dearer father
in my love.
[Exeunt.]

Scene VI. A Chamber in a Farmhouse adjoining the Castle.
[Enter Gloucester, Lear, Kent, Fool, and Edgar.]

GLOU.

Here is better than the open air; take it thankfully. I will
piece out the comfort with what addition I can: I will not be
long from you.

KENT.

All the power of his wits have given way to his impatience:—
the gods reward your kindness!
[Exit Gloucester.]

EDG.

Frateretto calls me; and tells me Nero is an angler in the lake
of darkness.—Pray, innocent, and beware the foul fiend.

FOOL.

Pr'ythee, nuncle, tell me whether a madman be a gentleman or a
yeoman.

LEAR.

A king, a king!

FOOL.

No, he's a yeoman that has a gentleman to his son; for he's a mad
yeoman that sees his son a gentleman before him.

LEAR.

To have a thousand with red burning spits
Come hissing in upon 'em,—

EDG.

The foul fiend bites my back.

FOOL.

He's mad that trusts in the tameness of a wolf, a horse's health,
a boy's love, or a whore's oath.

LEAR.

It shall be done; I will arraign them straight.—
[To Edgar.] Come, sit thou here, most learned justicer—
[To the FOOL.] Thou, sapient sir, sit here. Now, you she-foxes!—

EDG.

Look, where he stands and glares!—Want'st thou eyes at trial,
madam?
Come o'er the bourn, Bessy, to me,—

FOOL.

Her boat hath a leak,
And she must not speak
Why she dares not come over to thee.

EDG.

The foul fiend haunts poor Tom in the voice of a nightingale.
Hoppedance cries in Tom's belly for two white herring. Croak not,
black angel; I have no food for thee.

KENT.

How do you, sir? Stand you not so amaz'd;
Will you lie down and rest upon the cushions?

LEAR.

I'll see their trial first.—Bring in their evidence.
[To Edgar.] Thou, robed man of justice, take thy place;—
[To the FOOL.] And thou, his yokefellow of equity,

Bench by his side:—[To KENT.] you are o' the commission,
Sit you too.

EDG.

Let us deal justly.
Sleepest or wakest thou, jolly shepherd?
Thy sheep be in the corn;
And for one blast of thy minikin mouth
Thy sheep shall take no harm.
Purr! the cat is gray.

LEAR.

Arraign her first; 'tis Goneril. I here take my oath before
this honourable assembly, she kicked the poor king her father.

FOOL.

Come hither, mistress. Is your name Goneril?

LEAR.

She cannot deny it.

FOOL.

Cry you mercy, I took you for a joint-stool.

LEAR.

And here's another, whose warp'd looks proclaim
What store her heart is made on.—Stop her there!
Arms, arms! sword! fire!—Corruption in the place!—
False justicer, why hast thou let her 'scape?

EDG.

Bless thy five wits!

KENT.

O pity!—Sir, where is the patience now
That you so oft have boasted to retain?

EDG.

[Aside.] My tears begin to take his part so much
They'll mar my counterfeiting.

LEAR.

The little dogs and all,
Tray, Blanch, and Sweetheart, see, they bark at me.

EDG.

Tom will throw his head at them.—Avaunt, you curs!
Be thy mouth or black or white,
Tooth that poisons if it bite;
Mastiff, greyhound, mongrel grim,
Hound or spaniel, brach or lym,
Or bobtail tike or trundle-tail,—
Tom will make them weep and wail;
For, with throwing thus my head,
Dogs leap the hatch, and all are fled.
Do de, de, de. Sessa! Come, march to wakes and fairs and market-
towns. Poor Tom, thy horn is dry.

LEAR.

Then let them anatomize Regan; see what breeds about her
heart. Is there any cause in nature that makes these hard
hearts?—[To Edgar.] You, sir, I entertain you for one of my
hundred; only I do not like the fashion of your garments: you'll
say they are Persian; but let them be changed.

KENT.

Now, good my lord, lie here and rest awhile.

LEAR.

Make no noise, make no noise; draw the curtains:
So, so. We'll go to supper i' the morning.

FOOL.

And I'll go to bed at noon.
[Re-enter Gloucester.]

GLOU.

Come hither, friend: where is the king my master?

KENT.

Here, sir; but trouble him not,—his wits are gone.

GLOU.

Good friend, I pr'ythee, take him in thy arms;
I have o'erheard a plot of death upon him;
There is a litter ready; lay him in't
And drive towards Dover, friend, where thou shalt meet
Both welcome and protection. Take up thy master;

If thou shouldst dally half an hour, his life,
With thine, and all that offer to defend him,
Stand in assured loss: take up, take up;
And follow me, that will to some provision
Give thee quick conduct.

KENT.

Oppressed nature sleeps:—
This rest might yet have balm'd thy broken sinews,
Which, if convenience will not allow,
Stand in hard cure.—Come, help to bear thy master;
[To the FOOL.] Thou must not stay behind.

GLOU.

Come, come, away!
[Exeunt Kent, Gloucester, and the Fool, bearing off LEAR.]

EDG.

When we our betters see bearing our woes,
We scarcely think our miseries our foes.
Who alone suffers suffers most i' the mind,
Leaving free things and happy shows behind:
But then the mind much sufferance doth o'erskip
When grief hath mates, and bearing fellowship.
How light and portable my pain seems now,
When that which makes me bend makes the king bow;
He childed as I fathered!—Tom, away!
Mark the high noises; and thyself bewray,
When false opinion, whose wrong thought defiles thee,
In thy just proof repeals and reconciles thee.
What will hap more to-night, safe 'scape the king!
Lurk, lurk.
[Exit.]

Scene VII. A Room in Gloucester's Castle.
[Enter Cornwall, Regan, Goneril, Edmund, and Servants.]

CORN.

Post speedily to my lord your husband, show him this letter:—
the army of France is landed.—Seek out the traitor Gloucester.
[Exeunt some of the Servants.]

REG.

Hang him instantly.

GON.

Pluck out his eyes.

CORN.

Leave him to my displeasure.—Edmund, keep you our sister
company: the revenges we are bound to take upon your traitorous
father are not fit for your beholding. Advise the duke where you
are going, to a most festinate preparation: we are bound to the
like. Our posts shall be swift and intelligent betwixt us.
Farewell, dear sister:—farewell, my lord of Gloucester.
[Enter Oswald.]
How now! Where's the king?

OSW.

My lord of Gloucester hath convey'd him hence:
Some five or six and thirty of his knights,
Hot questrists after him, met him at gate;
Who, with some other of the lord's dependants,
Are gone with him towards Dover: where they boast
To have well-armed friends.

CORN.

Get horses for your mistress.

GON.

Farewell, sweet lord, and sister.

CORN.

Edmund, farewell.
[Exeunt Goneril, Edmund, and Oswald.]
Go seek the traitor Gloucester,
Pinion him like a thief, bring him before us.
[Exeunt other Servants.]
Though well we may not pass upon his life
Without the form of justice, yet our power
Shall do a courtesy to our wrath, which men
May blame, but not control.—Who's there? the traitor?
[Re-enter servants, with Gloucester.]

REG.

Ingrateful fox! 'tis he.

CORN.

Bind fast his corky arms.

GLOU.

What mean your graces?—Good my friends, consider
You are my guests: do me no foul play, friends.

CORN.

Bind him, I say.
[Servants bind him.]

REG.

Hard, hard.—O filthy traitor!

GLOU.

Unmerciful lady as you are, I'm none.

CORN.

To this chair bind him.—Villain, thou shalt find,—
[Regan plucks his beard.]

GLOU.

By the kind gods, 'tis most ignobly done
To pluck me by the beard.

REG.

So white, and such a traitor!

GLOU.

Naughty lady,
These hairs which thou dost ravish from my chin
Will quicken, and accuse thee: I am your host:
With robber's hands my hospitable favours
You should not ruffle thus. What will you do?

CORN.

Come, sir, what letters had you late from France?

REG.

Be simple-answer'd, for we know the truth.

CORN.

And what confederacy have you with the traitors
Late footed in the kingdom?

REG.
To whose hands have you sent the lunatic king?
Speak.

GLOU.
I have a letter guessingly set down,
Which came from one that's of a neutral heart,
And not from one oppos'd.

CORN.
Cunning.

REG.
And false.

CORN.
Where hast thou sent the king?

GLOU.
To Dover.

REG.
Wherefore to Dover? Wast thou not charg'd at peril,—

CORN.
Wherefore to Dover? Let him first answer that.

GLOU.
I am tied to the stake, and I must stand the course.

REG.
Wherefore to Dover, sir?

GLOU.
Because I would not see thy cruel nails
Pluck out his poor old eyes; nor thy fierce sister
In his anointed flesh stick boarish fangs.
The sea, with such a storm as his bare head
In hell-black night endur'd, would have buoy'd up,
And quench'd the stelled fires; yet, poor old heart,
He holp the heavens to rain.
If wolves had at thy gate howl'd that stern time,
Thou shouldst have said, 'Good porter, turn the key.'

All cruels else subscrib'd:—but I shall see
The winged vengeance overtake such children.

CORN.

See't shalt thou never.—Fellows, hold the chair.
Upon these eyes of thine I'll set my foot.
[Gloucester is held down in his chair, while Cornwall plucks out one
of his eyes and sets his foot on it.]

GLOU.

He that will think to live till he be old,
Give me some help!—O cruel!—O ye gods!

REG.

One side will mock another; the other too!

CORN.

If you see vengeance,—

FIRST SERV.

Hold your hand, my lord:
I have serv'd you ever since I was a child;
But better service have I never done you
Than now to bid you hold.

REG.

How now, you dog!

FIRST SERV.

If you did wear a beard upon your chin,
I'd shake it on this quarrel. What do you mean?

CORN.

My villain!
[Draws, and runs at him.]

FIRST SERV.

Nay, then, come on, and take the chance of anger.
[Draws. They fight. Cornwall is wounded.]

REG.

Give me thy sword [to another servant.]—A peasant stand up thus?
[Snatches a sword, comes behind, and stabs him.]

FIRST SERV.

O, I am slain!—My lord, you have one eye left
To see some mischief on thim. O!
[Dies.]

CORN.

Lest it see more, prevent it.—Out, vile jelly!
Where is thy lustre now?
[Tears out Gloucester's other eye and throws it on the ground.]

GLOU.

All dark and comfortless.—Where's my son Edmund?
Edmund, enkindle all the sparks of nature
To quit this horrid act.

REG.

Out, treacherous villain!
Thou call'st on him that hates thee: it was he
That made the overture of thy treasons to us;
Who is too good to pity thee.

GLOU.

O my follies! Then Edgar was abus'd.—
Kind gods, forgive me that, and prosper him!

REG.

Go thrust him out at gates, and let him smell
His way to Dover.—How is't, my lord? How look you?

CORN.

I have receiv'd a hurt:—follow me, lady.—
Turn out that eyeless villain;—throw this slave
Upon the dunghill.—Regan, I bleed apace:
Untimely comes this hurt: give me your arm.
[Exit Cornwall, led by Regan; Servants unbind Gloucester and lead
him out.]

SECOND SERV.

I'll never care what wickedness I do,
If this man come to good.

THIRD SERV.

If she live long,

And in the end meet the old course of death,
Women will all turn monsters.

SECOND SERV.

Let's follow the old earl, and get the Bedlam
To lead him where he would: his roguish madness
Allows itself to anything.

THIRD SERV.

Go thou: I'll fetch some flax and whites of eggs
To apply to his bleeding face. Now heaven help him!
[Exeunt severally.]

Act IV

Scene I. The heath.
[Enter Edgar.]

EDG.

Yet better thus, and known to be contemn'd,
Than still contemn'd and flatter'd. To be worst,
The lowest and most dejected thing of fortune,
Stands still in esperance, lives not in fear:
The lamentable change is from the best;
The worst returns to laughter. Welcome, then,
Thou unsubstantial air that I embrace!
The wretch that thou hast blown unto the worst
Owes nothing to thy blasts.—But who comes here?
[Enter Gloucester, led by an Old Man.]
My father, poorly led?—World, world, O world!
But that thy strange mutations make us hate thee,
Life would not yield to age.
Old Man.
O my good lord,
I have been your tenant, and your father's tenant,
These fourscore years.

GLOU.

Away, get thee away; good friend, be gone:
Thy comforts can do me no good at all;
Thee they may hurt.
Old Man.
You cannot see your way.

GLOU.

I have no way, and therefore want no eyes;
I stumbled when I saw: full oft 'tis seen
Our means secure us, and our mere defects
Prove our commodities.—O dear son Edgar,
The food of thy abused father's wrath!
Might I but live to see thee in my touch,
I'd say I had eyes again!
Old Man.
How now! Who's there?

EDG.

[Aside.] O gods! Who is't can say 'I am at the worst?'
I am worse than e'er I was.
Old Man.
'Tis poor mad Tom.

EDG.

[Aside.] And worse I may be yet. The worst is not
So long as we can say 'This is the worst.'
Old Man.
Fellow, where goest?

GLOU.

Is it a beggar-man?
Old Man.
Madman and beggar too.

GLOU.

He has some reason, else he could not beg.
I' the last night's storm I such a fellow saw;
Which made me think a man a worm: my son
Came then into my mind, and yet my mind
Was then scarce friends with him: I have heard more since.
As flies to wanton boys are we to the gods,—
They kill us for their sport.

EDG.

[Aside.] How should this be?—
Bad is the trade that must play fool to sorrow,
Angering itself and others.—Bless thee, master!

GLOU.

Is that the naked fellow?

Old Man.

Ay, my lord.

GLOU.

Then pr'ythee get thee gone: if for my sake
Thou wilt o'ertake us, hence a mile or twain,
I' the way toward Dover, do it for ancient love;
And bring some covering for this naked soul,
Which I'll entreat to lead me.

Old Man.

Alack, sir, he is mad.

GLOU.

'Tis the time's plague when madmen lead the blind.
Do as I bid thee, or rather do thy pleasure;
Above the rest, be gone.

Old Man.

I'll bring him the best 'parel that I have,
Come on't what will.

[Exit.]

GLOU.

Sirrah naked fellow,—

EDG.

Poor Tom's a-cold.
[Aside.] I cannot daub it further.

GLOU.

Come hither, fellow.

EDG.

[Aside.] And yet I must.—Bless thy sweet eyes, they bleed.

GLOU.

Know'st thou the way to Dover?

EDG.

Both stile and gate, horseway and footpath. Poor Tom hath been
scared out of his good wits:—bless thee, good man's son, from
the foul fiend! Five fiends have been in poor Tom at once; of

lust, as Obidicut; Hobbididence, prince of dumbness; Mahu, of
stealing; Modo, of murder; Flibbertigibbet, of mopping and
mowing,—who since possesses chambermaids and waiting women. So,
bless thee, master!

GLOU.

Here, take this purse, thou whom the heavens' plagues
Have humbled to all strokes: that I am wretched
Makes thee the happier;—heavens, deal so still!
Let the superfluous and lust-dieted man,
That slaves your ordinance, that will not see
Because he does not feel, feel your power quickly;
So distribution should undo excess,
And each man have enough.—Dost thou know Dover?

EDG.

Ay, master.

GLOU.

There is a cliff, whose high and bending head
Looks fearfully in the confined deep:
Bring me but to the very brim of it,
And I'll repair the misery thou dost bear
With something rich about me: from that place
I shall no leading need.

EDG.

Give me thy arm:
Poor Tom shall lead thee.
[Exeunt.]

Scene II. Before the Duke of Albany's Palace.
Enter Goneril and Edmund; Oswald meeting them.]

GON.

Welcome, my lord: I marvel our mild husband
Not met us on the way.—Now, where's your master?

OSW.

Madam, within; but never man so chang'd.
I told him of the army that was landed;
He smil'd at it: I told him you were coming;
His answer was, 'The worse.' Of Gloucester's treachery

And of the loyal service of his son
When I inform'd him, then he call'd me sot
And told me I had turn'd the wrong side out:—
What most he should dislike seems pleasant to him;
What like, offensive.

                                        GON.
[To Edmund.] Then shall you go no further.
It is the cowish terror of his spirit,
That dares not undertake: he'll not feel wrongs
Which tie him to an answer. Our wishes on the way
May prove effects. Back, Edmund, to my brother;
Hasten his musters and conduct his powers:
I must change arms at home, and give the distaff
Into my husband's hands. This trusty servant
Shall pass between us; ere long you are like to hear,
If you dare venture in your own behalf,
A mistress's command. [Giving a favour.]
Wear this; spare speech;
Decline your head: this kiss, if it durst speak,
Would stretch thy spirits up into the air:—
Conceive, and fare thee well.

                                        EDM.
Yours in the ranks of death!
[Exit Edmund.]

                                        GON.
My most dear Gloucester.
O, the difference of man and man!
To thee a woman's services are due:
My fool usurps my body.

                                        OSW.
Madam, here comes my lord.
[Exit.]
[Enter Albany.]

                                        GON.
I have been worth the whistle.

                                        ALB.
O Goneril!

You are not worth the dust which the rude wind
Blows in your face! I fear your disposition:
That nature which contemns it origin
Cannot be bordered certain in itself;
She that herself will sliver and disbranch
From her material sap, perforce must wither
And come to deadly use.

GON.

No more; the text is foolish.

ALB.

Wisdom and goodness to the vile seem vile:
Filths savour but themselves. What have you done?
Tigers, not daughters, what have you perform'd?
A father, and a gracious aged man,
Whose reverence even the head-lugg'd bear would lick,
Most barbarous, most degenerate, have you madded.
Could my good brother suffer you to do it?
A man, a prince, by him so benefited!
If that the heavens do not their visible spirits
Send quickly down to tame these vile offences,
It will come,
Humanity must perforce prey on itself,
Like monsters of the deep.

GON.

Milk-liver'd man!
That bear'st a cheek for blows, a head for wrongs;
Who hast not in thy brows an eye discerning
Thine honour from thy suffering; that not know'st
Fools do those villains pity who are punish'd
Ere they have done their mischief. Where's thy drum?
France spreads his banners in our noiseless land;
With plumed helm thy slayer begins threats;
Whiles thou, a moral fool, sitt'st still, and criest
'Alack, why does he so?'

ALB.

See thyself, devil!
Proper deformity seems not in the fiend
So horrid as in woman.

Page | 1369

GON.

O vain fool!

ALB.

Thou changed and self-cover'd thing, for shame!
Be-monster not thy feature! Were't my fitness
To let these hands obey my blood.
They are apt enough to dislocate and tear
Thy flesh and bones:—howe'er thou art a fiend,
A woman's shape doth shield thee.

GON.

Marry, your manhood now!
[Enter a Messenger.]

ALB.

What news?

MESS.

O, my good lord, the Duke of Cornwall's dead;
Slain by his servant, going to put out
The other eye of Gloucester.

ALB.

Gloucester's eyes!

MESS.

A servant that he bred, thrill'd with remorse,
Oppos'd against the act, bending his sword
To his great master; who, thereat enrag'd,
Flew on him, and amongst them fell'd him dead;
But not without that harmful stroke which since
Hath pluck'd him after.

ALB.

This shows you are above,
You justicers, that these our nether crimes
So speedily can venge!—But, O poor Gloucester!
Lost he his other eye?

MESS.

Both, both, my lord.—
This letter, madam, craves a speedy answer;
'Tis from your sister.

GON.

[Aside.] One way I like this well;
But being widow, and my Gloucester with her,
May all the building in my fancy pluck
Upon my hateful life: another way
The news is not so tart.—I'll read, and answer.
[Exit.]

ALB.

Where was his son when they did take his eyes?

MESS.

Come with my lady hither.

ALB.

He is not here.

MESS.

No, my good lord; I met him back again.

ALB.

Knows he the wickedness?

MESS.

Ay, my good lord. 'Twas he inform'd against him;
And quit the house on purpose, that their punishment
Might have the freer course.

ALB.

Gloucester, I live
To thank thee for the love thou show'dst the king,
And to revenge thine eyes.—Come hither, friend:
Tell me what more thou know'st.
[Exeunt.]

Scene III. The French camp near Dover.
[Enter Kent and a Gentleman.]

KENT.

Why the king of France is so suddenly gone back know you the
reason?

GENT.

Something he left imperfect in the state, which since his coming
forth is thought of, which imports to the kingdom so much fear
and danger that his personal return was most required and
necessary.

KENT.

Who hath he left behind him general?

GENT.

The Mareschal of France, Monsieur La Far.

KENT.

Did your letters pierce the queen to any demonstration of grief?

GENT.

Ay, sir; she took them, read them in my presence;
And now and then an ample tear trill'd down
Her delicate cheek: it seem'd she was a queen
Over her passion; who, most rebel-like,
Sought to be king o'er her.

KENT.

O, then it mov'd her.

GENT.

Not to a rage: patience and sorrow strove
Who should express her goodliest. You have seen
Sunshine and rain at once: her smiles and tears
Were like, a better day: those happy smilets
That play'd on her ripe lip seem'd not to know
What guests were in her eyes; which parted thence
As pearls from diamonds dropp'd.—In brief, sorrow
Would be a rarity most belov'd, if all
Could so become it.

KENT.

Made she no verbal question?

GENT.

Faith, once or twice she heav'd the name of 'father'
Pantingly forth, as if it press'd her heart;
Cried 'Sisters, sisters!—Shame of ladies! sisters!

Kent! father! sisters! What, i' the storm? i' the night?
Let pity not be believ'd!'—There she shook
The holy water from her heavenly eyes,
And clamour moisten'd: then away she started
To deal with grief alone.

KENT.

It is the stars,
The stars above us, govern our conditions;
Else one self mate and mate could not beget
Such different issues. You spoke not with her since?

GENT.

No.

KENT.

Was this before the king return'd?

GENT.

No, since.

KENT.

Well, sir, the poor distressed Lear's i' the town;
Who sometime, in his better tune, remembers
What we are come about, and by no means
Will yield to see his daughter.

GENT.

Why, good sir?

KENT.

A sovereign shame so elbows him: his own unkindness,
That stripp'd her from his benediction, turn'd her
To foreign casualties, gave her dear rights
To his dog-hearted daughters,—these things sting
His mind so venomously that burning shame
Detains him from Cordelia.

GENT.

Alack, poor gentleman!

KENT.

Of Albany's and Cornwall's powers you heard not?

GENT.

'Tis so; they are a-foot.

KENT.

Well, sir, I'll bring you to our master Lear
And leave you to attend him: some dear cause
Will in concealment wrap me up awhile;
When I am known aright, you shall not grieve
Lending me this acquaintance. I pray you go
Along with me.
[Exeunt.]

Scene IV. The French camp. A Tent.
[Enter Cordelia, Physician, and Soldiers.]

COR.

Alack, 'tis he: why, he was met even now
As mad as the vex'd sea; singing aloud;
Crown'd with rank fumiter and furrow weeds,
With harlocks, hemlock, nettles, cuckoo-flowers,
Darnel, and all the idle weeds that grow
In our sustaining corn.—A century send forth;
Search every acre in the high-grown field,
And bring him to our eye. [Exit an
OFFICER.]
What can man's wisdom
In the restoring his bereaved sense?
He that helps him take all my outward worth.

PHYS.

There is means, madam:
Our foster nurse of nature is repose,
The which he lacks; that to provoke in him
Are many simples operative, whose power
Will close the eye of anguish.

COR.

All bless'd secrets,
All you unpublish'd virtues of the earth,
Spring with my tears! be aidant and remediate
In the good man's distress!—Seek, seek for him;
Lest his ungovern'd rage dissolve the life
That wants the means to lead it.

[Enter a Messenger.]

MESS.
News, madam;
The British powers are marching hitherward.

COR.
'Tis known before; our preparation stands
In expectation of them.—O dear father,
It is thy business that I go about;
Therefore great France
My mourning and important tears hath pitied.
No blown ambition doth our arms incite,
But love, dear love, and our ag'd father's right:
Soon may I hear and see him!
[Exeunt.]

Scene V. A Room in Gloucester's Castle.
[Enter Regan and Oswald.]

REG.
But are my brother's powers set forth?

OSW.
Ay, madam.

REG.
Himself in person there?

OSW.
Madam, with much ado.
Your sister is the better soldier.

REG.
Lord Edmund spake not with your lord at home?

OSW.
No, madam.

REG.
What might import my sister's letter to him?

OSW.
I know not, lady.

REG.

Faith, he is posted hence on serious matter.
It was great ignorance, Gloucester's eyes being out,
To let him live: where he arrives he moves
All hearts against us: Edmund, I think, is gone,
In pity of his misery, to despatch
His nighted life; moreover, to descry
The strength o' the enemy.

OSW.

I must needs after him, madam, with my letter.

REG.

Our troops set forth to-morrow: stay with us;
The ways are dangerous.

OSW.

I may not, madam:
My lady charg'd my duty in this business.

REG.

Why should she write to Edmund? Might not you
Transport her purposes by word? Belike,
Something,—I know not what:—I'll love thee much—
Let me unseal the letter.

OSW.

Madam, I had rather,—

REG.

I know your lady does not love her husband;
I am sure of that: and at her late being here
She gave strange eyeliads and most speaking looks
To noble Edmund. I know you are of her bosom.

OSW.

I, madam?

REG.

I speak in understanding; you are, I know't:
Therefore I do advise you, take this note:
My lord is dead; Edmund and I have talk'd;
And more convenient is he for my hand

Than for your lady's.—You may gather more.
If you do find him, pray you give him this;
And when your mistress hears thus much from you,
I pray desire her call her wisdom to her
So, fare you well.
If you do chance to hear of that blind traitor,
Preferment falls on him that cuts him off.

OSW.

Would I could meet him, madam! I should show
What party I do follow.

REG.

Fare thee well.
[Exeunt.]

Scene VI. The country near Dover.
[Enter Gloucester, and Edgar dressed like a peasant.]

GLOU.

When shall I come to the top of that same hill?

EDG.

You do climb up it now: look, how we labour.

GLOU.

Methinks the ground is even.

EDG.

Horrible steep.
Hark, do you hear the sea?

GLOU.

No, truly.

EDG.

Why, then, your other senses grow imperfect
By your eyes' anguish.

GLOU.

So may it be indeed:
Methinks thy voice is alter'd; and thou speak'st
In better phrase and matter than thou didst.

EDG.

You are much deceiv'd: in nothing am I chang'd
But in my garments.

GLOU.

Methinks you're better spoken.

EDG.

Come on, sir; here's the place:—stand still.—How fearful
And dizzy 'tis to cast one's eyes so low!
The crows and choughs that wing the midway air
Show scarce so gross as beetles: half way down
Hangs one that gathers samphire—dreadful trade!
Methinks he seems no bigger than his head:
The fishermen that walk upon the beach
Appear like mice; and yond tall anchoring bark,
Diminish'd to her cock; her cock a buoy
Almost too small for sight: the murmuring surge
That on the unnumber'd idle pebble chafes
Cannot be heard so high.—I'll look no more;
Lest my brain turn, and the deficient sight
Topple down headlong.

GLOU.

Set me where you stand.

EDG.

Give me your hand:—you are now within a foot
Of th' extreme verge: for all beneath the moon
Would I not leap upright.

GLOU.

Let go my hand.
Here, friend, 's another purse; in it a jewel
Well worth a poor man's taking: fairies and gods
Prosper it with thee! Go thou further off;
Bid me farewell, and let me hear thee going.

EDG.

Now fare ye well, good sir.
[Seems to go.]

GLOU.

With all my heart.

EDG.

[Aside.] Why I do trifle thus with his despair
Is done to cure it.

GLOU.

O you mighty gods!
This world I do renounce, and, in your sights,
Shake patiently my great affliction off:
If I could bear it longer, and not fall
To quarrel with your great opposeless wills,
My snuff and loathed part of nature should
Burn itself out. If Edgar live, O, bless him!—
Now, fellow, fare thee well.

EDG.

Gone, sir:—farewell.—
[Gloucester leaps, and falls along.]
And yet I know not how conceit may rob
The treasury of life when life itself
Yields to the theft: had he been where he thought,
By this had thought been past.—Alive or dead?
Ho you, sir! friend! Hear you, sir?—speak!—
Thus might he pass indeed:—yet he revives.—
What are you, sir?

GLOU.

Away, and let me die.

EDG.

Hadst thou been aught but gossamer, feathers, air,
So many fathom down precipitating,
Thou'dst shiver'd like an egg: but thou dost breathe;
Hast heavy substance; bleed'st not; speak'st; art sound.
Ten masts at each make not the altitude
Which thou hast perpendicularly fell:
Thy life is a miracle.—Speak yet again.

GLOU.

But have I fall'n, or no?

EDG.

From the dread summit of this chalky bourn.
Look up a-height;—the shrill-gorg'd lark so far
Cannot be seen or heard: do but look up.

GLOU.

Alack, I have no eyes.—
Is wretchedness depriv'd that benefit
To end itself by death? 'Twas yet some comfort
When misery could beguile the tyrant's rage
And frustrate his proud will.

EDG.

Give me your arm:
Up:—so.—How is't? Feel you your legs? You stand.

GLOU.

Too well, too well.

EDG.

This is above all strangeness.
Upon the crown o' the cliff what thing was that
Which parted from you?

GLOU.

A poor unfortunate beggar.

EDG.

As I stood here below, methought his eyes
Were two full moons; he had a thousand noses,
Horns whelk'd and wav'd like the enridged sea:
It was some fiend; therefore, thou happy father,
Think that the clearest gods, who make them honours
Of men's impossibility, have preserv'd thee.

GLOU.

I do remember now: henceforth I'll bear
Affliction till it do cry out itself,
'Enough, enough,' and die. That thing you speak of,
I took it for a man; often 'twould say,
'The fiend, the fiend:'—he led me to that place.

EDG.

Bear free and patient thoughts.—But who comes here?
[Enter Lear, fantastically dressed up with flowers.]
The safer sense will ne'er accommodate
His master thus.

LEAR.

No, they cannot touch me for coining;
I am the king himself.

EDG.

O thou side-piercing sight!

LEAR.

Nature's above art in that respect.—There's your press money.
That fellow handles his bow like a crow-keeper: draw me a
clothier's yard.—Look, look, a mouse! Peace, peace;—this piece
of toasted cheese will do't. There's my gauntlet; I'll prove it
on a giant.—Bring up the brown bills. O, well flown, bird!—i'
the clout, i' the clout: hewgh!—Give the word.

EDG.

Sweet marjoram.

LEAR.

Pass.

GLOU.

I know that voice.

LEAR.

Ha! Goneril with a white beard!—They flattered me like a dog;
and told me I had white hairs in my beard ere the black ones were
there. To say 'ay' and 'no' to everything I said!—'Ay' and 'no',
too, was no good divinity. When the rain came to wet me once, and
the wind to make me chatter; when the thunder would not peace at
my bidding; there I found 'em, there I smelt 'em out. Go to, they
are not men o' their words: they told me I was everything; 'tis a
lie—I am not ague-proof.

GLOU.

The trick of that voice I do well remember:
Is't not the king?

LEAR.

Ay, every inch a king:
When I do stare, see how the subject quakes.
I pardon that man's life.—What was thy cause?—
Adultery?—

Thou shalt not die: die for adultery! No:
The wren goes to't, and the small gilded fly
Does lecher in my sight.
Let copulation thrive; for Gloucester's bastard son
Was kinder to his father than my daughters
Got 'tween the lawful sheets.
To't, luxury, pell-mell! for I lack soldiers.—
Behold yond simpering dame,
Whose face between her forks presages snow;
That minces virtue, and does shake the head
To hear of pleasure's name;—
The fitchew nor the soiled horse goes to't
With a more riotous appetite.
Down from the waist they are centaurs,
Though women all above:
But to the girdle do the gods inherit,
Beneath is all the fiend's; there's hell, there's darkness,
There is the sulphurous pit; burning, scalding, stench,
consumption; fie, fie, fie! pah, pah!
Give me an ounce of civet, good apothecary, to sweeten my
imagination: there's money for thee.

GLOU.

O, let me kiss that hand!

LEAR.

Let me wipe it first; it smells of mortality.

GLOU.

O ruin'd piece of nature! This great world
Shall so wear out to naught.—Dost thou know me?

LEAR.

I remember thine eyes well enough. Dost thou squiny at me?
No, do thy worst, blind Cupid; I'll not love.—Read thou this
challenge; mark but the penning of it.

GLOU.

Were all the letters suns, I could not see one.

EDG.

I would not take this from report;—it is,
And my heart breaks at it.

LEAR.

Read.

GLOU.

What, with the case of eyes?

LEAR.

O, ho, are you there with me? No eyes in your head, nor no money
in your purse? Your eyes are in a heavy case, your purse in a
light: yet you see how this world goes.

GLOU.

I see it feelingly.

LEAR.

What, art mad? A man may see how the world goes with no eyes.
Look with thine ears: see how yond justice rails upon yond simple
thief. Hark, in thine ear: change places; and, handy-dandy, which
is the justice, which is the thief?—Thou hast seen a farmer's
dog bark at a beggar?

GLOU.

Ay, sir.

LEAR.

And the creature run from the cur? There thou mightst behold
the great image of authority: a dog's obeyed in office.—
Thou rascal beadle, hold thy bloody hand!
Why dost thou lash that whore? Strip thine own back;
Thou hotly lust'st to use her in that kind
For which thou whipp'st her. The usurer hangs the cozener.
Through tatter'd clothes small vices do appear;
Robes and furr'd gowns hide all. Plate sin with gold,
And the strong lance of justice hurtless breaks;
Arm it in rags, a pygmy's straw does pierce it.
None does offend, none.—I say none; I'll able 'em:
Take that of me, my friend, who have the power
To seal the accuser's lips. Get thee glass eyes;
And, like a scurvy politician, seem
To see the things thou dost not.—Now, now, now, now:
Pull off my boots: harder, harder:—so.

EDG.

O, matter and impertinency mix'd!
Reason, in madness!

LEAR.

If thou wilt weep my fortunes, take my eyes.
I know thee well enough; thy name is Gloucester:
Thou must be patient; we came crying hither:
Thou know'st, the first time that we smell the air
We wawl and cry.—I will preach to thee: mark.

GLOU.

Alack, alack the day!

LEAR.

When we are born, we cry that we are come
To this great stage of fools—This a good block:—
It were a delicate stratagem to shoe
A troop of horse with felt: I'll put't in proof;
And when I have stol'n upon these sons-in-law,
Then kill, kill, kill, kill, kill, kill!
[Enter a Gentleman, with Attendants].

GENT.

O, here he is: lay hand upon him.—Sir,
Your most dear daughter,—

LEAR.

No rescue? What, a prisoner? I am even
The natural fool of fortune.—Use me well;
You shall have ransom. Let me have surgeons;
I am cut to the brains.

GENT.

You shall have anything.

LEAR.

No seconds? all myself?
Why, this would make a man a man of salt,
To use his eyes for garden water-pots,
Ay, and for laying Autumn's dust.

GENT.

Good sir,—

LEAR.

I will die bravely, like a smug bridegroom. What!
I will be jovial: come, come, I am a king,
My masters, know you that.

GENT.

You are a royal one, and we obey you.

LEAR.

Then there's life in't. Nay, an you get it, you shall get it
by running. Sa, sa, sa, sa!
[Exit running. Attendants follow.]

GENT.

A sight most pitiful in the meanest wretch,
Past speaking of in a king!—Thou hast one daughter
Who redeems nature from the general curse
Which twain have brought her to.

EDG.

Hail, gentle sir.

GENT.

Sir, speed you. What's your will?

EDG.

Do you hear aught, sir, of a battle toward?

GENT.

Most sure and vulgar: every one hears that
Which can distinguish sound.

EDG.

But, by your favour,
How near's the other army?

GENT.

Near and on speedy foot; the main descry
Stands on the hourly thought.

EDG.

I thank you sir: that's all.

GENT.

Though that the queen on special cause is here,
Her army is mov'd on.

EDG.

I thank you, sir.
[Exit Gentleman.]

GLOU.

You ever-gentle gods, take my breath from me;
Let not my worser spirit tempt me again
To die before you please!

EDG.

Well pray you, father.

GLOU.

Now, good sir, what are you?

EDG.

A most poor man, made tame to fortune's blows;
Who, by the art of known and feeling sorrows,
Am pregnant to good pity. Give me your hand,
I'll lead you to some biding.

GLOU.

Hearty thanks:
The bounty and the benison of heaven
To boot, and boot!
[Enter Oswald.]

OSW.

A proclaim'd prize! Most happy!
That eyeless head of thine was first fram'd flesh
To raise my fortunes.—Thou old unhappy traitor,
Briefly thyself remember:—the sword is out
That must destroy thee.

GLOU.

Now let thy friendly hand
Put strength enough to it.
[Edgar interposes.]

OSW.

Wherefore, bold peasant,
Dar'st thou support a publish'd traitor? Hence;
Lest that the infection of his fortune take
Like hold on thee. Let go his arm.

EDG.

Chill not let go, zir, without vurther 'casion.

OSW.

Let go, slave, or thou diest!

EDG.

Good gentleman, go your gait, and let poor voke pass. An chud
ha' bin zwaggered out of my life, 'twould not ha' bin zo long as
'tis by a vortnight. Nay, come not near the old man; keep out,
che vore ye, or ise try whether your costard or my bat be the
harder: chill be plain with you.

OSW.

Out, dunghill!

EDG.

Chill pick your teeth, zir. Come! No matter vor your foins.
[They fight, and Edgar knocks him down.]

OSW.

Slave, thou hast slain me:—villain, take my purse:
If ever thou wilt thrive, bury my body;
And give the letters which thou find'st about me
To Edmund Earl of Gloucester; seek him out
Upon the British party: O, untimely death!
[Dies.]

EDG.

I know thee well: a serviceable villain;
As duteous to the vices of thy mistress
As badness would desire.

GLOU.

What, is he dead?

EDG.

Sit you down, father; rest you.—
Let's see these pockets; the letters that he speaks of
May be my friends.—He's dead; I am only sorry
He had no other death's-man. Let us see:—
Leave, gentle wax; and, manners, blame us not:
To know our enemies' minds, we'd rip their hearts;
Their papers is more lawful.
[Reads.] 'Let our reciprocal vows be remembered. You have many
opportunities to cut him off: if your will want not, time and
place will be fruitfully offered. There is nothing done if he
return the conqueror: then am I the prisoner, and his bed my
gaol; from the loathed warmth whereof deliver me, and supply the
place for your labour.
Your (wife, so I would say) affectionate servant,
Goneril.'
O indistinguish'd space of woman's will!
A plot upon her virtuous husband's life;
And the exchange my brother!—Here in the sands
Thee I'll rake up, the post unsanctified
Of murderous lechers: and in the mature time
With this ungracious paper strike the sight
Of the death-practis'd duke: for him 'tis well
That of thy death and business I can tell.
[Exit Edgar, dragging out the body.]

GLOU.

The king is mad: how stiff is my vile sense,
That I stand up, and have ingenious feeling
Of my huge sorrows! Better I were distract:
So should my thoughts be sever'd from my griefs,
And woes by wrong imaginations lose
The knowledge of themselves.

EDG.

Give me your hand:
[A drum afar off.]
Far off methinks I hear the beaten drum:
Come, father, I'll bestow you with a friend.
[Exeunt.]

Scene VII. A Tent in the French Camp.
[Lear on a bed, asleep, soft music playing; Physician, Gentleman, and others attending.]

[Enter Cordelia, and KENT.]

COR.

O thou good Kent, how shall I live and work
To match thy goodness? My life will be too short
And every measure fail me.

KENT.

To be acknowledg'd, madam, is o'erpaid.
All my reports go with the modest truth;
Nor more nor clipp'd, but so.

COR.

Be better suited:
These weeds are memories of those worser hours:
I pr'ythee, put them off.

KENT.

Pardon, dear madam;
Yet to be known shortens my made intent:
My boon I make it that you know me not
Till time and I think meet.

COR.

Then be't so, my good lord. [To the Physician.] How, does the
king?

PHYS.

Madam, sleeps still.

COR.

O you kind gods,
Cure this great breach in his abused nature!
The untun'd and jarring senses, O, wind up
Of this child-changed father!

PHYS.

So please your majesty
That we may wake the king: he hath slept long.

COR.

Be govern'd by your knowledge, and proceed
I' the sway of your own will. Is he array'd?

GENT.

Ay, madam. In the heaviness of sleep
We put fresh garments on him.

PHYS.

Be by, good madam, when we do awake him;
I doubt not of his temperance.

COR.

Very well.

PHYS.

Please you draw near.—Louder the music there!

COR.

O my dear father! Restoration hang
Thy medicine on my lips; and let this kiss
Repair those violent harms that my two sisters
Have in thy reverence made!

KENT.

Kind and dear princess!

COR.

Had you not been their father, these white flakes
Had challeng'd pity of them. Was this a face
To be oppos'd against the warring winds?
To stand against the deep dread-bolted thunder?
In the most terrible and nimble stroke
Of quick cross lightning? to watch—,poor perdu!—
With this thin helm? Mine enemy's dog,
Though he had bit me, should have stood that night
Against my fire; and wast thou fain, poor father,
To hovel thee with swine and rogues forlorn,
In short and musty straw? Alack, alack!
'Tis wonder that thy life and wits at once
Had not concluded all.—He wakes; speak to him.

DOCT.

Madam, do you; 'tis fittest.

COR.

How does my royal lord? How fares your majesty?

LEAR.

You do me wrong to take me out o' the grave:—
Thou art a soul in bliss; but I am bound
Upon a wheel of fire, that mine own tears
Do scald like molten lead.

COR.

Sir, do you know me?

LEAR.

You are a spirit, I know: when did you die?

COR.

Still, still, far wide!

PHYS.

He's scarce awake: let him alone awhile.

LEAR.

Where have I been? Where am I?—Fair daylight,—
I am mightily abus'd.—I should e'en die with pity,
To see another thus.—I know not what to say.—
I will not swear these are my hands:—let's see;
I feel this pin prick. Would I were assur'd
Of my condition!

COR.

O, look upon me, sir,
And hold your hands in benediction o'er me.—
No, sir, you must not kneel.

LEAR.

Pray, do not mock me:
I am a very foolish fond old man,
Fourscore and upward, not an hour more nor less;
And, to deal plainly,
I fear I am not in my perfect mind.
Methinks I should know you, and know this man;
Yet I am doubtful: for I am mainly ignorant
What place this is; and all the skill I have
Remembers not these garments; nor I know not
Where I did lodge last night. Do not laugh at me;
For, as I am a man, I think this lady
To be my child Cordelia.

COR.

And so I am. I am.

LEAR.

Be your tears wet? yes, faith. I pray, weep not:
If you have poison for me, I will drink it.
I know you do not love me; for your sisters
Have, as I do remember, done me wrong:
You have some cause, they have not.

COR.

No cause, no cause.

LEAR.

Am I in France?

KENT.

In your own kingdom, sir.

LEAR.

Do not abuse me.

PHYS.

Be comforted, good madam: the great rage,
You see, is kill'd in him: and yet it is danger
To make him even o'er the time he has lost.
Desire him to go in; trouble him no more
Till further settling.

COR.

Will't please your highness walk?

LEAR.

You must bear with me:
Pray you now, forget and forgive: I am old and foolish.
[Exeunt Lear, Cordelia, Physician, and Attendants.]

GENT.

Holds it true, sir, that the Duke of Cornwall was so slain?

KENT.

Most certain, sir.

GENT.

Who is conductor of his people?

KENT.

As 'tis said, the bastard son of Gloucester.

GENT.

They say Edgar, his banished son, is with the Earl of Kent
in Germany.

KENT.

Report is changeable. 'Tis time to look about; the powers of
the kingdom approach apace.

GENT.

The arbitrement is like to be bloody.
Fare you well, sir.
[Exit.]

KENT.

My point and period will be throughly wrought,
Or well or ill, as this day's battle's fought.
[Exit.]

Act V
Scene I. The Camp of the British Forces near Dover.
[Enter, with drum and colours, Edmund, Regan, Officers, Soldiers,
and others.]

EDM.

Know of the duke if his last purpose hold,
Or whether since he is advis'd by aught
To change the course: he's full of alteration
And self-reproving:—bring his constant pleasure.
[To an Officer, who goes out.]

REG.

Our sister's man is certainly miscarried.

EDM.

Tis to be doubted, madam.

REG.

Now, sweet lord,
You know the goodness I intend upon you:
Tell me,—but truly,—but then speak the truth,
Do you not love my sister?

EDM.

In honour'd love.

REG.

But have you never found my brother's way
To the forfended place?

EDM.

That thought abuses you.

REG.

I am doubtful that you have been conjunct
And bosom'd with her, as far as we call hers.

EDM.

No, by mine honour, madam.

REG.

I never shall endure her: dear my lord,
Be not familiar with her.

EDM.

Fear me not:—
She and the duke her husband!
[Enter, with drum and colours, Albany, Goneril, and Soldiers.]

GON.

[Aside.] I had rather lose the battle than that sister
Should loosen him and me.

ALB.

Our very loving sister, well be-met.—
Sir, this I heard,—the king is come to his daughter,
With others whom the rigour of our state
Forc'd to cry out. Where I could not be honest,
I never yet was valiant: for this business,
It toucheth us, as France invades our land,

Not bolds the king, with others whom, I fear,
Most just and heavy causes make oppose.

EDM.

Sir, you speak nobly.

REG.

Why is this reason'd?

GON.

Combine together 'gainst the enemy;
For these domestic and particular broils
Are not the question here.

ALB.

Let's, then, determine
With the ancient of war on our proceeding.

EDM.

I shall attend you presently at your tent.

REG.

Sister, you'll go with us?

GON.

No.

REG.

'Tis most convenient; pray you, go with us.

GON.

[Aside.] O, ho, I know the riddle.—I will go.
[As they are going out, enter Edgar disguised.]

EDG.

If e'er your grace had speech with man so poor,
Hear me one word.

ALB.

I'll overtake you.—Speak.
[Exeunt Edmund, Regan, Goneril, Officers, Soldiers, and Attendants.]

EDG.

Before you fight the battle, ope this letter.
If you have victory, let the trumpet sound
For him that brought it: wretched though I seem,
I can produce a champion that will prove
What is avouched there. If you miscarry,
Your business of the world hath so an end,
And machination ceases. Fortune love you!

ALB.

Stay till I have read the letter.

EDG.

I was forbid it.
When time shall serve, let but the herald cry,
And I'll appear again.

ALB.

Why, fare thee well: I will o'erlook thy paper.
[Exit Edgar.]
[Re-enter Edmund.]

EDM.

The enemy's in view; draw up your powers.
Here is the guess of their true strength and forces
By diligent discovery;—but your haste
Is now urg'd on you.

ALB.

We will greet the time.
[Exit.]

EDM.

To both these sisters have I sworn my love;
Each jealous of the other, as the stung
Are of the adder. Which of them shall I take?
Both? one? or neither? Neither can be enjoy'd,
If both remain alive: to take the widow
Exasperates, makes mad her sister Goneril;
And hardly shall I carry out my side,
Her husband being alive. Now, then, we'll use
His countenance for the battle; which being done,
Let her who would be rid of him devise

His speedy taking off. As for the mercy
Which he intends to Lear and to Cordelia,—
The battle done, and they within our power,
Shall never see his pardon: for my state
Stands on me to defend, not to debate.
[Exit.]

Scene II. A field between the two Camps.
[Alarum within. Enter, with drum and colours, Lear, Cordelia, and
their Forces, and exeunt.]
[Enter Edgar and Gloucester.]

EDG.

Here, father, take the shadow of this tree
For your good host; pray that the right may thrive:
If ever I return to you again,
I'll bring you comfort.

GLOU.

Grace go with you, sir!
[Exit Edgar].
[Alarum and retreat within. R-enter Edgar.]

EDG.

Away, old man,—give me thy hand,—away!
King Lear hath lost, he and his daughter ta'en:
Give me thy hand; come on!

GLOU.

No further, sir; a man may rot even here.

EDG.

What, in ill thoughts again? Men must endure
Their going hence, even as their coming hither;
Ripeness is all:—come on.

GLOU.

And that's true too.
[Exeunt.]

Scene III. The British Camp near Dover.
[Enter, in conquest, with drum and colours, Edmund; Lear and
Cordelia prisoners; Officers, Soldiers, &c.]

EDM.

Some officers take them away: good guard
Until their greater pleasures first be known
That are to censure them.

COR.

We are not the first
Who with best meaning have incurr'd the worst.
For thee, oppressed king, am I cast down;
Myself could else out-frown false fortune's frown.—
Shall we not see these daughters and these sisters?

LEAR.

No, no, no, no! Come, let's away to prison:
We two alone will sing like birds i' the cage:
When thou dost ask me blessing I'll kneel down
And ask of thee forgiveness: so we'll live,
And pray, and sing, and tell old tales, and laugh
At gilded butterflies, and hear poor rogues
Talk of court news; and we'll talk with them too,—
Who loses and who wins; who's in, who's out;—
And take upon's the mystery of things,
As if we were God's spies: and we'll wear out,
In a wall'd prison, packs and sects of great ones
That ebb and flow by the moon.

EDM.

Take them away.

LEAR.

Upon such sacrifices, my Cordelia,
The gods themselves throw incense. Have I caught thee?
He that parts us shall bring a brand from heaven
And fire us hence like foxes. Wipe thine eyes;
The goodyears shall devour them, flesh and fell,
Ere they shall make us weep: we'll see 'em starve first.
Come.
[Exeunt Lear and Cordelia, guarded.]

EDM.

Come hither, captain; hark.
Take thou this note [giving a paper]; go follow them to prison:
One step I have advanc'd thee; if thou dost

As this instructs thee, thou dost make thy way
To noble fortunes: know thou this,—that men
Are as the time is: to be tender-minded
Does not become a sword:—thy great employment
Will not bear question; either say thou'lt do't,
Or thrive by other means.
Capt.
I'll do't, my lord.

EDM.

About it; and write happy when thou hast done.
Mark,—I say, instantly; and carry it so
As I have set it down.
Capt.
I cannot draw a cart, nor eat dried oats;
If it be man's work, I'll do't.
[Exit.]
[Flourish. Enter Albany, Goneril, Regan, Officers, and Attendants.]

ALB.

Sir, you have show'd to-day your valiant strain,
And fortune led you well: you have the captives
Who were the opposites of this day's strife:
We do require them of you, so to use them
As we shall find their merits and our safety
May equally determine.

EDM.

Sir, I thought it fit
To send the old and miserable king
To some retention and appointed guard;
Whose age has charms in it, whose title more,
To pluck the common bosom on his side,
And turn our impress'd lances in our eyes
Which do command them. With him I sent the queen;
My reason all the same; and they are ready
To-morrow, or at further space, to appear
Where you shall hold your session. At this time
We sweat and bleed: the friend hath lost his friend;
And the best quarrels, in the heat, are curs'd
By those that feel their sharpness:—
The question of Cordelia and her father
Requires a fitter place.

ALB.

Sir, by your patience,
I hold you but a subject of this war,
Not as a brother.

REG.

That's as we list to grace him.
Methinks our pleasure might have been demanded
Ere you had spoke so far. He led our powers;
Bore the commission of my place and person;
The which immediacy may well stand up
And call itself your brother.

GON.

Not so hot:
In his own grace he doth exalt himself,
More than in your addition.

REG.

In my rights
By me invested, he compeers the best.

GON.

That were the most if he should husband you.

REG.

Jesters do oft prove prophets.

GON.

Holla, holla!
That eye that told you so look'd but asquint.

REG.

Lady, I am not well; else I should answer
From a full-flowing stomach.—General,
Take thou my soldiers, prisoners, patrimony;
Dispose of them, of me; the walls are thine:
Witness the world that I create thee here
My lord and master.

GON.

Mean you to enjoy him?

ALB.

The let-alone lies not in your good will.

EDM.

Nor in thine, lord.

ALB.

Half-blooded fellow, yes.

REG.

[To Edmund.] Let the drum strike, and prove my title thine.

ALB.

Stay yet; hear reason.—Edmund, I arrest thee
On capital treason; and, in thine arrest,
This gilded serpent [pointing to Goneril.],—For your claim, fair
sister,
I bar it in the interest of my wife;
'Tis she is subcontracted to this lord,
And I, her husband, contradict your bans.
If you will marry, make your loves to me,—
My lady is bespoke.

GON.

An interlude!

ALB.

Thou art arm'd, Gloucester:—let the trumpet sound:
If none appear to prove upon thy person
Thy heinous, manifest, and many treasons,
There is my pledge [throwing down a glove]; I'll prove it on thy
heart,
Ere I taste bread, thou art in nothing less
Than I have here proclaim'd thee.

REG.

Sick, O, sick!

GON.

[Aside.] If not, I'll ne'er trust medicine.

EDM.

There's my exchange [throwing down a glove]: what in the world he is

That names me traitor, villain-like he lies:
Call by thy trumpet: he that dares approach,
On him, on you, who not? I will maintain
My truth and honour firmly.

ALB.

A herald, ho!

EDM.

A herald, ho, a herald!

ALB.

Trust to thy single virtue; for thy soldiers,
All levied in my name, have in my name
Took their discharge.

REG.

My sickness grows upon me.

ALB.

She is not well. Convey her to my tent.
[Exit Regan, led.]
[Enter a Herald.]
Come hither, herald.—Let the trumpet sound,—
And read out this.

OFFICER.

Sound, trumpet!
[A trumpet sounds.]

HER.

[Reads.] 'If any man of quality or degree within the lists of
the army will maintain upon Edmund, supposed Earl of Gloucester,
that he is a manifold traitor, let him appear by the third sound
of the trumpet. He is bold in his defence.'

EDM.

Sound!
[First trumpet.]

HER.

Again!
[Second trumpet.]

HER.

Again!

[Third trumpet. Trumpet answers within. Enter Edgar, armed,
preceded by a trumpet.]

ALB.

Ask him his purposes, why he appears
Upon this call o' the trumpet.

HER.

What are you?
Your name, your quality? and why you answer
This present summons?

EDG.

Know, my name is lost;
By treason's tooth bare-gnawn and canker-bit.
Yet am I noble as the adversary
I come to cope.

ALB.

Which is that adversary?

EDG.

What's he that speaks for Edmund Earl of Gloucester?

EDM.

Himself:—what say'st thou to him?

EDG.

Draw thy sword,
That, if my speech offend a noble heart,
Thy arm may do thee justice: here is mine.
Behold, it is the privilege of mine honours,
My oath, and my profession: I protest,—
Maugre thy strength, youth, place, and eminence,
Despite thy victor sword and fire-new fortune,
Thy valour and thy heart,—thou art a traitor;
False to thy gods, thy brother, and thy father;
Conspirant 'gainst this high illustrious prince;
And, from the extremest upward of thy head
To the descent and dust beneath thy foot,
A most toad-spotted traitor. Say thou 'No,'

This sword, this arm, and my best spirits are bent
To prove upon thy heart, whereto I speak,
Thou liest.

EDM.

In wisdom I should ask thy name;
But since thy outside looks so fair and warlike,
And that thy tongue some say of breeding breathes,
What safe and nicely I might well delay
By rule of knighthood, I disdain and spurn:
Back do I toss those treasons to thy head;
With the hell-hated lie o'erwhelm thy heart;
Which,—for they yet glance by and scarcely bruise,—
This sword of mine shall give them instant way,
Where they shall rest for ever.—Trumpets, speak!
[Alarums. They fight. Edmund falls.]

ALB.

Save him, save him!

GON.

This is mere practice, Gloucester:
By the law of arms thou wast not bound to answer
An unknown opposite; thou art not vanquish'd,
But cozen'd and beguil'd.

ALB.

Shut your mouth, dame,
Or with this paper shall I stop it:—Hold, sir;
Thou worse than any name, read thine own evil:—
No tearing, lady; I perceive you know it.
[Gives the letter to Edmund.]

GON.

Say if I do,—the laws are mine, not thine:
Who can arraign me for't?

ALB.

Most monstrous!
Know'st thou this paper?

GON.

Ask me not what I know.
[Exit.]

ALB.

Go after her: she's desperate; govern her.
[To an Officer, who goes out.]

EDM.

What, you have charg'd me with, that have I done;
And more, much more; the time will bring it out:
'Tis past, and so am I.—But what art thou
That hast this fortune on me? If thou'rt noble,
I do forgive thee.

EDG.

Let's exchange charity.
I am no less in blood than thou art, Edmund;
If more, the more thou hast wrong'd me.
My name is Edgar, and thy father's son.
The gods are just, and of our pleasant vices
Make instruments to plague us:
The dark and vicious place where thee he got
Cost him his eyes.

EDM.

Thou hast spoken right; 'tis true;
The wheel is come full circle; I am here.

ALB.

Methought thy very gait did prophesy
A royal nobleness:—I must embrace thee:
Let sorrow split my heart if ever I
Did hate thee or thy father!

EDG.

Worthy prince, I know't.

ALB.

Where have you hid yourself?
How have you known the miseries of your father?

EDG.

By nursing them, my lord.—List a brief tale;—
And when 'tis told, O that my heart would burst!—
The bloody proclamation to escape,
That follow'd me so near,—O, our lives' sweetness!

That with the pain of death we'd hourly die
Rather than die at once!)—taught me to shift
Into a madman's rags; to assume a semblance
That very dogs disdain'd; and in this habit
Met I my father with his bleeding rings,
Their precious stones new lost; became his guide,
Led him, begg'd for him, sav'd him from despair;
Never,—O fault!—reveal'd myself unto him
Until some half hour past, when I was arm'd;
Not sure, though hoping of this good success,
I ask'd his blessing, and from first to last
Told him my pilgrimage: but his flaw'd heart,—
Alack, too weak the conflict to support!—
'Twixt two extremes of passion, joy and grief,
Burst smilingly.

                         EDM.
This speech of yours hath mov'd me,
And shall perchance do good: but speak you on;
You look as you had something more to say.

                         ALB.
If there be more, more woeful, hold it in;
For I am almost ready to dissolve,
Hearing of this.

                         EDG.
This would have seem'd a period
To such as love not sorrow; but another,
To amplify too much, would make much more,
And top extremity.
Whilst I was big in clamour, came there a man
Who, having seen me in my worst estate,
Shunn'd my abhorr'd society; but then, finding
Who 'twas that so endur'd, with his strong arms
He fastened on my neck, and bellow'd out
As he'd burst heaven; threw him on my father;
Told the most piteous tale of Lear and him
That ever ear receiv'd: which in recounting
His grief grew puissant, and the strings of life
Began to crack: twice then the trumpets sounded,
And there I left him tranc'd.

ALB.

But who was this?

EDG.

Kent, sir, the banish'd Kent; who in disguise
Follow'd his enemy king and did him service
Improper for a slave.
[Enter a Gentleman hastily, with a bloody knife.]

GENT.

Help, help! O, help!

EDG.

What kind of help?

ALB.

Speak, man.

EDG.

What means that bloody knife?

GENT.

'Tis hot, it smokes;
It came even from the heart of—O! she's dead!

ALB.

Who dead? speak, man.

GENT.

Your lady, sir, your lady: and her sister
By her is poisoned; she hath confess'd it.

EDM.

I was contracted to them both: all three
Now marry in an instant.

EDG.

Here comes KENT.

ALB.

Produce their bodies, be they alive or dead:—
This judgement of the heavens, that makes us tremble
Touches us not with pity. [Exit Gentleman.]

[Enter KENT.]
O, is this he?
The time will not allow the compliment
That very manners urges.

KENT.

I am come
To bid my king and master aye good night:
Is he not here?

ALB.

Great thing of us forgot!
Speak, Edmund, where's the king? and where's Cordelia?
[The bodies of Goneril and Regan are brought in.]
Seest thou this object, Kent?

KENT.

Alack, why thus?

EDM.

Yet Edmund was belov'd.
The one the other poisoned for my sake,
And after slew herself.

ALB.

Even so.—Cover their faces.

EDM.

I pant for life:—some good I mean to do,
Despite of mine own nature. Quickly send,—
Be brief in it,—to the castle; for my writ
Is on the life of Lear and on Cordelia:—
Nay, send in time.

ALB.

Run, run, O, run!

EDG.

To who, my lord?—Who has the office? send
Thy token of reprieve.

EDM.

Well thought on: take my sword,
Give it the Captain.

ALB.

Haste thee for thy life.
[Exit Edgar.]

EDM.

He hath commission from thy wife and me
To hang Cordelia in the prison, and
To lay the blame upon her own despair,
That she fordid herself.

ALB.

The gods defend her!—Bear him hence awhile.
[Edmund is borne off.]
[Re-enter Lear, with Cordelia dead in his arms; Edgar, Officer, and others following.]

LEAR.

Howl, howl, howl, howl!—O, you are men of stone.
Had I your tongues and eyes, I'ld use them so
That heaven's vault should crack.—She's gone for ever!—
I know when one is dead, and when one lives;
She's dead as earth.—Lend me a looking glass;
If that her breath will mist or stain the stone,
Why, then she lives.

KENT.

Is this the promis'd end?

EDG.

Or image of that horror?

ALB.

Fall, and cease!

LEAR.

This feather stirs; she lives! If it be so,
It is a chance which does redeem all sorrows
That ever I have felt.

KENT.

O my good master! [Kneeling.]

LEAR.

Pr'ythee, away!

EDG.

'Tis noble Kent, your friend.

LEAR.

A plague upon you, murderers, traitors all!
I might have sav'd her; now she's gone for ever!—
Cordelia, Cordelia! stay a little. Ha!
What is't thou say'st?—Her voice was ever soft,
Gentle, and low,—an excellent thing in woman.—
I kill'd the slave that was a-hanging thee.

OFF.

'Tis true, my lords, he did.

LEAR.

Did I not, fellow?
I have seen the day, with my good biting falchion
I would have made them skip: I am old now,
And these same crosses spoil me.—Who are you?
Mine eyes are not o' the best:—I'll tell you straight.

KENT.

If fortune brag of two she lov'd and hated,
One of them we behold.

LEAR.

This is a dull sight. Are you not Kent?

KENT.

The same,
Your servant Kent.—Where is your servant Caius?

LEAR.

He's a good fellow, I can tell you that;
He'll strike, and quickly too:—he's dead and rotten.

KENT.

No, my good lord; I am the very man,—

LEAR.

I'll see that straight.

KENT.

That from your first of difference and decay
Have follow'd your sad steps.

LEAR.

You are welcome hither.

KENT.

Nor no man else:—All's cheerless, dark, and deadly.—
Your eldest daughters have fordone themselves,
And desperately are dead.

LEAR.

Ay, so I think.

ALB.

He knows not what he says; and vain is it
That we present us to him.

EDG.

Very bootless.
[Enter a OFFICER.]

OFF.

Edmund is dead, my lord.

ALB.

That's but a trifle here.—
You lords and noble friends, know our intent.
What comfort to this great decay may come
Shall be applied: for us, we will resign,
During the life of this old majesty,
To him our absolute power:—[to Edgar and Kent] you to your
rights;
With boot, and such addition as your honours
Have more than merited.—All friends shall taste
The wages of their virtue, and all foes
The cup of their deservings.—O, see, see!

LEAR.

And my poor fool is hang'd! No, no, no life!
Why should a dog, a horse, a rat, have life,
And thou no breath at all? Thou'lt come no more,

Never, never, never, never, never!—
Pray you undo this button:—thank you, sir.—
Do you see this? Look on her!—look!—her lips!—
Look there, look there!—
[He dies.]

                         EDG.

He faints!—My lord, my lord!—

                         KENT.

Break, heart; I pr'ythee break!

                         EDG.

Look up, my lord.

                         KENT.

Vex not his ghost: O, let him pass! he hates him
That would upon the rack of this rough world
Stretch him out longer.

                         EDG.

He is gone indeed.

                         KENT.

The wonder is, he hath endur'd so long:
He but usurp'd his life.

                         ALB.

Bear them from hence.—Our present business
Is general woe.—[To Kent and Edgar.] Friends of my soul, you
twain
Rule in this realm, and the gor'd state sustain.

                         KENT.

I have a journey, sir, shortly to go;
My master calls me,—I must not say no.

                         EDG.

The weight of this sad time we must obey;
Speak what we feel, not what we ought to say.
The oldest have borne most: we that are young
Shall never see so much, nor live so long.
[Exeunt, with a dead march.]

2.13.4 Reading and Review Questions

1. What do his sonnets suggest are matters of importance to Shakespeare? What purpose(s), if any, do they serve? How do you know? How does the subject matter of Shakespeare's sonnets compare with Wyatt's, Surrey's, or Sydney's?

2. With its aristocratic milieu, masques, veils, and people spying on each other, the wit of *Much Ado About Nothing* is based a good deal on sight. What does this play suggest about the problem of seeing? What does it suggest is the relationship (real and ideal) between appearances and reality? What do the play's series of "plays" (masques, acting) suggest about art's relationship to truth and reality?

3. What metaphorical or symbolic purposes does "blindness" serve in *King Lear*, and why? What metaphorical or symbolic purposes does "madness" serve, and why? What connection, if any, exists between them?

4. In *King Lear,* what is the effect of Edmund's viewing himself as a "natural man," that is, a man without the grace that allows humans to distinguish between "right" and "wrong?" What motivates him? How does his character connect with others in the play; consider not only Goneril and Regan but also Edgar and Gloucester.

5. Is there any justice, or moral, in *King Lear*? How do you know?

2.14 KEY TERMS

- The Areopagus
- Allegory
- The Battle of Bosworth Field
- Blank Verse
- Catherine of Aragon
- counter-reformation
- Edward VI
- English Epic
- English Sonnets
- Elizabeth I
- Henry VII
- Henry VIII
- Iambic Pentameter
- King Arthur
- King's Council, or Star Chamber

- London
- Mary I
- Mary, Queen of Scots
- New Men
- ottava rima
- pastoral eclogue
- Petrarch
- Plantagenets
- The Printing Press
- The Reformation
- recognisances
- Renaissance Humanism
- rondeau
- Rhyme Scheme
- English sonnet
- Sonnet Conventions
- Spenserian sonnet
- Spenserian stanza
- terza rima
- The Spanish Armada
- The Wars of the Roses
- Vernacular, or native English, Literature
- William Caxton

CPSIA information can be obtained
at www.ICGtesting.com
Printed in the USA
LVHW082033191219
641008LV00006B/13/P